IT Career FastTrack with CompTIA A+ Certification for Exams 220-701 / 702

L1201eng verM020

Acknowledgements

Course Developer.. James Pengelly

This courseware is owned, published, and distributed by **gtslearning**, the world's only specialist supplier of CompTIA learning solutions.

✉ sales@gtslearning.com
☎ +44 (0)20 7887 7999   📠 +44 (0)20 7887 7988
🏢 Three Elysium Gate, 126-128 New Kings Road, London, SW6 4LZ, UK

COPYRIGHT

This courseware is copyrighted © 2010 gtslearning. Product images are the copyright of the vendor or manufacturer named in the caption and used by permission. No part of this courseware or any training material supplied by the publisher to accompany the courseware may be copied, photocopied, reproduced, or re-used in any form or by any means without permission in writing from the publisher. Violation of these laws will lead to prosecution.

All trademarks, service marks, products, or services are trademarks or registered trademarks of their respective holders and are acknowledged by the publisher.

LIMITATION OF LIABILITY

Every effort has been made to ensure complete and accurate information concerning the material presented in this course. Neither the publisher nor its agents can be held legally responsible for any mistakes in printing or for faulty instructions contained within this course. The publisher appreciates receiving notice of any errors or misprints.

Information in this course is subject to change without notice. Companies, names, and data used in examples herein are fictitious unless otherwise noted.

Where the course and all materials supplied for training are designed to familiarize the user with the operation of software programs and computer devices, the publisher urges the user to review the manuals provided by the product vendor regarding specific questions as to operation.

There are no warranties, expressed or implied, including warranties of merchantability or fitness for a particular purpose, made with respect to the materials or any information provided herein. Neither the author nor publisher shall be liable for any direct, indirect, special, incidental, or consequential damages arising out of the use or the inability to use the contents of this course.

EDITION

US Second Edition (verM020). Printed in the USA.

ISBN 978-1-84005-307-4

Table of Contents

Course Introduction   1

About CompTIA A+ Certification 2
Course Organization 3
Course Website 3
Studying the Course 4
Finding a Job 6
CompTIA Authorized Quality Curriculum Program 7

Module 1 Personal Computer Components   9

Unit 1.1 Motherboards 15
Form Factors and System Cases 15
Components, Slots, and Sockets 18
Expansion Bus 22
Drive Controllers 28

Unit 1.2 Processors 34
Processor Generations 34
CPU Features 35
Intel CPUs 42
AMD CPUs 44
CPU Packaging 46

Unit 1.3 Memory 50
Memory Types 50
Memory Configurations 55

Unit 1.4 Storage Devices 59
Floppy Disk Drives 59
Hard Disk Drives 60
Optical Drives 62
Removable Storage 67

Unit 1.5 Peripheral Devices 71
Peripheral Ports 71
PS/2 Port 71
Parallel Port 72
Serial Port 73
USB 74
Firewire 75
I/O Devices 76
Input Devices 76

© 2010 gtslearning   IT Career FastTrack with CompTIA A+ Certification   Page iii

Course Introduction

Communication Devices 81

Unit 1.6 Sound and Video Devices 83
Display Devices 83
Video Adapters 89
Audio Devices 95
Other Multimedia Devices 99

Unit 1.7 Power Supplies 104
Power Supply Unit (PSU) 104
Power Rating 105
Form Factors and Outputs 106
Air Cooling Systems 108
Liquid Cooling Systems 110

Unit 1.8 Laptops and Portable Devices 112
Portable Device Types 112
Laptop Components 117
Laptop Expansion Devices 120
Laptop Communication Connections 124
Laptop Power Devices 125

Module 2 Operating Systems   127

Unit 2.1 Windows Versions and Features 128
Microsoft Windows 128
Windows 2000 129
Windows XP 133
Windows Vista 140
Other Operating Systems 147

Unit 2.2 Installing and Upgrading Windows 150
Installation Steps and Processes 150
Windows Setup 154
Upgrading Windows 163
Deploying Windows 167

Unit 2.3 Windows Administrative Tools 170
Windows Architecture and Components 170
Windows Administration Tools 173
Remote Administration Tools 183

Unit 2.4 Windows Disk and File Management 189
Managing File Systems 189
Managing Disks 192
Managing Folders 193
Command Prompt Folder Management 205
Managing Files 208

Page iv   IT Career FastTrack with CompTIA A+ Certification   © 2010 gtslearning

Unit 2.5 Configuring Windows 218

Installing and Configuring Peripheral Devices...218

Managing Applications..223

Managing Services...228

Configuring Power Management...230

Configuring Regional and Language Options 234

Unit 2.6 Optimizing Windows...236

System Performance and Optimization..236

System Monitor 238

Task Manager 239

Performance Monitor 242

Reliability and Performance Monitor 247

Configuring Startup Services and Applications...248

Optimizing Drives and the File System 250

Configuring Performance Settings 257

Module 3 Operational Procedures   265

Unit 3.1 Communication and Professionalism 266

Customer Service 266

Communication Skills..267

Professionalism..270

Dealing with Difficult Situations 278

Unit 3.2 Troubleshooting Techniques...282

Troubleshooting Theory 282

Diagnostic Procedures..284

Troubleshooting Resources 289

Unit 3.3 Safety and Environmental Issues...293

Safety Hazards...293

Materials Handling...300

ESD Precautions..301

RFI / EMI 304

Power Problems...305

Safe Disposal and Recycling...309

Unit 3.4 Security..311

Security Concepts 311

Authorization 314

Authentication 317

Accounting and Incident Reporting..319

Social Engineering..320

Malware...323

Data Sensitivity and Security...325

Course Introduction

Module 4 Installation, Troubleshooting, and Maintenance 329

Unit 4.1 Preventative Maintenance.. 330
Repair Tools 330
Scheduling Preventative Maintenance 331
Ensuring the Proper Environment.. 332
Performing Preventative Maintenance 335
Windows Preventative Maintenance Schedule 339
Configuring Backup Procedures 345

Unit 4.2 Installing and Configuring Components 353
General Installation and Upgrade Advice 353
Installing and Upgrading Storage Devices..................................... 354
Configuring RAID 363
Installing and Upgrading Adapter Cards 368
Installing and Configuring Display Devices.................................... 370
Installing and Upgrading System Components 376
Installing and Configuring Input and Multimedia Devices......... 386

Unit 4.3 Windows Startup and Recovery.. 393
Windows Boot Process.. 393
Startup Options and Recovery Tools 403
Emergency Repair.. 410
Troubleshooting Boot Problems 417

Unit 4.4 Troubleshooting Windows 421
Diagnostic Tools.. 421
Troubleshooting Windows Errors and Lockups.......................... 428
Managing and Troubleshooting Devices 430
Troubleshooting Applications 437

Unit 4.5 Troubleshooting Components 444
Troubleshooting Basic Hardware Problems.................................. 444
Troubleshooting Power Problems... 448
Troubleshooting POST Problems 453
Troubleshooting Motherboard and CPU Problems.................... 458
Troubleshooting Memory Problems 461
Troubleshooting I/O Port Problems 462
Troubleshooting Hard Drive Problems.. 465
Troubleshooting Other Storage Device Problems...................... 469
Troubleshooting Peripheral Device Problems.............................. 472

Unit 4.6 Upgrading and Troubleshooting Laptops............................... 476
Upgrading Laptops 476
Troubleshooting Laptops 483

Page vi   IT Career FastTrack with CompTIA A+ Certification   © 2010 gtslearning

Course Introduction

Module 5 Networks and Printing   489

Unit 5.1 Networking Fundamentals 492
    Workgroups and Domains 492
    Network Technologies and Protocols 495
    TCP/IP 499
    NetBEUI / NetBIOS 510

Unit 5.2 Installing and Configuring Local Networks 511
    Installing a Local Network 511
    Configuring a Local Network 521
    Installing and Configuring a Wireless Network 528

Unit 5.3 File Sharing and Data Security 544
    Configuring Network Clients 544
    Security Policies 549
    Configuring Data and File System Security 559
    Implementing System Security 571

Unit 5.4 Configuring Internet Access 577
    Internet Connection Types 577
    Installing and Configuring Internet Connections 582
    Configuring the Browser 591
    Virtual Private Networks 594

Unit 5.5 Troubleshooting Network Links 596
    Network Troubleshooting Theory 596
    Troubleshooting Network Hardware 597
    Troubleshooting TCP/IP 604

Unit 5.6 Troubleshooting Network Applications 612
    Troubleshooting Client Connectivity 612
    Troubleshooting Firewalls 612
    Troubleshooting Web Browsers 621
    Troubleshooting Email Clients 631
    Troubleshooting FTP 633
    NET, Telnet, and Secure Shell (SSH) 636
    Troubleshooting Voice-over-IP 638

Unit 5.7 Configuring Malware Protection 642
    Malware Symptoms 642
    Preventing Malware Infections 646
    Anti-virus Software 648
    Removing Backdoor Applications 657
    Repairing Boot Blocks 658
    Windows Defender 660
    Parental Controls 661

© 2010 gtslearning   IT Career FastTrack with CompTIA A+ Certification   Page vii

Unit 5.8 Printers 662

Windows Print Process 662
Printer Technologies 664
Installing and Configuring Printers 672
Maintaining Printers 682
Troubleshooting Printers 688

Module 6 Taking the Exams   695

Preparing for the Essentials Exam 695
Registering for the Exam 697
Arriving for the Exam 697
Taking the Essentials Exam 698
After the Exam 699
Taking the Practical Application Exam 700

Module 7 Career Advice   701

Making a Career Plan 701
IT Support Job Roles 702
Searching for Vacancies 706
Approaching Employers 707
Career Paths 712

Index   713

Course Introduction

CompTIA A+ Certification is the essential qualification for beginning a career in IT Support. In this CompTIA approved course, you will learn everything you need to know about PC support:

- Install and configure PC hardware, such as CPUs, memory, hard disks, and graphics cards.
- Install, configure, and optimize Microsoft Windows.
- Configure printers and networking technologies.
- Troubleshoot PC, printer, and networking problems.
- Understand vital PC and internet security concepts.
- Communicate effectively and professionally with customers.

This fully illustrated course covers every exam objective in the CompTIA A+ syllabus, making it easy for you to learn everything you need to know to pass the CompTIA A+ Essentials and CompTIA A+ Practical Application exams.

This guide has been specially developed with your IT career in mind. Your career might begin with A+ Certification but it doesn't end there, so we've included a special section dedicated to helping you find a job in PC support. There's an overview of the industry, advice on where to look for job opportunities, plus practical advice on writing your resume or job application and attending an interview.

Course Introduction

About CompTIA A+ Certification

The CompTIA A+ certification is the industry standard for computer support technicians. The international, vendor-neutral certification proves competence in areas such as installation, preventative maintenance, networking, security and troubleshooting. CompTIA A+ certified technicians also have excellent customer service and communication skills to work with clients.

CompTIA A+ is part of the certification track for corporations such as Microsoft, Hewlett-Packard, Cisco and Novell. Other technology companies, including CompuCom and Ricoh, have made CompTIA A+ certification mandatory for their service technicians. More than 700,000 people worldwide have become CompTIA A+ certified since the program's inception in 1993.

CompTIA website (www.comptia.org)

The first step in achieving CompTIA A+ Certification is to pass the **Essentials** exam, which has the exam code **220-701** (the exam code is used when you book your test). The Essentials exam contains questions based on objectives and example content listed in the exam blueprint, published by CompTIA.

The objectives are divided into six **domains**, as listed below:

A+ Certification Essentials Domain Areas
1.0 Hardware
2.0 Troubleshooting, Repair, and Maintenance
3.0 Operating System and Software
4.0 Networking
5.0 Security
6.0 Operational Procedure

Having passed the Essentials exam, to become A+ Certified you must also pass the **Practical Application** exam (220-702). This exam covers the same sort of domains as the Essentials exam, but the objectives within the domains are sometimes more detailed and are generally more oriented to tasks and applied knowledge.

A+ Certification Practical Application Domain Areas
1.0 Hardware
2.0 Operating Systems
3.0 Networking
4.0 Security

Page 2   IT Career FastTrack with CompTIA A+ Certification   © 2010 gtslearning

Course Introduction

Course Organization

The course is divided into six **modules**. Each module is organized into several **units** to cover the domain objectives in *both exams*.

This means that when you are preparing for the Essentials exam, you will have studied a little bit *more* than you need to. We feel that this approach makes the topics more readable and easier to understand than would be the case if they were divided between the two sets of exam objectives. It also means that you will already be very well prepared to take the second exam!

There are also a couple of extra modules at the end of the book, which are designed to help you to prepare for the exams (module 7) and start your job search (module 8).

Course Website

Purchasing this book gives you free access to the course support website (www.aplus-fast.com). The website is designed to help you to learn and practice the basic study content found in the modules. At the end of each unit, you should browse the website and complete the extra content associated with that unit. For each unit, you can complete **review questions** to test what you have learned and follow guided **activities** to help to build your practical skills. There is a **glossary** of terms that you can use while reading the book or as a revision aid.

The website also contains **practice tests** to help you in your final preparations to take the CompTIA A+ exams and resources to help you to **search for a job** in PC or IT Support.

To register for the website, visit www.aplus-fast.com and create an account. You will need Internet Explorer 7 or later to browse the site. You will also need Microsoft Word (or other word processing software) and Adobe Reader to access some of the sample resources.

© 2010 gtslearning   IT Career FastTrack with CompTIA A+ Certification   Page 3

Course Introduction

Studying the Course

Each module contains a general introduction to the topics in the domain. The rest of the content, divided into units, is focused on explaining the exam objectives and content examples and telling you what you need to *know* and how you need to *think* to pass the exam and become a good PC technician. Each unit starts with a list of the CompTIA A+ domain objectives and content examples to be covered.

The course website contains links to other websites and articles that you can visit or read to broaden your experience of PC and software technologies. This reading is not essential to passing the exam but you will find it useful, especially to learn about newer products and standards (A+ focuses on well-established technologies rather than the "cutting-edge"). The course website also contains ideas about how to gain practical experience of PC support tasks.

HOME

IT Career FastTrack with CompTIA A+ Certification

CompTIA A+ Certification is the essential qualification for beginning a career in IT Support. In this CompTIA approved course, you will learn everything you need to know about PC support:

- Install and configure PC hardware, such as CPUs, memory, hard disks, and graphics cards.
- Install, configure, and optimize Microsoft Windows.
- Configure printers and networking technologies.
- Troubleshoot PC, printer, and networking problems.
- Understand vital PC and internet security concepts.
- Communicate effectively and professionally with customers.

This fully illustrated course covers every exam objective in the CompTIA A+ syllabus, making it easy for you to learn everything you need to know to pass the CompTIA A+ Essentials and CompTIA A+ Practical Application exams.

www.aplus-fast.com support website

Course Introduction

Getting started

The best way to approach this course, as with most courses, is to *read through* the whole thing quite quickly. On this first reading, do not worry if you cannot recall facts, get two similar technologies mixed up, or do not completely understand some of the topics.

The idea is to get an overview of everything you are going to need to know. The first reading shouldn't take you too long either - a few hours is plenty of time. You don't have to do it at one sitting, but try to complete the read through within about a week.

Making a study plan

When you have completed your first read through, you should make a **study plan**. We've put a sample study plan on the course website, but you'll need to adjust it to account for:

- How much you know about PCs *already*.

- How much *time* you have to study each day or each week.

- *When* you want to (or have to) become A+ Certified.

In your study plan, you'll identify how much time you want to spend on each unit and when you're going to sit down and do that study. We recommend that you study no more than one or two units per day. Studying the unit means reading it closely, making notes about things that come to mind as you read, using the glossary on the course website to look up terms you do not understand, then using the review questions and practical activities on the course website to test and reinforce what you have learned.

Only you can decide how long you need to study for in total. A+ Certification is supposed to represent the knowledge and skills of someone with 500 hours of practical PC support experience. On the course website, we have outlined some ideas for getting hands-on experience. If you cannot get that experience, you will need to do a corresponding amount of study to make up. We have included practice tests for the course; these should give you a good idea of whether you are ready to attempt the exams.

You also need to think about *where* you are going to study. You need to find somewhere comfortable and where you are not subject to interruptions or distractions. You will also need a computer with an internet connection for the review and practical activities.

© 2010 gtslearning   IT Career FastTrack with CompTIA A+ Certification   Page 5

Course Introduction

Preparing for the exams

When you've completed reading the units in detail, you can start to prepare for the Essentials exam. Module 6 and the support website contain tips on booking the test, the format of the exam, and what to expect. The next phase of study will then be to prepare for the Practical Application exam. Module 6 and the notes on the support website will help you to focus on the appropriate parts of the course book.

Course prerequisites

We have made the assumption that you don't know much about how computers or software *work*, but that you do know a little about how to *use* them. You should be able to use a mouse and keyboard and perform typical Windows and PC tasks, such as moving and copying files, using Drag-and-Drop, and browsing the web.

On the course website, you will find a **Prerequisites Test**. If you start reading the book and simply feel lost, take the test and see how you do. If you cannot answer the questions in the test, you should try to read about some more basic PC knowledge before continuing with this course. gtslearning's course book for the **CompTIA Strata** exam is designed to provide this sort of entry-level knowledge.

When working with computers, it also helps to know a little about electricity and mathematics. The introduction chapter provides a very brief overview, with everything you need to know as it relates to A+, but you may need to get your old physics and math school books out to refresh your memory on these subjects. Again, we've put some simple questions in the Prerequisites Test; if you can answer those you should be ready to start studying with this book.

Finding a Job

CompTIA A+ Certification is a great thing to have to prove to employers that you know a lot about PC support, but it is not a golden ticket into employment. To get a job, you need to know where to look, how to write an effective resume and application letter, how to prepare for an interview, and generally how to impress potential employers.

Page 6   IT Career FastTrack with CompTIA A+ Certification   © 2010 gtslearning

Course Introduction

Knowing that this can be just as daunting as sitting down to take the A+ exams, we've put together a guide to doing these things in Module 8 of this book and put resources such as a sample resume and application letter on the course website, to help you get started.

There's also advice on the next steps you might take in your career and an overview of the certification options available to help to progress a career in IT support.

CompTIA Authorized Quality Curriculum Program

This course has been approved under CompTIA's Authorized Quality Curriculum Program (CAQC). The following text is provided by CompTIA in acknowledgement of this.

The logo of the CompTIA Authorized Quality Curriculum Program and the status of this or other training material as "Authorized" under the CompTIA Authorized Quality Curriculum Program signifies that, in CompTIA's opinion, such training material covers the content of CompTIA's related certification exam.

The contents of this training material were created for the CompTIA **A+ Certification Essentials** exam (exam code: **220-701**) and CompTIA **A+ Certification Practical Application** exam (exam code: **220-702**) covering CompTIA certification exam objectives that were current as of **August 7, 2009**.

CompTIA has not reviewed or approved the accuracy of the contents of this training material and specifically disclaims any warranties of merchantability or fitness for a particular purpose. CompTIA makes no guarantee concerning the success of persons using any such "Authorized" or other training material in order to prepare for any CompTIA certification exam.

How to become CompTIA certified

This training material can help you prepare for and pass a related CompTIA certification exam or exams. In order to achieve CompTIA certification, you must register for and pass a CompTIA certification exam or exams.

Course Introduction

In order to become CompTIA certified, you must:

1. Select a certification exam provider. For more information please visit certification.comptia.org/resources/registration.aspx

2. Register for and schedule a time to take the CompTIA certification exam(s) at a convenient location.

3. Read and sign the Candidate Agreement, which will be presented at the time of the exam(s). The text of the Candidate Agreement can be found at certification.comptia.org/resources/candidate_agreement.aspx

4. Take and pass the CompTIA certification exam(s).

For more information about CompTIA's certifications, such as their industry acceptance, benefits, or program news, please visit certification.comptia.org

CompTIA is a not-for-profit information technology (IT) trade association. CompTIA's certifications are designed by subject matter experts from across the IT industry. Each CompTIA certification is vendor-neutral, covers multiple technologies, and requires demonstration of skills and knowledge widely sought after by the IT industry.

To contact CompTIA with any questions or comments, please call (1) (630) 678 8300 or email questions@comptia.org.

Tip

It is CompTIA's policy to update the exam regularly with new test items to deter fraud and for compliance with ISO standards. The exam objectives may therefore describe the current "Edition" of the exam with a date different to that above. Please note that this training material remains valid for the stated exam code, regardless of the exam edition. For more information, please check the FAQs on CompTIA's website (certification.comptia.org/customer_service).

Module 1 Personal Computer Components

This module lists the basic information you need to know about the components of a personal computer; what each component does, how it relates to the other components, and how different models and versions of components compare as regards features and performance.

Personal Computers (PC)

The term **"Personal Computer"** is generally understood to apply to versions of the IBM PC, developed in 1981. The IBM PC was based on a microprocessor (or Central Processing Unit [CPU]) designed by Intel. This is also called the x86 architecture or platform.

While technologies and performance have completely transformed what we know as PCs from the boxes available in 1981, most desktop computers are still based on the IBM PC design and x86 platform.

As this PC platform matured, it came to be associated with use of Microsoft's **Windows operating system** software. Now, hardware and software development for PCs is often done with Windows compatibility in mind.

Mainstream PCs were developed as business machines, with the home computer market dominated by cheaper versions of the microcomputer. Through the 1990s, cost and ease-of-use improved to the point where PCs are mainstream consumer devices used in business, education, and the home.

How a PC works

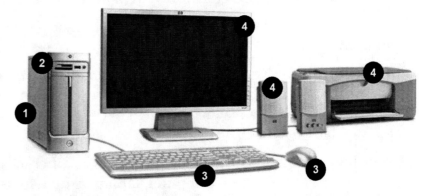

HP Pavilion PC system showing 1) Processing components (within case); 2) Storage components (within case); 3) Input components (keyboard and mouse); 4) Output components (display, speakers, printer)

PCs use *hardware* and *software* components. Hardware components are often classed according to usage (input, output, storage, processing, or network/communications). Software components include the operating system and applications.

A good way to understand the functions of the different components of the PC is to think of them working as *interfaces*. Input and output hardware devices provide an interface between the user and the computer; the operating system provides an interface between hardware components and software applications.

HP Pavilion laptop and peripherals showing how a PC works: 1) Hardware allows the user to interact with the computer; 2) The Operating System provides the interface between hardware and applications; 3) The user creates and modifies files using applications

Essentially, a PC works as follows:

- When a user selects a **command** (perhaps using a mouse to click an icon on the application toolbar), the **software application** receives the command and, using the functions of the **operating system**, converts it into a series of **instructions**, which are stored in **system memory**.

- The **Central Processing Unit (CPU)** retrieves each instruction from memory and processes it.

- The CPU then writes the result back to memory (RAM) and directs other components to perform actions (for example, it may instruct the display subsystem to update the image shown to the user or the storage subsystem to save data to a disk).

PCs for home and office use come in a number of different shapes and sizes. The main types are **desktop computer**, **laptop**, **handheld devices**, and **servers**.

Module 1 Personal Computer Components

Personal Computer Components

PC vendors

PCs and even laptops are a fully commoditized product, meaning that margins are low and vendors must achieve *market share* by differentiating on support and customer service and *profitability* by leveraging economies of scale.

While there are many vendors serving local and special interest markets, globally PC manufacture is dominated by Dell, Hewlett-Packard (HP)/Compaq, Lenovo (previously IBM's PC division), Acer, and Fujitsu/Siemens with Sony, Toshiba, and ASUS also strong in the laptop market.

Another personal computer vendor, Apple, ship Macintosh computers with a different operating system (Apple Mac OS) and (up until 2006) a different hardware platform to the IBM PC-compatible vendors.

Computer data units (binary)

You need to understand the terminology and units used to describe computer storage, signaling, and networking. The following notes will help you to understand binary and hexadecimal notation and the terms used to speak about data size values.

Computers work with *binary* data. The fundamental unit of data storage is the **bit** (binary digit) which can represent 1 or 0. A bit can be measured in multiples using Kilobit (Kb) and Megabit (Mb). However, in terms of today's computers, these values represent tiny amounts. Larger units are more typically used to describe file sizes, memory capacity, and disk storage capacity:

- 8 bits form a byte (B).

- 1024 bytes make a kilobyte (that is 2^{10} bytes).

- 1024 kilobytes (KB) make a Megabyte (MB) or 1,048,576 bytes.

- 1024 MB make 1 Gigabyte (GB) or 1,073,741,824 bytes.

- 1024 GB make 1 Terabyte (TB).

The units listed above conflict with the SI labels for unit multiples. Under the SI system, kilo should mean 1,000, mega should mean 1,000,000, and giga should mean 1,000,000,000. The use of KB to mean 1,204 or GB to mean 1,073,741,824 is shorthand used only in the PC industry.

© 2010 gtslearning   IT Career FastTrack with CompTIA A+ Certification   Page 11

| Module I | Module I Personal Computer Components |

To try to clear this up, a system of labels for binary units has been devised (kibibyte [KiB], mebibyte [MiB], and gibibyte [GiB]). In practice however, no part of the computer industry has taken this distinction on board. Therefore the old units have been used throughout this course book and will be the ones used in the A+ exams. Consequently, you should understand what is generally meant by terms such as MB and GB in different contexts.

- File sizes and memory capacity are always quoted as *binary* measurements. For example, when you see that Windows reports 2 GB memory, this means 2048 MB, *not* 2000 MB.

- Storage capacity is typically quoted by vendors in *decimal* measurements. For example, a hard disk advertised with a capacity of 300 GB has an "actual" capacity of 286 GiB.

You also need to be familiar with values used to talk about transferring data between components or over a network. Data transfer rates are recorded as units per second; for example, bit per second (bps), Megabits per second (Mbps), Megabytes per second (MBps), or Gigabytes per second (GBps). When used to speak about network transfer rates, kilo, mega, and giga are *decimal* measurements. For example, 56 Kbps means 56,000 bits per second *not* 57,344 bits per second.

Hexadecimal notation

It is often necessary to refer to memory or network addresses. To a computer, these addresses are represented as binary values, but because binary has only two values for each position and the values are typically very large, this would require a long string of characters. This is difficult enough to read but even harder to type accurately into configuration dialogs.

Binary values are often converted to decimal but hexadecimal notation is another convenient way of referring to long binary strings. Hexadecimal has 16 characters (0...9 plus A, B, C, D, E, F). Therefore it only takes 1 hexadecimal character to represent 4 binary characters.

For example, the memory address for the component COM2 (a serial port) is 02F8. In binary, this is 0000 0010 1111 1000. Hex notation is therefore much more compact.

The following table summarizes the equivalent representations of decimal values from 1-16 in binary and hex.

Page 12   IT Career FastTrack with CompTIA A+ Certification   © 2010 gtslearning

Module 1 Personal Computer Components

Decimal	Hexadecimal	Binary	Decimal	Hexadecimal	Binary
0	0	0000	8	8	1000
1	1	0001	9	9	1001
2	2	0010	10	A	1010
3	3	0011	11	B	1011
4	4	0100	12	C	1100
5	5	0101	13	D	1101
6	6	0110	14	E	1110
7	7	0111	15	F	1111

Signaling

Another subject you need to understand is how PC components exchange information. Computers transmit data using electrical signals and store it using components called **transistors**. The electrical pathways within the computer or through cabling that carry the signals are referred to as the bus. However, numerous *different* bus technologies have been and are used to build computers. Also, there are many different signaling methods.

Generally speaking, older computer bus types (such as serial and PS/2 ports or VGA display connectors) use a method called **single ended** signaling. Newer buses (such as USB, Firewire, and PCI Express) use **differential** signaling. The advantage of differential signaling is that it allows the use of lower voltages, reducing power consumption and heat.

Another distinction between signaling methods is between parallel and serial communications. Some bus types transfer data in parallel, which means that there are multiple physical wires to carry the signals. While parallel communications were popular for technologies in the 1990s, improved signaling methods mean that bus technologies developed in the last few years use serial communications.

An important characteristic of signaling is the supported frequency (or speed), measured in **hertz** (cycles per second) or, more commonly, megahertz (MHz) or gigahertz (GHz). Finally, signaling can either be digital or analog. Computers use digital signaling, where changes in the electrical signal refer to discrete binary values (ones and zeros). With analog signaling, the signal represents a continuous value. For some types of communication, a computer needs to translate between digital and analog signals (for example, for video or audio signaling on analog equipment).

Module 1   Module 1 Personal Computer Components

Electrical circuits

The last bit of preparatory information you need to master is the fundamental principles of electrical circuits and components. Electricity is the flow of electrons through a conductor. The characteristics of the electricity supply are measured as voltage, current (amperage), resistance, and power.

- **Voltage** - the potential difference between two points (often likened to pressure in a water pipe) measured in Volts (V).

- **Current** - the actual flow of electrons, measured in Amps (I). A current flows in a **circuit**, which is made when conductors from a continuous path between the positive and negative terminals of a power source. The size of the current is determined by the conductivity of the circuit (for example, a larger current can flow in a thicker wire than can in a thinner one).

- **Resistance** - the conductivity of the media, measured in Ohms (Ω or R).

- **Power** - the energy drawn from the supply per second by the device using it, measured in Watts. Power is equal to the Voltage multiplied by the Current (W=V*I).

In a **Direct Current (DC)** circuit, the charge flows in one direction from the positive to negative terminals of the power source at a constant voltage. DC is used for electronic circuits, which require stable voltages. Mains electricity is supplied as **Alternating Current (AC)**, which means that the current flows in both directions around the circuit and the voltage alternates. In the UK, mains power is supplied at 220-240V. In the US, mains power is 110-120V. AC is a cheap way to distribute electrical power over long distances but is incompatible with PC electronics. A **transformer** in the PC's power supply is used to convert AC to DC voltages.

IT Career FastTrack with CompTIA A+ Certification   © 2010 gtslearning

Module 1 Personal Computer Components | *Motherboards*

Unit 1.1 Motherboards

CompTIA A+ Essentials Objectives

☐ **701.1.2 Explain motherboard components, types and features**
Form Factor (ATX / BTX, micro ATX, NLX) • Bus architecture • Bus slots (PCI, AGP, PCIe, AMR, CNR) • PATA (IDE, EIDE) • SATA, eSATA • Chipsets • BIOS / CMOS / Firmware (POST, CMOS battery) • Riser card / daughterboard

Form Factors and System Cases

The **motherboard** (or main board or system board) is a **Printed Circuit Board (PCB)** containing chips, circuitry, connectors, and power regulators. The motherboard provides interfaces for the other components of the computer. The motherboard **form factor** means its size and shape and the location of components on it. When building a system, the motherboard must be matched to a suitable **case** (or **chassis**) and **power supply** of the same form factor.

System case types

There are three types of personal computer case: **desktop, tower**, and **Small Form Factor (SFF)**. The case provides connection points for the motherboard, power supply, and disk drives. Disk drives are fitted into drive bays or drive cages and come in two sizes: 5.25" and 3.5".

Cases can be **full height** or **slimline**. Tower case sizes are **full, mid**, or **mini**. Larger cases support more drive bays and expansion cards. Full tower cases are generally used for servers while mid or mini tower are the most popular choices for PCs. Desktop cases are comparatively rare these days.

SFF cases are semi-portable, space-saving designs typically used for domestic entertainment "Media Center" systems. They are usually cube-like or super slimline. SFF cases can only fit a limited number of components.

Motherboard form factors

There are a great many motherboard manufacturers, including Abit, AOpen (Acer), ASUSTek, Chaintech, Gigabyte, Intel, MSI, Shuttle, Tyan, and Via but most developed boards based on a standard **form factor**.

© 2010 gtslearning | IT Career FastTrack with CompTIA A+ Certification | Page 15

Most motherboards are based on a variant of the **ATX (Advanced Technology eXtended)** form factor, which replaced the obsolete AT design in 1996.

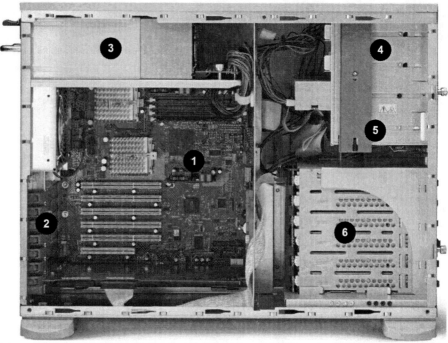

HP Compaq Proliant tower case (cover removed) showing 1) Motherboard; 2) Expansion slots; 3) Power supply; 4) 5.25" Drive bays; 5) Floppy disk drive bay; 6) 3.5" Drive bays (for hard drives)

Shuttle XPC Small Form Factor PC chassis

In 2004, Intel introduced the **BTX (Balanced TX)** specification, designed to reduce heat and be scalable to different sizes. BTX is used by some of the major PC vendors, including HP and Dell, but has not gained wider acceptance (in fact, Intel has suspended development of retail versions of the boards).

The following table summarizes some of the main form factors still in general use:

Standard	WidthxHeight	Description
ATX	12x9.6" 305x244 mm	Full size layout with up to seven expansion slots.
MicroATX	9.6x9.6" 305x244 mm	SFF layout with up to four expansion slots (though can typically be fitted to a standard ATX case).
FlexATX	9x7.5" 229x191 mm	Intel developed addendum to MicroATX.
BTX	12.8x10.5" 325x267 mm	Full size layout with up to seven expansion slots.
MicroBTX	10.4x10.5" 264x267 mm	Supports up to four expansion slots.
NanoBTX	8.8x10.5" 224x267 mm	Up to two expansion slots.
PicoBTX	8x10.5" 203x267 mm	Supports just one expansion slot.
Mini-ITX	6.7x6.7" 170x170 mm	SFF design created by VIA Technologies, supporting one expansion slot. There are also even smaller Nano- and Pico- versions with no support for expansion cards.

Some PC case designs are *slimline*, meaning that there is not enough space for full height expansion cards. This problem is addressed by providing a **riser card** (or **daughter board**) at right-angles to the main board. Historically, the LPX and NLX form factors were designed as riser architectures, but most manufacturers just use the ATX riser card specification (which specifies a 2x11 connector plus a PCI connector for the riser card), a spare PCI connector, or low profile adapter cards.

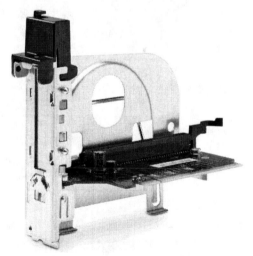

Riser card providing full height PCIe slot for HP Compaq Ultraslim Desktop

You can obtain more information about motherboard form factors at www.formfactors.org.

Unit 1.1   Module 1 Personal Computer Components

Components, Slots, and Sockets

The layout of components on the motherboard is one of the main things that distinguishes different motherboard form factors.

Intel ATX motherboard showing 1) CPU slot; 2) Memory slots; 3) Power connector; 4) PATA connector; 5) Floppy drive connector; 6) SATA connectors; 7) PCI connectors; 8) PCI Express connectors; 9) I/O ports

Compare the position of the CPU socket and memory slots in the ATX specification shown above with the BTX motherboard shown overleaf. The main components of the motherboard are as follows:

- The **processor socket** provides a connection point for a supported CPU[1]. There are several different socket designs. CPUs are covered in unit 1.2.
- **Memory slots** (typically DIMMs) provide connection points for system memory. The number and type of slots determines the type and maximum amount of memory that can be installed. Memory is covered in unit 1.3.

---

[1] Some motherboards may feature two sockets, allowing the use of two CPUs (Symmetric Multiprocessing [SMP]).

Module 1 Personal Computer Components · Motherboards

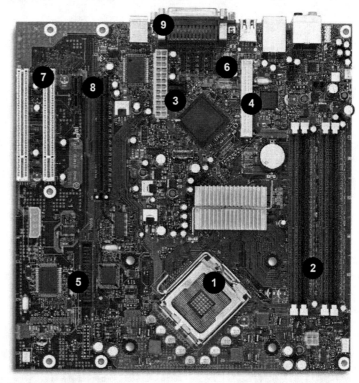

Intel BTX motherboard showing 1) CPU slot; 2) Memory slots; 3) Power connector; 4) PATA connector; 5) Floppy drive connector; 6) SATA connectors; 7) PCI connectors; 8) PCI Express connectors; 9) I/O ports

- The **chipset** provides interfaces between the CPU and the components on the motherboard (see below). It may also provide "onboard" or "integrated" expansion features.

- **Drive controllers** provide interfaces for different types of storage device (see below).

- An **expansion bus** provides the means to install adapter (or expansion) cards to add functionality to the computer (see below).

- **I/O (Input / Output) ports**, such as USB, serial, parallel, and PS/2, provide a point for peripheral devices to be connected to the computer. They are positioned in a standard layout on the motherboard so as to match up to slots or holes in the chassis[2]. The different ports and connectors will be covered in unit 1.5. Additional I/O ports can be added by installing a suitable expansion card.

---

[2] Historically, I/O ports have always been on the back of the case. Newer designs duplicate some ports (such as audio and USB) on the front of the case to make them more accessible to users. Cabling connects the ports to headers on the motherboard.

Unit 1.1   Module 1 Personal Computer Components

Chipset

The **chipset** is circuitry that connects the CPU to the rest of the motherboard.
The chipset is soldered onto the motherboard and cannot be replaced. A
chipset supports a particular range of CPU models only.

> **Tip**
>
> PC CPUs are manufactured by Intel and AMD. Chipsets are manufactured
> by a wider range of vendors, including Intel, Via, SiS, NVIDIA, ATI (now
> owned by AMD), and Broadcom.

The main function of the chipset is *I/O control* between the CPU and
components such as system memory, expansion buses, peripheral ports, and
storage drives.

Another function of the chipset is to provide the **clock signal** that
synchronizes the different components of the PC. The CPU, memory, and
buses can all run at different multiples of the base clock speed. The chipset
also provides the **Real Time Clock** to keep track of the date and time.

Historically, the chipset was split between two microprocessors. The
"northbridge" connects to the CPU via the **Front Side Bus (FSB)**. It provides
the system memory controller and a fast video I/O connection (AGP or PCI
Express). The "southbridge" chip handles slower connections, such as USB,
disk controllers, the expansion buses, and so on[3]. The southbridge may also
provide integrated adapters, such as an audio controller or network
controller[4].

The latest AMD and Intel CPUs feature a memory controller as part of the
CPU chip ("on die") rather than being part of the chipset. Also, components
within the chipset and bus tend to use point-to-point links rather than a
shared bus. AMD refer to this as **Direct Connect Architecture** with
HyperTransport links; Intel call it **QuickPath Interconnect**.

> **Tip**
>
> The key thing to remember is that the chipset determines the model of
> CPU and type of system memory that can be installed plus support for any
> integrated adapters.

---

[3] In later Intel Hub Architecture chipsets, the northbridge is called the Memory Controller Hub or Graphics and
Memory Controller Hub and the southbridge the I/O Controller Hub.

[4] These are called "integrated" adapters because these functions would previously have been provided by installing
an expansion card.

Page 20   IT Career FastTrack with CompTIA A+ Certification   © 2010 gtslearning

Module I Personal Computer Components   *Motherboards*

Cache memory

Cache memory is a small block of fast memory designed to correct
performance imbalances between different computer components (**latency**).
For example, the CPU can work far faster than system memory so, instead of
fetching data from system memory all the time, it stores some data that get
used repetitively in cache memory.

At one point in the history of CPU designs, cache memory could be supplied
as a chip on the motherboard. This is no longer usually the case, except with
some server systems. Nowadays, cache is integrated onto the CPU chip itself
("on die"). There are also different levels of cache (typically 1 and 2). The
CPU's internal architecture determines the way different cache levels are used
to optimize performance (see unit 1.2).

Despite CPU cache disappearing from the motherboard, many other
components feature cache to speed up processing (for example, storage
devices feature cache memory). Also, chipsets can now make use of flash
memory as non-volatile cache to reduce disk access. This has the twin benefits
of being faster and reducing power consumption.

BIOS, CMOS, and firmware

BIOS (Basic Input Output System) is the firmware that starts ("bootstraps") a
PC. **Firmware** refers to software that is embedded in a hardware device. It is
usually stored in **Read Only Memory (ROM)**. This type of memory is *non-
volatile*; that is, it does not require a power source to preserve data.

Note that a PC motherboard is not the only type of computer component that
comes with firmware. Some expansion cards (notably SCSI adapters) and
printers have firmware.

BIOS contains industry standard code that enables the main components of
the PC to communicate and accept user input. It also contains the **Power On
Self Test (POST)** program that runs when the computer is started. This
program checks that all the required components (CPU, graphics adapter,
memory, keyboard) are present and working.

© 2010 gtslearning   IT Career FastTrack with CompTIA A+ Certification   Page 21

One of the other functions of BIOS is to run a low-level setup configuration program. Information entered using this program is stored in a **CMOS (Complementary Metal Oxide Semiconductor) RAM** chip (though the "chip" is more typically part of the southbridge chipset). CMOS is *volatile* memory and so needs to be supplied power by a battery when the computer is switched off. The battery is a coin cell type, which can either be rechargeable (VL or ML models) or non-rechargeable (CR, BR, or DR).

We'll look more closely at functions of BIOS and configuring CMOS Setup when it comes to troubleshooting PC startup (unit 4.5).

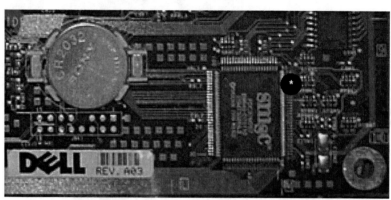

CMOS coin cell battery (non-rechargeable CR2032 lithium battery)

Expansion Bus

A **bus** is the circuitry that connects the various microprocessors (chips) and other components on the motherboard. If you look closely at a motherboard, you will see many tiny wires; this is the circuitry that makes up a bus imprinted on the **Printed Circuit Board (PCB)** that is the basis of a motherboard (there are actually multiple layers of circuitry in addition to what you can see on the surface). A bus carries four things:

- **Data** - the information being transferred between components.
- **Address** information - where the data is located in memory.
- **Timing** signal - as different components can work at different speeds, the system clock synchronizes the way they communicate over the bus.
- **Power** - electricity to run the component.

A PC system has two or three main types of bus: the system bus, the expansion bus, and a dedicated video bus.

- The **system** bus (also referred to as the **Front Side Bus [FSB]** or **local bus**) provides connections between the CPU and system memory.

Module I Personal Computer Components   *Motherboards*

- The **expansion** bus (also called the **Input / Output [I/O]** bus) provides connections between the CPU and add-on components, which can be integrated onto the motherboard, installed as expansion cards, or connected as peripheral devices.

- The **video** bus provides a faster connection between the CPU and the graphics adapter and the graphics adapter and system memory than would be possible with the expansion bus.

The architecture of the bus depends on what generation the motherboard and CPU platform are[5]. The oldest type of PC bus is **Industry Standard Architecture (ISA),** which has been obsolete for some years[6]. Broadly speaking, since 1993, PC architecture has been based on one of PCI, PCI with AGP, and latterly PCI Express (PCIe) with legacy support for PCI.

PCI bus

The **Peripheral Component Interconnect (PCI)** bus was designed to replace the 16-bit ISA AT bus. PCI was introduced in 1993 but gained widespread adoption with the introduction of Intel's 32-bit Pentium processor and Microsoft's Windows 95 operating system. Information about PCI standards (including AGP and PCIe) is published at www.pcisig.org.

PCI supports up to 5 devices (though each device can have up to 8 different functions) and allocates **system resources** using **Plug-and-Play**[7]. Bandwidth on the PCI bus is *shared* between all devices, which use bus mastering and arbitration to determine which component has "control" of the bus at any time.

The first commercial version of PCI (2.0) worked at 33 MHz, meaning that it could support a maximum transfer rate of 133 MBps (32 bits multiplied by 33.3 MHz and divided by 8 to get units in megabytes). The mainstream version (2.1), released in 1995, introduced 64-bit data transfers and 66 MHz signaling (up to 533 MBps). 64-bit cards and slots were more widely used on server systems than on desktop PCs though[8]. A 32-bit card can be installed in a 64-bit slot.

---

[5] CPUs that introduce a new internal architecture are said to be of a new generation. CPUs from Intel and AMD also have different architectures.

[6] You may see ISA expansion slots on older machines (two are shown unlabelled on the ATX motherboard picture earlier). They are usually colored black and distinctively larger than any other type of expansion slot.

[7] System resources allow the device to signal the CPU (using an interrupt or IRQ) and the CPU to address the device, using a specified location in memory. Prior to Plug-and-Play, these settings had to be configured manually using device jumpers (switches) or software.

[8] A variant of PCI technology (PCI-X) was developed for use on server systems. It uses 3.3V signaling only and supports clock speeds of 66, 133, 266, and 533 MHz. Do not confuse PCI-X with PCI Express (PCIe).

© 2010 gtslearning   IT Career FastTrack with CompTIA A+ Certification   Page 23

> **Note**
> As with other quoted transfer rates, these are the maximum possible peak transfer rates. The sustained transfer rate would be a lot lower. Also, remember that PCI bus bandwidth is *shared* between all connected devices.

PCI 2.1 also specified lower voltage (3.3V) signaling. PCI 2.1 cards can support either 5V or 3.3V or both (**universal PCI**). Support for 5V-only signaling was dropped in version 2.3 (2002). The type of signaling for a slot or adapter is identified by the position of a "key" (a gap with no connector pins).

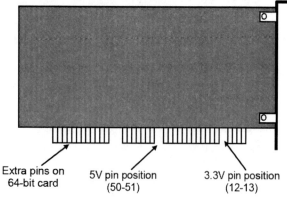

PCI card form factors; universal cards and connectors have both keys

PCI connectors are typically color-coded either white or yellow.

AGP

The fact that the bandwidth of PCI is shared meant that it soon became a performance bottleneck when PCs started to be used for multimedia applications and games demanding 3D graphics. The **Accelerated Graphics Port (AGP)** was released in 1997 to circumvent PCI by providing direct connections between the CPU, system memory, and graphics adapter.

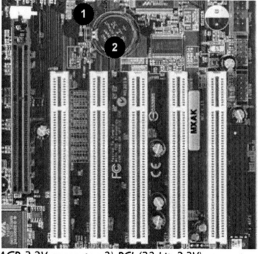

AGP graphics card and motherboard showing 1) AGP 3.3V connector; 2) PCI (32-bit, 3.3V) connectors

Several AGP standards have been introduced over the years:

Standard	Type	Effective Speed[9]	Max Transfer Rate	Other Notes
AGP 1.0	AGP 1x	32-bit @ 66 MHz	266 MBps	3.3V signaling
	AGP 2x	32-bit @ 133 MHz	533 MBps	
AGP 2.0[10]	AGP 4x	32-bit @ 266 MHz	1066 MBps	1.5V signaling
AGP 3.0	AGP 8x	32-bit @ 533 MHz	2133 MBps	0.8V signaling

Unless both card and connector support universal signaling, the card's signaling must be matched to the slot (1.5V and 0.8V are interchangeable though). Cards and connectors are keyed to prevent incorrect insertion.

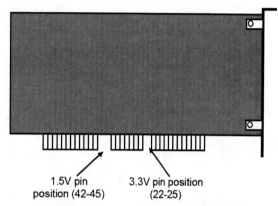

Key positions for AGP; universal <u>cards</u> have **both** keys but universal <u>connectors</u> have **neither** key

> **Note**
> The use of keys on cards and connectors is not always reliable for AGP (some cards and motherboards were incorrectly manufactured). Check the documentation for the card and motherboard carefully.

The AGP connector is typically color-coded brown or maroon.

---

[9] AGP speeds are synchronized to the PCI bus speed (66 MHz) but "pumped" or "strobed" meaning that data is transferred more than once on each clock cycle. The clock speeds quoted in the table are therefore *effective* speeds. Standards documentation has started to use the units Megatransfers per second (MT/s) in place of MHz to quote these speeds.

[10] AGP Pro is an adaptation of AGP 4x for high-end CAD (Computer Aided Design) cards that require more power. Pro50 and Pro110 deliver up to 50 and 110 watts of power respectively (compared to the usual 25W). AGP Pro slots are larger than normal and require extra space on either side for cooling. Ordinary AGP cards can be fitted in Pro slots (subject to the signaling restrictions listed above) but Pro cards do not fit in standard slots.

AMR and CNR

Intel's **Audio/Modem Riser (AMR)** slots were designed to overcome the expense and difficulty of supporting sound and modem functions directly on the motherboard or using separate PCI slots.

The updated specification (**Communications Network Riser [CNR]**) adds support for a network adapter, Plug-and-Play, and USB. A rival interface (**Advanced Communication Riser [ACR]**) also adds support for wireless connections and is backwards compatible with AMR.

Support for the slots is patchy compared to PCI. Most motherboard manufacturers preferred to integrate sound and network functions on the board and provide modems as plug-in cards or external units.

CNR slot

PCIe bus

As CPU and memory bus speeds increased over the years, PCI represented a substantial bottleneck to computer performance. PCI and AGP are both *parallel* interfaces. Parallel interface speeds are limited by the problem of timing each signal (**data skew**). They are also more complex and costly to implement. Another performance barrier is the fact that the bandwidth of the PCI bus is *shared* between all the components connected to it and only one component can make use of the bus at any one time. This is a particular problem for video, disk access, and networking.

Various fixes were implemented to remove critical bottlenecks (such as using AGP for graphics or providing dedicated southbridge links for drive controllers or networking). These fixes added to the complexity of chip design and over time the PCI bus simply became inadequate.

PCI Express (PCIe) was released by Intel in 2004 as the replacement for the PCI/AGP architecture. PCIe uses point-to-point *serial* communications, meaning that each component can have a dedicated connection to any other component. Connections are made via a **switch**, which routes data between components and can provide **Quality of Service (QoS)** to any component that needs it (for example, to prioritize real-time video over non-time critical data).

Each point-to-point connection is referred to as a **link**. The link sends both data and control and timing instructions. A link can make use of one or more **lanes**. Each lane consists of two wire pairs (four wires in total) using low voltage differential signaling. One pair is used to transmit and the other to receive (bi-directional). A given component can support a specific number of lanes (x1, x2, x4, x8, x16, or x32) and the switch negotiates the maximum possible number of lanes to use (for example, a x16 device could only use 8 lanes to communicate with a x8 device).

Each lane supports a transfer rate of 250 MBps in each direction[11]. A x32 link therefore supports up to 8 GBps in each direction. A x8 link is roughly equivalent to AGP 8x. Most graphics cards use x16 links (4 GBps in each direction).

A card will fit in any connector with an equal or greater number of lanes. For example, a x8 card will fit in a x8 or x16 socket, but *not* in a x1 or x4 socket.

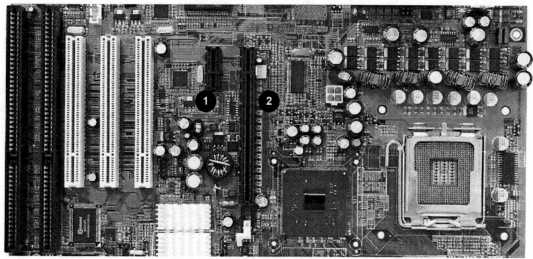

Motherboard with 1) x1 PCIe connector; 2) x16 PCIe connector

As well as providing an expansion bus, PCIe is used for local bus connections under Intel architectures[12]. PCIe is software-compatible with PCI, meaning that PCI connectors can be included on a motherboard (to support legacy adapter cards) but PCI cards *cannot* be fitted into PCIe sockets.

---

[11] The current version of the standard is 1.1. PCIe 2.0 (released in 2007) specifies a 500 MBps base transfer rate. PCIe 2.0 is backward compatible with PCIe 1.1.

[12] AMD-based systems use the rival Direct Connect architecture with HyperTransport links between components. However, AMD chipsets also support PCIe connectors for graphics and other expansion cards.

PCIe can supply up to 75W to a device via the motherboard slot. An extra 75W power (as is typically required by graphics adapters) can be supplied via a 6-pin PCIe power connector (150W-ATX 1.0 Specification[13]). PCIe also features power management functions and support for hot swappable and hot pluggable adapters[14].

HP PCIe video (x16 slot) and LAN (x1 slot) cards

PCI Express 2.0 compatible motherboards and adapters support transfer rates of 500 MBps per lane. Version 2.0 motherboards and adapters are interchangeable with earlier version 1.1 devices, though the added performance benefits are only realized if both components support 2.0. Version 2.0 allows for slots with a smaller *footprint* than previously (a 2.0 x8 slot delivers the same performance as a 1.1 x16 slot).

PCIe 2.0 also specifies a power draw from the slot of up to 150W and an 8-pin auxiliary power connector delivering another 150W.

Drive Controllers

Drive controllers provide a connection point for internal **mass storage devices**, such as hard drives, CD/DVD drives, and tape drives. The interface between the drive, controller, and the rest of the system is a type of bus. There are three main bus standards for attaching internal storage devices to a PC: EIDE/PATA, SATA, and SCSI.

---

[13] Some top-end cards requiring more than 150W use two extra connectors.

[14] A hot pluggable card can be added when the system is active but cannot be removed until the system is shut down. A hot swappable card can be added or removed while the system is powered up. Note that not many desktop cards actually support hot plugging or hot swapping. This technology is usually a feature of devices designed for servers.

Parallel ATA

The **Parallel Advanced Technology Attachment (PATA)** interface was the principal interface for desktop PCs for many years[15].

Most PCs supporting PATA come with two drive controllers (IDE1 and IDE2, or primary [PRI IDE] and secondary [SEC IDE]). A single controller is now more typical if the motherboard also supports SATA. Each controller supports two devices (**master** and **slave**).

IDE connectors on the motherboard - note the labels printed to the right of the connectors

A PATA drive features a 40-pin port. PATA cabling typically has three connectors. Shielded cables have 80 wires and are required for UDMA4 or better transfer modes (see below). PATA cable is supposed to be up to 45 cm (18") long. Most new cables are "Cable Select", allowing the master and slave device to be identified by the use of a color-coded connector (rather than setting jumpers on the device itself).

PATA has supported a number of standards over the years. The following table lists non-obsolete ATA standards[16]:

Interface Standard	DMA Mode[17]	Maximum Transfer Rate	Special Features
ATA/ATAPI-4	UDMA 0, 1, 2 (UDMA-33)	33 MBps	Ultra DMA, 80 conductor cable, and Cyclic Redundancy Checking
ATA/ATAPI-5	UDMA 3, 4 (UDMA-66)	66 MBps	
ATA/ATAPI-6	UDMA 5 (UDMA-100)	100 MBps	48-bit LBA expansion[18] and disk noise reduction
ATA/ATAPI-7	UDMA 6 (UDMA-133)	133 MBps	Multimedia streaming, SATA 1.0 (see below)

Regardless of the interface, PATA connections are limited to the throughput of the PCI bus.

---

[15] The interface was (and still is) also referred to as IDE (Integrated Drive Electronics) or EIDE (Extended IDE).

[16] ATAPI stands for ATA Packet Interface and is an extension to ATA to support CD/DVD drives and tape drives.

[17] DMA (Direct Memory Access) mode refers to the way that data is transferred to and from system memory.

[18] In the early days of the EIDE interface, BIOS versions severely restricted maximum drive capacity. 32-bit driver software in the OS now handles drive addressing. Logical Block Addressing (LBA) is a method of telling the drive how to address a particular place on the disk surface. 48-bit LBA supports drives up to a (theoretical) 144 Petabytes. Windows 2000 must be patched to SP3 to use 48-bit addressing (otherwise the maximum partition size is limited to 137 GB).

SATA

Serial ATA (SATA) was developed to address the limitations of PATA. It is now the most popular means of attaching internal hard drives, though other types of device (such as DVD drives or tape drives) are not well-established, meaning that most motherboards retain at least one PATA controller.

4 SATA motherboard connectors in front of an IDE connector on an Intel D945 motherboard

As the name suggests, SATA transfers data in *serial* format. This allows for thinner, longer, more flexible cables (up to 1m [39"]) with smaller, 7-pin connectors. Each port supports a single device.

SATA cable for HP workstations

The original SATA standard (1.5 or SATA/150) supports speeds of up to 150 MBps. This standard was quickly augmented by SATA 3.0 (or SATA/300), which specifies a 300 MBps transfer rate (well beyond what is actually possible with current drive technologies).

There is also an **eSATA** standard for the attachment of external drives, with a 2m (78") cable. The main drawback of eSATA compared to a dedicated peripheral bus such as USB or Firewire is that power is not supplied over the cable. This is not so much of an issue for 3.5" drives, which require a separate power supply anyway, but limits the usefulness of eSATA for 2.5" portable drives.

More information on SATA standards can be obtained from www.sata-io.org.

SCSI

The **Small Computer System Interface (SCSI)** has been in use as an expansion bus since the 1980s. There have been many revisions to the standard. While SCSI supports any type of internal or external device (including scanners, printers, and CD drives), it is most commonly used as a hard disk interface, particularly on server systems. The main advantages of SCSI over PATA are higher transfer rates and support for a larger number of devices. Like PATA, the older types of SCSI are parallel interfaces. The main SCSI standards and configuration issues are summarized below.

Interface Protocol	Bus Speed Max	Bus Width (bits)	Max Cable Length (m) Single-ended	LVD	HVD	Devices per Bus
SCSI-1	5 MBps	8	6	12	25	8
Fast SCSI	10 MBps	8	3	12	25	8
Fast-Wide SCSI	20 MBps	16	3	12	25	16
Ultra SCSI	20 MBps	8	1.5	12	25	8
Wide Ultra SCSI	40 MBps	16	-	12	25	16
Ultra2 SCSI	40 MBps	8	-	12	25	8
Wide Ultra2 SCSI	80 MBps	16	-	12	25	16
Ultra3 (160) SCSI	160 MBps	16	-	12	-	16
Ultra320 SCSI	320 MBps	16	-	12	-	16

- Host adapter - SCSI can be implemented via a host adapter card connected to a PCI, PCI-X, or PCIe slot or as a host adapter integrated onto the motherboard. The host adapter must be installed and recognized by the system for drives to be detected.

- Signaling - SCSI specifies three signaling methods. Most buses and devices use LVD (Low Voltage Differential). SE (Single Ended) devices can be added to an LVD bus, but it reduces the performance of the whole bus. H(igh)VD is incompatible with the other two and must not be mixed with them.

- Connectors - there are numerous SCSI connectors. The most common are 68-pin High Density (HD) internal and external connectors or 80-pin Single Connector Attachments (SCA), which incorporate a power connector and configuration wires, allowing for hot swappable drives.

Internal (left) and external HD connectors

- Termination - a SCSI bus must be terminated at both ends by enabling termination on the first and last devices in the chain. Termination may either be enabled internally on the device by setting a switch or by physically connecting a terminator pack to a device or the host adapter[19].

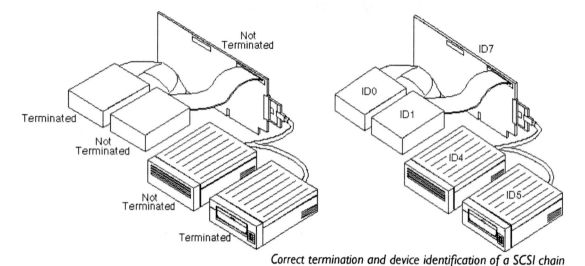

Correct termination and device identification of a SCSI chain

- ID - each SCSI device must be allocated a unique ID, from 0 to 7 (or 15 for wide SCSI). IDs may be allocated automatically or by setting a jumper or click-wheel on the device itself. The order of SCSI ID priorities (from highest to lowest) is 7 through to 0 then 15 through to 8.

Tip

Firewire (see unit 1.5) is a type of serial SCSI. **Serial Attached SCSI (SAS)** is also very popular in the sever market. It supports over 16,000 devices, offers point-to-point links (as opposed to shared bandwidth), has no termination issues, and supports higher bandwidths (up to 3 Gbps).

---

[19] There are passive and active terminators. Passive terminators are generally used with older devices (pre-Ultra SCSI). When installing a terminator pack, the terminator must match the signaling type (SE, LVD, HVD, or SE/LVD). Termination is also made more complex if there is a mix of narrow (8-bit) and wide (16-bit) devices on the bus.

Summary

The motherboard form factor (ATX, BTX, or small form factor) and components determine the compatibility of all the other components (including chassis, power supply, CPU, memory, and support for expansion cards). The motherboard chipset provides memory and I/O controllers plus any integrated adapters (such as sound and video) and ports (such as USB, parallel, serial, and network). The chipset and connectors provide support for different I/O bus (PCI, PCIe, and AGP) and disk standards (PATA, SATA, and SCSI).

Tip

To review what you have learned in this chapter, you should now visit the course website. This contains review questions and bonus material to help you to learn more and practice the topics covered in this unit.

Practical Activities

You should try to acquire a good understanding of the market for PC components. While the latest technologies do not always appear on the A+ exams, you need to be able to keep up-to-date with new developments.

The best place to do this of course is using the web or by subscribing to one of the many magazines devoted to PC and portable technologies. Some good examples include:

- PC World - venerable magazine dedicated to personal computing.
- PC Magazine - long-standing magazine with a business focus (published by Ziff Davis).
- Wired - devoted to new technologies.
- Slashdot - "open source" news and forum.

Visit the support site to test what you have learned and complete practical activities

| Unit 1.2 | Module 1 Personal Computer Components |

Unit 1.2 Processors

CompTIA A+ Essentials Objectives

☐ **701.1.2 Explain motherboard components, types and features**
Processor sockets • Chipsets

☐ **701.1.4 Explain the purpose and characteristics of CPUs and their features**
Identify CPU types (AMD, Intel) • HyperThreading • Multi core (Dual core, Triple core, Quad core) • On-chip cache (L1, L2) • Speed (real vs. actual) • 32bit vs. 64 bit

Processor Generations

A **microprocessor** (usually shortened to "processor") is a programmable **integrated circuit (IC)**. An IC is a silicon chip embedded on a ceramic plate. A silicon chip is a wafer of purified silicon doped with a metal oxide (typically copper or aluminum). The doping process creates millions of transistors and signal pathways within an area called the **die**, which provide the electrical on/off states that are the basis of binary computer systems.

The process used to create the transistors is referred to as an n-micron or n-nanometer (nm) process, reflecting the size of the *features* (a transistor for instance) that can be created. A micron is a millionth of a meter; a nanometer is a billionth of a meter. This process has developed over 20 years from 1 micron to 0.065 micron (or 65nm). Scaling down the process allows reduced voltages and therefore more speed with less heat. It also allows more components to be added to the package, which has enabled innovations such as on-die cache and multi-core CPUs.

PCs contain a number of processors, but the most important is the **Central Processing Unit (CPU)**. The CPU is commonly described as the "brains" of a computer; in fact, it is better thought of as a very efficient sorting office. The CPU cannot *think*, but it can process instructions very, very quickly and efficiently. A computer is only as "clever" as its software. There have been numerous CPU architectures, developed by the vendors **Intel** and **AMD**, and, within each architecture, a number of different models. The following table represents the generations of Intel and AMD desktop CPU models[20] and when they were introduced:

---

[20] The model names are used to market a CPU to consumers, but a model may go through several different versions. The "core" used for a version is given a codename, such as "Prescott", "Smithfield", or "Clawhammer". You will see these names used on PC tech websites and in magazines.

Page 34   IT Career FastTrack with CompTIA A+ Certification   © 2010 gtslearning

Module 1 Personal Computer Components | Processors

Time	Intel	AMD	Bus Speeds	Clock Speeds
1978-1989	1st-3rd generation (8086, 2086, 3086)		5-40 MHz	5-40 MHz
1989 - 1993	4th generation (486)	AMD486	25-50 MHz	25-120 MHz
1993 - 1997	5th generation (Pentium, Pentium MMX)	K5	60-66 MHz	75-233 MHz
1996 - 1999	6th generation (P6 [Pentium Pro], Pentium II, Pentium III, Celeron)	K6, K6-2, K7 (Athlon, Duron)	66-133 MHz	150-1400 MHz
2000 - 2005	7th generation ("NetBurst") (Pentium 4, Pentium D, Pentium 4 EE, Celeron)	Athlon XP, Athlon MP, Athlon XP-M	400-1066 MHz[21]	1.3-3.8 GHz
2003 -		K8 (Athlon 64, Turion 64, Sempron, Opteron)	800-1000 MHz	1.4-3.0 GHz
2006 -	8th generation (Core, Core 2, Celeron, Xeon)		800-1333 MHz	1.8-3.0 GHz
2009-	9th generation (Atom, Core i3, i5, i7)	10th generation (Phenom, Phenom II, Athlon II)	1.6-2.5 GHz	1.8-3.4 GHz

CPU Features

The CPU is designed to run software programs. When a software program runs (whether it be an operating system, BIOS firmware, anti-virus utility, or word processing application) it is assembled into instructions utilizing the fundamental **instruction set** of the CPU and loaded into system memory. The CPU then performs the following operations on these instructions:

- The **Control Unit** fetches the next instruction in sequence from system memory to the **pipeline**.

- The control unit decodes each instruction from the pipeline in turn and either executes it itself or passes it to the **Arithmetic Logic Unit (ALU)** or **Floating Point Unit (FPU)** for execution.

---

[21] From this point on, the bus is "quad-pumped", meaning data is transferred four times per clock cycle, or uses point-to-point links. The units Megatransfers per second (MT/s) sometimes replace the inaccurate use of MHz.

© 2010 gtslearning   IT Career FastTrack with CompTIA A+ Certification   Page 35

Unit 1.2   Module 1 Personal Computer Components

- The result of the executed instruction is written back to a **register** or to system memory. A register is a temporary storage area available to the different units within the CPU.

This overview is grossly simplified of course. Over the years, many different internal architectures have been developed to optimize the process of fetch, decode, execute, and writeback, while retaining compatibility with the basic x86 instruction set, which defines a CPU as IBM PC compatible.

HyperThreading

One way to make instruction execution more efficient is to improve the way the pipeline works. The basic approach is to do the most amount of work possible in a single clock cycle (**multitasking**). There are various ways to achieve this goal though.

CPUs process multiple instructions at the same time (for example, while one instruction is fetched, another is being decoded, another is being executed, and another is being written back to memory). This is referred to as a **superscalar** architecture, as multiple execution units are required. Superscalar architectures also feature longer pipelines with multiple stages but shorter actions (micro-ops) at each stage, referred to as **superpipelining**. The original Pentium has a 5-stage pipeline; by contrast, the Pentium 4 has up to *31* stages (NetBurst architecture). NetBurst actually proved relatively inefficient in terms of power and thermal performance, so Intel reverted to a modified form of the P6 architecture it used in Pentium IIs and IIIs for its current Core and Core 2 CPUs (with around 14 stages).

Another approach (introduced on some Pentium 4 models) is **Simultaneous Multithreading (SMT)**, called **HyperThreading** by Intel. A **thread** is a stream of instructions generated by a software application **process**. Most applications run a single process in a single thread; software that runs multiple parallel threads within a process is said to be **multithreaded**. SMT allows the threads to run through the CPU at the same time. It duplicates many of the registers of the CPU. This reduces the amount of "idle time" the CPU spends waiting for new instructions to process. To the OS, it *seems* as though there are two CPUs installed.

The main drawback of SMT is that it works best with multithreaded software. As this software is more difficult to design, it tends to be restricted to programs designed to run on servers. Most desktop applications software cannot take full advantage.

Page 36   IT Career FastTrack with CompTIA A+ Certification   © 2010 gtslearning

Module 1 Personal Computer Components   *Processors*

HyperThreading was implemented on premium models in the Pentium 4 range but is not used on the Intel's Core 2 chips. It has however been *reintroduced* as a feature of Core i7 and Atom processors from Intel.

Microcode improvements

Another approach to improving CPU efficiency is to *extend* the basic instruction set. Many applications (such as games, video decompression, or speech recognition) make repetitive use of the same *instructions* with different *data*. Intel and AMD both introduced instruction set extensions to support this kind of **Single Instruction, Multiple Data (SIMD)** programming:

- MMX - supported by Intel (Pentium MMX and later) and AMD (K6 and later) CPUs.

- 3DNow! - supported by AMD K6-2 and later processors.

- SSE (Streaming SIMD Extensions) - supported by Intel Pentium III and AMD Athlon XP CPUs. The original version has been updated several times (SSE2, SSE3, and SSE4).

In all cases, software needs to be specifically developed to take advantage of the microcode.

Multiprocessing and dual-core

Yet another approach to making a computer system faster is to use two or more physical CPUs, referred to as **Symmetric Multiprocessing (SMP)**. A SMP-aware OS can then make efficient use of the processing resources available to run application processes on whichever CPU is "available". This approach is not dependent on software *applications* being multithreaded to deliver performance benefits.

Traditionally, SMP was provided by physically installing two or more CPUs in a multi-socket motherboard. Obviously, this adds significantly to the cost and so is only implemented on servers and high-end workstations.

However, improvements in CPU manufacturing techniques have led to another solution: dual-core CPUs (or **Chip Level Multiprocessing [CMP]**). A dual-core CPU is essentially two processors combined on the same die.

© 2010 gtslearning   IT Career FastTrack with CompTIA A+ Certification   Page 37

The market has quickly moved beyond dual-core CPUs to **multi-core** packages with 3, 4, or 8 processors. For desktop computing however, the performance benefits of multi-core are unlikely to increase dramatically unless backed up by improved software design.

Cores	Intel	AMD
2	Core Duo, Core 2 Duo, Core i3, i5, Xeon, Celeron, Pentium D	X2 models of Athlon 64, Sempron, Turion 64, Phenom, Phenom II, and Opteron
3		X3 models of Athlon II, Phenom, Phenom II
4	Core 2 Quad, Core i5, i7, Xeon	X4 models of Athlon II, Phenom, Phenom II, and Opteron
6		Opteron
8	Xeon	

Tip

Dual-core is not quite the same as SMP and software has to be specially written or updated to take advantage of the architecture. Only Windows XP SP2 and Vista provide full support. Running Windows 2000 on a dual-core system will not realize the full potential of the processor.

Instruction set (32- versus 64-bit)

The instruction set used by IBM PC compatible CPUs is called **x86-32** or **IA-32** (Intel Architecture). As described above, this has been extended with SIMD instructions and the way the instructions are processed internally has been modified and optimized by various different CPU architectures, but otherwise the same platform has been in use for the last 30 years[22]. Most CPUs are optimized to run 32-bit code. This means that each instruction can be up to 32-bits in length. A 32-bit CPU's **General Purpose (GP)** registers are also 32-bits wide[23]. However, since 2004, most desktop CPUs (and from 2006, most mobile CPUs) released to the market have been capable of running 64-bit code.

Intel first developed a 64-bit instruction set for its Itanium server CPU platform in 2001. This platform (IA-64) has never gained acceptance in the PC market.

---

[22] IA-32 updated the 16-bit x86 instruction set, first launched in 1978.

[23] Note that 32-bit Pentium-compatible CPUs feature additional larger registers for floating point calculations (80-bit) and SIMD processing (64- or 128-bit). They also feature a 64-bit *data bus*. It is the **GP register** size that makes a CPU 32- or 64-bit.

Module I Personal Computer Components   *Processors*

AMD's 64-bit instruction set (AMD64) has proved more popular and was adopted by Intel for its 64-bit desktop and mobile line. Intel refers to it as EM64T or IA-64. The same instruction set is also called x86-64 or x64.

Despite the availability of the hardware and 64-bit operating systems, the vast majority of installed desktop OS and applications software is 32-bit and this situation seems likely to persist for some time.

Cache

Complex superscalar architecture depends on routines that predict which instructions will be used repeatedly and in what sequence. If these instructions are readily available to the control unit, overall throughput is greatly enhanced. Fetching instructions from system memory is relatively slow, so CPU designs incorporate at least two levels of **cache memory** to trace and store instructions. This reduces the **latency** of fetching instructions from system memory. Level 1 cache is a small block (typically around 64 KB); level 2 cache is larger (between 512 KB and 2 MB).

Cache design becomes even more important with multi-core CPUs as multiple components are contending for use of a single resource (system memory). At each level, cache can either be **discrete** (available to one core only) or **shared** (available to all cores) depending on the processor model.

Clock speed and overclocking

Despite the architectural features discussed above, the *speed* at which the CPU runs is generally seen as a key indicator of performance. This is certainly true when comparing CPUs with the same architecture but is not necessarily the case otherwise. Core CPUs run slower than Pentium 4s, but deliver better performance. The *core clock speed* is the speed at which the CPU runs internal processes and accesses L1 and L2 cache[24]. The **Front Side Bus** speed is the interface between the CPU and system memory.

Overclocking increases the clock speed, improving performance. When a manufacturer releases a new chip, it sets an optimum clock speed based on systems testing. This clock speed will be set at a level where damage to the chip is not likely to occur during normal operation.

---

[24] L2 cache access speed actually depends on the CPU architecture but full-speed access to L2 cache has been standard for some years.

© 2010 gtslearning   IT Career FastTrack with CompTIA A+ Certification   Page 39

Unit 1.2   Module 1 Personal Computer Components

Increasing this speed (overclocking) is done using CMOS Setup by adjusting the **CPU Speed** or **Advanced Chipset Features** properties[25]. Increasing the clock speed requires more power and generates more heat. Therefore, an overclocked system must have a suitable power supply and sufficient cooling. The operating environment (the warmth of the room and build-up of dust) must also be quite carefully controlled.

Overclocking is generally performed by hobbyists and games enthusiasts but it is also a means to build a PC more cheaply by specifying lower cost components then boosting their performance.

Without cooling, overclocking increases the risk of thermal damage to components and may increase the frequency of system lockups. It also invalidates the warranty. OEM (Original Equipment Manufacturer) PC and laptop vendors generally try to prevent overclocking by disabling custom settings in the computer's CMOS Setup program so overclocking can only typically be done with retail versions of the motherboard.

Addressing

The system bus between the CPU and memory consists of a *data* bus and an *address* bus. The width of the data bus (64-bit on all current CPUs) determines how much data can be transferred per clock cycle; the width of the address bus determines how many memory locations the PC can access.

The address bus for most 32-bit CPUs is either 32- or 36-bits wide. A 32-bit address bus can access a 4 GB address space; 36-bit expands that to 64 GB. In theory, a 64-bit CPU could implement a 64-bit address space (64 Exabytes). In practice, the current generation of x64 CPUs are "restricted" to 40-bit address spaces (1 TB) to reduce the complexity of compatibility with 32-bit software.

Power management (throttling)

Rising energy costs and environmental legislation are placing power efficiency at the top of the agenda for IT buyers. In terms of CPU performance, more speed means greater power consumption and heat production. To deal with this, CPUs can implement power management to enter lower power states, referred to as **throttling**.

---

[25] You can either increase the core clock speed (multiplier) or the FSB speed (overclocking the memory chips) or both.

Module I Personal Computer Components   Processors

Intel chips implement throttling using their **SpeedStep** technology. The original version simply allowed high and low frequency modes. **Enhanced SpeedStep** allows the CPU to step up or down through a range of voltages. See unit 2.5 for details on configuring power management.

Another aspect of power management is protection for the CPU. If a processor runs too hot, the system can become unstable or damage can occur. Some Intel CPUs provide Thermal Monitor (TM) modes, triggered by a temperature gauge (the activation point depends on the processor, but tends to be around 50-65°C). Intel CPUs work in one of two modes, depending on the age of the model:

- TM1 (SpeedStep) - the CPU inserts idle cycles between instructions (implemented on early Pentium 4 models).

- TM2 (Enhanced SpeedStep) - the CPU lowers the actual clock speed (used on later P4s and current mobile and desktop CPUs).

Power management on AMD CPUs is referred to as **PowerNow!** (mobile CPUs) or **Cool'n'Quiet** (desktop CPUs).

Virtualization support

Virtualization software allows a single computer to run multiple operating systems (or Virtual Machines [VM]). Intel's Virtualization Technology (VT) and AMD's AMD-V provide processor extensions to support virtualization. This makes the VMs run much more quickly.

These extensions are usually features of premium models in a given processor range.

Malware protection

Computer viruses (and other malware) can use various techniques to infect a computer. One is a so-called buffer overflow attack, where the virus "tricks" another program into executing it when the other program thinks it is just processing some data.

CPUs and operating systems supporting AMD's **No Execute (NX)** technology are more resilient to this type of attack because they prevent areas in memory marked for data storage from executing code (running a new program). Intel call this feature **Execute Disable (XD)**; in Windows, it is referred to as **Data Execution Prevention (DEP)**.

© 2010 gtslearning   IT Career FastTrack with CompTIA A+ Certification   Page 41

Intel CPUs

Intel developed the first x86 processors and continues to be most closely associated with PC CPUs.

Legacy Intel processors

Intel CPU models go back to 1978 (the 8088) but one of the most significant developments was the 5th generation Socket 7 Pentium, introduced in 1995. While not the first 32-bit CPU, the Pentium did most to maximize the benefits of the PCI bus, SDRAM, and the Windows 95 OS.

The 6th generation Pentium II and Pentium III, developed from the server-based Pentium Pro architecture, continued to dominate the market for the next five years.

Intel Pentium II CPU

Intel also introduced the Celeron budget CPU brand alongside the Pentium II. Celeron models were clocked at lower speed than the equivalent Pentium and featured less L2 cache. Intel's line-up also featured Xeon versions, designed for servers and workstations (the Xeons support SMP).

Pentium 4

Intel's 7th generation architecture (NetBurst) was the basis for the Pentium 4. Different Pentium 4 models saw the introduction of many features (such as SSE2 and SSE3, HyperThreading [HT], and 64-bit chips). As with earlier Pentiums, the budget Celeron and server/workstation brand Xeon were developed alongside the P4.

Some P4 models also support **Execute Disable Bit (XD)**, a technology designed to limit the effect of malicious software. Some later models feature **Virtualization Technology (VT)**.

Intel Pentium 4 CPU

Pentium D and Pentium Extreme Edition

The last models using the Pentium brand, the Pentium D and Pentium Extreme Edition (EE), are dual-core processors based on the same NetBurst architecture as the P4. All these chips are multi-core and support 64-bit, MMX/SSE/SSE2/SSE3, and XD. Some models also support VT. The Pentium Extreme Edition supports HyperThreading but the Pentium D does not.

Core 2

Intel's 7th generation NetBurst architecture suffered from power consumption and thermal problems. Its 8th generation architecture (Core) was first developed for mobile chips and based on the P6 design. The first generation of desktop CPUs using this architecture was branded Core 2.

All Core 2 chips are multi-core and support 64-bit, MMX/SSE/SSE2/SSE3, and XD but *not* HyperThreading. All but the cheapest models support VT.

Intel Core 2 Duo processor

Core i7

The premium **Core i7** models are quad-core chips supporting HyperThreading, meaning that each CPU has 8 logical processors. The Core i7 features a redesigned memory bus. The memory controller is implemented on the CPU package (rather than the motherboard chipset) and the memory bus is implemented using the new QuickPath Interconnect bus. Each core has dedicated L1 and L2 cache and all cores share a L3 cache. There is also an update to an SSE4 SIMD instruction set.

The **Core i3** and **Core i5** series represent budget and mid-range models based on the same general architecture. HyperThreading is disabled on these models.

Xeon

The Xeon brand remains in Intel's line-up as models designed for servers and workstations. Xeons use the same architecture as the desktop model (Core 2 or Core i7) but are SMP-capable (on most models) and come with more cache.

AMD CPUs

Advanced Micro Devices (AMD) has competed alongside Intel for a share of the x86 CPU market since it introduced its Pentium competitor the K5 and currently occupies around 20% of the x86 market.

Legacy AMD processors

AMD developed a Pentium clone, the K5, in 1996. The K6 saw the introduction of support for MMX while the K6-2 introduced a competing version of SIMD called 3DNow!.

AMD's first great market success came with the Athlon (K7) and its low-cost "Celeron"-type models, the Duron and Sempron. The Athlon was the first CPU to support Double Data Rate (DDR) SDRAM (see unit 1.3). It also provided support for SSE (Athlon XP) as well as an enhanced version of 3DNow!.

Athlon 64

The Athlon 64 was AMD's 8th generation CPU architecture and the first x86 CPU to introduce 64-bit instructions. It features an on-die memory controller, implemented using AMD's HyperTransport bus.

The Athlon 64 supports SSE and SSE2 (with later models also supporting SSE3) as well as MMX and 3DNow! plus No Execute (NX) bit protection against malware and AMD-V.

AMD Athlon 64 X2 CPU

The Athlon 64 X2 is a dual-core version. "FX" models represent the premium brand in the range. The most recent FX models (the 70 series using Socket F) are quad-core processors.

AMD Phenom / Phenom II

AMD's 10th generation architecture (the 9th generation was never produced) is represented in its Phenom and Phenom II chips. The X2 models are dual core, the X3 models are triple core, and the X4s are quad core. There is support for SSE4. Like the Core i7, each core has its own L1 and L2 cache and there is a shared L3 cache.

AMD Opteron

The Opteron is AMD's server / workstation produce, positioned against Intel's Xeon line of chips. Like the Xeon, Opterons share the same basic features with AMD's Athlon and Phenom CPUs, but provide support for multiprocessor configurations as well as multiple cores.

CPU Packaging

CPU packaging refers to the CPU's form factor and how it is connected to the motherboard.

The most popular type of CPU package has been the **Pin Grid Array (PGA)** chip, designed to fit in a **Zero Insertion Force (ZIF)** socket on the motherboard. As the name suggests, a PGA chip has a number of pins on the underside of the processor. These plug into corresponding holes in the socket. Care must be taken to orient the CPU correctly with the socket and to insert it so as not to bend or break any of the pins.

For a while, Intel packaged CPUs (the Pentium II and Pentium III) in a slot-based form factor (**Single Edge Contact Cartridge [SECC]**[26]). The CPU was mounted on a card (much like an expansion card) fitted to a slot on the motherboard.

Pentium II motherboard with SECC slot

The cartridge design is not very space-efficient so for the Pentium 4 and Core CPUs Intel reverted to a socket approach. The initial socket designs used a slightly modified type called **Flip Chip PGA (FC-PGA)**. This reverses the orientation of the CPU die to make better contact with the heatsink. The FC-PGA2 also added a heat spreader to the package.

---

[26] AMD also experimented with slot-based CPUs but quickly reverted to sockets.

The next socket type used by Intel, **Land Grid Array (LGA)**, saw the pins move from the CPU to the socket, reducing the likelihood of damage to the CPU but increasing the chance of damaging the motherboard. AMD have adopted this form factor for their Opteron CPUs and the latest Athlons (Socket F).

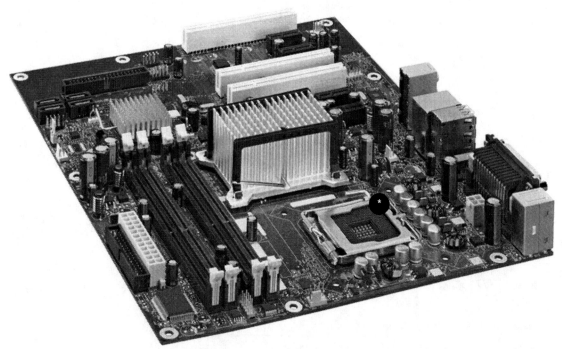

Intel G965 motherboard for Core 2 Duo CPUs with Socket T [LGA 775] socket

Processor sockets also feature **voltage regulators**. These step down the power supplied to the processor (typically 12V) to the core voltage used within the CPU (around 1-2V). Voltage regulators are the barrel-like components positioned around the socket. They automatically detect the required voltage using a **Voltage ID (VID)** code from the CPU.

Early socket designs featured replaceable **Voltage Regulator Modules (VRM)**. On most motherboards however, **Voltage Regulator Downs (VRD)** are soldered to the board.

The following table summarizes the various socket and slot types that have been used over the years:

Unit 1.2 Module 1 Personal Computer Components

Designation	Type	Supported Processors	Memory	Memory Speeds (MHz)
Socket 7 (321 pins)	PGA	Pentium, Pentium MMX, K5, K6, K6-2	SDRAM	66
Intel sockets and slots				
Socket 8 (387 pins)	PGA	Pentium Pro	SDRAM	66
Slot 1 (242 pins)	SECC	Pentium II, Pentium III, Celeron	SDRAM	66-133
Slot 2 (330 pins)	SECC2	Pentium II Xeon, Pentium III Xeon	SDRAM	100-133
Socket 370	FC-PGA	Pentium III, Celeron	SDRAM	66-133
Socket 423	FC-PGA	Pentium 4	RDRAM	100 (x4)
Socket 478	FC-PGA2	Pentium 4, Celeron	DDR / RDRAM	100-200 (x4)
Socket 603	PGA	Xeon	DDR	100 (x4)
Socket 604	PGA	Xeon	DDR	100-200 (x4)
Socket T (775 pins)	LGA	Pentium 4, Pentium D, Celeron D, Core 2, Xeon	DDR / DDR2	133-266 (x4)
Socket J (771 pins)	LGA	Xeon	DDR / DDR2	133-266 (x4)
Socket B (1366 pins)	LGA	Core i7, Xeon	DDR3	2.4-3.2 GHz
Socket H (1156 pins)	LGA	Core i3, i5, i7	DDR3	2.5 GHz
AMD sockets and slots				
Slot A (242 pins)	PGA	Athlon	SDRAM	100
Socket A (462 pins)	PGA	Athlon MP, Athlon XP, Duron, Sempron	SDRAM	100-166 (x2)
Socket 754	PGA	Athlon 64, Sempron	DDR	800
Socket 939	PGA	Athlon 64, Athlon 64 FX, Athlon 64 X2	DDR	800-1000
Socket F (1207 pins)	LGA	Athlon 64 FX 70 Series	DDR2	1 GHz
Socket AM2 (940 pins)	PGA	Athlon 64 X2 / Athlon 64 FX	DDR2	1 GHz
Socket AM2+ (940 pins)	PGA	Athlon 64 X2 / Phenom	DDR2	2.6 GHz
Socket AM3 (941 pins)	PGA	Athlon II / Phenom II / Sempron / Opteron	DDR2 / DDR3	3.2 GHz

Gigabyte motherboard for Athlon 64 X2 CPU with ZIF-type AM2 socket

Summary

CPU performance is measured by a combination of its clock speed and internal architecture (with a key distinction between 32-bit and 64-bit modes). Multiple CPUs (SMP), multi-core CPUs (CMP), and HyperThreading represent other ways to boost performance. The CPU fits in a socket or slot on the motherboard and the particular model of CPU must be supported by the motherboard chipset and BIOS.

Tip

To review what you have learned in this chapter, you should now visit the course website. This contains review questions and bonus material to help you to learn more and practice the topics covered in this unit.

Unit 1.3

Module I Personal Computer Components

Unit 1.3 Memory

CompTIA A+ Essentials Objectives

☐ **701.1.2 Explain motherboard components, types and features**
Memory slots (RIMM, DIMM, SIMM)

☐ **701.1.6 Compare and contrast memory types, characteristics and their purpose**
Types (DRAM, SRAM, SDRAM, DDR / DDR2 / DDR3, RAMBUS) • Parity vs. Non-parity • ECC vs. non-ECC • Single sided vs. double sided • Single channel vs. dual channel • Speed (PC100, PC133, PC2700, PC3200, DDR3-1600, DDR2-667)

Memory Types

System memory is the main storage area for programs and data when the computer is running. System memory is necessary because it is much faster than accessing data in a mass storage system, such as a hard disk.

System memory is a type of *volatile* memory called **RAM (Random Access Memory)**. Volatile means that data is only retained in the memory chips while there is a power source.

Note

Non-volatile memory does not require a constant power source to store data. Examples include Read Only Memory (ROM) used to store firmware (see unit 1.1) and flash memory (see unit 1.4).

A large quantity of system memory is essential for running a PC. It determines its ability to work with multiple applications at the same time and larger files. Each new generation of software tends to take up more memory space. If there is not enough system RAM, the memory space can be extended by using disk space (virtual memory), but as noted above, accessing the disk is very slow compared to accessing RAM.

Some notable RAM vendors include Kingston, Crucial (Micron), Corsair, PNY, and Integral.

DRAM

System RAM is a type of RAM called **Dynamic RAM (DRAM)**. DRAM stores each data bit as an electrical charge within a single **bit cell**. A bit cell consists of a **capacitor** to hold a charge (the cell represents 1 if there is a charge and 0 if there is not) and a **transistor** to read the contents of the capacitor.

The electrical charge gradually discharges, causing the memory cell to lose its information. In order to preserve the information, dynamic memory has to be refreshed periodically by accessing each cell at regular intervals. The refresh cycles slow down the operation of DRAM but it is the basis for all system memory, mainly because of its high-density (MB per chip) and low price.

DRAM is packaged in modules called **Single Inline Memory Modules (SIMM)**. SIMMs for Pentium systems have 72 pins and a 32-bit data bus. Consequently, they must be installed in pairs to match the Pentium's 64-bit data bus.

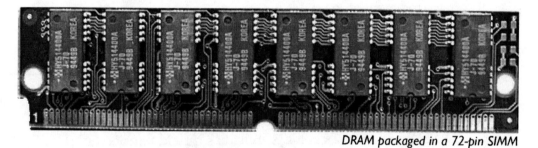

DRAM packaged in a 72-pin SIMM

You are unlikely to encounter standard DRAM. PC systems have generally used updated DRAM technologies over the years, with DDR2 and DDR3 SDRAM being the current standards.

SDRAM

Many different types of DRAM have been developed and become obsolete. In the mid-1990s, variants of **S(ynchronous)DRAM** were used for system memory. SDRAM is so-called because it is synchronized to the system clock (FSB). It has a 64-bit data bus.

Model	Clock Speed	Bandwidth
PC66	66 MHz	533 MBps
PC100	100 MHz	800 MBps
PC133	133 MHz	1066 MBps

SDRAM works with the Pentium, Pentium MMX, Pentium II, and Pentium III Intel CPUs (and their AMD K5/6/7 and Athlon equivalents).

SDRAM for desktop PCs is packaged in 168-pin **DIMMs (Dual Inline Memory Module)**. The notches (keys) on the module prevent it from being inserted into a slot the wrong way around.

SDRAM packaged in a 168-pin DIMM

Tip

Memory slots look quite like expansion slots but have catches on each end to secure the memory modules.

Rambus (RDRAM)

Rambus DRAM (RDRAM)[27] is a proprietary memory technology developed by the Rambus corporation. It was used with some Pentium 4 motherboards (all socket 423 and some socket 478) but was quickly superseded by DDR SDRAM (see below).

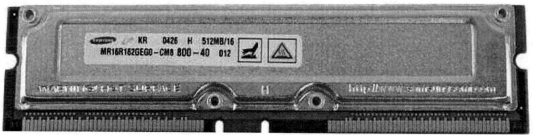

Samsung RDRAM packaged in a 184-pin RIMM

RDRAM has a 16-bit (single channel) or 32-bit (dual channel) bus width but runs at much higher speed than SDRAM (300 MHz and more) as well as being "double-pumped", meaning data is transferred twice per clock cycle.

16-bit RDRAM is packaged in 184-pin RIMMs while 32-bit modules are packaged in 232-pin RIMMs, both of which feature heatsinks because of the high clock speeds.

---

[27] Technically, it is actually called Direct Rambus DRAM (or DRDRAM).

Model	Type	Clock Speed	Bandwidth
PC600	Single channel (16-bit)	300 MHz	1200 MBps
PC700	Single channel (16-bit)	355 MHz	1420 MBps
PC800	Single channel (16-bit)	400 MHz	1600 MBps
PC1066	Single channel (16-bit)	533 MHz	2133 MBps
RIMM 3200	Dual channel (32-bit)	400 MHz	3200 MBps
RIMM 4200	Dual channel (32-bit)	533 MHz	4200 MBps

Most motherboards supporting RDRAM are dual channel (see below). Single channel RIMMs have to be installed in matching pairs in a dual channel motherboard, but dual channel modules can be installed singly. Regardless of single or dual channel modules, unused slots need to be filled with a terminator, called **Continuity RIMM (CRIMM)**.

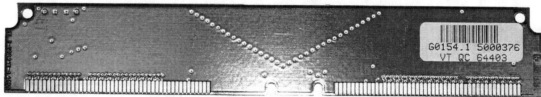

CRIMM terminator (public domain image courtesy en.wikipedia.org/wiki/RDRAM)

Double Data Rate SDRAM (DDR SDRAM)

Double Data Rate SDRAM (DDR SDRAM, or just DDR) is an updated type of SDRAM featuring "double pumped" data transfers. DDR is very popular and used on many motherboard designs for both Intel and AMD CPUs.

Corsair ValueSelect DDR SDRAM in 184-pin DIMM

There are four DDR standards, matching different system clock speeds:

Model	Clock Speed	Bandwidth
DDR-200 / PC-1600	100 MHz	1600 MBps
DDR-266 / PC-2100	133 MHz	2133 MBps
DDR-333 / PC-2700	166 MHz	2667 MBps
DDR-400 / PC-3200	200 MHz	3200 MBps

DDR is being replaced by **DDR2** and **DDR3** SDRAM. These increase bandwidth by doubling (or quadrupling) the *bus* speed (as opposed to the speed at which the actual memory chips work). This produces scalable speed improvements without making the chips too unreliable or hot. The drawback is increased **latency**, as data takes longer to access on each chip. Latency is offset by improving the memory circuitry[28].

Model	Memory Speed	Bus Speed	Bandwidth
DDR2-400 / PC2-3200	100 MHz	200 MHz	3.2 GBps
DDR2-533 / PC2-4200	133 MHz	266 MHz	4.3 GBps
DDR2-667 / PC2-5300	166 MHz	333 MHz	5.3 GBps
DDR2-800 / PC2-6400	200 MHz	400 MHz	6.4 GBps
DDR2-1066 / PC2-8500	266 MHz	533 MHz	8.5 GBps
DDR3-1066 / PC3-8500	133 MHz	533 MHz	8.5 GBps
DDR3-1333 / PC3-10600	166 MHz	667 MHz	10.66 GBps
DDR3-1600 / PC3-12800	200 MHz	800 MHz	12.8 GBps

DDR for desktop system memory is packaged in 184-pin DIMMs; DDR2 and DDR3 are both packaged in 240-pin DIMMs but are *not* compatible (the modules and slots are keyed differently). Faster modules typically feature heatsinks, because of the higher clock speeds.

Corsair ValueSelect DDR2 SDRAM in 240-pin DIMM

---

[28] When specifying high performance RAM you may want to compare the performance timings. These are quoted as a series of numbers in the form 5-5-5-15. Each number represents a different timing statistic. The lower the numbers, the better the performance.

Corsair XMS DDR3 SDRAM in 240-pin DIMM - note the different pin position and heatsink

More information on SDRAM standards can be obtained from www.jedec.org.

SRAM

Another type of RAM used in computer components is **Static RAM (SRAM)**. SRAM stores data in an electronic circuit called a **flip-flop**, which does not need to be constantly refreshed. SRAM is faster than DRAM but because every bit cell requires four or more transistors to function, compared to one per bit for DRAM, SRAM modules are larger and more expensive. They are normally reserved for speed critical functions, such as cache and buffers.

Memory Configurations

Given the main memory types (SDRAM, DDR, and RDRAM) there are also different types of memory and ways of implementing system memory on the motherboard.

Chips

The capacity of a memory module is determined by the number of chips and the size of each chip. Most SDRAM and DDR RAM modules are configured with 8 or 16 chips. Each chip typically has a size (or **density**) of either 64 MB or 32 MB. Typical total capacities for modules are 128, 256, 512, and 1024 MB.

The way a chip stores data is expressed as the depth of the chip by its width. For example, 64Mx8 means the storage locations in the chip are organized into 64 rows and 8 columns with a total capacity of 512 mega*bits*. If there were 8 such chips on a module, the module would be 64Mx64 and have a capacity of 512 MB (mega*bytes*). x4 chips are cheaper than x8 or x16 chips but can cause problems with some motherboards, especially in high capacity modules (1 GB).

Unit 1.3   Module 1 Personal Computer Components

The number and layout of chips on a memory board does not generally affect system performance, except when a **dual channel** motherboard is used (see below). That said, for optimum stability, use the same density (and brand) of memory in all sockets.

Memory banks

When memory is installed, it must fill a **bank**, which is the amount of data the memory controller expects to fetch. All current PC motherboards support a 64-bit data bus, matching the 64-bit data bus of DIMMs (older technologies sometimes required the 64-bit data bus to be matched with 32-bit modules)[29].

Single- and double-sided memory

Single-sided (or more properly single *rank*) memory is a module that fills a single bank (that is, the computer can access all of the memory chips on the module at the same time).

Double-sided (or dual *bank* or dual *rank*[30]) memory divides the memory chips on a single module into two "ranks"; the controller can access one rank or the other, but not both simultaneously. This makes the memory lower cost and higher density but degrades performance slightly. There are also quad rank modules, though these are usually designed for server-level hardware.

The memory controller on the motherboard will only be able to support a given number of ranks. Consequently, DIMM slots may not always support dual rank modules or may only support one dual rank module (typically this must be installed in the first slot) - check the motherboard documentation carefully. In some cases, support for dual or quad rank memory may be enabled through a BIOS update.

Dual-channel motherboards

The increasing speed and architectural improvements of CPU technologies have led to memory becoming a bottleneck to system performance. To address this, Intel and AMD developed a **dual-channel** memory architecture for DDR and DDR2 RAM. Dual-channel was originally used primarily on server-level hardware but is now often being employed on desktop and laptop systems.

---

[29] The exception is motherboards supporting ECC memory, where 8 extra bits are transmitted for parity calculations.

[30] The term "rank" is preferred by JEDEC but "sided", "bank", and "rank" are not used consistently across the industry. Double-sided is often used to refer to a module that has chips physically located on both sides of the board. A "double-sided" module in this sense could be single rank.

Page 56   IT Career FastTrack with CompTIA A+ Certification   © 2010 gtslearning

| Module 1 Personal Computer Components | Memory |

With a dual-channel memory controller on the motherboard, there can effectively be two pathways between the CPU and system memory, meaning that 128 bits of data can be transferred per "transaction" rather than 64 bits. Ordinary RAM modules are used (that is, there are no "dual channel" DDR memory modules[31]).

A dual-channel motherboard will have four DIMM slots arranged in color-coded pairs. Each pair represents one **channel**; each slot represents one of the two **sockets** in each channel. The memory modules installed must be identical in terms of speed and capacity and chip number, density, and location. If only two slots are used, the modules must be installed in socket 1 of each channel (that is, slot 1 and slot 3 in most motherboard layouts[32]).

Adding an odd number of modules or adding mismatched DIMMs will cause the system to operate in single-channel mode. Dual channel mode may also need to be enabled via CMOS Setup (see unit 4.5).

Intel's latest Core i7 CPUs and supporting chipsets have a triple channel memory controller.

| ECC |

Motherboards used to use a simple error detection method called **parity checking**. In the parity system, each byte of data in memory is accompanied by a ninth bit. This bit is set to 1 or 0 to make the total number of bits set to 1 in the byte an odd or even number, depending on the type of parity checking being performed.

When the byte is read, its parity is checked to ensure that the parity value is still odd (or even). If this is not the case, a bit must have become corrupted.

Error Checking and Correcting (ECC) memory has *enhanced* parity circuitry that can detect internal data errors and make corrections.

ECC will detect and correct single-bit errors and allow the system to continue functioning normally. It will also detect errors of 2, 3 or 4 bits but will not correct them; instead, it will generate an error message and halt the system.

ECC memory has an extra chip and a 72-bit data bus rather than 64-bit.

---

[31] There are dual-channel RDRAM chips but RDRAM uses a different architecture.

[32] Unfortunately there is no standardized color-coding. As well as using different colors, some motherboard manufacturers use the same color for the same channel; others use the same color for the same socket. Check the documentation carefully.

© 2010 gtslearning   IT Career FastTrack with CompTIA A+ Certification   Page 57

ECC memory is often used in mission critical systems, such as high-performance servers. It can only be installed on motherboards supporting ECC RAM. It cannot be mixed with non-parity modules.

Registered memory

Most SDRAM (and DDR SDRAM) designed for desktop systems is **unbuffered**.

Registered memory has an extra component that stores address information, taking some load off the memory controller. This is slightly slower but increases system stability when a large amount of memory (2 GB or more) is installed. Most, but not all, ECC RAM is registered. Non-ECC registered chips are also available, at higher cost than unbuffered chips.

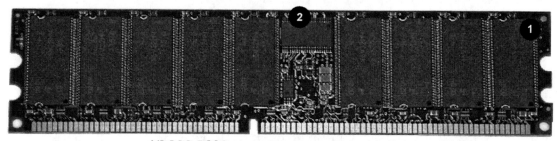

HP DDR ECC Registered memory module with 1) Extra ECC chip; 2) Register chip

Registered RAM must be supported by the motherboard. Registered and unbuffered modules **cannot** be mixed.

Summary

The amount of system memory affects the ability of the computer to open multiple applications and work efficiently with larger files. The main types of memory are SDRAM, RDRAM, and DDR/DDR2/DDR3. A motherboard will support a number of modules, inserted into DIMM (or RIMM) slots. Memory may need to be installed in particular configuration (such as on a dual channel motherboard). ECC/registered memory presents another compatibility issue.

Tip

To review what you have learned in this chapter, you should now visit the course website. This contains review questions and bonus material to help you to learn more and practice the topics covered in this unit.

Module 1 Personal Computer Components | Storage Devices

Unit 1.4 Storage Devices

CompTIA A+ Essentials Objectives
- **701.1.1 Categorize storage devices and backup media**
  FDD • HDD (Solid state vs. magnetic) • Optical drives (CD / DVD / RW / Blu-Ray) • Removable storage (Tape drive, Solid state [e.g. thumb drive, flash, SD cards, USB], External CD-RW and hard drive)

Floppy Disk Drives

A **floppy disk** (or "diskette") is a plastic disk coated with a magnetic substance. The surface of the disk is low-level formatted with circular **tracks** and each track contains a number of 512-byte **sectors**. Data is stored on the magnetized disk surface using an encoding scheme called **Modified Frequency Modulation**. The disc is enclosed in a rigid plastic case (for protection) with a metal shutter (so that the drive can access the disk contents). Disks also feature a write protect tab (when the tab is open, the disk contents cannot be changed).

The only type of floppy disk in any sort of use is the 3.5" HD (High Density) double-sided disk, with a maximum storage capacity of "1.44 MB" (that is, it has 80 tracks each with 18 sectors of 512 bytes on both sides of the disk[33]). Floppy disks support a transfer rate of 62.5 KBps.

Floppy disk with 1) Shutter; 2) Spindle; 3) Write protect tab; 4) HD tab

Diskettes are read and written via a **Floppy Disk Drive (FDD)**. A drive consists of a spindle motor to spin the disk, read/write heads (moved by a head actuator) to access the disk and read and write data, connectors for power and data transfer, and a disk eject mechanism. The FDD is connected to the PC's FDD **controller** on the motherboard using a 34-pin cable.

---

[33] There are also Double Density (720 KB) and Extra HD (2.88 MB) formats plus 5.25" formats, but these are obsolete. The capacity is always referred to as 1.44 MB but this is actually a mistake derived from combining binary and decimal measurements (assuming the sector size is 500 bytes (0.5 KB) rather than 512 bytes). The actual capacity is 1.47 MB or 1.41 MiB (binary "mebibytes"), with the latter value being reported by software such as Windows, which uses the binary measurements.

Unit 1.4 — Module 1 Personal Computer Components

34-pin FDD connector (below two 40-pin IDE connectors) and FDD cable

Many new PCs and almost all laptops are no longer shipped with FDDs, though external units are available. With their limited storage capacity, floppy disks are used almost exclusively for troubleshooting.

Hard Disk Drives

Hard Disk Drives (HDD) are the mainstay of PC storage. Every PC has at least one internal HDD (or "fixed drive"). The HDD stores OS and application files plus user data.

HDD construction

HDDs feature the same sort of components as FDDs. However, instead of a plastic disk, data is stored on a number of metal or glass platters coated with a magnetic substance. The top and bottom of each platter is accessed by its own read/write head, moved by an actuator mechanism. Unlike a FDD, the heads do not actually touch the surface of the platters. The platters are mounted on a spindle and spun at high speed and the heads "float" above them at a distance of less than a millionth of an inch.

HDD with drive circuitry and casing removed showing 1) Platters; 2) Spindle; 3) Read/write heads; 4) Actuator

The disk unit is kept sealed to maintain a constant air pressure (important for keeping the drive heads at the correct distance from the platters[34]) and to prevent the entry of dust.

Stack of platters on spindle

Like a floppy disk, each side of each platter is divided into circular **tracks** and each track contains a number of **sectors**, each with a capacity of 512 bytes. The collection of tracks in the same place on each platter is called a **cylinder**. This low-level formatting is also referred to as the drive *geometry*.

There are two main formats for HDDs: 3.5" units are the mainstream type used in PCs; 2.5" form factors are used for laptops and as portable external drives.

HDD capacity and performance

HDDs are available in a range of capacities, from 20 GB up to 1 TB (1000 GB).

HDD performance is largely a measure of how quickly it can read and write data. One factor is the speed at which the disks can spin (measured in **Revolutions Per Minute [rpm]**). The higher the rpm, the faster the drive is. High performance drives can reach 15,000 rpm; average performance is typically 5400 or 7200 rpm.

rpm is one factor determining **access time** (measured in milliseconds), which is the delay that occurs as the read/write head locates a particular position on the drive. A high performance drive will have an access time below 4 ms; a typical drive might have an access time of around 9 ms.

The **internal transfer rate** (or data or disk transfer rate) of a drive is a measure of how fast read/write operations are performed on the disk platters. The **external** transfer rate (often simply described as the transfer rate) measures how fast data can be transferred to the CPU across the bus and is governed by the type of **controller** used (see unit 1.1). Cache memory can help to sustain better transfer rates. A high performance disk may feature a 4 MB or larger cache.

---

[34] A head touching a platter is called a head crash. This can damage the platter and / or the head.

Unit 1.4   Module 1 Personal Computer Components

> **Tip**
>
> Some HDDs are now being fitted with a substantial cache of **flash memory** (see below) to improve performance. These are referred to as **hybrid** drives.

The other crucial factor that impacts HDD performance is *reliability*. Reliability is rated by various statistics, including **Early-life Failure Rate**, **Mean Time Between Failures (MTBF)**, which is the number of hours that a device should operate (under optimum conditions) before a critical incident can be expected, and **life expectancy**, which is the duration for which the device can be expected to remain reliable. All drives now feature **Self Monitoring Analysis and Reporting Technology (SMART)** to pass status information and alerts back to monitoring software. This can provide advance warning that a drive is about to fail.

Some of the major hard drive vendors include Seagate, Western Digital, Maxtor, Hitachi, Fujitsu, Toshiba, and Samsung.

HDD interfaces

Over the years, there have been several different standards for the controller and bus connecting a hard disk to a PC. These standards (EIDE/PATA, SATA, and SCSI) are covered in detail in unit 1.1. HDDs are also available as external units, interfaced to the PC via a USB or Firewire port (see unit 1.5). External units may be designed for desk use or to be portable.

Optical Drives

CDs (Compact Disc) and **DVDs (Digital Video** or **Versatile Disc**, depending on who you believe) are mainstream storage formats for consumer multimedia, such as music and video. Both formats have also been adapted for data storage with PC systems. The CD / DVD drives used with PCs can also play consumer versions of the discs[35].

The data version of the CD (CD-ROM) became ubiquitous on PC systems as it has sufficient capacity (700 MB[36]) to deliver most software applications.

---

[35] Some commercial discs have been produced with copy protection systems, making them unplayable in PC drives.

[36] Audio CDs can store up to 80 minutes of music (assuming 16-bit stereo encoded at 44.1 KHz). Originally, CDs could only store 650 MB (74 minutes) but improved manufacturing techniques have increased that to 700 MB.

Page 62   IT Career FastTrack with CompTIA A+ Certification   © 2010 gtslearning

Module 1 Personal Computer Components | Storage Devices

DVD is an improvement on CD technology and delivers substantially more capacity (up to about 17 GB). DVDs are used for some software installs (Windows Vista for instance) and for games and multimedia. The latest optical disc format (Blu-ray) can support 50 GB discs.

CD construction

A CD is a layer of aluminum foil encased in protective plastic, which can also incorporate a label or screen-printed image on the non-playing side. The foil layer contains a series of **pits** and spaces in-between (called **lands**) arranged in a spiral. The changes between pits and lands are used to encode each bit. A standard CD is 120 mm in diameter[37] and 1.2 mm thick.

Recordable CDs

A **recordable** version of the CD (CD-R) was developed in 1999. Rather than a premastered layer of foil with pits and lands, CD-Rs feature a layer of photosensitive dye. A special laser is used to transform the dye, mimicking the pits and lands of a normal CD, in a process called **burning**. Most ordinary CD players and drives can read CD-Rs but they may not playback properly on older equipment.

CD-R is a type of **Write Once Read Many (WORM)** media. Data areas once written cannot be overwritten[38]. However, a **rewritable** (or multisession) disc format (CD-RW) has also been developed. This uses a heat sensitive compound whose properties can be changed between crystalline and amorphous by a special laser.

There is some concern over the lifetime of recordable CD (and DVD) media. Cheaply manufactured discs have shown a tendency to degrade and become unusable (sometimes over the space of just a few years).

CD standards

Standards for different types of CD are published as the rainbow books:

---

[37] There are also 80mm discs, playable in most CD-ROM drives.

[38] If there is space, a new session can be started on the disc. However, this makes the disc unreadable in ordinary CD-ROM drives.

© 2010 gtslearning | IT Career FastTrack with CompTIA A+ Certification | Page 63

Standard	CD Type
Red book	Audio CDs (16-bit sampled at 44.4 Hz).
Yellow book	Data CDs (Mode 1) and compressed audio CDs (Mode 2, which defines 5 stages of compression).
Orange book	Defines the unused CD-MO and the more popular CD-R and CD-RW.
Green book	Phillips' CD-I(nteractive) product.
White book	Video CD.

CD drives

A CD drive consists of a spindle motor (to spin the disc) and a laser (to read the disc). The mechanism for inserting a CD is either tray or slot based. A drive may feature audio play and volume controls and a headphone jack. The drives are considerably larger than hard disks (5.25" form factor).

Note

Drives also feature a small hole that accesses a disc eject mechanism (insert a paper clip to activate the mechanism). This is useful if the standard eject button will not work or if the drive does not have power.

CD drives are rated according to their data transfer speed. The original drives had a data transfer rate of 150 KBps. Subsequently, drives have been available that offer multiples of the original rate; this would be around 52x for new models, offering transfer rates in excess of 7 MBps.

Many CD drives also function as recordable / rewritable CD burners (or writers). Such drives feature three speeds, always expressed as the Read/Record/Rewrite speed (for example, 52X/24X/16X). One feature to look out for on such drives is BURN-proof technology, which prevents discs being ruined by buffer under-run errors (where the software cannot supply the drive the data to write quickly enough).

DVD media

DVD is similar to CD but with a different encoding method, higher density discs, and a shorter wavelength laser. DVD discs are also thinner and can be dual-layer and / or double-sided (a DVD is two 0.6 mm discs sandwiched together). The different permutations result in these storage capacities:

Module I Personal Computer Components   _   *Storage Devices*

Standard	Capacity	Description
DVD-5	4.7 GB	Single layer / Single sided
DVD-9	8.5 GB	Dual layer / Single sided
DVD-10	9.4 GB	Single layer / Double sided[39]
DVD-18	17.1 GB	Dual layer / Double sided
DVD-Video	Up to 17.1 GB	Commercially produced DVDs using mpeg encoding and chapters for navigation (can be single or dual layer and single or double sided)
DVD-Audio		Format for high quality audio (superior sampling rates and 5.1 surround sound for instance)

DVDs also feature a higher transfer rate, with multiples of 1.38 MBps (equivalent to 9X CD speed). The fastest models feature 16X read speeds.

Like CD, there are recordable and rewritable versions of DVD, some of which support dual layer recording. There are two slightly different standards for recordable and rewritable DVDs, referred to as DVD-R / DVD-RW versus DVD+R / DVD+RW. Most drives can read all formats but write in either + or - format. Many consumer DVD players can play DVD±R discs.

Consumer DVDs feature copy protection mechanisms (Digital Rights Management) and region coding. Region coding, if enforced, means that a disc can only be used on a player from the same region.

The following codes are used:

- Region 0 - no coding (that is, playback is unrestricted).

- Region 1 - Canada and the US.

- Region 2 - EMEA and Japan.

- Region 3 - SE Asia.

- Region 4 - South America, Australia, and New Zealand.

- Region 5 - Russia, Africa, and parts of Asia.

- Region 6 - China.

Some DVD players are multi-region but some discs feature protection mechanisms to disable playback in such machines. PC software is not usually region coded, with the exception of some PC game discs.

---

[39] Double-sided discs need to be turned over to play or record to the second side.

© 2010 gtslearning   IT Career FastTrack with CompTIA A+ Certification   Page 65

Blu-ray Discs

Blu-ray Discs (BD) have emerged as the next generation format for distributing consumer multimedia and are also likely to be used to distribute high-bandwidth applications, such as video games[40].

Blu-ray is principally required to cope with the demands of High Definition video recording and playback. HD requires much more bandwidth and storage space because it uses a higher resolution picture (1920x1080 compared to 720x480 [NTSC] or 720x576 [PAL]) and better quality audio (digital surround sound). Video and audio terminology and formats are covered in more detail in unit 1.6.

A Blu-ray Disc works on fundamentally the same principle as DVD but with a shorter wavelength laser (a 405nm blue laser compared to DVD's 650nm red laser). This means discs can be much higher density; though the cost of components to make the drives is considerably higher.

A standard BD has a capacity of 25 GB per layer; mini-discs (8cm) can store 7.8 GB per layer. Currently, only dual-layer discs are standard though quad-layer 100 GB discs have been demoed. There are currently no double-sided formats.

The base speed for Blu-ray is 36 MBps and the maximum theoretical rate is 12x (432 MBps). At the time of writing, most drives are 2x or 4x; 2x is the minimum required for movie playback.

Generally speaking, BD players are also capable of CD and DVD playback. Recordable (BD-R) and re-recordable (BD-RE) drives and discs are also available. BD-R is often available at the same speed as playback while BD-RE is usually half playback speed.

HP Blu-ray / DVD / CD drive

Like DVDs, consumer Blu-ray Discs (BD-ROMs) are likely to be DRM-protected and may be region coded:

- Region A - America, Japan, and SE Asia.

---

[40] Its competitor, High Definition DVD (HD DVD), was discontinued in 2008.

Module 1 Personal Computer Components

- Region B - EMEA, Africa, Australia, and New Zealand.
- Region C - Russia and Central Asia (including China).

Removable Storage

Floppy disks and optical media are types of **removable storage**. Removable storage contrasts with the one or more fixed hard disks within the computer, which cannot be removed (at least in the course of normal operations). Removable storage is used to *transfer* data between computers and make *backup* copies of data and system files.

FDDs, HDDs, and optical drives are typically integrated into a desktop computer's chassis as internal units. Versions of all these types of drive can be purchased as external units, connected to the computer via a USB or Firewire port (see unit 1.5).

External units provide *portability* between computer systems, a means of *expanding* a computer system that has no room for more internal units, or a simpler way for home users to *upgrade* storage (without having to install an internal drive).

There are several more types of removable storage used with PCs and consumer electronics...

Tape drives

Magnetic tape drives provide a low cost method of creating data **backups**. They may be internal or external units, supplied with PATA, SATA, SCSI, USB, or Firewire interfaces.

Some of the more popular formats are summarized below[41]:

- **Digital Audio Tape (DAT)** - this ⅛" (4 mm) tape uses a digital format with two magnetic heads: one to read and one to write. DAT backup systems conform to a standard called **Digital Data Storage (DDS)** and support up to 36 GB uncompressed capacity[42].

---

[41] All tape formats have a range of standards associated with them. A tape drive will be incompatible with later standards and may not be compatible with earlier standards (or may have read-only compatibility).

[42] Compression increases tape capacity (approximately doubling it) but also makes backup jobs slower to complete.

© 2010 gtslearning   IT Career FastTrack with CompTIA A+ Certification   Page 67

- **8 mm Tape** - offers high-capacity (up to 200 GB) data storage in a cartridge that appears identical to ¼" video tapes, although it uses higher quality magnetic media. The 8 mm standard is mainly being developed by the **Advanced Intelligent Tape (AIT)** forum, sponsored notably by Sony.

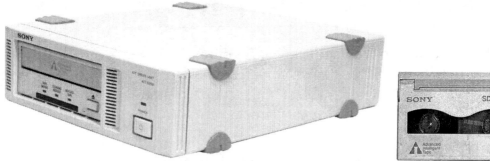

Sony AIT-3 drive and tape cartridge

- **Digital Linear Tape (DLT)** - this ½" (12 mm) tape technology is a popular format for mini-computers, large servers, and enterprise networks.

    DLT was originally developed by DEC but the standard is now maintained by Quantum, Fujitsu, Hitachi, and Imation. The standard has **VS (Value Series)** and **Super-DLT** variants, with capacity up to 300 GB. Another DLT format, **Linear Tape-Open (LTO)**, was set up by HP and IBM. LTO-based products go under the brand name **Ultrium**. Tapes have up to 400 GB uncompressed capacity.

Flash memory

Solid state storage uses a type of non-volatile **Electrically Erasable Programmable Read-Only Memory (EEPROM)** technology called **flash memory**. Flash memory is *non-volatile* because it does not need a power source to retain information. Compared to other types of storage, flash memory is very small and light. Mass manufacturing has seen prices fall to very affordable levels. Storage capacity ranges from 512 MB to 256 GB.

Data transfer rates vary quite widely between different devices, which are rated on the same system as CDs, using multiples of 150 KBps, with the fastest devices working at up to 200x read speeds (or 38 MBps; the write speed is typically about two-thirds of the read speed).

There are many ways of packaging flash memory. One of the most popular is the USB drive (or "thumb" drive). This type of drive simply plugs into any spare USB port (see unit 1.5 for more information on USB). Some USB drives may come with security features, such as encryption or fingerprint recognition.

HB USB flash drive

Another popular type of packaging is the **memory card**, used extensively in consumer digital imaging products, such as digital still and video cameras. There are several proprietary types of memory card. Some popular examples include CompactFlash (CF), Secure Digital (SD), and Sony Memory Stick. The largest cards have up to 64 GB capacity. Many PCs are fitted with **Memory Card Readers** with 2 or 3 slots that between them will accommodate most of the sticks on the market.

Memory card reader on an HP Pavilion PC

Another use for flash memory is as the main storage for electronics devices such as PDAs, cellphones, mp3 players, handheld games consoles, and so on.

Solid State Drives

Flash memory is also being incorporated onto a new generation of **Solid State Drives (SSD)** designed to replicate or supplement the function of the hard drive. The lack of moving parts in flash memory-based SSDs make them quieter, more power efficient, and less prone to catastrophic failure. Read times are better because seek time, and consequently the effect of file fragmentation, is eliminated[43]. They are also less susceptible to data loss in the event of power failure[44].

---

[43] Writing to a drive is always slower than reading, so when performing write operations the OS selects the most easily available part of the drive rather than trying to keep a file in contiguous sectors. This means that over time data for a file can become fragmented over different physical locations on the drive, reducing read performance on a hard disk. Flash memory locations can be accessed without having to move a read head so do not suffer degraded performance when the file system is fragmented.

[44] Most drives still feature DRAM-based write cache to improve performance. In the event of a power failure, unwritten cache would be lost. However, the DRAM cache may be backed up by a battery to cover this eventuality.

Unit 1.4	Module 1 Personal Computer Components

The main disadvantage is the high cost; SSDs are about 3-4x the cost of HDDs. SSDs are not available in the same range of capacities (up to about 30 GB). SSDs can also perform worse than HDDs when writing data and when serving large (GB) files. Flash chips are also susceptible to their own type of degradation over the course of many write operations, so the operating system must use **wear leveling** routines to optimize the usable life of the device[45].

SSDs are available as either standalone units or hybrid drives. In a hybrid drive, the SSD portion functions as a large cache, containing data that is accessed frequently. The magnetic disc is only spun up when non-cached data is accessed. This reduces power consumption but can degrade performance.

Summary

Internal hard disks (or fixed disks) provide the main storage capacity for personal computers. A number of types of removable drive and media provide extra storage capacity, backup, and data transfer. Some examples include CD/DVD/BD (read-only, recordable, and rewritable), flash memory, tape drives, and the long-lasting floppy disk drive.

Tip

To review what you have learned in this chapter, you should now visit the course website. This contains review questions and bonus material to help you to learn more and practice the topics covered in this unit.

---

[45] Windows Vista supports booting from flash memory USB, SSDs, or hybrid drives (ReadyDrive) but doesn't support wear leveling. Support for wear leveling has been included in Windows 7.

Module I Personal Computer Components — *Peripheral Devices*

Unit 1.5 Peripheral Devices

CompTIA A+ Essentials Objectives

☐ **701.1.2 Explain motherboard components, types and features**
I/O interfaces (USB 1.1 and 2.0, Serial, IEEE 1394 / Firewire, Parallel, NIC, Modem, PS/2)

☐ **701.1.8 Install and configure peripherals and input devices**
Mouse • Keyboard • Bar code reader • Biometric devices • Touch screen • KVM switch

Peripheral Ports

One of the functions of the motherboard is to provide the standard ports used to attach peripheral devices and cabling to the computer.

Motherboard I/O ports 1) PS/2 mouse; 2) PS/2 keyboard; 3) Parallel port; 4) Serial port; 5) USB ports; 6) RJ-45 network port; 7) Audio ports [audio in, audio out, and microphone in]

Tip

Ports and connectors are described as male (pins) or female (holes). Connectors are usually male (with pins); ports are usually female (with holes).

PS/2 Port

The **PS/2** (or mini-DIN) port is used to connect a keyboard and mouse to the PC. Both PS/2 keyboard and mouse ports are 6-pin female. To avoid confusion the system case usually has symbols and color coding (green for mouse; purple for keyboard) to differentiate them. PS/2 is a serial bus.

PS/2 ports

Parallel Port

The **parallel** port (also known as the **printer** or **Centronics** port) is so-called because data is transferred simultaneously over 8 wires, each of which carries 1-bit of data (there are extra "handshake" wires for controlling the signals). This restricts the maximum length of cabling as tiny differences in the properties of the wires cause delays in the signal (data skew), which get worse the farther the signal travels.

Parallel port

The parallel port was used to connect devices such as printers and scanners but is now close to being completely obsolete. It has largely been replaced by USB.

The original interface developed by Centronics was *unidirectional* (that is, the computer could send data to a printer but the printer could not send data back). IEEE 1284 standards[46] defined new interfaces, using the same type of connectors and cabling:

- **Compatibility/Centronics/Standard Mode** - data transfer is unidirectional from PC to peripheral 8 bits at a time at a maximum possible rate of 150 KBps.

- **Nibble (4-bit) / Bi-tronics Mode** - this mode supports 4-bit input back to the PC. The transfer rate into the PC is limited to 50 KBps. It is suitable for sending printer status messages (for example, Out of Toner or Paper Jam), but not for CD-ROMs or disk drives.

- **Byte (8-bit) Mode** - this mode allows transfer speeds of approximately 150 KBps in both directions.

- **Extended Capabilities Port (ECP)** - supports half-duplex data transfer rates of up to 2 MBps. Half-duplex means that the devices cannot send and receive at the *same time*.

- **Enhanced Parallel Port (EPP)** - supports half-duplex data transfer rates of up to 2.5 MBps and support for multiple (daisy-chained) peripherals.

The parallel port on the PC is a 25-pin female DB25 (or D-sub) type, which accepts a male DB25 connector[47].

---

[46] IEEE is the Institute of Electronic and Electrical Engineers; a professional body that oversees the development and registration of electronic standards.

[47] New PCs may not ship with a parallel port. Laptops no longer feature these ports. Adapters are available for parallel to USB connections.

The port on the printer or scanner is typically a 36-pin Centronics edge connector[48].

Printer cable with Centronics (left) and DB25 (right) male connectors

Parallel connections are not suitable for long-distance operation; the official maximum length for *standard* parallel cable is 5m (15 feet). Some high-quality, screened cables will work over greater distances, but devices known as line drivers are required for reliable long cable runs. In enhanced modes, the quality of the cable is very important. If the cable is of poor quality or not to IEEE 1284 specification, problems may be encountered, such as data errors on tape units or corrupted printouts. The official maximum length of IEEE 1284 cable is 10m (30 feet).

In software terms, the parallel port is referred to as an **LPT (Line Printer)** port.

Serial Port

The **serial** port (or **RS-232**) is so-called because data is transmitted over one wire one bit at a time. Start, stop, and parity bits are used to format and verify data transmission. The port supports data rates up to about 115 Kbps.

Serial ports are generally associated with connecting external modems. This function has largely been superseded by USB. Some very old computers may use a serial port to attach the mouse.

Serial port

The RS-232 standard for serial ports specified a 25-pin interface but in practice PC manufacturers use the cheaper 9-pin D-sub male port shown above with a female connector on the device. Without line drivers to improve the signal, serial cable can generally extend to around 10m (30 feet).

In software terms, the serial port is referred to as a **COM (Communications)** port.

---

[48] Some models of HP printer featured a mini-Centronics (or Type C) connector, which has the same number of pins but is more compact.

USB

The **Universal Series Bus (USB)** has become the standard means of connecting peripheral devices to a PC. Unlike serial and parallel ports, it supports compact connectors and high data rates.

A USB bus consists of a **host** (the PC) and up to 127 devices, which may either be **hubs** or **functions**. Functions are divided into classes, such as human interface, mass storage, printer, audio device, and so on.

USB devices are **Plug-and-Play**. This means that when a device is connected via the port, Windows can identify the device and try to install a **driver** for it (make the device usable) automatically. Another feature of USB is that devices are **hot swappable**. This means that Windows can detect and configure a device without requiring a restart.

USB ports

USB supplies power of up to 2.5 watts over the cable. This is enough power for small peripherals (such as portable hard drives and webcams) but devices such as CD writers or printers that require more power must be connected to a mains supply or battery.

There are two types of standard USB connector:

- **Type A** - for connection to the host or to hub ports. The connector and port are shaped like flat rectangles.

- **Type B** - for connection to a device. The connector and port are square, with a beveled top. USB On-the-Go (USB-OTG) also defines a compact **mini-Type B** connector for small devices (such as digital cameras).

Type A (left) and Type B (right) USB connectors

USB connectors are always inserted with the USB symbol (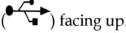) facing up.

Cabling can be screened or unscreened. Screened cables can be up to 5m (about 16.5 feet).

The data rate for USB 1.1 is 12 Mbps for a screened cable and 1.5 Mbps for an unscreened cable (used for low bandwidth devices such as keyboards and mice).

> **Tip**
> Note that this is peak, theoretical bandwidth and that it is *shared* between all devices attached to the same host.

Most USB hosts and devices now conform to the **USB 2.0 (Hi-Speed)** standard, with a nominal data rate of 480 Mbps. USB 2.0 uses the same connectors as USB 1.1 and is completely compatible with the older standard. A USB 1.1 device can be plugged into a USB 2.0 bus, but will operate at the lower speed.

Firewire

The **Firewire** bus, based on the IEEE 1394 standard, is another modern series bus. IEEE 1394 was developed from SCSI but uses serial rather than parallel communications and much smaller connectors.

Firewire is similar to USB but is not quite so well-supported. All PCs and laptops have USB ports while only some models have Firewire. If the motherboard does not provide Firewire ports, an I/O expansion card can be fitted. There are also more USB devices than Firewire devices.

A single bus can connect up to 63 devices. Like USB, the bus is powered and supports Plug-and-Play and hot swapping.

The maximum transfer rate is 400 Mbps. Firewire supports **isochronous** transfer mode, where the data rate to a particular device is guaranteed, making it very well matched to the transfer of real-time data such as video.

There are unpowered 4-pin cables in addition to 6-pin powered connectors. The maximum cable length between two devices is 4.5 meters (14.85 feet).

The IEEE 1394b (Firewire 800) standard supports transfer rates up to 800 Mbps and increased power from the bus (up to 45 watts) to support larger devices without the need for a separate power source. The new standard uses 9-pin connectors and cabling but is backward compatible with IEEE 1394a.

Firewire cables

6-pin (left) and 4-pin (right) Firewire ports

I/O Devices

Most Input / Output bus functions are provided on the motherboard, which will typically have USB, PS/2, PATA/SATA, parallel, and serial ports in various numbers. An adapter card can be installed to provide additional ports or a bus type that is not supported on the motherboard (for example, a SCSI host adapter, a card with extra USB and Firewire ports, or a card supporting wireless ports, such as Bluetooth or IrDA).

HP Ultra320 SCSI host adapter for PCI-X slot

Input Devices

Input devices (or **Human Interface Devices [HID]**) are peripherals that enable the user to enter data and select commands.

Keyboard

The **keyboard** is the longest serving type of input device. Historically, keyboards were connected via a 5-pin mini-DIN port called PS/2. This is colored purple to differentiate it from the identical mouse connector. Keyboards can also use USB or wireless (infrared or Bluetooth) connections though.

Extended PC keyboards feature a number of special command keys (ALT and CTRL plus keys such as PRINT SCREEN, NUM LOCK, SCROLL LOCK, START, SHORTCUT, and FUNCTION). Multimedia keyboards may also feature programmable keys and buttons that can be used for web browsing, playing CD/DVDs, and so on.

HP PS/2 Easy Access keyboard with programmable function buttons (across the top)

Mouse

The **mouse** is the main type of input device for graphical software. Mice use the same interfaces as keyboards (the PS/2 port is color-coded green though).

There are three distinct types of mice:

- Mechanical mouse - this contains rollers to detect the movement of a ball housed within the mouse case. As the user moves the mouse on a mat or other firm surface, the ball is moved and the rollers and circuitry translate that motion to move a cursor on the screen.

- Optical mouse - this uses LEDs to detect movement over a surface.

- Laser mouse - this uses an infrared laser, which gives greater precision than an optical mouse.

Another distinguishing feature of different mouse models is the number of buttons (between two and four), which can be customized to different functions, and the presence of a scroll wheel, used (obviously) for scrolling and as a clickable extra button. Mice are also distinguished by their size and shape. Smaller mice are useful with portable systems; some mice are marketed on the basis of their ergonomic shape.

HP laser mouse with wireless dongle

A **trackball** is basically an upside-down version of a mechanical mouse. Rather than moving the mouse to move the cursor, you can spin the ball. This arrangement is easier for some people to use.

Keyboard, Video, Mouse (KVM)

A **Keyboard, Video, Mouse (KVM)** switch allows multiple computers (typically servers) to be controlled via a single keyboard, mouse, and monitor. Some switches designed for home use also support speaker and microphone ports.

Each computer's ports are cabled to the switch then a single cable runs from the switch to the input and output devices.

HP KVM cables for USB (left) and PS/2 (right)

Simple desktop KVM switches support two devices; control is usually switched using a key sequence such as **SCROLL LOCK-SCROLL LOCK-ARROW KEY**. Server-level KVM switches may support tens of ports and have more sophisticated controls.

Module I Personal Computer Components   *Peripheral Devices*

Touch screen

A **touch screen** can be used for input where a mouse and/or keyboard are impractical. Typically, touch screens are used on handheld portable devices but they are also useful in industrial environments or for public terminals, such as kiosks, where mice or keyboards could be damaged, stolen, or vandalized.

There are three main ways of implementing a touch screen:

■ **Resistive** screens use panels that convert pressure (applied by a finger or stylus) to electrical signals. This is the cheapest method but dims the image from the display device (**clarity**) by up to 25%.

■ A **capacitive** touch screen has a panel with a small electrical charge; when a user touches the panel the charge is dissipated. Circuitry detects this change in charge and calculates the co-ordinates of the touch. Capacitive systems have clarity of up to 90% but require a conductive pointer (such as a finger or specially designed stylus).

■ A **Surface Acoustic Wave** system beams ultrasonic waves across the surface of the screen. An object touching the screen disrupts the waves and the circuitry works out the co-ordinates of the touch accordingly. SAW systems offer 100% clarity.

Computing devices may use an enhanced type of touch screen called a **digitizer**. A digitizer only works with a special stylus or pen, meaning that the user can rest his or her hand on the screen surface without it being interpreted as input[49]. Most digitizers are manufactured by Wacom, who produce drawing tablets (based on the same technology) for art and design applications as well.

The stylus also replicates mouse functionality in the following ways:

■ Tap - a single short tap represents a mouse click.

■ Tap-and-Drag - to select text.

■ Tap-and-Hold - display a shortcut menu.

Another advanced type of touch screen is one that supports **gesture control** (or **multi-touch**). This means that a gesture using two or more fingers at the same time is interpreted as a command (to scroll in or out for instance).

---

[49] On hybrid devices, you can enable or disable touch input as required.

© 2010 gtslearning   IT Career FastTrack with CompTIA A+ Certification   Page 79

Joystick / game pad

PC games are mostly designed for use with the mouse and keyboard but some games (flight simulators for instance) benefit from the use of a **joystick** or **gamepad**. Historically, joysticks used a DA-15 game port, usually located on the sound card, but new devices use USB connectors.

Joysticks can also be used as input devices by people who have difficulty using a mouse or keyboard.

Bar code reader

A **bar code reader** is a handheld or pen-shaped device designed to scan bar codes.

HP USB bar code scanner

A bar code is a pattern of different sized parallel bars, typically representing a product number, such as an ISBN, EAN, or UPC. The reader uses a sensor mechanism (either a photo diode, laser, or Charge Coupled Display [CCD]) to read the intensity of light reflected back by the bar code. The reader then reports the number back to application software, which links it to a product database.

Bar code readers are interfaced using USB or the PS/2 keyboard port.

Biometric devices

Biometric devices are used to perform authentication (identifying someone as a valid user of the computer or network).

Biometric devices associated with computer equipment tend to be thumb- or fingerprint readers. These may be standalone devices connected via a USB port or incorporated onto the computer chassis, keyboard, or mouse.

Biometric authentication is covered in more detail in unit 3.4.

Communication Devices

Communication devices allow computers to be connected together in a computer **network**. A **network adapter** provides a direct connection to a local network. A **modem** is used to connect to a remote computer using the telephone system.

Network adapters

Most motherboards come with an onboard **network adapter**; alternatively one can be installed as a PCI or PCIe expansion card. Most computer networks are based on **Ethernet**. There are different types of Ethernet, though the most commonly implemented are 100 Mbps or 1000 Mbps (Gigabit) over copper wire (UTP)[50], which uses **Registered Jack (RJ)** connectors and ports.

RJ-45 connector (left) and port (right)

RJ-45 (or 8P8C) connectors are used with 4-pair (8-wire) network data cables.

Cards that can support other types of Ethernet, notably fiber optic, or other network standards (such as wireless) can be obtained if necessary.

Networking is covered in more detail in module 5.

Modems

A **modem** connects the computer to another computer over a telephone line. To do this, it converts digital signals to an analog carrier signal (modulation) and transfers it over the telephone cable, making a distinctive screeching noise. The modem at the other end converts the analog signal back to digital (demodulation) and processes the data.

Most modems support the V.90 or V.92 standards, defined by the International Telecommunications Union (ITU). These support theoretical speeds of up to 56 Kbps, though actual throughput is often much less.

---

[50] Unshielded Twisted Pair is a type of copper cabling where pairs of insulated conductors are twisted around one another, to minimize electrical interference.

A modem may be installed either as an internal adapter card or as an external device. Early modems were connected using the serial (COM) port. Most external modems now use USB connections.

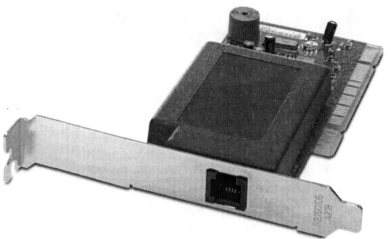

HP Connexant 56K modem PCI card with RJ-11 port

A modem is connected to the phone point[51] by 2-pair cable (often a "silver satin" cable) with RJ-11 connectors.

RJ-11 (left) and BT (right) connectors

In the UK, BT 631A connectors are used to connect equipment to telephone points. Modems designed for UK use come with a cable with an RJ-11 connector at one end and a BT connector at the other.

Summary

Ports provide connectivity for peripheral devices. USB and Firewire represent the main way of connecting newer devices, with PS/2, serial, and parallel ports providing compatibility for older hardware. Network and modem cables are connected via RJ-45 and RJ-11 ports respectively.

Peripheral devices provide input (mouse, keyboard, and touch screen for instance), audio/multimedia, I/O, and network/communications functions.

---

[51] It is important not to plug a modem into a digital phone system as the digital signaling can damage the modem.

Module 1 Personal Computer Components   *Sound and Video Devices*

Unit 1.6 Sound and Video Devices

CompTIA A+ Essentials Objectives

☐ **701.1.2 Explain motherboard components, types and features**
I/O interfaces (Sound, Video)

☐ **701.1.7 Distinguish between the different display devices and their characteristics**
Projectors, CRT and LCD • LCD technologies (Resolution [e.g. XGA, SXGA+, UXGA, WUXGA], Contrast ratio, Native resolution) • Connector types (VGA, HDMi ,S-Video, Component / RGB, DVI pin compatibility) • Settings (Refresh rate, Resolution, Multi-monitor, Degauss)

☐ **701.1.8 Install and configure peripherals and input devices**
Multimedia (e.g. web and digital cameras, MIDI, microphones)

☐ **701.1.9 Summarize the function and types of adapter cards**
Video (PCI, PCIe, AGP) • Multimedia (Sound card, TV tuner cards, Capture cards)

Display Devices

The **display subsystem** is the main type of output provided with a PC. Display output is provided by some sort of **Visual Display Unit (VDU)** - a CRT, LCD, or projector - plus a **video (or graphics) adapter**, which generates the signals to send to the VDU.

Some notable manufacturers of display devices include Viewsonic, Iiyama, Sony, Panasonic, Toshiba, LG, Acer, Sanyo, and Mitsubishi.

CRT monitors

A **Cathode Ray Tube (CRT)** monitor was the main type of display output device used with computers for most of the PC's history.

A color CRT is a vacuum tube with three electron guns at one end (the "neck") and a phosphor coated glass screen at the other. Electron beams ("cathode rays") are directed from the guns onto the screen. The screen is coated with differently colored phosphors (red, blue, and green) arranged in triangular dot clusters (triads[52]). When an electron beam strikes a dot, it glows.

---

[52] This is for a shadow mask type CRT. Another CRT type uses an aperture grill (based on the Sony Trinitron), where the phosphors are arranged in thin strips. Such CRTs have a faint line running across the top third of the screen.

© 2010 gtslearning   IT Career FastTrack with CompTIA A+ Certification   Page 83

The intensity of the beam on the combination of red, green, and blue phosphors produces a range of millions of colors (the **gamut**). The beam intensity is varied by analog signals received from the video adapter (graphics card).

Magnetic coils within the CRT are used to "aim" the beam at each triad. The beams are scanned across and down the screen very quickly (raster) to produce the image.

Mass production makes CRTs cheap. On the best models, color reproduction is extremely good and CRTs can display sharp images at a range of resolutions (see below). The main drawbacks of CRTs are that the monitors are bulky and heavy and tend to consume more power and generate more heat than "flat panel" equivalents.

CRT monitor

Liquid Crystal Displays

Liquid Crystal Displays (LCD) (or "flat panel") displays have largely replaced CRTs as the standard display type for PC systems. Mass production has driven prices down to the level of CRTs and quality has improved to close to the level of CRTs.

Liquid crystals are chemicals whose properties change with the application of voltage. In the **Thin Film Transistor (TFT) Twisted Nematic (TN)** type of LCD used for most computer displays[53], voltages "twist" the molecules in the liquid crystal to block the passage of light to some degree. Each picture element (pixel) in a color LCD comprises cells (or subpixels) with filters to generate the three primary colors (red, green, and blue) and transistors to vary the intensity of each cell, so creating the gamut (range of colors) that the display can generate. The whole panel is illuminated by a fluorescent or **Light Emitting Diode (LED)** backlight. LED backlights are starting to replace fluorescents as they are brighter and use less power.

---

[53] TFTs are also called active matrix displays, because each element in the matrix has its own transistors. Some old, low quality screens used passive matrix displays. Passive matrix displays are refreshed on a row and column basis, rather than pixel-by-pixel. This makes them subject to poor response times (ghosting) and viewing angles.

HP Compaq desktop with TFT display

Tip

CRTs are considered better at accurate color reproduction and so still widely used in the design and publishing industries. However, production of top-end CRTs is tailing off, making them more and more expensive.

Projectors

A **video projector** is a large format display, suitable for use with a presentation or at a meeting. The image is projected onto a screen or wall using a lens system. Some types of projector are portable; others are fixed in place.

There are CRT and LCD versions but the top end of the market is dominated by **Digital Light Processing (DLP)**, developed by Texas Instruments. Each pixel in a DLP device is represented by a mirror, which can be tilted towards or away from a light source and color filters to create the required shade.

Unit 1.6　　　　　　　　　　　　　　　　　　　　　Module 1 Personal Computer Components

HP DLP Projector

Apart from cost, portability, and reliability, the basic ratings for a projector include the display resolution, the size of the image, and how bright it is, measured in lumens (lm). The brightness required depends on the ambient light in the room and the size of the image. Where the projector is to be used in full daylight, a lumens rating of between 1500 and 3000 is required, depending on the image size.

Comparing display technologies

Output displays are evaluated on the following characteristics:

- **Resolution** - a device's **native resolution** is determined by dot pitch[54]. A CRT can support a number of output resolutions without losing quality (the "crispness" of an image). LCDs only support lower resolutions by interpolating the image, which makes it look "fuzzy".

- **Screen size** - for CRTs, this is the diagonal size of the tube, measured in inches. For CRTs, screen size is not always the same as *viewable area*, because part of the tube is hidden by the monitor's plastic casing (bezel). For flat panels, the quoted screen size is always the viewable area. Most screens are 15" or 17", with 19" or 21" also available.

---

[54] On a shadow mask CRT, dot pitch is the diagonal distance between two phosphors of the same color; in an aperture grill CRT, dot pitch is the horizontal distance between two phosphors of the same color. However, some shadow mask CRTs were advertised using the horizontal dot pitch, giving a misleading indication of the quality of the monitor. On an LCD, dot pitch is the diagonal distance between cells of the same color, though most LCDs are simply marketed using the native resolution in pixels.

Viewable area of a CRT is not always the same as the quoted screen size

This HP TFT can pivot between portrait and landscape modes

- **Aspect ratio** - this is the width of the screen divided by the height. CRT monitors for PC use are all 4:3. Flat panels are either 4:3 or widescreen (16:9 or 16:10[55]). One feature of some flat panels is the ability to pivot the display through 90 degrees (making it 3:4 or 9:16).

- **Refresh rate** - this is the speed at which the display device redraws the image, measured in hertz (Hz). If the refresh rate of a CRT is not high enough (below about 70 Hz), there will be a noticeable flicker as the image is redrawn. This can cause eyestrain and headache. LCDs are not refreshed in the same way and do not suffer from flicker but the refresh rate in an LCD still has an impact on the *quality* of the image (in particular, how smoothly objects in motion are displayed).

---

[55] Consumer widescreen (for DVD movies) is 16:9 but many PC widescreen display formats are 16:10 to leave room for on-screen controls above or below the movie.

Unit 1.6   Module 1 Personal Computer Components

- **Response rate** - this is the time taken for a pixel to change color, measured in milliseconds (ms). The best quality LCDs have a response rate of 8 ms or lower. High response rates (over 20 ms) can lead to "ghosting" or "trails" when the image changes quickly. CRTs do not have problems with response rate (except for the very cheapest or oldest models).

- **Luminance** - this is the brightness of an LCD, measured in candelas per square meter (cd/m²). Typically, LCDs are between 200 and 300 cd/m² though panels designed for home entertainment or gaming may be 500 cd/m² or better.

- **Contrast ratio** - this is a measure of luminance of white compared to black. Higher ratios (above 600:1) indicate that LCDs can display "true blacks" and better saturated (more intense) colors.

- **Viewing angle** - the image on a flat panel darkens and distorts to some degree if not viewed straight on. While this is not an issue for desktop use, it can affect use of the screen for viewing movies or as a presentation device. Manufacturers may quote acceptable viewing angles in marketing literature, but these values are not usually comparable to one another.

Note

LCDs can suffer from stuck or dead pixels. These cause a fixed bright or dull spot on the display. Manufacturers will usually refuse to replace a flat panel on the basis of a small number of dead pixels and it is worth reading the vendor's policy carefully before purchase. Another quality issue to consider is how much the backlight "bleeds" from the frame into the image.

Adjusting the image

Display settings, such as screen size and position and brightness, can be changed using push-button controls on the monitor case. These may bring up a simple on-screen menu. You may also be able to change these settings via Display properties in Windows or using software supplied with the monitor. The following settings apply to both CRTs and LCDs:

- Brightness and contrast - adjust the image.

- Color - calibrate the monitor to display colors accurately.

- Reset - apply the factory default settings.

The following settings apply only to CRT monitors:

Page 88   IT Career FastTrack with CompTIA A+ Certification   © 2010 gtslearning

Module I Personal Computer Components   *Sound and Video Devices*

- Display area - size and position of the image.

- Geometry - adjust the orientation of the picture and make edges straight as possible (pincushion and keystone).

- Moiré - cancel interference patterns (wavy lines); this is usually set to automatic.

- Convergence - adjust if there are colored "shadows" around text and lines.

- Degauss - use if the picture is "fuzzy" (this demagnetizes the monitor).

Note
A monitor is degaussed when it is switched on. Do not degauss a monitor more than twice within a 20-30 minute period.

- V-hold - adjust if the picture scrolls uncontrollably.

Video Adapters

The **video adapter** (or **graphics card**) generates the signal to send to the display output device. The video adapter may make use of the system CPU and memory, but most add-in cards are highly sophisticated pieces of equipment, essentially computers in their own right.

Low-end video adapters are likely to be included with the motherboard chipset. If a computer is to be used for 3D gaming or multimedia work, a better quality adapter is required. This can be installed via a PCIe slot (though older cards use AGP or even PCI).

Most graphics adapters are based on chipsets by ATI[56] (Radeon chipset), nVIDIA (GeForce and nForce chipsets), SiS, VIA, and Intel.

VGA standards

IBM created **VGA (Video Graphics Array)** as a standard for the resolution and color depth of computer displays. VGA specifies a resolution of 640x480 with 16 colors (4-bit color[57]) at 60 Hz.

---

[56] ATI are now owned by AMD, the CPU manufacturer.

[57] VGA also specified other lower resolution modes with more colors but 640x480 is what is commonly referred to as "VGA".

© 2010 gtslearning   IT Career FastTrack with CompTIA A+ Certification   Page 89

A computer image is made up of a number of **pixels**. The number of horizontal and vertical pixels gives the resolution of the image. Each pixel can be a different color. The total number of colors supported in the image is referred to as the **color depth** (or **bit depth**). The standard color depths are:

- 4-bit (16 colors)

- 8-bit (256 colors)

- 16-bit (65,536 colors)

- 24-bit (16,777,216 colors)

- 32-bit (24-bit color with support for 8-bit alpha channels, used for special effects).

The other important component of video is the speed at which the display is refreshed, measured in Hertz (Hz).

Increasing any one of these factors increases the amount of bandwidth required for the video signal and therefore the amount of processing that the CPU or GPU (Graphics Processing Unit) must do and the amount of system or graphics memory required.

The VGA standard is long obsolete[58] but was further developed by the **Video Electronics Standards Association (VESA)** as **Super VGA (SVGA)**. SVGA was originally 800x600 @ 4-bit or 8-bit color. This was very quickly extended as the capabilities of graphics cards increased with the de facto **XGA** standard providing 1024x768 resolution, better color depths, and higher refresh rates.

Resolutions for modern display systems use some variant of the XGA "standard" (in fact, these are labels rather than standards).

Some of the more popular XGA resolutions in use are:

Standard	Resolution	Aspect Ratio
SXGA (Super XGA)	1280x1024	5:4
SXGA+	1400x1050	3:4
WSXGA+	1680x1050	Widescreen (16:10)[59]
UXGA (Ultra XGA)	1600x1200	3:4
WUXGA	1920x1200	Widescreen (16:10)

[58] The resolution (640x480) referred to as "VGA" is popular on handheld devices such as PDAs and smartphones but at 16- or 24-bit color depth.

[59] Widescreen on consumer devices means a 16:9 ratio. For example, HDTV resolutions are 1280x720 and 1920x1080.

Module 1 Personal Computer Components | Sound and Video Devices

Video adapter GPU

The core of a video adapter is the **Graphics Processing Unit (GPU)**. This is a microprocessor like the CPU, but designed and optimized for processing instructions that render 2D and 3D images on-screen. High-end cards are differentiated based on the following features:

- Clock speed - as with the CPU, the clock speed is the basic measure of performance but the internal architecture (pipeline) of the GPU is another important factor.

- Shader units - support the special effects built into games and other software. These units perform calculations that allow for 3D shading, realistic shadows and lighting, surface textures, translucency, and so on.

- Frame rate - the basic test for a GPU is the frame rate it can produce for a particular game or application. 25 fps is about the minimum to make a game playable. A powerful GPU might generate a faster frame rate than the output device's refresh rate can handle. V-sync synchronizes the frame rate to the refresh rate[60].

Video memory

3D cards need a substantial amount of memory for processing and texture effects. A dedicated card may be fitted with between 128 and 512 MB GDDR RAM[61]. The width and speed of the memory bus between the graphics RAM and GPU is also important. Low end cards use shared memory (that is, the adapter uses the system RAM). Some cards may use a mix of dedicated and shared memory[62].

---

[60] The frame rate is the number of times the image in a video stream changes per second and can be expressed in Hertz or Frames per Second (fps). Refresh rate is the number of times the display device updates the display (regardless of whether the image is changed or not) expressed in Hertz. The refresh rate needs to be synched to the frame rate. For example, a display device with a 120 Hz refresh rate displays a 30 fps video stream at a ratio of 4:1.

[61] GDDR is very similar to DDR GDDR3 and GDDR4 are based on DDR2 while GDDR5 is based on DDR3. See unit 1.3 for more information on RAM types. Older cards would use ordinary DDR or SDRAM.

[62] Some of the literature and vendor terminology can be misleading. ATI call shared memory "HyperMemory" and nVIDIA call it "TurboCache". Some marketing literature may even describe shared memory as "video memory".

© 2010 gtslearning | IT Career FastTrack with CompTIA A+ Certification | Page 91

Adapter interface

Most modern cards are PCIe x16, though some AGP cards remain on the market. Dual cards, using two slots, are also available. With nVIDIA cards this is accomplished using Scalable Link Interface (SLI); ATI dual cards are branded CrossFire.

nVIDIA Quadro PCIe adapter card with single DVI-D dual link connector

Video port

There are several types of interface between the display device and the computer's video card. The display device and/or the video card may support more than one type of interface.

- **VGA** - the distinctive blue, 15-pin Video Graphics Array port (HD15F) is the standard video interface for PC devices. The connector is a D-sub type (HD15M). The interface is analog, meaning that it carries a continuous, variable signal.

VGA connector

Note

CRTs are analog devices but flat panel devices are digital. A TFT supporting VGA needs an analog-digital converter.

Component (top) and S-Video ports

- **S-Video** - this uses a 4-pin mini-DIN connector and carries an analog video signal. S(eparate)-Video is commonly used on consumer Audio/Visual (A/V) equipment in North America and Japan. In Europe, the SCART connector is used for consumer devices but SCART is not supported on PC equipment.

- **Component (RGB) video** - this uses three RCA jacks (one each for the red, blue, and green analog or digital video signals). Component video has high bandwidth and is widely found on better quality A-V equipment.

The more widespread use of digital displays (LCDs) has led to the development of new digital interfaces. Another factor is the increased bandwidth required to support High Definition TV and video (HDTV).

- **Digital Visual Interface (DVI)** - this is a high quality digital interface designed for flat panel display equipment and now standard on video adapters. There are five types of DVI, as described below. The pin configuration of the connectors identifies what type of DVI is supported:

    □ **Single-** or **dual- link** - DVI bandwidth in single-link mode is 3.7 Gbps, enough for HDTV (1920x1080) at a frame rate of 60 fps. More bandwidth can be obtained through connectors that support dual-link mode. Dual-link supports over 7.4 Gbps, enough for HDTV @ 85 fps. A single-link connector can be plugged into a dual-link port, but not vice versa.

    □ **Analog** and / or **digital** - DVI-I supports analog equipment (such as CRTs) and digital. DVI-A supports only analog and DVI-D supports only digital.

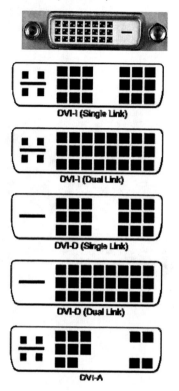

DVI-D dual-link port (top) and DVI interface diagrams

- **High Definition Multimedia Interface (HDMI)** - this supports both video and audio streams, plus remote control (CEC) and digital content protection (HDCP). It uses a proprietary 19-pin connector[63]. HDMI cabling is specified to different HDMI versions (from v1.0, supporting 4.9 Gbps, up to v1.3, which supports 10.2 Gbps).

HDMI connector

Tip
HDMI is backwards compatible with DVI using a suitable adapter cable. This means that (for example) a DVI graphics adapter could be connected to an HDMI port on the display device.

---

[63] This is the Type A connector. The Type B connector supports dual-link connections but it is not widely used.

ATI Radeon x800 AGP graphics adapter with VGA, S-Video, and DVI-I ports

> **Note**
> DVI and HDMI both use a signaling method called **Transition Minimized Differential Signaling (TMDS)**.

Having two connectors on the card also allows for the attachment of two display devices, even if the connectors are different types.

Graphics API

To work with 3D games and design applications, graphics cards need to be compliant with the specified version of one of the major graphics APIs:

- DirectX - Microsoft's specification, currently on version 9 for Windows XP or version 11 for Windows Vista SP2 and Windows 7. DirectX also specifies sound and multimedia APIs.

- OpenGL - developed by Silicon Graphics, currently on version 2.0.

Module 1 Personal Computer Components   *Sound and Video Devices*

Audio Devices

A computer's **audio subsystem** is made up of a **sound card** (to process audio signals and provide interfaces for connecting equipment) and one or more input (**microphone**) and output (**speaker**) devices[64].

Sound card

The basis of a sound (or audio) card is the **Digital Signal Processor (DSP)** chip, which contains one or more **Digital-to-Analog Converters (DAC)**. DACs convert the digital signals generated by the CPU to an analog electrical signal that can drive the speakers[65]. The DSP also provides functions for playing digital sound (synthesis) and driving MIDI-compatible devices.

A basic sound chip may be provided as part of the motherboard chipset but better quality sound functions can be provided as a PCI or PCIe expansion card.

Pro-level cards may also feature onboard memory, ROMs storing sound samples (wave tables), and multiple jacks for different input sources.

As with graphics cards, sound cards are designed to support sound APIs. Cards designed for use with Windows should support Microsoft's DirectSound3D (part of DirectX). Cards designed for use with games should also support Open AL and EAX, which provide extensions to DS3D for special sound effects.

Creative, Terratec, RealTek, and Turtle Beach are the most notable vendors of consumer sound cards, while E-MU, Yamaha, and Creative are noted for their professional-level cards.

Audio ports

Audio or "multimedia" ports are used to play and record audio from different inputs and outputs. One distinction that can be made between different types of multimedia port is whether they are *analog* or *digital*. Analog signals need to be converted to digital to be processed by the computer, which can degrade the signal.

---

[64] Most PCs also have a simple internal speaker capable of producing beeps. This is used for troubleshooting.

[65] An Analog-to-Digital chip converts analog audio input (such as from a microphone) to digital signals.

© 2010 gtslearning   IT Career FastTrack with CompTIA A+ Certification   Page 95

Most analog audio connectors are 3.5 mm (⅛") mono or stereo **phone plugs** (or **jacks**). A standard sound card will have a number of color-coded plugs for different equipment:

- **Audio in (light blue)** - audio in (or line in) is a low-level (1V) stereo signal as supplied by most tape decks, video players, tuners, CD players, and so on.

- **Microphone input (pink)** - this is generally a mono analog input.

- **Audio out (lime)** - audio out (or line out) is a low-level (1V) analog signal suitable for feeding into an amplifier. It does not have enough power to drive speakers directly. Connecting a low-level audio out signal directly to a pair of passive speakers (speakers without a built-in amplifier) will not work. An extra jack (color-coded black) may also be provided for rear speakers.

- **Headphones/Speaker out (orange)** - some sound cards include an amplifier internally, which can drive passive speakers or headphones.

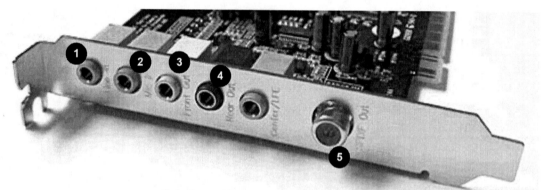

1) Audio in; 2) Mic in; 3) Audio out; 4) Speaker out; 5) S/PDIF RCA connector

Higher end sound cards will include an **S/PDIF (Sony/Phillips Digital Interface)** jack. S/PDIF can either use coax cabling with **RCA** (or **phono**) connectors or **fiber optic** cabling and connectors. S/PDIF is most often used to carry digital data for surround-sound speaker systems.

Tip

RCA connectors are distinguished by a collar surrounding the connector, which makes the fit between plug and socket more secure.

Audio playback

Sound cards supporting multiple output channels[66] with an appropriate speaker system can provide various levels of playback, from mono (on legacy systems) or stereo to some type of **surround sound**.

Surround sound uses multiple speakers positioned around the listener to provide a "cinematic" audio experience. A 5.1 digital system (**Dolby Digital** or **Digital Theatre System [DTS]**) has three front center, left, and right speakers, two left and right rear speakers, and a subwoofer for bass sounds. A 7.1 system (**Dolby Digital Plus** or **DTS-HD**) has two extra side speakers[67].

A speaker system will usually have controls for adjusting volume, bass, and treble plus optionally EQ or preset sound effects.

Another feature of a sound card is the audio cable connector to interface with the CD drive. This is provided so that audio CD playback can be achieved without using the CPU, which can make the sound "choppy" is the CPU is busy.

Audio cable connector (1) and 1/8" jacks (2) on a Creative X-Fi XtremeGamer PCI sound card

The quality of audio playback is determined by the card's **frequency response**, which is the volume that can be produced at different frequencies.

---

[66] A sound card will also feature internal channels (or voices). These represent the number of sounds that the card can play and mix at once (polyphony). This is important for music recording and working with sound effects used by some games.

[67] There are actually many more types of surround sound, but these are the two most popular digital formats.

Recording sound

Prosumer and professional-level cards are likely to feature numerous inputs, including ¼" phone plugs to connect musical equipment (such as professional quality microphone or amplifier equipment), extra RCA connectors, S/PDIF connectors, and 5-pin DIN connectors for MIDI equipment (see below).

These ports are often provided through a "breakout" box connected to the card and installed in a 5.25" drive bay. This reduces electrical interference from PC components when making recordings.

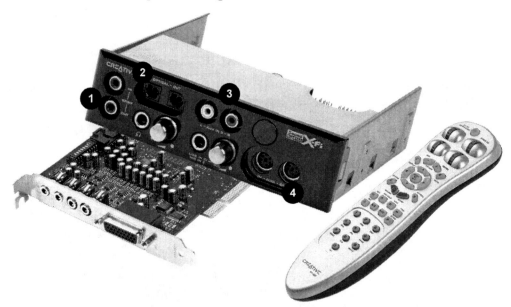

Creative Sound Blaster Audigy X-Fi Platinum with breakout box with 1) ¼" jacks; 2) Optical S/PDIF connectors; 3) RCA connectors; 4) MIDI DIN connectors

Tip
When using a PC to record music, the acoustic performance of components such as the hard drive and fans is very important, so as not to cause interference with analog inputs. Locate the sound card in the slot farthest from any other components.

To record an analog sound wave, the sound card must **sample** the wave. The sampler divides the wave up into a number of slices per second (sampling rate) and records information about each slice (resolution). The higher the sampling rate (measured in Kilohertz [KHz]) and resolution (measured in bits), the better the representation of the source is. CD-quality audio is sampled at 16-bit / 44.1 KHz but professional cards may sample at up to 24-bit / 192 KHz or better.

Module 1 Personal Computer Components

Sound and Video Devices

The card's circuitry and cabling introduce some degree of noise or distortion into the sampled audio. Noise levels are measured using **Total Harmonic Distortion (THD)** and **Signal-to-Noise Ratio (SNR)**. THD is measured as a percentage and SNR in decibels (dB). For both, smaller values represent better performance.

Tip

The acoustic performance and internal layout of all the PC components needs to be carefully specified and considered in a computer designed for professional sound recording.

MIDI

As well as playing sound via speakers, a card supporting **MIDI (Musical Instrument Digital Interface)** functions can be used to control MIDI equipment (such as a synthesizer or drum machine). Instead of exchanging the sound wave, the devices exchange information about how to play a sound (in terms of sample [sound pattern], volume, pitch, tempo, and so on). For example, you could use a keyboard to play with samples stored on the PC or use sequencing software to program a drum machine.

MIDI devices can use various ports (programmable 3.5mm jack, 5-pin DIN connector, 15-pin D-sub connector, or USB/Firewire).

Other Multimedia Devices

A number of other multimedia devices can be connected to a PC.

Digital cameras

Digital cameras are still cameras[68] that record an image using a light-sensitive **Charge Coupled Device (CCD)** array and store it on digital media (a flash memory card). Properties of 35mm film, such as ISO sensitivity, can be set through software. As well as the traditional viewfinder, the image can be displayed on a small TFT screen on the back of the camera. In other respects, digital cameras have the same features and functions as film cameras.

---

[68] Many digicams can record video too.

© 2010 gtslearning   IT Career FastTrack with CompTIA A+ Certification   Page 99

 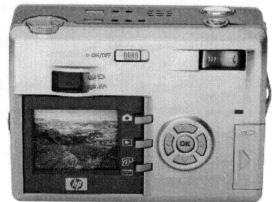

Front and back views of HP's Photosmart 935 digital camera - note the TFT viewfinder

The digicam market is divided into consumer models (replicating the features of compact 35mm film cameras), professional **Digital Single Lens Reflex (DSLR)** models (providing much better image quality, replaceable lenses, and manual adjustments), and "prosumer" models (ranging from high end compacts to entry-level DSLRs). Additionally, many cellphones now come with a camera function.

Apart from its lens, shutter speed, and feature set, the basic quality measurement of a digital camera is its resolution, expressed in megapixels (MP). The following table lists the best output that can be expected from images of a particular resolution:

Resolution	Uses
< 1 MP	Onscreen viewing only
1 - 2 MP	Onscreen and small prints (up to about 7")
3 MP	Larger prints (up to about 12" [Letter])
4 - 8 MP	Poster prints (30" and more)
8 - 15 MP	Prosumer and professional use

Another important factor is the type of **memory card** used by the camera (see unit 1.4 for a list of standard makes of flash card). Cameras can only use one type of card. Most cameras convert images to compressed (JPEG) file format to save space. JPEG is a *lossy* compression algorithm, meaning that even at the highest quality setting, some image information is discarded. Professional and prosumer models can typically record uncompressed (RAW) data, but this requires about 2-3 times as much space per picture.

Picture files can be transferred to a PC using the removable memory card or the camera can be connected directly using USB. Many printers also support memory card slots or connectivity for *direct printing* from a camera without requiring a PC.

Webcams

Webcams record video images using a CMOS or CCD sensor and may also feature a microphone to record audio. Most are low resolution (under 1 MP), record about 25 fps (frames per second), and have quite low quality lenses. Webcams are used for online video conferencing, as feeds for websites, and as surveillance devices.

HP USB webcam

Webcams are sometimes built into a laptop computer chassis but are more normally connected via USB.

TV tuners

A **TV tuner** is the basis for using a computer as a **Media Center**. A TV tuner allows the computer to receive broadcast TV (and radio) signals. Typically, a card will support analog and digital broadcasts, with the latest models supporting High Definition (HD) TV. The main TV broadcast signal formats are:

- NTSC - analog format used in North America and parts of South America.
- PAL - analog format used everywhere else.
- ATSC - digital format used in North America.
- DVB-T / DVB-S / DVB-C - digital formats (Terrestrial, Satellite, and Cable) used everywhere else.

Most cards also enable video capture using MPEG video encoding, allowing the PC to be used as a **Digital Video Recorder (DVR)**[69].

Some adapters feature two tuners so that a program other than the one being watched can be recorded.

The major card vendors are Hauppauge, ATI, and nVIDIA.

TV tuners are either fitted as PCIe or PCI adapter cards or external units connected via a USB or Firewire port.

Cards generally interface with a set-top box (used for satellite, cable, or digital TV reception) using S-Video or component connectors (or possibly DVI or HDMI) or directly with the reception antenna using a coax connector. Some cards have a built-in reception antenna.

The tuner is usually supplied with an infrared remote control, though not all remotes can be used to operate the set-top box.

HP external TV tuner

Video capture cards are similar but do not feature any sort of reception antenna. They take a video feed directly from playback equipment, such as a camcorder or VHS tape deck, and convert to a suitable multimedia file format for editing on the computer.

---

[69] MPEG (Moving Pictures Expert Group) is an ISO standards committee for audio and video compression and playback. There have been numerous MPEG standards over the years. From MPEG-1, the mp3 audio compression format remains very popular. MPEG-2 is widely used for film and broadcast delivery. MPEG-4 extends the MPEG-2 specification, notably providing support for Digital Rights Management (DRM), which enables playback to be tied to particular hardware devices.

Module 1 Personal Computer Components | *Sound and Video Devices*

Summary

The main display types are CRT monitor and flat panel LCD (or TFT). There are a number of video interfaces, including VGA, DVI, HDMI, and S-Video. The display signal is generated by the graphics adapter, which will determine the supported resolution, color depth, and 3D capabilities of the system.

A sound card allows for audio playback and recording. Audio ports come in different sizes and types to allow the connection of equipment such as microphones, speakers, and MIDI musical equipment.

Tip

To review what you have learned in this chapter, you should now visit the course website. This contains review questions and bonus material to help you to learn more and practice the topics covered in this unit.

Unit 1.7

Module 1 Personal Computer Components

Unit 1.7 Power Supplies

CompTIA A+ Essentials Objectives

☐ **701.1.3 Classify power supplies types and characteristics**
AC adapter • ATX proprietary • Voltage, wattage and capacity • Voltage selector switch • Pins

☐ **701.1.5 Explain cooling methods and devices**
Heat sinks • CPU and case fans • Liquid cooling systems • Thermal compound

Power Supply Unit (PSU)

The **Power Supply Unit (PSU)** delivers **DC (Direct Current)** low voltage power to the PC components. Mains electricity is supplied as **Alternating Current (AC)** at high voltage (110V or 240V, depending on which country you are in) because it is a cheap, efficient way of transmitting electricity over long distances. Computer components require low, stable voltage to work properly. The PSU contains transformers (to step down to lower voltages), rectifiers (to convert AC to DC), and filters and regulators (to ensure a "clean" output; or steady voltage). The other important component in the PSU is the fan, which dissipates the heat generated. Better quality models feature low noise fans.

Warning

The PSU is not user-serviceable - do not attempt to open the casing without the proper tools, knowledge, and experience. The PSU contains capacitors, which can store lethal electrical charges for long after the unit is disconnected from the power supply.

A PSU is plugged into an electrical outlet using a suitable power cable. The plug should suit the outlet type of the country you are in, though "travel plug" converters are commonly available. Some PSUs also have an outlet to plug a monitor power cable into. The plug should always be fitted with a working fuse of the correct rating (typically 3A or 5A).

A critical point to recognize if you are taking a computer to a different country is to ensure that the PSU is set to the correct input voltage. Some PSUs can accept different input voltages and are auto-switching (or auto-sensing); some have a switch to select the correct voltage; others can only accept one type of input voltage (fixed). The input operating voltages should be clearly marked on the unit and accompanying documentation.

Page 104   IT Career FastTrack with CompTIA A+ Certification   © 2010 gtslearning

Module 1 Personal Computer Components — Power Supplies

Autoswitching PSU (left) and PSU with manual voltage selector (between the power points)

Power Rating

A PSU must be able to supply adequate power to all the PC's components. The **power rating** of a PSU is measured in **watts** (calculated as voltage multiplied by current [V*I]). A 300W PSU is adequate for most desktop PCs. A system configured for gaming however could require 500W or even more, depending on the graphics subsystem installed.

> **Tip**
> The power requirement of different components varies widely (for example, CPUs can range from 17W to over 100W, depending on the model). If you are building or upgrading a system, the simplest way to work out the power requirement is to use an online calculator. Examples of these tools include outervision.com and journeysystems.com.

When specifying a PSU for a system that needs a lot of power, it is also important to look closely at the *power distribution* of each unit. Power distribution refers to how much power is supplied over each rail. A rail is a wire providing current at a particular voltage. For example, the following chart shows the maximum output for a PSU rated at 450W:

Output Rail	Max Load	Max Output
+3.3V	20A	130W[70]
+5V	20A	
+12V	33A	396W
-12V	0.8A	9.6W
+5V (Standby)	2.5A	12.5W

[70] The output of +3.3V and +5V has a combined limit. Note that no combination of values actually add up to 450W but PSU outputs are self-certified by the manufacturers so this situation is not uncommon.

Unit 1.7

Module 1 Personal Computer Components

For a modern computer, the output rating of the +12V rail (or rails) is the most important factor, as 12V is the most heavily used. Also note that as with bus bandwidth, *peak* output is only achieved under optimum conditions; *sustained* (or *continuous*) power output represents "real world" performance.

The power *output* is not the same as the power the PSU *draws* from the supply. PSUs typically work at around 75% efficiency, meaning a 300W supply draws 400W from the outlet. The energy is lost mainly as heat.

Tip

As power becomes more expensive, power efficiency is an increasingly important criterion to use when selecting a PSU. From 2007, an **ENERGY STAR** compliant PSU must be 80% efficient at 20-100% of load (many vendors only display the efficiency obtained under low load). **80 PLUS** is a similar rating scheme.

Another consideration when selecting a PSU is the circuitry used for **Power Factor Correction (PFC)**. In many countries, PFC is required to be provided for in electronic equipment by environmental legislation. Because of the way it works, a PSU can generate a large amount of *reactive* power, which is not used but "pushed back" to the electricity generator. The power factor is measured as the ratio of *active* to reactive power. PSUs with no PFC circuitry have a power factor of around 60%; **Passive PFC** circuitry can improve this to around 70% while **Active PFC** can improve it to between 95 and 99%.

Note that power factor is *not* the same thing as the efficiency of the PSU. Power factor affects the distribution of electricity rather than the efficiency of the device itself. However, PFC does reduce overall power consumption (which is why it is often required by environmental legislation) and brings cost-savings to organizations that purchase electricity on an industrial scale.

Form Factors and Outputs

Most PSUs are based on the ATX form factor, which can also be used with full-size BTX motherboards. The form factor determines both the size of the unit and position of the fan (allowing it to be screwed into a standard case) and the standard pin-outs for the power connectors.

The connectors supply various combinations of 3.3V, 5V, and 12V positive and negative current. Not all components use power at precisely these voltages. **Voltage regulators** on the motherboard are used to correct the voltage supplied from the PSU to the voltage required by the component.

Page 106   IT Career FastTrack with CompTIA A+ Certification   © 2010 gtslearning

The ATX PSU standard has gone through a number of revisions. The original ATX PSU has one 20-pin **P1** connector for the motherboard, a number of 4-pin **Molex** connectors for peripheral devices, and a 4-pin **mini-Molex** for the FDD.

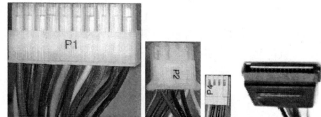

20-pin P1 motherboard, 4-pin Molex, 4-pin floppy (Berg), and 15-pin SATA power connectors

Tip

Modular PSUs have cables that are detachable from the PSU unit, allowing only the connectors actually required to be used. This reduces clutter within the chassis, improving air flow and cooling.

In 2000, Intel produced an updated ATX12V specification with an additional +12V connector to support the Pentium 4 CPU[71]. This can be provided either as an extra, square 4-pin connector (**P4**)[72]. An update to this specification defined optional support for SATA power connectors (to power hard disk drives)[73].

In 2003, the ATX12V specification was updated to version 2, which defined a 24-pin P1 connector to replace the 20-pin one. Power distribution was changed to favor the 12V circuits. It also made the provision of SATA connectors compulsory. The ATX12V 2.2 specification adds a 6-pin connector to supply extra power to PCIe graphics cards[74].

The general compatibility of different ATX PSU specifications to systems based on different CPUs is as follows:

PSU Type	CPU		
	Pre-P4 / Athlon	P4 / Athlon	Core / Athlon 64
ATX	Good	Incompatible	Incompatible
ATX12V v1	OK	Good	Incompatible
ATX12V v2	Poor / Incompatible	Good	Good

---

[71] This is often misleadingly referred to as Dual 12V Output, which implies separately generated outputs (giving better stability). In fact, most PSUs only generate one 12V output and split it between two or four rails, to comply with electrical safety standards (overcurrent protection).

[72] ATX12V v1 power supplies rated over 250W may also feature a 6-pin Aux connector.

[73] If a PSU has no SATA connectors, Molex-to-SATA converters are available.

[74] PSUs designed for dual card systems will feature two PCIe connectors. PSUs supporting the PCIe 2.0 specification have 8-pin connectors delivering 150W.

Some vendors may use *proprietary* designs, which can sometimes closely resemble a "standard" ATX PSU, but may use different pin-outs for the power connectors. An example of this is some of the systems produced by Dell. When upgrading or replacing a power supply, it is critical to check the documentation accompanying the system carefully. Another use of non-ATX PSUs is in SFF (Small Form Factor) PCs. There are a number of SFF PSU specifications from Intel (CFX, SFX, LFX, and TFX) but such systems are equally likely to use proprietary designs (such as Shuttle or AOpen). You can check www.formfactors.org for complete descriptions of the Intel specifications.

Air Cooling Systems

Heat is a by-product of pushing electric current through the various electronic components in the computer. The faster the components work, the more heat is produced. Excessive temperatures can cause the components to malfunction or even damage them. PC designs have to employ thermal management to counteract this effect.

PSU (1) and chassis (2) fans on an HP Compaq PC

Heatsinks

A **heatsink** is a block of metal with fins. As the fins expose a larger surface area to the air around the component, a greater cooling effect by convection is achieved.

The heatsink is "glued" to the surface of the chip using a **thermal pad** (or **compound** on earlier models) to ensure the best transfer of heat. In order to work well, a heatsink requires good airflow around the PC.

Fans

A **fan** improves *air flow* and so helps to dissipate heat. Fans are used for the power supply and chassis exhaust points. Smaller fans may be used to improve the performance of the heatsink on CPU and GPUs.

Fan assembly on a CPU (left) and ATI Radeon graphics processor (right)

Plastic shroud (1) covering the CPU and channeling the air to the fan exhaust (2) on an HP PC system

Unit 1.7

Module 1 Personal Computer Components

The main problem with fans, especially at the lower end of the market, is that they generate *noise*. A fan also needs to be matched to the CPU model to ensure that it is powerful enough to cope with the processor's thermal output.

Some fan or chassis designs incorporate a plastic shroud to cover the CPU and channel the flow of air to the fan.

Heat pipes and heat spreaders

A **heat pipe** is a sealed tube containing some type of coolant (water or ethanol). The liquid close to the heat source evaporates then condenses at a cooler point in the pipe and flows back towards the heat source. The cool parts of the pipe are kept so by convection.

This mechanism is more effective than a simple heatsink and fan assembly. It is necessary for a CPU that runs particularly hot or where there is not much space for airflow within the chassis. A **dual heat pipe** has two tubes, providing better cooling.

A **heat spreader** uses the same design but is a flat container rather than a pipe (this design is better suited to portable computers).

Liquid Cooling Systems

PCs used for high-end gaming (those with twin graphics cards for instance) and with overclocked components may generate more heat than basic thermal management can cope with. PCs used where the ambient temperature is very high may also require exceptional cooling measures.

Liquid cooling refers to a system of pumping water around the chassis. Water is a much more effective coolant than air convection and a good pump can run more quietly than numerous fans. Liquid cooling makes maintenance and upgrades more difficult, requires quite a lot of power to run, and is costly.

Page 110

IT Career FastTrack with CompTIA A+ Certification

© 2010 gtslearning

Module I Personal Computer Components — Power Supplies

Liquid-cooled Alienware PC

Summary

The power supply needs to meet the power requirements of the components installed in the computer. The quality of a power supply is determined by a combination of total power output, power distribution, and efficiency. Noise and cooling are other factors to consider. The power supply needs to be matched to the motherboard and chassis form factor. A supply will feature a number of connectors, including the P1 for connection to the motherboard, Molex connectors for drives, and auxiliary connectors for CPUs and graphics cards.

Computer components generate a lot of heat during operation and this needs to be dissipated by a cooling system. Most systems are based on air cooling, with a heatsink to draw heat from the component and a fan to provide circulation. Higher performance systems may use liquid cooling.

| Unit 1.8 | Module 1 Personal Computer Components |

Unit 1.8 Laptops and Portable Devices

CompTIA A+ Essentials Objectives

☐ **701.1.2 Explain motherboard components, types and features**
Memory slots (SODIMM) • Bus slots (PCMCIA)

☐ **701.1.10 Install, configure and optimize laptop components and features**
Expansion devices (PCMCIA cards, PCI Express cards, Docking station) • Communication connections (Bluetooth, Infrared, Cellular WAN, Ethernet, Modem) • Power and electrical input devices (Auto-switching, Fixed input power supplies, Batteries) • Input devices (Stylus / digitizer, Function keys, Point devices [e.g. touch pad, point stick / track point])

Portable Device Types

The market for portable computers is one of the faster growing areas of IT. There are three main types of portable technology, categorized in ascending order of size:

■ **Handheld devices** - including Personal Data Assistants (PDA) and smartphones (cellphones with PDA functionality). These devices are a few inches in size and weigh only a few ounces (or a few hundred grams).

■ **Tablet PCs** - larger than handhelds but operated using a touch screen rather than a pointing device and keyboard.

■ **Laptops** - still coming in a range of sizes, but closest to the functionality of a desktop PC.

Laptops are eating into the market share enjoyed by desktop PCs, driving prices closer and closer. Most vendors now expect to sell more laptops than desktops each year. Another important driver is network *convergence*. This means use of the same network to deliver different types of communications (voice, video, data, and so on). Portable devices commonly integrate the functions of phone, TV, radio, and computer.

The main features distinguishing portable computers from desktop PCs are:

■ **Size and weight** - laptops weigh between around 2 and 4 kg (4 - 9 lbs) and handhelds even less.

■ **Display type** - portable computers use flat-panel display technologies to provide lightweight, slimline screens that are built into the case.

Page 112   IT Career FastTrack with CompTIA A+ Certification   © 2010 gtslearning

- **Input devices** - the main input devices are integrated into the unit, such as a built-in keyboard, touchpad instead of mouse, or touch screen.

- **Cost** - laptops cost from 1½-2x as much as a similarly-specified desktop computer. Handhelds can cost as much as a low-end desktop.

- **Power source** - portable computers can be run from internal battery packs as well as from mains power.

- **Components** - portables often use different components that are smaller, lighter, and draw less power than desktop versions.

Types of laptop

HP Compaq Presario laptop computer with 1) Built-in TFT screen; 2) Integrated keyboard; 3) Touchpad pointer control; 4) I/O ports [on both sides and rear of chassis]

Like desktops, laptops come in many different models and specifications. You could broadly categorize laptops as follows:

- Budget / Mid-level - basic models featuring average components and a happy trade-off between features and portability.

- Desktop Replacement - a powerful machine with similar performance, capacity, and peripherals to a desktop PC. The trade off is being less portable and less able to run for a long period on battery power.

- Ultra Portable - very small and light machines offering extended operating time on battery power. The trade off here is smaller screen size, lower capacity drives, and fewer peripherals.

- Media Center - portable home entertainment systems, featuring large screens, storage capacity, media features (such as TV tuner, video recording, and surround sound), and components capable of running the latest games.

- Gaming Laptop - an increasingly popular class of machine. ATI and nVIDIA are producing more laptop graphics adapters designed for gaming, though they cannot match the power of the top-range desktop cards.

Tablet PC

A **Tablet PC** (or **slate**) is similar to an ultra portable laptop but has a touch sensitive screen that supports handwriting recognition. This makes the device ideal for professions where note-taking is important (doctors, nurses, teachers, scientists, and so on).

HP Compaq Tablet PC

A tablet PC may come with a keyboard (typically the screen is attached with a hinge) or may require a USB keyboard.

Netbook

Netbooks fit between traditional laptops and PDAs. Just as laptops have consumed a large part of the desktop market share, netbooks are starting to consume laptop market share. Unlike laptops, they only have limited functionality and performance (typically restricted to running two or three applications simultaneously) but unlike PDAs they have a full keyboard, touchpad, and large (7-9") screen.

Netbooks are designed primarily for internet access and communications. While they can run standard desktop / laptop operating systems and software, they are often used to access software hosted on the internet (referred to as **cloud computing**) rather than locally-installed applications.

HP Mini 1000 netbook

Personal Digital Assistants (PDAs) and smartphones

A PDA is an instant-access miniature computer, but PDAs are not as versatile as laptops or tablets. Only software designed specifically for the mobile operating system can be installed.

Many PDAs use **Windows Mobile** (or **Pocket PC**), and so provide a familiar user interface. Other machines use their own proprietary operating system; for example, the Palm and HandSpring series of PDAs, which use Palm OS.

Increasingly, PDA functionality is being integrated with cellphones, called **smartphones**. As well as Windows Mobile, the Apple iPhone OS, RIM BlackBerry, and Symbian OS are used for these devices.

- Storage - PDAs use ROM and flash memory, rather than a magnetic disk drive, to store the operating system and user data. One of the resulting benefits is that the operating system is available as soon as the user turns on the device.

- Power - PDAs can use battery or mains power (via an AC adapter or docking cradle). However, the battery in a PDA is not always user replaceable, in which case it is not possible to carry a spare battery, as you might with a laptop. Due to their lack of moving parts, PDAs last considerably longer on a single charge than laptops.

- Input and Output Devices - PDAs use small but high quality TFT touch screen displays. The latest models use high color (64K) 640x480 screens[75]. Using touch screen technology, a user can select icons and menu options and write on the screen. Text can also be entered using a touch-screen keyboard. Some devices (such as a BlackBerry) have a miniature keyboard; others can be fitted with a removable, fold-up keyboard.

HP iPAQ with a foldable Bluetooth keyboard

- Communications - many PDAs provide some kind of docking system and software (such as Microsoft ActiveSync) which enable users to synchronize data between their PDA and desktop computer. Push email (where a mail server sends messages to the device automatically), once the preserve of BlackBerries, is now commonly found on Pocket PCs and smartphones (using features in Microsoft Exchange Server).

- Internet connectivity - a standard PDA can connect to a cellphone via infrared or Bluetooth then use the phone's cellular dial-up or broadband service. The vast majority of PDAs on sale these days are smartphones though. Another option is to use a Wi-Fi adapter in the PDA and connect via a public wireless "hot spot".

---

[75] The PDA detects when the device is tilted, switching between landscape (480x640) and portrait mode automatically.

| Module I Personal Computer Components | Portable Devices |

Laptop Components

While there are a few "barebones" laptop vendors, most laptops are proprietary systems produced by (notably) HP, Dell, Lenovo, Sony, Toshiba, and ASUS). The chassis and motherboard are not designed in such a way as to allow the simple upgrade and replacement of components, as PCs are. The designs emphasize size, weight, and thermal efficiency over upgrade potential.

Motherboard and processor

A laptop's chipset is likely to contain more integrated features than a desktop's, including wireless networking (Wi-Fi) and connectivity and a modem. Components that would be replaceable in a desktop system, such as CPU, graphics card, and sound card, are often soldered to the motherboard or provided as part of the chipset. A laptop does not feature expansion slots as such.

Intel and AMD produce mobile versions of their processor models or (more recently) dedicated mobile CPU brands. The mobile versions tend to be clocked at lower speeds to reduce power consumption[76].

Apart from the legacy mobile versions of Pentiums II, III, 4, the Celeron, and AMD's mobile Athlon processors, there are four main types of mobile CPU in general use:

- **Intel Pentium M** - this CPU was the first to be part of Intel's **Centrino** mobile platform (also incorporating the chipset and wireless adapter) and was designed to be far more power efficient than the desktop Pentium 4 (the microarchitecture design is actually based on the Pentium III). There is support for Enhanced SpeedStep, MMX, SSE1, SSE2, and XD (on some models). It uses DDR memory.

- **Intel Core** - the original version of Intel's rebadged mobile CPUs consisted of Core Solo (uniprocessor) and Core Duo (dual-core) models. There is support for Enhanced SpeedStep, MMX, SSE1, SSE2, and XD (on some models). It uses DDR or DDR2 memory.

---

[76] You will often see the Thermal Design Power (TDP) quoted for mobile CPUs. This is the most amount of power (and therefore cooling) the chip will require during "ordinary use".

| © 2010 gtslearning | IT Career FastTrack with CompTIA A+ Certification | Page 117 |

- **Intel Core 2** - mobile versions of Intel's 64-bit, dual-core and quad-core CPUs. There is support for Enhanced SpeedStep, MMX, SSE1, SSE2, SSE3, VT (on some models), and XD. It uses DDR or DDR2 memory.

- **Intel Core i3, i5, i7** - mobile versions of Intel's latest generation of CPUs. They support SSE4 and use DDR3 memory.

- **AMD Turion 64** - AMD's 64-bit mobile CPUs. Dual-core models are branded as Turion X2. There is support for 3DNow!, MMX, SSE1, SSE2, SSE3, NX, and AMD's virtualization technology, plus the PowerNow! power management technology. It uses DDR or DDR2 memory.

- **AMD Turion II** - mobile version of AMD's Phenom CPU design. It supports SSE4 and DDR3 system memory.

- **Intel Atom** - low-cost processor designed for the netbook market.

Memory

Laptop memory uses the same technologies as desktop (SDRAM, DDR/DDR2/DDR3) but in different packaging. The most commonly used type is called **Small Outline DIMM (SODIMM)**.

Corsair ValueSelect SODIMM

Older SDRAM chips used 144-pin chips; DDR and DDR2 chips use 200-pin packages, which are differently keyed to prevent DDR modules from being installed in a DDR2 slot and vice versa. DDR3 uses a 204-pin package.

Drives

Laptop hard drives use the 2.5" form factor also used for external portable drives. Capacities range from 20 GB up to 160 GB. Speeds are usually either 5400 rpm or 7200 rpm (high performance desktop drives can be 10K rpm or better). The drive is connected to the motherboard using either a modified PATA connector (that combines the data and power connectors) or SATA connections, though some manufacturers use proprietary connections.

Most laptops also have an optical drive installed or the laptop may feature a **media bay**, which can accept a variety of pluggable drives or a second battery.

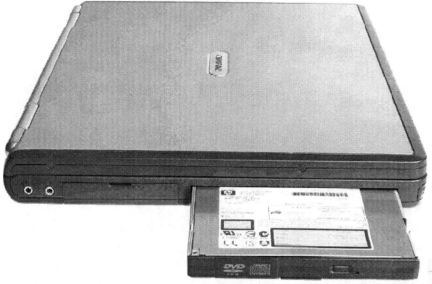

Swappable drive bay on a Compaq Presario

Additional storage options can be provided by connecting external drives via USB or Firewire ports or the PC Card / ExpressCard interfaces (see below).

Input devices

Laptops have built-in keyboards. On smaller laptops, the keyboard may not feature full size keys, which can make typing difficult. Laptop keyboards do not often have **numeric keypads** either. Instead, the keypad functions are accessed using the **FN** (Function) key. The **FN** key also accesses laptop specific functions indicated by distinctive blue icons. These include switching the display output between the built-in screen and a connected monitor, adjusting the screen brightness, switching to battery power, disabling wireless functions, and so on.

A laptop also has a built-in **touch pad** or (on IBM / Lenovo[77] machines) a **point stick**, replicating the function of the mouse. To use a pad, you move your finger over the surface to move the cursor and tap the pad to click. Touch pads also come with buttons and (usually) scroll areas to replicate the function of a mouse's scroll wheel.

---

[77] Lenovo purchased IBM's personal computer division in 2005.

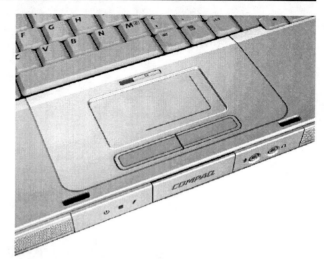

Compaq Touchpad - note the scroll areas and left and right buttons

A point stick (referred to as TrackPoint by IBM/Lenovo) is a mini-joystick located in the middle of the keyboard. Unlike a trackpad, it is responsive to the *amount* of pressure applied, making it easier to move the cursor long distances. Its proximity to the keyboard also assists touch typists.

None of the input devices on a laptop are really suitable for sustained use. An external keyboard and/or mouse can of course be connected using a USB or wireless port (or on older laptops, a PS/2 port).

Tablet PCs have integrated **touch screens**. These allow the user to control software by pointing at the screen (with a finger or stylus) and can be used for handwriting input.

Laptop Expansion Devices

Laptops ship with a number of standard wired ports for connectivity. Typically these will include VGA and DVI for an external display device, a number of USB ports, possibly a Firewire port, microphone and speaker jacks, possibly a memory card reader, and RJ-11 (modem) and RJ-45 (Ethernet) for communications. Laptops produced in the last couple of years usually do not support legacy ports (parallel, serial, and PS/2).

As mentioned above, there is not much scope for adding expansion cards within the chassis (with the exception of mini PCI [see below]). Laptops have two means of connecting add-on devices externally however: PCMCIA and ExpressCard.

PCMCIA

The **Personal Computer Memory Card Industry Association (PCMCIA)** was founded to provide a standard bus (**PC Card**) for laptop computers.

Initially, the standard was devised for flash memory cards (Type I), but it was subsequently extended to cover other types of expansion card, such as modems and network cards (Type II) and removable hard disks and devices that require larger external connectors, such as network adapters (Type III).

PC Card (adding modem functionality to a laptop)

All card types use the same 68-pin connector. The major difference between the slots is the thickness of card that can be supported:

- Type I cards can be up to 3.3 mm thick.
- Type II cards can be up to 5 mm thick.
- Type III cards can be up to 10.5 mm thick.

All slots are backwards compatible, so a Type III slot can take a Type II or a Type I card. Most laptop computers offer multi-purpose slots; for example, one Type III slot that takes 1 x Type III card or 2 x Type II or Type I cards.

PCMCIA 2.0 cards have a 16-bit interface and 5V signaling. The current standard (PCMCIA 2.1 [**CardBus**]) defines a 32-bit interface (supporting a maximum transfer rate of 132 MBps) and 3.3V signaling. CardBus slots also support PCMCIA 2.0 cards but PCMCIA 2.0 slots do not support CardBus. Slots are keyed to prevent use of the wrong card.

Xircom CardBus Ethernet adapter

PCMCIA cards use software known as socket services and card services:

- Socket services are like device drivers and handle the interaction between the PC and the card.
- Card services handle higher-level functions and control transfer of information from card memory to the CPU.

Like USB peripherals, PCMCIA cards are hot swappable.

ExpressCard

If you think of CardBus as PCI then ExpressCard is PCI Express for laptops. The bus operates at 1.5V, reducing power consumption and thermal output. The connector interfaces with either a PCI Express bus (using one lane) or a USB 2.0 bus on the motherboard.

Standard ExpressCards use a 26-pin, 34 mm connector. A wider card form factor, ExpressCard/54, has the same connector but a 54 mm "body", making an "L" shape. The wider cards cannot be used in 34 mm slots, but 34 mm cards can be used in 54 mm slots. Both types of card are 75 mm long and 5 mm deep.

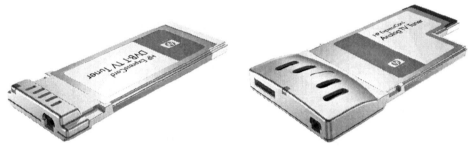

HP TV tuner ExpressCards - /34 (left) and /54 (right)

ExpressCard slots are not backwards compatible with CardBus.

Mini PCI / PCIe

Mini-PCI wireless adapter card

Mini PCI is a standard for adding upgradable cards to the motherboard. Mini-PCI is a Small Form Factor version of PCI 2.2. It supports 32-bit data transfer at 33 MHz using 3.3V signaling.

It is mostly used to add internal network, wireless, and modem adapters, making more external CardBus or ExpressCard slots available.

There are three types of mini-PCI card[78]:

---

[78] Also, each type is defined with A and B sizes. The cards are 45mm wide and between 60 and 70 mm long and 2.4 to 7.5 mm thick (though type IIB can be thicker to accommodate the external port).

- Type I - uses a 100-pin stacking connector (at right-angles to the card).
- Type II - as Type I but designed to be positioned on the chassis (with an integrated RJ-45 port for example).
- Type III - uses a 124-pin SO-DIMM style edge connector.

There are also PCI Express (PCIe) mini cards, supporting one lane (see unit 1.1 for more detail on PCIe). The cards have a 52-pin edge connector and are 30 mm wide by 56 mm or 32 mm long.

Port replicators and docking stations

A **port replicator** usually attaches to a special connector on the bottom of a portable computer. It provides a full range of ports for devices such as keyboards, monitors, mice, and network connections. A replicator does not normally add any functionality to the portable computer.

HP laptop connected to a port replicator

A **docking station** is a sophisticated port replicator that may support add-in cards or drives via a **media bay**. When docked, a portable computer can function like a desktop machine or use additional features, such as a full size expansion card.

HP docking station

Laptop Communication Connections

As mentioned above, most laptops feature a modem and Ethernet port on the motherboard. However, as portable devices, the use of **wireless technologies** for networking and peripheral connections is particularly useful. Wireless is a means of connecting peripheral devices or making network connections without cables. While there are products for desktop systems, the use of wireless adapters is more closely associated with mobile computing.

There are four main products in use with computer systems:

- IrDA Ports - these use infrared lasers (to transmit) and photodiodes (to receive) to transfer data at a reasonable rate (up to about 4 Mbps) at close range (up to 1 m or 3 feet). IrDA is used for input devices and wireless printing. Devices must have "line-of-sight" between one another.

- Bluetooth - this is a short-range radio-based technology, working at up to 10 m (30 feet) at up to 1 Mbps (or 3 Mbps for devices supporting version 2.0 of the standard). The advantage of radio-based signals is that devices do not need line-of-sight. Bluetooth has similar applications to IrDA, though is also used for connectivity with smartphones.

- Wi-Fi (802.11) Ports - this is a set of standards developed by IEEE for radio-based Wireless Local Area Network (WLAN) products. The main standard in use is 802.11g, which supports up to 54 Mbps at a range of up to about 30m (100 feet). A Wi-Fi adapter allows a laptop to join a wireless network.

- Cellular - internet access can be gained through the cellular network. A **W-CDMA** or **HSPA (High-Speed Packet Access)** adapter fitted in the laptop (or connected via ExpressCard or USB) enables the laptop to use cellular broadband internet access using the selected telecom provider's network.

These functions can be provided by add-in cards but are increasingly incorporated as standard features on the motherboard. Wireless and networking technologies are covered in more detail in module 5.

Laptop Power Devices

Portable computers offer both mains power and battery operation.

Mains power

To operate from mains power, the laptop needs a power supply that can convert from the AC (Alternating Current) supplied at the outlet to the DC (Direct Current) voltages used by the laptop's components. The power supply is provided as an external **AC adapter**.

Mains AC adapters are normally **universal** (or **auto-switching**) and can operate from any 110-240V 50/60Hz supply (check the label to confirm). Some adapters (notably some sold with US machines) are **fixed-input** (for instance, they only work with a 110V supply or have to be **manually switched** to the correct input).

AC adapter with US-style plug

AC adapter input and output information

AC adapters are also rated for their power output (ranging from around 65 - 120W). Again, this information will be printed on the adapter label (as shown above). Output (W) is calculated by multiplying voltage (V) by current (I). Obviously, a larger output will be able to power more devices and more powerful components.

Note that the power output of adapters and batteries can vary, so using an adapter designed for an ultra-mobile model probably won't work with a desktop replacement, even if it's the same brand.

Note
Plugging a fixed-input 240V adapter into a 110V supply won't cause any damage (though the laptop won't work), but plugging a fixed-input 110V adapter into a 240V supply will.

Battery power

Laptop computers use removable, rechargeable battery packs. There have been several different battery technologies in use over the years. Older technologies, such as Ni-Cad and NiMH, have been replaced by **Lithium ion (Li-ion)**. Li-ion batteries have good storage capacity and slower loss of charge. The metals used in their manufacture are slightly less damaging to the environment. They are typically available in 6, 9, or 12 cell versions, with more cells providing for a longer charge.

Summary

Laptop upgrade options are usually more limited than for desktop PCs, as the system design prioritizes size, weight, power consumption, and thermal management. Add-in devices are provided either through USB/Firewire ports or slot cards. A laptop can be powered from a removable battery pack or from mains power via an AC adapter.

Module 2 Operating Systems

A PC requires an **Operating System (OS)** in order to function. The operating system provides interfaces between the **hardware, application programs**, and the **user**.

The operating system handles many of the basic system functions, such as interaction with the system hardware and input/output. This allows **application software designers** to concentrate on application functions and makes the PC more reliable. One consequence of this is that there are relatively few operating systems, as it takes a lot of work to produce software applications that will work with different OS's. Also, changes to an operating system have to be made very carefully in order to remain compatible with previous generations of software and hardware.

For the **user** an operating system provides:

- A standard method to execute application programs.

- A number of utility programs which are useful in organizing data, troubleshooting, and optimizing the PC.

An operating system is generally made up of a number of core files (the **kernel**) with additional **device drivers** and programs to provide extended functionality. The earliest operating systems for PCs used a command-line interface or simple menu systems. Windows and later applications were marked by the use of a **Graphical User Interface (GUI)**[79]. This helped to make computers easier to use by non-technical staff and home users.

The market for operating systems is divided into three main functions:

- Business client - OS designed to work as a client in business networks.

- Network Operating System (NOS) - OS designed to run on servers in business networks.

- Home client - OS designed to work on standalone or workgroup PC in a home or small office.

---

[79] Actually, some DOS applications presented a GUI (of a kind). Windows is sometimes described as a WIMP (Window, Icon, Menu, Pointing device) interface.

Unit 2.1   Module 2 Operating Systems

Unit 2.1 Windows Versions and Features

CompTIA A+ Essentials Objectives

☐ **701.3.1 Compare and contrast the different Windows Operating Systems and their features**
Windows 2000, Windows XP 32bit vs. 64bit, Windows Vista 32 bit vs. 64bit (Side bar, Aero, UAC, minimum system requirements, system limits, Terminology [32bit vs. 64bit - x86 vs. x64], User interface, Start bar layout)

☐ **701.3.2 Given a scenario, demonstrate proper use of user interfaces**
Taskbar / systray • Start menu

Microsoft Windows

Windows is the dominant client OS, estimated to be installed on 90% of the world's desktop and laptop computers.

Early versions of Windows

Microsoft provided the command-line **Disk Operating System (DOS)** for the first IBM compatible PCs and followed this with the first commercial version of Windows (3x), running "on top" of DOS. In 1995, Microsoft released **Windows 95**, which was followed by the versions **Windows 98** and **Windows Millennium Edition (Me)**. These marked a move away from having a separate operating system and graphical user interface, though some DOS features were still present. Windows 9x added support for 32-bit applications, but was not a fully 32-bit operating system.

Alongside the development of Windows 9x, in 1993 Microsoft released **Windows NT 3.1**. Windows NT was not based on a 16-bit DOS kernel but rather fully optimized to take advantage of new 32-bit processors. Windows NT was positioned as an operating system for business PCs, with better reliability, security, and user management than Windows 9x. Windows 9x maintained greater support for games and multimedia. Windows NT was produced in client (Workstation) and server editions. In 1996, **Windows NT 4** updated the NT GUI to match that of Windows 95.

These early versions of Windows are now obsolete, with no continued support available from Microsoft. The subsequent versions of Windows however are still widely deployed.

Page 128   IT Career FastTrack with CompTIA A+ Certification   © 2010 gtslearning

| Module 2 Operating Systems | Windows Versions and Features |

Windows licensing

A condition of installing Microsoft Windows is accepting the **End User License Agreement (EULA)**[80]. The EULA controls how you may deploy the software and whether you may transfer it to another computer. There are several different types of license, summarized below:

- **OEM (Original Equipment Manufacturer)** - this is for pre-installed versions of Windows sold with new PCs. The license is not transferable and the software may not be installed on a different PC.

- **Retail** - these are subdivided into **Full** and **Upgrade** versions of software. Generally the software may be transferred but may only be installed on one computer at any one time. Upgrade versions require a valid license and setup media for a qualifying upgrade product.

- **Volume** - these are schemes to simplify license administration in small to large organizations and enterprises. Microsoft operates Open License, Select License, and Enterprise Agreement schemes here.

- **Server** - licensing for servers is different to licensing desktop software. As well as a license for the software installed on the server, **Client Access Licenses (CAL)** are required (based on the number of clients accessing the software services). CALs can be sold per server (limiting the number of simultaneous accesses) or per seat (specifying each unique device or user).

Breaching the terms of a software license is a criminal offence and leaves the individual or organization liable to pay damages.

Windows 2000

Windows 2000, despite dropping the NT name, was based on the same architecture, and provided further improvements to reliability, support for new hardware, and a cosmetically updated interface, similar to Windows 98. New features included support for power management and Plug-and-Play and support for new disk management features. Like Windows NT, there were client ("Windows 2000 Professional") and various server editions.

---

[80] Volume licensing customers agree to the Product Use Rights (PUR).

| © 2010 gtslearning | IT Career FastTrack with CompTIA A+ Certification | Page 129 |

Desktop

One of the main functions of an OS is to provide an interface between the user and the computer hardware and software. Windows has a number of interface components, some designed for general use and others for more technical configuration and troubleshooting. Collectively, the user interface is referred to as the **shell**.

Tip
Make sure you know how to navigate Windows and know the routes to open the various administration and file management tools.

Windows 2000 desktop showing 1) Shortcut icons; 2) Start button; 3) Quick Launch toolbar; 4) System Tray

The top level of the user interface is the **desktop**. This is displayed when Windows starts and the user logs on. The desktop contains icons to launch applications and possibly user data files. The desktop also contains the Start menu and taskbar, which are used to launch and control applications.

The desktop (and the Windows UI generally) are highly configurable. For example, icons can be opened in classic style (double-clicking) or web style (single click to open and point to select). Another option is Active Desktop, which displays a web page as the desktop wallpaper.

Start menu, taskbar, and systray

The **Start menu** lists all the programs installed on the computer within **Program Groups**, represented as submenus. There are also items for accessing recently-used programs and documents, searching for files and folders, accessing the help system, and shutting down.

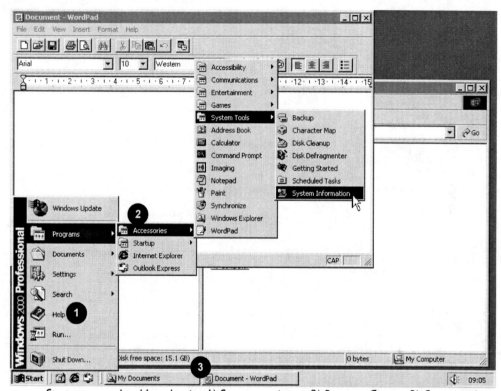

Start menu and taskbar showing 1) Start menu items; 2) Program Groups; 3) Open windows

Next to the Start button is the **Quick Launch** toolbar. This contains shortcuts for frequently used programs such as email and web browser. It contains a **Show Desktop** toggle button that minimizes or restores all open windows.

Apart from containing the Start button, the **taskbar's** main function is to show the programs (windows) currently running on the desktop. The user can click the window icons to switch between them or use the taskbar's shortcut menu to arrange them on the desktop.

The area on the right-hand side of the taskbar is called the **systray** or **system tray**. This displays the current time and icons for programs that run without a window, such as anti-virus software, volume control, battery meter, network status, and so on. These icons have shortcut menus for enabling, disabling, and configuring the related application or setting.

The Start menu and taskbar can be customized by alt-clicking and selecting **Properties**. This allows you to show or hide various options and add or remove program shortcuts. You can also use drag-and-drop to add or remove shortcuts from the menu.

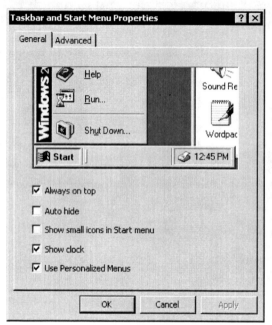
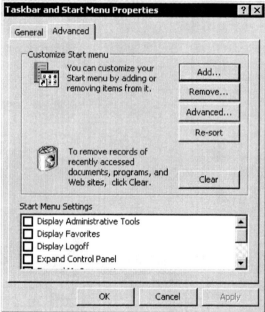

Configuring taskbar and Start menu Properties

Windows 2000 system requirements

Before installing or deploying an OS, it is necessary to ensure that the computer meets the minimum hardware specification.

The minimum requirements quoted in the table below will allow you to install and run Windows 2000 Professional, but you should not expect outstanding performance at the minimum specification. For good workstation throughput, you should consider a high-end Pentium or Pentium II and 128 MB RAM or more. System requirements will be considerably higher for many *software applications*.

In addition to the system requirements outlined above, you must ensure your system and all attached devices are on the **Hardware Compatibility List (HCL)**. This is available from the Microsoft website.

For hardware devices that Microsoft does not provide a driver for, you should contact the hardware vendor directly. Most provide a website with a support page for driver downloads.

Component	Minimum and Recommended Specification
Processor	Pentium 133 MHz (Pentium II recommended).
RAM	32 MB minimum (64 MB+ recommended).
Hard disk / capacity	2 GB with 650 MB free required for the system files (2 GB free space recommended).
Display adapter	VGA (SVGA recommended).
Network card / modem	Required for networking or dial-up.
CD-ROM	12X speed or faster CD-ROM is recommended. This is not required if a network installation is performed.
Floppy drive	Required if the computer does not boot from a CD-ROM.
Input devices	Keyboard and mouse.

Windows 2000 Professional system limits

Windows 2000 Professional supports 2-CPU SMP configurations, dual-core CPUs, and up to 4 GB system RAM.

There is no support for 64-bit hardware or software. There is also no support for advanced processor features, such as Data Execution Prevention, hardware-assisted virtualization (VT-x / AMD-v), or HyperThreading[81].

Third-party software is required to support DVD playback and recording, Wi-Fi networking, and Bluetooth.

Windows XP

In 2002 Microsoft united the "business" and "home" client versions of Windows in **Windows XP**. XP is based on Windows 2000 but adds enhanced versions of many of the multimedia features of Windows 9x.

Compared to Windows 9x, Windows XP is much more reliable and stable and can integrate properly into a Windows Active Directory / Domain network (see unit 5.1). For home users, there is a Home Networking Wizard and updates of the media tools for playing audio and video files.

---

[81] Windows 2000 will recognize a dual-core or HyperThreading CPU as two processors but is not optimized for HT use and so will not perform as well. Windows 2000 is restricted to 2 CPUs, whether implemented logically or physically.

Windows XP desktop

Compared to Windows 2000, XP adds better hardware support (including better support for wireless technologies) and internet/remote connectivity options. The desktop has also been updated with a more colorful interface.

The "standard" version of Windows XP for business clients is **Windows XP Professional**. This is the preferred client for Windows Active Directory (Domain) networks.

Microsoft released several editions alongside the Professional edition, designed for different markets.

Windows XP Home Edition

Windows XP Home Edition is a cheaper, stripped down version of Windows XP Professional. It does not support an Active Directory client, Remote Desktop[82], or file encryption and has a simplified user access control model. It supports up to 5 clients in a workgroup rather than Professional's 10.

---

[82] Remote Desktop enables the computer to be controlled from another computer over a network. See unit 2.3 for more details.

Module 2 Operating Systems   *Windows Versions and Features*

Windows XP Media Center Edition (MCE)

Only available to OEMs, this version makes the computer a "digital media hub" capable of TV reception and recording. MCE is based on Windows XP Professional, but features an extra shell that can be operated using a TV-style remote control. The use of a suitable tuner card allows TV and radio reception and playback, as well as DVD/CD playback and management of the digital libraries.

There have been several versions of MCE (one each year from 2002 in fact). The last version (2005) cannot be used as to join a domain but does feature a tweaked desktop color theme and supports the other features of the Professional edition.

Windows XP Tablet PC Edition

Windows XP Tablet PC Edition is a version optimized for Tablet PCs. It provides support for handwriting recognition and the touchscreen interface through its "Ink" features. Otherwise it is identical to Windows XP Professional Edition.

Windows XP x64 Edition

Windows XP x64 is a version of the Professional edition optimized for 64-bit CPUs. This is only available to OEMs and volume license customers.

The 64-bit edition drops support for legacy applications (DOS, Win16, OS/2, and POSIX [UNIX]).

Windows XP with Advanced Security Technologies (SP2)

In 2004, Windows XP SP2 was released. This service pack introduced a significant number of new features, including a **Security Center** applet for the Control Panel, an improved **Internet Connection Firewall** (activated by default and renamed **Windows Firewall**), and improvements to the web browser Internet Explorer, including a **pop-up window blocker** and an **Information Bar** to warn about potentially harmful content.

© 2010 gtslearning   IT Career FastTrack with CompTIA A+ Certification   Page 135

| Unit 2.1 | Module 2 Operating Systems |

Changes to the desktop, taskbar, and Start menu

The appearance of the desktop and windows can be customized more easily using preset themes (one of which is the Windows Classic, "vanilla" interface used in Windows 2000).

The System Tray is now referred to as the **notification area** and as well as showing icons for background processes displays alerts, such as warning that disk space is low or that anti-virus software is not installed or updated.

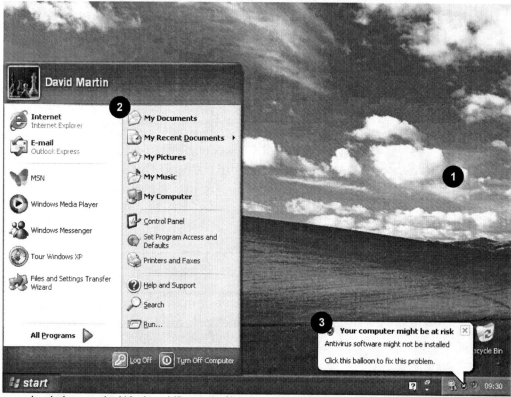

Changes to the desktop under Windows XP include 1) Removing most of the shortcuts; 2) 2-column layout for the Start menu; 3) Use of the notification area to display alerts

The Start menu has been changed to a 2-column layout. The left-hand column contains "pinned" items at the top[83] and recently used programs at the bottom. Other shortcuts can be displayed via the **All Programs** link. The right-hand column contains links to document folders and control panel, help, and so on[84].

---

[83] To pin an item in one of the program groups, alt-click it and select **Pin to Start menu**.

[84] The option to shut down is called "Turn Off Computer" if the computer is not joined to a domain. A standalone or workgroup PC can also configure Fast User Switching. This saves data in the currently logged on profile before logging on another user. The previous user's desktop can then be restarted more quickly.

Module 2 Operating Systems *Windows Versions and Features*

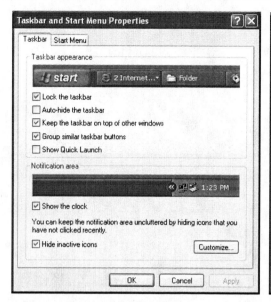 

 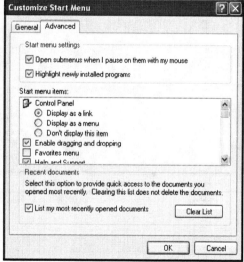

Customization options for the taskbar and Start menu in Windows XP

As you can see, among the settings is the option to use the "classic" Windows 2000 Start menu.

Some other new configuration options include:

- Locking the taskbar so that it cannot be moved or resized by drag-and-drop.

- Grouping document windows belonging to the same application (when there is not enough room on the taskbar).

- Hiding inactive icons from the notification area.

Unit 2.1 — Module 2 Operating Systems

- Enabling the Quick Launch menu (it is disabled by default).

Windows XP MCE features an alternative interface (EHSHELL.EXE), designed to be controlled via a TV-style remote.

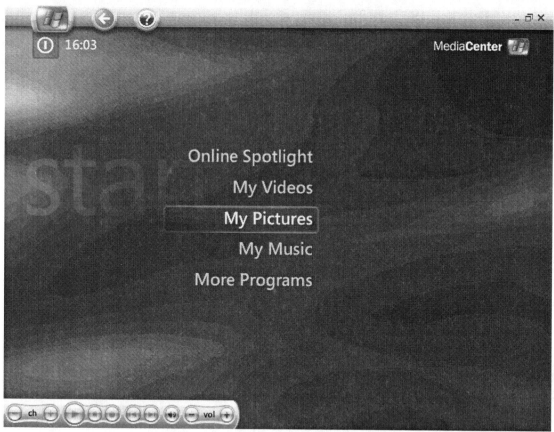

Media Center interface

Windows XP system requirements

The following requirements are for Windows XP Professional and Home editions. For good workstation throughput, you should be considering a high-end Pentium and 128 MB RAM or more.

As well as determining the system unit's ability to support Windows XP, ensure that any third-party hardware devices you have will also support XP. Not everything that runs under Windows 98 or Windows 2000 will run correctly under Windows XP. Microsoft publish a **Hardware Compatibility List (HCL)** at www.microsoft.com/hcl. If in doubt, contact the hardware vendor for additional drivers.

Component	Minimum and Recommended Specification
CPU	32-bit x86 (P233 or higher). 300 MHz (or better) recommended.
Memory	64 MB RAM (128 MB+ recommended).
Display	SVGA or higher (800 x 600).
Hard disk	1.5 GB free disk space + paging space. It is therefore recommended that you have at least 2 GB of free space available.
Installation Media	CD-ROM or cross-network.
Input devices	Keyboard and mouse.

The following additional requirements apply to the various editions of XP:

■ x64 - CPU supporting AMD64 or EM64T and 256 MB system memory.

■ Tablet - runs only on dedicated Tablet PC hardware.

■ MCE - this requires considerably more computing power (a 1.6 GHz CPU and 256 MB memory at *least*) and disk space for good usability. It also requires a TV Tuner card (the latest version supports multiple cards) and an IR receiver for the remote control.

Windows XP system limits

The various editions of Windows XP have different restrictions in terms of CPU types and features and memory supported:

Feature	Home	Professional	MCE	Tablet Edition
64-bit (x64) Edition	No	Yes	No	No
SMP	No	2-way	No	2-way
Multi-core	Yes	Yes	Yes	Yes
HyperThreading	Yes	Yes	Yes	Yes
Virtualization (VT-x / AMD-V)	Yes (SP2)	Yes (SP2)	Yes (SP2)	Yes (SP2)
Data Execution Prevention	Yes (SP2)	Yes (SP2)	Yes (SP2)	Yes (SP2)
Physical Memory (32-bit)	4 GB	4 GB	4 GB	4 GB
Physical Memory (64-bit)	N/A	128 GB	N/A	N/A

Third-party software is required to support DVD / Blu-ray playback and recording.

Windows Vista

In 2007 Microsoft released **Windows Vista,** the successor to Windows XP. It features a new graphics system (called Aero), better suited to scaling to different resolutions and capable of displaying windows in 3D. It also comes with updated media tools, a reworked desktop search engine, and a greater selection of mini-applications for home use.

Vista also refocuses on security, with greater control over use of the local administrator account (User Account Control) and use of privilege restrictions to try to defeat malware.

There are numerous editions of Vista (including Home/Home Premium, Business/Enterprise, and Ultimate)[85].

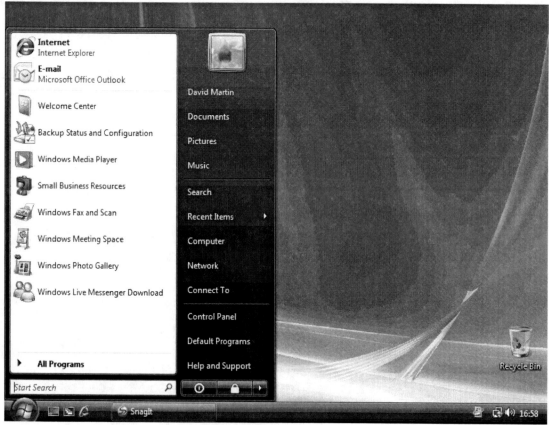

Windows Vista desktop

---

[85] Editions such as Home "N" released in the European Union do not feature tools such as Media Player or Movie Maker as part of Microsoft's settlement with the EU over monopolistic trade practice.

Module 2 Operating Systems — *Windows Versions and Features*

Windows Vista Home Editions

Like Windows XP Home Edition, the Vista Home Editions are aimed at workgroup users. There is no support for joining Active Directory networks. There are Home Basic and Home Premium versions.

Home Premium supports more network clients (10 compared to 5) and touchscreen and tablet (ink) input, and comes with some extra tools (notably Media Center, Meeting Space (a conferencing application for local networks), High Definition video editing, and DVD authoring). Also, the Home Basic edition does not include advanced features of the Aero interface, such as Aero Glass (see below).

Windows Vista Professional Editions

The Active Directory client editions of Vista are Business and Enterprise. These include fax / scan tools, file encryption, and a Remote Desktop server.

The Enterprise edition is only available to Software Assurance licensing customers (that is, it is not available for retail purchase). Compared to the retail Business edition, it adds drive encryption (BitLocker) and support for UNIX applications.

Windows Vista Ultimate

The "professional" editions of Vista do not include the multimedia tools supplied with the "home" editions, such as Media Center, DVD Maker, Movie Maker, and games. The Ultimate edition comes with all the features of Vista Home Premium and Vista Enterprise.

Changes to the desktop

The Vista desktop is broadly similar to Windows XP in terms of layout but its appearance has been reworked and there are a number of extra features.

© 2010 gtslearning   IT Career FastTrack with CompTIA A+ Certification   Page 141

Unit 2.1 · Module 2 Operating Systems

Vista desktop showing 1) New Start button; 2) Switch Between Windows button; 3) Welcome Center; 4) Sidebar with clock, slide show, and RSS news feed gadgets

Aero

As mentioned previously, Vista features a new graphics engine. Aero specifies a number of improvements to the way the desktop works and looks (themes). It includes new specifications for things such as configuration wizards and notifications, but the following features are most obvious to users:

- Scalable icons and previews of window / file contents.
- Aero Glass theme - translucent title bars and window borders.
- Flip3D window manager, displaying 3D previews of open windows (activated by pressing **START+TAB**).

Module 2 Operating Systems   Windows Versions and Features

Windows Aero theme and Flip3D window selection

These effects require a fairly substantial graphics adapter but Windows selects appropriate settings on installation and individual effects can be customized and enabled or disabled by the user. The special effects are not included in the Home Basic edition.

Sidebar

The **Sidebar** is a strip that can be positioned on the right (default) or left of the desktop. It hosts mini-applications (referred to as **gadgets**).

Default gadgets include things such as a clock, calendar, RSS news ticker, weather report, and so on.

You can configure the Sidebar by alt-clicking it or by selecting its taskbar icon.

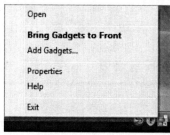

Configuring the Sidebar

Unit 2.1   Module 2 Operating Systems

Start menu

The Start button has been replaced by a round button with the Windows logo. The menu itself is similar to that of XP. The main change is that "All Programs" displays a scrollable list within the left-hand pane rather than cascading across the screen.

Vista Start menu - note that all program links are shown within the left pane by default rather than as a cascading menu

The "power" icon can be customized to perform different actions (for example, hibernate rather than shut down). There is now an option to lock the computer.

In terms of properties, there are now tabs for customizing the notification area and mini-toolbars. You can still revert to the "classic" Start menu if preferred. The taskbar has a new option to enable or disable window previews if you point to the taskbar icon. The taskbar can no longer be reduced to zero size.

User Account Control and Windows Defender

User Account Control (UAC) is Vista's solution to the problem of elevated privileges. In order to change important settings on the computer (such as installing drivers or software), administrative privileges are required. Previous versions of Windows make dealing with typical administrative tasks as an ordinary user very difficult, meaning that most users were given administrative privileges as a matter of course. This makes the OS more usable but it also makes it much more vulnerable, as any malicious software infecting the computer would run with the same administrative privileges.

UAC counters this by first extending some system privileges to ordinary users but then running accounts in a sandbox mode.

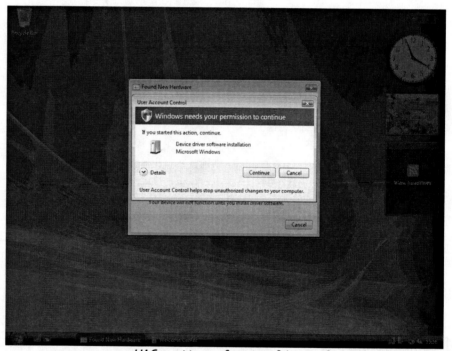

UAC requiring confirmation of the use of administrator privileges

When a user needs to exercise administrative rights, s/he must explicitly confirm use of those rights by entering the administrator's credentials or by clicking through an authorization dialog (the desktop also darkens into a special secure mode to prevent third-party software from imitating the authorization dialog).

Vista is also bundled with an anti-spyware tool (Windows Defender) and an improved firewall product.

| Unit 2.1 | Module 2 Operating Systems |

Windows Vista system requirements

As with other versions of Windows, Vista really needs to be configured with the recommended system components rather than the minimum.

Component	Minimum and Recommended Specification
CPU	800 MHz (1 GHz 32-bit or 64-bit recommended).
Memory	512 MB RAM (1 GB recommended for all editions other than Home Basic).
Display	SVGA or higher (800 x 600). Support for DirectX9 graphics and 32 MB graphics memory recommended. Aero requires 128 MB graphics memory, pixel shader 2.0, and 32-bits / pixel.
Hard disk	20 GB with 15 GB free space (40 GB recommended for all editions other than Home Basic)
Installation Media	DVD-ROM or cross-network.
Audio	Sound card and speakers are recommended.

As well as determining the system unit's ability to support Windows Vista, ensure that any third-party hardware devices you have will also support it (www.microsoft.com/hcl). At launch, third-party support for Vista was quite patchy. While the situation is greatly improved as regards newly released devices, older hardware may not have suitable drivers.

The following additional requirements apply to specific features:

- x64 - CPU supporting AMD64 or EM64T.

- Tablet / touchscreen - runs only on dedicated hardware.

- Media Center - requires a TV Tuner card and an IR receiver for the remote control.

Windows Vista system limits

The various editions of Windows Vista have different restrictions in terms of CPU types and features and memory supported. All editions support HyperThreading, hardware-assisted virtualization, and Data Execution Prevention. DVD playback and recording is supported[86] but Blu-ray requires third-party software.

---

[86] All editions can use DVD as a data disc; the Home Premium and Ultimate editions include a DVD Maker tool for creating video or picture DVDs with navigation menus.

Feature	Home Basic	Home Premium	Business	Enterprise	Ultimate
64-bit (x64) Edition	Yes	Yes	Yes	Yes	Yes
SMP	No	No	2-way	2-way	2-way
Multi-core	Yes	Yes	Yes	Yes	Yes
Physical Memory (32-bit)	4 GB	4 GB	4 GB	4 GB	4 GB
Physical Memory (64-bit)	8 GB	16 GB	128 GB	128 GB	128 GB

Other Operating Systems

Windows has a massive market share in terms of desktop operating systems. For the CompTIA A+ exam, you only need to know the features of Windows 2000 / XP / Vista but it is worth being aware of other operating systems.

UNIX and Linux

UNIX is one of the first operating systems and continues to be used as a client OS (mostly in universities) and server OS. It is usually configured using a command-line interface.

Linux is an open source version of UNIX. Open source means that the programming code used to design the software is freely available. Open source doesn't necessarily mean available for free (although many distributions are); it means that developers are free to make changes to the way the operating system works, so long as they make the changes they have made available in turn.

Linux can be used as a desktop or server OS. There are many **distributions** (notably SUSE, Mandriva, Fedora Core, Debian, SimplyMEPIS, PCLinuxOS, and Ubuntu) though all are based on the same **kernel**. Linux does not require a graphical interface, though most distributions provide one. Linux with GUIs tend to be less demanding than Windows. Some types of Linux support a broad range of computing platforms (whereas Windows is restricted to x86- and x64-based CPUs). The latest version of the Linux kernel supports the features found on the latest Intel and AMD CPUs (64-bit, multi-core, and so on).

Linux is not supported by Microsoft or Adobe, though there is plenty of good software available for the system (such as Open Office / Star Office).

Unit 2.1 Module 2 Operating Systems

Apple Mac OS

Mac OS X Leopard

The main difference between Apple Mac OS and other operating systems is that the OS is only supplied with Apple-built computers. You cannot purchase Mac OS and install it on an ordinary PC. This helps to make Mac OS very stable but does mean that there is far less choice in terms of buying extra hardware.

Mac OS is supported by the software vendors Microsoft and Adobe, amongst others. Apple computers are very popular in the creative and design industries.

Windows 7

Windows 7 was released in July 2009. Most of the changes compared to Windows Vista improve usability, with tweaks to the desktop / taskbar and UAC prompts. There is also better support for touchscreens (notably multitouch events where the screen can interpret gestures as well as simple taps) and Solid State Drives.

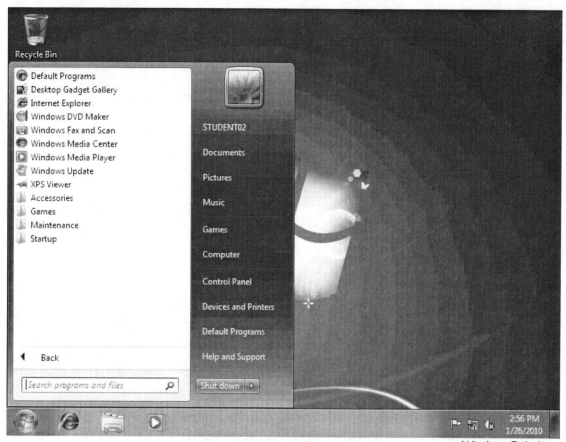

Windows 7 desktop

Windows 7 is not covered on the CompTIA A+ syllabus and will not be tested in the exam and therefore is not covered in this course. Many of the configuration and management tools are identical to those in Vista however.

Summary

The main versions of Windows are 2000, XP, and Vista. Windows XP and Vista have a number of different editions with different functionality, designed for different markets. Make sure you know the minimum specification for each version, but also remember that for good performance the PC should exceed the recommended specification. Alternative operating systems include the newly released Windows 7, Apple Mac OS, and the various types of Linux.

| Unit 2.2 | Module 2 Operating Systems |

Unit 2.2 Installing and Upgrading Windows

CompTIA A+ Essentials Objectives

☐ **701.3.1 Compare and contrast the different Windows Operating Systems and their features**
Windows 2000 and newer - upgrade paths and requirements

☐ **701.3.3 Explain the process and steps to install and configure the Windows OS**
Verification of hardware compatibility and minimum requirements • Installation methods (Boot media such as CD, floppy or USB, Network installation, Install from image) • Operating system installation options (File system type, Network configuration) • Disk preparation order (Format drive, Partition, Start installation) • User data migration - User State Migration Tool (USMT)

Installation Steps and Processes

There are two ways of installing Windows:

■ **Clean install** - means installing to a new computer or completely replacing the software on an old one.

■ **Upgrade** - means installing on top of an existing version of Windows, retaining applications, user settings, and data files.

A clean install is generally seen as more reliable than upgrading. In a corporate network environment, installations are done using **images** (a template containing the OS and required software) so that machines contain consistent set of software and configuration options. PC vendors also use images to install new equipment.

Upgrades are generally designed for home users. Upgrade software can be purchased at a discount.

A clean install should be carefully planned. It will consist of the following phases:

1. Check hardware compatibility (that the core components of the computer are sufficient to run the OS and that peripheral devices have drivers suitable for use with the OS).

2. Select an installation method.

3. Back up any existing user data or settings.

Page 150   IT Career FastTrack with CompTIA A+ Certification   © 2010 gtslearning

| Module 2 Operating Systems | Installing and Upgrading Windows |

4. Text mode setup (prepare the hard disk and copy setup files to the target).

5. Graphical mode setup (configure installation options).

6. Verify installation (check logs and complete tests to confirm that installation has succeeded).

These stages are described in more detail in the following topics.

Hardware compatibility

The first step in checking hardware compatibility is to verify that the system exceeds the *recommended* requirements. The *minimum* requirements will not usually deliver adequate performance. See unit 2.1 for a description of the minimum hardware required to install different versions of Windows.

The second step is to verify that peripheral devices and expansion cards will work under the OS. Effectively this means, "Has the manufacturer released a stable driver for the OS?" Microsoft maintains a list of compatible hardware called the **Hardware Compatibility List (HCL)**. The HCL is located on the setup CD or at www.microsoft.com/hcl (for the most up-to-date version[87]). If a device is not on the HCL, you should check the device vendor's website to confirm whether there is a driver available.

> **Note**
>
> If a device is not on the HCL, the driver is likely to be unsigned (not guaranteed by Microsoft). See unit 4.4 for more information about driver signing.

Unsupported hardware can cause problems during the setup process and should be physically uninstalled from the PC.

It is also worth obtaining the latest drivers for various devices from the vendor's website. The Windows setup media ship with default drivers for a number of products, but these are often not up-to-date nor are they comprehensive.

> **Tip**
>
> Store the latest drivers for your hardware on a CD or network location so that you can update hardware efficiently.

---

[87] The HCL for Windows 2000 is no longer available from this web page but you can download it at ftp://ftp.microsoft.com/services/whql/hcl/win2000hcl.txt.

| Unit 2.2 | Module 2 Operating Systems |

Installation methods

- CD / DVD - most manual installations are run by booting from the setup CD or DVD. You can also run a clean install or upgrade from an existing Windows installation.

- Floppy - the earliest OS software was supplied on floppy disks, but that is no longer an option. You may need to use setup floppies if the computer does not support booting from CD (extremely unlikely for all but the oldest machines). For Windows XP, you will need to download **WinXP_EN_PRO_BF.EXE** from the Microsoft website to enable creation of these disks. For Windows 2000, you use the **MAKEBT32.EXE** application in the **\bootdisk** directory on the Setup CD.

- USB - one problem with disc-based installs is that the setup disc quickly becomes out-of-date and post-installation tasks for installing drivers, updates, and service packs can take longer than the original installation. One way around this is to build **slipstreamed** media, with all the various patches and drivers already applied[88]. The media could be CD, DVD, or USB (if the computer supports booting from USB).

- Network - a network install means connecting to a shared folder containing the installation files (which could be slipstreamed). The target PC must have a usable partition on the hard disk in which to store temporary files. There also needs to be some means of booting with networking software. This could mean a network boot disk (floppy, CD, or USB) or a PXE-compliant network adapter, which supports booting from a network with a suitably configured server.

- Imaging - as mentioned above, any installation involving more than a few PCs makes using imaging technology worthwhile. An image is a clone of an existing installation stored in one file. The image can contain the base OS and configuration settings, service packs and updates, applications software, and whatever else is required. An image can be stored on DVD or USB media or can be accessed over a network.

Unless using imaging, installation is quite time-consuming, as you need to monitor the setup program and input information at various points (**attended** installation). To simplify this process, Windows supports the use of **answer files**, allowing for fully or partially **unattended** installations. Creating and configuring answer files is done using **Setup Manager**.

---

[88] Check the web for articles (search for "slipstream windows setup").

Page 152   IT Career FastTrack with CompTIA A+ Certification   © 2010 gtslearning

| Module 2 Operating Systems | *- Installing and Upgrading Windows* |

Drive preparation

Windows must be installed into a partition of a suitable size and formatted with an appropriate file system. The system partition cannot be changed (except by using third-party tools) so it is important to plan this step in accordance with the way the computer will be used. File systems are covered in detail in unit 2.4 but the main considerations for Windows setup are:

- Will the computer have multiple operating systems installed (multi-boot)? If so, it is best practice to create a partition for each OS.

- Will partitioning achieve better performance? A very large disk (80 GB+) may benefit from being partitioned but in other cases the performance benefits may be minimal.

- Does the boot partition have spare capacity for growth? Running out of space will cause serious problems so leave plenty of overhead.

The other choice is whether to use NTFS or FAT32. Choose NTFS unless there are good reasons for using FAT32 (compatibility in a multi-boot environment). Vista can only be installed to an NTFS partition.

There are various tools available to partition a disk (including the FDISK program supplied with Windows 9x). However, the Windows Setup program includes a text-mode disk management program that should be suitable for most uses.

Backing up data and settings

This is obviously not necessary if installing to a new computer, but is a vital step if you are updating (rather than upgrading) an existing installation. While it takes more time, performance and reliability can be improved by performing a clean install. The general process will be as follows:

- Back up data from the existing target system. You can use the NTBACKUP program supplied with Windows, a third-party backup program, the Files and Settings Transfer Wizard / User State Migration Tool.

- Install the new OS, overwriting the existing target (optionally reconfiguring the disk partition and file system structure too).

- Reinstall software applications and utilities.

- Restore data from the previous system.

© 2010 gtslearning IT Career FastTrack with CompTIA A+ Certification Page 153

Unit 2.2	Module 2 Operating Systems

Joining a network

To join a network, you must install the appropriate protocol and client software and configure it to obtain a valid network address. In most cases, the typical installation settings for Windows will do this. The typical settings install the TCP/IP network protocol suite, set the computer to obtain a network address automatically (via a service called DHCP), install Microsoft Client software, and install File and Printer Sharing software. A local Windows network can either be configured as a workgroup or as a domain:

- Workgroup - up to 10 computers in a "peer-to-peer" configuration. This means that user details are held on each PC but resources can be shared between the PCs.

- Domain - computers connect to a domain server, which holds the user logon details and other information about network resources in an Active Directory database. Member servers may host other applications, such as email.

Assuming you are running a "Professional" or "Business / Enterprise" version of Windows, you can join a domain at any time, move between domains, or migrate back to a workgroup.

Networking is discussed in detail in Module 5.

Windows Setup

The following topics cover installation as it applies to Windows 2000/XP while installing Vista is covered later on.

Text mode setup

The installation process is straightforward: after booting from the disc, the **WINNT** setup process loads a minimal version of Windows and you will complete the following tasks:

1. Press **ENTER** to acknowledge the welcome screen and start setup[89].

2. Acknowledge the **End User License Agreement (EULA)** by pressing **F8**.

---

[89] Before you are prompted to press ENTER, you can press F6 to install third-party drivers. This is necessary if you have a SCSI boot disk, attached to a host adapter for which Windows does not have a relevant driver.

Page 154　　　　IT Career FastTrack with CompTIA A+ Certification　　　　© 2010 gtslearning

Module 2 Operating Systems   *Installing and Upgrading Windows*

3. If using upgrade *media* and no previous version of Windows has been installed, you will be prompted to insert a qualifying product CD. Remember to swap the install disc back when you have finished.

4. Optionally, follow the prompts to delete and create partitions on the target disk.

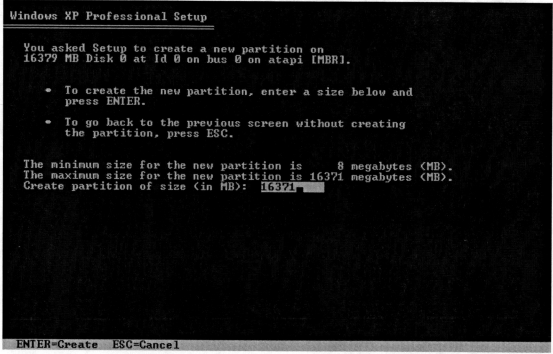

Creating a partition using the setup program

5. Select the target partition and choose the file system to use.

Note

Deleting partitions or re-formatting an existing partition deletes any data stored in the partition. If you are installing "over the top" of an existing Windows installation *without* reformatting the volume, the contents of system folders will be overwritten but other folders will remain intact. This is not a recommended way to proceed.

Note

You can also choose between **quick** and **full** formats. A quick format just rewrites the file table; a full format overwrites all data and checks for bad sectors, and is therefore more reliable.

Unit 2.2   Module 2 Operating Systems

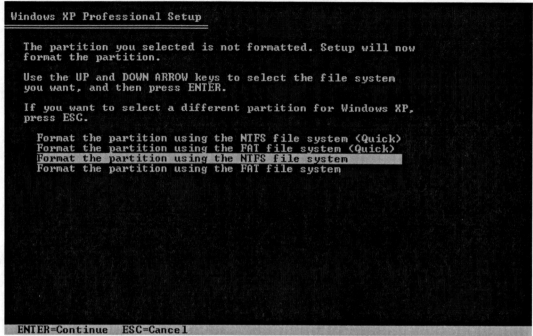

Selecting a file system using the setup program

Once you have partitioned and formatted the disk, setup begins the file copy stage (copying files from the installation folder (I386) to a temporary folder on the target volume). Once this is complete, the computer reboots and enters the graphical setup mode.

Graphical mode setup

Unless you have configured an answer file, the next phase of setup requires you to enter configuration information using the Setup Wizard. The following steps comprise the Windows XP Professional setup routine.

1. **Initial setup** - the installation process proceeds automatically, detecting and configuring hardware.

2. **Regional and language options** - define the keyboard layout, input locales, and other regional information.

3. **Personalize your software** - for licensing purposes; enter the registered user and organization details.

4. **Product key** - ensures the legitimacy of your software; this five-part (20 digit) code is located on the CD sleeve.

| Module 2 Operating Systems | Installing and Upgrading Windows |

5. **Computer name and local administrator password** - each computer name should be up to 15 characters (with no spaces) and unique, at least within the network. See unit 5.3 for more information about use of computer names. The password is case-sensitive.

6. **Date and time settings** - define the date, time, and time zone.

7. **Networking settings** - *Typical Settings* will load the Client for Microsoft Networks, the TCP/IP network transport, and the File and Print Sharing for Microsoft Networks service for the detected network adapter. In addition, TCP/IP will be set to automatic configuration (DHCP). If you wish to change or add to these settings, choose *Custom Settings.*

8. **Workgroup or computer domain** - enter the name of the workgroup or domain you wish to join. To join a domain, you will need a computer account configured in that domain, or else the administrator will need to give you account credentials that will enable you to add your machine to the domain during installation. This will require a domain controller to be online and accessible during installation.

9. **Start menu configuration** - an automated process that builds the Start menu.

10. **Registering components** - an automated process that configures various system components.

11. **Save Settings** - final settings are saved.

12. **Remove Temporary Files** - the disk is cleaned up.

Depending upon the speed of your computer, installation will take approximately 45 minutes.

After you have installed Windows, the system will restart and load.

| Verify installation |

When you run Windows XP for the first time, a **Welcome to Windows** screen displays. This wizard-driven component will guide you through the final phases of system configuration. During this process, you might be asked to:

Tip

There is no Welcome to Windows process for Windows 2000 and no requirement for product activation.

© 2010 gtslearning | IT Career FastTrack with CompTIA A+ Certification | Page 157

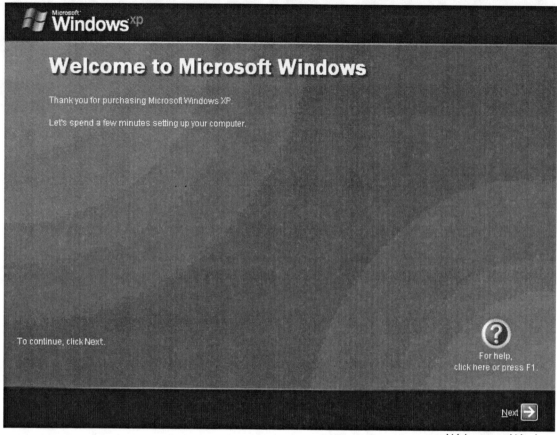

Welcome to Windows

- **Configure your internet connection** - details will include proxy settings and so forth. Your internet connection is needed for product activation but you can configure this later (see unit 5.4).

> **Tip**
> An unpatched installation of Windows is very vulnerable to malware (specifically the Blaster and Sasser worms). If possible, obtain and install service packs on CD before connecting to the internet. If using SP2 media, additional steps prompt you to configure Automatic Updates and enable the firewall before proceeding.

- **Activate Windows** - Microsoft require that Windows XP be activated. This can be done via the web or over the phone, now or later, but must be completed within 30 days in order that Windows continues to function.

| Module 2 Operating Systems | Installing and Upgrading Windows |

- **Defining users of this computer** - you must define at least one name. This is only relevant if the machine will remain in a workgroup (that is, if the machine is to be part of a domain, you will not use the user account you are adding at this stage).

Windows will now load and you will be prompted to log on. Any hardware devices not installed during setup will be detected and you will be prompted to select a driver (see unit 2.5).

When you have gotten this far, it is a good sign that the installation has succeeded. You might want to check the log files (see below), check Device Manager to confirm all hardware has been recognized, and test each hardware device to verify functionality. You can use **Add or Remove Programs** (in **Control Panel**) to install any optional Windows components (see unit 2.5).

Tip

Update the system documentation with details of the installation. Keeping up-to-date documentation is important for system maintenance and troubleshooting.

Setup recovery

Windows uses a variety of detection methods to determine the hardware configuration of the PC. In most cases, this process is completely successful. However, some PCs **hang** (stop responding) during the detection process. The setup program includes a safe recovery mechanism to ensure that it subsequently skips the stage that caused the PC to hang.

Tip

If performing an upgrade, anti-virus software can also cause setup to hang. Disable the software before starting setup.

If you are sure that the PC is not responding, turn it off. Pressing CTRL+ALT+DEL to reboot does not have the same result.

Tip

Pressing CTRL+ALT+DEL reboots a computer if Windows has not fully loaded (referred to as a "warm boot" where starting from a power-off state is a "cold boot"). A memory flag means that the BIOS routine does not run a full POST routine after a warm boot.

© 2010 gtslearning   IT Career FastTrack with CompTIA A+ Certification   Page 159

Turning off the PC has the following effect:

- Setup restarts and recognizes that there has been a failed setup.

- Setup prompts you to confirm that it should **Recover from a failed installation**.

- Setup bypasses the stage that caused the problem.

In some cases you may have to repeat this process more than once. Each time, the setup skips the offending stages. The setup may prompt for hardware details to allow it to complete the system configuration.

Setup records information into the following log files to allow it to recover and to assist troubleshooting:

Log File	Use
%SystemRoot%\Setupact.log	Records actions completed during the graphical phase of setup.
%SystemRoot%\Setuperr.log	Records any errors.
%SystemRoot%\Debug\Netsetup.log	Record the process of joining a domain or workgroup.
%SystemRoot%\Repair\Setup.log	Used by the repair process to recover from a failed installation.

Windows Vista setup

Installation of Windows Vista covers broadly the same steps but in a slightly more efficient order, reducing the amount of time you have to monitor the process during an attended install. Also, the whole installation process takes place within a GUI. The process SETUP.EXE replaces the WINNT process used by Windows 2000/XP. You can start the installation from within an existing version of Windows or by booting from the product disc.

1. The first step is to select your location and regional settings.

2. Setup then prompts you to enter the product key. If you don't enter a product key, choose the edition of Vista you are installing. You will need to input the key later to activate Windows:

Module 2 Operating Systems   Installing and Upgrading Windows

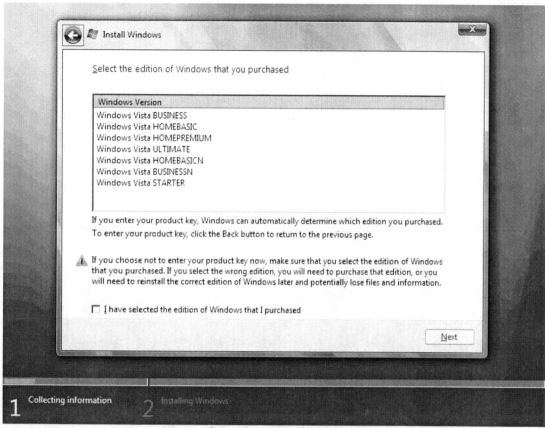

Select the edition of Vista that matches your product key during setup

Tip

The installation media for the various editions of Windows Vista are identical (though 32-bit and 64-bit versions use different discs[90]). The edition that gets installed is determined by the product key. An installed edition can be upgraded by purchasing an upgrade license key.

3. The next step is to accept the EULA. Having done that, choose whether to upgrade the current installation or perform a clean (custom) install.

4. If performing a custom install, you are presented with tools to create and modify partitions on the disk(s). Note that the partition you select will automatically be formatted using NTFS.

---

[90] There are also retail and volume license versions of the discs; the retail discs do not include the Enterprise edition while the volume license discs only include Business and Enterprise.

Unit 2.2   Module 2 Operating Systems

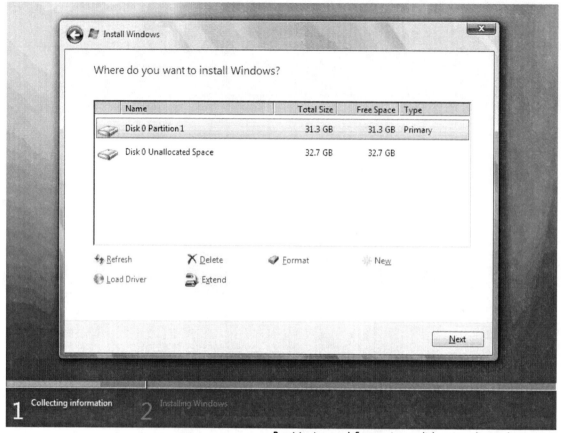

Partitioning and formatting a disk using the tools in setup

5. Once you have configured the disk, setup proceeds with the file copy, installation, and configuration phases. This will take between 30 and 60 minutes, depending on system performance.

Note

There is no option to join a domain or workgroup though Windows will detect connected networks after installation. Domain settings can be configured as part of an image-based installation (see later), which is how most domain network clients would be deployed.

Tip

Vista's setupact.log and setuperr.log files are stored in c:\windows\panther.

Module 2 Operating Systems | *Installing and Upgrading Windows*

Upgrading Windows

Broadly speaking, an upgrade can take place in two ways:

- In-place - the existing OS is upgraded. This preserves the existing applications, data files, and user settings.

- Clean install - an ordinary installation is performed over the existing OS (which would normally be deleted first). If data or settings from the old system need to be preserved, these would need to be backed up and migrated to the new environment. Applications would also need to be re-installed.

Generally speaking, in an enterprise environment upgrading client machines is probably pretty inefficient; most network administrators tend to favor performing installations over the top of the old operating system (often using drive imaging). Since it is best practice to avoid storing data of any type on local hard disks of workstations, this should have no discernible drawbacks.

On smaller networks or for home use, in-place upgrades are simpler. It is more important to make a backup of the existing system in this scenario, so that the old system can be recovered if the upgrade fails.

Note
Make a full backup of the system and data files before proceeding with the upgrade.

When you upgrade from one operating system to another, you need to follow a defined **upgrade path**. Some versions of Windows cannot be upgraded directly to the latest version, usually for licensing reasons.

Upgrade paths to Windows 2000

The following products can be directly upgraded to Windows 2000 Professional:

- Windows 95

- Windows 98 / Windows 98 Second Edition

- Windows NT 3.51 or later

Earlier versions of Windows must be first upgraded to one of the above. Windows *Me* (*Millennium Edition*) cannot be upgraded to Windows 2000.

© 2010 gtslearning | IT Career FastTrack with CompTIA A+ Certification | Page 163

Upgrade paths to Windows XP

For Windows XP, the table below summarizes the in-place upgrade paths:

Product	Upgrade Path
Windows 95	Upgrade to Windows 98 or Windows 2000 then Windows XP Professional or Home Edition
Windows 98 / Windows 98 Second Edition	Windows XP Professional / Windows XP Home
Windows Me	Windows XP Professional / Windows XP Home
Windows NT Workstation 3.51	Upgrade to Windows NT 4.0 (SP5) then Windows XP Professional
Windows NT4 Workstation (SP5)	Windows XP Professional
Windows 2000 Professional	Windows XP Professional
Windows XP Home Edition	Windows XP Professional
Windows Media Center Edition (MCE)	None

You cannot "upgrade" from Windows XP Professional to Home Edition. You cannot upgrade any product to MCE, which is available only to OEMs.

Upgrading from Windows 2000 to Windows XP

When you perform the upgrade, you will be presented with a choice:

Module 2 Operating Systems   *Installing and Upgrading Windows*

- **Upgrade** - in which Windows will make most decisions for you regarding your upgrade. Most, if not all, applications and settings will be retained during the upgrade.
- **Installation** - Windows will replace any existing operating systems and then you can configure options such as:
    - (a) Installation partition and folder
    - (b) File system
    - (c) Language and locale settings

Transferring settings using the USMT

If performing a clean install or providing a user with a new computer, you may want to retain the user's settings from the old PC. These may include desktop and browser configuration, application settings, and even data. The **User State Migration Tool (USMT)** will assist in this process as part of a large scale deployment. The files for USMT are found in the **\VALUEADD\MSFT\USMT** folder on the Windows XP Professional product CD (it is not available with the Home edition).

Transferring settings using the File and Settings Wizard

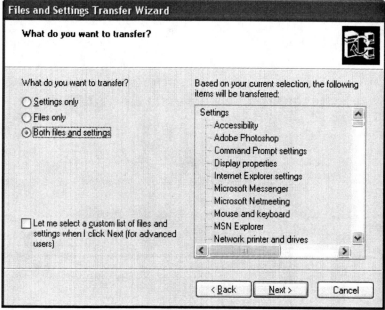

File and Settings Transfer Wizard

| Unit 2.2 | Module 2 Operating Systems |

This graphical program provides a friendly interface to the USMT, designed for home users. Again, it is useful if you are planning to do a clean install or for users that have bought a new computer and want to transfer settings from the old one. You can run the utility from the product disc (**Perform Additional Tasks > Transfer files and settings**) or run it on a current Windows XP installation (**Start > All Programs > Accessories > System Tools**).

Upgrade paths to Windows Vista

Windows Vista only supports in-place upgrades from Windows XP 32-bit versions and other editions of Vista[91]. The table below summarizes the in-place upgrade paths for the various editions:

Product	Upgrade Path
Windows XP Professional	Windows Vista Business or Ultimate
Windows XP Home Edition	Windows Vista Home Basic, Home Premium, Business, or Ultimate
Windows XP Media Center Edition (MCE)	Windows Vista Home Premium or Ultimate
Windows XP Tablet PC	Windows Vista Business or Ultimate
Windows Vista Starter	Windows Vista Home Basic, Home Premium, Business, or Ultimate
Windows Vista Home Basic	Windows Vista Home Premium, Business, or Ultimate
Windows Vista Home Premium	Windows Vista Ultimate
Windows Vista Business	Windows Vista Ultimate
Windows Vista Enterprise	Windows Vista Ultimate

An upgrade from one edition of Vista to another can be performed over the web using the **Windows Anytime Upgrade** tool.

Note

You cannot upgrade from a 32-bit version of Windows to a 64-bit version nor can you upgrade from Windows XP x64 Edition to any 64-bit edition of Vista.

In Vista, the **Windows Easy Transfer (WET)** tool replaces the Files and Settings Transfer Wizard. It has essentially the same functionality except that it can collect data files and settings from Windows XP or data files only from Windows 2000. Older versions of Windows are not supported.

---

[91] If you have purchased Windows Vista upgrade media, any previous version of Windows 2000 or XP is valid for licensing purposes but will require a clean install if an in-place upgrade option is not available.

Page 166   IT Career FastTrack with CompTIA A+ Certification   © 2010 gtslearning

Deploying Windows

Performing a manual installation is time-consuming. While the setup process has been streamlined since the very early versions of Windows, an attended installation still requires the installer to monitor the setup program and input information for the first 20-30 minutes or so.

When it comes to **deploying** large numbers of installations (whether at the same time or over a period of months), there are several options for completing fully or partially **unattended** installations. As with ordinary installs, these can be completed using a variety of media.

Setup Manager

In Windows 2000/XP, the **Setup Manager** is used to create answer files[92]. An **answer file** contains the information input during setup, such as product key, computer name, language and network settings, and so on. This file is accessed automatically during setup, meaning that an installer does not have to be present.

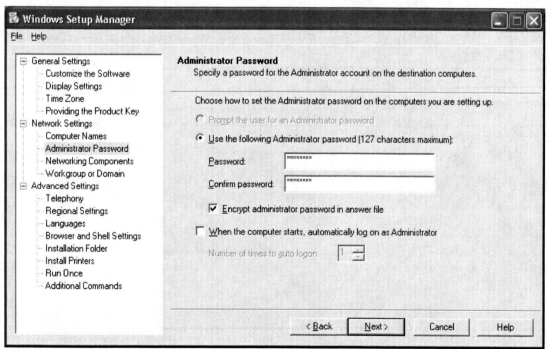

Configuring setup choices using Setup Manager

---

[92] The Setup Manager and Sysprep tools are included on the setup CD in **\SUPPORT\TOOLS\DEPLOY.CAB**.

Drive cloning and sysprep

If Windows is to be deployed to multiple machines with similar hardware specifications, the most common method of deployment is to use disk imaging software to clone an installation from one PC to the rest. This has the advantage that a full system can be built, including applications, service packs and patches, and default user settings.

> **Note**
> Windows 2000/XP PCs must have the same HAL. In most cases, the ACPI HAL will work (ACPI is a power management interface). A different image may be required for multiprocessor platforms. Windows Vista setup can deal with different processor platforms more easily.

Third-party disk imaging software, such as Symantec's Ghost, is used to duplicate the disk contents. However, duplicating the disk exactly causes problems, as it repeats the SID (a unique identifier for each machine) and assumes that the machines have exactly the same hardware configuration, which may not be the case.

Microsoft's Sysprep utility should be run before imaging the disk to side-step these problems.

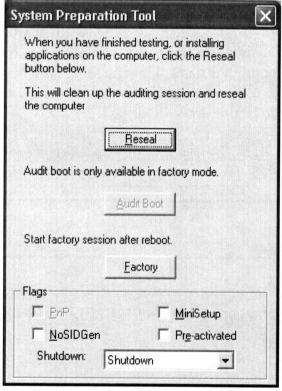

Resealing your computer using SYSPREP

> **Tip**
> The Sysprep utility has gone through several updates with different Windows versions and service packs.

Module 2 Operating Systems | *Installing and Upgrading Windows*

Windows System Image Manager

Vista introduces a new deployment tool - the **Windows System Image Manager** . The System Image Manager is packaged with the **Windows Automated Installation Kit (WAIK)** available from Microsoft's website.

Remote Installation Service (RIS) / Windows Deployment Services

A basic network installation can be setup by putting the installation files in a network share, booting the machine to the network, then accessing the installation program from the share.

The **Remote Installation Service (RIS)** is a Windows Server component used to implement network installs more effectively. As well as file-based installs RIS can create and deploy its own RIPrep images. Setup Manager and Sysprep can be used to configure the setup process for RIS.

From Windows Server 2003 SP2 and up, RIS has been replaced by **Windows Deployment Services**. This works only with image-based installs, using Microsoft new image format (**Windows Imaging Format [WIM]**).

Summary

If planned carefully, Windows installations and upgrades are usually straightforward. Make sure you check compatibility, back up any existing data, and verify the installation. Setup for a clean install can be started using any boot method supported by the PC (CD/DVD, floppy, USB, or network). Make sure you know the upgrade paths from earlier versions of Windows.

There are numerous tools for deploying Windows using a network share of the installation media or image-based setup.

The desktop, Start menu, taskbar, and Windows Explorer are the main user interfaces for Windows, allowing access to programs and files on the local computer and on the network.

Tip

To review what you have learned in this chapter, you should now visit the course website. This contains review questions and bonus material to help you to learn more and practice the topics covered in this unit.

© 2010 gtslearning | IT Career FastTrack with CompTIA A+ Certification | Page 169

Unit 2.3 Windows Administrative Tools

CompTIA A+ Essentials Objectives

- **701.3.2 Given a scenario, demonstrate proper use of user interfaces**
  My Computer • Control Panel • Run line utilities (CMD) • taskbar / systray • Administrative tools (Computer Management) • MMC • Start menu

CompTIA A+ Practical Application Objectives

- **702.2.1 Select the appropriate commands and options to troubleshoot and resolve problems**
  [command name] /?

- **702.2.3 Given a scenario, select and use system utilities / tools and evaluate the results**
  Administrative tools (Computer Management) • Remote Desktop Protocol (Remote Desktop / Remote Assistance)

Windows Architecture and Components

The core files of an operating system provide the basic level of services required by software applications. Microsoft Windows is designed to be *robust* (meaning that it is not subject to crashes or security problems). It tries to achieve this by defining levels of abstraction between the OS and hardware and between the OS kernel and software applications.

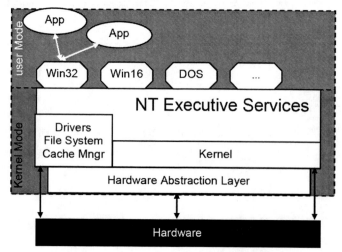

Simplified Windows NT architecture

Modes

Windows allows systems to run in one of two modes: **user** and **kernel**. In user mode, direct access to the computer's hardware is strictly limited (that is, there is no direct access, except to specified memory addresses).

| Module 2 Operating Systems | Windows Administrative Tools |

User mode is where various operating system environments and applications can run. The main operating system environment is Win32 (32-bit Windows applications). There is also support for DOS, Win16, and (in Windows 2000 only) OS/2 (an old IBM operating system) and POSIX (a UNIX standard).

Kernel mode provides direct access to the computer's hardware. When a user-mode component needs to access the hardware, it makes a **call** to one of the components making up the **NT Executive** (some examples of which are I/O Manager, Virtual Memory Manager, and Process Manager). These components use the **kernel**, which in turn uses the **Hardware Abstraction Layer (HAL)** to interact with the hardware.

As 64-bit capable CPUs have been released to market so versions of Windows have been developed to support them. 64-bit versions of Windows have the same basic architecture but support different user mode environments. For example, DOS and Win16 are not supported, but POSIX supported has been reintroduced for the Windows Vista x64 Enterprise and Ultimate Editions.

Hardware Abstraction Layer

Windows provides support for different platforms (CPU architectures) through the **Hardware Abstraction Layer (HAL)**. The **HAL.dll** file provides an **API (Application Programming Interface)** for NT Executive to use a specific platform. In theory, to support a different platform, vendors can develop a new version of HAL.dll without having to change NT Executive code. In practice, support for 32-bit processors is limited to Intel x86 and compatible AMD CPUs, though there are different HAL versions for single and multiprocessor systems. Windows XP x64 supports 64-bit CPUs based on the x64 architecture (variously called AMD64 or Intel EM64T).

Device drivers

A **device driver** is an interface between a hardware component and software. Essentially, the driver makes the commands that will be recognized by the device available in a format that the OS understands.

Poorly written drivers have historically been a major cause of system lockups and crashes. Microsoft publishes the **Windows Driver Foundation** SDK (Software Development Kit) and has a process of certifying **signed drivers** to try to ensure stability.

© 2010 gtslearning   IT Career FastTrack with CompTIA A+ Certification   Page 171

Most components have user-mode drivers to limit the instability that a poorly-written kernel mode driver could cause in the OS itself.

64-bit Windows *requires* signed 64-bit device drivers; 32-bit drivers cannot be installed and nor can unsigned 64-bit drivers. There are also more security features in terms of restricting access to the kernel by both Windows processes and third-party software.

See unit 4.4 for more information about configuring devices.

Registry

The Windows **registry** stores the computer's configuration information. The registry is structured as a set of five subtrees (or **keys**) that contain computer and user databases. The **computer** database includes information about hardware and software installed on the specific computer. The **user** database includes the information in user profiles, such as desktop settings, individual preferences for certain software, and personal printer and network settings.

See unit 4.4 for more information about modifying the registry.

NT Executive and virtual memory

NT Executive is a number of services that provide interfaces between the user mode environment and OS functions. Executive services include things like managing I/O (Input / Output), power management, Plug-and-Play, object management, window (application interface) management, and GDI (Graphics Device Interface - responsible for drawing graphics elements and some print functions)[93].

Another service provided by the NT Executive is **virtual memory**. Virtual memory is an area of disk space called a **pagefile** that data can be "paged" to when the physical memory installed in the computer is full. This allows the computer to work with more applications or open files simultaneously than would otherwise be the case, but impacts performance (as disk I/O is much slower than system memory).

See unit 2.6 for more information on configuring virtual memory.

---

[93] With Windows Vista, subsystems such as audio, display and print, and networking and communications have been redesigned. Display and print are both implemented by the Windows Presentation Foundation, which replaces GDI.

Windows Administration Tools

Administrative tools allow general users (for some tasks) and users with administrative privileges (for most tasks) to configure Windows settings and install and remove devices, applications, and services.

Windows Explorer

Windows Explorer (or simply "Explorer") is the file management interface. You use it to view, create, rename, and delete folders and files on local disks, removable drives, and the network. You can open an Explorer window by alt-clicking a folder object and selecting **Explore**. There is also a shortcut in the Start menu's **Accessories** group or you can press **START+E**. Alternatively, you can run **EXPLORER.EXE** from a command prompt.

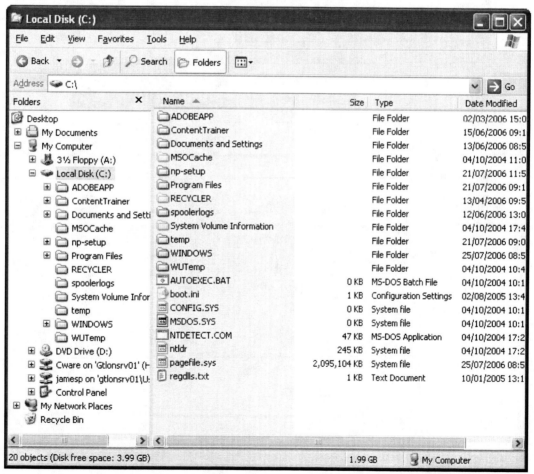

Windows Explorer

Control Panel

The **Control Panel** is the best place to start configuring your system. Each icon in the Control Panel represents an **applet** used to configure some part of the system. Most applets are added by Windows but some software applications, such as anti-virus software, add their own applets.

Configuration information is stored in the registry on a **per system** or **per user** basis, and the icons within Control Panel reflect this, although some parts of some applets contain both system and user settings.

You can access Control Panel through the Start menu[94] or through (My) Computer.

In addition, certain applets are accessible by viewing object properties straight from the desktop or from Explorer.

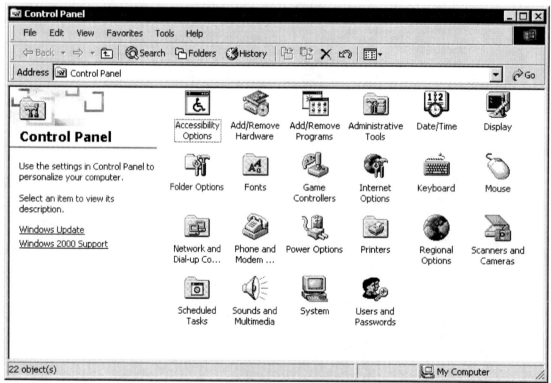

Windows 2000 Control Panel

---

[94] Start menu properties allow this link to be enabled or disabled and shown as either a link to the Control Panel home page or as a menu of control panel applets.

The applets available in Control Panel vary from version-to-version of Windows and sometimes applets with the same sort of function are renamed. This course covers the applets mentioned specifically in the CompTIA A+ content examples but you should try to learn the function of all of them.

Control Panel classic and category views

Under Windows XP, Control Panel can be viewed in either Category View or Classic View. Category view presents a simplified wizard style interface for home users. Classic view replicates the Windows 2000 Control Panel.

Windows XP Control Panel - Category View

Windows Vista displays a task-based list of the most commonly-used Control Panel options and can also be switched to Classic View if necessary.

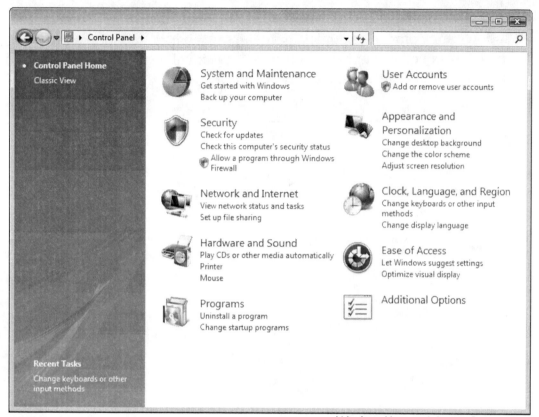

Windows Vista task-based Control Panel

Note that options with the 🛡 icon on or next to them will require you to authorize use of the command through User Account Control (UAC).

My Computer and system settings

My Computer provides access to your local drives (whether hard, floppy, optical, or flash-based [USB or memory card]), printers, and any network drives that have been **mapped**.

> **Tip**
> One of the cosmetic changes in Vista is that the "My" designation has been dropped; so "My Computer" is listed simply as "Computer", "My Documents" just appears as "Documents", and so on.

To browse resources, open **My Computer** then the icon that represents the resource you want to view.

By alt-clicking the My Computer icon itself and selecting the **Properties** option from the menu, you can access the **System** properties. Alternatively, you can open the **System** icon in Control Panel. System settings include network identification and domain membership, hardware settings and configuration, user and hardware profiles, and performance and recovery options.

The **General** tab in System Properties gives information about the system, such as the processor type, and registered owner.

Under Windows Vista, the General tab is replaced by a System Properties home page displaying additional summary information about the computer, including the Windows edition, product key, and activation status.

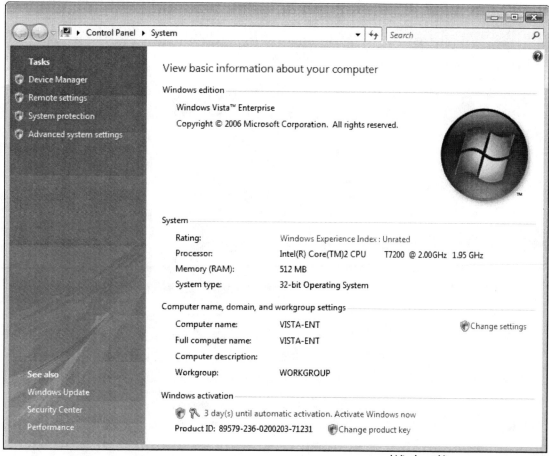

Windows Vista system properties

You would click the **Tasks** or **Change settings** links to access the configuration dialogs.

Run and the command prompt

Using the **Start > Run** dialog, you can open any file or program by typing the **path** to the file. In the case of registered programs and utilities, you simply need to type the program file name or utility name.

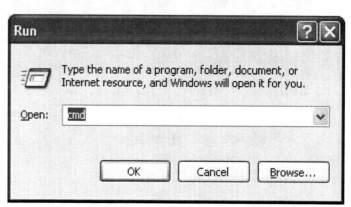

Run dialog box

As well as the basic command or program name, you can include **switches** to control the operation of the program.

In Windows Vista, the **Search** box at the bottom of the menu replaces the Run command[95] and will execute programs and configuration options using simple names.

> **Tip**
> Display the Run dialog quickly by pressing START+R. Activate Windows Vista Search even more simply by pressing the START key.

You can also execute **commands** from the **Run** dialog. If a command is interactive, it will open a command prompt window for input. If a command is non-interactive, the command prompt window will open briefly and close again as the command executes.

The **command prompt** itself is used for some non-GUI utilities or for any system configuration task where you can work more quickly by typing commands than you can by going through the menus.

You can open a command prompt from the **Accessories** program group in **Start menu** or by selecting the **Run** command and entering **CMD**[96].

---

[95] You can still access the Run command by entering "run" into the search box or by opening the shortcut in the Accessories program group.

[96] **COMMAND** opens a DOS command interpreter. This could be used to work with legacy applications but you would not use it for system management. In Windows Vista, you may need to run the command prompt with **elevated privileges** in order to execute a command. To do this, alt-click the command prompt shortcut and select **Run as administrator** then confirm the UAC (User Account Control) prompt.

You can use CMD with a number of switches. One of the most useful is
CMD /f:on, which enables directory and file name completion (press **CTRL+D**
or **CTRL+F** when typing to complete the directory or file name as
appropriate). **/c** and **/k** can be used to execute a particular command (**/c** closes
the prompt when the command has run).

Command prompt

Tip
The Windows command interface is not case-sensitive. Commands are listed here in upper case and switches in lower case to make them easier to read.

/a and **/u** switch between ANSI and Unicode output text formats. The **/t:***fg*
switch lets you set the foreground and background colors. Check Windows
help for the color identifiers and for other switches to use with CMD.

The command prompt includes a rudimentary help system. If you type **HELP**
at the command prompt then press **ENTER**, a list of available commands is
displayed. If you enter **HELP *CommandName***, help on that command is
displayed, listing the syntax and switches used for the command. You can also
display help on a particular command by using the **/?** switch (for example,
CMD /? displays help on the CMD command).

Tip
If you need to copy output from the command prompt, alt-click the title bar and select **Edit > Select All** then press ENTER. You can now paste the output into a text editor (CTRL+V).

You can run registered commands and programs from the command prompt. For unregistered applications, you need to switch the focus to the folder containing the program (see unit 2.4) or type the full path to the executable file.

Microsoft Management Consoles and Administrative Tools

One of the options in Control Panel is the **Administrative Tools** shortcut[97].

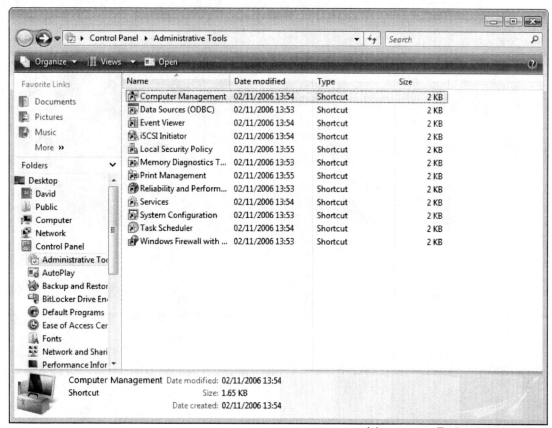

Administrative Tools in Windows Vista

Administrative Tools contains a number of shortcuts, giving you the ability to define and configure various advanced system settings and processes. There are also several tools to assist with troubleshooting the system.

Administrative Tools is a collection of pre-defined **Microsoft Management Consoles (MMC)**. Each console contains one or more **snap-ins** that are used to modify various settings. The principal consoles are:

---

[97] Administrative Tools can also be displayed on the Start menu by adjusting its properties.

- **Computer Management** - configure users and groups, disks, services, devices and so on, and view the event log.

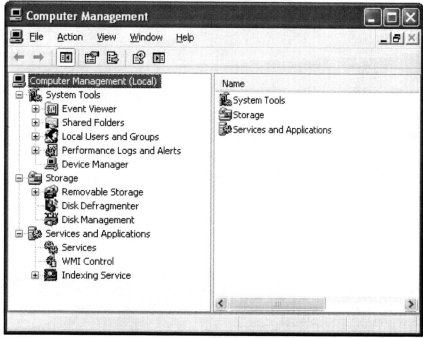

Local computer management in Windows XP

- **Event Viewer** - allows monitoring of Windows logs. System, security, and application events are recorded in these logs. Events are categorized as informational, warning, or error (along with success or failure security audit events). Event Viewer allows you to view and filter events by category, source, date, and so on. This is a critical troubleshooting tool and the first port of call when you are attempting to diagnose a problem.

- **Local Security Policy** - define security options.

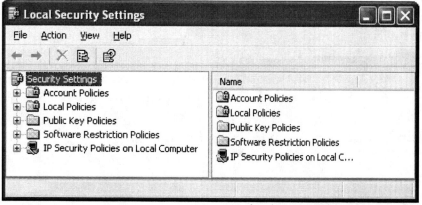

Local security policy in Windows XP

- **Performance monitoring** - measure the performance of the local computer. Vista has an improved **Reliability and Performance Monitoring** tool and also a **Memory Diagnostic Tool**.

- **Services** - start, stop, and pause services.

Customizing MMCs

As well as using the default consoles, you may find it useful to create your own. To access management console itself, click **Start > Run**, type **MMC** and click **OK**. The standard, empty console appears. You can now use the **Console** menu to add or remove any **snap-ins**.

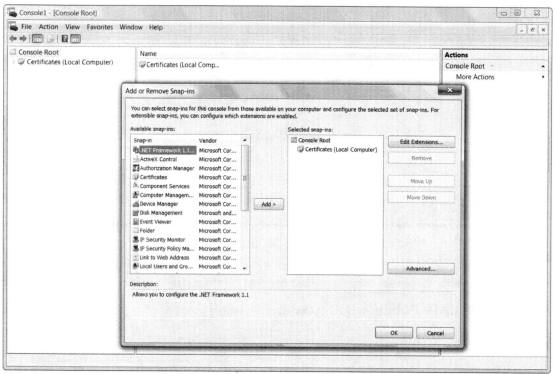

Windows Vista Microsoft Management Console

It may help to think of Management Console as a Swiss Army knife without blades or tools and snap-ins as blades and tools. Consoles may be configured for the convenience of each administrator and the details saved as a file with an **MSC** extension in their Start menu folder.

Remote Administration Tools

One of the key improvements in IT support in the last few years is the ability to provide remote configuration and troubleshooting. Windows XP and Vista come with a number of remote access features[98]. These are:

- **Remote Desktop** - allows a remote user (perhaps a dial-in user) to connect to their desktop machine. The desktop machine functions as a terminal server, and the dial-in machine as a Windows terminal. This allows the user to work as if physically connected to their workstation.

- **Remote Assistance** - allows a user to ask for help from a technician or co-worker. The "helper" can then connect and establish a session with the user. This session can include an interactive desktop, whereby the helper can control the system of the user.

Remote Desktop

To turn on **Remote Desktop**, open the **System Properties** sheet, and click the **Remote** tab. Check the box to enable remote desktop.

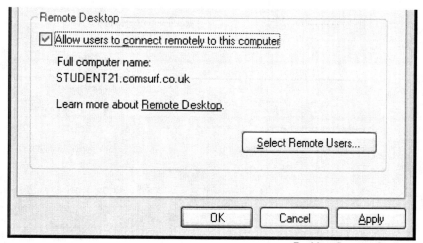

Enabling Remote Desktop

---

[98] To access a Windows 2000 Professional system, you would need to use third-party software such as PCAnywhere or VNC (Virtual Network Computing). You can use Windows 2000 (or Windows 9x or Windows NT4 for that matter) to access a Windows XP/Vista host if you install the Remote Desktop client (MSRDPCLI.EXE) on the other PC (downloadable from the Microsoft website).

> **Note**
>
> Windows Home editions do not include the Remote Desktop server so you cannot connect *to* them but they do include the client so you can connect to other computers *from* them.

Click the **Select Remote Users** button to define which users can connect remotely. The local user already has this property. You can select from local accounts or from the domain of which your machine is a member.

To utilize an established remote facility, open the **Remote Desktop Connection** shortcut, from the **Communications** menu in **Accessories**. You will need to define logon credentials, as above.

Remote Desktop - Logon properties

In addition, you might need to define display properties. You can use either full screen or a windowed display. Also, you can configure the quality of the color scheme.

Module 2 Operating Systems — Windows Administrative Tools

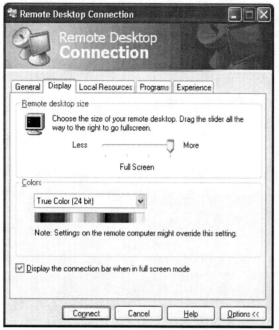

Remote Desktop - Display and Local Resources properties

The **Local Resources** tab allows you to define how key combinations (such as **ALT+TAB**) function - that is, will they affect the local computer, the remote computer, or the remote computer in full screen mode.

Because the connection may be over a slow link, such as dial-up, you can configure optimization based on the line speeds (modem, LAN, and so on) using the **Experience** tab. This affects bitmap caching and video options.

Once you have your remote desktop connection established, you can work quite normally, as if physically adjacent to the target machine - but be aware that no one else can use the target system while in remote mode. The system becomes locked and can be unlocked by the administrator or the remotely connected user only.

Remote Assistance

Remote support means taking control of the user's desktop or computer application to resolve a problem. This can result in an extremely quick resolution to a problem; with the additional bonus that the user can watch the solution being performed (a technician can also use this method to demonstrate procedures to a user).

Remote Assistance uses the same protocols as Remote Desktop. Unlike Remote Desktop, both the local and remote user can see the desktop at the same time. There are also chat tools to allow them to talk and text message each other.

To enable Remote Assistance, open the **System Properties** sheet and click the **Remote** tab. Check the box for remote assistance and if you wish, click **Advanced** to configure the invitation duration.

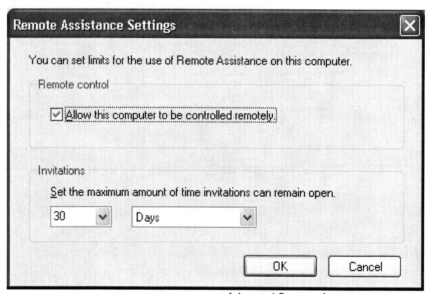

Advanced Remote Assistance properties

1. To request assistance, from the Start menu, select **Programs > Remote Assistance** or from the **Help and Support Center**, click **Invite a friend to connect to your computer with Remote Assistance**[99].

2. Click the option to **Invite someone to help you**.

3. You can then choose how the invitation is to be sent - by email, Windows Messenger, or by file.

4. Enter a message and then define some security about the request, such as a password that the helper must know to enable remote assistance.

5. Define the invitation expiration and then an optional password. Send your invitation.

    Your colleague receives the email message. If they wish to assist, they can double-click the attachment.

---

[99] Remote Assistance can also be offered without being requested. This is known as Unsolicited Help. This is achieved through the Help and Support program (search for "Offer Remote Assistance").

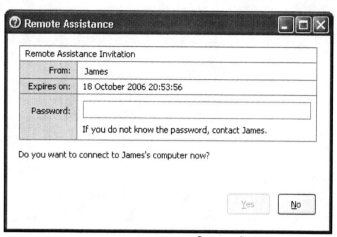

Remote Assistance invitation

Your assistant enters the password you specified (you will need to let them know what this is) and then chooses whether to assist.

You can exchange text messages and files or chat if the PCs are equipped with microphone and sound card. Click the **Take Control** button to use the remote PC's desktop (the remote user must click **Yes** to grant control).

6. Click **Disconnect** to end the session.

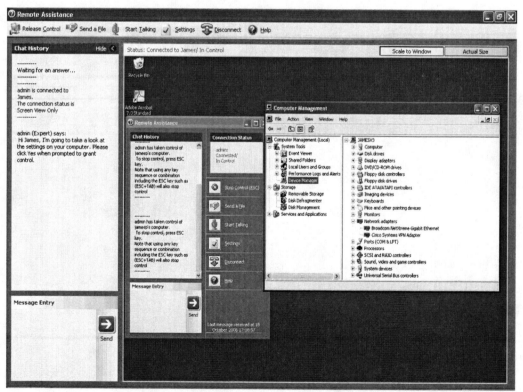

Remote Assistance

| Unit 2.3 | Module 2 Operating Systems |

Note

Because of the way that remote assistance invitations work, the process will only function reliably when used within a private network. Remote assistance connections on the internet may prove unreliable. Remote Assistance uses port 3389 (as does Remote Desktop). This port may well be blocked on firewalls, as it is not a well known port. Refer to unit 5.6 for more information about firewalls and internet security issues.

Summary

To protect against crashes and badly written software, Windows has kernel and user modes. Almost all access to the computer hardware is through user mode drivers making calls to kernel mode services. The registry is a system configuration database, organized into keys and subkeys (a folder-like structure). Virtual memory utilizes one or more paging files on disk drives to supplement system memory (RAM).

The main administrative tools are Control Panel, Computer Management Console, the Administrative Tools folder, and the Command Prompt.

Remote maintenance utilities such as Remote Desktop and Remote Assistance make providing customer support far more cost-effective.

Tip

To review what you have learned in this chapter, you should now visit the course website. This contains review questions and bonus material to help you to learn more and practice the topics covered in this unit.

Page 188   IT Career FastTrack with CompTIA A+ Certification   © 2010 gtslearning

Module 2 Operating Systems

File Management

Unit 2.4 Windows Disk and File Management

CompTIA A+ Essentials Objectives

☐ **701.3.2 Given a scenario, demonstrate proper use of user interfaces**
Windows Explorer

☐ **701.3.3 Explain the process and steps to install and configure the Windows OS**
File systems (FAT32 vs. NTFS) • Directory structures (Create folders, Navigate directory structures) • Files (Creation, Extensions, Attributes, Permissions)

CompTIA A+ Practical Application Objectives

☐ **702.2.1 Select the appropriate commands and options to troubleshoot and resolve problems**
DIR • CHKDSK (/f /r) • EDIT • COPY (/a /v /y) • XCOPY • FORMAT • MD / CD / RD

☐ **702.2.2 Differentiate between Windows Operating System directory structures (Windows 2000, XP and Vista)**
User file locations • System file locations • Temporary files • Program files

☐ **702.2.3 Given a scenario, select and use system utilities / tools and evaluate the results**
Disk Manager (Active, primary, extended and logical partitions, Mount points, Mounting a drive, FAT32 and NTFS)

Managing File Systems

Non-volatile computer storage is based around hard disk drives. The main disk in the computer is the primary hard drive. Whether this drive is PATA, SATA, or SCSI, it is managed in the same way under Windows. The computer may also have a number of other storage devices, such as a secondary hard drive, an optical drive or writer, a floppy drive, external drives, or flash memory drives.

Partitions

A single physical hard disk may be divided into multiple **partitions**. This may be done to improve the performance of the disk, to install multiple operating systems, or to provide a logical separation of different data areas. Removable media, such as floppy disks, CD/DVD/BDs, or flash memory, cannot be partitioned.

© 2010 gtslearning

IT Career FastTrack with CompTIA A+ Certification

Page 189

| Unit 2.4 | Module 2 Operating Systems |

Under Windows **basic** storage management, a disk can be divided into up to *four* **primary** partitions. Each partition can be formatted with a different **file system**. If four "drives" is insufficient, an **extended** partition can replace one of the primary partitions. The extended partition can be subdivided into as many **logical drives** as required. On the primary hard disk, one of the partitions must be made active (bootable).

The **partition table** storing information about how the disk is divided is stored on the disk itself in the first sector in area called the **Master Boot Record (MBR)** or **boot sector**.

Note

You should be familiar with the terminology Microsoft use for boot drives. On the main hard drive, the partition containing the *boot files* (the active primary partition) is labeled drive C and referred to as the "system" partition. The drive containing the *operating system files* (the system root) is referred to as the "boot" partition. The boot partition can be in a different primary partition to the system partition or located on an extended partition or a different physical disk.

Tip

The term **volume** refers to a storage area formatted with the same file system. This is loosely interchangeable with the term "drive" and could be a floppy disk or a partition on a hard disk. Volume can also refer to an area spanning multiple disks. Under Windows, multiple disks are configured using **Dynamic Storage**. Using multiple disks in one volume is referred to as **RAID (Redundant Array of Independent Disks)**.

File systems

Each volume can be formatted with a different file system. Under Windows, there is a choice between FAT and NTFS.

- FAT (File Allocation Table) - this was used for older versions of Windows and is preserved under Windows 2000/XP for compatibility. Typically the 32-bit version (FAT32) is used. This permits a maximum file size of 4 GB and a maximum volume size of 32 GB (under Windows XP)[100].

---

[100] FAT16 is restricted to 2 GB volumes. FAT32 can support up to 2 TB but the Windows XP setup program restricts this to 32 GB. Windows 2000 has no such restriction and Windows XP can *access* larger volumes formatted using a third-party program.

Page 190 · IT Career FastTrack with CompTIA A+ Certification · © 2010 gtslearning

| Module 2 Operating Systems | – | File Management |

- NTFS (New Technology File System) - as a 64-bit addressing scheme, NTFS allows much larger partitions (up to 2 TB) than FAT[101]. NTFS also supports extended attributes, allowing for file-level security permissions, compression, and encryption. These features make NTFS much more stable and secure than FAT.

Under Windows 2000 and XP, either of these file systems will support the system/boot partition. NTFS would be the automatic choice for new installations unless there were dual-boot considerations or the primary hard disk capacity was less than 10 GB[102]. Windows Vista *only* supports installation on an NTFS boot partition, though it can read and write to FAT/FAT32 drives and the system partition (if different) can use FAT or FAT32.

FAT is used for formatting most removable drives and disks as it provides the best compatibility between different types of computers and devices.

CDs and DVDs are often formatted using **Universal Disk Format (UDF)** though the older CD format ISO 9660 offers the best compatibility with legacy drives.

| Clusters / allocation units |

One of the functions of formatting with a file system is to define **clusters** (or **allocation units**) on the disk. A cluster is the smallest unit on the disk readable by the OS. For example, a 512 byte cluster size results in a 1:1 mapping between sectors and clusters, whereas 4096-byte clusters each take up 8 sectors.

Large cluster sizes make for better performance, as it is easier to locate the clusters on the disk and causes less file fragmentation. However, larger clusters can waste disk space if the cluster size is larger than the average file size. When formatting a drive, you can choose to specify the allocation unit size, but it is usually best left to the default setting.

---

[101] This is the limit for basic disks. NTFS supports volumes up to 256 TB minus 64 KB but only if the disks are configured for dynamic storage and the cluster size is set to 64 KB. The maximum file size is 16 TB minus 64 KB.
[102] A typical dual-boot configuration would be to have a 1.5 GB system partition formatted using FAT then partitions for each operating system, formatted with whatever file system is most suitable.

© 2010 gtslearning   IT Career FastTrack with CompTIA A+ Certification   Page 191

Managing Disks

Under Windows, disks are managed using the **Disk Management** snap-in, part of the default Computer Management console.

Volumes are shown in the top pane while physical disks and their partitions plus any unpartitioned space are shown at the bottom. Alt-clicking an object brings up the shortcut menu, with options such as **Delete**, **Format**, **Mark Partition as Active**, **Change Drive Letter**, and **Properties**.

Note however, that you cannot change or delete the boot or system partitions. Also, once created, a basic partition cannot be resized. These sorts of operation require a third-party disk manager, such as Acronis Disk Director or Norton PartitionMagic.

> **Warning**
> Deleting a partition or reformatting deletes the data stored in the partition. Once the command is confirmed, the data becomes unrecoverable.

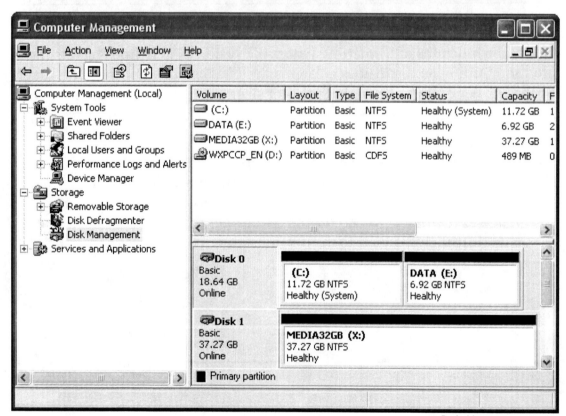

Disk Management utility

Module 2 Operating Systems	File Management

You can format a floppy disk (or other removable drive) by alt-clicking the **A:** drive in Windows Explorer and selecting the **Format** command from the shortcut menu.

Another option is to use the FORMAT command from the command prompt. This process deletes any data existing on the volume[103]. The basic command is FORMAT *volume*, where *volume* is a drive letter or volume name. The main switches are as follows:

Switch	Use
/fs:	Specify the file system (NTFS, FAT, or FAT32).
/v:	Enter a label for the volume. If you do not include this switch, you are prompted for a label when format is complete.
/q	Perform a quick format (does not scan for bad sectors).
/a:	Specify the size of allocation units (512, 1024, 2048, 4096, 8192, 16K, 32K, 64K). If omitted, the default size depends on the size of the volume.
/x	Force the volume to dismount. This will cause file errors for users with files open on the volume.
/c	Enable file compression if using NTFS[104].

Managing Folders

The purpose of a drive or volume is to store files. **Directories** are a means of organizing files on a drive to make them easier to find.

The first level of the hierarchy is called the **root** directory. This is created when the volume is formatted. The root directory is identified by the volume label and a backslash. For example, the root directory of the C: drive is **C:**

The root directory can contain files and named subdirectories. The **path** to a subdirectory is also separated by backslashes. For example, in C:\WINDOWS\System32\, "WINDOWS" is a subdirectory of the root and "System32" is a subdirectory of "WINDOWS".

Tip

Under Windows, directories are referred to as folders.

---

[103] You can convert a FAT drive to NTFS without losing data using the command CONVERT *volume* /fs:ntfs. This command is not reversible; you cannot convert from NTFS to FAT without reformatting.

[104] It's not usually a good idea to enable compression on the drive root, especially if the drive contains system files. Use folder properties to enable compression on a case-by-case basis.

Windows system folders

Under Windows, system objects are presented to the user via Windows Explorer in a slightly different hierarchy to the storage of folders on the boot volume.

In Windows 2000/XP, the **desktop** is at the top of the Explorer hierarchy and contains shortcuts, files, **My Computer**, **My Network Places**, **Recycle Bin**, and the current user's **My Documents** object. My Computer contains local, removable, and network drives plus the Control Panel.

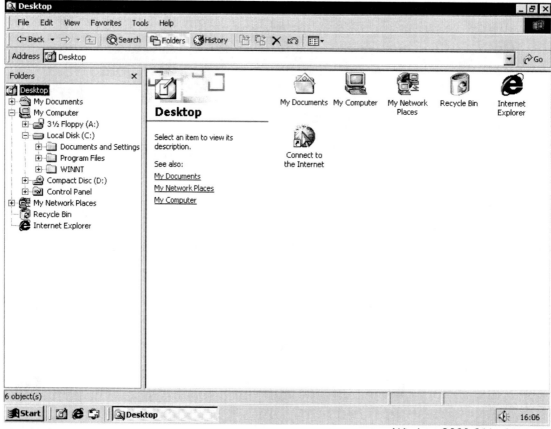

Windows 2000 folder hierarchy

Within My Computer, drives are referred to by letters and optional labels. As described above, a "drive" can be a single physical disk or a partition on a disk. A drive can also point to a shared network folder "mapped" to a drive letter. By convention, the A: drive is the floppy disk and the C: drive is the active (bootable) partition on the primary hard disk.

Standalone or workgroup installations of Windows XP also include a "Shared Documents" folder that is accessible to all users of the computer.

Module 2 Operating Systems Zoom File Management

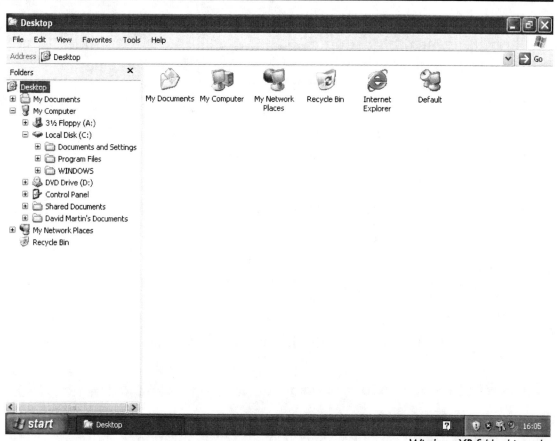

Windows XP folder hierarchy

The system / boot partition (assuming they are the same) contains the following system folders and files:

- **Windows**[105] - the system root, containing drivers, logs, add-in applications, system and registry files (notably the System32 subdirectory[106]), fonts, and so on.

- **Program Files** - subdirectories for installed applications software.

- **Documents and Settings** - storage for users' profile settings and data. Each user has a folder named after their user account. This subfolder contains NTUSER.DAT (user-specific settings in the registry), My Documents, Temporary Internet Files, Cookies, recent file shortcuts, desktop shortcuts, Start menu shortcuts, temporary files created by applications, and so on.

---

[105] If the computer is running (or was upgraded from) Windows 2000, this folder is called WINNT.

[106] System32 contains most of the applications and utilities used to manage and configure Windows. This is true even of 64-bit versions of Windows (32-bit Dynamic Link Libraries [DLL] running under 64-bit Windows are stored in the SYSWOW64 folder).

| Unit 2.4 | Module 2 Operating Systems |

This folder also includes "All Users", which contains desktop and Start menu shortcuts for all users of the computer. Windows XP also uses this profile's Documents folder to share files between users (Shared Documents). It also contains a folder called "Default User", which is the template for new user profiles.

- **Inetpub** - if the web server Internet Information Services (IIS) is installed, this folder is created to store the default website and settings.

- **NTLDR** - OS loader.

- **NTDETECT.COM** - hardware recognizer.

- **BOOT.INI** - multi-boot OS loader menu.

- **pagefile.sys** - Virtual Memory pagefile.

- **hiberfil.sys** - current configuration saved when putting the computer into hibernation power-saving mode.

- **System Volume Information** - hidden folder containing System Restore data.

- **RECYCLER** - hidden folder containing deleted files and folders (Recycle Bin).

- **IO.SYS / MSDOS.SYS / CONFIG.SYS / COMMAND.COM / AUTOEXEC.BAT** - Windows 9x boot and configuration files (these may be present if the PC is configured to dual boot or was upgraded).

Vista has the same sort of hierarchy but some different terminology and organizational principles. The **desktop** is still the container object but within that are a **User** folder (named after the user account), a **Public** folder, the **Computer** object, the **Network** object, **Control Panel**, and the **Recycle Bin**. The User object contains numerous subfolders, including Documents, Pictures, Videos, Downloads, Contacts, and so on[107].

Other changes to the system folder structure include:

- **Boot** - this folder contains the **Boot Configuration Database (BCD)** and log files. This replaces BOOT.INI.

- c:\Windows\System32\WINLOAD.EXE - OS loader; replaces NTLDR.

- c:\Windows\System32\WINRESUME.EXE - OS loader invoked when the computer has been put into hibernation.

---

[107] Various hidden "Junction Points" are created using the old folder terminology ("My Documents", and so on). These are used for compatibility with pre-Vista applications. If junction points are unhidden, they appear like shortcut icons. Clicking one results in an "Access Denied" message however.

Page 196   IT Career FastTrack with CompTIA A+ Certification   © 2010 gtslearning

Module 2 Operating Systems | File Management

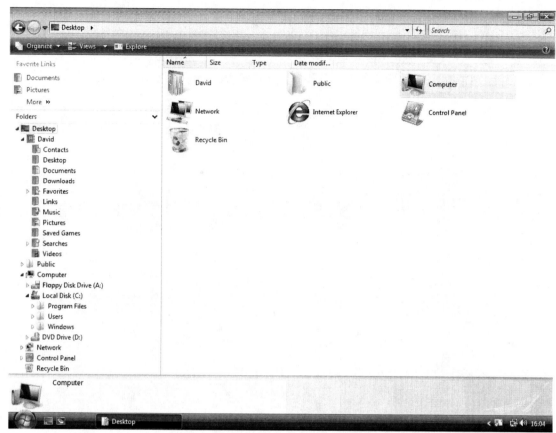

Windows Vista folder hierarchy

System variables

When entering directory paths as arguments to command line functions or scripts, you may not know exactly which locations were chosen for installation. The command prompt recognizes a number of system variables and replaces the correct path when one of these is used. Some of the common variables include:

- %SystemDrive% - for example, "c:"
- %SystemRoot% - for example, "c:\Windows"
- %SystemDirectory% - for example, "c:\Windows\System32"
- %UserName% - for example, "george"
- %HomeDrive% - for example, "c:"
- %HomePath% - for example, "\Documents and Settings\george"

You can view the full list of variables using the **SET** command (without switches) at the command prompt. **SET** also lets you create and modify new variables. You can also view variables through the **Advanced** page of the **System Properties** dialog by clicking the **Environment Variables** button.

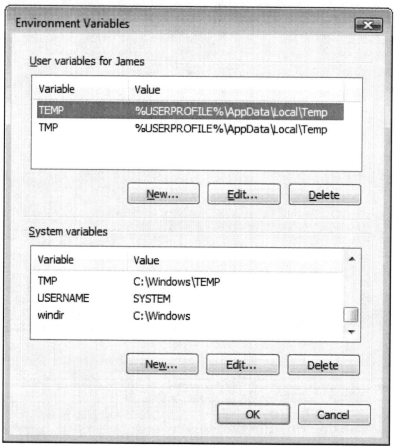

Environment Variables dialog

Windows Explorer

Windows Explorer provides a visual means of navigating the system objects and disks / folders / files.

In the main pane, you can double-click a folder to open it. You can also use the Explorer pane on the left to expand (+) and collapse (-) objects or the **Back**, **Forward**, and **Up One Level** buttons on the toolbar. You can use the shortcut or File menus to create a new folder within another object.

Module 2 Operating Systems File Management

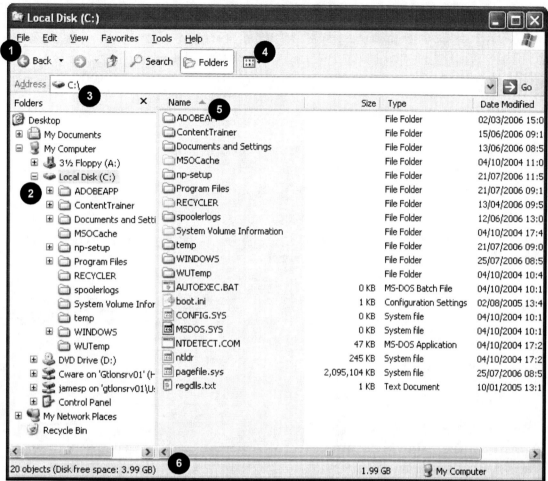

Windows Explorer with 1) Navigation buttons (Back, Forward, Up); 2) Expand and collapse folders; 3) Address bar (enter a file path to open a location or file); 4) View button (change how icons are displayed); 5) Clicking column headers in Detail view allows you to sort icons; 6) Status bar shows information about the selected object

Windows has various folder naming rules that must be followed when modifying the directory structure:

- No two subdirectories within the same directory may have the same name (subdirectories of *different* directories may have the same name though).

- Directory names may not contain the following reserved characters:
  \ / : * ? " < > |

- The full path to an object (including any file name and extension) may not usually exceed 260 characters.

A warning message is displayed if these rules are not followed and the user is prompted to enter a new folder name.

> **Tip**
>
> Directories and file names on a FAT volume are *not* case sensitive. Names on an NTFS volume are *case aware*, which means that the system preserves case in the name as entered by the user but does not regard the case as significant for operations such as detecting duplicate file names, indexing, and so on.

The display options in Explorer are highly configurable[108]. You can select different view modes (small or large icons, file details, thumbnail previews, and so on) via the toolbar button or **View** menu.

You can sort icons using the **Arrange Icons By** command in the shortcut menu or **View** menu or using the column buttons in Detail view. Use the **Choose Details** command from the **View** menu to select which file attributes are shown.

Options affecting how folders and files are displayed in Explorer (such as whether to show hidden files or file extensions) are controlled through the **View** tab in **Folder Options** (open from **Control Panel** or the **Tools** menu in Explorer). View settings are retained on a per-folder basis but can be reset using the buttons on the **View** tab.

Folder Options View settings

---

[108] Windows XP and Vista have more options than Windows 2000, including new filmstrip view mode for pictures. You can also apply view templates to a folder (use the **Customize** tab under folder **Properties**).

Module 2 Operating Systems | File Management

Searching for folders and files

The Windows **Search** utility is a tool for locating files. In addition to searching by file name, the utility can locate files that *contain* a specific text string, that were created or modified within a range of dates, or that are within specific sizes.

1. To open the **Search** tool, select **Start > Search**, or press **START+F**, or click the **Search** button [Search] in an Explorer window

2. In the **file name** field, enter the name (or part of the name) of the required file; for example, LETTER.DOC, *.DOC or LET*. If you are not sure of the name, or plan to search for files using other criteria, leave this entry blank.

3. Optionally, enter text that you want to search for *within* the file. Note that this will take a long time if you select a large number of files to search.

4. Select *where* you want to search from the **Look in** box. This displays a list of drives and locations such as **My Documents**. To search a specific folder only, choose the **Browse** option at the end of the list.

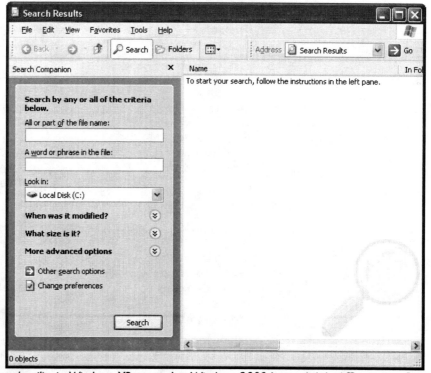

Search utility in Windows XP - note that Windows 2000 has a slightly different interface

5. Click **Search**.

> **Tip**
> By default, Windows XP displays a simplified search interface and a "Search Companion". To use the advanced interface, select **Change Preferences > Change Files and Folders Search Behavior > Advanced > OK**. To get rid of the companion, click it and select **Turn Off**.

As files and folders matching the criteria you set are located, they appear in the right-hand pane. When **Search** is complete, the number of files located is displayed in the Status bar.

You can open, rename, delete, move, and copy files from the search results as normal.

6. To set other options, click the links to expand the **Search** pane (or check the boxes if using Windows 2000).

7. Select from any of the options you want then click **Search**.

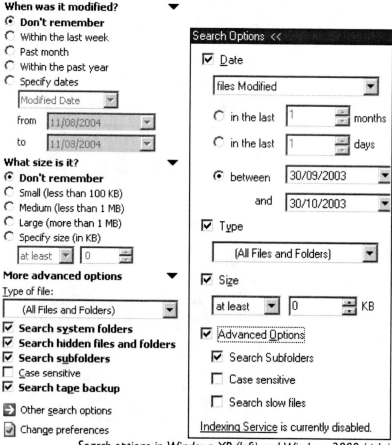

Search options in Windows XP (left) and Windows 2000 (right)

Module 2 Operating Systems — File Management

Managing folders using Windows Vista

While based on the same fundamental principles, Windows Vista contains numerous tweaks to the way folder management works. There are too many changes to detail fully here but the main enhancements are:

- The Search tool is always available as a search box in Explorer and makes automatic use of file and folder properties (or metadata) and file contents[109].

> **Tip**
> Pressing the START key accesses the Instant Search box on the Start menu.

- More powerful options for grouping, stacking, filtering, and sorting files across multiple folders, including saving searches as Search Folders and applying filters from column headers.

Windows Vista Instant Search - note the options to save the search and sort, group, and stack by fields shown in the column headers plus the Details pane at the bottom of the window

---

[109] Vista uses Microsoft's new Desktop Search engine. This relies heavily on the Windows Search service, which indexes files and folders in the background. Indexing (and re-indexing) files can slow the computer down so you may need to configure Indexing Options from Control Panel.

Unit 2.4   Module 2 Operating Systems

- Display enhancements, including file previews and additional view options.

- "Breadcrumb" style address bar where each part of the file location is clickable.

- The menu bar is not displayed by default - press **ALT** to show it[110].

Mount points

A **mount point** means that rather than allocating the drive a letter, it is accessed from a designated folder in the file system. For example, you might partition and format a removable hard disk then mount it as a TOOLS volume within a user's Documents folder.

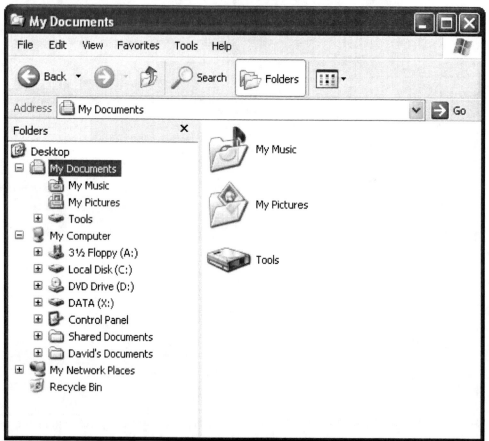

TOOLS volume mounted within the Documents folder - notice the drive does not appear under any of the drive letters

---

[110] To keep the menu bar visible all the time, click the Organize button on the toolbar and select Menu Bar from Layout options.

To assign a volume to a mount point, first create a folder at the point in the file system you want to mount the drive. This folder must be empty. Next, open the **Disk Management** snap-in and either run the **New Partition Wizard** or unassign the drive letter from an existing partition and mount it (use the **Change Drive Letter and Paths** shortcut menu to do this).

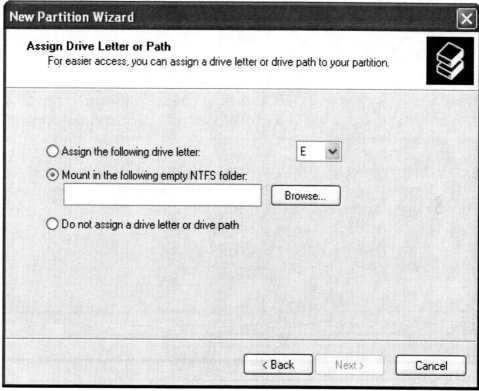

Mounting a drive

Command Prompt Folder Management

You can also manage folders from the command prompt.

Navigating between directories

If the root directory of the C: drive is selected, the command prompt will display **C:\>** The greater than sign (**>**) at the end of the prompt separates the prompt information from your input. If you change from the current directory (in this example, the root directory) to a first-level directory called WINDOWS, the prompt would become **C:\WINDOWS>**

Unit 2.4   Module 2 Operating Systems

Changing to a second-level directory called SYSTEM32 would change the prompt to **C:\WINDOWS\SYSTEM32>**

A backslash (\ ) is used to separate each directory level.

Each drive is assigned its own letter. To change the drive, simply enter the drive letter followed by a colon. For example, to change to the floppy drive, enter A:.

When using the command prompt from Windows, the default path will be %HomePath% (for example, c:\Documents and Settings\George). The CD (CHDIR) command is used to change the current directory. If the current directory is **C:** and you want to change to **c:\Windows**, enter CD windows. If the current directory is **c:\Windows** and you want to change to the root directory of the drive, enter: CD\

It is not possible to move across from one directory to another at the same level. To reach c:\Windows from c:\Documents and Settings, the command has to return to the root directory and then select the chosen branch. The command CD*DirectoryName* includes the two steps in one - for example, CD\windows. Moving up one directory is referred to as moving to the **parent** directory. A shortcut for doing this is CD..

Listing files and directories (DIR)

To find a particular file, it is often necessary to display the contents of a directory. Use the DIR command to list the files and subdirectories from either the current drive and directory or from a specified drive and directory. A subdirectory will be listed with **<DIR>** next to it in normal view or with square brackets **[Windows]** around the name if DIR /w is used to list in wide view.

If the current directory has more than one screen of files and directories, type:

- DIR /w (lists files using wide format with no file details).
- DIR /p (lists files one screen at a time).
- DIR /w/p (both of the above).

To view the files and directories in the root directory of the A: drive when your current drive is C: enter: DIR a:\. The \ following the a: is important. Typing just DIR a: or DIR c: would list the files present in the *current* directory for that drive (the last one used). To view files in a specific directory on drive A, you must type the full path; for example, DIR a:\backups.

Page 206   IT Career FastTrack with CompTIA A+ Certification   © 2010 gtslearning

Module 2 Operating Systems   *File Management*

```
C:\WINDOWS\system32\cmd.exe                                    _ □ x

Microsoft Windows XP [Version 5.1.2600]
(C) Copyright 1985-2001 Microsoft Corp.

C:\Documents and Settings\jamesp.STONEWALL>cd\

C:\>dir
 Volume in drive C has no label.
 Volume Serial Number is 9C54-2A5E

 Directory of C:\

24/05/2004  15:40                     0 AUTOEXEC.BAT
04/07/2005  16:21                   211 boot.ini
24/05/2004  15:40                     0 CONFIG.SYS
14/08/2006  15:52        <DIR>          Documents and Settings
10/08/2006  15:00        <DIR>          Inetpub
04/04/2006  17:46                   188 INSTALL.LOG
09/08/2006  20:47        <DIR>          Program Files
17/03/2005  12:47                   327 system.ini
18/08/2006  09:59        <DIR>          Temp
17/08/2006  10:03        <DIR>          WINDOWS
               5 File(s)            726 bytes
               5 Dir(s)   1,226,096,640 bytes free

C:\>
```

DIR command

A wildcard character allows you to use unspecified characters with the command. **?** means a single unspecified character. The asterisk (*****) is used to indicate an unknown number of unspecified characters.

DIR can be used with a number of other switches. Some of the most useful are listed below:

- **/a:** - list files with a specified attribute (see below). For example, **DIR /a:r** lists only Read-Only files. **DIR /a:-a** lists only files that are *not* ready for archiving.

- **/o:** - list files with a specified sort order (**n** for name, **s** for size, **e** for extension, **d** for date, **g** for directories, and **-** for reverse order) Use **/t:** to specify the date field used for sorting (**c** for created, **a** for accessed, and **w** for modified).

- **/s** - list all files and folders in subdirectories of the specified folder.

- **/x** - display 8.3 compatibility names. Microsoft DOS was restricted to 8 character file names with a three character extension (see below). Windows maintains versions of those file names for compatibility with legacy applications.

Creating and removing directories

To create a directory, use the command **MD (MKDIR)**. The syntax of this command is: **MD [*drive:*]*path***

© 2010 gtslearning   IT Career FastTrack with CompTIA A+ Certification   Page 207

Unit 2.4   Module 2 Operating Systems

For example, to create a directory called "Data" in the current directory, type **MD Data**. To create a directory called "Docs" in a directory called "Data" on the **A** drive, when the current path is c:\ type **MD a:\Data\Docs**.

To delete an empty directory, type **RD** *directory* (or **RMDIR** *directory*). If the directory is *not empty* you can remove files and subdirectories from it using the **RD /s** command.

You can also use the **/q** switch to suppress confirmation messages (quiet mode).

Tip

If a folder (or file) name contains spaces, enter the name using quotes when supplying it as an argument to a command. For example, to delete a folder named "My Files", enter RD "my files".

Managing Files

Files are the "containers" for the data that is used and modified through the operating system and applications. Files store either **text** or **binary** data; text data is human-readable while binary data can only be interpreted by the correct software application.

Files follow a similar naming convention to folders, except that the last part of the file name represents an extension, which describes what type of file it is and is used by Windows to associate the file with an application.

The extension is divided from the rest of the file name by a period. By convention, extensions are three characters. The following table lists some well known file extensions:

Extension	File Type	Text / Binary
TXT	Plain text	Text
.EXE	Application	Binary
.DLL	Dynamic Link Library (software code shared between applications)	Binary
.INF	Configuration settings (usually for device drivers)	Text
.INI	Configuration settings (usually for applications)	Text
.MSI	Package used to install applications	Binary
.DAT	Data file using an application-specific format (such as comma delimited)	Text

Page 208   IT Career FastTrack with CompTIA A+ Certification   © 2010 gtslearning

Module 2 Operating Systems | File Management

Extension	File Type	Text / Binary
.TMP	Temporary file created by an application while processing data	Binary
.ZIP	Archive containing one or more compressed files	Binary
.HLP	Help file	Text
.CHM	Compiled help file	Binary
.HTM / .HTML	Web page	Text
.OCX	ActiveX Control (website plug-in)	Binary
.VBS / .JS / .BAT	VBScript, JavaScript, and batch files	Text
.BMP / .JPG / .GIF / .PNG / .TIFF	Image file formats	Binary
.WAV / .MP3 / .WMA	Audio file formats	Binary
.AVI / .WMV / .MP4	Video file formats	Binary
.DOC / .RTF	Word processing files (DOC files are used by Microsoft Word while Rich Text Format is generic)	Binary

Creating and opening files

System and application files are created when you install programs. User files are created when you use the **Save** or **Save As** function of a program.

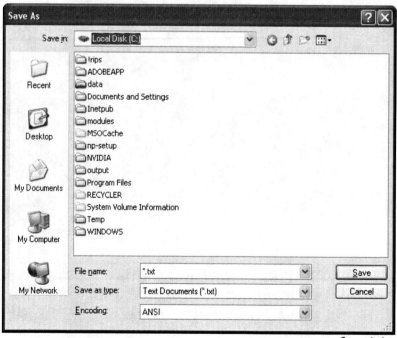

Save dialog

The **Save In** box and the side panel allow the selection of system objects and locations. Folders can be opened from the main window or you can move back and up using the buttons next to the **Save In** box. Most applications let you save the file in one of several file types, accessed through the **Save as type** box.

You can also create certain types of file (and folders) in the Windows shell by alt-clicking in a folder and selecting **New**, followed by the type of file you want to create.

When creating and editing text files, you must be careful to use a plain text file format, such as that used by Notepad (a Windows accessory). If you convert a plain text system file to a binary format, it will become unusable.

Files are opened by double- or single-clicking them (depending on the desktop style specified in **Folder Options**). You may want to open a file in a software product other than the default. When you alt-click a file, the shortcut menu displays a list of suitable choices, or you can choose **Open With** and browse for different application.

EDIT command

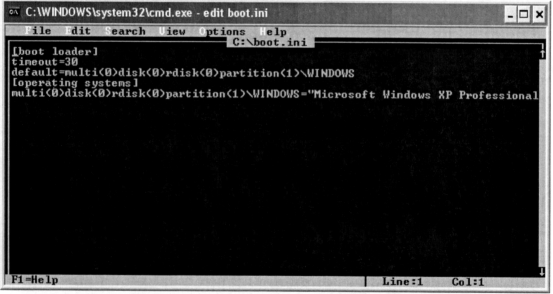

Command prompt text file editor

The command prompt text editor (**EDIT**) is a plain text editing application. It is a suitable application for changing text format system files. Unlike a word processor, it does not convert the file to a binary format and make it unreadable by the OS.

The utility can either be used to create a new file (simply enter **EDIT** or **EDIT Filename**[111]) or to edit an existing file: **EDIT c:\boot.ini**. You can use the **/r** switch to load a file in Read-Only mode.

The menu will respond to mouse clicks or you can use **ALT** to navigate it using the keyboard. Basic keyboard shortcuts, such as **CTRL+V** to paste, are also supported.

When you have finished editing, remember to save the file. The program will prompt you if there are unsaved changes.

Deleting files and the Recycle Bin

To delete a file using Explorer, select it then press **DEL** (or use the shortcut menu). Confirm the action using the prompts.

If you accidentally delete a file from a local hard disk, you can retrieve it from the **Recycle Bin**. A retrieved file will be restored to the location from which it was deleted. The size of the Recycle Bin is limited by default to 10% of the drive's capacity. If large numbers of files are deleted, those files that have been in the Recycle Bin the longest will be permanently deleted to make room for the newly deleted files.

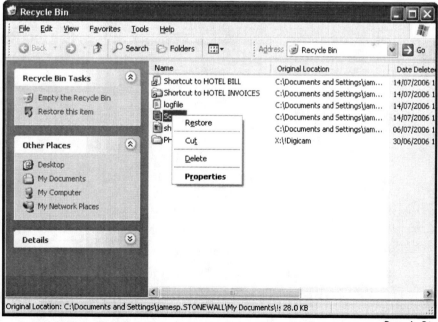

Recycle Bin

---

[111] Obviously if you enter an existing file name, the file will be opened for editing. Using a file name does not automatically create the file. You need to save the file first.

To recover a file, open the **Recycle Bin**, alt-click the file to recover, and select **Restore**. You can recover a folder (and its contents when deleted) in the same way or recover everything by alt-clicking the Recycle Bin icon itself.

If disk space is low, the Recycle Bin can be emptied (alt-click the **Recycle Bin** icon and select **Empty Recycle Bin** from the shortcut menu). This process will permanently remove deleted files.

Note

From a security point-of-view, note that the data is not actually erased until that area of disk is overwritten by different data. Third-party utilities can recover files that have been "deleted" in this way. Other file "shredding" utilities are available to properly erase confidential data.

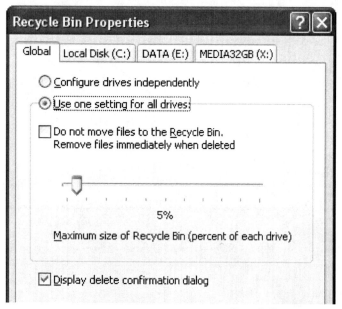

Recycle Bin properties

You can set the amount of space to use on a per-drive basis or set one Recycle Bin for all local drives. You can also choose to suppress the use of delete confirmation dialogs.

To set these options, alt-click the **Recycle Bin** and select **Properties**.

At a command prompt, use **DEL** or **ERASE**. The following switches are available:

Switch	Use
/p	Prompt to delete for each file.
/f	Suppress prompt for read-only files.
/q	Suppress prompt on wildcard delete.
/s	Delete files from subdirectories.
/a:	Delete files with particular attributes (for example, /a:r) or without particular attributes (for example, /a:-r).

Files deleted using the command line are *not* sent to the Recycle Bin.

Module 2 Operating Systems | File Management

Copying and moving files

Windows Explorer supports multiple methods of moving or copying files, including:

- Use the **Edit > Cut / Copy / Paste** commands from the main menu or shortcut menu or their keyboard shortcuts (CTRL+X, CTRL+C, CTRL+V).

- Drag-and-drop the object, holding down CTRL to copy or SHIFT to move (or CTRL+SHIFT to create a shortcut[112]).

> **Tip**
> The default action (no key press) for drag-and-drop is to **move** the selection if the destination is a **local** drive or **copy** it if the destination is a **network** or **removable** drive.

- Alt-drag the object and select an option from the shortcut menu displayed when you release the mouse button.

- Use the **Edit > Move to Folder / Copy to Folder** commands.

- Use the **Send To** command from the main menu or shortcut menu to copy a file to a disk or send it by email.

In Vista, paste operations allow for preserving a file with the same name in the destination folder.

File move / copy displays this dialog when there are files with the same name in the destination folder

---

[112] It is simplest to have the destination folder visible before you start to drag-and-drop, but you can cause a window to scroll up or down during the drag process or make a minimized window active by dragging the selection over the window's taskbar icon.

| Unit 2.4 | Module 2 Operating Systems |

At a command prompt, the MOVE and COPY commands provide the ability to copy and move files from one disk or directory to another. Both commands use a three-part syntax: *COMMAND source destination*. You can enter a different path (including filename) for *destination*. If you use COPY with the same folder but different file name, it will create a duplicate in the same directory.

The following switches are available to use with COPY:

Switch	Use
/y /-y	Enable (the default) or disable quiet mode. Disabling suppresses a warning if the operation will overwrite an existing file[113].
/v	Verifies each file as it is written to the destination file to make sure that the destination files are identical to the source files.
/z	Copy network files in restartable mode (if the network connection is lost, the utility will wait for it to be restored before restarting the copy process).
/b /a	Switch between binary (the default) and ASCII text mode.
/d	Decrypt an encrypted source file at the destination.

XCOPY is a utility that allows a user to copy the contents of more than one directory at a time and retain the directory structure. The table below explains some of the different parameters and switches.

Parameter	Notes
source	The location and names of the files to be copied. Source must include either a drive or a path.
destination	The destination where the files are to be copied. Destination can include a drive letter and colon, a directory name, a filename, or a combination.
/i	Specifies that the destination is a directory[114].
/exclude:	Lists file paths that should **not** be copied.
/u	Copies only files that already exist in the destination.
/a	Only copies a file if it has its archive file attribute set. This switch does not turn off the archive attribute, which means that if a backup was performed afterwards which relied on the archive attribute, the files would still get backed up.
/m	Only copies a file if it has its archive file attribute set but does turn off the archive attribute.
/h	Copies hidden files (XCOPY does not do this by default).

---

[113] Obviously you can use this switch with the MOVE command as well as with COPY.

[114] If the destination does not end in a backslash and is not an existing directory and source contains multiple files, XCOPY prompts you to confirm whether destination is a file or directory.

Parameter	Notes
/r	Copies read-only files.
/k	Retains read-only attribute of source file at destination (*not* the default).
/d:*date*	Copies files modified on or after the specified date.
/p	Prompts you to confirm whether you want to create each destination file.
/s	Copies directories and subdirectories, unless they are empty. Without this switch XCOPY will only copy the contents of one directory.
/e	Copies any subdirectories, even if they are empty.
/t	Copies directory structure but not files. Use with /e to recreate empty directories.
/w	Displays a prompt and waits for a response before starting to copy files.
/q	Enables quiet mode (does not display file names while copying).
/f	Displays full file path while copying.
/v /y /z	As for COPY command.

Renaming a file (REN)

In Explorer, you can rename an object by selecting it and pressing F2 or using the shortcut menu. At the command prompt, use REN to change a file or folder name. The syntax of this command is: REN *OldName NewName*. To rename multiple files, wildcard characters may be used. For example, REN *.txt *.doc will rename all files with an extension of TXT to DOC.

File attributes

A file's name is just one of its **attributes**. Other attributes include things like the date the file was created, accessed, or modified, its size, its description, and the following markers, which can be enabled or disabled:

Attribute	Usage
Read-only (R)	Prevent changes being saved back to the file. The user will be prompted to create another file containing the modified data.
Hidden (H)	Specifies whether the file is visible in the default view (it is possible to adjust Windows to display hidden files and folders though the Folder Options applet though).
System (S)	Specifies that the file should not be modified.
Archive (A)	Shows whether a file has changed since the last backup.

Unit 2.4

Module 2 Operating Systems

You can set some attributes manually using the file or folder's property dialog or the ATTRIB command. A full list of the switches available with ATTRIB is shown in the table below.

Switch	Description
+r	Marks the file as read-only.
-r	Clears the read-only attribute.
+a	Sets the archive attribute.
-a	Clears the archive attribute.
+h	Marks the file as hidden, so that it will not be visible in a normal directory listing.
-h	Clears the hidden attribute.
+s	Marks the file as a system file.
-s	Clears the system attribute.
/s	Applies the command to files in subdirectories.

NTFS file and folder permissions and extended attributes

Files stored on an NTFS volume have **extended attributes**, including permissions, compression, and encryption. To create, modify, or delete a file in a folder, you may need the correct permissions on that folder. Permissions can also be applied to individual files. See unit 5.3 for more information about permissions and user accounts.

Extracting a file

Setup files are often stored in compressed archives named CABs. Archives may be split over more than file stored on more than one floppy disk. The installation procedure extracts the files automatically, but on some occasions it may be necessary to retrieve a file manually. You can do this using the **EXPAND** command. For example, to extract a single file (**ReadMe.txt**) from **Install.cab** on the floppy drive to the root of c:\, type: EXPAND a:\install.cab -f:readme.txt c:\. To extract all files from a cab to a folder **c:\Temp**, type: EXPAND a:\install.cab c:\temp. You can also use these switches:

■ /r - rename expanded files.

■ /d - locate or list files.

Page 216   IT Career FastTrack with CompTIA A+ Certification   © 2010 gtslearning

Module 2 Operating Systems   *File Management*

Summary

Hard disks can be divided into a number of partitions and each partition can be formatted with either FAT or NTFS to make a drive or volume accessible under Windows. Each volume is assigned a drive letter, with the system (or active) volume always labeled "C". FAT provides compatibility with dual-boot system but NTFS would be the choice for most installations. Disks can be configured using the Disk Management program.

There are differences between the versions of Windows in the names of system folders and files.

Files and folders can be managed using Windows Explorer or the command prompt utilities (DIR, CD, MD, XCOPY, and so on). Files are associated with applications using a period plus three-character extension on the end of the file name. Files also have attributes, such as Read-Only or Archive.

Tip

To review what you have learned in this chapter, you should now visit the course website. This contains review questions and bonus material to help you to learn more and practice the topics covered in this unit.

| Unit 2.5 | Module 2 Operating Systems |

Unit 2.5 Configuring Windows

CompTIA A+ Essentials Objectives

☐ **701.1.1 Categorize storage devices and backup media**
Removable storage (Hot swappable devices and non-hot swappable devices)

☐ **701.3.1 Compare and contrast the different Windows Operating Systems and their features**
Application compatibility, Installed program locations [32bit vs. 64bit], Windows compatibility mode

☐ **701.3.2 Given a scenario, demonstrate proper use of user interfaces**
Run line utilities (MSINFO32, DXDIAG) • Administrative tools (Services) • Start menu

☐ **701.3.3 Explain the process and steps to install and configure the Windows OS**
Configure power management (Suspend, Wake on LAN, Sleep timers, Hibernate, Standby) • Demonstrate safe removal of peripherals

CompTIA A+ Practical Application Objectives

☐ **702.2.3 Given a scenario, select and use system utilities / tools and evaluate the results**
Administrative tools (Services) • System Information • Regional Settings and Language Settings

Installing and Configuring Peripheral Devices

Peripheral devices for Windows computers[115] are **Plug-and-Play**. This means that they can be added to the computer and the operating system will detect the device automatically and prompt you to configure it using the **Add Hardware Wizard**. Most devices also come with setup programs which will do the same job (they are required if the OS does not ship with the drivers required by the device).

System resources

When you install a new device, such as a network card, sound card, or internal modem into a PC, it must be allocated a set of system **resources** that enable it to communicate with the processor and system memory without conflicting with other devices.

---

[115] That is, Windows 2000/XP/Vista computers. Devices for older versions of Windows (such as Windows 95) would sometimes require manual resource configuration.

Page 218   IT Career FastTrack with CompTIA A+ Certification   © 2010 gtslearning

Module 2 Operating Systems

Configuring Windows

Memory range / I/O address

Every device in the PC has its own set of unique memory addresses in an area called the I/O address map. The I/O address is a means for the CPU to communicate with a device. The address map is a block of system memory 65,536 bytes (64KB) in size.

The I/O port is referred to using its hexadecimal (or port) address in the range of 0000-FFFF. References to I/O ports are usually made using the start address only. For example, the I/O port of COM1 is referred to as 03F8, although it uses the range 03F8-03FF. Standard notation omits the leading zero and puts an "h" after the address to indicate the number is hexadecimal (3F8h).

Interrupts (IRQ)

An I/O address tells the CPU where to look in memory to communicate with a device, but it must also know *when* to communicate with it! This is accomplished by the device raising an **Interrupt Request (IRQ)**. Under the early PC architecture, each device was allocated an IRQ "line" from 0 to 15. Allocating two devices the same IRQ was the cause of many problems on these early computers.

Modern PCs use more advanced interrupt controllers to facilitate interrupts from multiple devices on a bus such as PCI or PCIe. Some core system components are still allocated IRQs from the 0 to 15 range though.

Installing a device

Most devices with USB or Firewire connections are **hot swappable**. This means that the device can be added to or removed from the computer while it is switched on. Devices attached via a parallel, serial, or PS/2 interface may need the PC to be shut down and restarted.

Tip

You may also see the term hot pluggable used. Technically, a hot pluggable device can be installed while the system is running but can not necessarily be removed safely without shutting down the computer. A fully hot swappable device can be added or removed without an OS restart.

© 2010 gtslearning   IT Career FastTrack with CompTIA A+ Certification   Page 219

| Unit 2.5 | Module 2 Operating Systems |

Before connecting a device, you may need to install its **drivers** using the vendor-supplied software. A driver is software that creates an interface between the device and the operating system. It may also include tools for configuring and optimizing the device. Many devices have drivers that are shipped along with Windows, but even in that case the vendor may be able to supply a more up-to-date driver.

Bear the following points in mind when adding or removing peripherals:

- Always read the manufacturer's instructions and check that the device is compatible with the PC and operating system.

- Hold the connector not the cable when removing a lead.

- Inspect the connector and port for damage (notably broken or bent pins) before attaching a lead.

- Take care to align the connector carefully and do not use excessive force, to avoid damaging the pins (PS/2 connectors are particularly fragile)[116].

- Check whether the device requires an external power source.

- If you plug a USB 2.0 device into a USB 1.1 port, a notification message will be displayed, helpfully telling you that the device could perform faster if plugged into a High Speed port.

If the driver is installed, the OS will detect and configure the device automatically when it is plugged in. You can then use Device Manager, Control Panel, or the vendor-supplied software to adjust user settings.

Removing a device

Before removing a storage device, close any applications that might be using it then double-click the **Safely Remove Hardware** icon (or) in the **notification area** on the taskbar and choose the option to stop the device.

This ensures that any pending data writes are completed before the device is remove; simply pulling the plug could cause a file or file system corruption.

If a device does not support hot swapping, you should uninstall it using Device Manager and shut down the computer before removing it. See unit 4.4 for more information about configuring hardware.

---

[116] USB and Firewire have simple push/pull connectors that are keyed to prevent incorrect insertion. Serial, parallel, and display connectors have screws to hold them in place. RJ-11 and RJ-45 connectors have a plastic clip that must be pushed in to remove.

System Information

The **System Information (MSINFO32)** application provides a report of some of the configuration information contained in the registry.

Folder	Information
System Summary	Information about operating system and BIOS versions and registration details.
Hardware Resources	I/O, DMA, IRQ, and memory settings.
Components	A detailed list of all running devices including configuration information such as IRQ.
Software Environment	Various information including drivers, environment settings, network connections.
Internet	Internet connection settings.
Applications	Microsoft application settings

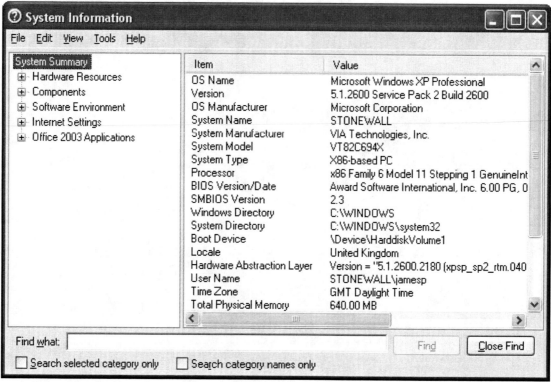

System Information

Note that you can run several troubleshooting tools from the Tools menu in the Windows 2000/XP version, including Net Diagnostics, System Restore, File Signature Verification, DirectX Diagnostics, and Dr Watson. In Windows Vista, shortcuts to these kinds of tools have been moved to the MSCONFIG utility.

You can run the `MSINFO32` utility with a number of switches[117].

- `/category` *CategoryName* - start with the named category selected.
- `/report` *FileName* - output to a text file.
- `/computer` *ComputerName* - display information for the named workstation.

DirectX diagnostic tool

The `DXDIAG` tool displays a report on the system's DirectX configuration, which determines its ability to support 3D graphics and sound.

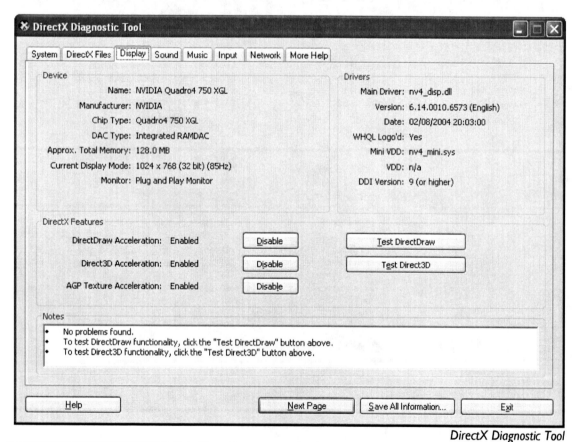

DirectX Diagnostic Tool

[117] You can also use the WINMSD command to launch System Information. By default, the utility is installed to **Program Files\Common Files\Microsoft Shared\MSInfo**.

Module 2 Operating Systems   *Configuring Windows*

In Windows 2000/XP, it can test that DirectX drivers are signed and that settings such as 3D acceleration, sound output, and so on are working properly. The Windows Vista version is informational only.

On the other hand, Vista does come with the **Performance Information and Tools** applet (see unit 2.6).

Managing Applications

Local applications are installed to the **Program Files** directory on the boot volume (for example, c:\Program Files). Most applications will also write configuration data to the registry and may add folders and files to the user's home directory (or to the All Users directory for settings shared by all users).

Applications should be installed and removed using the supplied Setup program or the applet in Control Panel.

Windows 2000/XP Add or Remove Programs

Add or Remove Programs allows an administrator to:

- **Add new programs** - run setup programs to install new software (though you can also run the program's setup file or installer from Windows Explorer).

> **Note**
>
> In order to install a program successfully, you should exit any other applications or files[118]. You may also need to disable anti-virus software.

- **Add/Remove Windows Components** - such as networking or other services.

---

[118] Application installation and removal under legacy versions of Windows could cause problems as an application changed or removed DLL (Dynamic Link Library) files used by other applications, causing them to malfunction. With Windows 2000, Microsoft introduced the Windows File Protection and the Installer Service to mitigate these problems. Most application vendors use setup programs that are compliant with Windows Installer (Windows Installer packages have .MSI extensions). Under Windows XP, System Restore can also be configured to create a Restore Point automatically upon application installation, adding a further measure of protection.

© 2010 gtslearning   IT Career FastTrack with CompTIA A+ Certification   Page 223

Unit 2.5 Module 2 Operating Systems

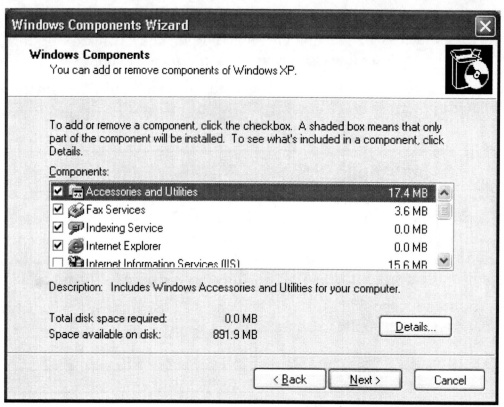

Adding/removing Windows components

- **Change or Remove Programs** - uninstall a program or add or remove component features of software such as Microsoft Office. Under Windows XP, if you check the **Show updates** box, the list will also display patches or hotfixes installed for a particular application (or conversely hide them if you uncheck it). You can use the wizard to uninstall a patch (see unit 4.1 for more notes on Windows Update).

> **Note**
> In order to uninstall a program successfully, you should exit any applications or files that might lock files installed by the application or the PC will need to be restarted. You may also need to disable anti-virus software. If the uninstall program cannot remove locked files, it will normally prompt you to check its log file for details (the files and directories can then be deleted manually).

- **Set Program Access and Defaults** - configure which applications to use for tasks such as web browsing and email (Windows XP only).

Module 2 Operating Systems │ Configuring Windows

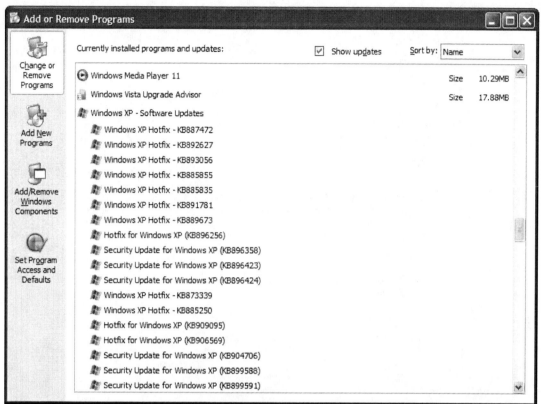

Add or Remove Programs with Show updates checked (displaying updates installed for Windows)

Windows Vista Programs and Features

As you can see from the screenshot below, the basic uninstall / configure functionality of **Programs and Features** is unchanged from **Add or Remove Programs**. You can switch between viewing Windows updates and installed programs by clicking the link on the left.

In Vista, the option to add or remove Windows components is called "Turn Windows features on or off". There are also some extra options for purchasing and managing online software (**Windows Marketplace**).

The **Set Program Access and Defaults** functionality is provided by the **Default Programs** applet. You can also use this applet to set file associations (choosing which application is used to open files with a particular extension).

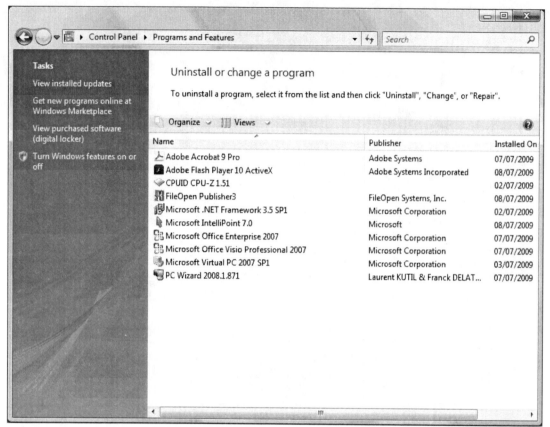

Windows Vista Programs and Features

Application compatibility

One of the challenges for Microsoft in releasing a new version of Windows is to provide compatibility for hardware and software developed for previous versions.

Windows 2000 and XP provide support for legacy DOS and Windows NT and 9x programs[119]. Shortcuts to such programs have a **Compatibility** tab.

This allows you to configure the program's original operating system environment and force it to use compatible display settings.

Windows Vista features such as User Account Control and its greater protection for system folders (Program Files and the system root) plus the redesigned desktop compositing engine (Aero Glass) have made application compatibility even more challenging.

---

[119] Windows 2000 compatibility modes were added in SP2 and need to be enabled by executing the command `regsvr32 %systemroot%\apppatch\slayerui.dll`. Refer to support.microsoft.com/kb/279792 for more information.

Module 2 Operating Systems
Configuring Windows

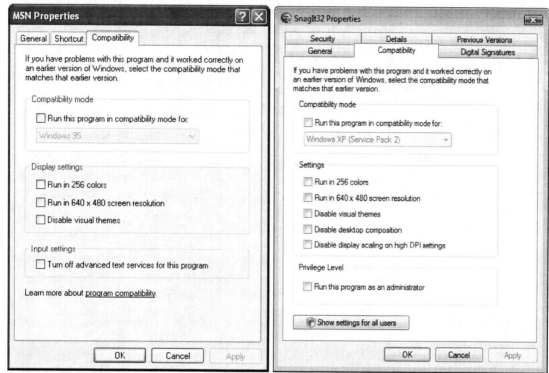

Windows XP and Windows Vista compatibility options

UAC problems can be solved by running the program as an administrator and there is an option to turn off advanced desktop compositing effects.

64-bit Windows and 32-bit applications

Many of the software applications available for Windows are still 32-bit. These applications can usually be installed under 64-bit versions of Windows. They run within a special application environment called WOW64 (Windows on Windows 64-bit). This environment replicates the 32-bit environment expected by the application and translates its requests into ones that can be processed by the 64-bit CPU, memory, and file subsystems.

One of the confusing points to note is that Windows' 64-bit shared system files (DLLs and EXEs) are stored in **%SystemRoot%\system32**; that is, the *same* system folder as 32-bit versions of Windows. Files for the *32-bit* versions are stored in **%SystemRoot%\syswow64**.

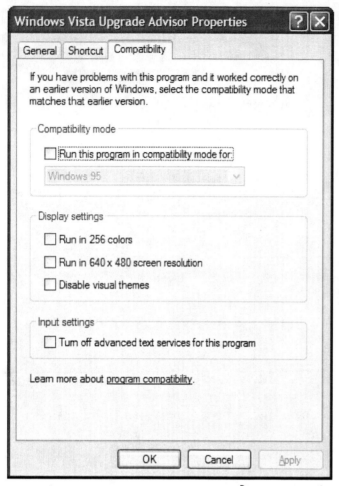
Program properties

When an application is installed, you may experience difficulties getting it to run. If this is the case, you can inspect the properties of the executable file (or a shortcut to the executable). The **Version** tab is useful for troubleshooting as it will let you know whether you are running a version with the latest patches. The **Compatibility** tab can be used to run the program in a compatibility mode (for Windows 98 for instance) and adjust the display settings.

Program shortcuts are added to the Start menu and (optionally) the desktop. Each user's Start menu is built from items in the **All Users** Start menu and the user's own Start menu.

Program shortcuts may be added to either, depending on how the installer has been written. The **Startup** folder in the Start menu contains program shortcuts that are run automatically at boot time.

Managing Services

Services provide functionality for many parts of the Windows OS, such as allowing logon, browsing the network, or indexing file details to optimize searches. Services may be installed by Windows and by other applications, such as anti-virus, database, or backup software.

You might want to disable non-essential services to improve performance or security. If something is not working properly, you should check that any services it depends upon are started.

To configure services, alt-click **(My) Computer** and select **Manage**. Expand **Services and Applications** from the tree and click the **Services** icon. This displays a list of installed services in the right-hand panel. Clicking a service displays information about it in the middle panel. The shortcut menu for a service allows you to start, stop, pause/resume, or restart (stop then start).

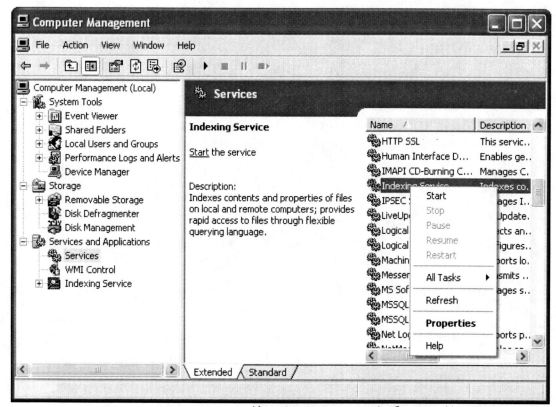

Managing services using the Computer Management console

Service properties allow you to configure the following options:

- **General** - shows information about the service and lets you choose the startup type (Automatic, Manual, or Disabled).
- **Log on** - specify which user account the service should run under.
- **Recovery** - specify what to do when a service fails to start.
- **Dependencies** - shows how the service is related to other services.

Configuring Power Management

Power management requires three compatible components:

- Hardware - devices that support power management are often labeled **Energy Star** (after the US Environmental Protection Agency scheme). It is important for the CPU, motherboard, hard disks, and display screen to support the same standard.

- BIOS - almost all BIOS support the standard ACPI (Advanced Configuration and Power Interface) but you may need to check that it has been enabled.

- Operating System - Windows provides full ACPI compatibility.

One basic feature of ACPI is to support different **power saving modes**. The computer can be configured to enter a power saving mode automatically (for example, if there is no use of an input device for a set period). The user can also put the computer into a power saving state rather than shutting down.

Windows implements the following ACPI power modes:

- **Standby (2000 / XP) / Suspend to RAM** - cuts power to most devices (for example, the CPU, monitor, disk drives, and peripherals) but maintains power to the memory. This is also referred to as ACPI mode S3.

- **Hibernate / Suspend to Disk** - saves any data in memory (open files) to disk then turns the computer off. This is also referred to as ACPI mode S4.

- **Sleep (Vista)** - in Windows Vista, standby is replaced by sleep, which functions differently depending on whether the computer is a laptop or desktop:

  □ A laptop goes into the standby state as normal; if running on battery power, it will switch from standby to hibernate before the battery runs down

  □ A desktop creates a hibernation file then goes into the standby state (this is referred to as hybrid sleep mode); it can also be configured to switch to the full hibernation state after a set time

Tip

You can also set a specific device (such as the display or hard drive) to enter a power-saving state if it goes unused for a defined period (sleep timers). Note that monitors still consume quite a lot of power in standby mode.

Configuring power management in Windows 2000/XP

Modern operating systems are able to switch off the monitor (and hard disk) after a specified period to conserve power. These options are configured through the **Power** applet in **Control Panel**. Alternatively, click the **Power** button from the **Screen Saver** tab of **Display Properties** or access power properties via the **Power Meter** (or depending on whether the computer is on AC or battery power) in the notification area.

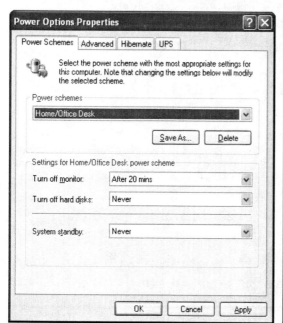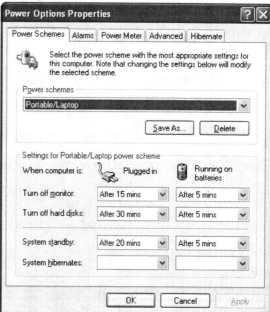

Power Management Properties for desktop (left) and laptop (right) computers

You can choose from the predefined power schemes or configure custom settings using the boxes. The **Power Meter** tab shows you the status of the battery[120] and the **Advanced** tab is used to set default responses to user actions such as pressing the power button (typically shut down) or closing the laptop lid (typically go to standby).

The **Hibernate** tab lets you disable the hibernation option (useful if the computer is low on disk space).

You can also configure alarms to (dis)play when battery power is low, configure soft power behavior, and choose whether to display the battery power meter on the taskbar.

---

[120] There will usually be a vendor-supplied utility providing more information about battery status and health.

| Unit 2.5 | Module 2 Operating Systems |

To re-activate the computer from a screen saver or power-saving mode, press a key or move the mouse.

In addition to the schemes defined for ACPI, you may be able to adjust the properties of the CPU and graphics card to enter power saving modes. Intel CPU SpeedStep and AMD PowerNow! under Windows XP is automatically enabled if you select certain power schemes[121]:

Power Scheme	CPU Powersaving Mode	
	AC (Mains)	DC (Battery)
Home/Office Desk	None	Adaptive
Portable/Laptop	Adaptive	Adaptive
Presentation	Adaptive	Degrade
Always On	None	None
Minimal Power Management	Adaptive	Adaptive
Max Battery	Adaptive	Degrade

Adaptive mode means the processor responds to demand from applications, speeding up and down as necessary; **degrade** means that it starts in the lowest performance state and is further slowed through software manipulation. Graphics card throttling is configured via the vendor's driver.

Another option is the ability to disable power-hungry wireless components, such as a Wi-Fi or Bluetooth adapter. This can usually be done quickly via a FN key shortcut or the laptop vendor's driver or software utility.

Configuring power management in Windows Vista

Vista extends the degree to which power management can be customized. Firstly, there is a system of **power plans**, enabling the user to switch between a different set of preconfigured options easily. Each power plan can be customized or new plans can be defined and saved.

Secondly, as well as configuring events for the power button or closing the lid of a laptop, the "shut down" option in Start menu can be customized; so clicking the button could make the computer sleep while closing the lid could activate the hibernate routine. These settings can be defined for all plans (use the "Choose what the power button does" link in the bar on the left shown in the dialog below) or on a per-plan basis (click the plan then configure advanced settings).

---

[121] Windows 2000 requires a driver to work with Intel SpeedStep and AMD PowerNow!.

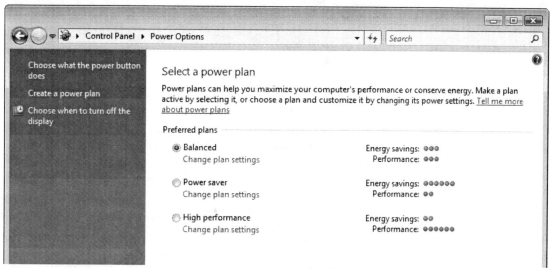

Configuring power management in Windows Vista

Thirdly, advanced settings allow you to configure a very wide range of options, including CPU states, search and indexing behavior, display brightness, and so on.

Wake on LAN (WoL)

Wake on LAN (WoL) allows an administrator to start up a computer remotely. When the computer is switched off, the network card (NIC), powered by a battery, remains active. The administrator would use network software to broadcast a "magic packet" to the NIC; when it receives it, the NIC initiates the computer's boot process. The general steps to setting up Wake on LAN are as follows:

1. Enable WoL in the BIOS (any motherboard released in the last few years should support WoL).

2. Open the adapter's **Properties** dialog in **Device Manager**. Select the **Advanced** tab then enable the option for WoL[122]. Again, older NICs might not support WoL but these would be the exception rather than the rule now.

3. Configure the network software to send magic packets. This type of software is often provided with systems and network management suites or you can obtain standalone utilities.

---

[122] This option may be described as many different things: WoL, power management, wake up, and so on. Check the vendor documentation.

Configuring Regional and Language Options

The **Regional and Language Options** applet in Control Panel lets you change the settings for applications (date format, currency, and so on) and the input language(s) for the keyboard from those chosen during setup.

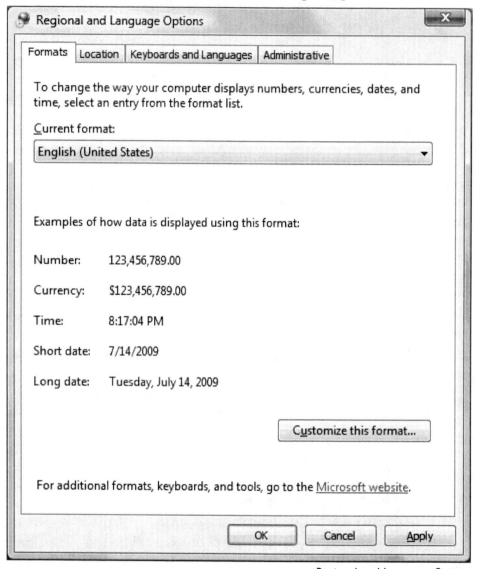

Regional and Language Options

In Windows XP and Vista, the **Location** tab allows web services such as weather reporting or traffic news to default to your current location.

If you want to use multiple input languages (both US and UK keyboard layouts for instance), you can install them using the **Keyboards and Languages** tab and switch between them using the Language Bar or a defined keystroke combo. If you have the appropriate language pack, you can also display Windows' and compatible applications' menus in the selected language.

> **Note**
> If troubleshooting a keyboard issue, make sure the keyboard is set to the correct input language.

Configuring input languages

Summary

Make sure you know the procedures for adding and removing devices and the tools for managing software, services, power options (including standby modes and timers), and regional settings in the various versions of Windows.

Unit 2.6 | Module 2 Operating Systems

Unit 2.6 Optimizing Windows

CompTIA A+ Essentials Objectives

☐ **701.3.2 Given a scenario, demonstrate proper use of user interfaces**
Run line utilities (MSCONFIG) • Administrative tools (Performance Monitor) • Task Manager

☐ **701.3.3 Explain the process and steps to install and configure the Windows OS**
Virtual memory

☐ **701.2.5 Given a scenario, integrate common preventative maintenance techniques**
Scheduling preventative maintenance (Defrag, Scandisk, Check Disk, Startup programs)

CompTIA A+ Practical Application Objectives

☐ **702.2.1 Select the appropriate commands and options to troubleshoot and resolve problems**
MSCONFIG

☐ **702.2.3 Given a scenario, select and use system utilities / tools and evaluate the results**
Disk management tools (DEFRAG, Check Disk) • System monitor • Administrative tools (Performance Monitor) • Task Manager (Resource usage) • Task Scheduler

☐ **702.2.4 Evaluate and resolve common issues**
System Performance and Optimization (Aero settings, Indexing settings, UAC, Sidebar settings, Startup file maintenance, Background processes)

System Performance and Optimization

When you install or purchase a computer for a given purpose, you will have tried to anticipate what sort of demands and software application requirements you have for the machine's intended usage and specified the appropriate hardware resources.

As time goes by, a user's demands on the system may increase, making additional demands on resources until a point is reached where application responsiveness is compromised to such an extent that the user begins to experience problems. You may be able to optimize settings to solve the problem temporarily but if demand increases at some point the machine will need a hardware upgrade or replacing with a better specified computer.

A user's opinion about performance is largely subjective. While it may not always be wrong, stating that a system is "slow" does not explain why it is slow. Performance Monitoring allows you to measure whether the key resources are being stretched to the point where they need to be upgraded or replaced.

Page 236 | IT Career FastTrack with CompTIA A+ Certification | © 2010 gtslearning

Understanding resource usage

A computer has four key resources: Processor, Memory, Disk, and Network. These are the resources that determine a computer's performance in a given situation. Which of these is the most important is dependent upon several factors. What the optimum configuration is for each is also variable.

Computer resources

- Processors - desktop performance is very much governed by processor performance. The speed of the main CPU and its ability to multiprocess (for example, whether it is dual core) will usually be the most important factor in determining system speed. However, for certain applications, such as games, the performance of the GPU on the graphics card is almost as important.

- Memory - a fast memory bus and the capacity of the memory modules are both important for performance. Higher clock speeds and technologies such as dual-channel improve throughput while memory capacity determines the ability to work with multiple applications and large files. If memory runs out, the system starts to use disk-paged memory, which is very slow in comparison with system memory.

- Disks - on a client computer, the storage capacity of disks is probably more important than their speed, especially if the system has plenty of memory. Technologies such as Windows Vista ReadyBoost and SuperFetch can improve performance by pre-caching code and data in system memory or flash memory.

- Network - bandwidth of the network or modem link is self-evidently important when accessing a LAN or the internet. There is not often too much scope to upgrade this however.

Establishing a baseline

You may have experienced a situation where a computer suddenly stops performing well. Perhaps it takes minutes to boot or loading a document that previously took a few moments now takes several minutes. This is (informal) performance monitoring, with comparison to a **baseline**. In this case, the baseline is your personal experience of the responsiveness of the computer under a given load.

An administrator needs to establish a more accurate baseline for comparison, in order to measure system responsiveness at a later date. Changes to the system require a new baseline to be taken. For instance, this could be done when hardware or software is upgraded or installed.

System Monitor

A **System Monitor** (or Health Monitor or Diagnostics Tool) can be used to provide early warning of problems such as device temperature, fan speeds, disk failure, chassis intrusion, component failure, and so on.

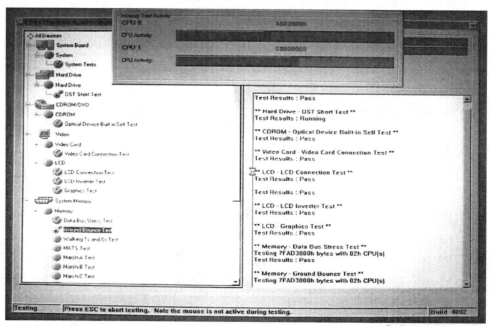

Dell diagnostic utility

Most PC and laptop vendors supply their own tool, accessible either as a boot option (press **F12** at startup or similar) or as a Windows application.

Task Manager

The **Task Manager** utility (`TASKMGR`) allows the user to shut down applications that are not responding. In addition to this functionality, Task Manager can be used to monitor the PC's key resources.

The quickest way to open Task Manager is to press `CTRL+SHIFT+ESC`. Other ways to open Task Manager include pressing `CTRL+ALT+DEL` and selecting Task Manger or alt-clicking the taskbar.

Click the **Performance** tab to view resource usage. In Windows 2000/XP, this shows graphs of CPU and pagefile utilization. On a system with multiple processors, you should see two graphs for CPU Usage (one for each CPU)[123].

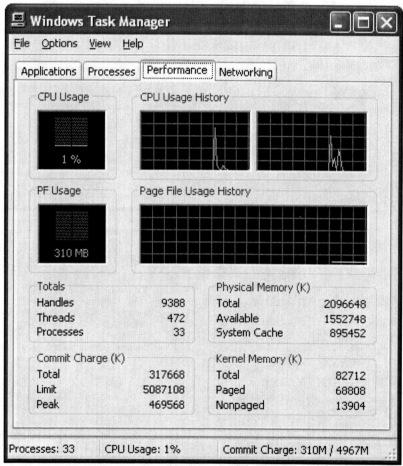

Windows XP Task Manager - Performance tab

---

[123] If this is not the case, select View > CPU History > One Graph per CPU.

The following memory usage is also displayed:

- **Physical Memory** - usage of system RAM (not including pagefile).
- **Commit Charge** - overall memory usage (including physical memory and pagefile).
- **Kernel Memory** - physical and paged memory used by Windows core files.

High peak values are nothing to worry about, but *consistently* high utilization means that you should consider adding more resources to the system (or run fewer processes!). CPU and physical memory obviously require physical upgrades. If pagefile usage is very high, Windows will normally change the pagefile dynamically. If it has been set manually, you should increase it (see below).

In Vista, the graphs show CPU and system memory utilization plus the stats for physical and kernel memory. In place of the commit charge information, there is a system summary showing handles, threads, and processes (software objects being managed by the CPU), system uptime, and pagefile usage.

Under Windows XP and Vista (not Windows 2000) the **Networking** tab shows the status and utilization of network links.

The **Processes** tab shows CPU utilization and memory usage for each process. You would examine these values to discover whether a particular application was misbehaving (for example, an application may "leak" memory by not freeing it up when it has finished using it). To show more than the default CPU and Memory Usage, select **View > Select Columns** and check the items that you want to look at.

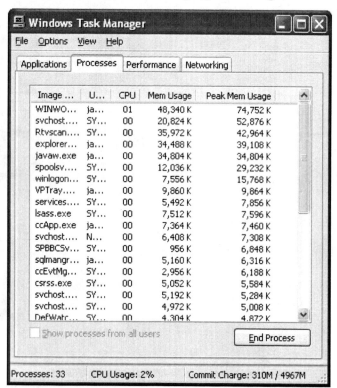

Task Manager - Processes tab

Under Windows Vista, there are also **Services** and **Users** tabs. You can use the **Services** tab to show which services are running, start and stop services, or open the services management console. The **Users** tab shows who is logged on to the machine. An administrator can disconnect or log off other users.

Windows Vista Task Manager - Users tab

Note

As with other Vista administrative tools, some settings in Task Manager are not available unless you run the tool with administrative privileges.

Task Manager is useful for viewing system resources at a *point-in-time*. For more in-depth performance analysis, you can record historical logs and track usage over time using a tool such as **Performance Monitor** or a third-party tool.

Performance Monitor

Windows **Performance Monitor** (found in the **Administrative Tools** menu[124]) can be used to provide real-time charts of system resources or can be used to log information to a file for viewing at a later date.

By monitoring different resources at different times of the day, you can detect bottlenecks that are causing problems and hopefully specify the most effective upgrade.

It may be that a particular application starts freezing for longer and longer periods. This could be caused by a number of things. By using Performance Monitor, you can decide what is causing it. Perhaps it is that the processor is too slow, which would cause the requests to take longer; perhaps the hard disk is too slow, which would mean that it takes too long for the computer to open and save files; perhaps the application uses a network link that has become faulty or congested.

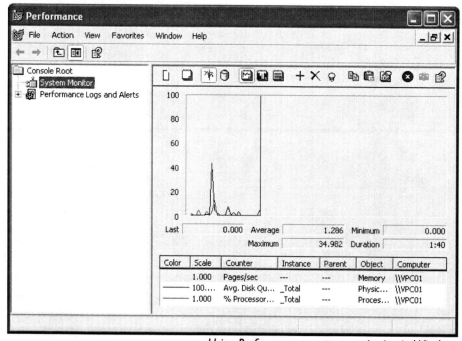

Using Performance - system monitoring in Windows

The computer's performance could be increased by upgrading any or all of these components, but Performance Monitor will help determine which is critical.

---

[124] You can also run perfmon.exe. This topic first discusses Performance Monitor as supplied with Windows 2000/XP and then looks at the version provided with Windows Vista.

Objects, counters, and instances

Resources, such as memory and disk, are collected into **objects**. Objects have **counters**, representing different performance statistics, and where there are several of the same type of object, multiple **instances** are listed. For example, disk performance can be measured using the Physical Disk Object and the best counter to use is the Average Queue Length. If there are two disks, three instances of this object can be viewed: disk 0, disk 1, and disks Total.

Interval

As well as selecting objects and counters to monitor, you also need to define an appropriate sampling interval. If you are logging data for a few minutes, a short interval (of a few seconds) is fine; if measuring over a longer period (hours), you should set a longer interval (15 - 60 seconds) to avoid overloading the computer and generating an unmanageably large log file.

Monitoring counters

You can monitor different parts of your system by adding different counters to your monitor chart. To add a counter click the **Add** + button.

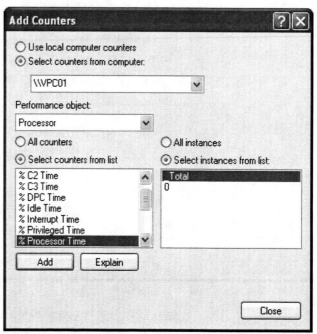

Adding a counter

| Unit 2.6 | | Module 2 Operating Systems |

Some of the most commonly used counters are listed below:

Object	Counter	Description
Processor	% Processor Time	The percentage of time that the processor is executing a non-idle thread. In general terms this should be low. If it is greater than 85% for a sustained period, you may have a processor bottleneck.
	% Privileged Time % User Time	If overall processor time is very high (over 85% for sustained periods), it can be helpful to compare these. Privileged time represents system processes while user time is software applications. If privileged time is much higher, it is likely that the CPU is underpowered (it can barely run Windows core processes efficiently).
Physical Disk	% Disk Time	The percentage of elapsed time that the selected disk drive is busy servicing read or write requests. This is a good overall indicator of how busy the disk is. Again, if the average exceeds 85% for a sustained period, you may have a disk problem.
	Average Disk Queue Length	The number of requests outstanding on the disk at the time the performance data is collected. Taken with the preceding counter, this gives a better indicator of disk problems. For example, if the disk queue length is increasing and disk time is high, then you have a disk problem.
Memory	Available Bytes	The amount of memory available - this should not be below about 10% of total system RAM. It can also be instructive to compare available bytes to committed bytes; if available bytes does not rise as committed bytes falls, there could be a memory leak.
	Pages/sec	The number of pages read from or written to disk to resolve hard page faults. This means your system is using the paging file. Nothing wrong so long as this is not excessive (averaging above about 50). You probably also want to check the paging file's usage by viewing the paging object itself.
Paging File	% Usage	The amount of the pagefile instance in use in percent. If your paging file is currently 1000 MB on the disk and this figure averages 50%, then it means you might benefit from adding memory (about 500 MB in fact). Don't forget that if your system pages excessively, then disk performance will suffer - paging is disk intensive.

Page 244   IT Career FastTrack with CompTIA A+ Certification   © 2010 gtslearning

Notice that it is not always immediately apparent which component is causing a problem. Many counters are interrelated and must be viewed with other counters in mind. For instance, if you system memory is low, then the disk will likely be slow because of excessive paging. Conversely, if you have plenty of memory, then caching is enhanced, allowing the disk sub-system to run more efficiently.

You'll also notice that no objects/counters have been defined for network problems. That's primarily because there are more appropriate methods of determining network performance. You can collect statistics about the network interface, including packets sent or received per second; but in reality, they tell you little about whether there is a bottleneck in the network. It is usually better to use Network Monitor or a third-party analyzer.

When you have more than one counter running it can be hard to distinguish between them. This problem is solved by using the highlight button.

To highlight a counter, select it from the list at the bottom and click the **Highlight** button.

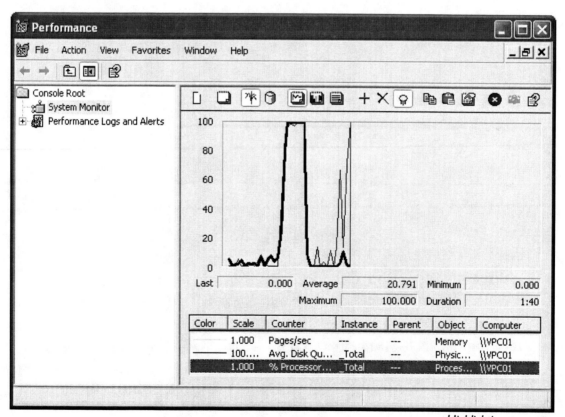

Highlighting a counter

Logging performance

In Performance Monitor you can create counter log files which will record information for viewing at a later date. By using this feature, you can generate a library of log files taken at different times of the day, week or even year. This information can provide a system baseline and then be used to give a longer term view of system performance.

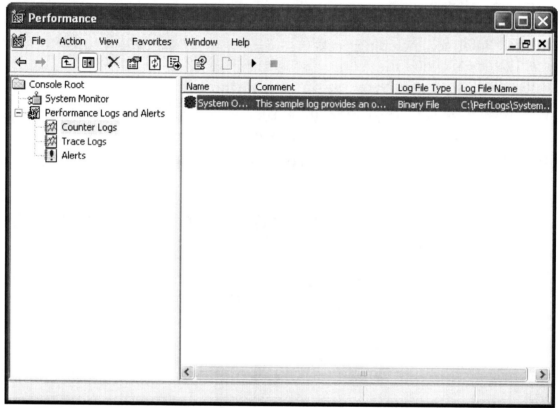

Viewing logs

There are two types of logs: counter and trace:

- **Counter logs** allow you to collect statistics about resources, such as memory, disk, and processor. These can be used to determine system health and performance.

- **Trace logs** can collect statistics about services, providing you with detailed reports about resource behavior. In essence, trace logs provide extensions to the Event Viewer, logging data that would otherwise be inaccessible.

Reliability and Performance Monitor

Windows Vista ships with the improved **Reliability and Performance Monitor** utility, accessed via **Administrative Tools**.

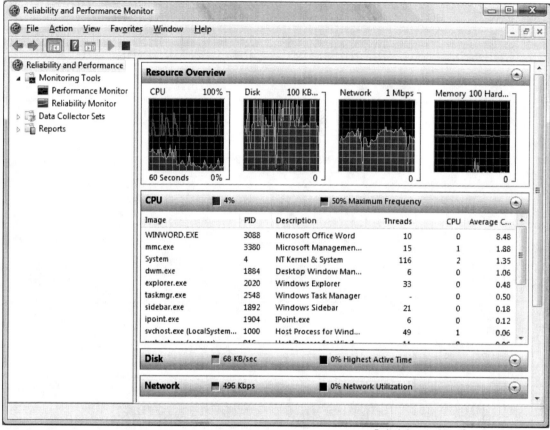

Reliability and Performance Monitor

The default page (Resource View) shows an enhanced version of the sort of monitoring provided by Task Manager. You can see graphs of resource performance along with key statistics, such as threads started by a process or hard page faults / second (continually rising numbers of either of these can indicate a problem).

Under **Monitoring Tools**, there are options to open **Performance Monitor** itself (which works much as the 2000/XP version) and **Reliability Monitor**, which displays a log of "system stability" events, so you can see at a glance whether a particular application has stopped responding frequently.

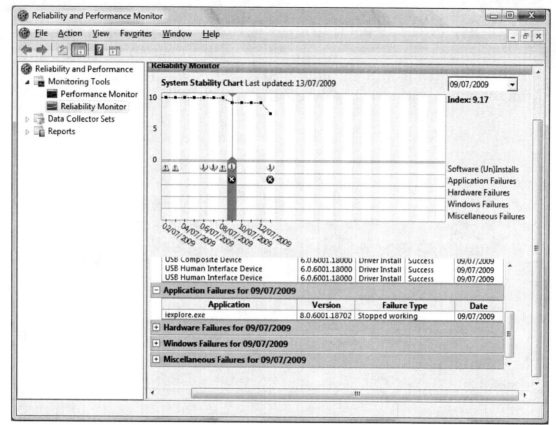

Reliability Monitor

The other options are for creating reports and collecting data for analysis.

Configuring Startup Services and Applications

One frequently experienced performance problem associated with Windows is the boot time. Slow boot problems can have any number of causes, many of which are either malware or networking problems. However, slow boots can also be caused by the number of programs and services that load at startup.

The **System Configuration Utility (MSCONFIG)** is a control panel allowing you to view and configure startup settings from one location.

You can adjust settings in the legacy startup files (SYSTEM.INI and WIN.INI)[125], change BOOT.INI (multi-boot) settings, and enable or disable Services and Startup (programs).

---

[125] These files provide backward-compatibility for Windows 9x programs. MSCONFIG is not included with Windows 2000, though the executable shipped with XP will work if copied to a Windows 2000 PC.

Startup items are either registry entries or shortcuts in the Start menu's Startup folder[126].

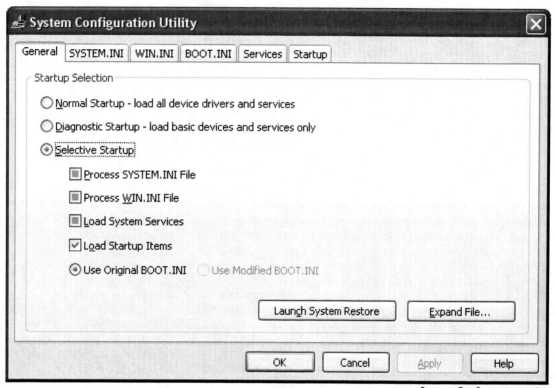

System Configuration utility

The Vista version of MSCONFIG displays a bit more information, such as when a service was disabled, to make troubleshooting easier. It also includes a **Tools** tab containing shortcuts to various useful utilities including System Information, Configuring UAC, Registry Editor, and so on.

> **Tip**
> Startup performance can also be improved by hibernating the computer (or using a Vista Sleep mode) rather than shutting down. This means that the desktop is restored much more quickly when the computer is switched back on. Power-saving modes do tend to cause problems with some hardware devices or applications however.

---

[126] The Start menu is built from a template containing settings for all users plus shortcuts customized for the current user profile. In Windows 2000/XP, the template is stored in c:\Documents and Settings\All Users\Start Menu and user-specific settings in c:\Documents and Settings*UserName*\Start Menu. In Vista, the template is stored in C:\ProgramData\Microsoft\Windows\Start Menu and the user-specific shortcuts are in C:\Users*UserName*\AppData\Roaming\Microsoft\Windows\Start Menu

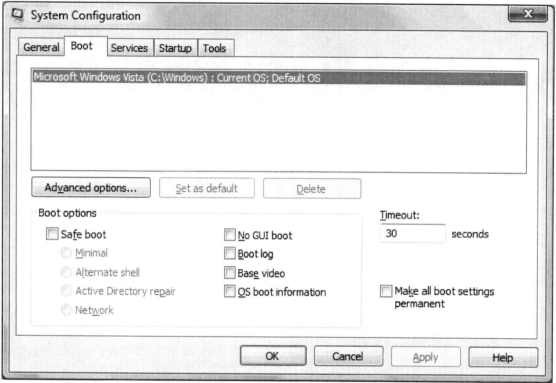

The MSCONFIG utility can be used to modify boot configuration under Windows Vista

Optimizing Drives and the File System

Of all the computer's subsystems, hard disk drives and the file system probably require the most attention to keep in optimum working order. They are subject to three main problems:

- Fragmentation - ideally, each file would be saved in contiguous clusters on the disk. In practice, files are saved using the nearest available cluster, to improve write performance. Over time, as files grow they become defragmented, reducing read performance[127].

- Capacity - typically, much more file creation occurs on a computer than file deletion. This means that capacity can reduce quickly over time. If the system disk has less than 15% free space, performance can be impaired. When space drops below 200 MB, a **Low Disk Space** warning is generated.

---

[127] NTFS is more efficient than FAT in this respect though NTFS volumes still need periodic defragmentation.

- Damage - hard disk operations are physically intensive and the platters of the disk are easy to damage, especially if there is a power cut. If the disk does not recognize that a sector is damaged, files can become corrupted.

These problems can be addressed by the systematic use of disk performance tools. These tools should be run regularly (at least every month and before installing software applications).

Task Scheduler

Task Scheduler, as its name suggests, sets tasks to run at a particular time. Tasks can be run once at a future date or time or according to a recurring schedule.

A "task" can be a simple application process or (more commonly) a batch file or script.

Task Scheduler is accessed via **Control Panel** in Windows 2000/XP and through **Administrative Tools** in Windows Vista. Apart from defining the path to the file or script you want to execute and setting the schedule, you should also enter the credentials that the task will run under - if the selected user account does not have sufficient permissions the task will not run.

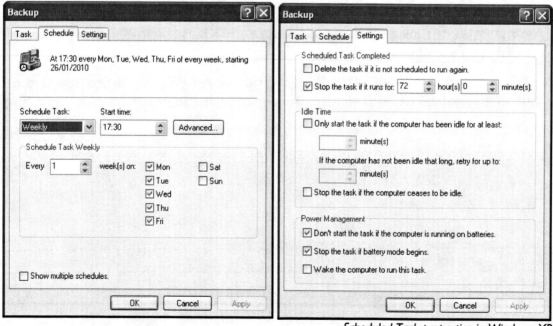

Scheduled Task properties in Windows XP

Vista's Task Scheduler comes with numerous enhancements.

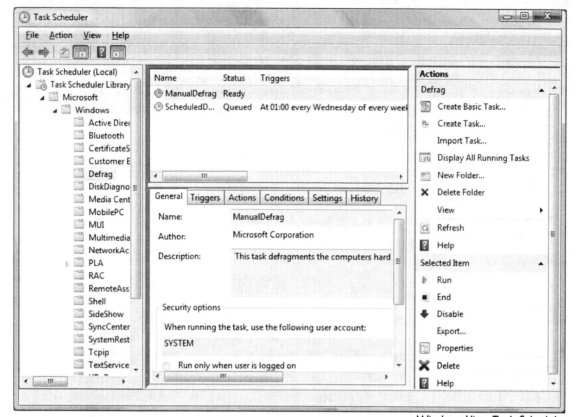

Windows Vista Task Scheduler

Many of Windows' processes come with predefined task schedules (Disk Defragmenter, for instance, is now configured to run automatically by default). Other enhancements include:

- You can define triggers other than a simple schedule (running a task when the machine wakes from sleep or hibernation for instance).
- You can add multiple actions under a single task.
- You can view a log of events connected to the task.
- You can organize tasks in folders and there are more tools for managing them.

Batch files and scripts

A **batch file** is a plain text file saved with a .BAT or .CMD extension. The file should contain commands entered onto separate lines. When the batch file is run, each command executes in sequence.

The command **@ECHO OFF** is usually added to the top of the file to suppress the display of commands. A batch file can also accept user input, by entering an argument as a **variable** of the form **%1**.

A **script** can be used to create a mini-program, working with all the functionality of the chosen scripting language. Scripts can automate many functions of Windows. Most Windows scripts use VBScript (Visual Basic Script), which are given the extension .VBS. JavaScript (.JS) is also used, though more often on websites than with Windows.

Batch files and scripts are commonly used to set up the user environment or copy files for backup. They can be run manually, automatically at logon (as part of a login profile), or automatically at any time using the Task Scheduler.

Disk Defragmenter (DEFRAG)

Defragmenter is a snap-in found in the default management console. It reorganizes a volume by moving files into contiguous clusters. There must be at least 15% free space on the volume[128].

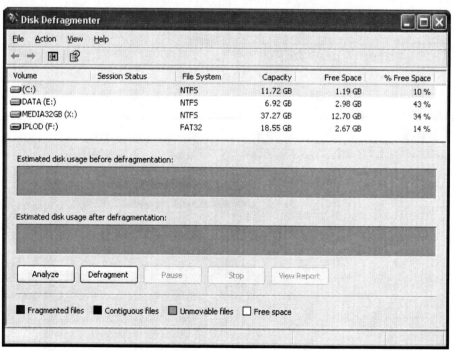

Disk Defragmenter

---

[128] Disk Defragmenter cannot defragment some types of file (notably the pagefile and hibernation file). Third-party defragmentation or disk utilities can be used instead. Alternatively, you can defragment the pagefile by setting it to 0, restarting (check pagefile.sys has been deleted), defragment, then re-enable the pagefile and set it to a fixed size.

> **Tip**
>
> Although it is possible to run this utility in the background while you work, it will slow your machine and prevent defragmentation of open files. It is usually better to defragment when your computer is not being used. It may also be necessary to disable applications that run in the background, such as anti-virus software, Task Scheduler, or a Screen Saver.

> **Note**
>
> Defragmenter in Vista is set to run automatically by default. There is no visual feedback on progress and you need to install SP1 before you can select which drive to defragment via the GUI.

You can also run the tool from a command prompt. The basic command is DEFRAG *volume*, where *volume* is a drive letter or volume name. The main switches are as follows:

Switch	Use
/a	Analyze the volume and display a report.
/f	Force the volume to be defragmented.
/v	Display complete analysis and defragmentation reports.

Disk Cleanup (CLEANMGR)

As well as files the user *intends* to create, a disk can get clogged up with temporary and cached files created by applications and software installers. **Disk Cleanup** identifies these files, divides them into different categories, and allows you to choose whether to retain or delete them.

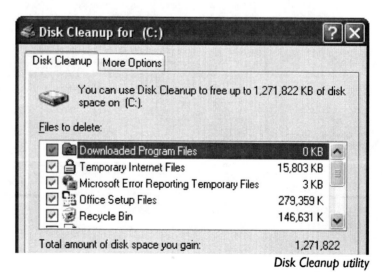

Disk Cleanup utility

On an NTFS volume, it can also automatically compress files that have not been accessed recently (though not in the Windows Vista version of the tool).

You can run Disk Cleanup from the **General Properties** page of the disk or from the **Systems Tools** folder in the **Accessories** group on the Start menu.

Check Disk (CHKDSK)

Check Disk (CHKDSK) can scan for and correct file system errors and detect bad sectors (damaged parts of the disk). To run it, open the **Properties** sheet for the drive and select the **Tools** tab. Click the **Check Now** button. It can run in three modes:

- **No option selected** - CHKDSK runs in Read-Only mode.
- **Automatically fix file system errors** - file system errors are caused by crashes, power loss, and the like.
- **Scan for and attempt recovery of bad sectors** - bad sectors are damage to the actual drive. If a drive has many bad sectors, it is probably nearing the end of its useful life.

CHKDSK cannot fix open files, so you may be prompted to schedule the scan for the next system restart. CHKDSK will also run automatically if the system detects file system errors. Recovered data can be saved as files to the root of the drive.

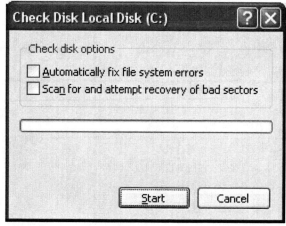

CHKDSK utility

Note
CHKDSK can take a *long* time to scan and fix errors on a large disk. You cannot cancel once started. Run a Read-Only scan first.

Again, you can run this tool from the command prompt. `CHKDSK volume` performs a scan only. The main parameters and switches are as follows:

Switch	Use
path	Specify a path (and optionally file name) to check.
/f	Automatically fix errors.
/r	Locate bad sectors. You are prompted to save any recoverable data, which is copied to the root directory as **file*nnn*.chk** files.
/x	Force the volume to dismount. This will cause file errors for users with files open on the volume[129].
/i /c	On NTFS volumes only, skips parts of the checking process.

Backup

Another important file system operation is to make backups of the system configuration and data files. The NTBACKUP or a third-party utility can be used for this. See unit 4.1 for more information.

Disk performance settings

Many fixed and removable hard disks support **write caching** on the drive; you can also use Windows cache if not supported on the drive. Using write cache improves performance, but comes with an increased risk of data loss in the event of a power outage.

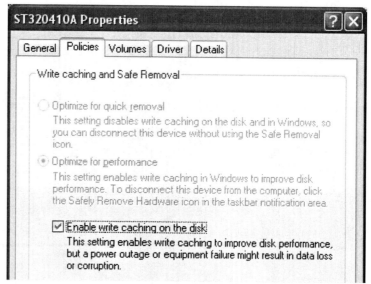

Hard Disk policies

To configure caching properties, locate the disk in **Device Manager** or **Disk Management**, alt-click and select **Properties**. Select the appropriate option on the **Policies** tab.

---

[129] If the volume is in use and you use the /f or /r switches without /x, you are prompted to schedule CHKDSK for the next system restart.

> **Tip**
>
> If you have a DVD or Blu-ray drive, you can set the device's region via the Properties dialog. The firmware on most drives restricts the number of times the region can be changed.

Configuring Performance Settings

There are a number of configuration options and settings you can change to best suit Windows to the installed hardware.

Performance options and virtual memory

Performance options allow the administrator to fine-tune settings that can make the computer run faster. Some of these settings require the computer to be restarted. You would only need to adjust these on a computer with the minimum system requirements or just above.

To configure performance options, from **System Properties**, click the **Advanced** tab then the **Settings** button under **Performance**.

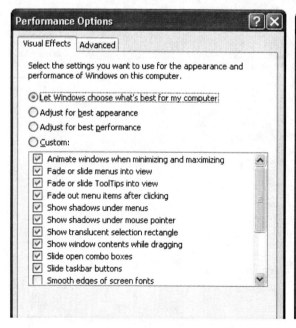 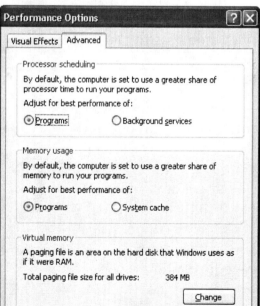

Performance options for Windows XP

The **Visual Effects** tab lets you enable or disable effects that consume CPU and GPU resources. The **Advanced** tab lets you optimize processor scheduling and memory usage for a PC role (select **Programs**) or server (select **Background services** and **System cache**).

> **Tip**
> In Vista, the Aero interface comes with several processor-intensive features, such as Flip-3D and translucent title bars. Best performance will turn these off.

> **Tip**
> If your processor supports XD (Execute Disable Bit), there will also be a **Data Execution Protection** tab allowing you to enable or disable the feature. XD help to protect the computer against a type of malware attack called a "Buffer Overflow" (where executable code is supplied to a program as data causing it to run without permission).

To configure Virtual Memory settings, click the **Change** button.

Windows uses the equation *1.5 times Total System RAM* to calculate the initial (minimum) pagefile. The maximum pagefile size is configured to prevent disk space being exhausted. The typical value for maximum is twice the initial value.

You can normally leave this set to the default but you may want to adjust it if the volume is critically short of disk space or if multiple physical disks are installed, in which case it boosts performance to have a pagefile configured on each disk[130].

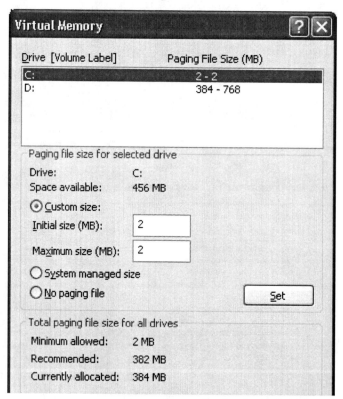

Configuring virtual memory

---

[130] Performance may also be improved by setting the pagefile to a fixed size, which prevents it defragmenting over time. However, this approach may use up more disk space than is necessary or make less memory available than the system needs.

| Module 2 Operating Systems | Optimizing Windows |

> **Note**
>
> If the pagefile is fixed size but too small, Windows might run out of memory, which could cause programs to crash.

The pagefile is created as a system file named **pagefile.sys** in the root of the drive.

> **Note**
>
> It is possible that secure information will be paged. If security is a concern, then the paging file content can be deleted during shut down by configuring local security settings.

SuperFetch and ReadyBoost

Vista has a redesigned memory subsystem. Vista uses a service called **SuperFetch** to pre-cache frequently-used programs in system memory. While previous versions of Windows implemented a similar process (prefetcher), SuperFetch is more "aggressive" in terms of utilizing free memory and "intelligent" in terms of identifying typical patterns of application use[131].

Windows Vista also implements **ReadyBoost**. This allows a flash memory Solid State Drive (SSD), hybrid HDD/SSD, or USB or ExpressCard flash drive to be used as a system cache. If the flash drive is suitable for the task (it must support low seek times and be at least the same size as the amount of installed system RAM), this can produce significantly faster load times compared to hard disk, especially if there is not much system RAM (under 2 GB).

There is nothing to configure for either option, though the services can be disabled. Windows will detect the addition of a compatible flash memory device and prompt whether you want to use it with ReadyBoost.

---

[131] If you observe Vista's memory usage, it may seem high compared to the number of programs you have running.

Performance Information and Tools

Windows Vista comes with an additional utility that provides an alternative route for configuring some of the settings listed above (plus a few others).

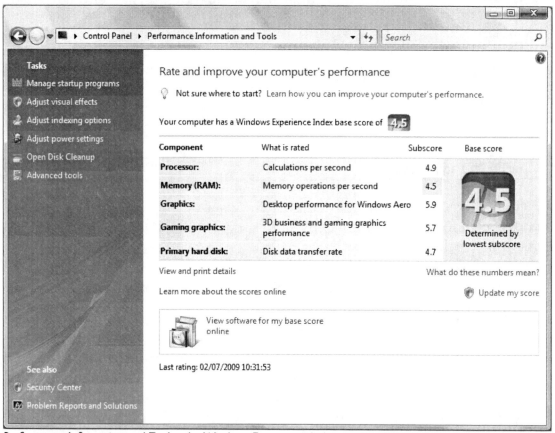

Performance Information and Tools - the Windows Experience Index gives a snapshot of computer performance

The default page of **Performance Information and Tools** (accessed via Control Panel) shows the "Windows Experience Index". This tests all the hardware on the computer and determines a rating from 1 to 5.9. Each subsystem (CPU, memory, disk, graphics, and so on) is given its own subscore. The overall score is the lowest of these. Vista automatically configures performance settings for the computer based on this report.

The links allow you to adjust startup programs via the Windows Defender anti-spyware tool, start Disk Cleanup, open the Visual Effects dialog, and manage indexing.

Module 2 Operating Systems   Optimizing Windows

User profiles

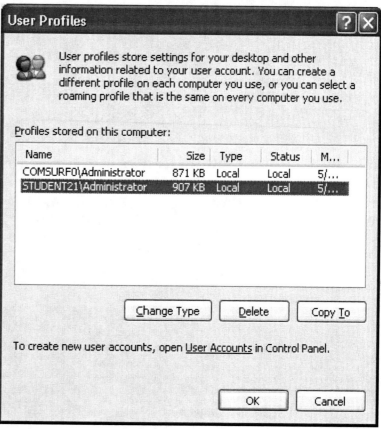

User profiles

Every user's desktop settings are stored in a local (or cached) profile. This is in fact a series of files and folders, together with registry settings, stored under the **Documents and Settings** folder (Windows 2000 / XP) or **Users** folder (Windows Vista) on the boot partition. If you wish, you can copy or delete these local profiles using the dialog above.

Tip
When a new user account is created, the initial profile is copied from the one called "Default User" (or just "Default" in Vista).

Index settings

The index service is important to the search functions of Windows 2000 and XP but is *critical* to the performance of Vista's new Instant Search tools. Indexing takes place in the background; when files are added and changed, more indexing and re-indexing will take place. By default, only user data folders are monitored. You can add other locations, but obviously the more locations that are added the more indexing that is required to keep track of files in them.

The default dialog shows the current index status (complete in the example below) and the locations currently being monitored. Click **Modify** to add or remove locations or **Advanced** to rebuild the index and select which file types will be indexed.

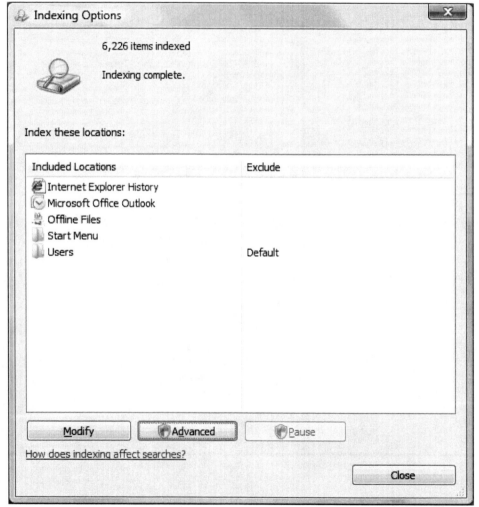

Indexing Options

User Account Control

User Account Control (UAC) protects the system from malware running with elevated administrator privileges. This is a good thing, but if you need to perform a number of system administration tasks at the same time, UAC can prove very frustrating. UAC also does not work particularly well with Explorer and command prompt permissions

There are a number of ways to disable UAC. The GUI methods are either to use **MSCONFIG** (disable for all users) or the **User Accounts** applet (disable for a specific user).

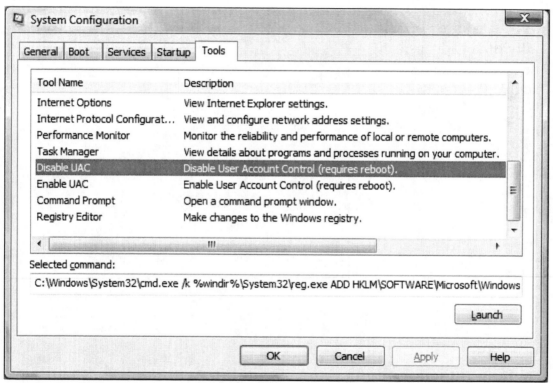

Using MSCONFIG to disable UAC

Both methods require a restart. Vista will nag you (perhaps properly[132]) to re-enable UAC, which you can do from the notification area prompt or using MSCONFIG again.

---

[132] You can disable security notifications via the Security Center in Control Panel.

Sidebar

Where Windows 2000 and Windows XP had the little used Active Desktop (allowing the display of a live webpage on the desktop), Vista has its **Sidebar** and **Gadgets**. Obviously, while charming, each gadget takes up its own little slice of system resources.

You can configure the Sidebar using the **Windows Sidebar Properties** applet in Control Panel.

You can add or remove individual gadgets using the alt-click menu on the Sidebar itself or through its notification area task icon .

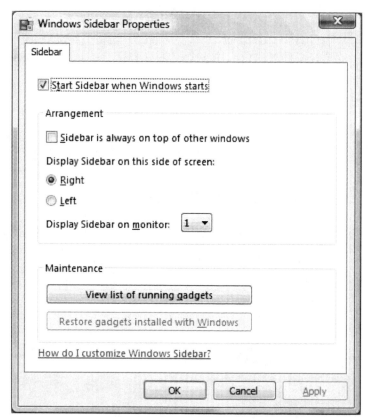

Windows Sidebar Properties

Summary

Windows optimization is mostly about keeping the disk subsystem well maintained and managing applications and services. You can view a snapshot of performance using Task Manager or evaluate over a longer period using Performance Monitor. Disk management tools (CHKDSK, Defragmenter, Disk Cleanup) maintain drive performance. Tweaking the performance settings and virtual memory settings may be worthwhile on systems with a low-spec CPU, graphics card, or limited memory.

Module 3 Operational Procedures

Operational procedures refers to "soft skills" elements of PC support. This includes competencies such as customer service, troubleshooting procedures, health and safety, and security.

PC support employers value customer contact skills as highly as technical knowledge of PC components or Windows subsystems.

You have to master communication skills as well as technical ones

Unit 3.1   Module 3 Operational Procedures

Unit 3.1 Communication and Professionalism

CompTIA A+ Essentials Objectives

☐ **701.6.2 Given a scenario, demonstrate the appropriate use of communication skills and professionalism in the workplace**
Use proper language - avoid jargon, acronyms, slang • Maintain a positive attitude • Listen and do not interrupt a customer • Be culturally sensitive • Be on time (If late contact the customer) • Avoid distractions (Personal calls, Talking to co-workers while interacting with customers, Personal interruptions) • Dealing with a difficult customer or situation (Avoid arguing with customers and/or being defensive, Do not minimize customers' problems, Avoid being judgmental, Clarify customer statements, Ask open-ended questions to narrow the scope of the problem, Restate the issue or question to verify understanding) • Set and meet expectations / timeline and communicate status with the customer (Offer different repair / replacement options if applicable, Provide proper documentation on the services provided, Follow up with customers / user later date to verify satisfaction) • Deal appropriately with customers' confidential materials (Located on computer, desktop, printer, etc)

Customer Service

A service technician should not only understand technical matters, but must also be a good communicator. It is easy to pick up facts and information, but it can be much harder to use this information in a troubleshooting scenario requiring customer interaction, whether face-to-face or over the telephone.

Learning how to deal with customers, interpret the information they give you, and respond to their queries can be difficult, but logical problem diagnosis and successful techniques for working with customers go hand-in-hand. A person with only one of these skills is not likely to impress as a professional customer service technician.

Remember that "customer" need not refer to someone who buys something; it can include any users or clients of a support service.

Four simple rules can be applied to good customer service:

- Be in control and drive the issue towards resolution.

- Be positive and confident without being aggressive or rude.

- Be clear, concise, and direct.

- Be consistent, fair, and respectful.

Page 266   IT Career FastTrack with CompTIA A+ Certification   © 2010 gtslearning

Module 3 Operational Procedures
Communication and Professionalism

Communication Skills

There are five key aspects that contribute to the art of communication: the words you use, listening effectively, your inflection (or tone), empathy, and your body language and appearance. You must use all five together to give the best possible impression to your customer.

Using proper language

When speaking to a customer, you need to make sense. Obviously you must be factually accurate, but it is equally important that the customer understands what you are saying[133]. Not only does this show the customer that you are competent, it also proves that you are in control of the situation and gives the customer confidence in your abilities.

You need to use clear and concise statements that avoid jargon, abbreviations, acronyms, and other technical language that a user might not understand. For example compare:

"Looking at the TFT, can you tell me whether the driver is signed?"

...with:

"Is a green tick shown on the icon?"

The first statement depends on the user understanding what a signed driver might be and knowing that a green tick indicates one. The second statement gives you the same information without having to rely on the user's understanding.

While you do not have to speak very formally, avoid being *over-familiar* with customers. Try not to use very informal language (slang) and do not use any language that may cause any sort of offence. For example, you should greet a customer by saying "Hello" or "Good morning" rather than "Whassup?" or "Hey!"

---

[133] Understanding is not only affected by technical knowledge. You are likely to encounter situations where there are language or dialect barriers between you and the customer. In an extreme case, you may need to get the help of an interpreter. If an interpreter is not available, try to find workarounds, such as drawing diagrams, giving a practical demonstration, or using hand gestures.

© 2010 gtslearning   IT Career FastTrack with CompTIA A+ Certification   Page 267

Unit 3.1	Module 3 Operational Procedures

Listening

You must listen carefully to what is being said to you; it will give you clues to the customer's technical level, enabling you to pace and adapt your replies accordingly.

Active listening is the ability to listen to an individual so that you give them your full attention and are not trying to argue with, comment on, or misinterpret what they have said. With active listening, you make a conscious effort to keep your attention focused on what the other person is saying (as opposed to being distracted by thinking what your *reply* is going to be or by some background noise or interruption). Some of the other techniques of active listening are to reflect phrases used by the other person or to summarize what they have said. This helps to reassure the other person that you have attended to what they have to say.

Listening carefully will help you to get the most information from what a customer tells you. It is also important to understand that you must not *interrupt* customers when they are speaking. Also, do not ignore what they have said. If you are rude in this sort of way, the customer will form a poor opinion of you and may become less willing to help with troubleshooting.

If a customer is not getting to the point, take charge of the conversation or call at the earliest opportunity by asking a "closed" question. For example, compare:

> *"It's been like this for ages now and I've tried pressing a key and moving the mouse but nothing happens."*
>
> "What does the screen look like?"
> *"It's dark. I thought the computer was just resting and I know in that circumstance I need to press a key, but that's not working and I really need to get on with..."*

...with:

> *"It's been like this for ages now and I've tried pressing a key and moving the mouse but nothing happens."*
>
> "OK, pressing a key should work normally but as it isn't I'd like to investigate something else first. Can you tell me whether the light on the monitor is green?"
> *"No, there's a yellow light though."*

Page 268   IT Career FastTrack with CompTIA A+ Certification   © 2010 gtslearning

Module 3 Operational Procedures   *Communication and Professionalism*

In the first example, the technician asks an open question, which just lets the user focus on what they perceive as the problem, but which isn't producing any valuable troubleshooting information. Using a closed question, as in the second example, allows the technician to start working through a series of symptoms to try to diagnose the problem.

Inflection

The tone of your voice is an important factor for successful communication.

Your tone of voice will tell the customer whether you are bored, confused, keen to help, tired, angry, or impatient. Make sure that the customer gets the right message.

Empathy

Empathizing with a customer means understanding the situation and reacting accordingly. This means identifying whether the customer is confused, annoyed, or upset and understanding the customer's priorities.

For example, a customer may call to complain that a new monitor stopped working the day after it was purchased, and he or she is very annoyed. An empathic response would include the following:

- Understanding why the customer is annoyed. Would you feel angry in that situation?

- Understanding what you would want done if it were your monitor.

- Responding in the best way possible to assist the customer (within the scope of your ability, warranties, and so on).

Your response should prove to the customer that you are in control and can help.

> "I'm sorry to hear that, let's see what we can do about it..."

Sympathy is being in a like-minded emotional state and, unlike empathy, is not usually helpful or productive. For example, in the above situation, you may react sympathetically in the following ways:

- Complete sympathy:

> "Damn monitor! You'd think they'd make them better than that."

Unit 3.1　　　　　　　　　　　　　　　　　　Module 3 Operational Procedures

- Lack of sympathy (for example, you may be annoyed, and wonder why the customer is shouting at you):

> "Hey, wait a minute - it's not my fault your monitor's broken..."

Lack of sympathy makes the situation more confrontational. Complete sympathy leads you to denigrate the products and services that your company has supplied or is supporting and creates a very poor impression.

Body language and dress code

Face-to-face, "body language" and what you wear are also important. They tell the customer many things about you as a person and help the customer to form an opinion of you. Body language means things such as your stance, hand gestures, and making eye contact.

- The customer will use visual and verbal clues to judge your confidence and competence to do the job.

- Look at the customer for visual and verbal clues as to his or her state of mind. This will enable you to develop empathy with him or her. Try to make regular eye contact when speaking with someone (without staring at them threateningly).

If you are poorly dressed, a customer is likely to infer that you are not very competent. On the other hand, if you are well-dressed, the customer is more likely to assume that you are keen, able, and attentive. Either impression may be false, but the customer's *perception* governs how they respond to you and the company you represent.

Professionalism

Professionalism means taking pride in one's work and in treating people fairly. Some of the procedures and attitudes that contribute to professional working practices in IT support are discussed below.

Advertizing the support service

One of the key points of providing an effective support service is making it easy for customers to contact it. Most support takes place either over the telephone or through an email / web contact form. More advanced options include text messaging and Remote Assistance-style desktop sharing.

| Module 3 Operational Procedures | Communication and Professionalism |

Whatever the method used, the contact information and hours of operation should be well advertized, so that the customer knows what to do. The service should also have proper documentation, so that the customer knows what to expect in terms of items that are supported, how long incidents may take to resolve, when they can expect an item to be replaced instead of repaired, and so on.

Problem management

Problem management means tracking and auditing support requests. Whatever the tools and resources used to implement problem management, the basic process of receiving a support request, resolving the problem, and verifying the solution remains much the same.

On receiving the request (whether it is a call, email, or face-to-face contact), acknowledge the request and set expectations. For example, repeat the request back to the customer, then state the next steps, such as "I have assigned this problem to [person or department]. If you don't hear from us by [specific time], please call me".

The course of action that you agree must be realistic and achievable. Each request must be logged as an **incident** or **ticket** so that progress on resolving it can be documented. Most support departments use a Call Management or Problem Management System for this. Examples include FrontRange's HEAT, AIM's HelpDesk Expert, BMC's Remedy, and HP OpenView's Help Desk module.

The following information will form the core of a job ticket:

Information	Notes
Job ID	Job IDs are often referred to as tickets.
Contact	Name, organization, department, email address, telephone number. In a database, the job could be linked to a contact record.
Priority	Assessed from caller's description and customer's service level.
Problem description	Including information about platform (hardware, OS, application [including version and update number], and what the user was doing).
Asset	Hardware component or software application associated with the problem, linked to an asset management database.
Resolution	What was attempted during the first contact.
Follow up	Date and description of follow up actions.
Dates	Dates when the ticket was opened, updated, and closed.

© 2010 gtslearning   IT Career FastTrack with CompTIA A+ Certification   Page 271

As with any communications, job tickets should be completed professionally, with due regard for spelling, grammar, and clarity. Remember that other people may need to take action using just the information in the ticket and that analysis of tickets will take place as part of quality assurance procedures. It is also possible that tickets will be forwarded to customers as a record of the jobs performed.

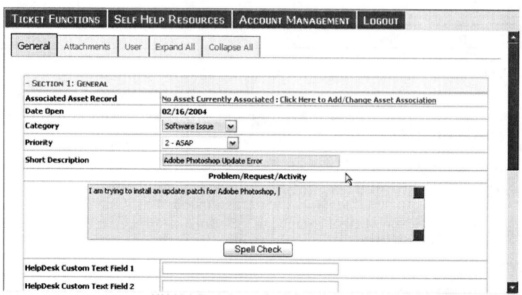

AIM HelpDesk Expert for IT Support management tool (helpdesktools.com)

If possible, the request should be resolved in one call. If this is not possible, the call should be dealt with as quickly as possible, and escalated to a senior support team if a solution cannot be found promptly.

What is important is that you drive problem acceptance and resolution, either by working on a solution yourself or ensuring that the problem is accepted by the assigned person or department.

If a problem cannot be resolved within the course of a single call, it is imperative to manage the customer's expectations of when the problem will be resolved. Customers should not feel the need to call you to find out what's happening. This is irritating for them to do and means time is wasted dealing with an unnecessary call.

When the solution has been tested and verified and the customer has expressed satisfaction with the resolution of the problem, log the problem as closed.

Record the solution and send verification to the customer via email or phone call.

Module 3 Operational Procedures

Communication and Professionalism

Escalation

There will be times when you will be unable to resolve the customer's enquiry using the resources at your immediate disposal. As soon as you run into problems resolving a customer's enquiry, you should take steps to identify your next source of assistance and **escalate** the issue.

There is no shame in admitting to the customer that you cannot answer their enquiry, provided that you escalate the problem correctly and see the enquiry through to a close (this relates to being in control and driving the issue forward).

You may also find yourself in a situation where you need to refer your support call to your manager or supervisor; for example, if the customer complains or becomes difficult or abusive or demands help with an unsupported item.

Ownership

Ownership is the question of who is responsible for a ticket if the problem is escalated. There are two types of ownership to consider: *actual* and *perceived*.

- Actual ownership - the person who is dealing with the problem; if you have escalated it to someone else, they have ownership.

- Perceived ownership - as you initially took the call, your customer perceives that you have ownership even though you may be handing ownership to another level or area of expertise. So the customer expects you to keep in touch with them and keep them informed at each phase of the problem-solving process.

Prioritizing work

Time is an invaluable factor in the service industry because workload usually outweighs staff resources. Time management practices impact the level of service you are able to provide to your customers.

Anybody who requests support will hope that their problem can be resolved immediately. However this is not always possible for a number of reasons and the customer's idea of an acceptable response time may vary greatly from your own.

© 2010 gtslearning

IT Career FastTrack with CompTIA A+ Certification

Page 273

| Unit 3.1 | Module 3 Operational Procedures |

Assigning a priority can depend upon several factors, not all of them representing best practice...

- Your understanding of the severity of the problem (*impact*).

- The seniority of the customer (*urgency*).

- Service support levels agreed with a customer in a Service Level Agreement.

- How well you like the customer.

- How much the customer yells at you.

- How able you feel to resolve the problem (*effort*).

- How "easy" the problem is to resolve (*effort*).

A formal call management system will usually allow a priority code to be assigned to a call. Open tickets can be monitored and re-prioritized to ensure that they do not fail to meet the agreed service and performance levels.

| Punctuality and accountability |

If a customer expects a visit (or call or email) from a service technician at a certain time, it is reasonable to assume that the technician will respond as promised. If it becomes obvious that the technician is not going to be on time, then the customer should be informed as soon as possible. A customer may make special arrangements to be with the technician at the allotted time and changes can be very annoying.

Be accountable for your actions, both before you arrive on site and while on site. This usually means being honest and direct about issues, but make sure this is done in a positive manner. For example:

> "I'm sorry I'm late - show me this faulty PC and I'll start work right away."
>
> "The printer needs a new fuser - and I'm afraid that I don't have this type with me. What I will do is call the office and find out how quickly we can get one..."
>
> "I've not seen this problem before but I have taken some notes and I'll check this out as soon as I get back to the office. I'll give you a call this afternoon - will that be OK?"

Module 3 Operational Procedures

Communication and Professionalism

Flexibility and compromise

As a service technician, you want to ensure your customer receives the best possible attention at all times but, unfortunately, saying no is sometimes inevitable:

- The customer may ask (or demand) that you do something beyond your control or perhaps beyond the terms of the service contract.

- The customer may ask you to confirm a fact or detail beyond your control.

Consider the following examples; which approach is better?

> *"My printer is broken again - I want a replacement"*
> 1. "I'm sorry, we can't do that..."
> 2: "I can arrange for a technician to be with you first thing tomorrow and I'll mention to my supervisor that this is the second time this has occurred."

> *"Can you guarantee that the technician will be with me before 3pm?"*
> 1: "Sorry, I can't guarantee a specific time"
> 2: "I'll ask the technician to try and visit before 3pm if possible and I'll call you around 2pm if it looks like the technician will be later than that - is this OK?"

Tip

The key to saying no in a positive way is to offer an alternative.

Respect

Respect means that you treat others (and their property) as you would like to be treated. Respect is one of the hallmarks of professionalism. At a bare minimum, respect means not being rude or offensive. Some of the other elements are listed below.

Respect for property and confidentiality

- Do not treat customers' property carelessly. Do not use equipment or services such as PCs, printers, web access, or phones without permission and *never* for personal use.

© 2010 gtslearning　　　IT Career FastTrack with CompTIA A+ Certification　　　Page 275

| Unit 3.1 | Module 3 Operational Procedures |

- If you are visiting someone's home or office do not help yourself to food or drink, ask before using the bathroom, and do not attempt to snoop around other areas[134].

- If you find printed copies of confidential materials while performing a support task (bank statements or personal letters for instance), do not look at them, make the customer aware of them, and allow time for them to be tidied away.

- If making a site visit, keep the area in which you are working clean and tidy and leave it as you found it.

Avoid distractions

Do not allow interruptions when you are working at a customer's site. Do not take calls from colleagues unless they are work related, urgent, and important. Do not take personal calls unless they relate to some sort of family emergency.

If speaking with a customer on the telephone, always ask their permission before putting them on hold or transferring their call.

Cultural sensitivity

Cultural sensitivity means being aware of customs and habits used by other people. It is easy to associate culture simply with national elements, such as the difference between the way Americans and Japanese greet one another. *Within* each nation, there are many different cultures however, created by things such as social class, business opportunities, leisure pursuits, and so on.

You need to realize that though a person may be *influenced* by several cultures, their behavior is not *determined* by culture. Customer service and support requires consideration for other people. You cannot show this if you make assumptions about their cultural background without treating them as an individual (**stereotyping**).

Accent, dialect, and language are one of the crucial elements of cultural sensitivity. These can make it hard for you to understand a customer and perhaps difficult for a customer to understand you. When dealing with a language barrier, use questions, summaries, and restatements to clarify customer statements. Consider using visual aids or demonstrations rather than trying to explain something in words.

---

[134] Do not be tempted to snoop around data files on someone else's PC either!

| Page 276 | IT Career FastTrack with CompTIA A+ Certification | © 2010 gtslearning |

Module 3 Operational Procedures

Communication and Professionalism

Quality assurance

Quality Assurance is a process of setting and measuring performance targets in terms of an organization's goals. A system of quality assurance, setting performance targets and using metrics to analyze performance, maintains and improves the level of customer care offered.

Most service contracts are governed by a **Service Level Agreement (SLA)**.

The SLA is beneficial to both parties as it establishes the scope of the support to be offered and the scope of the support that can be expected by the customer. The SLA helps to ensure that no dispute arises about what incidents are covered and what level of response can be expected.

Service **standards** cover aspects of dealing with a customer that are not appropriate to put in a SLA. They allow the service organization to define its own ways of working in order to measure how effectively it is conforming to its target levels of customer service quality.

Service Level Agreement

Metrics are measurements of performance based on statistics. These are used for improving business procedures. Some **Key Performance Indicators (KPI)** used for technical support include:

- **Quantity** measures the total number of incidents handled over a specific period, as well as the percentage of customers that hang up before their call is taken (referred to as Abandonment Rate [ABA]).

- **Quality** measures the percentage of calls that are resolved during the first call; sometimes referred to as One Call Resolution (OCR).

- **Cost** is measured as the relationship between the cost of running support services against the cost of the lost working time of the customers. For external customers this will also include loss of business income.

- **Time** measures the average time it takes to answer a call from the queue, or Average Speed of Answer (ASA).

Unit 3.1	Module 3 Operational Procedures

- **Talk time** is the amount of time spent on a call and can help to measure advisors' performance and problem complexity.

- **Availability** is the percentage of the work day that a support person was available to take a call (that is, not on a call or on a break). This can be used to measure productivity. High availability means that if agents are available for long periods, they are not doing useful work. Low availability will result in higher ASA and ABA.

Customer satisfaction can be determined through feedback such as call monitoring and customer surveys. Surveys need to be well-designed to ensure that they contain specific answers which will help to determine *performance* and *improvements,* rather than act as a means for customers to vent complaints.

Dealing with Difficult Situations

All customer **complaints**, whether they are valid or not, should be treated with equal seriousness.

Do not take complaints personally

Understand that an angry customer is usually frustrated that things are not working properly or feels let down (perhaps the technician arrived late). Empathizing with the customer is a good way of developing a positive relationship towards resolving their problem. Saying you are sorry does not necessarily mean you agree with what the customer is saying, just that you can understand their point of view.

> "I'm sorry you're having a problem with your new PC. Let's see what we can do to sort things out..."

Arguing with the customer, denying that a problem exists, or being judgmental (assuming that the problem is of the customer's making because they do not understand the system properly) will only tend to lower the customer's impression of the service you offer.

Do not try to dismiss the problem out of hand or minimize its importance. If the customer has taken it to the point of complaining then clearly they feel that it *is* important; whether you consider the matter trivial is not the issue.

| Module 3 Operational Procedures | Communication and Professionalism |

Listen while the customer explains the problem and let them know that you are listening.

On the phone, use confirmatory phrases such as "Yes", "I see", and "Uh-huh" from time to time to make sure the customer knows you are paying attention. Do not just repeat the same phrase every few seconds - the customer may think you are mocking them.

If you are face-to-face with the customer, maintain eye contact and nod your head frequently but watch your body language. Do not fold your arms as this puts up a barrier.

Be accurate and honest

A common problem when dealing with customer complaints is feeling that you have to defend every action of your company or department.

If the customer makes a true statement about your levels of service (or that of other employees), do not try and think of a clever excuse or mitigating circumstance for the failing; you will sound as though you do not care.

If you have let a customer down, it is probably best to empathize while including some positive actions:

> "You're right - I'm sorry the technician didn't turn up. I guarantee that a technician will be with you by 3pm and I'll let my supervisor know that you have had to call us. Shall I ring you back just after 3 to make sure that things are OK?"

On the other hand, if the customer is incorrect in their understanding of the situation, empathy and correction is in order:

> "I'm sorry the replacement disk hasn't arrived, but I know it made the post. Would you be happy to wait to see whether it arrives tomorrow or should I mail another one to you?"

Agree on the steps to be taken

Having acknowledged the complaint and worked out how to take the matter forward, tell the customer what you are going to do and confirm that your plan is acceptable to them.

© 2010 gtslearning IT Career FastTrack with CompTIA A+ Certification Page 279

Unit 3.1   Module 3 Operational Procedures

You may not be able to offer the customer a complete solution on the phone if you need to obtain further information or talk to other personnel; you should tell the customer this.

Your plan to drive the problem forward should be realistic; do not make promises you may not be able to keep. If the customer is annoyed that your organization has not returned a faulty printer in time, he or she will become extremely angry if you say that it will arrive within the next few days and it does not.

Follow the call through

Contact the customer later to make sure the problem has been resolved to his or her satisfaction.

If the customer had a valid cause to complain about levels of service or any aspect of your company's operation, resolve the problem and then investigate what can be done to ensure this type of problem never occurs again.

Dealing with angry or abusive customer

It is never easy to talk to someone who is being unreasonable, abusive, or shouting down the telephone but it is important to be able to deal with these situations professionally.

1. Identify signs that a customer is becoming angry early (for example, raised voice, speaking too quickly, interrupting, and so on). Try to calm the situation down by using a low voice, soothing language, and focusing on positive actions.

2. Do not take complaints personally - provided that you haven't deliberately caused the problem about which the customer is complaining, they are using you as a representative of your organization and any anger expressed in your direction is not personal but a symptom of their anger and frustration.

Page 280   IT Career FastTrack with CompTIA A+ Certification   © 2010 gtslearning

Let the customer vent

3. Listen and let the customer explain the problem - draw out the facts and use them as a positive action plan to drive the conversation forward.

4. Hang up - if a customer is persistently abusive or threatening, issue a caution, then warn them about their behavior, then end the call or contact if they do not act reasonably. For example:

> "I'd like to deal with your problem but I'm afraid I can't do that if you're going to use that kind of language - could we start again and I'll see if I can help"
> "!"
>
> "I'm sorry, but as I said, I am having problems with the language you are using, and if you continue I will have to end this call!"
> "!"
>
> "I'm afraid that I cannot continue with this conversation. I will refer this call to my manager/supervisor and ask them to call you back." - CLICK!

Summary

Make sure that you understand the factors that could make communication between you and a client difficult. You should appreciate that professionalism means using procedures and technology to manage problems, taking pride in the quality and consistency of your work, and showing respect for customer's concerns, time, and property.

Unit 3.2   Module 3 Operational Procedures

Unit 3.2 Troubleshooting Techniques

CompTIA A+ Essentials Objectives

☐ **701.2.1 Given a scenario, explain the troubleshooting theory**
Identify the problem (Question user and identify user changes to computer and perform backups before making changes) • Establish a theory of probable cause (question the obvious) • Test the theory to determine cause (Once theory is confirmed determine next steps to resolve problem, If theory is not confirmed re-establish new theory or escalate) • Establish a plan of action to resolve the problem and implement the solution • Verify full system functionality and if applicable implement preventative measures • Document findings, actions and outcomes

☐ **701.2.2 Given a scenario, explain and interpret common hardware and operating system symptoms and their causes**
Use documentation and resources (User / installation manuals, internet / web based, Training materials)

Troubleshooting Theory

Troubleshooting is a process of **problem solving**. It is important to realize that problems have *causes*, *symptoms*, and *consequences*. For example:

- A computer system has a fault in the hard disk drive (cause).

- Because the disk drive is faulty, the computer is displaying a "bluescreen" (symptom).

- Because of the fault, the user cannot do any work (consequence).

From a business point-of-view, resolving the consequences of the problem is more important than solving the original cause. For example, the most effective solution might be to provide the user with another workstation, *then* get the drive replaced.

It is also important to realize that the cause of a *specific* problem might be the *symptom* of a larger problem. This is particularly true if the same problem recurs. For example, you might ask why the disk drive is faulty - is it a one-off error or are there problems in the environment, supply chain, and so on?

Tip

This is called **root cause analysis**. There are several models to help with root cause analysis (such as the 5 Whys model or the Ishiwaka / Fishbone Diagram.

Page 282   IT Career FastTrack with CompTIA A+ Certification   © 2010 gtslearning

Module 3 Operational Procedures   *Troubleshooting Techniques*

Problem management

Any organization that has to deal with more than a few problems every week will have a system in place for problem management. The basis of problem management is the *identification, prioritization,* and *ownership* of incidents. The typical process of problem management is as follows:

- A user contacts the help desk, typically by phone or email. An operator or technician is assigned to the incident and a job **ticket** is generated.

- The user describes the problem to the operator, who may ask clarifying questions. The operator categorizes the problem, assesses how urgent it is, and how long it will take to fix.

- The operator may take the user through initial troubleshooting steps. If these do not work, the job may be *escalated* to deskside support or a senior technician.

- Troubleshooting continues until the problem is resolved. At that point, the user is contacted to *confirm* that the problem has been fixed. The job ticket is updated with details of the problem and how it was resolved. The ticket is then considered *closed.*

At each stage, the problem management system can track the ownership of the problem (who is dealing with it) and its status (what has been done).

Troubleshooting models

When approaching a particular problem, it can help to apply a structured troubleshooting methodology. The CompTIA A+ troubleshooting model refers to the following steps:

1. Identify the problem:

    (a) Question user and identify user changes to computer

    (b) Perform backups before making changes

2. Establish a theory of probable cause (question the obvious).

3. Test the theory to determine cause:

    (a) Once theory is confirmed determine next steps to resolve problem

    (b) If theory is not confirmed, re-establish new theory or escalate

© 2010 gtslearning   IT Career FastTrack with CompTIA A+ Certification   Page 283

| Unit 3.2 | Module 3 Operational Procedures |

4. Establish a plan of action to resolve the problem and implement the solution.

5. Verify full system functionality and if applicable implement preventative measures.

6. Document findings, actions, and outcomes.

These steps and the approach and attitude you should apply when troubleshooting are explained in a bit more detail below.

Tip

A methodical process is the ideal, but troubleshooting in help desk and IT support departments is often a time-critical process. In the real world, you often have to balance being methodical with being efficient.

Diagnostic Procedures

Diagnosis is the process of identifying the **symptoms** and from the symptoms the **cause** (or causes) of a problem. There are two main sources of information: the system itself and the user of the system.

Be prepared

Before you visit a user or customer to fix a problem, ensure that you have all of the necessary hardware and software tools, documentation, and any other information you may need to avoid repeated and unnecessary trips between your office and the customer's location.

If you are instructing a user over the phone or by email, make sure you offer clear, concise, and accurate instructions.

If troubleshooting requires that the system be taken offline, make sure that this is scheduled appropriately and sensitively. Remember that troubleshooting may involve more than fixing a particular problem; it is about maintaining the resources that users need to do their work.

Consider the importance of data stored on the local computer when performing troubleshooting or maintenance. Check when a backup was last made. If a backup has not been made, perform one before changing the system configuration, if at all possible. The simplest way of making a backup before troubleshooting is to use drive imaging software (such as Norton Ghost).

Page 284   IT Career FastTrack with CompTIA A+ Certification   © 2010 gtslearning

Module 3 Operational Procedures   *Troubleshooting Techniques*

Investigating a computer system

You diagnose a problem by identifying the symptoms. From knowing what causes such symptoms, you can test each possible cause until you find the right one. Sometimes symptoms derive from more than one cause; while this type of problem is rarer, it is much harder to troubleshoot.

A computer system comprises a number of components. Fault finding needs to identify which component is faulty. There are two good ways to consider a computer problem systematically:

- Step through what *should* happen and identify the point at which there is a failure or error.

- Work up or down layers (for example, power, hardware components, drivers / firmware, software, network, user actions).

Unless a problem is trivial, break the troubleshooting process into compartments or categories. For example, when troubleshooting a PC you might work as follows:

1. Decide whether the problem is hardware or software related (Hardware).

2. Decide which hardware subsystem is affected (Disk).

3. Decide whether the problem is in the disk unit or connectors and cabling (Connector).

4. Test your theory.

When you have drilled down like this, the problem should become obvious. Of course, you could have made the wrong choice at any point, so you must be prepared to go back and follow a different path.

Be careful about making casual assumptions. A problem may be reported that is similar to one that you have experienced before, but you should not assume that the problem is identical. Although the symptoms may be similar, the problem and its solution could be completely different. Always treat each problem as a new challenge.

Do not overlook the obvious - sometimes seemingly intractable problems are caused by the simplest things. Always run through what *should* happen to verify that there has not been a user or configuration error.

There are a number of tools to use to diagnose faults in computers:

© 2010 gtslearning   IT Career FastTrack with CompTIA A+ Certification   Page 285

Unit 3.2

Module 3 Operational Procedures

- Look and listen - you may be able to see or hear a fault (scorched motherboard, "sick"-sounding disk drive, no fan noise, and so on).

- Hardware tools - diagnosis tools such as multimeters help to reveal faults.

- Software tools - a PC may come with diagnostic software or you can obtain third party software. You should also examine the configuration (Device Manager) and reporting (Event Viewer) utilities of the operating system.

- Error messages - some types of problem may display an error message or sound an alarm. Remember that the error could reveal a symptom not a cause though.

If the symptoms of the problem are no longer apparent, a basic technique is to *reproduce* the problem (that is, repeat the exact circumstances that produced the failure or error). Some problems are *intermittent* though, which means that they cannot be repeated reliably.

Another technique is to reduce a system to the minimum configuration required to start the computer. If that works, subsystems can be reinstalled until the one that produces an error is discovered. This process is obviously time-consuming though.

Questioning the user

Employers value "soft skills", such as being able to communicate and use questioning, as highly as technical skills. Troubleshooting is one area where soft skills are vital:

- A user may be upset or angry (perhaps they have lost work or cannot get an expensive, new computer to work).

- A user may not be technically knowledgeable.

It is your job to calm the user and to help them give you the information you need to diagnose and solve the problem. You need to be able to ask them questions that they can answer simply (without having to know anything about the computer or its software) and guide them through basic troubleshooting steps.

When speaking with users, try to be calm and polite. Do not interrupt when the user is speaking. Do not use technical language (jargon) or abbreviations that are likely to confuse them.

The basis of getting troubleshooting information from users is asking good *questions*. Questions are commonly divided into two types:

Page 286

IT Career FastTrack with CompTIA A+ Certification

© 2010 gtslearning

Module 3 Operational Procedures   *Troubleshooting Techniques*

- Open questions invite someone to explain in their own words. Examples are, "What is the problem?" or "What happens when you try to switch the computer on?"

- Closed questions invite a Yes/No answer or a fixed response. Examples include, "Can you see any text on the screen?" or "What does the error message say?"

Open questions are good to start with as they help to avoid making your own assumptions about what is wrong and encourage the user to give you all the information they are able to. However, you should not trust the user's judgment completely. The user may be inexperienced or have formed a false impression of what is going wrong. Try to establish factual information rather than asking for the user's opinion.

Closed questions can be used to "drill down" into the nature of the problem and guide a user towards giving you information that is useful.

One of the first questions you should answer is "What has changed?" If something worked previously, it is likely that the problem has arisen because of some user-initiated change (excepting mechanical failures). If something has never worked, a different approach is required.

Test components and evaluate results

When you have formed a theory of the probable cause of the problem, you need to devise tests to confirm whether you are correct. Tests could involve any of the following:

- Trying to use a component.

- Substituting the component for a "known good" one.

- Inspecting a component to see whether it is properly connected or damaged or whether any status or indicator lights show a problem.

- Disabling or uninstalling the component (if it might be the cause of a wider problem).

- Consulting documentation and software tools such as Device Manager to confirm a component is configured properly.

- Updating software or a device driver.

When you test, change one thing at a time and check functionality. If there is no improvement, you may want to reverse what you did and try something else.

© 2010 gtslearning   IT Career FastTrack with CompTIA A+ Certification   Page 287

Unit 3.2   Module 3 Operational Procedures

Tip

If you are really unlucky, two (or more) components may be faulty. Another difficulty lies in assessing whether a component itself is faulty or whether it is not working because a related component is broken.

If you cannot solve a problem yourself, it is better to escalate it than to waste a lot of time trying to come up with an answer. Possible escalation routes include senior technicians or support staff, warranty or support contract, or vendor help line or web contact tools.

Tip

Troubleshooting is often less about knowing how to solve a problem yourself than knowing where to find an answer. Identify websites and support forums that can be useful sources of answers.

Resolve the problem and verify the system

When you have a confirmed the cause of the problem you next need to identify a plan of action to put a solution in place. There are typically three solutions to any PC problem:

- **Repair** - you need to determine whether the cost of repair makes this the best option.

- **Replace** - often more expensive and may be time-consuming if a part is not available. There may also be an opportunity to **upgrade** the part or software.

Tip

If a part or system is under warranty, you can return the broken part for a replacement. To do this, you normally need to obtain a Returned Materials Authorization (RMA) ticket from the vendor.

- **Ignore** - as any software developer will tell you, not all problems are critical. If neither repair nor replace is cost-effective, it may be best either to find a workaround or just to document the issue and move on.

When you consider solutions you have to assess the cost and time required. Another consideration is how the solution will impact the rest of the system. A typical example is applying a software patch, which might fix a given problem but cause other programs not to work.

| Module 3 Operational Procedures | Troubleshooting Techniques |

When you apply a solution, test that it fixes the reported problem **and** that the system as a whole continues to function normally.

As mentioned earlier, you should also be confident that you have solved any underlying causes of a problem by putting **preventative measures** in place. For example, if a computer crashes because the disk drive is full, you might consider making sure the user knows how to delete unwanted files and schedule the disk cleanup program to run automatically.

Document activities

If you work in a help desk environment, each support incident will be accompanied by a log. You can use the log to detail the troubleshooting steps you took and identify the eventual cause of, and solution to, the problem.

One value of a log is that it assists troubleshooting efforts. The log can be analyzed to identify recurring incidents and update hardware or software systems as a result. Troubleshooting steps can be gathered into a "Knowledge Base" or Frequently Asked Questions (FAQ) of support articles.

The other value of a log is that it demonstrates what the support department is doing to help the business. This is particularly important for third-party support companies, who need to prove the value achieved in service contracts.

When you complete a log, remember to be professional about spelling and terminology. You may not be the only person who reads or relies upon it.

Troubleshooting Resources

When troubleshooting a problem, if you can identify the symptoms then you can search for those symptoms in various kinds of documentation and hopefully find the likely cause much more quickly than you could be testing the system from first principles.

Windows Help and Support

Windows 2000 has a help system with basic configuration and troubleshooting articles plus a few interactive troubleshooters. Windows XP/Vista Help and Support is greatly expanded, with links to online topics and articles and troubleshooting tools. You can also use it to launch Remote Assistance requests (see unit 2.3).

© 2010 gtslearning   IT Career FastTrack with CompTIA A+ Certification   Page 289

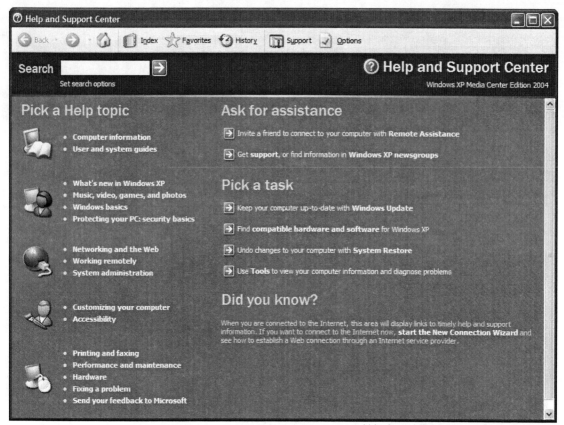

Windows XP Help and Support Center

Knowledge Base

A vendor's Knowledge Base is an extremely useful troubleshooting tool. A Knowledge Base is a searchable collection of troubleshooting articles and known issues.

Most vendors also have fully featured support sites. Many of the services available from them are free, though assisted support is sometimes only provided under warranty. Typical options include:

- Product troubleshooters.
- Software and driver downloads.
- User and technical documentation.
- Email, chat, or telephone assisted support.
- Newsgroups.

Microsoft Knowledge Base, communities, and Technet

Windows does not ship with printed product documentation (other than a basic user guide) but Microsoft's support website support.microsoft.com hosts solution centers for each product. You can access troubleshooting articles and (if applicable) assisted support via phone, email, or chat. More advanced articles plus product documentation and online books can be found at technet.microsoft.com.

If you are looking for a solution to a specific problem, the Microsoft Knowledge Base (KB) at support.microsoft.com/search should be the first point-of-call.

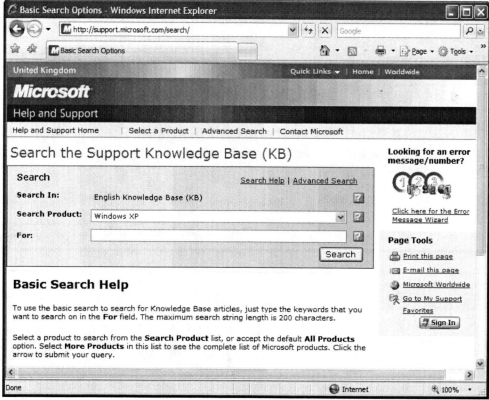

Microsoft Knowledge Base

Select the appropriate product then enter a search phrase.

The communities site (www.microsoft.com/communities) features newsgroups, blogs, webcasts, and forums dedicated to different Microsoft products. These resources are generally monitored by **Microsoft Most Valued Professionals (MVP)** volunteers. mvps.org contains links to useful sites maintained by MVPs.

Unit 3.2   Module 3 Operational Procedures

There are plenty of third-party "expert help" sites and forums, some of which provide information for free or for a subscription. You should naturally be a little bit cautious about the advice given but most of the sites support feedback on the authors and the community standards of professionally run sites will not allow rogues to hang around for too long. There are also some subscription-based sites. Some well known ones include theeldergeek.com, experts-exchange.com, windowsitpro.com, petri.co.il, and winsupersite.com (Paul Thurrott).

Tip
When posting a problem to any newsgroup or forum, remember that people are responding to you out of goodwill. Pick the appropriate forum, do not "cross-post" problems to multiple forums, describe the problem accurately, and be patient.

Other resources

User and installation manuals are of most use when setting up and configuring a system but may also contain troubleshooting information. You may need the system documentation to investigate error codes or find the route to some obscure configuration option.

Tip
Some systems ship with a very simple user guide, designed for end users, and a more in-depth administration or systems configuration guide. In most cases, the latter will be of more use in troubleshooting.

You could also consider referring back to any training manuals or products (elearning or Computer Based Training) - if they are comprehensive and have an effective index you may be able to discover the answer to your problem quite easily(!)

Summary

When troubleshooting, assess the problem systematically using an appropriate troubleshooting model. Understand how to obtain information about the problem from the user, from investigating the system, and from sources such as documentation or the web. Test solutions and confirm with the user that the problem has been fixed. Document problems and their resolutions.

Page 292   IT Career FastTrack with CompTIA A+ Certification   © 2010 gtslearning

Module 3 Operational Procedures

Safety and Environmental Issues

Unit 3.3 Safety and Environmental Issues

CompTIA A+ Essentials Objectives

☐ **701.6.1 Outline the purpose of appropriate safety and environmental procedures and given a scenario apply them**

ESD • EMI (Network interference, Magnets) • RFI (Cordless phone interference, Microwaves) • Electrical safety (CRT, Power supply, Inverter, Laser printers, Matching power requirements of equipment with power distribution and UPSs) • Material Safety Data Sheets (MSDS) • Cable management (Avoiding trip hazards) • Physical safety (Heavy devices, Hot components) • Environmental - consider proper disposal procedures

Safety Hazards

Most countries have **Health and Safety** laws designed to protect employees and the public from dangerous working conditions or practices.

Obviously the specific requirements of legislation vary depending on the local laws and regulations and usually by the type of industry. However, in the general scheme of these laws, *employers* are responsible for providing a safe and healthy working environment for their employees. *Employees* have a responsibility to use equipment in the workplace in accordance with the guidelines given to them and to report any hazards. Employees should also not interfere with any safety systems, including signs or warnings or devices such as firefighting equipment. Employees should not introduce or install devices, equipment, or materials to the workplace without authorization or without making a health and safety assessment of the installation

A company's health and safety procedures should be set out in a handbook, possibly as part of an employee's induction handbook. Health and safety procedures should:

- Identify what to do in the event of a fire or other emergency.

- Identify responsible persons (for example, for overall health and safety, nominated first aiders, fire marshals, and so on).

- Identify hazardous areas in the workspace and precautions to take when entering them.

- Describe best practice for use and care of the workspace and equipment.

- Establish an incident reporting procedure for detecting and eliminating workplace hazards and accidents.

© 2010 gtslearning

IT Career FastTrack with CompTIA A+ Certification

Page 293

Unit 3.3	Module 3 Operational Procedures

Dealing with emergencies

The general procedure for an **emergency** situation is as follows:

1. Raise the **alarm** and contact the **emergency services**, giving them a description of the emergency and your location.

2. If possible, make the scene **safe**. For example, if faced with a fire, establish that you have an escape route or if faced with electrical shock, disconnect the power (if it is safe for you to do so).

3. If you have **training** and it is **safe** to do so, do what you can to **tackle** the emergency (for example, give first aid or use firefighting equipment).

Of course, circumstances could dictate that you do something differently. It is vital that you keep calm and do not act rashly.

Incidents, accidents, or hazards have to be reported to the person responsible for health and safety, using the appropriate procedure. The incident should then be investigated to ensure that the hazard has been made safe.

Fire safety

Fire safety means ensuring that sources of *ignition* (such as electrical equipment, heat, or fire) are kept as separate as possible from sources of *combustion* (such as paper, wood, cloth, and so on). The likeliest causes of fires in offices are discarded cigarettes and overloaded or faulty electrical equipment.

The other elements of fire safety include:

■ Having well-rehearsed evacuation procedures.

■ Keeping fire exits unobstructed, clearly signed, and well-lit.

■ Installing and testing fire and smoke detectors and alarms and firefighting equipment.

Firefighting equipment

Firefighting equipment requires training to use properly. In an office workspace, this equipment will normally consist of a number of **fire extinguishers**. A fire extinguisher should only be used to tackle a small fire. The first consideration should be to identify a clear route to an emergency exit.

Page 294	IT Career FastTrack with CompTIA A+ Certification	© 2010 gtslearning

In the US (and most other countries), fires are divided by class under the NFPA (National Fire Protection Association) system, according to the combustible material that fuels the fire.

- Class A - ordinary combustible materials such as paper, wood, cardboard, and most plastics.
- Class B - flammable or combustible liquids, solids (notably oils, paints, alcohol), and gases.
- Class C - electrical equipment.
- Class D - combustible metals, such as those found in a laboratory.
- Class K - highly flammable materials, such as cooking oils or fats.

Fire extinguisher

Note

Under the European classification system, "electrical" fires are **Class E** and cooking oil files **Class F**.

Extinguishers come in several different types; each type being designed for fighting a particular class of fire. Using the wrong type of extinguisher on a fire can have catastrophic effects.

Class	Color	Symbol	Pictogram
A	Silver	Green Triangle	
B	Red	Red Square	
C	Red	Blue Circle	
D	Yellow	Yellow Star	
K	Red	Black Hexagon	

Special Dry Power extinguishers can be used for Class D fires. Wet Chemical extinguishers can be used against Class F fires. The color code can refer either to the color of the extinguisher unit itself or to a predominant block or strip on an otherwise red unit.

Fire blankets can also be used to smother a small fire (such as a pan fire or where someone's clothing has caught fire).

| Unit 3.3 | Module 3 Operational Procedures |

Electrical safety

As well as being a fire risk, electrical equipment can give an **electric shock** if it is broken, faulty, or installed incorrectly. An electric shock can cause severe burns or even kill. Electrical currents can pass through metal and most liquids, so neither should be allowed to come into contact with any electrical device installations.

Power supplies such as those inside the system unit, CRT monitors, LCD displays (inverter), and laser printers can carry extremely high levels of voltage. Charges held in capacitors can persist for hours after the power supply is turned off. You should not open up these units unless you have been specifically trained to do so. Adhere to all printed warnings, and never remove or break open any safety devices that carry such a warning.

> **Warning**
>
> Before performing work within a PC, always remove the power cord. After removing the cord, hold down the power button for a few seconds to ensure that the circuits are de-energized. Similarly, before opening the chassis of a laptop, remove the AC adapter and the battery.

Damaged components or cables are also a risk and should be replaced or isolated immediately. It is important to test electrical devices regularly (the frequency will depend on the environment in which the device is used). **Portable Appliance Testing (PAT)** carried out by a qualified electrician or technician ensures that a device is safe to use.

An electrical device must be fitted with a **fuse** appropriate to its power output. A fuse blows if there is a problem with the electrical supply, breaking the circuit to the power source. Fuses come in different ratings, such as 3A, 5A, and 13A. A device's instructions will indicate what rating of fuse to use, but most computer equipment is rated at 3A or 5A.

If the fuse fitted is rated too low, it will blow too easily; if the rating is too high, it may not blow when it should (it will allow too much current to pass through the device, which may overload its circuits and cause a fire).

If multiple devices need to be attached to a single power point, an appropriate **strip** of sockets should be used. If too many devices are attached to a single point, there is a severe risk that they will overheat and cause a fire. "Daisy-chaining" one strip to another is not recommended.

Page 296   IT Career FastTrack with CompTIA A+ Certification   © 2010 gtslearning

Overloaded (left) and properly used power strips

Strips may be fitted with a **surge suppressor**, which provides some protection for equipment against surges in the supply.

Lifting and manual handling

Lifting a heavy object in the wrong way can damage your back, but lifting and manual handling risks are not limited to particularly heavy objects. An object that is large or awkward to carry could cause you to trip over or walk into something else. An object that has sharp or rough edges or contains a hot or corrosive liquid could cause you to cut or hurt yourself. If necessary, you should obtain protective clothing (gloves and possibly goggles).

To lift a heavy object safely, plant your feet around the object with one foot slightly toward the direction in which you are going to move. Bend your knees to reach the object while keeping your back as straight as is possible and comfortable and your chin up. Find a firm grip on the object then lift smoothly by straightening your legs - do not jerk the object up. Carry the object while keeping your back straight. To lower an object, reverse the lifting process; keep your chin up and bend at the knees. Take care not to trap your fingers or to lower the object onto your feet.

If you cannot lift an object because it is too awkward or heavy, get help. If you need to carry an object for some distance, make sure that the route is unobstructed and that the pathway (including stairs or doorways) is wide and tall enough.

Moving parts and device safety

Devices with moving parts such as fans, gears, and motors represent a hazard as fingers or clothing could be caught in the mechanism, though most PC equipment will not apply sufficient force to cause serious injury. Also take care with components that generate heat as they may cause scalding if touched. One of the properties of logic devices is that the faster they run the hotter they become. Take care when handling the heat sink if the computer has been running for any length of time.

The fuser unit in a laser printer uses very high temperatures and could cause serious burns if handled after use. When maintaining a laser printer, allow at least 30 mins after powering down the device before attempting to remove it.

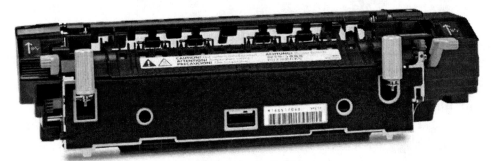

HP LaserJet fuser- the rollers (near the yellow warning label) become extremely hot

Another common hazard associated with PC equipment is laser light sources. These are used in fiber optic ports, optical drives, and laser printers. Take care not to look directly at the light source to avoid damaging your eyesight. Protective goggles should be used if such devices are to be disassembled.

Safe work environment

A number of health hazards are associated with the use of computer equipment. PCs should be installed in an ergonomic way (designed for maximum comfort and safety). The principal hazards are:

- Posture - typing and mouse use is associated with **Repetitive Strain Injuries (RSI)**. To minimize the risk to health, equipment should be installed and used properly:
    - ☐ Adjust the seat so that feet are flat on the floor, the back is straight or inclined slightly backward, and the display is at eye level.

- Type with arms parallel to the keyboard (or pointing slightly downwards) and keep wrists straight (do *not* bend them to use a wrist rest). Hands should move freely above the keyboard, using any wrist rest present only for breaks between typing spells.
- Take regular short breaks to stretch and walk around.

Check your posture when using mouse, keyboard, and monitor

Note

Symptoms of RSI can include muscle pain, numbness, tingling, prickly heat, and loss of strength. Users with those symptoms should consult their doctor.

- Eyestrain - if reflections make the display difficult to read, use anti-glare screens or coating. Ensure that ambient lighting is at the correct level and that refresh, brightness, and contrast controls are set correctly.
- Trips and falls - position equipment so that it is not a topple hazard or could be knocked off a desk. Use cable tidies to prevent trips. If cabling must be run across a walkway, use a cord protector to secure it.

Built-in cable management such as on this HP LCD display make it less likely trailing wires will cause an accident

- Air quality - computer equipment emits fumes and heat. Ensure that there is plenty of fresh air circulating (to improve the health of the person and the computer!) Users should drink plenty of fresh water to avoid dehydration.

Materials Handling

Employers are obliged to assess the risk to their workforce from hazardous substances at work and to take steps to eliminate or control that risk. No work with hazardous substances should take place unless an assessment has been made.

Suppliers of chemicals are required to identify the hazards (or dangers) of the substances they supply. If a chemical is dangerous, the supplier must provide information about the hazards that it presents.

Some hazard information will be provided on labels, but the supplier must also provide more detailed information in a **Material Safety Data Sheet (MSDS)**. An MSDS will contain information about:

- Ingredients.
- Health hazards, precautions, and first aid information.
- Safety precautions and protection.
- What to do if the material is spilt or leaks.

MSDS for an HP toner cartridge

The principal materials hazard for PC support is laser printer toner. Toner is composed of very fine particles. These are a health hazard if breathed in and can cause irritation to the skin. Only clean up toner spills using an approved toner vacuum (a vacuum where the dust bag is fine enough to capture the toner particles) or wipes. If toner is spilled on skin, wash it off with *cold* water.

Module 3 Operational Procedures   *Safety and Environmental Issues*

ESD Precautions

Static electricity is a very high voltage stored in an insulated body. Although the voltage is high, the amount of current that it can sustain is very low, so static electricity is not harmful to health when it discharges into a conductor (**ElectroStatic Discharge [ESD]**). It can, however, be slightly painful; you may have felt a small shock when reaching for a metal door handle[135]. The human body is mostly water and so does not generate or store static electricity very well. Unfortunately, our clothes are often made of synthetic materials, such as nylon and polyester, which act as good generators of static electricity and provide insulating layers that allow charges to accumulate. A clothed person may hold a very high static charge, especially if he or she has just walked across a synthetic carpet.

Humidity and climate also affect the likelihood of ESD. The risk increases significantly during dry, cool conditions when humidity is low. In wet conditions, such as before or during a storm, the residual charge will bleed into the environment before it can increase sufficiently to be harmful to electrical components.

An electronic component, such as a memory or logic chip, is composed of fine, conductive metal oxides. Its dimensions are measured in fractions of a micron (one millionth of a millimeter). Any static electricity discharged into this structure will flash-over between the conductive tracks, damaging or even vaporizing them. This may make the chip completely unusable. If not, it is likely to fail at some later time. Damage occurring in this way can be hidden for many months and may only manifest itself in occasional failures. Memory chips and processors are especially susceptible to damage by ESD[136].

Personal anti-static methods

To protect components and equipment from ESD damage, make sure that your body and clothing are drained of static electricity before starting work. The simplest (but least effective) way to achieve this is to touch a grounded point (such as the case of your PC while it is plugged into the wall) briefly before you begin.

---

[135] You can feel a discharge of over about 2500V. A discharge of 20,000V or more could produce a visible spark. Walking over an untreated carpet in dry conditions could create a charge of around 35,000V.

[136] A transistor designed to work with 1-3V can be damaged by a charge of under 100V (though most have ESD protection circuits that improve this tolerance). CMOS can typically withstand a charge of 2000-5000V.

© 2010 gtslearning   IT Career FastTrack with CompTIA A+ Certification   Page 301

This is only a temporary solution and the static charge soon builds up again. Several items of service equipment are available to dissipate the static charge. They are designed to dissipate the static charge.

Anti-static service kit

Basic ESD protection is provided by wearing an **anti-static wrist strap**, which is attached to a grounded point. A ground is made either using a grounding plug, which plugs into a wall socket, or a crocodile clip to attach to the computer's metal chassis.

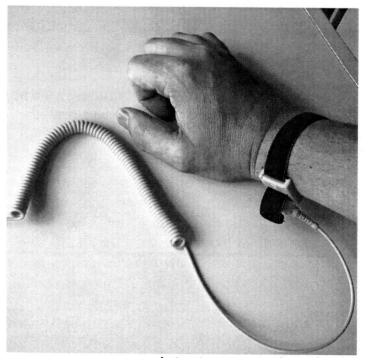

Anti-static wrist strap and grounding cord

Note
The wrist band should fit snugly around your wrist to maximize contact with the skin. Do not wear it over clothing. Ensure that the strap has a working current-limiting resistor for safety (straps should be tested daily).

Warning
Do not touch the cabling or pins on a monitor while wearing a wrist strap. Do not handle any high voltage equipment while using anti-static protection. Test wrist straps daily (before use!) with a multimeter or dedicated wrist strap tester.

A more advanced device is a service mat, which has its own grounding cord and plug. Sensitive items can be placed on the mat safely.

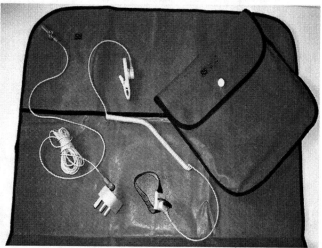

Anti-static service kit with mat

Anti-static packaging

Electronic components, assemblies, and spare parts (known as **Field Replaceable Units** [or **FRUs**]) are often shipped in protective packaging to protect them from ESD damage.

- Anti-Static Shielding - this packaging reduces the risk of ESD because it is coated with a conductive material (such as a nickel compound). This material prevents static electricity from discharging through the inside of the bag. These bags are usually a shiny grey metallic color. To protect the contents of the bag fully, you should seal it, or at least fold the top over and seal that down.

- Dissipative Packaging - this light pink or blue packaging reduces the build-up of static in the general vicinity of the contents by being slightly more conductive than normal. A plastic bag or foam packaging may be sprayed with an anti-static coating or have anti-static materials added to the plastic compound. This is used to package non-static-sensitive components packed in proximity to static-sensitive components.

ESD-safe cleaning materials

Use cleaning pads and cloths designed for use with PCs. You can obtain anti-static spray to eliminate any residual charge on cleaning products.

| Unit 3.3 | Module 3 Operational Procedures |

Other ways of controlling ESD

Wrist straps are a useful means of controlling localized sources of ESD, such as the human body. Manufacturing and repair companies often take additional steps to reduce the build-up of electrostatic charge within the entire workshop area. Preventative measures include:

- Anti-static floor treatments or special carpeting to dissipate any static before it can build up.

- Humidifier units to stabilize the levels of moisture in the air: dry air is less conductive and assists the build-up of static charges (around 35-50% humidity is ideal).

RFI / EMI

Radio Frequency Interference (RFI) is electromagnetic "noise". Noise in this context is anything that interferes with the signal you want to transmit (or receive). Typical man-made sources of electromagnetic noise include power lines, generators, transformers, magnets, fluorescent lights, fans, air-conditioning units, cordless phones, baby monitors, and microwave ovens. The signal from another device also counts as interference when it disrupts another device - for example, if you use a cell phone in proximity to stereo speakers you may be able to hear the interference. Similarly, the signals from two access points can interfere with one another in some circumstances.

RFI has the potential to disrupt wireless communications. Microwaves and cordless phones are a particular problem because they use the same general part of the spectrum as 802.11b/g (2.4 GHz).

When electromagnetic noise affects electronic equipment, it is often referred to specifically as **ElectroMagnetic Interference (EMI)**. To affect an electronic circuit, the source of EMI would have to be quite close to the component. Examples include a fan positioned next to a monitor or a network cable running next to a fluorescent light. If a troublesome EMI source is identified and cannot be relocated, the only option is to install some sort of shielding.

> **Note**
> Do not confuse ESD with EMI. Unlike ESD, EMI does not cause permanent damage; once the cause is identified, the problem should disappear.

Page 304 IT Career FastTrack with CompTIA A+ Certification © 2010 gtslearning

Module 3 Operational Procedures   *Safety and Environmental Issues*

Power Problems

Environmental power problems are those caused by failures in the mains power supply rather than failures in the computer's power supply unit, AC adapter, or battery pack.

Environmental power problems

- **Surge** (or **spike**) - an abrupt, but very brief, change in the value of the voltage. It can be caused by a light being turned off or a nearby lightning storm. Many spikes are very small and of too short a duration to cause problems, but some can take the supply several hundred volts over its normal value and cause sufficient interference to a computer's power supply to crash, reboot, or even damage it.

- **Sag** - some electrically powered devices require very high starting, or inrush, current. When this kind of device is turned on, the large current surge into the device may cause the available voltage within the locality to dip for a brief period of time. A sag of longer than about 10 to 20 milliseconds can cause computer equipment to malfunction.

- **Brownout** - a sag that lasts for longer than a second. Overloaded or faulty mains distribution circuits sometimes cause brownouts.

- **Blackout** - a complete power failure. A blackout may be caused by a disruption to the power distribution grid (an equipment failure or the accidental cutting of a cable during construction work, for example), or may simply happen because a fuse has blown or a circuit breaker has tripped.

Dealing with power problems

All the above power problems can have disastrous effects on computer equipment. A range of power protection devices is available to either reduce the symptoms of the power problem or to eliminate it altogether.

So-called **passive protection devices** can be used to filter out the effects of spikes and surges. The simplest devices (**surge suppressors**) come in the form of adapters, trailing sockets, or filter plugs, with the protection circuitry built into the unit. These devices offer low-cost protection to one or two pieces of equipment.

© 2010 gtslearning   IT Career FastTrack with CompTIA A+ Certification   Page 305

The maximum current that can be carried by a filter unit ranges from 3A to 13A. You must always make sure that the device is of the correct rating and will not be overloaded in use.

HP Power Distribution Unit (PDU) with monitoring functionality

Larger industrial power filter units (**line conditioners** or **Power Distribution Units [PDU]**) can be used to protect entire power circuits from the effects of surges or brownouts, but they are unable to remove or reduce the effects of blackouts.

However, line conditioners are generally built into **Uninterruptible Power Supplies (UPS)**, which do eliminate the effects of complete power failure.

> **Note**
> Telephone lines and modem connections are also vulnerable to surges, especially lightning strikes. Better quality protection devices also have jacks for telephone/modem connections. Very few devices will provide complete protection from lightning strikes. The safest option during a severe electrical storm where there is a risk of lightning strike is to disconnect computer equipment from mains and network cabling.

Choosing a UPS

A UPS is generally used to protect server-level equipment. It consists of a bank of batteries that can continue to supply power to the computer for a few minutes (sometimes as much as an hour). This allows time for either the power to be restored, a backup generator to be brought online, or for the computer to be shut down gracefully.

Choosing the right type of UPS is relatively straightforward. The following guidelines assist the choice but should be used in conjunction with the information available from the equipment and UPS manufacturers.

Module 3 Operational Procedures — Safety and Environmental Issues

APC desktop UPS

The maximum power rating (and hence cost) of a UPS is determined by the battery specification and the power handling of the inverter and other circuitry. Each UPS is rated according to the maximum VA (power) they can supply without overloading.

To calculate the required VA rating for a UPS, simply add up the VA ratings of all the equipment to be connected to the unit. These may be calculated by taking the number of watts used by each device and multiplying by 1.6.

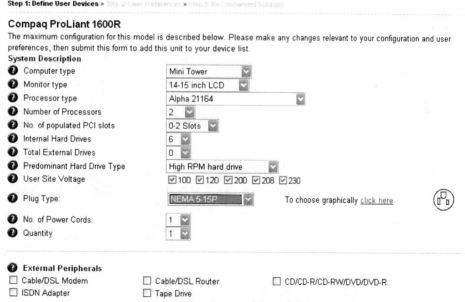

Choosing the UPS - defining the computer and peripherals

Most UPS vendor websites have a configuration wizard which you can complete to determine which UPS models suit your IT infrastructure.

| Unit 3.3 | Module 3 Operational Procedures |

As you can see, you also specify the maximum duration of battery power (10 minutes for instance) which enables you to determine how much charge the unit must be able to hold to supply your needs.

UPS Selector

Step 1: Define User Devices > **Step 2: User Preferences** > Step 3: Recommended Solutions

Please set your preferences below, then click the "Show Solution" button to view a list of of solutions. If you would like to have more control over your preferences click here for ⦿Advanced Preferences

- ❷ Extra Power for future expansion: 30% ☑
- ❷ Desired run time during power fail: 0 ☑ : 10 ☑ (Hours : Minutes)
- ❷ Do you require a Rackmountable UPS?   ○ Yes ⦿ No
- ❷ Do you require a Redundant solution?   ○ Yes ⦿ No
- ❷ User Site Voltage: International - 230V system (& 400V) ☑

[Show Solution]

Defining the power requirements

Configuring a UPS

To use a UPS, just connect the power leads from the PC to the ports on the UPS then plug the UPS into the mains.

> **Note**
>
> A UPS is only designed to power a computer and its monitor. Do not plug printers (especially laser printers) into a UPS as they will drain the batteries in seconds.

A UPS normally also connects to the PC via a serial or USB port in order to provide status information and alerts to the operating system. Any configurable settings can be made either via the driver or Control Panel applet (the UPS may add a tab under Power Management).

If mains power is lost, the UPS will sound an audible alarm (beep) to indicate that the battery is being drained.

UPS batteries are recharged automatically while the unit is connected to the mains. If the UPS is disconnected from the mains for any length of time, the batteries should be conditioned and stored according to the manufacturer's instructions. As with any type of battery, UPS batteries hold less charge as they age and so may only have a usable life of a couple of years. Most vendors operate trade-in programs for old batteries and obsolete UPS models.

Module 3 Operational Procedures

Safe Disposal and Recycling

Many countries are also passing environmental legislation to ensure that companies demonstrate good energy efficiency and waste disposal practice.

Materials safety and environmental legislation require that environmental hazards be disposed of correctly. In the UK, the main piece of relevant legislation is the **Environmental Protection Act (1990)**; there are also a number of European Community directives (EC member states have to implement directives through national legislation). The most notable of these is the recently introduced EC Directive on **Waste Electrical and Electronic Equipment (WEEE)**. This makes collection and disposal of equipment purchased after 13 August 2005 the responsibility of the producer of the new equipment. In the US, environmental matters are the responsibility of the **Environmental Protection Agency (EPA)**.

IT equipment contains several components and materials that can cause environmental damage if disposed of as ordinary refuse.

Batteries

Generally, batteries should be recycled where possible. Failing this, they should always be disposed of in accordance with local and national regulations. The disposal of rechargeable batteries is often regulated.

Manufacturers should offer advice on the correct disposal of batteries and cells. In most cases they will either be shipped back to the manufacturer or taken to an approved recycling center. There can be high penalties for illegal disposal.

Toner kits and cartridges

Toner may be disposed of as normal waste, though it should be placed in a sealed bag to retain the fine powder. However, most manufacturers and third-party organizations offer a toner cartridge recycling and disposal service. Remember to check whether the use of recycled cartridges affects a printer's warranty.

© 2010 gtslearning   IT Career FastTrack with CompTIA A+ Certification   Page 309

Unit 3.3   Module 3 Operational Procedures

Computers

PCs contain few hazardous waste products and disposal of old equipment should not be a major issue. However, there are other disposal matters that may need to be considered:

- Recycling components could reduce the sheer bulk generated by mass disposal in landfill.

- Donating systems for educational or charitable use provides environmental and social benefits. Some companies also offer resale programs, offering employees the option to purchase decommissioned equipment.

- Some precious metals (such as gold and silver from the motherboard and switch contacts) can be recovered and have recyclable value; however, the quantities involved are very small.

Chemical solvents and cans

The disposal of all chemicals and cans should always be carried out in accordance with the manufacturer's instructions. Generally, the following rules apply to the disposal of solvents and cans:

- Do not pour solvents into household waste water systems.

- Do not puncture cans, even when empty.

- Do not burn waste solvents, cans, or aerosols.

- Do not re-fill empty cans or aerosols except where they are designed to be refillable and always re-fill them with exactly the same chemical.

- Do not mix waste solvents, even in containers designed for waste disposal.

- Only use licensed waste disposal companies.

Summary

Make sure you know the proper responses to emergency and hazardous situations. You should be able to identify the impacts adverse environmental conditions (heat, humidity, ESD, power, and EMI) have on computers. Learn the use of disposal and recycling facilities.

Module 3 Operational Procedures   *Security*

Unit 3.4 Security

CompTIA A+ Essentials Objectives

☐ **701.5.1 Explain the basic principles of security concepts and technologies**
Encryption technologies • Data wiping / hard drive destruction / hard drive recycling • Software firewall (Port security, Exceptions) • Authentication technologies (User name, Password, Biometrics, Smart cards) • Basics of data sensitivity and data security (Compliance, Classifications, Social engineering)

☐ **701.5.2 Summarize the following security features**
Malicious software protection (Viruses, Trojans, Worms, Spam, Spyware, Adware, Grayware) • Biometrics (Fingerprint scanner)

Security Concepts

Security is the practice of controlling access to something (a **resource**). Computer security has become a vital competency as the risks from threats such as malware, hacking, and identity fraud become better recognized and increasingly serious.

Basic security concepts

Security is always balanced against **accessibility**; if a system is completely secure, then no-one has access to it and it is unusable. Secure information has three properties, often referred to as the "CIA triad":

- **Confidentiality** - this means that certain information should only be known to certain people.

- **Integrity** - this means that information is stored and transferred as intended and that any modification is authorized.

- **Availability** - this means that information is accessible to those authorized to view or modify it.

Another triad ("AAA") describes the characteristics of a security system: **Authorization** (Access Control), **Authentication**, and **Accounting** (or Auditing).

© 2010 gtslearning   IT Career FastTrack with CompTIA A+ Certification   Page 311

| Unit 3.4 | Module 3 Operational Procedures |

- Authorization means creating one or more barriers around the resource such that only authenticated users can gain access. Each resource has an access control list specifying what users can do. Resources often have different access levels (for example, being able to read a file or being able to read and edit it).

- Authentication means one or more methods of proving that a user is who s/he says s/he is.

- Accounting means recording when and by whom a resource was accessed.

One of the key points to note from the above is "one or more". A security system that depends on one mechanism only is often not very effective.

Threats

Threats are all the things that could steal or damage a resource. Typical threats include:

- Disaster - fire, flood, earthquake, war, disease, and so on.

- Theft - physical theft of equipment and printed documents.

- Espionage - theft of computer data (or information generally)[137].

- Vandalism - deliberate damage to systems or data.

It is important to realize that threats can be *accidental* or *malicious* and arise from *within* or *without* an organization. Threats can also be characterized as *targeted* or *untargeted*. For example, mass mailing a virus to millions of computers is an untargeted threat; emailing a Trojan Horse with some message that relates specifically to the employees of a particular business is a targeted threat. Targeted threats are increasingly common and often carry much higher risk than untargeted threats.

Threats are identified by performing a **risk assessment** for each resource. Where there is risk, an appropriate form of access control must be put in place.

---

[137] A cracker (or "black hat") is someone who breaks into a computer system (or more generally gains unauthorized access to one) with the intent of causing damage or theft. A hacker (or "white hat") is someone interested in network security, though of course the media tend to refer to crackers as hackers indiscriminately.

| Page 312 | IT Career FastTrack with CompTIA A+ Certification | © 2010 gtslearning |

Module 3 Operational Procedures   *Security*

Compliance

Compliance is the process of identifying and adhering to legislation and professional best practice relevant to a business. Compliance affects all levels of an organization. Most responsibility for compliance falls at the managerial level, but ordinary employees may have numerous rights and responsibilities.

Some of the types of legislation that have the most effect are:

- Health and Safety - this ensures that the working environment is properly managed. In offices, it mostly refers to the installation and use of ICT equipment.

- Data Protection - this type of legislation controls what information a company can gather and store on individuals and sets standards for how it can be stored and processed.

- Privacy - businesses use a lot of technology that traces and records activity (both from customers and their own staff). Privacy legislation sets boundaries on the sort of monitoring that a company can perform.

- Equal Opportunities - this legislation prevents employers from discriminating against their employees on the basis of disability, gender, race, or beliefs. The legislation also applies to services provided to customers and the public.

- Consumer Protection - this type of legislation controls the sales process, ensuring that companies advertise goods and services honestly and handle customer transactions fairly. Consumer protection is usually particularly strong in retail sales and financial services.

- Software Licensing - piracy costs vendors billions every year. It is vital to respect the terms of software licenses and to educate customers that may not properly understand their responsibilities.

Failure to comply with legislation can result in serious penalties, ranging from fines to imprisonment or suspension of trading.

As well as legislation, a business may also adhere to professional standards through membership of some sort of trade association:

© 2010 gtslearning   IT Career FastTrack with CompTIA A+ Certification   Page 313

Authorization

Authorization is about creating barriers around protected resources.

Physical security

The concept of **restricted spaces** refers to the fact that an organization's premises and equipment should be *physically* secured against theft or damage. To do this, a number of zones can be identified (such as external, perimeter, public, restricted, and secure) and barriers and gateways set up to control movement between spaces. In IT terms, the most restricted space is usually the "computer room" containing server and networking equipment.

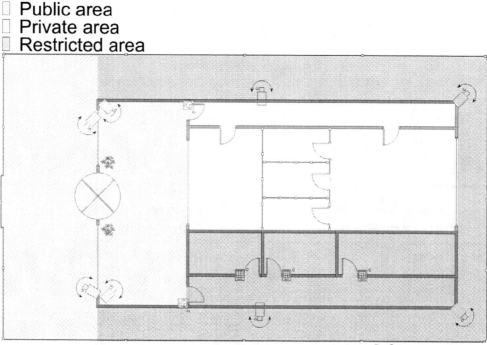

Defining security zones

Component security can be enforced using device locks (physically chaining a device to a desk or cabinet) or using some sort of theft-prevention ID system. Mobile device protection is best enforced by secure log on and encryption of data stored on the device. Computer systems may also feature lockable faceplates, to prevent access to the on/off switch, disk drives, and ports (to prevent the attachment of unauthorized equipment), though these tend to be features of servers rather than workstations.

Module 3 Operational Procedures   Security

Data / file security

In terms of software or data security, operating systems and security
applications can provide a number of solutions to controlling access to
systems configuration settings and confidential or secret data. In Windows, a
person is associated with a user account and the user account is granted
permissions to configure the system and access files (see unit 5.3).

Encryption

Encryption refers to *encoding* data. An **algorithm** (or **cipher**) based on a
complex value (the "key") is applied to the characters in the data to scramble
them. The result is that the data message cannot be read or modified without
access to the correct "key". This means that even if the "message" is stolen or
intercepted, it still cannot be read (or modified).

There are two main types of encryption used in data transfer and storage
systems[138]:

■ **Symmetric encryption** is where the same key is used to encrypt and
decrypt data. This encryption technology is fast (it can encode large
amounts of data quickly) but raises the problem of *distributing* the key
securely.

■ **Asymmetric encryption** is where the encryption key is different to the
decryption key but the keys are linked by some mathematical property.
Data encrypted with one key can only be decrypted by the related key (and
vice versa). One key cannot be derived from the other, so one can be made
publicly available while the other is kept private. This solves the key
distribution problem, but asymmetric encryption is more complex, and so
typically only used on small amounts of data.

Encryption has many uses in IT security. Asymmetric encryption is used in
smart cards and on websites (digital certificates) to authenticate users and
services.

---

[138] A third type of encryption is used to store passwords securely as an encrypted hash. Once encrypted, a hash
cannot be decrypted (the encryption process is not reversible).

© 2010 gtslearning   IT Career FastTrack with CompTIA A+ Certification   Page 315

Public Key Infrastructure (PKI)

Asymmetric encryption is an important part of **Public Key Infrastructure (PKI)**. PKI is a solution to the problem of authenticating unknown users or servers on public networks.

Under PKI, users are validated by a **Certificate Authority (CA)**, which issues the user with a digital certificate[139]. The digital certificate contains a public key associated with the user embedded in it. The certificate has also been signed by the CA, guaranteeing its validity. Therefore, if a third-party trusts the signing CA, they can also trust the user.

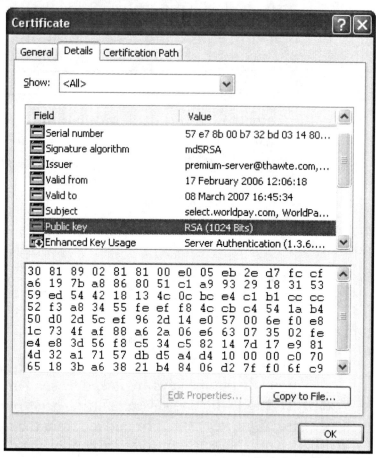

Digital certificate details

The third-party (a customer for example) can then send the user (Amazon.com for example) data (their credit card details for example) encrypted using the public key, safe in the knowledge that only the user will be able to decrypt it (using their secret private key).

Digital certificates are also used for secure authentication to computer networks.

---

[139] User in this sense is usually something like a website or software developer, though digital certificates can be used for personal email communications too.

Module 3 Operational Procedures | Security

Firewalls

Connecting an organization to the internet is a major security worry. There have been many articles in the press regarding hackers breaking into organizations and gaining access to important information and systems. A **firewall** describes hardware or software used to filter packets of data as they pass through the system.

The packets can be filtered on the following parameters:

- Direction (both inbound and outbound).

- IP addresses (individual addresses or a range of IP addresses).

- Well-known port number (for example, SMTP uses port 25).

This configuration is referred to as an **Access Control List (ACL)**. The firewall may provide the option to accept all packets *except* for those on the reject list or, alternatively, it may provide the option to reject all packets *except* for those on the accept list. Generally the latter is the best choice, since it is more secure and involves less configuration.

Authentication

Authentication is the process of allowing legitimate users through the barriers set up for access control. There are many different authentication technologies. They can be categorized as something you **know** (such as a password), something you **have** (such as a smart card), or something you **are** (such as a fingerprint). Each has advantages and drawbacks.

Something you know

The typical something you know authentication technology is the log on: this comprises a user name and a password. The user name is typically not a secret (though it doesn't do to go round publishing it) but the password must be known only to the one user.

Under Windows, this method of authentication is implemented by default. The computer or domain administrator sets up user accounts and their permissions. Passwords should be known only to users and each user is responsible for selecting a secure password and keeping it secret.

© 2010 gtslearning | IT Career FastTrack with CompTIA A+ Certification | Page 317

This type of authentication is generally considered to be "weak", because it can easily be compromised by user error (writing passwords down, selecting easily guessable passwords, sharing passwords, and so on).

Something you have

There are various ways to authenticate a user based on something they have. The most common is a **smart card** or **USB fob**, which contains a chip with authentication data, such as a **digital certificate**. The card must be presented to a card reader before the user can be authenticated (this is typically combined with a user name/password logon or Personal Identification Number [PIN] code).

Another hardware authentication device is the SecurID token, developed by RSA. This generates a number code synchronized to a code on a server for the user to enter to log on (usually combined with a secret PIN, in case the device is stolen). The code changes every 60 seconds or so. This is an example of a **one-time password**.

RSA SecurID key fob token generator

> **Note**
> A really secure system will always use a combination of authentication methods. This is referred to as two-factor authentication or strong authentication.

The main concerns with something you have technologies are loss and theft and the chance that the device can be counterfeited. There are also extra setup and maintenance costs.

Something you are

Something you are authentication means employing some sort of **biometric** recognition system. Many types of biometric information can be recorded, including fingerprint patterns, signature recognition, iris or retina recognition, or facial recognition.

The chosen biometric information is scanned and recorded in a database (the **template**). When the user wants to access a resource, s/he is re-scanned and the scan compared to the template. If they match, access is granted.

Microsoft IntelliMouse with fingerprint reader

The main problems with biometric technology are that users find it intrusive and threatening to privacy, the setup and maintenance costs, and the chance that the technology can be counterfeited. Biometrics can also be prone to false negatives (where a valid user is refused access) and false positives (where an intruder is misidentified as a valid user or one user is mistaken for another).

Tip
The same authentication concepts apply to physical barriers too. For example, you could control access to the server room using a key (something you have), PIN code combination lock (something you know), or an iris scanner biometric lock (something you are).

Accounting and Incident Reporting

Access control puts barriers around resources while authentication allows users to pass through access control. The third part of the AAA triad is **accounting** (or **auditing**). The purpose of auditing is to track what has happened to a resource over time. As well as keeping a log of authorized access and edits, this can also reveal suspicious behavior and attempts to break through security.

Auditing is generally performed by **logging** actions automatically. In Windows, this can be done by configuring event logging (see unit 5.6). Software applications such as databases can also be configured with event logs. There is also a class of security software called **Intrusion Detection (or Prevention)** designed to monitor the system state and prevent unauthorized changes. In other circumstances, auditing may mean deploying surveillance systems or security guards to monitor restricted spaces.

| Unit 3.4 | Module 3 Operational Procedures |

Incident reporting means informing the relevant person that there has been a security breach. Auditing software might do this automatically (for example, by emailing the administrator). For situations not covered by software, there needs to be a clear policy for employees to follow:

- What is an incident? What should I report?
- To whom do I make the report?
- How quickly should I report an incident?

Social Engineering

An effective security system is *multi-layered*. This means that an attacker must successfully penetrate several barriers to compromise the system. Information security can be enforced using operating system policies and tools, but physical barriers and user education/training are just as important. One way for security to be compromised is for users to make mistakes; another is for them to be tricked. **Social engineering,** pioneered by Kevin Mitnick (see his book "The Art of Deception"), refers to means of getting users to reveal confidential information.

Social engineering attacks

The classic attack is for an attacker to phone into a department, claim they have to adjust something on the user's system remotely, and get the user to reveal their password. Such attacks can also be launched via email or instant messaging[140]. Another example is getting a user to hold open a door into a controlled area.

For social engineering to be effective, the attacker generally needs some inside information. For example, the dial-in attack is much more effective if the attacker knows the user's name. As most companies are set up towards customer service rather than security, this information is typically quite easy to come by.

---

[140] Phone, email, and IM all feature relatively weak authentication (they rely on the user to identify the person). Email and IM can be improved using security systems such as digital certificates, but the correspondents have to pre-agree to use the same security system.

| Page 320 | IT Career FastTrack with CompTIA A+ Certification | © 2010 gtslearning |

Information that might seem innocuous of itself, such as department employee lists, job titles, phone numbers, diary, invoices, or purchase orders, can help an attacker penetrate an organization through *impersonation*.

Do you really know who's on the other end of the line?

Attackers will generally try one of the following methods:

- Intimidate the target by pretending to be someone senior in rank.
- Intimidate the target by using spurious technical arguments and jargon.
- Coax the target by engaging them in friendly chat.

Another technique for gathering information is "Dumpster Diving", which refers to combing through an organization's (or individual's) refuse to try to find useful documents (or even files stored on discarded removable media).

Defeating social engineering attacks

Social engineering is best defeated by training users to recognize and respond to these kinds of situations. Users should understand what constitutes secure information and know in what circumstances (if any) it should be revealed to other people. Users should also have a good understanding of the technical support process, so that it cannot be compromised.

Train or educate users in secure behavior

In terms of physical security, employees need to be trained to be confident enough to challenge unrecognized persons or those without an appropriate security badge. Care should be taken when moving between areas not to leave security doors open or unlocked and to be alert to "shoulder surfing", where an intruder tries to pass through a door just behind you.

> **Tip**
> Users cannot be expected to do these things without clear guidance. There needs to be a written security policy, explaining how users should behave in these types of situation. Ideally, this should also be backed up by training.

Users should also know not to introduce unauthorized hardware or software to the computer system and not to tamper with the system configuration or security software. There should be a reporting system for detecting unrecognized devices or software appearing on a computer or on the network. Employees should also follow acceptable use policies when accessing the internet or receiving personal email through their employer's message system. These measures will help to defeat malware and network attacks.

Other measures include ensuring documents and information are destroyed before disposal and using multi-factor access control, to put more than one or two barriers between an attacker and his or her target.

Module 3 Operational Procedures   *Security*

Malware

Malware is a catch-all term to describe malicious software threats and social engineering tools designed to vandalize or compromise computer systems.

Computer viruses

Computer viruses are programs designed to *replicate* and spread amongst computers. Viruses are classified by the different ways they can infect the computer. For example:

- **Boot sector viruses** - these attack the boot sector information, the partition table, and sometimes the file system.

- **Program viruses** - these are sequences of code that insert themselves into another executable program or script. When the application is executed, the virus code becomes active.

- **Macro viruses** - these viruses affect Microsoft Office documents using the macro programming language (Visual Basic for Applications [VBA]) used to provide macro functionality.

- **Worms** are memory-resident viruses that replicate over network resources.

Viruses are classified as software that attempts to self-replicate to other files, disks, computers, or networks. However, a virus's **payload** can be programmed to perform many different actions, especially in the case of program and macro viruses. A virus payload may be programmed to display silly messages, corrupt or delete documents, damage system files, or to install some sort of spyware (see below).

Most viruses must be activated by the user and so need some means to trick the user into opening the infected file. **Email attachment viruses** (usually program or macro viruses in an attached file) often use the infected host's electronic address book to **spoof** the sender's address when replicating (for example, Jim's computer is infected with a virus and has Alan's email address in his address book. When Sue gets an infected email apparently sent by Alan, it is the virus on Jim's computer that has sent the message).

Viruses can also use **application exploits** to replicate without user intervention. This is why it is imperative to apply security patches to OS and applications software (especially web browser and email software) promptly.

© 2010 gtslearning   IT Career FastTrack with CompTIA A+ Certification   Page 323

| Unit 3.4 | Module 3 Operational Procedures |

Trojan Horse and spyware

Other types of malware are not classed as viruses as they do not necessarily try to make copies of themselves. They can be just as much of a security threat as viruses however.

A **Trojan Horse** is a program that pretends to be something else. For example, an amusing screen saver may also install a **key logger**.

Most Trojans are of a type also referred to as **backdoor** applications; that is, the program opens a backdoor to your computer giving access to it to an attacker. A related term is **rootkit**, which is a set of tools designed to gain complete control of a computer without revealing its presence (they often attack the kernel-level operating system code).

Trojans are often used to compromise a number of computers (**botnets**) for the purpose of carrying out widescale **Denial of Service (DoS)** attacks against internet hosts. Trojans are also used by attackers to conceal their actions (attacks appear to come from the corrupted computer system).

Spyware and **adware** are classes of program that monitor internet activity and send the information to someone else. If the user is not informed then it's spyware; if the user accepts the use of their data, then it's adware[141]. Aggressive spyware or Trojans known as **key loggers** actively attempt to steal confidential information (for example, capturing a credit card number by recording key strokes entered into a web form). **Ransomware** refers to another aggressive type of malware, which may encrypt files or spawn browser pop-up windows to make the system unusable, unless the user gives in and pays a "release fee".

Phishing is a technique for tricking a user into revealing confidential information by requesting it in an official-looking email (perhaps pretending to come from a bank or genuine service provider). The email will contain a link to a counterfeit site or to a valid site that is vulnerable to a **cross-site scripting** attack. The user is prompted to input confidential data, such as online bank account numbers and passwords, which are then stolen by the attacker. A related attack (**pharming**) attempts to redirect web traffic to a counterfeit page, usually by corrupting the way the computer processes DNS addresses (see unit 5.1).

---

[141] The distinction can be blurred somewhat if the "acceptance" is buried in a lengthy terms and conditions notice or software license agreement that few users are likely to read. Trend Micro, an anti-virus and internet security vendor, refers to this type of software as "grayware".

Module 3 Operational Procedures   *Security*

Spam

Spam is unsolicited email messages, the content of which is usually advertising pornography, miracle cures for various unpleasant medical conditions, or bogus stock market tips and investments. Spam is also used to launch phishing attacks and spread viruses, Trojans, and worms, either through a file attachment or using a link to a malicious website.

Spam needs to be filtered before it reaches the user's inbox. Most email applications now ship with junk mail filters or you can install a filter at the organization's mail gateway.

The main problem with spam filters is that they can block genuine messages too, leading to missed communications. Spammers also develop ways to circumvent filters, such as using images or PDF file attachments.

Data Sensitivity and Security

Most documents go through one or more draft stages before they are published. As a draft, a document will be subject to a **workflow**, which describes how editorial changes are made and approved. The workflow will specify who are the authors, editors, and reviewers of the document.

As part of the creation process, the document must be **classified** depending on how sensitive it is. Classification restricts who may see the document contents. Classification is generally divided into several levels, following military usage:

- Unclassified - there are no restrictions on viewing the document.

- Classified (internal use only / official use only) - viewing is restricted to the owner organization or to third-parties under a Non-disclosure Agreement (NDA).

- Confidential - the information is highly sensitive, for viewing only by approved persons within the organization (and possibly by trusted third-parties under NDA).

- Secret - the information is too valuable to permit any risk of its capture. Viewing is severely restricted.

- Top-Secret - this is the highest level of classification.

Confidential, secret, and top-secret information should be securely protected (encrypted) for storage and transmission.

© 2010 gtslearning   IT Career FastTrack with CompTIA A+ Certification   Page 325

Over its lifecycle, information may change in sensitivity, typically becoming less sensitive over time. A document may be downgraded to a lower security level or eventually declassified. In this circumstance, there needs to be a clear process of authorization and notification, so that confidentiality is not breached.

> ## Note
> Data security is a very difficult problem to solve. Copy and paste makes it easy for users to transfer information from one document file to another or into an email message. There are various information management products to try to prevent this misuse but effective training is generally the most cost-effective option for all but the most highly classified information.

Backups

There are two types of backup:

- **Security** backups are made regularly so that data can be recovered in the event that the original is lost or damaged in some way.

- **Archive** backups are made if the data is no longer required for day-to-day use but must be retained for business or legal purposes.

With both types of backup, security and access control are still primary concerns. Data is no less confidential just because it has been copied to a tape! Windows includes Backup and Restore account privileges for users that would not normally be permitted to view the data that they are backing up.

Thought also needs to be given to the storage of backup media. There is little point having a security backup if it is subject to the same risks as the live data. Backup systems work on the basis of tape rotation, so that backup media can be stored securely (often off-site). It is also important to prevent unauthorized users from accessing the media.

Hardware deconstruction and recycling

Data stored on media such as hard drives or removable disks can present a security risk when the device or media is removed from service. When a device is obsolete, it may either be disposed of as general waste, recycled to recover useful materials, donated for charitable or educational use, or sold on.

| Module 3 Operational Procedures | Security |

In each of these scenarios, if confidential data is not removed from the media, there is the chance that it could be intercepted. This exposes an organization to risks:

- An organization's own confidential data could be compromised.

- Third-party data that the organization processes could be compromised, leaving it liable under Data Protection legislation (in addition to contracts or Service Level Agreements).

- Software licensing could be compromised.

The main issue is understanding the degree to which data on different media types may be recoverable. Data "deleted" from a magnetic-type disk (such as a hard disk) is not erased[142]. With the proper tools, up to 60% of a drive's deleted information can be recovered.

Remnant removal

Remnant removal refers to fully erasing decommissioned media (including old hard disks, removable disks, flash drives, tape media, CD and DVD ROMs, and so on). The problem has become particularly prominent as organizations recycle their old PCs, either by donating them to charities or by sending them to a recycling company, who may recover and sell on parts.

There are several approaches to the problem of data remnants on magnetic disks:

- Full format using Windows - this is the simplest method but is not completely reliable.

- Overwriting - disk wiping software ensures that old data is destroyed by writing to each location on the media in a random pattern, usually multiple times. This is suitable for all but the most confidential data, but is time consuming and requires special software.

- Use a reputable recycling company - this requires a degree of trust in the third-party to erase the data properly.

- Destruction - a magnetic disk can be degaussed or even obliterated using acid. Obviously, this is costly and renders the disk unusable (so it cannot be recycled).

---

[142] The problem also affects Flash Memory media.

© 2010 gtslearning   IT Career FastTrack with CompTIA A+ Certification   Page 327

Unit 3.4   Module 3 Operational Procedures

- Disk encryption - this method encrypts *all* the information on the disk, so that any remnants could not be read. This requires third-party software under most versions of Windows[143] and there will be an impact on performance.

Optical media cannot be reformatted. Discs should be destroyed before discarding them. Shredders are available for destroying CD and DVD media.

Summary

You can classify security systems as providing authorization (access control), authentication, and accounting (auditing). Make sure you know the technologies associated with each of these groups.

Learn the different types of malware and social engineering attacks and what risks they pose for computer and internet users.

Tip

To review what you have learned in this chapter, you should now visit the course website. This contains review questions and bonus material to help you to learn more and practice the topics covered in this unit.

---

[143] A disk encryption product (BitLocker) is included in the Enterprise and Ultimate editions of Windows Vista.

Module 4 Installation, Troubleshooting, and Maintenance

The preceding modules and units should have given you a solid understanding of the types of components used in PCs and the utilities and commands used to administer and configure Windows.

The next step is to apply that knowledge to practical PC installation, upgrade, repair, and troubleshooting tasks.

| Unit 4.1 | Module 4 Installation, Troubleshooting, and Maintenance |

Unit 4.1 Preventative Maintenance

CompTIA A+ Essentials Objectives

☐ **702.2.3 Given a scenario, select and use system utilities / tools and evaluate the results**
Disk management tools (NTBACKUP)

☐ **701.2.5 Given a scenario, integrate common preventative maintenance techniques**
Physical inspection • Updates (Driver, Firmware, OS, Security) • Scheduling preventative maintenance (Defrag, Scandisk, Check disk, Startup programs) • Use of appropriate repair tools and cleaning materials (Compressed air, Lint free cloth, Computer vacuum and compressors) • Power devices (Appropriate source such as power strip, surge protector or UPS) • Ensuring proper environment • Backup procedures

☐ **702.1.4 Given a scenario, select and use the following tools**
Specialty hardware / tools • Anti-static pad and wrist strap • Extension magnet

Repair Tools

A PC technician should use appropriate tools to perform maintenance and upgrade tasks. Using inappropriate tools or cleaning materials can damage components.

Some of the main elements of a PC technician's toolkit are listed below:

- ESD service kit - to prevent static discharge damage when working inside a PC.

- Phillips (or cross-) head screwdriver - for use with most screws used in PC equipment. Different sized heads may be required, especially when working with laptops.

- Other screwdrivers - flat-head, TORX (star-shaped), or hex drivers may be required for some systems.

- Tweezers/grips - for grabbing items such as screws or jumpers that have been dropped and are difficult to pick up.

- Extension magnet - magnet on a telescopic arm that can be used to pick up small metal objects.

- Flashlight and/or magnifying glass - useful for inspecting motherboard and device labels.

Page 330   IT Career FastTrack with CompTIA A+ Certification   © 2010 gtslearning

Module 4 Installation, Troubleshooting, and Maintenance   *Preventative Maintenance*

- Containers - for small objects such as screws and jumpers. Anti-static packaging and containers are required to store static-sensitive components, such as memory modules.

- Key puller - for removing keys from a keyboard for cleaning.

- Multimeter - for testing power output (see unit 4.5 for details).

- Cleaning materials - PC vacuum, compressed air blaster, natural bristle brushes, and approved cleaning solutions.

- Network service and diagnostic tools - such as a cable crimper (to attach connectors to cabling) and cable verifiers (see unit 5.5).

In addition to the above, it is also useful to have software tools and utilities easily available. Depending on size, these could be stored on a CD/DVD, USB stick, on a separate partition on the local disk, or the network:

- OS setup disc with service packs and patches.

- Up-to-date vendor drivers for hardware devices.

- Boot disk / Recovery Console - for booting with the minimal configuration.

- Diagnostic software.

- Online documentation and service information.

Scheduling Preventative Maintenance

Preventative maintenance is about forestalling the conditions that can cause problems with computer operation. This includes making sure that environmental conditions are suitable for PC use and maintaining the software environment. To be effective, preventative maintenance must take place according to a schedule, someone must be assigned to do the work, and completion of the work must be recorded in some sort of log.

The typical tasks involved are as follows:

- Inspection - check that equipment is installed and maintained satisfactorily:

    □ Look for dust or dirt in ventilation slots or on keyboards or the display screen.

    □ Check that equipment and cabling is installed safely (double-check that power points and strips are not overloaded) and that food or drink is not being used nearby.

© 2010 gtslearning   IT Career FastTrack with CompTIA A+ Certification   Page 331

| Unit 4.1 | Module 4 Installation, Troubleshooting, and Maintenance |

- ☐ Listen for unusual sounds (fans not working or making unusual noise; disk drives making unusual "grinding" or clicking noise).

- Cleaning - establish a schedule for basic cleaning of computer and printer equipment, using the proper tools:

    - ☐ Use an air blaster to remove dust and debris from a keyboard.

    - ☐ Use approved products to clean surfaces, such as casing and the display screen.

    - ☐ Use a computer vacuum to remove dust from ventilation slots.

The above tasks should be performed quite regularly (every month for instance[144]). It may also be necessary to clean dust from within the computer case, but this would be done far less frequently (annually or bi-annually for instance).

- Software - establish a procedure for identifying, testing, and installing software updates, driver updates, and firmware updates. This should be done regularly (bi-weekly or monthly) or using an alerting service. Other software tasks include running disk optimization tools and managing startup items (see unit 2.6 for more information on these).

Ensuring the Proper Environment

The environment in which computer equipment is installed, used, and stored is important for maintaining the equipment in working condition and maximizing its usable life. It is also vital to comply with relevant national or local health and safety or workplace legislation

Power

Computers need a stable power supply to operate. Power problems can occur through faults in the mains supply, faulty components or wiring, and in extreme weather conditions, such as a lightning storm.

---

[144] The frequency depends on the environment. If a workstation is used by one person and the surrounding area is kept clean, maintenance may only be required every 2-3 months.

APC Smart-UPS for workstations and entry-level servers

If power is removed, even very briefly, the computer will crash. An **Uninterruptible Power Supply (UPS)** protects computers against this. UPS are more commonly used to protect server systems, but desktop models are available.

Another problem is *too much* power (a spike or surge). Protection can be provided by a surge suppressor, though these are never completely reliable. UPS typically have line conditioners built in, which provide for a higher level of reliability.

Static electricity

Static charges can build up on non-conductive surfaces, such as carpeting, clothing, or skin. If the surface is brought into proximity with a conductive surface, the charge will drain into the conductor (flash over). Components such as processors and memory chips are extremely sensitive to static discharge and can be damaged very easily.

Computer casing should prevent static damage during normal use, but care needs to be taken when handling components during maintenance, upgrades, or troubleshooting.

Heat

Excessive heat can make a computer unreliable. Computers generate plenty of heat just by running. Direct sunlight or proximity to a radiator can cause heat to build up too easily. It is vital to ensure there is space for air to flow around the case, especially around the ventilation holes.

| Unit 4.1 | Module 4 Installation, Troubleshooting, and Maintenance |

Dust

Dust is drawn into the computer via ventilation holes and clogs up keys and mice. Dust and smears can also make the display hard to read. Excessive dust can cause shorts and interferes with heat dissipation. Dust can be controlled by cleaning, but also ensure that the surrounding environment is kept clean.

Humidity

High humidity can cause condensation to form; low humidity promotes static charges. The ideal level is around 50%.

Condensation can also form as a result of sudden warming. When installing new equipment that has just been delivered, it is important to leave it in its packaging for a few hours (depending on the outside temperature) to allow it to adjust to room temperature gradually.

Light

As mentioned above, computer components should not be left in direct sunlight. Reflected light can also make displays hard to read. This can be controlled by careful placement of equipment, adjusting the angle of the display, or using non-reflective displays or screen overlays.

User

Health and safety legislation requires that office equipment be installed and used in a way that reduces the risk of long term injury. The user should be provided with adjustable display and seat positions. Equipment and cabling should be installed so that it does not present trip or topple hazards.

Page 334   IT Career FastTrack with CompTIA A+ Certification   © 2010 gtslearning

Performing Preventative Maintenance

Preventative maintenance should be performed carefully and methodically and with the proper tools and equipment, to avoid causing damage to the components you are trying to maintain! In particular, the use of household cleaning products should be avoided. These can damage the materials used in component and case manufacture or leave residues. Specialist computer non-scratch, low residue, cleaning products are available from many vendors.

- PC vacuum - vacuum cleaners that can be used safely around computer components as they do not generate static charges.

- Toner vacuum - cleaner for use with laser printers. These vacuums feature fine filters and bags that can hold the microscopic toner particles.

Mr PC Clean fine particle, ESD safe vacuum cleaner (mrpcclean.co.uk)

- Air blaster - compressed air for blowing debris from ventilation slots and keyboards.

- Natural bristle brush - for sweeping away dust without scratching.

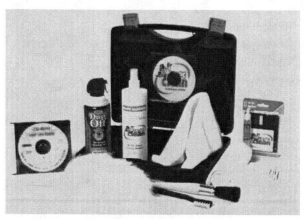

Mr PC Clean complete computer cleaning kit

- Pads, cloths, and swabs - non-abrasive, lint-free cleaning products that will not leave fibers behind.

- Alcohol-based wipes - for cleaning smears or stubborn dirt; alcohol (typically isopropyl solution) evaporates very quickly, unlike water. Special wipes are also available for picking up spilled toner.

| Unit 4.1 | Module 4 Installation, Troubleshooting, and Maintenance |

- LCD cleaner - solutions formulated for cleaning LCDs without damaging the plastic surface or anti-static coating.

- Disk cleaning kits - special solutions and media for cleaning the heads on a floppy drive or the lens on an optical drives.

Cleaning external components

The general procedure for cleaning the external components of a desktop computer is as follows:

1. Make sure that your hands are clean and dry and you have all the necessary tools and cleaning products close by.

2. Disconnect the computer and display screen from the mains power supply. Disconnect peripheral devices.

3. Use a PC vacuum or air blaster to remove dust from the ventilation slots on the PC and monitor.

4. Wipe the casing of the PC and monitor using a damp, non-abrasive cloth. Use a mild detergent for stubborn deposits.

5. Use an appropriate cleaning solution or wipes to clean the monitor or LCD screen[145]. Wipe horizontally, then vertically (*not* in a circular motion), cleaning into the corners.

Note

Always apply solution to the cloth or pad not directly to the surface. Do not use sprays around ventilation slots.

6. To clean the keyboard, first shake it over a piece of paper to dislodge any debris. Use a PC vacuum with a suitable attachment or an air blaster to dislodge dust and dirt from between the keys. Wipe the surface with a soft damp cloth and (if necessary) mild detergent or alcohol-based cleaning solution.

Tip

If a keyboard requires more substantial cleaning, you can remove the keys using a key puller.

---

[145] A monitor can usually be cleaned using glass cleaner, but check the manufacturer's recommendations. LCDs can be cleaned using approved products or isopropyl solution if using a dry cloth does not work. Make sure that you use a non-abrasive cloth (not a paper towel) to prevent scratches.

7. To clean a trackball, open the clip on the underside of the mouse and let the ball fall into your hand. Clean it using a soft cloth if necessary. Inspect the rollers and use a swab to clean any dirt off (you may need to loosen debris using a toothpick or tweezers but take care not to damage the rollers).

Cleaning the trackball compartment

8. Clean a touchpad or touch screen as you would an LCD screen.

9. Reconnect peripheral devices and the mains power supply. Verify that the computer boots normally. Update the maintenance schedule or log to show that cleaning has been completed.

Cleaning inside the case

When working inside the computer case, make sure to take anti-static precautions and to disconnect the computer from mains power.

Use a soft bristle brush or compressed air to remove dust from components, fans, and heatsinks. Remove excess dust from the chassis using a PC vacuum with a suitable attachment hose.

If a card edge or slot is visibly dirty, use a lint-free swab and PC cleaning solution to clean it.

Cleaning drives and media

When cleaning the heads of magnetic media devices (for example, floppy disk drives and tape drives) or the lens of an optical drive, you should use a purpose-designed cleaning product, such as a cleaning disk or cartridge. If this type of cleaning product is not available, use a lint-free cloth or approved cleaning pad or swab.

Clean optical discs using a lint-free cloth, wiping out from the center of the disc. Always store discs in their case, and avoid exposing them to extremes of temperature and bending.

Unit 4.1   Module 4 Installation, Troubleshooting, and Maintenance

Recovering from spills

If liquid is spilled over an electrical device, it is likely that the device will short circuit. A short circuit is likely to cause an increased amount of current to flow, which can damage components or cause a fire. Obviously, electrical equipment should not be used in damp or wet areas unless it is designed for that purpose (take care with laptops and portable devices for instance). A spill hazard is created by placing any unsealed liquid container (such as a cup of coffee) near electrical equipment. Most users will ignore injunctions not to bring drinks to their desks, so spills on keyboards, mice, and portable devices are relatively frequent.

If there is a spill, disconnect the power supply or unplug the device if this can be done safely. In the case of a laptop or portable computer, remove the battery and any peripherals or plug-in devices. Drain as much excess liquid as you can from the device then allow it to dry for 24 hours[146]. Once dry, if not irreparably damaged, it will probably require thorough cleaning before it can be used again.

Laptop preventative maintenance

Most of the preventative maintenance procedures that apply to desktops also apply to laptops. Use approved solutions and materials for cleaning, especially for the screen, to reduce the risk of scratching or damaging surfaces. Laptops are not subject to internal cleaning because the chassis is relatively inaccessible but do keep the vents clear using compressed air or a PC vacuum.

Care should be taken to use a laptop in a suitable environment. Actually using a laptop as a "laptop" can lead to overheating, as the exhaust vents can be blocked by clothing. The best environment is a flat surface with plenty of airflow around the chassis. Laptops are also obviously susceptible to damage from spills, dust, and debris.

Laptops are relatively fragile (especially the screen, which is easy to scratch or crack). Consequently, laptops should be transported in specially designed bags, which have padding and straps to protect against damage.

---

[146] You can accelerate drying times using a hairdryer set to cool. Do not connect the device to a power source unless you are sure that it is completely dry.

Page 338   IT Career FastTrack with CompTIA A+ Certification   © 2010 gtslearning

Module 4 Installation, Troubleshooting, and Maintenance | Preventative Maintenance

The same warning applies to transportation and shipping; it is a good idea to retain the original packing materials if possible, so that the laptop can be securely packed. Remove any peripherals, media bays, adapter cards, and batteries to avoid accidental damage.

Windows Preventative Maintenance Schedule

To keep Windows working well, you should perform the following maintenance activities:

- Make data backups (typically daily or weekly, depending on how the computer is used[147]).

- Review event logs for alerts and warnings (weekly).

- Perform a full anti-virus scan (weekly). Note that anti-virus software should also be configured to provide *on-access* file and email message and attachment scanning. Also verify that security software such as anti-virus and firewalls are correctly configured and have not been disabled. See unit 5.7 for more details.

- Update security software (anti-virus or anti-spyware) with latest definitions (weekly).

- Update Windows with latest security and critical patches (weekly).

- Perform disk maintenance (monthly). This should include defragmenting the volume, cleaning up temporary files, and checking for errors. See unit 2.6 for more details.

- Check for operating system service packs and non-critical updates and application software and driver updates (either monthly or using an alerting service).

- Make system configuration backups (before installing applications or devices or monthly).

Windows comes with a number of tools to help you keep the system up-to-date.

---

[147] On a network, it is best practice to store data on a server, so that it can be backed up by the network backup system.

© 2010 gtslearning   IT Career FastTrack with CompTIA A+ Certification   Page 339

Windows Update

Windows Update is a website (update.microsoft.com) hosting maintenance updates for different versions of Microsoft Windows and Internet Explorer[148]. An ActiveX control installed on the computer enables it to browse the site and select updates for download and installation, using the **Background Intelligent Transfer Services (BITS)** protocol[149].

Windows Update hosts critical updates and security patches (code to fix security vulnerabilities in Windows and its associated software) plus optional software and hardware updates to add or change features or drivers[150].

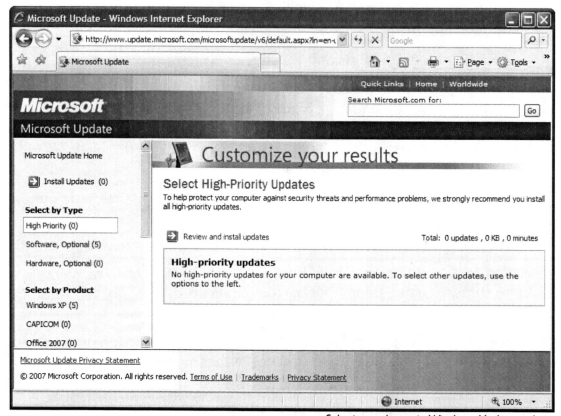

Selecting updates via Windows Update website

---

[148] There is also a complementary program, called Microsoft Update, which can be used to keep Microsoft Office software patched at the same time. On a corporate network, updates can also be served using a **Windows Software Update Services (WSUS)** server. This allows the network administrator to approve updates for selected computer groups.

[149] Windows Update is also being used by Microsoft as a privacy-deterrence tool. It requires the installation of **Windows Genuine Advantage**, which checks that a valid license has been installed before authorizing any updates.

[150] Hotfixes are released to fix problems being experienced in specific circumstances. They are not available through Windows Update but can be requested via the Microsoft Knowledge Base article describing the problem.

The **WindowsUpdate.txt** log (stored in the **%SystemRoot%** folder) records update activity and can be used to troubleshoot failed updates. %SystemRoot% also contains **KB??????.txt** log files listing which updates have been installed and hidden uninstall folders for the updates (**$NtUninstallKB??????$**). If these folders are deleted, the updates cannot be uninstalled.

During Setup, Windows XP/Vista can be configured to check for system updates (via the internet) and download them as needed. You might want to turn this feature off in a corporate environment, because most systems administrators want to know what changes are being made to the computers they support and schedule time to test and deploy these updates.

The **Automatic Updates** applet (opened from **Control Panel** or on a tab in the **System Properties** dialog box[151]) allows you to configure when updates are scheduled and what level of user interaction is required.

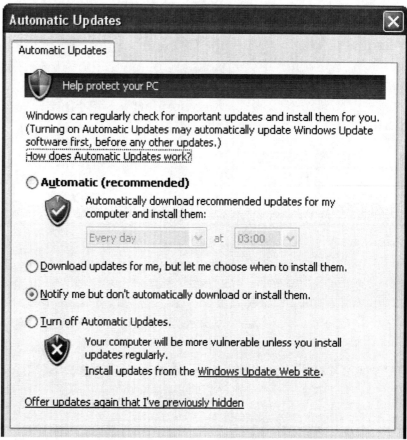

Automatic Updates configuration

---

[151] Under Windows 2000, Automatic Updates is only available from Control Panel (not from System Properties).

| Unit 4.1 | Module 4 Installation, Troubleshooting, and Maintenance |

Key features of service packs

A **Service Pack (SP)** is a collection of previous updates and hotfixes but may also contain new features and functionality. For this reason, service packs require you to follow the upgrade process to ensure that software and (to a lesser extent) hardware will be compatible. You should also make a backup before applying a service pack.

Service packs can be downloaded from Microsoft's website (Windows XP SP2 and Vista service packs are available through Windows Update) or shipped on disc. The later manufacturing releases of the setup media tend to include the latest service pack. You can also create customized setup media to include service packs and patches in new installations (search for "slipstreaming windows setup" on the web for details).

Microsoft service packs for Windows 2000 and Windows XP are cumulative, so there is no requirement to install them in sequence; you can simply apply the latest pack.

Windows 2000 is currently on SP4 with an update rollup of subsequent patches. No more service packs are planned for Windows 2000, though fixes for critical issues will continue to be released. SP1 added support for stronger encryption (128-bit); SP3 added support for 48-bit disk addressing, enabling partition sizes of over 137 GB.

Windows XP is currently on SP3. SP2 is a highly significant release, with security-related interface updates to Control Panel and the web browser Internet Explorer. Versions of Windows XP patched only to SP1 are no longer supported by Microsoft.

Windows Vista is on SP2 at the time of writing. Both service packs focus mostly on fixing reliability and performance issues (especially file copy performance) and solving specific hardware and application compatibility problems. Some notable changes in SP1 include being able to select which drive Defragmenter runs on, improvements to BitLocker, support for UEFI, and improvements to the System Recovery tool.

Note that installing a service pack often requires a large amount of free disk space.

Module 4 Installation, Troubleshooting, and Maintenance   *Preventative Maintenance*

Application updates

Software applications may also need updating with the latest patches. Applications can contain security vulnerabilities in the same way as the OS; in fact applications are targeted more aggressively than Windows itself as attackers recognize that they are less likely to be patched than the OS.

It is particularly important to update anti-virus software with the latest virus definitions or the software will not be able to do its job in identifying virus infections.

Driver updates

Windows ships with a number of core and third-party hardware drivers. Updates for these devices can be obtained via Windows Update, though they will be listed as optional updates and will not install automatically.

Most of the time, third-party drivers should be obtained from the vendor's website. To update, you download the driver and install them using the supplied setup program (or extract them manually and save them to the hard disk). You can then use the device's property dialog in Device Manager to update the driver. You can either scan for the update automatically or point the tool to the updated version you saved to the hard disk.

BIOS updates

System vendors and motherboard manufacturers may regularly update their BIOS in order to fix bugs, solve incompatibilities with operating systems or to add new features. You should visit the relevant support website regularly to check if and when upgrades are available. As upgrading the firmware is relatively risky (a failed motherboard update can leave the computer unbootable for instance), it is only worth doing if the update fixes a specific problem that you are encountering or if it is regarded as a **critical** update.

> **Note**
>
> You should check with the system (PC) vendor before the BIOS manufacturer. The PC vendor may use a modified version of the firmware to the retail one.

© 2010 gtslearning   IT Career FastTrack with CompTIA A+ Certification   Page 343

Before you start, record any custom CMOS settings (see unit 4.5), as updating the BIOS may reset the system configuration to the default. You will need to change the CMOS settings back after the update.

To perform the upgrade, download the upgrade program from the website. Either run the program or copy it to a floppy boot disk, then boot the computer using the floppy (follow the installation instructions carefully). If there is an option to backup the existing firmware configuration, use it. As a security feature, a jumper on the motherboard may have to be adjusted in order to allow BIOS upgrades to take place.

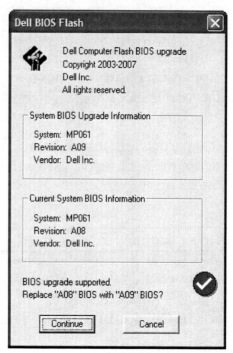

Dell BIOS Flash program

If a firmware update goes wrong (for example if there is a power cut during the flashing process), you may be able to re-install the old firmware from a backup. However, it is equally likely that the component will be unusable. If this is the case, you will have to contact the manufacturer for help or buy a new one.

> **Tip**
> In the case of failed motherboard BIOS updates, the motherboard may feature a recovery mode jumper. Set this then re-boot using the BIOS upgrade disk. There will be no video but you should hear the POST beep confirmation then hear disk activity. Wait for the disk activity to end, switch off the system, remove the disk, reset the flash recovery jumper, and reboot.

The CMOS reset jumper is to the left of the battery

As well as the PC BIOS, you may need to update the firmware on other devices, such as drive units, printers, and networking equipment. Devices directly attached to the PC (via USB or Firewire) can normally be updated from Windows using a setup utility provided by the vendor. A network device would typically be updated using its management software or web configuration interface.

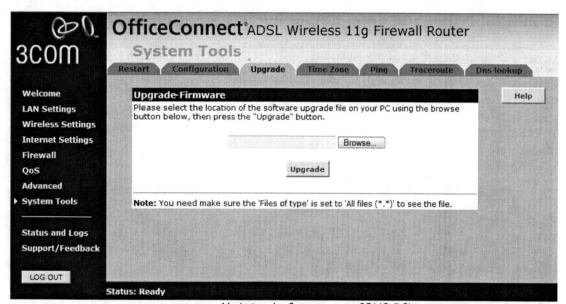

Updating the firmware on a SOHO DSL router using its web interface

Configuring Backup Procedures

One of the most important operations in IT is the creation of a **secure backup** of data files. Typically, network backups take place using a tape system, which has the advantages of high capacity, relatively low cost, and portability. For this type of backup, advanced backup software capable of backing up online databases and remote systems is required.

When a computer is connected to a network, it is bad practice for a user to store data locally (on the client PC's hard drive). Network home folders and the use of scripts to copy data can help users to transfer data to a file server, where it can be backed up safely.

Personal backups are necessary for home users or on workgroups, where no central file server is available. In this scenario, the backup software built into Windows 2000/XP (**NTBACKUP**) is serviceable.

Unit 4.1   Module 4 Installation, Troubleshooting, and Maintenance

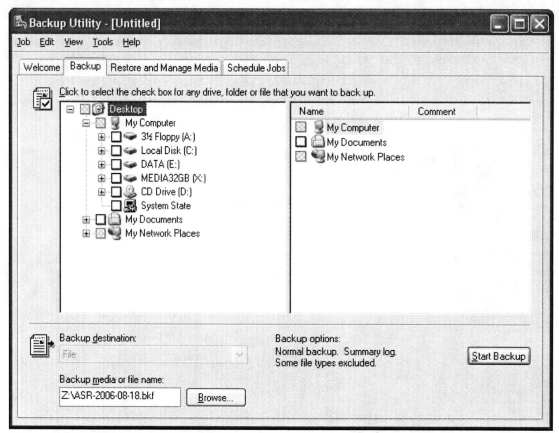

Performing a backup using NTBACKUP

Windows Vista supplies a simplified wizard driven tool with options to back up the whole system (an image) or just user data to an appropriate device (hard disk or recordable DVD)[152].

A network backup requires high capacity media (multiple gigabytes). This means the use of tape-based systems, such as DAT or DLT. For a workgroup or workstation, tape-based media might be too expensive. Alternatives include removable hard disks or even flash memory/USB drives[153].

---

[152] Image backup (Windows Complete PC Backup) is only available in the Business, Enterprise, and Ultimate editions.

[153] Another option is to use an online service provider to backup data over the internet.

Module 4 Installation, Troubleshooting, and Maintenance   Preventative Maintenance

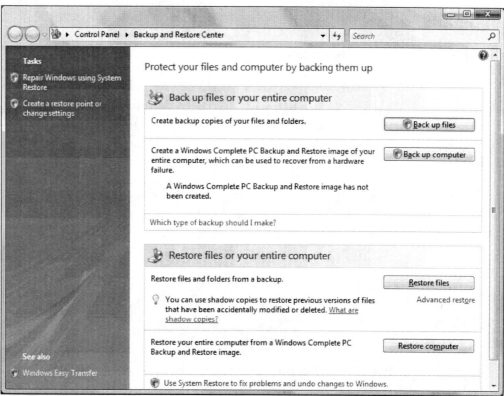

Windows Vista Backup and Restore Center

Backup types

A backup is usually performed using one of three main types: **full (normal)**, **incremental**, or **differential**[154].

A **full** backup includes all selected files and directories while **incremental** and **differential** backups check the status of the **archive attribute** before including a file.

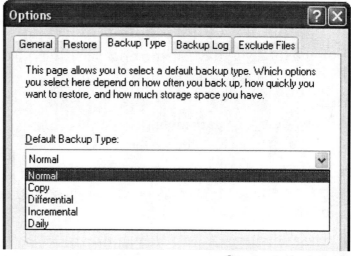

Choosing the backup type

---

[154] There is also the option to do **copy** backups. These are made outside the tape rotation system (ad hoc) and do not affect the archive attribute.

© 2010 gtslearning   IT Career FastTrack with CompTIA A+ Certification   Page 347

Unit 4.1   Module 4 Installation, Troubleshooting, and Maintenance

The archive attribute is *set* whenever a file is modified. This allows backup software to determine which files have been changed since the previous backup and therefore need to be copied.

The criteria for determining which method to use is based on the time it takes to *restore* versus the time it takes to *back up*. Assuming a backup is performed every working day, an incremental backup only includes files changed during that day, while a differential backup includes all files changed since the last full backup.

Incremental backups save backup time but can be more time-consuming when the system must be restored. The system must be restored from the last full backup set and then from each incremental backup that has subsequently occurred. A differential backup system only involves two tape sets when restore is required.

The following table summarizes the three different backup types:

Type	Data Selection	Backup / Restore Time	Archive Attribute
Full	All selected data regardless of when it has previously been backed up	High / low (one tape set)	Cleared
Incremental	New files and files modified since the last backup	Low / high (multiple tape sets)	Cleared
Differential	All data modified since the last full backup	Moderate / moderate (no more than 2 sets)	Not Cleared

Doing a full everyday backup on a large network takes a long time. A typical strategy for a network would be a *full weekly backup* followed by an *incremental* or *differential* backup at the *end of each day*.

- The advantage of using a full daily backup is that one tape set only is required to restore the system.

- The advantage of an incremental backup is that it takes less time to back up but several tape sets may need to be restored before the system is operational.

- The advantage of a differential backup is the balance of time for both restoring and backing up.

On a single PC, media rotation is less likely to be an issue and most backups can be performed as full backups.

Page 348   IT Career FastTrack with CompTIA A+ Certification   © 2010 gtslearning

Module 4 Installation, Troubleshooting, and Maintenance	Preventative Maintenance

Note

Do not combine differential and incremental backups. Use full backups interspersed with differential backups or full backups interspersed with incremental backups.

Media (tape) rotation

Once a suitable backup method has been determined, a **tape rotation** method must be established to minimize the number of tapes required for maintaining an adequate history of the backup points.

A commonly used tape rotation method is known as **Grandfather-Father-Son**. This method uses **three sets** of media in which **monthly**, **weekly**, and **daily** tapes correspond to the generations.

Before starting the system, a **full backup** of all media should be made. The system then proceeds as follows:

1. Daily backups, which may be incremental *or* differential, use the **son** tapes. These are *reused* each week and remain the youngest in rotation.

2. Weekly full backups are written to the **father** tapes. A father tape set is required for each week of the month except the last.

3. The **final weekly** backup is written to the monthly grandfather tape set.

Assuming a network is operational five days per week, the following tape sets are required:

Type	Frequency	Number of Sets
Son	Daily	4 sets
Father	Weekly	4 sets (plus one to be held off site)[155]
Grandfather	Monthly	12 sets

---

[155] Securely stored offsite media is essential to protect against data loss from disasters, such as theft, fire, flood, earthquakes, terrorism, and so on. Tapes held onsite should also be stored securely (normally in a safe if not using an AutoLoader or tape library).

Unit 4.1 | Module 4 Installation, Troubleshooting, and Maintenance

NTBACKUP commands

You can use the **NTBACKUP** utility at a command line (or more likely, as part of a script) to back up files but *not* to restore them. The basic command is:

NTBACKUP backup "@*SelectionFile*.bks" /j "*JobName*"
/f "*DestinationFile*.bkf"

This would back up files specified in *SelectionFile*.bks to the file path specified in *DestinationFile*.bkf using the supplied *JobName*.

It is also possible to back up to removable media using the **/p** (media pool) and **/t** (tape) switches. Media and tapes can be defined using the **Removable Storage** snap-in under **Computer Management**.

Some of the other main parameters and switches are as follows:

Switch	Use
/systemstate	Back up system state data (for ERD or ASR).
/d	Label the backup set.
/a	Append the data to the tape (as opposed to overwriting existing sets).
/v:yes	Verify data (or use /v:no to skip).
/m	Specify the backup type (normal, copy, differential, incremental, or daily).

Vista does not ship with the **NTBACKUP** program. Instead, the **WBADMIN** utility can be used at the command-line to script backup jobs

Maintaining tape drives

When installing or upgrading a tape drive, it is important to use the manufacturer's latest drivers, to ensure that the full set of features is supported.

Tape drives need periodic cleaning. Most drives feature built-in head cleaners.

Most media comes pre-formatted and should only be erased using the supplied software. From time-to-time, the tape may need re-tensioning to ensure reliability; again this can be done via the supplied software.

Page 350 | IT Career FastTrack with CompTIA A+ Certification | © 2010 gtslearning

| Module 4 Installation, Troubleshooting, and Maintenance | *Preventative Maintenance* |

Restoring data and verifying backups

It is *critical* to test that backup operations work properly. There can be no worse feeling in IT support than turning to the backup media you have been happily writing to and rotating for the last 8 months only to discover that a critical data folder has never been included in the job! The following represent some of the main backup security issues:

- **Compatibility** - a tape backup is useless without a drive capable of reading the media. Most drives can read from tape formats from the previous generation (or more). If a legacy drive fails and there is no replacement available, there is a very real risk to the security of the organization's data. These sort of issues need to be dealt with by data migration plans.

- **Error detection** - problems with the tape or configuration can cause backup jobs to fail. Depending on the error, the whole job may be cancelled or some data may not get backed up. Backup software usually has the facility to verify a backup (obviously this makes the backup operation longer though) and report errors to the log.

- **Configuration** - when setting up a new job (and periodically thereafter), it is wise to check the media catalog to ensure that all the expected data has been backed up.

- **Test restore** - another option is to test that a restore operation can be performed successfully. This is important when using new backup software, to test old tapes, to check a new job, and to carry out random spot checks. When you do a test restore, you *redirect* the data to a different folder, to avoid overwriting live data.

As well as completing test restores, you should also review the application event logs to confirm that the backup ran successfully. Backups can sometimes run into problems with permissions. The best option is to configure a user as a member of the **Backup Operators** group and to schedule the backup to run using this user's account. Another point to remember is the physical security of the backup media. The disk or tape should be removed as soon as possible after the backup is complete and stored in a secure location, ideally at a different site.

Tip

Of course, you need to balance backup security with the complexity and time required to complete restore operations. If all the backup media is stored offsite, restore operations will be very difficult. Plan a schedule for backups and use a mixture of media and storage locations.

| © 2010 gtslearning | IT Career FastTrack with CompTIA A+ Certification | Page 351 |

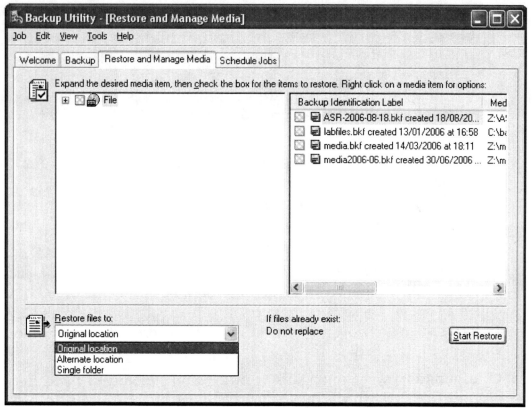

Redirecting file output for a restore operation

Summary

Learn the appropriate tools to use for PC maintenance and repair. Establish a clean and hazard free environment when installing a computer system. Apply a preventative maintenance cycle to keep the system clean and check its functionality regularly. When cleaning computer components, work carefully and use the appropriate tools and cleaning products.

Software maintenance tasks revolve around disk management and checking for updates to system files, drivers, malware detection, and applications. Windows Update provides an automated system for doing this for Windows systems.

Make sure you know the procedures for making backups and the differences between backup types.

Module 4 Installation, Troubleshooting, and Maintenance | *Installing and Configuring Components*

Unit 4.2 Installing and Configuring Components

CompTIA A+ Essentials Objectives

☐ **701.1.2 Explain motherboard components, types and features**
Contrast RAID (levels 0, 1, 5)

CompTIA A+ Practical Application Objectives

☐ **702.1.1 Given a scenario, install, configure, and maintain personal computer components**
Storage devices (HDD [SATA, PATA, Solid state], FDD, Optical drives [CD / DVD / RW / Blu-ray], Removable, External) • Motherboards (Socket types, Expansion slots, Memory slots, Front panel connectors, I/O ports [Sound, video, USB 1.1, USB 2.0, serial, IEEE 1394 / Firewire, parallel, NIC, modem, PS/2]) • Power supplies (Wattages and capacity, Connector types and quantity, Output voltage) • Processors (Socket types, Speed, Number of cores, Power consumption, Cache, Front side bus, 32-bit vs. 64-bit) • Memory • Adapter cards (Graphics cards - memory, Sound cards, Storage controllers [RAID cards - levels 0,1,5, eSATA cards], I/O cards [Firewire, USB, Parallel, Serial), Wired and wireless network cards, Capture cards [TV, video], Media reader]) • Cooling systems (Heat sinks, Thermal compound, CPU fans, Case fans)

General Installation and Upgrade Advice

Installing basic components is not difficult and does not require much equipment. For most jobs, a Phillips (cross-head) screwdriver and anti-static wrist strap should suffice (see unit 4.1 for more information about PC maintenance tools and anti-static procedures).

The most important step is to obtain up-to-date documentation on the system you are upgrading. PC chassis designs and cases are all different and you can make installation jobs go more smoothly by referring to the manufacturer's service handbook before you start (if you do not have a printed copy, these manuals can usually be downloaded from the PC vendor's website).

The PC documentation should also help you to identify and select suitable components to use for an upgrade. If the IT environment is well maintained, there should also be a service and configuration log for each system, which will also assist you in making upgrade decisions.

© 2010 gtslearning | IT Career FastTrack with CompTIA A+ Certification | Page 353

Unit 4.2 Module 4 Installation, Troubleshooting, and Maintenance

Accessing the chassis

1. Unplug any peripherals (pull connectors out by grasping the connector not the cable) and disconnect the power supply from the mains.

Tip
After disconnecting a power cable, hold down the power button on the PC for a few seconds to ensure that its circuits are completely de-energized.

2. Set up a work area so that the PC is at a comfortable height and that you have all the tools, components, and reference material required for the job within reach. Take anti-static precautions to minimize the chance of damaging static sensitive components (see unit 4.1).

Tip
A notepad and pen may be useful for making diagrams and notes. A digicam is also useful for recording the layout of components.

3. For a tower case, remove the main panel (the one opposite the I/O ports) by undoing the screws and sliding it out. If necessary, remove the front bezel by releasing the retaining clips. Finally (if necessary), remove the secondary panel (the one behind the motherboard) by unscrewing it and sliding out.

Installing and Upgrading Storage Devices

Storage devices include hard drives, optical drives, floppy drives, and flash memory readers.

The computer's storage system has two attributes: performance and capacity.

Performance

Run a PATA hard disk on a different IDE channel to the CD-ROM. Only one command at a time can be processed on an IDE channel. If two devices are using the same channel at the same time, one may have to wait while the other completes its command. CD-ROMs use the slower ATAPI protocol, which takes longer to complete commands than hard disk protocols.

Module 4 Installation, Troubleshooting, and Maintenance | *Installing and Configuring Components*

The following table summarizes the main storage device expansion technologies:

Technology	Date Rate	Cabling	Connector	Features
PATA	33 MBps - 133 MBps	40cm	40-pin (80-wire cable for UDMA-33 and above)	Each controller supports two devices
SATA	150 MBps / 300 MBps	1m	7-pin	Hot swapping; one device / controller
SCSI	Up to 320 MBps	12m (for LVD)	Usually 68-pin	Up to 16 devices (wide bus)

Note that external drives can also use USB, Firewire, SCSI, or external SATA (eSATA) connections.

If you already have a high-performing SATA or SCSI interface, you may still be able to improve performance by upgrading the disks themselves (from 5,400 rpm to 10,000 rpm models for instance).

Windows uses part of the disk to supplement system memory (the pagefile). If there is not enough room on the disk for the pagefile, performance will be significantly reduced. A Windows computer requires space for a pagefile on the hard disk of at least 1.5 times System Memory. Virtual memory is not nearly as fast as system memory however. If there is constant disk activity when using an application, this is a sign that virtual memory is being overused. Consider installing extra RAM.

Another option if you are running Windows Vista is to upgrade to a **hybrid** hard drive or fully **Solid State Drive (SSD)**. A hybrid drive has a large (multi-gigabyte) flash memory cache. Windows can cache startup files here to greatly improve loading times (**ReadyDrive**). It can also cache applications and data on any type of flash memory device (provided it is large and quick enough) to further improve performance (**ReadyBoost**).

Tip

The case for swapping HDDs with SSDs is not made; SSDs are a developing technology and true performance benefits will only be realized as products mature.

© 2010 gtslearning | IT Career FastTrack with CompTIA A+ Certification | Page 355

Unit 4.2   Module 4 Installation, Troubleshooting, and Maintenance

Run hard disk utilities, such as surface scans and defragmentation, regularly to optimize file system performance (fragmentation is when the data for a single file gets split between non-consecutive clusters, increasing the time required for read and write operations).

If hard disk performance is a real problem, you could consider a RAID (Redundant Array of Independent Disks) solution. RAID can improve performance and/or reliability. This is generally implemented on server systems rather than workstations.

Capacity

At a minimum, internal hard disk storage must have sufficient capacity for the OS and applications software. Beyond this, capacity requirements are determined by what the user needs to store. Capacity can be extended very simply by installing external devices and adding a second (or third) internal drive is usually straightforward too.

Note

When adding or removing storage devices (or performing any type of work inside the PC case), make sure that you take a backup of any data stored on local drives.

Installing a PATA hard drive

PATA supports two devices per **channel** and up to two channels. One device on each channel can be configured as **master** and the other as **slave**. The master device has priority over the slave device and the primary channel has priority over the secondary channel.

You can add optical and tape units via PATA, so some thought needs to be given to configuration in order to achieve the best performance.

The main hard disk (the boot disk) should always be configured as the *primary master*. An optical drive should then generally be added as the *secondary* master. A second hard disk should be added as the *primary slave*.

1. Locate a spare 3.5" drive bay or remove an existing unit by unplugging the cables from the back then unscrewing the drive from the chassis.

Page 356   IT Career FastTrack with CompTIA A+ Certification   © 2010 gtslearning

Module 4 Installation, Troubleshooting, and Maintenance Installing and Configuring Components

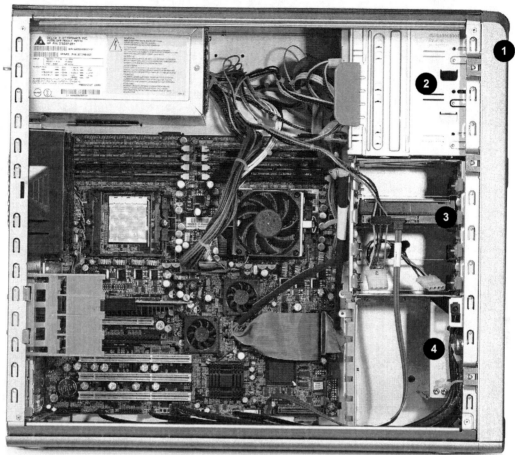

HP Compaq with main panel removed showing 1) Bezel; 2) 5.25" drive bays; 3) 3.5" drive bays; 4) Floppy drive bay

Some drives screw directly onto the chassis; others are screwed onto **rails** so that the drive can be slid in and out (this also usually means that you do not have to remove the secondary panel) or screwed into a removable **cage**. Hard drives can be oriented horizontally or vertically.

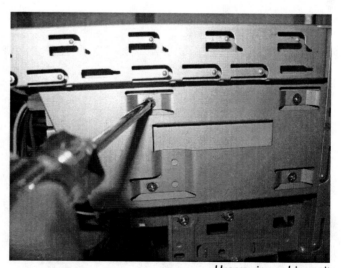

Unscrewing a drive unit

2. Set the jumpers on the drive to indicate whether it is master, slave, or cable select. A jumper is set by sliding the clip over two of the available pins (you can use fingers or needle nose pliers to position the clip). The jumper diagram is usually printed on the drive; otherwise, consult the drive vendor's documentation.

Hard drive with 1) Molex power connector; 2) Configuration jumper; 3) PATA connector

3. Screw the drive into the bay. Do not overtighten the screws.

4. Connect the PATA cable to the drive, taking care that pin 1 on the cable and connector are oriented correctly (most connectors have a notch to help orient the cable). If using a cable select cable, make sure you attach the correct connector:

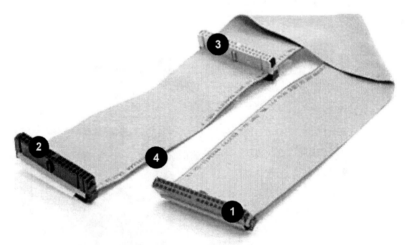

Cable Select PATA cable with 1) Motherboard (blue); 2) Master (black); and 3) Slave (grey) connectors plus 4) Red stripe indicating pin 1

5. Connect the other end of the PATA cable to the appropriate IDE channel connector on the motherboard.

IDE connectors on the motherboard - note the labels printed to the right of the connectors

6. Connect a spare Molex connector from the power supply to the 4-pin port on the drive. The connectors are keyed so that you cannot insert them the wrong way around.

7. Check that the cables are all secure then refit the parts of the case.

Tip

Make sure that cables do not restrict air flow around the case or obstruct the operation of fans, especially around the CPU, memory, and graphics adapter. Use cable ties to keep cabling neat and tidy.

Installing a SATA hard drive

SATA configuration is much simpler than PATA/IDE. Each drive is connected to a SATA port on the motherboard or on an SATA host adapter. The connectors are keyed to prevent incorrect insertion. There are no device settings to configure[156]. Generally speaking, you should install the boot drive into the lowest numbered port.

HP SATA drive with 1) SATA power connector; 2) SATA data connector

SATA specifies a new 15-pin power connector. A drive may feature the new connector *and* a Molex connector or just the new one. Also, the computer's power supply may not have SATA power connectors. In these circumstances, you can use a Molex-SATA converter cable.

---

[156] The only thing to check if the drive is not recognized is that the controllers are enabled (check the settings through CMOS).

| Unit 4.2 | Module 4 Installation, Troubleshooting, and Maintenance |

Installing a SCSI hard drive

Depending on the age of the equipment, SCSI configuration can be quite complex. You should refer to the vendor's setup instructions carefully. Try to ensure that configuration and service records for the equipment are kept up-to-date so that you have accurate documentation about the SCSI configuration.

1. Check that the drive is a SCSI type that is compatible with the host adapter.

2. If necessary, set the device ID to a unique number on the chain. On an internal device, the ID is usually configured via jumpers using the settings diagram provided by the vendor; external devices usually have click-wheels. The boot hard drive is usually set to ID 0. You should not use ID 7 as this is normally reserved for the host adapter.

Tip

The host adapter may configure device IDs automatically. This is likely to be the case if the drive uses a SCA connector.

3. Enable or disable termination on the device (the first and last devices in a chain must be terminated).This may be configured via a jumper setting or by physically installing a terminator onto the device.

4. Screw the drive into the bay and connect it to the host adapter using a suitable SCSI cable. Connect to the power supply using a Molex connector.

Installing a Solid State Drive

A **Solid State Drive (SSD)** uses flash memory instead of the glass patter and read/write heads of a normal HDD. A hybrid drive is a normal HDD with a large flash memory cache.

SSDs use the same connectors as HDDs (SATA or SCSI) and are installed in just the same way.

Installing an optical drive or tape drive

Installing an optical (CD, DVD, or Blu-ray) drive or tape drive is fundamentally the same as installing a hard drive, except that you will fit it to a 5.25" drive bay. You may also need to remove a faceplate from the front bezel. Most optical and tape drives need to be oriented horizontally.

Drives can be PATA, SCSI, or SATA. PATA and SCSI configuration on these devices is the same as for hard drives.

Installing a floppy drive

A floppy drive is installed in a 3.5" bay (obviously this needs to be a bay that is user-accessible via the front panel) and can be oriented horizontally or vertically. The floppy drive uses a single 34-wire cable to connect the drive to the motherboard or disk controller card. Each cable has connectors along its length; these connectors are commonly arranged in pairs. Most floppy drive cables twist seven wires before the last drive connector - the twist designates which connector is used for the bootable floppy drive (drive A:). Power is supplied via a mini-Molex (or Berg) connector.

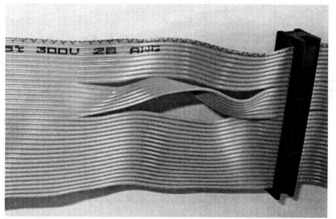

Floppy disk cable

Installing a memory card reader

A memory card reader is usually designed to replace the floppy disk, though some can be fitted to a 5.25" bay.

The reader then needs to be connected to a USB hub. Most motherboards have a 9-pin USB header for making internal connections or the reader may come with an expansion card (as with the HP model shown below). Alternatively, you may be able to run a USB converter cable from the reader to one of the external USB ports.

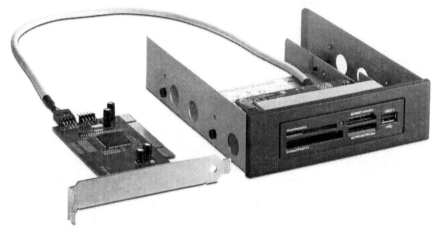

HP 16-in-1 Media Card Reader - note that connectivity is provided through the PCI card and the kit includes a bracket for installation in a 5.25" bay

Installing an external drive

Any of the different types of storage drive can also be supplied as external units. External disks are typically packaged in a **drive enclosure**. The drive enclosure provides USB[157] or Firewire ports, though some models support eSATA and some support network connections (referred to as **Network Attached Storage [NAS]**). The enclosure also provides for an external power supply, if the drive is too large to be powered over USB, and the casing protects the drive from damage.

Drive preparation

Once a hard disk drive has been physically installed, there are two further checks that need to be made before the device can be used.

Firstly, you should check that the device has been recognized by the computer's BIOS. If the drive is not listed in the startup configuration pages, enter CMOS Setup (see unit 4.5) and check that the drive's controller is enabled.

---

[157] Some drives use twin USB connectors to draw more power over the bus. 3.5" drives usually need a mains power supply.

| Module 4 Installation, Troubleshooting, and Maintenance | *Installing and Configuring Components* |

When the drive is recognized in BIOS, you can access it using the operating system to **format** and **partition** it. Partitioning the drive defines one or more discrete storage areas on the same physical disk. This is useful for installing multiple operating systems or for defining system and user data storage areas.

Tip

You may see references to "low-level formatting". This is the division of the disk surface into sectors. This is done at the factory by the manufacturer.

Each partition can be formatted using a different **file system** (under Windows, this means either FAT or NTFS). The choice of file system is driven by software compatibility.

Removable storage may also need formatting or re-formatting. For example, floppy disks come pre-formatted but can be re-formatted using Windows to correct any problems with the file system. Memory cards also come formatted and can be reformatted using the device software (for example, you would reformat a memory card using firmware in the digital camera rather than Windows). Recordable and writable optical discs are formatted during the write process. See unit 2.4 for more information on formatting and configuring hard drives and removable storage using Windows.

Configuring RAID

With **RAID (Redundant Array of Independent Disks)**[158], many disks can act as backups for each other to increase reliability and fault tolerance or they can act together as one very large drive.

The RAID advisory board defines RAID levels. The most common levels are numbered from 0 to 6 where each level corresponds to a specific type of fault tolerance. Only levels 0, 1, and 5 are of much relevance at the desktop however.

RAID Level	Fault Tolerance
Level 0	Striping without parity (**no** fault tolerance)
Level 1	Mirroring / duplexing
Level 5	Independent data disks with distributed parity blocks (striping with parity)

---

[158] RAID can also be said to stand for "Redundant Array of Inexpensive Disks" and the "D" can also stand for "devices".

© 2010 gtslearning   IT Career FastTrack with CompTIA A+ Certification   Page 363

RAID 0 (striping without parity)

Disk striping is a technique where data is divided into 64K blocks and spread in a fixed order among all the disks in the array. Because it provides no **redundancy**, this method cannot be said to be a true RAID implementation. If *any* disk in the set fails, **all** data is lost. It is used to improve *performance* by spreading disk I/O over multiple drives.

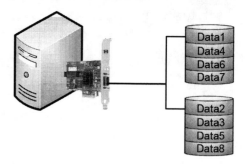

RAID 0 (striping) - data is spread across the array

This strategy requires between 2 and 32 hard disks. It provides the best performance when used with multiple disk controllers.

RAID 1 (mirroring / duplexing)

Mirroring requires an even number of hard disks and a single disk controller. It takes place at the partition level and any partition, including the boot/system partitions can be mirrored. Each write operation is duplicated on the second disk in the set.

This strategy is the simplest way of protecting a single disk against failure. If one disk fails, the other takes over. The failed disk can be replaced (ideally, as quickly as possible). In terms of cost per megabyte, disk mirroring is more expensive than other forms of fault tolerance because disk-space utilization is only 50%.

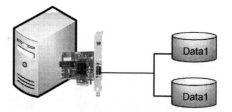

RAID 1 (mirroring) - data is written to both disks simultaneously

There can also be a loss in performance as each write operation has to be performed twice. However, disk mirroring usually has a lower entry cost because it requires only two disks. Stripe sets with parity (RAID level 5) require three or more.

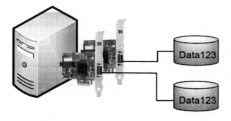

RAID 1 (duplex mirror)

Duplexing is simply a mirrored pair with an additional disk controller on the second drive. This potentially improves performance and protects against controller failures as well as media failures.

RAID 5 (striping with parity)

Striping with parity (RAID 5) is the most common strategy for fault tolerant designs. It differs from other levels in that it writes parity information across all the disks in the array. The data and parity information are managed so that the two are always on different disks. If a single disk fails, enough information is spread across the remaining disks to allow the data to be completely reconstructed.

Striping with parity requires a minimum of three drives.

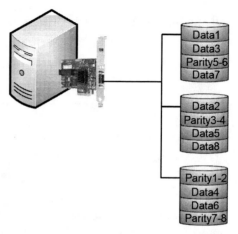

RAID 5 (striping with parity)

Stripe sets with parity offer the best performance for read operations. However, when a disk has failed, the read performance is *degraded* by the need to recover the data using the parity information. Also, all normal write operations require three times as much memory due to the parity calculation.

Implementing RAID

It is possible to implement RAID using either hardware or software.

Hardware solutions

Using hardware RAID (with either the motherboard's built-in support or a separate RAID card) means that a dedicated controller can service RAID operations. With software RAID this has to be performed by the CPU. Another advantage of hardware-based RAID is that the operating system sees the array as one disk. This allows you to install the operating system onto an array, which isn't usually possible when using software arrays.

In addition, hardware RAID is able to hot swap a damaged disk (replace the failed unit without shutting down Windows), thereby keeping the system operational all the time[159]. When the new disk is installed, the RAID controller transparently synchronizes it with the remaining disks in the set.

---

[159] Hot swapping is a feature of high-end hardware RAID solutions and requires a compatible controller *and* disk units.

| Unit 4.2 | Module 4 Installation, Troubleshooting, and Maintenance |

On the downside, hardware RAID is much more expensive than a software solution and may lock you into a single vendor solution.

Older hardware RAID solutions used SCSI disks and controllers in preference to IDE/ATA. Nowadays, entry-level hardware RAID may use SATA while **Serial Attached SCSI (SAS)** is a popular technology for server-class machines.

Software solutions

Windows provides the option to set up software-based RAID using standard disks and controllers, but desktop versions of Windows are restricted to striping, which provides no fault tolerance[160]. In a software solution, IDE/ATA and SCSI disks can be combined in an array. A software solution is also considerably cheaper, as RAID controller cards can be very expensive.

Configuring and troubleshooting software Windows dynamic storage

Dynamic storage is a feature of NTFS-formatted disks and the professional / business editions of Windows. It allows the creation of **volumes** spanning multiple disks that can be shrunk and expanded and therefore some approximation of RAID functionality. Dynamic disks can only be read by Windows 2000 / XP / Vista systems.

To convert a basic disk to dynamic, open the **Disk Management** snap-in, alt-click a disk, and select **Convert to Dynamic Disk**. Check the disks you want to add then click **Convert**.

The system will restart a couple of times while the configuration changes are completed.

Once the disk has been converted to dynamic, you can create new volumes[161]. These can be in the following configurations:

- **Simple** - occupies space on a single disk. Unlike partitions on basic disks however, simple volumes can be extended to claim additional disk space later (or conversely shrunk to reclaim disk space).

- **Spanned** - a volume using space on two or more disks. This arrangement is also referred to as **JBOD (Just a Bunch Of Disks)**.

---

[160] Windows Server versions support fault tolerant mirrored (RAID 1) and striping with parity (RAID 5) arrays.

[161] Any existing partitions are converted to simple volumes.

Module 4 Installation, Troubleshooting, and Maintenance   *Installing and Configuring Components*

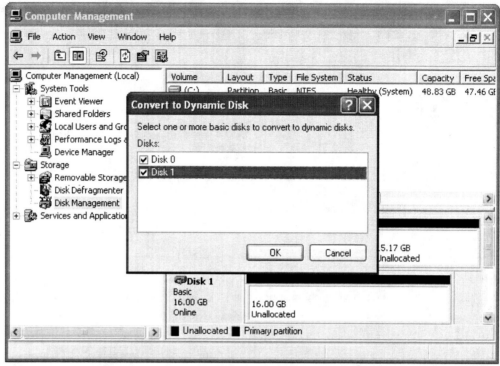

Creating a dynamic disk array

- **Striped** - a volume using space on two or more disks configured using RAID 0 to improve performance[162].

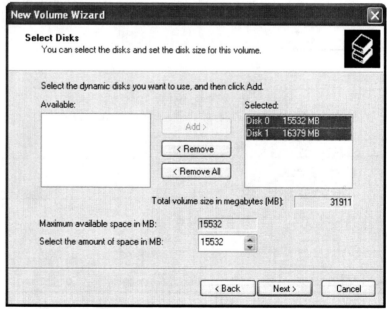

Creating a spanned volume

---

[162] Basically data is written across all disks whereas spanned just uses up space on the volume using the standard file access pattern

	Warning
	Spanned and striped volumes offer flexibility, but if *any* of the disks in the array fails, *all* data on the volume will be lost.

A dynamic disk can be converted back to basic, but the volumes (and any data on them) must be deleted first. As with basic partitions, volumes must be formatted (NTFS or FAT / FAT32) before they can be available to the OS.

Calculating usable storage

The following table shows how to calculate the amount of disk space available when using commonly implemented RAID configurations.

RAID Level	Usable Disk Space
Level 0	Total space of all disks in stripe set. For example, with 3 disks, each 80 GB in size, the administrator would have a 240 GB volume, all of which can be used for storing data or programs.
Level 1	Half of the disk space on the disks is available. One disk is a copy of the other. Therefore, if the administrator implements RAID1 with two 80 GB disks, he or she has 80 GB of storage available.
Level 5	The level of fault tolerance and available disk space are inverse. As you add disks to the set fault tolerance decreases but usable disk space increases. If the administrator configures a RAID 5 set using 3 disks, a ⅓ of each disk is set aside for parity. If four are used, ¼ is reserved on each disk. Using a three 80 GB disk configuration, the administrator would have a 160 GB usable volume.

Tip

If the disks are different sizes, the size used is that of the smallest disk. Extra disk space on larger drives is wasted.

Installing and Upgrading Adapter Cards

Bear the following in mind when connecting adapters:

- ISA is obsolete and you are unlikely to see them anymore.

- PCI has seen several revisions in terms of voltage and bus width. Different key positions on the card and slot are supposed to prevent insertion of an incompatible card but the vast majority of slots and cards you will come across will be 32-bit 3.3V

ISA (1), PCI (2), and PCI Express / PCIe (3) slots on a motherboard

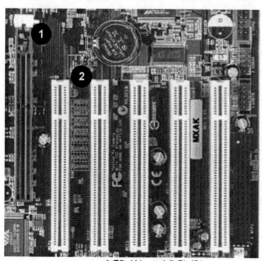

AGP (1) and PCI (2) connectors

- AGP is used for graphics adapters only.

- The size of PCIe slots corresponds to the number of lanes; you can (for instance) plug a x2 adapter card into a x8 slot but you cannot plug a x8 adapter card into a x2 slot.

Installing and Configuring Display Devices

The display subsystem consists of a graphics adapter and either a CRT or flat panel monitor.

If the machine is used for graphics work or games, updating the video card to the latest model may result in a fairly significant performance boost. Another option is to fit more memory on the graphics adapter.

ATI Radeon Crossfire graphics adapter

Using a better quality monitor is another way to improve productivity. High quality flat panel TFTs are now cheap compared to CRTs. They take up less space and consume less power. Larger viewable areas mean less scrolling and more work!

Installing a graphics adapter and connecting the display

1. If you are upgrading an existing adapter, uninstall the current driver. If the adapter is integrated in the motherboard chipset, reboot to CMOS Setup and disable the onboard graphics. Shut down the PC.

2. Unplug any peripherals (pull connectors out by grasping the connector not the cable) and disconnect the power supply from the mains.

3. Set up a work area so that the PC is at a comfortable height and that you have all the tools, components, and reference material required for the job within reach. Take anti-static precautions.

4. Remove the main panel (the one opposite the I/O ports) by undoing the screws and sliding it out.

5. If upgrading an expansion card, unscrew the blanking plate from the chassis, release any retaining clips on the card slot, and then lift the card from the slot. Otherwise, identify a suitable slot and remove the blanking plate.

Tip

If the card is difficult to release, rock it back-and-forth (*not* side-to-side). Handle the card by its edges; try to avoid touching any of the components.

6. Insert the new card into the slot, pushing it down firmly to ensure a good connection. If there is a retaining clip, ensure that this has clicked into place. Screw the blanking plate onto the chassis.

7. If necessary, connect a PCIe power connector from the PSU to the card.

Screwing an expansion card to the computer chassis - ensure that the card lines up with the slot and keep unused slots covered with blanking plates

8. Replace the access panel and reconnect the peripheral devices. Connect the cable from the monitor to a VGA or DVI port on the graphics adapter.

9. Connect the display device to mains power (or to an auxiliary power point on the computer PSU if available). Switch on the monitor then switch on the PC.

Installing display drivers

Unlike storage devices, a graphics adapter and the display need suitable drivers to work properly.

1. When the PC boots and you have logged on (using an Administrative account) Windows should detect that new hardware has been installed and will launch the **Found New Hardware Wizard**.

Found New Hardware Wizard in Windows XP

2. At this point you can either use the vendor's setup program, which may include extra utilities, or just search for a basic Windows driver. To use a setup program, click **Cancel** then run the installation program.

Tip
Browse the card vendor's website to download drivers or an updated Setup package.

3. Otherwise, choose whether to let the wizard use **Windows Update** to look for the latest drivers.

4. To proceed with the wizard, choose to **Install the software automatically** and wait while the wizard locates and installs the drivers. The screen may switch on and off during installation.

5. If Windows cannot locate a driver, you can specify the location of one or choose from a list of hardware models.

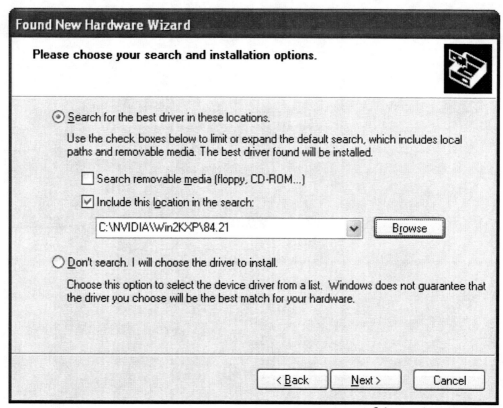

Selecting drivers manually

6. Once the driver has been installed, Windows will probably need to be restarted. You can then configure device properties using the vendor's setup program or the **Display** applet (Windows 2000 / XP) or **Personalization** applet (Windows Vista) in **Control Panel**.

The **Settings** tab allows you to configure the screen resolution and color depth. Use the **Advanced** button to change the monitor refresh rate, color management settings, view or change driver properties, or change the DPI[163].

---

[163] Increasing DPI makes text larger at a particular resolution. This is useful for TFTs that support high native resolutions (using a lower interpolated resolution would make the display "fuzzy"). However, this can cause graphics rendering problems with some software (notably Internet Explorer). Also, Windows may set a high DPI automatically when using a high resolution display device.

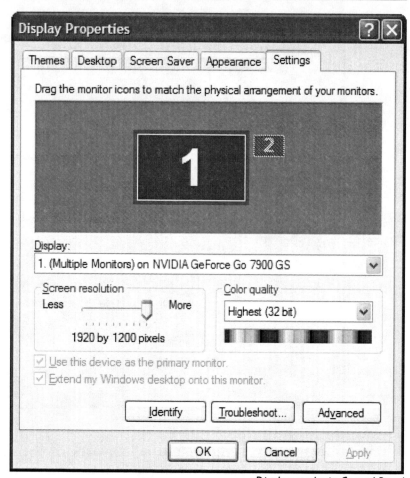

Display applet in Control Panel

Installing and configuring dual monitors

A PC (or laptop) can be set up to use two display devices. In terms of hardware, the PC requires either a graphics adapter with two display ports or two graphics adapters.

Connect the display devices to the two ports then open the **Display** applet in **Control Panel** and select the **Settings** tab. Dual monitors can be used in one of two modes:

- Display the same image on both devices - uncheck the **Extend my Windows desktop** box (this mode is useful for delivering presentations).

- Display the desktop over both devices - check the **Extend my Windows desktop** box (this mode makes more screen "real estate" available and is useful for design, publishing, and programming work).

In the first mode, you can set the resolution and color quality of each display device separately by choosing them from the **Display** list box.

Windows Vista displays a dialog when a new display device is connected. The options are the same (mirrored or extended) but you can also choose to use **Presentation Settings**, which disables screen savers and sleep timers.

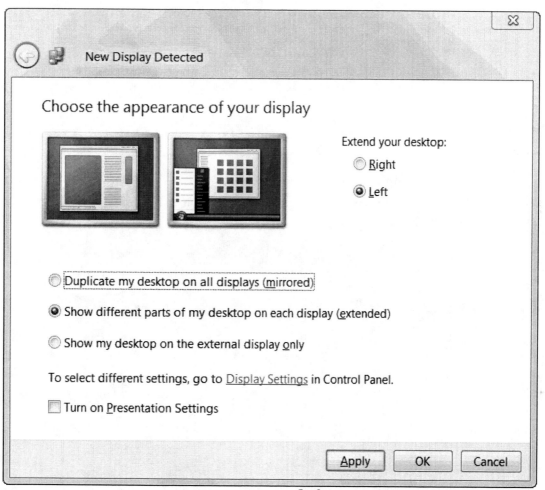

Configuring an additional display in Windows Vista

Unit 4.2   Module 4 Installation, Troubleshooting, and Maintenance

Installing and Upgrading System Components

Storage devices and adapter cards are relatively simple to change. Operations such as replacing the power supply or upgrading the CPU or memory can be more complex.

> ### Note
> CPU and memory and the chips on the motherboard are particularly sensitive to ESD. Make sure you take anti-static precautions when handling and storing these components. See unit 3.3 for more details.

Replacing or adding memory

Adding or upgrading system memory is often the cheapest and simplest way of increasing performance[164]. Most system memory is DDR, DDR2, or DDR3. The main standards in use are:

Type	Memory Speed	Bus Speed	Data Rate
PC-1600	100 MHz	100 MHz	1.6 GBps
PC-2100	133 MHz	133 MHz	2.1 GBps
PC-2700	167 MHz	167 MHz	2.7 GBps
PC-3200	200 MHz	200 MHz	3.2 GBps
PC2-3200	100 MHz	200 MHz	3.2 GBps
PC2-4300	133 MHz	266 MHz	4.3 GBps
PC2-5300	167 MHz	333 MHz	5.2 GBps
PC2-6400	200 MHz	400 MHz	6.4 GBps
PC2-8500	266 MHz	533 MHz	8.5 GBps
PC3-8500	133 MHz	533 MHz	8.5 GBps
PC3-10600	166 MHz	667 MHz	10.66 GBps
PC3-12800	200 MHz	800 MHz	12.8 GBps

If the motherboard supports it but the system is not configured to use it, enabling a dual-channel configuration is the best way of extracting more performance from existing components. Increasing the bus speed would require purchasing a new motherboard and memory modules (and possibly CPU).

---

[164] At around 2 GB or more of system RAM, you may need to consider using registered memory to maximize stability.

Page 376   IT Career FastTrack with CompTIA A+ Certification   © 2010 gtslearning

> **Tip**
> When purchasing a computer, it is a good idea to get the fastest memory bus you can afford, as this is the component that is most difficult to upgrade later.

Memory modules are quite easy to insert and remove (unless cabling within the case makes them inaccessible). The key point here is to ensure that the memory is suitable for the system and in the correct configuration. See unit 1.3 for a full discussion of the different memory technologies.

1. To remove DIMMs, release the catches at either end. Once you have released the catches, you can remove the memory module by hand (it should pop up out of the slot). Handle the module by the edges - avoid touching the chips.

2. If retaining the module, put it in anti-static packaging.

Retaining clips on DIMMs

3. To insert a module, line it up with the slot. There are notches at the bottom edge to ensure that the card is oriented correctly and compatible with the slot type. Check that the notches on the card are aligned correctly with the slot.

4. Push the module firmly into the socket. The catches should snap into place when the module is fully inserted.

Orient the module so that the notches on the card and slot match up then push down so that the retaining clips click into place

Unit 4.2

Module 4 Installation, Troubleshooting, and Maintenance

5. Reboot the PC and watch the RAM count during startup to verify the memory has been recognized. From Windows, you can check the installed RAM by looking at System properties or the System Information program (see unit 2.3).

Tip

When installing RAM, it is good practice to put the largest board in the first slot (slot 0).

Replacing the CPU

As the core of the PC, the CPU is obviously one of the decisive factors in determining overall system speed. That said, the scope for upgrading a CPU is limited by the motherboard and a board that is a couple of years old is unlikely to support the latest, fastest chips. Check the documentation carefully or confirm details on the motherboard manufacturer's website before ordering an upgrade. In some cases you may need to update (flash) the motherboard BIOS (obviously do this *before* removing the old CPU).

While clock speed increases can bring some performance benefit, increasing the number of processors can usually produce a dramatic improvement. Unfortunately, the scope to upgrade to SMP is limited:

- Install a second CPU - this requires having a dual-socket board and purchasing a CPU identical to the first (or two new CPUs).

- Upgrade to a dual-core CPU - this requires a motherboard with a chipset that supports the dual core CPU.

1. Unclip the fan's power connector then undo the fan and heatsink assembly from the motherboard (designs vary, but there will generally be plastic or metal clips holding this in place). If there is a liquid cooling system, remove it by following the manufacturer's instructions.

2. Release the CPU from its socket.

   □ ZIF - lift the lever to release the mechanism then lift the CPU out, taking care not to bend or touch the pins.

   □ Slot (SECC) - release the catches at either end of the slot then lift the cartridge out.

Page 378   IT Career FastTrack with CompTIA A+ Certification   © 2010 gtslearning

☐ LGA - release the lever and lift it up then flip the latch up. Lift the CPU out, handling it by the edges.

Removing a CPU from a ZIF socket (left) and LGA socket (right)

3. If retaining the CPU, put it in its protective packaging so that the pins or contacts do not get damaged or dirty. Store the CPU in anti-static packaging.

4. To insert a new CPU, first remove any packaging. Then orient the CPU correctly with the slot or socket. This means that pin 1 on the CPU orients with pin 1 on the socket. Pin 1 is usually indicated by a white or yellow marker or by a beveled corner.

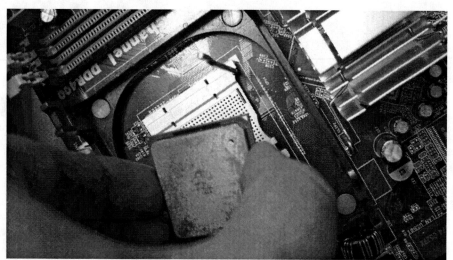

Orient the marker on the CPU with the marker on the socket - drop the CPU in lightly then close the lever to secure it

5. Put the CPU into the socket gently, making sure to keep it level. If aligned properly, it should fall easily into place. Press it down gently to make a good contact.

6. Secure the retaining mechanism:
   - ZIF - push the lever down until it clicks back into place.
   - Slot (SECC) - the retaining clips should click into place when the cartridge is properly seated.
   - LGA - close the latch then clip the lever back into place.
7. If you are replacing the original heatsink and fan assembly, clean off any existing thermal pad or compound and apply a new one. Otherwise, a boxed CPU will come with a heatsink with a thermal pad.
8. Put the heatsink over the CPU and secure it using the appropriate clips or fasteners. Connect the fan's power supply using the cable.
9. Reboot the PC and verify the new CPU has been recognized.

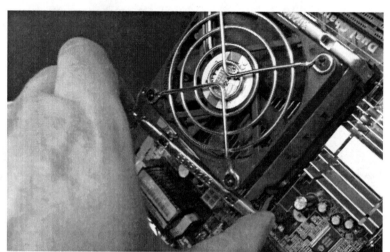

Replace the fan / heatsink assembly and secure using the clips then plug the fan's power connector into the motherboard header

Upgrading cooling devices

Different CPUs will run at different temperatures. Essentially though, the cooler you can make your CPU run the better. Many processors will still work quite happily running at temperatures up to 90°C. Some processors will be irreparably damaged if they reach temperatures above 60°C. By upgrading the cooling system on the processor you can decrease the temperature considerably. For example, a processor that is currently running at 60°C could be lowered to 30 or 40°C by replacing the heatsink or fan with a better model.

For systems where heat is a real problem, you could look at liquid cooling. These solutions also reduce noise. Water-based cooling systems obviously have to be removed and installed very carefully, following the manufacturer's instructions.

Installing or upgrading an SMP system

Some motherboards support two CPUs (**Symmetric Multiprocessing [SMP]**). In an SMP system, the CPUs must be identical in terms of clock speed, cache, and internal architecture.

The same brand of CPU (such as Pentium 4 and Xeon) will feature many different models, with different clock speeds and cache sizes. Different models cannot be mixed in an SMP system.

Furthermore, vendors release update versions of CPU models under different stepping numbers, consisting of a letter and number, starting with A-0. When a minor update is made, the number is incremented (for example, A-1). When a major update is made, the next letter is used (for example, B-0). Generally speaking, you need to use CPUs with identical stepping, though the vendor's website should have information about compatibility between steppings.

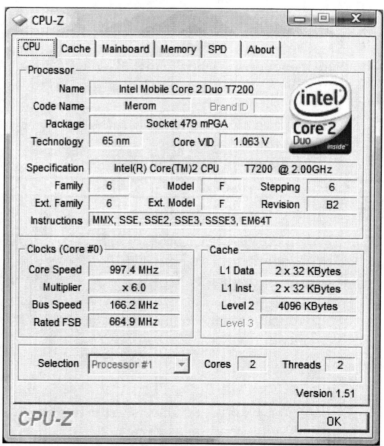

Checking CPU stepping and revision using the CPU-Z utility

When you upgrade a single processor system to SMP (or upgrade a single core CPU with a dual-core model), you need to update the computer's configuration manually (after installing the CPUs), as the OS will not recognize the change. To update the computer specification in Windows, complete the following steps:

1. Open **Device Manager** and expand the **Computer** icon.
2. Alt-click the current PC device and choose **Update Driver**.
3. Choose the options to locate a driver manually and select the appropriate option (for example, **ACPI Multiprocessor PC**).

Replacing the PSU

You may need to upgrade a power supply because you have added more drives and peripherals than the current one can cope with or replace a faulty supply.

Complete the following steps to install a new power supply:

1. To remove the existing supply, first disconnect all the connectors, and then unscrew the unit from the chassis.
2. Lift the unit out and put it in appropriate packaging (if retaining it).
3. Orient the new PSU correctly and screw it into the case. If the PSU features a manual voltage switch, ensure it is set to 110 or 240V as appropriate for the mains supply in your country.
4. Connect the cables:

Unscrewing the PSU from the chassis

- An ATX power connects to the motherboard using either a single 20-pin connector, a 20-pin + 4-pin connector, or a single 24-pin connector, depending on the ATX version supported. The connectors are keyed to prevent incorrect insertion.

This PSU supporting the P4 CPU has a 20-pin mainboard connector (1) and an auxiliary 4-pin +12V connector (2)

- Systems based on the Pentium 4 CPU may require a +12V 4-pin connector to power the CPU socket.

- Hard disks and optical drives can use any available Molex connector, as these all supply identical voltages. They are keyed to prevent incorrect insertion.

- Floppy drives generally use mini-Molex connectors, which are keyed to prevent incorrect insertion.

- SATA drives may require a special SATA power connector. If the PSU does not have these, you can obtain Molex-SATA converters.

- PCIe graphics cards may use a 6-pin or 8-pin power connector (or possibly a 6-pin + 2-pin connector designed to be compatible with both types of socket).

The PSU comes with its own fan for cooling. There may be additional case fans to install.

Also, do not forget to connect the power to the CPU fan and any graphics adapter fans.

Jumper settings and front panel connectors

Components on the front panel of the chassis connect to headers on the motherboard. Typically, front panel connectors can include:

- Power button (soft power)
- Hard disk LED
- USB ports
- Audio ports (headphones and microphone)

Replacing front panel connectors

When disassembling the system, you should have made a diagram of how these are plugged in. If you do not have a diagram, you will have to refer to the motherboard documentation or go by any labels printed on the wires and headers. These are not always very easy to follow however, which is why you should always make a diagram (or take a digital photo to refer to).

When upgrading components such as the CPU, you may also have to change the position of jumpers on the motherboard. A jumper is a small plastic clip that fits over two contacts on the motherboard. The position of the clip completes a circuit that configures the motherboard in one way or another.

Module 4 Installation, Troubleshooting, and Maintenance | *Installing and Configuring Components*

Tip

There may also be a motherboard reset jumper. Setting this may allow you to restore the system from a failed BIOS update, forgotten BIOS supervisor password, and so on.

Replacing the motherboard

There will be very few occasions where you actually need to replace the motherboard, as it is a time-consuming process and buying a new PC is usually more cost-effective.

1. Remove all cabling and components from the motherboard and chassis.

2. Remove the screws or lugs that secure the motherboard to the floor of the case. These can be difficult to remove but take great care not to crack the board. Make sure you retain the clips.

3. Lift or slide the motherboard out and (if storing it) put it in anti-static packaging.

4. Orient the new motherboard correctly so that it is positioned over the mounting holes and that expansion slots line up with the slots cut in the case.

5. Secure the new board using the screws or lugs - again, be careful not to apply excessive force.

6. Complete the following checks:

   ☐ The expansion slots and I/O ports should line up with the slots in the system case.

   ☐ The motherboard should not be touching the system case, except where attached by screws or stand-offs.

   ☐ The motherboard should be firmly attached and should not wobble.

   ☐ The motherboard should be flat and level with the floor of the chassis.

© 2010 gtslearning   IT Career FastTrack with CompTIA A+ Certification   Page 385

Unit 4.2   Module 4 Installation, Troubleshooting, and Maintenance

Installing and Configuring Input and Multimedia Devices

While easily overlooked, input devices are vital to productivity (a cheap keyboard can damage overall performance more than a slightly pedestrian CPU). Peripheral devices (whether installed internally or externally) add features rather than improve performance. As usual, ensure they are supported by the motherboard and OS and install the latest drivers. The following table summarizes the main peripheral and storage device expansion technologies:

Technology	Transfer Rate	Range	Connectors	Other Features
PS/2		~2m	6-pin	Mouse and keyboard only
Serial	~115 Kbps	~10m	9-pin or 25-pin	
Parallel (SPP)	~150 KBps	~5m	25-pin at host; 36-pin at device	Unidirectional
Parallel (ECP/EPP)	~2 MBps	~10m	25-pin at host; 36-pin at device	Bidirectional
USB 1.1	12 Mbps	5m	Type A at host; Type B or Mini-B at device	Up to 127 devices; supports hot swapping; up to 2.5W power
USB 2.0	480 Mbps	5m	As above	As above
Firewire (IEEE 1394)	400 Mbps	4.5m	6-pin or 4-pin (unpowered)	Up to 63 devices; hot swapping; up to 15W power
Firewire (IEEE 1394b)	800 Mbps	4.5m	9-pin	As above but up to 45W power
SCSI	Up to 320 MBps	12m (for LVD)	Usually 68-pin	Up to 16 devices (wide bus)
CardBus (PCMCIA)	132 MBps			Hot swapping
ExpressCard	Depends on bus (USB or PCIe)		26-pin	Hot swapping
IrDA	4 Mbps	1m	Wireless (Infrared)	
Bluetooth 1.0	1 Mbps	10m	Wireless (2.4 GHz radio)	
Bluetooth 2.0	3 Mbps	10m	Wireless (2.4 GHz radio)	

Page 386   IT Career FastTrack with CompTIA A+ Certification   © 2010 gtslearning

Mouse

Mice can be installed on PS/2, USB, or wireless ports depending on the model.

- PS/2 - connect the mouse to the PS/2 port marked with a mouse icon (usually color-coded green) then switch on the PC.

- USB - connect the mouse to any USB port. USB is hot swappable so you can attach the mouse when the computer is already switched on.

- Wireless - install the wireless adapter (using the same general procedure as for installing a graphics adapter) and put a charged battery in the mouse. The mouse generally needs to be synchronized with the receiver using a push button (check the instructions for details).

A standard mouse does not need a special driver installing and basic settings can be configured using the **Mouse** applet in **Control Panel**. However, to access and configure extra buttons on some mice you will need to install the manufacturer's driver.

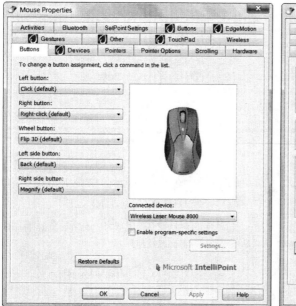 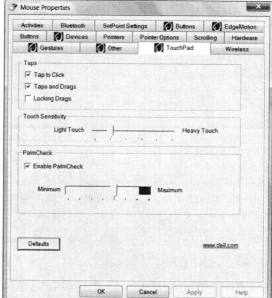

The Mouse applet in Control Panel allows you to configure both mice and touchpads - installing the vendor's driver makes extra configuration settings available

Tip

When using a touchpad, it is easy to brush the pad accidentally and for this to be interpreted as a click event. If this happens a lot, adjust the sensitivity setting or disable "Tap to click" completely.

Keyboard

A keyboard is connected in the same way as a mouse, except that you use the **Keyboard** applet in **Control Panel** to configure it.

The main options are to set the repeat rate and sensitivity for keys. Multimedia keyboards will also have programmable keys and key combos.

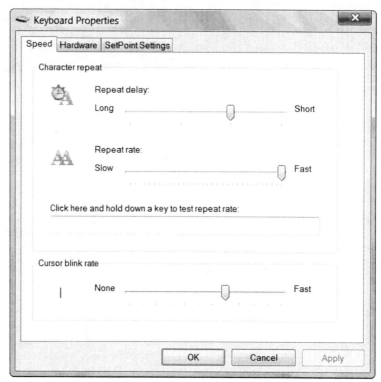

Keyboard applet in Control Panel

Keyboard regionalization

PC keyboards can vary from country-to-country. Where a country uses the Latin alphabet, the variations may be minor. For example, US and UK keyboards vary only in the location of some of the symbols. A keyboard that uses a non-Latin alphabet is considerably different of course.

The type of keyboard layout is configured through the **Keyboards and Languages** tab in the **Regional and Language Options** applet in **Control Panel** so that the computer knows which symbol to use when a particular key or key combination is pressed.

Module 4 Installation, Troubleshooting, and Maintenance — *Installing and Configuring Components*

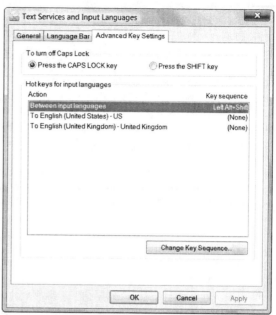

Make sure the keyboard is configured to use the correct layout - note that if multiple layouts are enabled, a key combo can be used to switch between them (and that this is quite easy to do by accident)

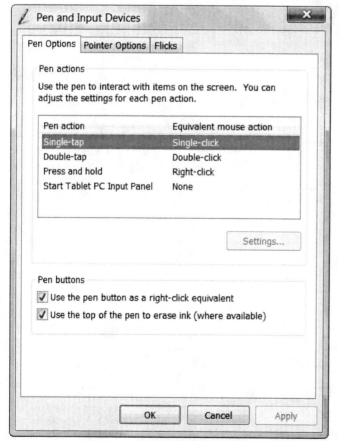

Configuring Pen and Input Devices

Configuring a pen / stylus

A **pen** (or **stylus**) can be used with a Tablet PC to operate Windows and enter text. Handwriting recognition software can then convert this into characters that can be edited in word processing software. You configure the pen via the **Pen and Input Devices** applet in Control Panel.

| Unit 4.2 | Module 4 Installation, Troubleshooting, and Maintenance |

Configuring a joystick / game pad

PC games are mostly designed for use with the mouse and keyboard but some games (flight simulators for instance) benefit from the use of a **joystick** or **gamepad**. Joysticks and game pads use USB connectors.

Joysticks can also be used as input devices by people who have difficulty using a mouse or keyboard.

Sound card and speakers

To set up audio, install the sound card (using the same general procedure as for the graphics adapter). There may be additional cables to connect the card to other devices in the PC. For example, most cards have a digital connector to interface with the CD/DVD drive[165]. Specialist recording adapters might feature more than one card, with the second (often a breakout box fitted in a drive bay) providing support for extra input jacks.

Tip

Try to locate the sound card in the farthest slot from disk drives and fans to minimize interference.

Connect the microphone and speakers to the appropriate ports on the card. Make sure you know the color-codes for the various ports (see unit 1.5).

Use the **Sounds and Audio Devices** applet in Control Panel to test the hardware and configure settings. Use the **Audio** and **Voice** tabs to configure speakers and microphones[166]. The **Sounds** tab configures sounds associated with Windows events.

---

[165] The advantage of making this connection is that the CD can playback through the sound card without having to use the CPU to decode the data.

[166] In Vista, the applet is just called "Sound" and the tabs are "Playback" and "Recording".

Module 4 Installation, Troubleshooting, and Maintenance   *Installing and Configuring Components*

Configure audio properties using the Sounds and Audio Devices applet - note the Test hardware option on the Voice tab

Other adapter cards

Other types of adapter card (I/O card, eSATA card, wired and wireless network cards, or TV / video capture cards) are installed using the same general procedure.

1. If the function of the card is also available on the motherboard chipset, you may want to disable the onboard adapter using CMOS setup.

   Tip
   This is not always necessary. A computer will quite happily support multiple I/O ports and network adapters.

2. Identify a suitable slot and install the card in it.

3. Make any other internal connections suggested by the vendor.

4. Make any external connections suggested by the vendor (connect a TV Tuner adapter to a set-top box for instance).

5. Restart Windows and install the drivers.

| Unit 4.2 | Module 4 Installation, Troubleshooting, and Maintenance |

6. Configure the adapter using the vendor supplied software.

Configuring network adapters (wired and wireless) is covered in more detail in unit 5.2.

Other USB and Firewire peripherals

To install a USB or Firewire device such as a webcam or external TV Tuner, install the device driver and software from the manufacturer's disk (or website) then simply plug the device into a spare port. USB/Firewire storage devices do not generally require special drivers. USB and Firewire devices are hot swappable, meaning that they can be connected and disconnected without restarting the computer.

Before removing a storage device, close any applications that might be using it then double-click the **Safely Remove Hardware** icon (or) in the **notification area** on the taskbar and choose the option to stop the device.

Summary

Make sure you know the options and compatibility issues when considering component upgrades. When installing equipment, work methodically and refer carefully to system documentation and installation guides. Test functionality when you have installed a component.

Tip

To review what you have learned in this chapter, you should now visit the course website. This contains review questions and bonus material to help you to learn more and practice the topics covered in this unit.

| Page 392 | IT Career FastTrack with CompTIA A+ Certification | © 2010 gtslearning |

Module 4 Installation, Troubleshooting, and Maintenance

Windows Startup and Recovery

Unit 4.3 Windows Startup and Recovery

CompTIA A+ Essentials Objectives

☐ **701.3.3 Explain the process and steps to install and configure the Windows OS**
Installation methods (Recover CD, Factory recovery partition) • Operating system installation options (Repair install)

☐ **701.3.4 Explain the basics of boot sequences, methods and startup utilities**
Disk boot order / device priority (Types of boot devices [disk, network, USB, other]) • Boot options (Safe mode, Boot to restore point, Recovery options [Automated System Recovery (ASR), Emergency Repair Disk (ERD), Recovery console])

CompTIA A+ Practical Application Objectives

☐ **702.2.3 Given a scenario, select and use system utilities / tools and evaluate the results**
System Restore

☐ **702.2.4 Evaluate and resolve common issues**
Error Messages and Conditions (Boot [Invalid boot disk, Inaccessible boot drive, Missing NTLDR], Startup [Device / service failed to start, Device / program in registry not found])

Windows Boot Process

The following notes describe the boot process for a typical Windows installation. It is important to have a good understanding of the normal boot process to be able to troubleshoot Windows startup.

Power On Self Test process

Intel machines have hardware based code that runs on power on. This code is executed before Windows initializes.

1. **POST (Power On Self Test)** - this is a routine that allows the system to recognize and test the required boot hardware, such as memory and keyboard.

2. **Adapter POST** - adapters (such as a SCSI host adapter) may also perform self test routines.

© 2010 gtslearning

IT Career FastTrack with CompTIA A+ Certification

Page 393

| Unit 4.3 | Module 4 Installation, Troubleshooting, and Maintenance |

```
AMIBIOS(C)2001 American Megatrends, Inc.
BIOS Date: 08/14/03 19:41:02  Ver: 08.00.02

Press DEL to run Setup
Checking NVRAM..

512MB OK
Auto-Detecting Pri Master..IDE Hard Disk
Auto-Detecting Pri Slave...Not Detected
Auto-Detecting Sec Master..CDROM
Auto-Detecting Sec Slave...
```

POST

3. **Locate boot device** - the BIOS tests each device configured for booting in the order specified in CMOS Setup, stopping when it locates a device with a valid boot sector. If no devices are found or if a device contains invalid media, an error message is displayed.

4. **The first sector of the boot device is read** - this contains the MBR (Master Boot Record). The MBR runs its internal code which scans the PBR (Partition Boot Record) to locate the active partition.

5. The boot sector loader from the active partition is loaded and run.

Windows bootstrap process

Once the pre-boot routines have been run, the system can start loading and running the Windows boot files[167]:

1. The boot sector loader finds and runs NTLDR. NTLDR completes the following functions:

   (a) Initializes 32-bit protected mode[168].

   (b) Loads the mini file system driver; this enables Windows to load the rest of the boot files including the actual file system driver.

   (c) If a SCSI disk is used, the NTBOOTDD.SYS mini-SCSI driver is loaded.

   (d) Checks for HIBERFIL.SYS - if present NTLDR resumes the previous session (from hibernation); otherwise it loads the BOOT.INI menu.

---

[167] This and the next few topics describe the boot process for Windows 2000/XP. The process for Windows Vista is described later.

[168] The CPU starts in real mode, which is a legacy of the earliest PC CPUs. Real mode can address only the first 1 MB of system memory.

| Module 4 Installation, Troubleshooting, and Maintenance | Windows Startup and Recovery |

2. If BOOT.INI contains more than one OS and the timeout parameter has not been set to zero, the menu is displayed to the user, who can select from one of the available choices. If no selection is made, the default OS is selected when the timeout expires (30 seconds by default)[169].

```
Please select the operating system to start:


    Microsoft Windows XP Professional
    Microsoft Windows

Use the up and down arrow keys to move the highlight to your choice.
Press ENTER to choose.
Seconds until highlighted choice will be started automatically: 28




For troubleshooting and advanced startup options for Windows, press F8.
```

Boot options menu

3. If the current version of Windows is not selected, BOOTSECT.DOS is loaded and run. This file contains the old boot sector loader from the previous operating system, created when Windows was installed.

4. If Windows has been selected from the menu, NTDETECT.COM loads and runs. This detects the hardware currently installed in the system and builds the volatile HKEY_LOCAL_MACHINE\System hive in the registry. A hardware list is generated.

5. NTLDR then loads the kernel NTOSKRNL.EXE into memory. The Kernel is not yet initialized.

6. At this point, if multiple hardware profiles are defined, the user is prompted to select one.

---

[169] At this point, the user can press F8 to invoke the **Advanced Options** menu. If the computer was not properly shut down, this menu is displayed automatically.

© 2010 gtslearning   IT Career FastTrack with CompTIA A+ Certification   Page 395

Windows load sequence

The final load phases of Windows are as follows:

1. The hardware list built by NTDETECT is passed to the kernel. The screen displays the Windows logo and a progress bar.

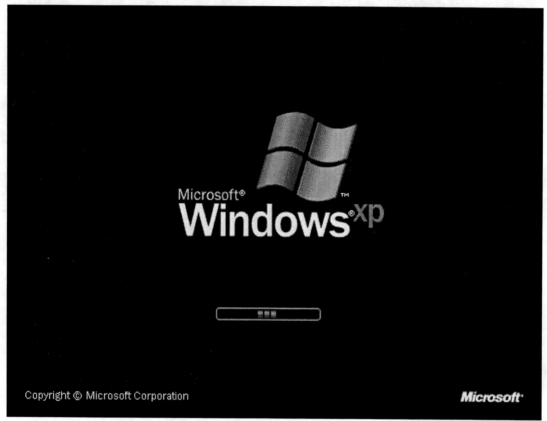

Windows load progress bar

2. HAL.DLL is loaded and initialized.

3. The registry system hive is scanned to determine which device drivers to load.

4. The system can now initialize the kernel (NTOSKRNL.EXE).

5. More device drivers are loaded via the registry.

6. Once the system drivers have been initialized the system loads and executes the Session Manager (SMSS.EXE). This performs several tasks, including creating the paging file, loading the Windows shell, and loading WINLOGON.

Module 4 Installation, Troubleshooting, and Maintenance   *Windows Startup and Recovery*

7. If a network connection is found, the "Preparing Network Connections" message is displayed while Windows loads the NETLOGON service.

8. The "Applying Computer Settings" message is displayed while the computer evaluates and configures system policies.

9. WINLOGON displays either the **Ctrl+Alt+Del** box (**Secure Attention Sequence [SAS]**) or **Welcome to Windows** screen, depending on the security and network configuration.

10. The user is then able to provide logon information. The **Local Security Authority (LSASS.EXE)** is loaded. This verifies the logon information provided (either against the local Security Account Manager or with a domain controller) and enforces the local security policy (assigning permissions to the user and so on).

11. If logon is accepted, the **Last Known Good** control set is updated to the copy used to boot. Personal settings are configured from the local profile. Any services, applications, or scripts set to run at startup are loaded, network connections are re-established, the logon chime is played, and the desktop is displayed.

Core boot files

The following is a list of the core Windows boot files named in the previous section and their locations.

File Name	Description	Location
NTLDR	NT Loader File	Root folder of the active partition
BOOT.INI	Operating System Menu	Root folder of the active partition
NTDETECT.COM	Hardware Recognizer	Root folder of the active partition
BOOTSECT.DOS	Alternative Boot Sector Loader	Root folder of the active partition
NTBOOTDD.SYS	Mini SCSI Disk Driver	Root folder of the active partition
NTOSKRNL.EXE	NT's Kernel	%SystemRoot%\System32
Device Drivers	Devices	Typically %SystemRoot%\System32
system, sam, security, software, default	Registry Hive Files	%SystemRoot%\System32\Config
ntuser.dat	Registry (User's Settings)	\Documents and Settings

© 2010 gtslearning   IT Career FastTrack with CompTIA A+ Certification   Page 397

| Unit 4.3 | Module 4 Installation, Troubleshooting, and Maintenance |

The BOOT.INI file

BOOT.INI is a hidden system file in the root folder of the active partition. It contains the OS menu displayed when the PC boots and the location of the system files.

A sample BOOT.INI file might look like this:

```
[Boot Loader]
timeout=30
default=multi(0)disk(0)rdisk(0)partition(1)\Windows
[Operating Systems]
multi(0)disk(0)rdisk(0)partition(1)\Windows="Windows XP Professional"
multi(0)disk(0)rdisk(0)partition(1)\Windows="Windows [VGA mode]"
/SOS /BASEVIDEO
C:\="Windows"
```

The first **[Boot Loader]** section of the file can either be edited directly or can be changed through the **System** icon in **Control Panel** (from the **Advanced** tab, under **Startup and Recovery** click **Settings**).

The second **[Operating Systems]** section contains the location of the boot files and the description, between the quotes, that will appear on the menu at boot time. This section can be modified using a plain text editor.

The naming convention used to specify the location of the Windows boot files is called the **ARC (Advanced RISC Computing)** naming convention. The information given is as follows:

ARC Name	Function
multi	Used if the drive is IDE or a SCSI drive that has BIOS enabled.
scsi	Used if the drive is SCSI but without BIOS enabled.
disk	The BUS ID of the SCSI disk.
rdisk	The LUN ID of the SCSI disk.
partition	The partition number that contains the boot files.
directory	The name of the directory containing the system root.

Several switches can be appended to the entries of the Operating System section of BOOT.INI to control some startup parameters of Windows.

Switch	Function
/basevideo	This forces Windows to load with only 640x480 16 color video support.
/bootlog	Enables boot logging to the %SystemRoot%\Ntbtlog.txt file.
/cmdcons	Boot to Recovery Console.
/crashdebug /debug	Converts the COM (serial) port to a debug port (for remote debugging of kernel errors). /crashdebug converts the COM port in the event of a crash only.
/fastdetect: comx	Turns off serial mouse detection for the specified COM port. This is useful for troubleshooting. It is also useful on serial ports that are providing UPS monitoring to prevent errors.
/hal	Specify an alternative HAL.dll file. This is useful for switching between single or multiprocessor modes.
/maxmem:nn	Specifies the amount of RAM that Windows will use; useful for isolating bad chips.
/nodebug	Specifies that no debugging information is to be generated.
/numproc	Sets the number of CPUs to utilize at startup (for troubleshooting defective chips).
/safeboot: minimal	Starts the computer in safe mode. The minimal(alternateshell) parameter starts in safe mode with command prompt. The network parameter adds networking support.
/sos	Displays the Start 0 device drivers as they are loaded.

UEFI

Windows Vista features a completely redesigned boot loader. Part of this is support for UEFI in 64-bit editions of the OS.

BIOS is starting to be replaced on some 64-bit client computers with the **Unified Extensible Firmware Interface (UEFI)**, developed from Intel's EFI specification used on Itanium servers[170]. The key features of UEFI are:

- Platform independence (the specification is not tied to a particular type of CPU).

- Boot manager - UEFI uses a designated system partition rather than a boot record.

- GUI - UEFI allows for full GUI implementations for boot selection and pre-boot authentication.

---

[170] Mac OS X and associated hardware has supported UEFI since 2006; there is Windows support in Vista SP1 and Server 2008.

Unit 4.3   Module 4 Installation, Troubleshooting, and Maintenance

- POST - UEFI can either run on top of BIOS or use its own implementation of the POST and CMOS Setup mechanism.

UEFI can be used for PC firmware and for other types of device; for example, HP use UEFI for the firmware on their 9000-series printers.

Windows Vista bootstrap

As with Windows 2000/XP, if using a traditional BIOS, the POST sequence checks the Master Boot Record (MBR) for the boot device but from that point a different set of files are invoked. The Windows Vista bootstrap files are as follows:

- Windows Boot Manager (BOOTMGR) - controls the boot process; it is located in the root of the system partition. If there are multiple operating systems, the Boot Manager displays the **OS Menu** to allow the user to choose which OS to boot (or to display the **Advanced Options** menu) then loads the appropriate boot loader. The BOOTMGR file is located in the root of the active (bootable) drive.

- Boot Configuration Database (BCD) - this contains information about the operating systems installed on the computer (replaces BOOT.INI). The database is stored as a file on the PC (the **\boot\bcd** file path in the root of the system partition). The database can be modified using the BCDEDIT command-line tool or MSCONFIG.

- OS loader (WINLOAD.EXE or WINRESUME.EXE) - the file that loads Windows Vista (replaces NTLDR); WINRESUME.EXE is used to restore a previous session if the OS was put into hibernation. These files are stored in the system root on the boot partition (in c:\Windows\System32 for example).

The OS load sequence is then fundamentally the same as for Windows 2000/XP.

The same files are used with EFI, but they are given .EFI file extensions and are stored in the **EFI System Partition (ESP)**.

Page 400   IT Career FastTrack with CompTIA A+ Certification   © 2010 gtslearning

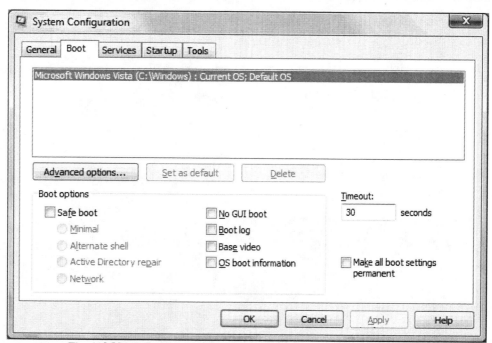

The MSCONFIG utility can be used to modify boot configuration under Windows Vista

Configuring boot devices

All PCs provide software that allows CMOS settings to be viewed or modified.

For most machines, you can use the **CMOS Setup** program that is part of your PC's BIOS. You can normally access this program with a keystroke during the power-on (boot) process. The key combination used will vary from system to system; typical examples are **ESC**, **DEL**, **F1**, **F2** or **F10**. The PC's documentation will explain how to access the CMOS setup; often a message with the required key is displayed when you boot the PC.

Many things can be configured in CMOS Setup, but the one that concerns us here is the **disk boot order** or **boot device priority**. This defines the sequence in which the BIOS searches drives for an operating system. You will usually be able to set 3 or 4 options in priority order. The typical choices are:

- Hard drive - this could be PATA, SATA, and / or SCSI. The master drive on the primary controller will be given priority under PATA and PATA is normally given priority over SATA or SCSI. If you have a mix of PATA and SATA / SCSI and want to use the latter, you will need to adjust the priority through CMOS.

- A SCSI boot disk is normally set to ID 0 while an SATA boot disk should be connected to the lowest numbered port.

- Floppy drive - this is a legacy option and not likely to be of use anymore.

- Optical drive (CD/DVD) - if you are performing a repair install, you will need to make this device highest priority.

- USB - some systems can boot from USB drives.

- Network - uses the network adapter to obtain boot settings from a specially configured server.

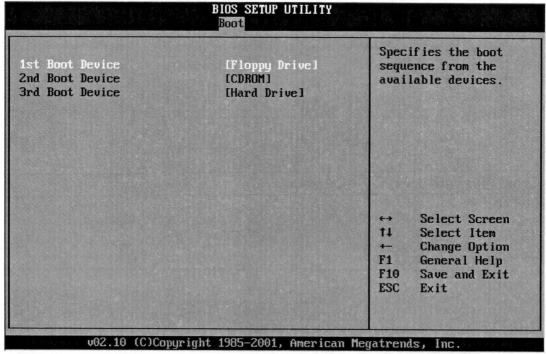

Choosing boot device priority in a CMOS Setup program

There is also usually an option to disable particular boot methods. This is a useful security feature.

Module 4 Installation, Troubleshooting, and Maintenance   *Windows Startup and Recovery*

Startup Options and Recovery Tools

Windows has a number of utilities designed to assist with startup problems or to recover the computer to a working state. You should be aware that there are a few differences between Windows 2000, Windows XP, and Windows Vista (and between the editions of Windows XP and Vista), which are highlighted below.

Advanced startup options

Advanced Startup Options allow the selection of different startup modes for troubleshooting. If you need to select a troubleshooting startup mode, press **F8** during startup (just before the Windows logo is displayed; try tapping repeatedly if the menu doesn't get displayed).

The **Advanced Options** menu contains the choices listed in the table below:

Option	Meaning
Safe Mode	Loads basic drivers and devices required to start the system.
Safe Mode with Networking	As above, but also includes networking drivers and services required to access the network.
Safe Mode with Command Prompt	As for safe mode, but does not load the graphical user interface.
Enable Boot Logging	Creates a log file (%SystemRoot%\Ntbtlog.txt).
Enable VGA Mode	Basic Video mode - VGA drivers in 640 by 480. Note that the display will look grainy.
Last Known Good Configuration	Rolls back to a previous control set.
Debugging Mode	Enables debugging.
Disable auto restart on system failure	Prevents the system restarting at a bluescreen. Selecting this option can give you time to read the error message[171].

Windows Vista adds options to boot to the Recovery Environment (see below) and to disable signed driver enforcement (to allow the use of unsigned drivers).

---

[171] You can set this as the default through System Properties > Advanced > Settings.

© 2010 gtslearning   IT Career FastTrack with CompTIA A+ Certification   Page 403

| Unit 4.3 | Module 4 Installation, Troubleshooting, and Maintenance |

Using the Last Known Good control set

Last Known Good is an effective way of recovering from a system configuration error. Typically it is used when a user has reconfigured or added a new device, which causes the system to fail to boot at all or to generate errors when booting.

When a configuration change is made, Windows modifies one version of the appropriate registry file but maintains a backup (referred to as Last Known Good). During the boot sequence, a user can opt to rollback and utilize this Last Known Good configuration.

> ### Note
> **DO NOT logon before shutting down the system, as this will overwrite the last known good configuration.** Last Known Good will only recover the SYSTEM portion of the registry and only if you have NOT logged in since making the change.

System Restore

Under Windows XP and Windows Vista, **System Restore** allows administrators to rollback from system configuration changes. Using Windows 2000, you would have to rely on **Last Known Good (LKG)** to recover from minor system changes, and thereafter, to recover the system from tape, or other backup media.

System restore points can be created automatically (following system configuration changes or software installation or according to a schedule) or created manually. In Windows XP, the **System Restore** tab (in the **System Properties** dialog) allows you to determine whether this feature is enabled, and if it is, how much disk space will be allocated to the rollback restore points.

Page 404   IT Career FastTrack with CompTIA A+ Certification   © 2010 gtslearning

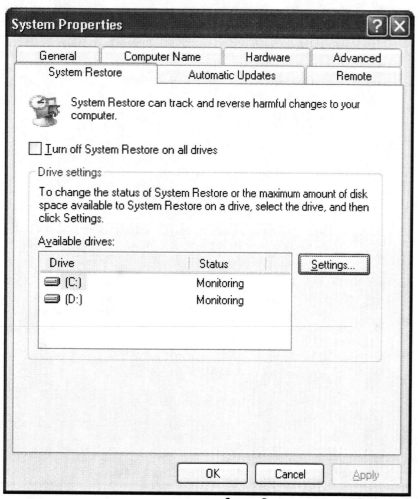

System Restore options in Windows XP

In Vista, the **System Protection** tab lets you select which disk(s) to enable for system restore but there is no configurable option to change the 15% of disk capacity used[172]. The disk must have a minimum of 300 MB free space.

> **Note**
> In Vista, System Restore can only be used on disks formatted with NTFS.

1. To create a system restore point manually in Windows XP, open the **System Restore** tool (**System Tools** folder in the **Accessories** group on the Start menu or from the **Tools** menu in **System Information** or from the **Help and Support Center**).

2. Select **Create a restore point** then click **Next**.

---
[172] You can change the amount of space used but you need to use the command-line tool VSSADMIN to do it.

3. Add a description and click **Create**.

> **Note**
> If the computer is infected with a virus, you should disable System Restore while removing the infected files and delete previous restore points; otherwise the virus could reinfect the computer if System Restore is used.

In Windows Vista, open the **System Protection** tab, select a disk, then click the **Create** button and add a description.

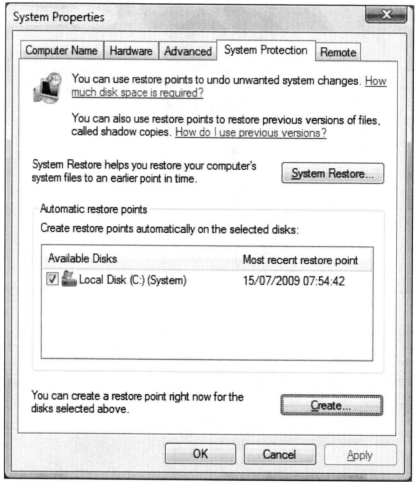

Creating a restore point in Windows Vista

To use a restore point, complete the following steps:

1. If the computer will not boot normally, try booting to Safe Mode to run System Restore.

2. Close and save any open files or applications.

3. Open the System Restore tool and select **Restore my computer to an earlier time**. Click **Next**.

The bold dates in the calendar represent restore points.

4. Pick a date then a restore point that undoes the change you think caused the problem. Click **Next**.

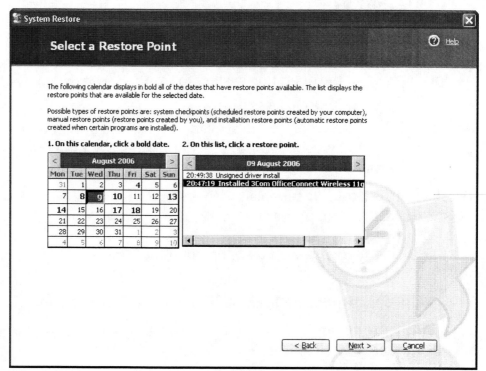

Selecting a restore point

5. To complete the restore, click **Next** again (or click **Cancel** if you have changed your mind).

If the restore is not successful, you can select the option to **Undo my last restoration**.

Tip
In Windows Vista, you can also run System Restore by booting from the product disc.

Note
System Restore will not restore (or delete) user data files. Under Windows XP, System Restore does not reset passwords but under Windows Vista, System Restore *does* reset the administrator password if you run it from the product disc.

| Unit 4.3 | Module 4 Installation, Troubleshooting, and Maintenance |

Tip

Use the Disk Cleanup utility to delete old restore points. If the allocated disk space is used up, System Restore will start overwriting old points automatically. If you disable System Restore, all restore points are deleted.

Using the recovery console

Windows cannot easily be booted from a floppy disk as DOS and Windows 9x could. However, if the system fails to boot, it is sometimes necessary to boot a minimal version of the operating system to troubleshoot the computer.

Most of the time, the Advanced Startup options (such as Safe Mode) should address this issue. Occasionally however, you will encounter a problem that cannot be resolved by booting into Safe Mode. This is where the recovery console comes in.

Use the recovery console to replace drivers or disable problematic services if the system fails to boot properly or generates a bluescreen during boot.

1. Boot from the product disc[173] then in the blue setup screen select **R** for Repair[174].

2. Optionally, press **ENTER** to select a non-US keyboard layout.

3. At the command prompt, select a Windows installation (normally **1**) and press **ENTER**.

4. Type the password for the local administrator account and press **ENTER**.

5. The Recovery Console is now loaded. It resembles the command prompt interface. However, by default, file access is restricted to the root and system root directories[175].

---

[173] You can install the Recovery Console so that it appears as an option on the boot menu. To do so, insert the product disc in your CD-ROM drive then use the Run command **x:\i386\winnt32 /cmdcons** (where x is your CD or DVD drive).

[174] Under Windows 2000, you choose R for repair then choose Recovery Console (as opposed to emergency repair). Also, there is no prompt to change the default keyboard layout.

[175] You can change this by enabling the relevant policy in the Local Security Policy. In the Recovery Console, you then need to use the SET command to change the environment variables AllowAllPaths and AllowRemovableMedia to True. Note that this makes data stored on the computer less secure.

| Module 4 Installation, Troubleshooting, and Maintenance | Windows Startup and Recovery |

Many of the commands usable at a command prompt are available through Recovery Console (**ATTRIB, CD, CHKDSK, COPY, DEL, DIR, FORMAT, MD (MKDIR), RD (RMDIR)**, and so on)[176].

Some additional commands are listed below:

Command	Usage
BATCH *FilePath*	Execute a batch file.
BOOTCFG	Scans the disk for Windows installations (NT, 2000, and XP) and can add them to (**/add** switch) or rebuild the BOOT.INI file (**/rebuild** switch).
DISABLE *ServiceName*	Disable a service or device. The **ENABLE** command starts a service or device.
DISKPART	Disk partition utility. Note that you cannot modify the system partition.
EXPAND	Extract a file from a compressed archive.
FIXBOOT	Repair the boot sector for a partition.
FIXMBR	Repair the Master Boot Record for a drive
LISTSVC	Display services and drivers available.
LOGON	Select a different Windows installation.
MAP	Display drive letter mappings.
NET USE	Map a network drive.

6. Type **EXIT** and press **ENTER** to exit Recovery Console and restart the computer.

Windows Vista RE Command Prompt

Vista also has a command prompt environment, accessed by booting from the product disc. This is not restricted as the Recovery Console is so you can use the usual command-line tools and access all the folders on the system drive and other partitions.

In Vista, the **BOOTCFG, FIXMBR**, and **FIXBOOT** commands are consolidated under the **BOOTREC** command. You can also use **BCDEDIT** to rebuild the boot configuration database.

---

[176] Note that the syntax and available switches for these commands is different under Recovery Console. Use the **/?** help command to check usage.

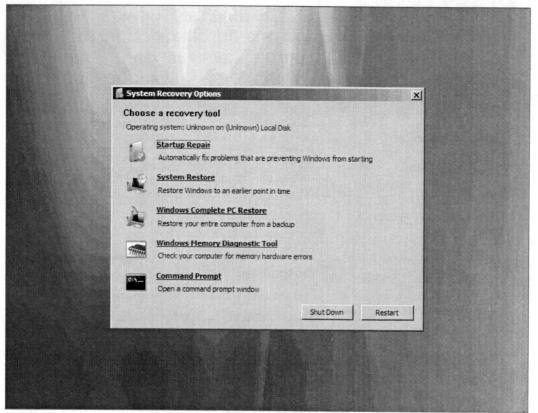

Windows Vista System Recovery Options, accessed by booting from the product disc

Emergency Repair

If a simple fix such as Last Known Good does not work and you cannot boot to a logon, the first thing to try is to see if the computer will boot in Safe Mode. If so, you should then be able to pinpoint the problem to a particular driver or service. Safe Mode loads Windows with a minimal set of drivers and services, so if this works it tells you that something is going wrong later on in the OS load.

If the computer will not boot at all, then you need to invoke a repair process. Under Windows XP/Vista, the best option is System Restore. Under Windows 2000/XP, a boot disk might help if the problem is restricted to the core boot files. Another option is to use the Recovery Console or Windows Vista RE command prompt to try to diagnose the problem manually. However, if you have made a system backup, you may be able to recover the system using that. The various versions of Windows use three different system backup processes for performing a **repair install**:

Module 4 Installation, Troubleshooting, and Maintenance Windows Startup and Recovery

- Under Windows 2000, you can use the **Emergency Repair** process, used in conjunction with an **Emergency Repair Disk (ERD)**. This process restores key system files and registry settings.

- Under Windows XP, the equivalent is the **Automated System Recovery (ASR)** process. ASR can back up and restore the boot partition.

- Under Windows Vista, you can restore the system from a **backup image**.

Creating and using a Windows 2000 Emergency Repair Disk

Windows 2000's backup program is used to create an emergency repair disk. You should update the repair disk prior to making significant system changes (such as updating a driver, installing components, or installing a service pack), as this provides for easier recovery in the event of a mistake.

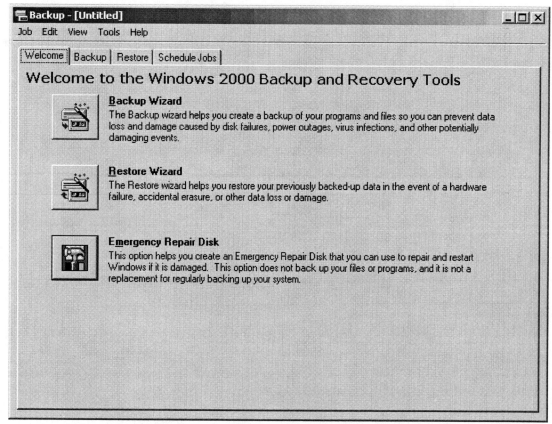

Creating a repair disk

| Unit 4.3 | Module 4 Installation, Troubleshooting, and Maintenance |

> ### Note
>
> The Emergency Repair Disk is **not** a boot disk. A Windows 2000 ERD contains the files SETUP.LOG, AUTOEXEC.NT, and CONFIG.NT. The system data is backed up to %SystemRoot%\Repair\RegBack. A boot disk requires BOOT.INI, NTDETECT.COM, NTLDR, and (if required) a SCSI device driver[177]. Also, ERD does not back up any application or user data.

If the system fails to boot using either the current or Last Known Good configuration, then you can use the emergency repair disk. Before you use this disk, remember the following:

- The emergency repair disk is computer-specific.

- You need the original system files.

- If you recreate the **SAM (Security Accounts Manager)** database, the Administrator password will be set to whatever it was when this disk was created.

- Any changes made since the disk was created will be lost.

To use the Emergency Repair Disk, follow these steps:

1. Boot into Windows 2000 setup then on the blue Setup screen select **R** for Repair.

2. You will be asked if you wish to perform an emergency repair, or access the recovery console. Choose **Repair**.

3. You can then either perform an automatic or manual repair. The former goes ahead and makes the necessary changes; the latter allows you to select from an options list of repair choices.

Windows XP Automated System Recovery

Under Windows XP, the **Automated System Recovery (ASR)** process replaces the Emergency Repair process. ASR is a wizard driven procedure for recovering your computer's configuration to a point in time. Use the Backup utility to run the wizard to create a recovery point. Note that a backup of data files stored outside the boot partition must be made separately.

---

[177] Windows Vista does not support boot disks. You need to use the product disc or recovery partition to boot to Windows RE and select the Startup Repair option.

1. Start the Backup Utility by entering **NTBACKUP** at a command line or selecting **Start > All Programs > Accessories > System Tools > Backup**[178].

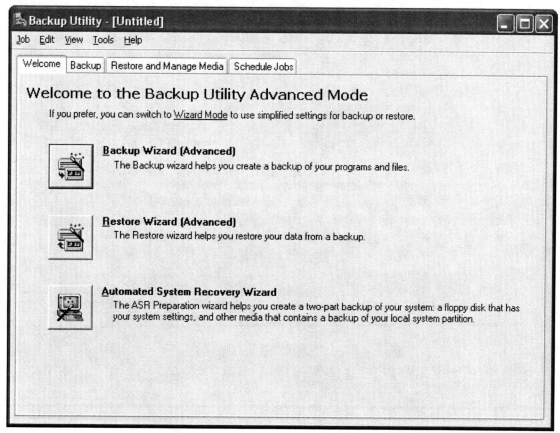

NTBACKUP utility

2. Click the **Automated System Recovery Wizard** icon then click **Next**.
3. Enter the path to create or update a backup file (.BKF)[179] then click **Next**.
4. Put a blank floppy disk in the A: drive and click **Finish**.

File copy will begin.

---

[178] NTBACKUP isn't readily accessible using XP Home Edition. You need to install it via \VALUEADD\MSFT\NTBACKUP on the setup CD. Also, the restore wizard won't work so you have to reinstall Windows then start ASR in Advanced mode. Note that using ASR by accident will destroy the Windows installation so hiding this functionality from inexperienced home users could be considered a good step.

[179] Do not backup system state data to drive C: as this will be formatted during the recovery process. You will need at least 2 GB space on the backup media.

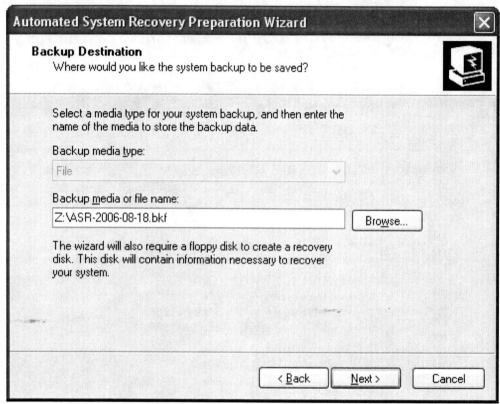

ASR Wizard

5. To start the recovery process, boot from the Windows XP Setup disc and press **F2** when prompted to run ASR.

6. Put the ASR floppy disk in the drive when prompted then press any key.

ASR will **re-format** the boot partition then start mini-setup. After a few moments, you will be prompted to select the backup media.

7. Enter the path to the .BKF file you created then click **Next** and **Finish**.

Windows Vista recovery tools

Windows Vista supports both Safe Mode and LKG; it also supports System Restore. Most of Vista's system recovery tools are accessed by booting from the product disc and selecting the **Repair** option. This boots to **Windows RE (Recovery Environment)**. It can also be installed to a recovery partition.

If the boot files are damaged, you can use the **Startup Repair** option to try to fix them. You can also launch System Restore from here.

Module 4 Installation, Troubleshooting, and Maintenance — Windows Startup and Recovery

Windows Complete PC Restore allows you to recover the complete system to a point-in-time backup image made using Vista's **Backup and Recovery** tool.

The last two options are a memory diagnostic and a command prompt (less restricted than the Recovery Console's command line).

Windows Vista image backup

Under Vista, the last resort recovery option is to make a complete backup of the system configuration and data files. This is called an **image**. This method is simple, but you do need a backup device with large capacity (the best option is usually a removable hard drive[180]) and you do have to keep the image up-to-date (or make a separate data backup).

To create an image, open the **Backup and Restore Center** from Control Panel and click the **Back up computer** button.

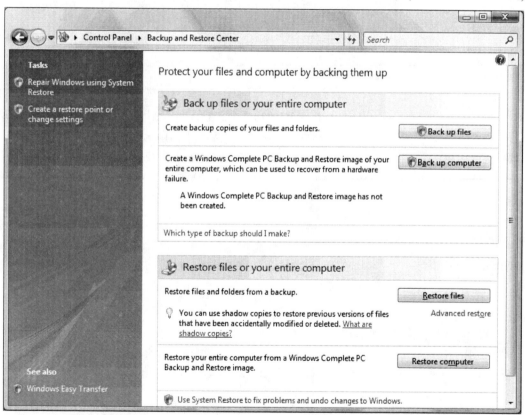

Windows Vista Backup and Restore Center

---

[180] The best compression ratio you can hope for is 2:1 (so a 20 GB system will create a 10 GB image) but if the system contains a lot of files that are already heavily compressed the ratio could be a lot lower. Windows Complete PC Backup is not included with the home editions of Vista.

| Unit 4.3 | Module 4 Installation, Troubleshooting, and Maintenance |

Select a backup device and give the image a suitable name.

To recover the system using the backup image, you can either use the dialog above, or if the system cannot be started, boot from the product CD and choose the repair option. Select **Windows Complete PC Restore** and follow the prompts.

Repair install

If none of the recovery options above works, the problem *may* be resolved by performing a **repair install**, which essentially means installing Windows over the top of the existing installation by selecting the in-place upgrade option during setup. This preserves applications and data files but is rarely a successful recovery method.

If every other recovery option fails, you can only try a clean install followed by reinstallation of applications and data files (from backup). This task may be made a little easier by using a vendor recovery disc or partition.

Recovery disc / partition

A **recovery disc** or **factory recovery partition** (also called a Rescue Disk) is a tool used by PC vendors to restore the OS environment to the same state in which it was shipped. The disc is used to boot the system then a simple wizard-driven process replaces the damaged installation with an image stored on a separate partition on the hard disk[181].

Recovery media will not usually recover user data or settings or applications installed - everything gets set back to the state in which the PC was shipped from the factory[182]. User data should be recovered from backup, which obviously has to be made before the computer becomes unbootable.

You could also create recovery media manually or using backup software or drive imaging. In this scenario, you can create images that reflect all the software and service packs that a typical machine should include. Most backup suites have a simple wizard-driven routine for creating recovery media.

---

[181] Another advantage for PC vendors and Microsoft is that they do not ship a full version of Windows with the PC. This cuts down on OEM license infringements (where an OEM version of Windows is installed on a different machine).

[182] Some discs are designed to repair the installation rather than replace it.

Page 416   IT Career FastTrack with CompTIA A+ Certification   © 2010 gtslearning

| Module 4 Installation, Troubleshooting, and Maintenance | *Windows Startup and Recovery* |

The advantages of using a recovery disc are that less time is required to re-build the machine and from a technical support point-of-view, recovery is much easier for end-users than re-installing Windows.

The main disadvantages with recovery media are that the disc only works if the original hard disk is still installed in the machine and will not include patches or service packs applied between the ship date and recovery date. The recovery image also takes up quite a lot of space and users may not feel that they are getting the hard disk capacity that they have paid for!

Note

A recovery partition is not usually allocated a drive letter so will not be obvious to the user. You can make the partition visible to Explorer through the Disk Management program.

Summary

The following table summarizes the different options for restoring different versions of Windows:

OS	Safe Mode	LKG	Boot Disk	System Restore	Repair Install	Command-Line
2000	Yes	Yes	Yes	No	ERD	Recovery Console
XP	Yes	Yes	Yes	Yes	ASR	Recovery Console
Vista	Yes	Yes	No	Yes	Image	Recovery Environment

Troubleshooting Boot Problems

Assuming there is no underlying hardware issue, the general technique for troubleshooting boot problems is to determine the failure point, and therefore the missing or corrupt file. This can then be *replaced*, either from the source files or using an emergency repair disk.

| © 2010 gtslearning | IT Career FastTrack with CompTIA A+ Certification | Page 417 |

Unit 4.3	Module 4 Installation, Troubleshooting, and Maintenance

If the system will not startup, you can try one of the system recovery tools described above. If available, use **Last Known Good** first, and then try startup menu options. Next, try **System Restore** (Windows XP/Vista only) and if that doesn't work then **Windows Complete PC Backup** (Windows Vista Business / Enterprise / Ultimate), **Automated System Recovery** (Windows XP Professional), or **Emergency Repair Disk** (Windows 2000). If none of these can resolve the problem, troubleshoot using the Recovery Console.

The following represent some typical startup problems:

- **Invalid boot disk** - the device selected for booting does not contain boot files. The most common cause of this error used to be leaving floppy disks in the drive on a restart; a modern symptom is for the BIOS to set to use USB for boot. Check for any removable disks and change the boot device priority if necessary. If this message occurs when booting from the hard disk, check the connections to the drive[183].

- **Inaccessible boot device (Stop 0x7b)** - if there is no obvious cause through change (for instance, if the disk has been repartitioned or converted to a dynamic disk recently), this could indicate a boot sector virus or a problem with the boot controller (resource conflict or driver problem). It could also indicate that the registry is corrupt.

Tip

If this error occurs during setup, it is most likely a problem with the drivers for the hard drive or drive controller (especially if it is a SCSI hard drive).

- **Unmountable boot volume** - this can be caused by using a 40-wire PATA cable in UDMA mode (replace with an 80-wire cable) but is more likely to indicate a corrupt boot sector. If the latter, you can try to repair the disk in Recovery Console using `CHKDSK` and `FIXBOOT`, however it could be that the disk is beyond repair.

- **NTLDR is missing** - replace the boot files (NTLDR, NTDETECT.COM, or BOOT.INI). If you are installing Windows on older equipment, this could indicate that the BIOS is not compatible. This could also be a symptom of a failing hard disk or virus infection.

---

[183] If the error is transitory (for example, if the message occurs a few times then the PC starts to boot OK), it could be a sign that the hard disk is failing. On an older system, it could be that the BIOS is having trouble detecting the drive.

Module 4 Installation, Troubleshooting, and Maintenance   *Windows Startup and Recovery*

Note

The equivalent in Vista is for WINLOAD or WINRESUME to be missing or corrupt. Use the Startup Recovery tool on the product disc to repair boot file problems.

- **BOOT.INI Errors** - if BOOT.INI is missing or corrupt, you will see boot errors such as "Invalid BOOT.INI", "Windows could not start", or "Hal.dll is missing or corrupt". If you do not have a backup of the file, boot to Recovery Console and use the `BOOTCFG / rebuild` command.

Note

The equivalent in Vista is for the BCD registry to be missing or corrupt. The `BOOTREC /fixboot` command can be used at the RE command prompt.

- **Windows could not start** - this indicates a missing or corrupt file (often BOOT.INI, NTOSKRNL.EXE, or a registry file (if the error points to %SystemRoot%\System32\Config).

- **System hive error** - corrupt registry file.

- **Service or device failed during system startup** - use LKG or System Restore to rollback a recent change. Otherwise, check Event Viewer to identify the problem then check the device or service's configuration.

- **Device / program in registry not found** - this is usually caused by a faulty uninstallation package that does not remove registry entries when uninstalling the device driver / program. Check the file listed; if the program is supposed to be there, try reinstalling it. If the program or device was removed, you can obtain a third-party registry cleaner product or check the vendor's website for instructions on manual removal.

  If the problem affects a core Windows file and prevents the system from booting, the best option is probably system restore or a repair install.

- **System hangs** - if this occurs up to the point the Windows logo is displayed, it is likely to indicate a problem with a device driver or the registry. Boot to Safe Mode and disable devices to try to identify the one that causes the problem. If the computer hangs at "Configuring Network Connection" or "Applying Computer Settings" the problem will be related to a service or network issue. You should also ensure the PC is free from malware.

© 2010 gtslearning   IT Career FastTrack with CompTIA A+ Certification   Page 419

Unit 4.3   Module 4 Installation, Troubleshooting, and Maintenance

Tip

System lockups could also be caused by hardware problems (typically hard disk, thermal, power, or memory problems) but try to discount software errors first.

Summary

The Windows boot process first initializes the core files (NTLDR, NTDETECT.COM, NTBOOTDD.SYS [SCSI drives], and NTOSKRNL.EXE), then loads device drivers, and finally starts services required to allow the user to log on and display the desktop. Additional services and applications configured to start automatically are also loaded. The BOOT.INI file allows the selection of a different operating system, if more than one is installed. Windows Vista uses the boot file BOOTMGR, BCD, and WINLOAD or WINRESUME and supports a new type of computer firmware for 64-bit platforms (UEFI).

The main tools used to troubleshoot boot problems are System Restore (Windows XP/Vista), Last Known Good, ASR / ERD / PC Complete Backup, Safe Mode, and Recovery Console.

Tip

To review what you have learned in this chapter, you should now visit the course website. This contains review questions and bonus material to help you to learn more and practice the topics covered in this unit.

Page 420   IT Career FastTrack with CompTIA A+ Certification   © 2010 gtslearning

Module 4 Installation, Troubleshooting, and Maintenance

Troubleshooting Windows

Unit 4.4 Troubleshooting Windows

CompTIA A+ Essentials Objectives

☐ **701.2.2 Given a scenario, explain and interpret common hardware and operating system symptoms and their causes**
OS related symptoms (Bluescreen, System lockup, Input / output device, Application install, start or load)

☐ **701.3.2 Given a scenario, demonstrate proper use of user interfaces**
Run line utilities (REGEDIT) • Administrative tools (Event Viewer)

☐ **701.3.3 Explain the process and steps to install and configure the Windows OS**
Device Manager (Verify, Install and update device drivers, Driver signing)

CompTIA A+ Practical Application Objectives

☐ **702.2.1 Select the appropriate commands to troubleshoot and resolve problems**
SFC

☐ **702.2.3 Given a scenario, select and use system utilities / tools and evaluate the results**
Administrative tools (Event Viewer) • Device Manager (Enable, Disable, Warnings, Indicators) • Task Manager (Process list, Process priority, Termination)

☐ **702.2.4 Evaluate and resolve common issues**
Operational Problems (Auto-restart errors, Bluescreen error, System lockup, Device driver failure [input / output devices], Application install, start or load failure, Service fails to start) • Error Messages and Conditions (Event Viewer [errors in the event log])

Diagnostic Tools

Several tools are available under Windows for checking the system configuration and tracking down errors.

Event Viewer

The **Event Viewer (EVENTVWR.EXE)** can be used to view log files, which are the starting point for most troubleshooting activity. The main logs are:

Log File	Description
System Log	Contains information about service load failures, hardware conflicts, driver load failures, and so on.
Security Log	This log holds the audit data for the system.
Application Log	Contains information regarding application errors.

© 2010 gtslearning   IT Career FastTrack with CompTIA A+ Certification   Page 421

The files (APPEVENT.LOG, SECURITY.LOG, and SYSTEM.LOG) are stored (by default) in the **%SystemRoot%\System32\Config** folder.

Open the Event Viewer from **Administrative Tools** or the Computer Management snap-in.

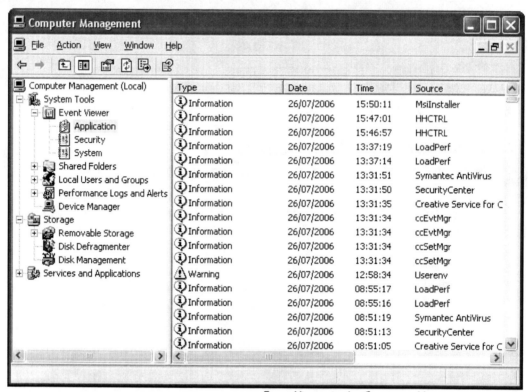

Event Viewer in the Computer Management console

Events are categorized as one of the following types:

Event	Description
Information	Significant events that describe successful operations, such as a driver starting or the event log service starting.
Warning	Events that may indicate future problems, such as when the system runs low on disk space.
Error	Significant problems, such as service failures and device conflicts.
Successful Audit	Security access attempts that were successful.
Failure Audit	Security access attempts that were unsuccessful. This may indicate a possible security breach or a mistyped password.

More information for each event can be displayed by double-clicking the event in question. This displays a screen that contains:

- Date and time of the event
- The user name
- The computer name
- An event ID
- A source
- An event type and category
- A description of the event
- The data in bytes and words

Under Windows XP, there may also be a link to the **Help and Support Center** displaying further information about the error and linking to any relevant Microsoft Knowledge Base articles.

The **View** menu has **Find** and **Filter** commands that you can use to track down particular errors or categories.

Windows Vista Event Viewer

Event Viewer in Windows Vista comes with a number of enhancements. Most notably, the default page shows a summary of system status, with recent error and warning events collected for viewing.

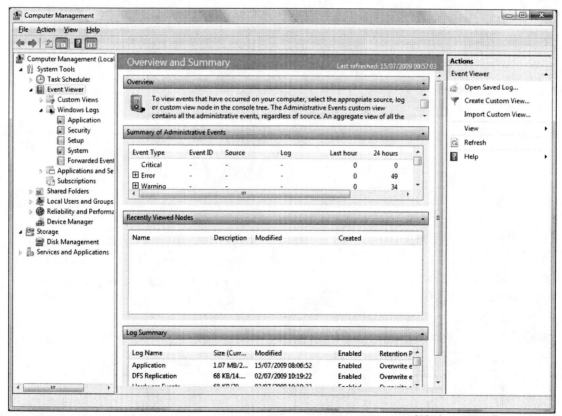

Windows Vista Event Viewer

There is also a new three-part pane view so you can view the details of the selected event in the bottom pane without having to open a separate dialog. The third pane contains useful tools for opening log files, filtering, creating a task from an event, and so on.

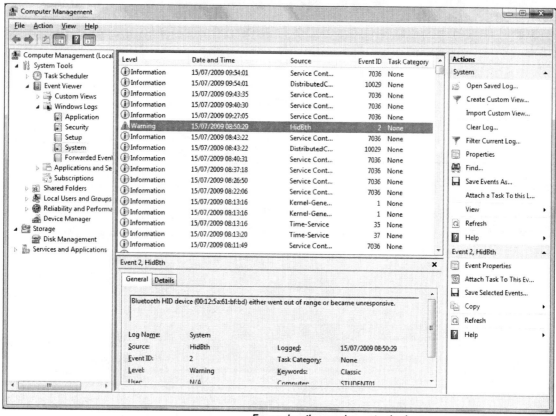

Event details are shown in the bottom pane in Windows Vista

System File Checker

Windows File Protection monitors the file signatures of system files. If a file is changed through a method other than Windows Update or installation of a hotfix or Service Pack, Windows either replaces the file automatically from **%SystemRoot%\System32\DLLCache** or from the installation media or displays a warning (when an administrator logs on). **System File Checker (SFC.EXE)** is a tool to initiate a scan and update the DLLCache. The program can be used from a command line or the Run dialog in several ways:

- SFC /*scannow* - runs a scan immediately.

- SFC /*scanonce* - schedules one scan when the computer is next restarted.

Module 4 Installation, Troubleshooting, and Maintenance   *Troubleshooting Windows*

- SFC */scanboot* - schedules scan whenever the PC boots.

If files are not found in the cache, the tool will prompt for the installation media.

Registry

The Windows **registry** stores the computer's configuration information. The registry is structured as a set of five subtrees (or **keys**) that contain computer and user databases. The **computer** database includes information about hardware and software installed on the specific computer. The **user** database includes the information in user profiles, such as desktop settings, individual preferences for certain software, and personal printer and network settings.

Root Key Name	Description
HKEY_LOCAL_MACHINE	Hardware and operating system data such as bus type, system memory, device drivers, and startup control data.
HKEY_CLASSES_ROOT	Object Linking and Embedding (OLE) and file-class association data.
HKEY_CURRENT_USER	Contains the profile for the user who is currently logged on, including environment variables, personal program groups, desktop settings, network connections, printers, and application preferences.
HKEY_USERS	Contains all actively loaded user profiles, including HKEY_CURRENT_ USER, which always refers to a child of HKEY_USERS, and the default profile.
HKEY_CURRENT_CONFIG	Contains system and software configuration information specific to this session. This section is built using the settings within HKEY_LOCAL_MACHINE and the hardware profiles set by the administrator.

The registry database is stored in binary files called **hives**. A hive comprises a single file (with no extension), a .LOG file (containing a transaction log), and a .SAV file (a copy of the key as it was at the end of setup). The system hive also has an .ALT backup file.

These files are stored in the *%SystemRoot%\System32\Config* folder, but hive files for user profiles are stored in the folder holding the user's profile.

The following table shows the standard hives for a computer running Windows[184]:

---

[184] HKEY_CLASSES_ROOT is not stored in a hive but built from the \SOFTWARE\CLASSES keys in CURRENT_USER and LOCAL_MACHINE.

© 2010 gtslearning   IT Career FastTrack with CompTIA A+ Certification   Page 425

Hive	Files
HKEY_CURRENT_CONFIG	system, system.alt, system.log, system.sav
HKEY_CURRENT_USER	ntuser.dat, ntuser.dat.log
HKEY_LOCAL_MACHINE\SAM	sam, sam.log, sam.sav
HKEY_LOCAL_MACHINE\SECURITY	security, security.log, security.sav
HKEY_LOCAL_MACHINE\SOFTWARE	software, software.log, software.sav
HKEY_LOCAL_MACHINE\SYSTEM	system, system.alt, system.log, system.sav
HKEY_USERS\DEFAULT	default, default.log, default.sav

Most changes to the registry are made via utilities, such as Control Panel applets or Device Manager. If necessary though, a change can be made directly using the Registry Editor.

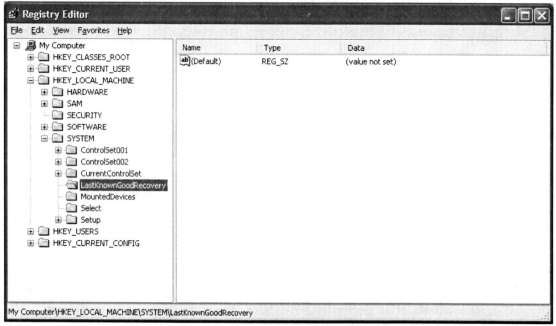

Registry Editor showing keys, subkeys, and values

Each individual key can contain data items called **value entries** and can also contain additional **subkeys**. In the registry structure, keys are analogous to folders, and the value entries are analogous to files.

A value entry has three parts: the name of the value, the data type of the value, and the value itself, which can be data of any length.

The following table lists the different data types:

Data Type	Description
REG_BINARY	Raw binary data. Most hardware component information is stored as binary data and displayed in hexadecimal format.
REG_DWORD	Data represented by a number that is 4 bytes long. Many parameters for device drivers and services are this type and can be displayed in binary, hex, or decimal format.
REG_SZ	A sequence of characters representing human-readable text.
REG_MULTI_SZ	A multiple string. Values that contain lists or multiple values in human readable text are usually this type. Entries are separated by NULL characters.
REG_EXPAND_SZ	An expandable data string, which is text that contains a variable to be replaced when called by an application. For example, the string %SystemRoot% would be replaced by the actual location of the folder containing the Windows system files.

The **Registry Editor** can be accessed from the **Start > Run** menu or the command prompt[185]. You can use it to view or edit the registry and back up and restore portions of the registry. Use the **Find** tool (**CTRL+F**) to search for a key or value. If you want to move portions of the registry database, and use them on other computers, use the **Export Registry File** option from the **File** menu. The file can be merged into another computer's registry by double-clicking it (or calling it from a script).

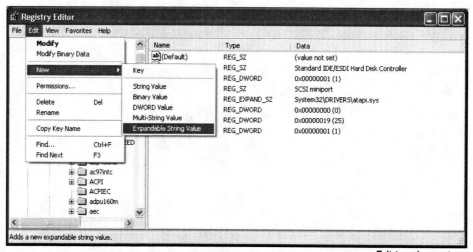

Editing the registry

---

[185] In Windows XP, typing either REGEDIT or REGEDT32 brings up the **same** Registry Editor (version 5.1). Note that this version is different to both REGEDIT and REGEDT32 from Windows 2000 (essentially it combines the functionality of both, except for not having the Read Only mode of REGEDT32). In Vista, both commands work but the Registry Editor is on version 6.

| Unit 4.4 | Module 4 Installation, Troubleshooting, and Maintenance |

The default export format is a plain text registration file. If you merge changes from a .REG file back to the registry, *additions* that you have made to the registry will not be overwritten. Use the **Registry Hive Files** format to create a **binary** copy of that portion of the registry. Restoring from the binary file will remove any additions you made as well as reversing changes.

Troubleshooting Windows Errors and Lockups

This topic lists some symptoms of common Windows errors and some possible solutions.

Bluescreens

Blue Screens (of Death or BSOD) during installation or following the addition of hardware usually indicate a hardware / driver problem. If Last Known Good or System Restore does not solve the problem, make a note of the stop error code (which will be in the form: **Stop: 0x0...**) and use the Microsoft Knowledge Base to troubleshoot.

Bluescreens at other times can be caused by file system errors, a corrupt pagefile, corrupt registry data, or faulty memory chips.

```
A problem has been detected and Windows has been shut down to prevent damage
to your computer.

If this is the first time you've seen this Stop error screen,
restart your computer. If this screen appears again, follow
these steps:

Disable or uninstall any anti-virus, disk defragmentation
or backup utilities. Check your hard drive configuration,
and check for any updated drivers. Run CHKDSK /F to check
for hard drive corruption, and then restart your computer.

Technical information:

*** STOP: 0x00000024 (0x001902FE,0xB994FB6C,0xB994F868,0xF8A2F746)


***        Ntfs.sys - Address F8A2F746 base at F8A1E000, DateStamp 41107eea

Beginning dump of physical memory
Physical memory dump complete.
Contact your system administrator or technical support group for further
assistance.
```

BSOD

| Page 428 | IT Career FastTrack with CompTIA A+ Certification | © 2010 gtslearning |

Module 4 Installation, Troubleshooting, and Maintenance   *Troubleshooting Windows*

Note

If the system autorestarts after a bluescreen and you cannot read the error, press F8 after POST to open the **Advanced Options** menu and select the **Disable automatic restarts** option.

Lockups and reboots

A **lockup** (or "hang") is where the computer stops responding to input. There are several scenarios:

- A single application stops responding.

- Multiple applications stop responding but the mouse cursor still moves.

- The computer does not respond to any sort of mouse or keyboard input.

Firstly, you should establish whether the system is actually locked or whether it is just slow to respond. If the latter, the usual cause is that too many programs are running. The only solution is to install more memory or run fewer programs.

If anti-virus software with on-access scanning is installed, check that it is configured to exclude the print spooler (%SystemRoot%\System32\Spool) and Windows Update (%SystemRoot%\SoftwareDistribution\Datastore) as online scanning of these can cause lockups. Also, Windows Update itself can cause lockup problems (100% CPU utilization), though installing the latest version of the Windows Update software should resolve this.

If an application is not responding, you can use **Task Manager** to close it (see "Troubleshooting Applications" below. If you cannot open Task Manager, then the system has crashed. If the computer is completely unresponsive, hold the power button down for a few seconds. The computer will switch itself off (this is called a hard reset). Wait for 10-20 seconds then switch the PC on again. Windows will run scandisk to check the hard disk for problems and display the Advanced Options menu. Again, if the problem persists, you will need to investigate the cause or restore the system from a backup.

Lockups are usually a sign of a hardware problem, such as overheating or unstable power supply. Spontaneous reboots (or auto-restarts) are also usually signs of a hardware problem. If you can rule out a hardware problem (which will typically be a disk, thermal, power, or memory problem), it could be a faulty driver or system/application file (a "memory leak").

© 2010 gtslearning   IT Career FastTrack with CompTIA A+ Certification   Page 429

Managing and Troubleshooting Devices

In order to install or configure devices and to install software you must have the proper **permissions**[186]. By default, installation tasks are performed by users in the **Administrators** security group, often using an account named "Administrator".

Adding a device

Almost all devices and expansion cards that you can connect to a Windows computer are **Plug-and-Play**. This means that Windows automatically detects when a new device is connected, locates drivers for it, and installs and configures it (with minimal user input).

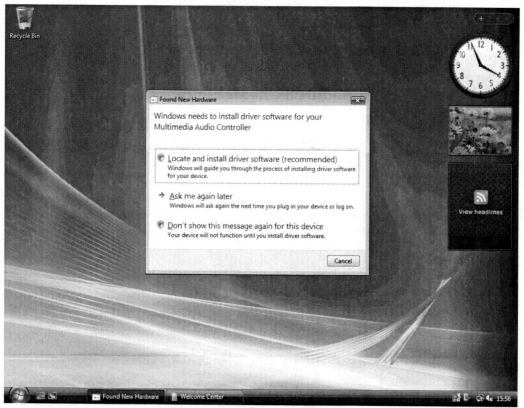

Detecting and installing a new device in Windows Vista

---

[186] You do not need to be an administrator to connect USB devices, though if the device requires driver installation you will need to supply administrative credentials.

Windows ships with drivers for some standard hardware devices but in some cases, you may need to install the hardware vendor's driver *before* connecting the device. The vendor usually provides a setup program to accomplish this.

> **Note**
> When using a 64-bit edition of Windows, you **must** obtain 64-bit device drivers. 32-bit drivers will **not** work.

There may also be circumstances where you need to install a device manually, disable or remove a device, or update a device's driver. The **Add Hardware** wizard supports the manual addition of devices while **Device Manager** is used to configure them.

Add Hardware Wizard

The precise stages in the **Add Hardware Wizard** are different between the various versions of Windows[187] but in all of them by selecting the appropriate options you can get to the point where you choose which hardware you want to install manually:

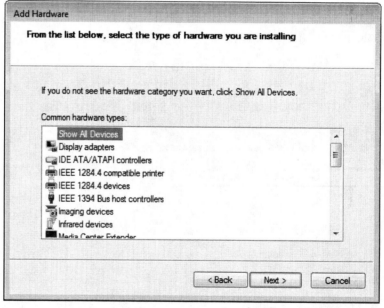

Installing a device manually

Choose the type of hardware from the list then select from the list of manufacturers and models, and Windows will attempt to allocate it resources.

---

[187] In Windows 2000, it is the Add/Remove Hardware wizard and as the name suggests you can also use it to remove devices. In later versions of Windows, you use Device Manager exclusively to do this. XP insists on searching for installed devices first (which typically takes quite a long time) while Vista allows you to go straight to the "manually install a device" step.

Using signed drivers

According to Microsoft, many problems experienced by users with Windows are actually related to poorly written device drivers. Driver signing (or Windows Logo testing) means that the driver has been tested by Microsoft. It also verifies that the driver has not been modified (to act as malware for instance).

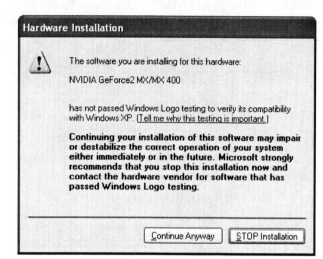

Unsigned driver warning

Unsigned drivers are not necessarily unsafe but you should find out from the vendor what sort of testing they have done.

In Windows 2000/XP, you can configure a policy to block or warn about unsigned drivers. Open **System Properties** then click the **Hardware** tab. Click the **Driver Signing** button and select **Ignore**, **Warn**, or **Block** as required.

Driver Signing Options

In Windows Vista, this policy is not configurable. In 32-bit versions, the system always prompts about unsigned drivers or ones with an untrustworthy certificate (Windows cannot verify the publisher) or ones where the driver has been altered subsequently to its being signed. 64-bit versions of Windows Vista **require** signed kernel mode drivers and will not install drivers where the publisher cannot be verified.

The **File Signature Verification (SIGVERIF)** utility is also useful in some circumstances. It provides a report about system files and device drivers that have not been digitally signed and may therefore be causing some sort of system instability.

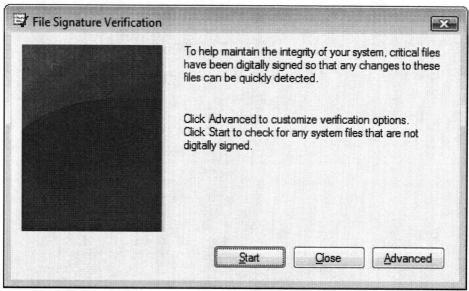

File Signature Verification (SIGVERIF) utility

Testing and configuring devices

When you have installed a device, the best way to test it is to try using it. If you suspect a problem with a device or want to update a driver, you can view and configure its properties via **Device Manager**.

You can open Device Manager (`DEVMGMT.MSC`) from the **Hardware** tab in **System Properties** or from the default **Computer Management** console.

The **View** menu allows you to sort devices in different ways (view devices or resources by connection or by type). Malfunctioning devices are shown with a yellow exclamation mark and may be listed as "Unknown Device".

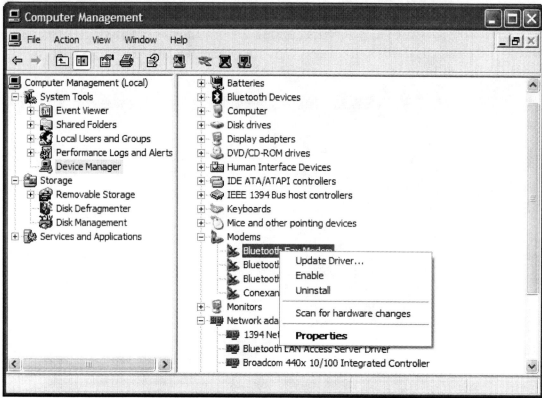

Device Manager - note the options in the shortcut menu for each device

If you alt-click a device you can select **Properties** from the context menu to configure it (there are also options to **Disable/Enable** and **Uninstall** the device and to **Update Driver**).

Driver details for a display adapter

The **Driver** tab contains an option to view **Driver Details**, useful if you want to find out the file name. A **signed driver** is indicated by an icon with a green tick. Other options on this page allow you to **Update Driver**, **Uninstall**, and (under Windows XP) **Roll Back Driver**, which allows you to revert to the previously installed driver.

A new driver may not work properly because it has not been fully tested or it may not work on your particular system[188].

The **Resources** tab shows information about which interrupt and memory settings the device is using. This can be used to troubleshoot resources conflicts (where two devices attempt to use the same resource), but these hardly ever happen under Plug-and-Play.

Viewing resource settings for a display adapter - note the "No conflicts" message

---

[188] When installing drivers, always check the notebook (or PC) vendor's site for an OEM version of the driver first. Devices used by system builders can be slightly different from retail versions and may need a different driver to work properly with the chipset and BIOS. This is more often the case with notebooks than desktop PCs.

| Unit 4.4 | Module 4 Installation, Troubleshooting, and Maintenance |

There may be other tabs to configure device settings, though most devices are controlled using a Control Panel applet or vendor software.

Note

Also check that the device is plugged in correctly. Check for loose or damaged cables / connectors. In the case of PS/2 and audio devices (microphones, headphones, and speakers) check that the device is plugged into the correct port (they are color-coded).

Uninstalling and disabling a device

If a device supports Plug-and-Play and is hot swappable, you can remove it from the computer without having to uninstall it. If however, you want to remove the drivers for the device, you can uninstall a device prior to physically removing it by alt-clicking in Device Manager and selecting **Uninstall**.

There is also an option to **Disable** a device, which you might use if it is not working with the current driver and want to make it inaccessible to users while you find a replacement or to improve system security by disabling unused devices (such as modems). Disabled devices are shown with a red cross in Windows 2000 / XP (in Vista they are shown with a down arrow). If you need to reactivate a disabled device, alt-click and select **Enable**.

Hardware profiles

Windows 2000 and XP provide support for **hardware profiles**. If your system operates in two or more very different configurations (perhaps you have a mobile computer, which you plug into a docking station in the office and at home use a modem to connect to the network) then by building two distinct configurations, you can choose between them during the boot sequence.

Windows Vista has dropped support for configurable profiles. Vista still creates a profile in some circumstances (for docked and undocked laptops for instance) but there is no user option to select a profile at boot time or configure which devices are available. It is still possible to choose which *services* run under a particular profile though.

Page 436 IT Career FastTrack with CompTIA A+ Certification © 2010 gtslearning

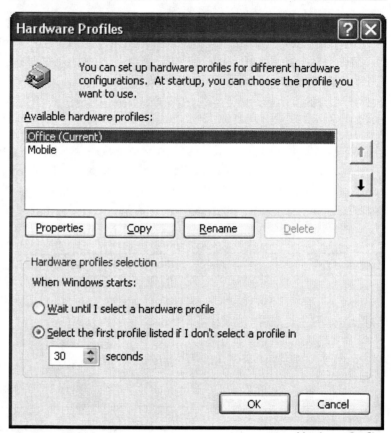
Hardware Profiles

Troubleshooting Applications

Installation

If an application will not install, the first thing to do is to check that the system meets the hardware and operating system requirements. If the proper requirements are met, check for any known issues in the software's ReadMe or through the vendor's website.

Load errors

If a correctly installed application (that is, one that appears in Add / Remove Programs / Programs and Features and has files installed to the Program Files folder) cannot be located, try searching for the shortcut.

| Unit 4.4 | Module 4 Installation, Troubleshooting, and Maintenance |

Some applications install shortcuts to the desktop; some to the Start menu only. The shortcut may appear in a Program Group or in the "root" of the Start menu. Also, in some circumstances a program may not be made available to all users of the computer; only the user that installed it. If the shortcut to a program has been deleted or moved by accident, it should be relatively simple to re-create.

If an application will not load, the best course is probably to try re-installing it (or use the Setup program's Repair feature), unless you can diagnose a specific problem. If the user receives an error such as "Access Denied", they need to be granted permissions on the folder containing the application[189].

Service problems

Some applications (and Windows subsystems) depend on **background services**. The system will display a message if a service fails to start. Check Event Viewer to see which one has failed. If a program is not working, you should also check that dependent services have not been disabled.

User errors

If you encounter an "Invalid working directory" or "File not found" error, the cause is likely to be either that the file or folder has been renamed or deleted or that the disk holding the file is not available (for example, a network connection has been lost or a removable disk has been ejected).

If files or folders are moved or renamed, shortcuts pointing to the resource may need to be updated manually.

Errors that occur through use of the product generally need to be assisted through specialist support. In the absence of any expert advice, check for a solution in the product's online help, Knowledge Base, or documentation.

---

[189] Windows developer best practice states that users should not need to write to the application's directory (which will be in "Program Files") as ordinary users do not have permission to do this. Some older or poorly written applications may not follow this practice however. In Vista, this can cause compatibility problems with User Account Control (UAC). If this is the case (and you are confident that the program is otherwise secure), use the program shortcut's Compatibility tab to configure it to Run as Administrator.

Page 438   IT Career FastTrack with CompTIA A+ Certification   © 2010 gtslearning

Program "Not Responding"

If a previously working application stops functioning, first try restarting it using **Task Manager** then try restarting the computer. If this doesn't fix the problem, it could be that files used by the application have been corrupted. Try re-installing the application. If this doesn't work, contact the application vendor.

Task Manager

Occasionally Windows programs will hang or stop responding. Sometimes they will recover without user intervention, but you may need to close them down manually. This can be done in **Task Manager**.

Press **CTRL+SHIFT+ESC** to open Task Manager (or run **TASKMGR.EXE**) and click the **Applications** tab. Note the running programs on your system.

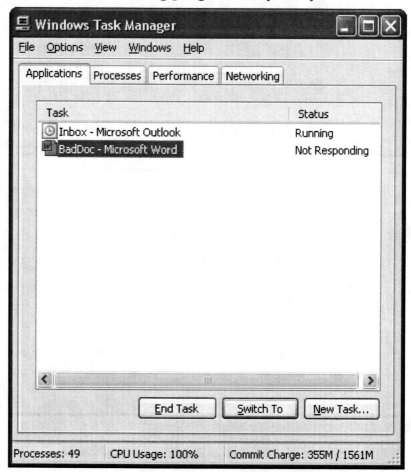

Windows Task Manager

Unit 4.4 Module 4 Installation, Troubleshooting, and Maintenance

Any that have stalled will be listed as **Not Responding**. Alt-click the offending program and choose **End Task** then click **End Now** in the confirmation dialog. The program should close and normal activity will resume[190].

> **Note**
>
> In most cases, you will lose any unsaved data that the program was processing. Some software (notably Microsoft Office) has the option to try to recover unsaved data. You can also configure most types of software to save files automatically.

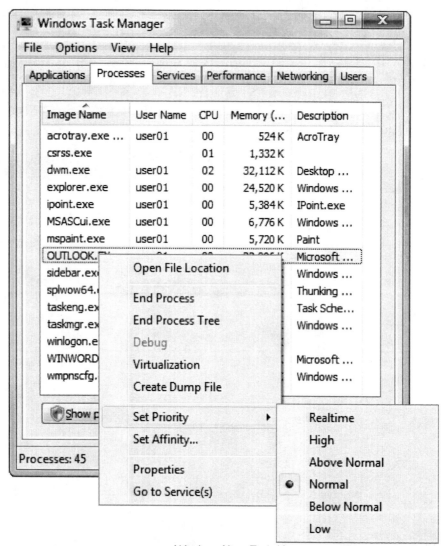

Windows Vista Task Manager - setting process priority

---

[190] An ordinary user can end unresponsive applications but administrative rights are required to end processes that were not started by the user. This protects the system as things like malware cannot disable anti-virus software.

The **Applications** tab only shows programs that have open desktop windows. If there is a problem with a background service, use the **Processes** tab to identify it. If a process is not responding or if you suspect it is faulty, you can alt-click and select **End Process** to terminate it.

In some circumstances, you may want to privilege one task over another (or conversely, set one task to have fewer resources than others). You can do this by alt-clicking the process and choosing an option from the **Set Priority** submenu.

For example, if you had a Voice over IP application and its priority was not already set to **Realtime**, changing its priority might improve call quality as the CPU would privilege that process over ones set to any other level.

Error reporting options

When a program stops responding or crashes, Dr Watson (DRWTSN32.EXE) will attempt to generate an error log (DRWTSN32.LOG).

The error log can be sent to the application developer to assist them in troubleshooting.

The default location for the log file is C:\Documents and Settings\All Users\Application Data\Microsoft\Dr Watson.

Windows XP allows you to define what action will be taken if it encounters an error while running a program.

Options include:

- Disable error reporting.
- Enable for Windows operating system.
- Enable for programs (which can then be specified via the **Choose Programs** button).

Error reporting

When errors occur, the report can be sent to Microsoft to enable them to enhance future products and perhaps to add features to a planned service pack.

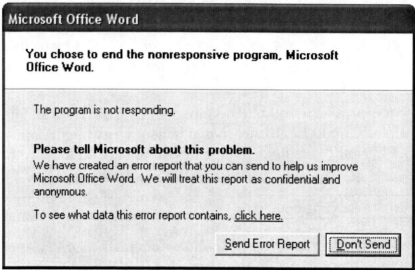

Microsoft Office error reporting

When the error has been reported, you may get a link to the relevant Microsoft Knowledge Base article with hints on how to avoid the problem in the future.

Problem Reports and Solutions

Windows Vista comes with a more advanced tool called **Problem Reports and Solutions**. Like XP, it prompts you to send a crash report over the internet but you can continue to monitor the status of the problem using the applet in Control Panel and discover whether any Windows or third-party updates have been made available to fix the problem.

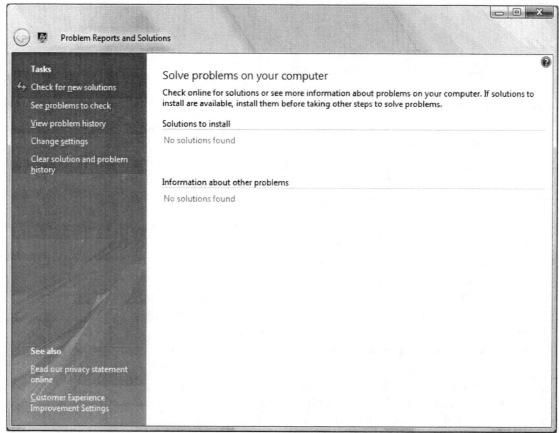

Problem Reports and Solutions

Summary

Windows and applications usually generate error messages, which you can investigate via Event Viewer.

Devices interface with the system using a device driver. If a device has a problem, the first step will usually be to check for an updated driver from the manufacturer. Driver signing confirms that a manufacturer's driver has been fully tested under Windows. Device Manager provides a central point for verifying and configuring devices. You can use it to update drivers, check device properties, configure system resource settings, and enable/disable devices.

Task Manager can be used to manage applications and faulty processes. Error Reporting generates crash debug files that can assist software developers with troubleshooting.

Unit 4.5   Module 4 Installation, Troubleshooting, and Maintenance

Unit 4.5 Troubleshooting Components

CompTIA A+ Essentials Objectives

☐ **701.2.2 Given a scenario, explain and interpret common hardware and operating system symptoms and their causes**

Hardware related symptoms (Excessive heat, Noise, Odours, Status light indicators, Alerts, Visible damage [e.g. cable, plastic])

CompTIA A+ Practical Application Objectives

☐ **702.1.1 Given a scenario, install, configure, and maintain personal computer components**

Motherboards (Jumper settings, CMOS battery, Advanced BIOS settings, Bus speeds, Chipsets, Firmware updates)

☐ **702.1.2 Given a scenario, detect problems, troubleshoot and repair/replace personal computer components**

Storage devices (HDD [SATA, PATA, Solid state], FDD, Optical drives [CD / DVD / RW / Blu-ray], Removable, External) • Motherboards (Jumper settings, CMOS battery, Advanced BIOS settings, Bus speeds, Chipsets, Firmware updates, Socket types, Expansion slots, Memory slots, Front panel connectors, I/O ports [Sound, video, USB 1.1, USB 2.0, serial, IEEE 1394 / Firewire, parallel, NIC, modem, PS/2]) • Power supplies (Wattages and capacity, Connector types and quantity, Output voltage) • Processors (Socket types, Speed, Number of cores, Power consumption, Cache, Front side bus, 32-bit vs. 64-bit) • Memory • Adapter cards (Graphics cards - memory, Sound cards, Storage controllers [RAID cards - levels 0,1,5, eSATA cards], I/O cards [Firewire, USB, Parallel, Serial), Wired and wireless network cards, Capture cards [TV, video], Media reader]) • Cooling systems (Heat sinks, Thermal compound, CPU fans, Case fans)

☐ **702.2.3 Given a scenario, select and use system utilities / tools and evaluate the results**

Disk Manager (Drive status [Foreign drive, Healthy, Formatting, Active, Unallocated, Failed, Dynamic, Offline, Online])

☐ **702.1.4 Given a scenario, select and use the following tools**

Multimeter • Power supply tester • Loopback plugs

Troubleshooting Basic Hardware Problems

When troubleshooting a suspected hardware problem, look for simple solutions first.

■ Find out if anything has changed.

■ Eliminate hardware issues as a cause first.

■ Try one thing at a time.

Module 4 Installation, Troubleshooting, and Maintenance   *Troubleshooting Components*

■ Take care to ensure that a user's data is backed up before proceeding.

Hardware symptoms

There are several externally observable symptoms that may help you to diagnose a hardware problem without having to open the computer chassis.

Status indicators

Most devices have a status Light Emitting Diode (LED) to indicate that the device is receiving power / switched on.

Some devices may have additional status indicators or show other functions. For example, a hard drive LED shows activity; normally this should flicker periodically - if a hard drive LED is solid for extended periods it can indicate a problem, especially if the PC is not doing any obvious processing.

Similarly, network adapters often have LEDs to indicate the connection speed and activity on the network.

Alerts

Most PC systems now have quite good internal monitoring systems (such as the internal thermometers). When these systems detect problems, they can display an administrative alert, either on the local system or to some sort of network management system.

The operating system may also be able to detect some kinds of hardware failure and display an appropriate alert.

Excessive heat

Excessive heat damages the sensitive circuitry of a computer very easily. If a system feels hot to the touch you should check that the fans are operating and are not clogged by dirt or dust.

As mentioned above, many systems now come with internal temperature sensors that you can check via driver or management software. Use the vendor documentation to confirm that the system is operating within acceptable limits.

© 2010 gtslearning   IT Career FastTrack with CompTIA A+ Certification   Page 445

| Unit 4.5 | Module 4 Installation, Troubleshooting, and Maintenance |

Thermal problems are also likely to cause symptoms such as spontaneous reboots or lockups. These will typically be cyclic - if you turn the system off and allow it to cool, the problem will only reappear once it has been running long enough for heat to build up again.

Noise

Devices may also start to fail over time - drives of most types are most prone to failure but sensitive chips such as memory and graphics adapters can also develop problems (often caused by some underlying thermal issue).

Unusual noises can often indicate that a device such as a fan or hard drive is failing. Note that these may not be caused by hardware problems alone. For example, a fan that sounds noisy may be spinning too fast because its driver software is not controlling it properly. You also need to be able to distinguish between "healthy" noises and "unhealthy" ones. For example, a hard disk may make a certain "whirring whine" when first spinning up and a "chattering" noise when data is being written[191], but clicking, squealing, loud noise, or continual noise can all indicate problems.

Odors

Unusual odors will almost always indicate something overheating (often at the point where it is too late to save the unfortunate component). The system should be shut down immediately and the problem investigated.

Visible damage

If a system has had liquid spilled on it or if fans or the keyboard are clogged by dust or dirt, there may be visible signs of this.

Actual physical damage to a computer system is usually caused to peripherals, ports, and cables. Damage to other components is only really likely if the unit has been in transit somewhere. Inspect a unit closely for damage to the case; even a small crack or dent may indicate a fall or knock that could have caused worse damage to the internal components than is obvious from outside.

---

[191] Newer and more expensive models make very little noise. There may also be a setting in BIOS to optimize disk performance to reduce noise.

If a peripheral device does not work, examine the port and the end of the cable closely for bent, broken, or dirty pins and connectors. Examine the length of the cable for damage.

Using diagnostic utilities

There are numerous test and benchmarking products available to help with diagnosing problems and establishing performance benchmarks and monitoring.

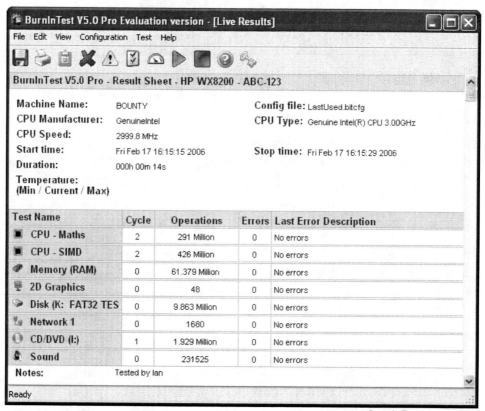

BurnInTest diagnostics

Vendors often sell individual test products for memory, buses, networks, and so on, as well as product suites. Some examples include Eurosoft's PC-Check, Micro2000's MicroScope, and PassMark's BurnInTest.

PCs built by the major vendors now tend to ship with built-in diagnostic utilities, as this facilitates the provision of remote support and reduces the number of units that have to be shipped "back to base" under warranty. These utilities typically run by pressing a function key at startup or can be installed as an application and run under Windows.

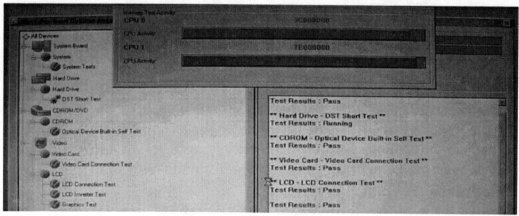

Dell diagnostic utility

Troubleshooting Power Problems

PC components need a constant, stable supply of power to run. If the computer will not start, it is likely to be due to a power problem. If the PC suddenly turns off or restarts, power problems are also likely.

Computer will not start

In the normal course of operations, the **Power Supply Unit (PSU)** converts the AC mains supply to DC voltages. DC voltage is used to power the internal drives and motherboard components. When the PSU is sure that it is providing a stable supply, it sends a **power good** signal to the processor.

The processor then begins to run the **Power On Self Test (POST)** program.

If none of the LEDs on the front panel of the system case are lit up and you cannot hear the fans or hard drives spinning, the computer is not getting power. This is likely to be one of a fault in the PSU, incoming mains electricity supply, power cables/connectors, or fuses. To isolate the cause, try the following tests:

- Check that other equipment in the area is working; there may be a blackout.

- Check that the PSU is connected to the PC and the wall socket correctly and that all switches are in the "on" position.

- Try another power cable - there may be a problem with the plug or fuse. Check that all of the wires are connected to the correct terminals in the plug. Check the fuse resistance with a multimeter (see below).

| Module 4 Installation, Troubleshooting, and Maintenance | Troubleshooting Components |

- Try plugging another piece of "known-good" equipment (such as a lamp) into the wall socket. If it does not work, the wall socket is faulty. Use another socket and get an electrician to investigate the fault.

- Check the voltages from the PSU with a multimeter. If these voltages are incorrect, the PSU has failed and must be replaced.

- Try disconnecting extra devices, such as optical drives. If this solves the problem, the PSU is underpowered and you need to fit one with a higher power rating.

Using a multimeter

A multi-purpose meter can be used to measure voltage, current, and resistance.

The original multimeters were analog devices; that is, they were based upon a mechanical moving coil with a pointer to indicate the value of the reading. Most modern meters are digital and have an LED or LCD readout. Digital meters are generally easier to read than analog types. They often have additional built-in testing functions, such as a transistor tester, conductance, thermometer, diode status, audio Wattmeter, and network cable tester.

1. Check the meter's leads before use. Do not use leads with damaged or broken probes or damaged insulation.

2. Where possible, connect the test meter before powering up the circuit and power down before removing the meter.

3. Connect the **black** test lead to the terminal on the meter marked **COM** or **REF**.

4. Connect the **red** lead to the terminal corresponding to the measurement to be taken. There may be more than one terminal for the red lead; examine the markings around the terminals. A typical arrangement is one terminal for measuring voltage and resistance and a separate one for current. There may also be a third 10A or high-current terminal.

5. Turn on the multimeter.

6. Adjust the switch so that it corresponds to the reading to be taken:

   □ Meters generally have settings for **Volts DC**, **Volts AC**, **Resistance**, and **Current (DC)**.

© 2010 gtslearning   IT Career FastTrack with CompTIA A+ Certification   Page 449

- Some meters have only one setting for each type of measurement. Some have multiple ranges; for example mV, Volts, 20V, 200V. Make sure the switch position corresponds to the maximum value likely to be measured.

> **Note**
> When measuring unknown voltages or current, always set the multimeter to its highest range first and then switch down if necessary to obtain a more accurate reading. The meter will probably not be damaged if the wrong range is selected, but it will not be able to display a correct reading.

7. Before taking a measurement, check that the leads are connected to the correct terminals and that all meter switches are in the correct position.

> **Note**
> Do not adjust switch settings while the meter is connected to an energized circuit; this can damage the meter.

8. To test PSU outputs, insert the **black** probe into a **ground** connector. Insert the other probe into the connector to be tested.

9. Turn on the PSU, ensuring that you are not touching any part of the PC, and take a reading from the multimeter. Use the diagrams below to determine whether the readings are correct.

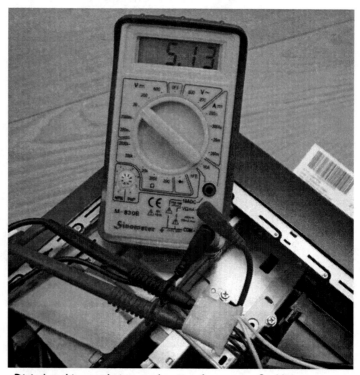

Digital multimeter being used to test the output of a Molex connector

The standard pin-outs for the ATX and ATX12V connectors are:

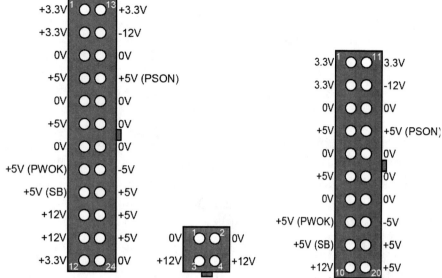

ATX 24-pin, ATX 12V 4-pin, and 20-pin connectors

For Molex connectors, the yellow cable supplies 12V, the red cable supplies 5V, and the black cable is ground (0V). For SATA power connectors, pins are as follows:

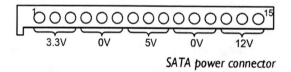

SATA power connector

PCIe power connectors are +12V on pins 1-3 or 1-4 (the yellow cables) and ground (0V) on the others (black cables).

Be aware that you may not get exactly the same results as those quoted in the diagrams. A degree of tolerance is allowed:

Supply line	Tolerance	Acceptable Values Minimum	Maximum
+5V	±5%	+4.75V	+5.25V
+12V	±5%	+11.4V	+12.6V
-5V	±5%	-5.25V	-4.75V
-12V	±10%	-13.2V	-10.8V
+3.3V	±5%	+3.14V	+3.47V

Also be aware that the PSU might not conform to the ATX specification and use different pin-outs. *Always refer to up-to-date documentation before starting any tests.*

> **Note**
> If you suspect that a power supply is faulty, do not leave it turned on for longer than absolutely necessary and do not leave it unattended. Keep watch for external signs of a problem (for example, smoke or fire). Turn off immediately if there are any unusual sights, smells, or noises.

If it seems that the PSU voltages are correct and that all power connectors are properly in place, then there may be a fault or overload on one of the peripheral devices (for example, the floppy or the hard disk). Remove one peripheral device at a time (turn OFF when removing and reconnecting devices) to confirm if the fault lies with one of these units. If you still cannot identify the fault, then the problem is likely to be the motherboard.

> **Tip**
> To test a fuse, set the multimeter to measure resistance and touch the probes to each end of the fuse. A good fuse should have virtually zero Ohms of resistance; a blown fuse will have virtually infinite resistance.

Power supply tester

A **Power Supply Tester** is a device designed (unsurprisingly) with the sole purpose of testing PSUs. It is much simpler to use than a multimeter as you do not have to test each pin in turn.

Typical models come with ports for the 20/24-pin P1, Molex, SATA, plus 8-pin, 6-pin, and 4-pin connectors found on different models of PSU. Usually each pin on each port has an LED to indicate whether the voltage supplied is good.

Casebuy EZ Power Supply Tester (www.casebuy.com.tw)

Module 4 Installation, Troubleshooting, and Maintenance   *Troubleshooting Components*

Troubleshooting POST Problems

Once the CPU has been given the power-good signal from the PSU, it loads the BIOS from ROM and performs the **Power-On Self Test (POST)**. The POST is a built-in diagnostic program that checks the hardware to ensure the components required to boot the PC are present and functioning correctly.

1. The POST starts by locating video card BIOS at the address C000 in memory. If found, the video card is initialized from its own BIOS. Information from the card manufacturer may also be displayed at this point.

2. A startup screen is displayed. More tests on the system, including counting through system RAM, are performed. If any errors are found, a text error message is displayed. Explanations of these messages are usually found in the system guide. Once numeric codes, these messages now tend to be descriptive, such as "key stuck".

3. You should be able to access the CMOS Setup routine from this point. This allows you to reconfigure the settings stored in CMOS RAM. The key used to invoke CMOS Setup varies according to the BIOS, but is usually **DELETE, F2, ESC, F10,** or **F1**.

4. Some PCs indicate that system checks have been successfully completed at this point with a single short beep but the trend for modern computers it to boot silently.

5. A search is made for further interfaces that may have ROM BIOS chips on them. This could include SCSI host adapters and network cards. Further information about these cards may be displayed at this point and their memory addresses reserved.

6. The BIOS may display a summary screen about the system configuration. This may scroll by quite quickly. Use the **PAUSE** key if you want to analyze it.

7. The operating system load sequence starts.

The sorts of things that can disrupt this process are described below...

© 2010 gtslearning   IT Career FastTrack with CompTIA A+ Certification   Page 453

| Unit 4.5 | Module 4 Installation, Troubleshooting, and Maintenance |

POST not running

If power is present, but the screen is blank and there are no beeps from the speaker it is likely that the POST procedure is not executing. The most likely causes are faulty cabling or a damaged or mis-seated CPU or other motherboard component. To troubleshoot, try the following tests and solutions:

- Ask what has changed - if the BIOS has been flashed and the PC has not booted since, the BIOS update may have failed. Use the reset procedure (see unit 4.1 for notes on updating firmware).

- Check cabling and connections, especially if maintenance work has just been performed on the PC. An incorrectly oriented PATA cable or a badly seated adapter card can stop the POST from running. Correct any errors, reset adapter cards, and then reboot the PC.

- Check for faulty interfaces and devices - it is possible that a faulty adapter card or device is halting the POST. Try removing one device at a time to see if this solves the problem (or remove all non-essential devices then add them back one-by-one).

- Check for logic errors - POST test adapter cards can interpret the debug codes given by the BIOS. The card displays the codes, so that you can check where the POST has stopped executing.

- Check for a faulty CPU or BIOS. If possible, replace the CPU and BIOS chips with known good ones.

- Some motherboards have jumpers to configure modes (such as BIOS recovery) or processor settings. If the jumpers are set incorrectly it could cause the computer to boot. If a computer will not work after being serviced, check that the jumpers have not been changed.

Tip

Remember to ask "What has changed" when troubleshooting. For example, it is best practice to check that a system works properly after performing any sort of servicing work (such as updating the BIOS) but not all technicians are so diligent. If a user complains that their previously working PC will not boot, find out what happened to it in the intervening period.

Module 4 Installation, Troubleshooting, and Maintenance | Troubleshooting Components

POST errors

If POST detects a problem, it generates an error message. As the error may prevent the computer from displaying anything on a screen, an error with a core component is often indicated by a series of beeps.

For a beep code, you must decode the pattern of beeps and take the appropriate action. Use resources such as the system documentation or the manufacturer's website to determine the meaning of the beep code[192].

The beep codes for the original IBM PC are listed below:

Code	Error
1 short beep	Normal POST - system is OK.
2 short beeps	POST Error - error code shown on screen.
No beep	Power supply or motherboard problem (but if the PC boots, use a multimeter to check the onboard speaker is functioning).
Continuous beep	Power supply or adapter card problem.
Repeating short beeps	Power supply or adapter card problem.
1 long, 1 short beep	Motherboard problem.
1 long, 2 short beeps	Legacy display adapter error (MDA, CGA).
1 long, 3 short beeps	Display adapter error (EGA, VGA).
3 long beeps	Keyboard error

Error messages on the screen are usually descriptive of the problem. In each case take the appropriate action.

CMOS Setup

To configure CMOS settings, press the appropriate key when the on-screen prompt is displayed (after the video adapter has been initialized). The key used to invoke CMOS Setup varies according to the BIOS, but is usually DELETE, F2, ESC, F10, or F1.

Tip

On some PCs, you may also be able to access a diagnostics program at this point (to run tests on the CPU, memory, drives, and I/O ports). Check the system documentation to find out whether one is included.

---

[192] Check the following websites for POST error meanings: www.ami.com, www.phoenix.com (Award), www.compaq.com, www.dell.com. Websites such as www.bioscentral.com provide a good summary and can be located easily through internet search engines.

© 2010 gtslearning | IT Career FastTrack with CompTIA A+ Certification | Page 455

| Unit 4.5 | Module 4 Installation, Troubleshooting, and Maintenance |

CMOS Setup layouts and options vary widely from vendor to vendor. You generally navigate the menus and options using the **ARROW** and **PGUP** and **PGDN** and **+** and **-** keys. Some of the standard options are as follows:

- System information - CMOS will contain information about core components such as CPU, chipset, memory, and battery (on a laptop).

- Date - the date and time stored in the PC's real time clock.

- Ports and peripherals - devices (integrated video/sound/network, PS/2, USB, wireless, SATA ports, and so on) can often be enabled or disabled through CMOS. There may be options to configure for some (such as the operating mode for a parallel port [SPP, ECP, or EPP]). On a laptop, there will also be settings for controlling the use of the Function key to turn the radio(s) on or off.

- Fast boot and POST errors - you may be able to configure which types of error halt the POST procedure. There may also be options for skipping some tests (such as memory count) to boot faster and for hiding or showing the test results (displaying a comforting logo instead).

- Boot order - set the priority of the different boot devices and enable or disable specific devices. You will usually be able to set 3 or 4 options in priority order. The typical choices are hard drive (choose between PATA, SATA, and / or SCSI), floppy drive, optical drive (CD/DVD), USB, and network[193].

- Performance - options for configuring features of the CPU, such as number of cores, cache, Execute Disable support, power performance (SpeedStep), and so on. In most cases, these features will be detected and enabled by default. You may want to disable them to perform troubleshooting however

- CPU / memory timing - allow you to overclock the PC to improve performance, at the risk of thermal damage and instability. Many of the larger PC vendors disable these options.

- Password - it is often possible to set passwords for the system (required to boot) and supervisor/administrator (required to enter CMOS Setup).

- Virus protection - some BIOS include low-level malware protection for the boot sector. This can cause problems with some types of genuine software. BIOS virus protection is no substitute for complete anti-virus software.

---

[193] A network boot option may be listed as PXE (Pre-boot Execution Environment).

- Power management - this can often be enabled or disabled through CMOS[194]. It is best to simply enable it then configure options through Windows. On a laptop, there may be options to check battery performance and configure default LCD brightness. There may also be power management options for USB, such as allowing USB devices to wake the computer from standby.

When closing CMOS Setup, there will be an option to exit and discard changes or exit and save changes. Sometimes this is done with a key (ESC versus F10 for instance) and but more often there is a prompt.

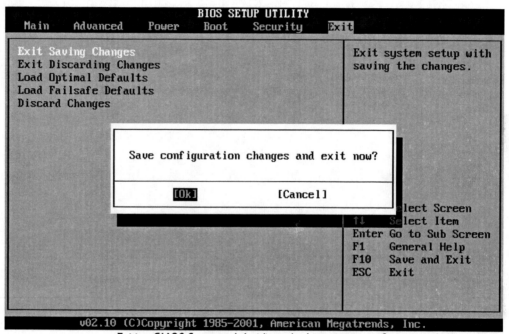

Exiting CMOS Setup and deciding whether to save configuration changes or not

There will also be an option to reload the default settings, in case you want to discard any customizations you have made.

CMOS battery

If the CMOS battery is losing power, settings stored in CMOS (such as the date and time or boot device order) will be lost or corrupted. If the computer is also losing the correct time, it can be a sign that the battery is failing.

---

[194] One interesting feature is an auto-on mode, which activates the computer automatically at a set time each day (or weekday).

| Unit 4.5 | Module 4 Installation, Troubleshooting, and Maintenance |

If this happens, the computer is likely to display the message **CMOS Checksum Error** during the boot process. If this is the case, replace the CMOS battery. Most use a coin cell, which will either be rechargeable or non-rechargeable[195]. Make sure you replace the battery with one of the *same type*. CMOS errors can also be caused by viruses or a faulty motherboard or power supply.

Operating system search

Once the POST tests are complete, the BIOS searches the devices as specified in the CMOS boot sequence. If the first device in the sequence is not found, it then moves on to the next; for example, if drive A: contains no disk, the boot sequence goes to drive C:. If a drive contains non-bootable media, it will prevent the PC from booting. If no boot device is found, the system displays an error message and halts the boot process.

The code from the boot sector on the selected device is loaded into memory and takes over from the BIOS. The boot sector code loads the rest of the operating system files into RAM. Error messages received after this point can usually be attributed to software (or driver), rather than hardware, problems.

Troubleshooting Motherboard and CPU Problems

Motherboard and processor failures are rare and most system faults are more likely to be caused by incorrect configuration, overheating, or problems with other failed components. Before assuming that the processor has failed, you should rule out other potential problems.

Unstable operation

Symptoms such as the system locking up, displaying a bluescreen error, or rebooting without warning are difficult to diagnose with a specific cause, especially if you are not able to witness the events directly. The most likely causes are software, disk problems, or malware.

---

[195] If the battery is a rechargeable type, try leaving the computer running for 24 hours to recharge it.

Page 458   IT Career FastTrack with CompTIA A+ Certification   © 2010 gtslearning

Module 4 Installation, Troubleshooting, and Maintenance
Troubleshooting Components

If you can discount these, try to establish whether there is a pattern to the errors; if they occur when the PC has been running for some time, it could be a thermal problem.

Next, check that the power supply is providing good, stable voltages to the system. If you can discount the power supply, you must start to suspect a problem with memory, CPU, or motherboard.

Inspect the CPU to ensure it is properly seated in its socket then look at the motherboard for any sign of damage. If a component has "blown" it can leave scorch marks. However, you will almost certainly need diagnostic software to run tests to confirm whether there is a problem. Testing by substituting "known good" components would be too time consuming and expensive.

The most likely causes of damage are heat, ESD, or a power surge or spike. It is worth investigating any environmental problems or maintenance procedures that could be the "root cause" of the error.

Heat

Insufficient cooling is the main cause of processor problems. Thermal faults are normally cyclic: a system works for some time, crashes, and then works again later, because powering down allows the processor to cool.

You should check the following:

- Ensure that the CPU fan is working. Proper cooling is vital to the lifespan and performance of the processor. If the processor is running too hot it can decrease performance. A processor that is overheating can cause crashes or reboot the machine.

  Is the fan's power cable properly connected? Is the fan jammed, clogged, or too small? If a processor upgrade is installed, the fan from the original CPU may not be suitable for the new device.

- Make sure the heatsink is properly fitted. It should be snug against the processor. Heatsinks are usually "stuck" to the processor using a special heat conductive paste. Some manufacturers use lower quality paste. In these cases it is possible to clean away the old paste and replace it with better paste, which will help the processor to run at a lower temperature.

- Always use blanking plates to cover up holes in the back or front of the PC. Holes can disrupt the airflow and decrease the effectiveness of the cooling systems.

© 2010 gtslearning IT Career FastTrack with CompTIA A+ Certification Page 459

Unit 4.5   Module 4 Installation, Troubleshooting, and Maintenance

- Speed - is the processor running at the correct speed? Running a processor at a higher clock speed can cause overheating.

- Voltage - double-check the voltage and timing settings in CMOS Setup.

- Environment - is the room unusually warm or dusty or is the PC positioned near a radiator or in direct sunlight?

Thermal problems may also affect system operation by causing loose connectors to drift apart, components to move in their sockets, or circuit board defects such as hairline cracks to widen and break connections.

Note

CPUs and other system components heat up while running. Take care not to scald yourself when handling internal components.

Processor appears not to work

If a new processor (or an upgrade) has just been installed, you should perform these simple diagnostic checks:

- Compatibility - check that the processor is supported by the motherboard.

- Orientation - make sure the processor has been inserted correctly into its socket.

- Voltage - double-check the voltage settings (through CMOS Setup). If the voltage has been set incorrectly (to overclock the CPU for instance), try correcting it and seeing if the CPU still works.

- Configuration - double-check the CMOS settings or motherboard jumpers to make sure they are correct.

- Swap - test by substitution: if the old processor works then the new one may be faulty.

Speed problems

If the system is slow or reports the wrong CPU speed at boot time, you should perform the following diagnostic checks:

- Setup - verify the CMOS configuration or (on a very old PC) motherboard jumper settings.

Page 460   IT Career FastTrack with CompTIA A+ Certification   © 2010 gtslearning

Module 4 Installation, Troubleshooting, and Maintenance | Troubleshooting Components

■ Throttling - most CPU models you will encounter will have protection circuitry to slow down when they get too hot. You should investigate why the CPU is overheating (for example, has the fan stopped working or is the heatsink clogged with dust?)

Tip

If a *user* complains that a system is slow, try to verify that it is not a software or network problem first. You can use Task Manager to display CPU and network utilization (see unit 2.6). If CPU utilization consistently runs at 90-100%, it is likely that a faulty application process is to blame.

Troubleshooting Memory Problems

If you suspect that memory is faulty, first check that it is seated properly in the connector and that the modules are compatible with the motherboard and with the slots in which they are installed. Next, use a diagnostic utility such as Memtest to verify the chips.

Lockups

Faulty memory chips can cause lockups and bluescreens. There are various troubleshooting utilities designed to test memory chips (**memtest** being one freeware example; Windows Vista is bundled with a startup memory scanner on the setup disc). The tests can take a long time to complete however and should normally be run several times to fully rule out a hardware failure.

New memory not recognized

After performing a memory upgrade, rebooting, and then checking the memory count (displayed during POST), the memory may not be recognized. You should first check that the modules have been installed correctly in their sockets. If this does not solve the problem, check the following:

■ Memory type

　□ Does the motherboard support the memory card capacity that you have installed (for example, a board may be restricted to 1 GB in total or may not support individual modules larger than 512 MB)?

© 2010 gtslearning | IT Career FastTrack with CompTIA A+ Certification | Page 461

| Unit 4.5 | Module 4 Installation, Troubleshooting, and Maintenance |

□ Does the motherboard chipset support the memory technology you have installed (for example, Registered, ECC)?

- Configuration

    □ Are the memory banks complete?

    □ Have the memory banks been filled in the correct sequence?

    □ Is the motherboard operating in dual-channel mode?

In all cases, refer to the motherboard guide.

ECC / parity errors

If an error occurs at boot-time, check CMOS settings to ensure that ECC has not been enabled with non-ECC memory cards installed.

If the error always occurs at the same address, there is likely to be a hardware fault with the memory. You can check this by booting several times to ensure that the error is always at the same address. If so, you should replace the memory modules.

If an error occurs during use and does not re-occur after reboot, it is likely to be a transient error. Allow the user to continue to work on the PC but ask them to report the error immediately if it happens again. If the error persists, you should run diagnostic tests or replace the memory modules.

Troubleshooting I/O Port Problems

Loopback tests

It is possible to perform "loopback" tests on all types of I/O and communications ports. Loopback tests are carried out using a special device, in the form of a connector plug which routes a port's output lines directly back to its input lines.

These are used in conjunction with third-party diagnostic programs (such as PC-Check and PassMark) that send test data to the port; the diagnostic software checks that the data is sent back correctly by the loopback plug.

Before you use these tools, you should check whether a loopback test is necessary.

PassMark BurnInTest USB loopback plug

Check connectors and cable

Check the connector at each end of the cable to ensure that it is clean and that none of the pins are bent and therefore not able to connect. Check along the length of the cable to ensure that it is not damaged. Ensure that the connectors are securely fastened to the port and to the device.

Check device

To ensure that the device is not causing the problem, try the device in another context. For example, plug a mouse or printer into a different PC.

Check CMOS settings

Check the port has not been disabled in the CMOS Setup and that the correct settings have been made for the port (for example, that a printer port is working in the correct mode [standard, ECP, or EPP]).

Resource conflicts

When you install a new device, such as a network card, sound card, or modem into a PC, it must be allocated a set of **system resources** that enable it to communicate with the processor and system memory without conflicting with other devices.

Resource conflicts are rare if all devices use **Plug-and-Play**. If the system contains legacy (manually configured) devices, using Windows Device Manager, check that the port is not using system resources that conflict with another device (see unit 4.4). Alternatively, just replace the card with one that does support Plug-and-Play!

| Unit 4.5 | Module 4 Installation, Troubleshooting, and Maintenance |

USB/Firewire ports

USB ports are designed to be very simple. If the device requires a driver or software, you should install that first (before connecting the device). Then you simply attach the device and it should be detected and installed. If a device is not recognized, it will appear as an "Unknown Device" in Device Manager. In this case, try reinstalling the driver, using a different port, or replacing the cable.

The connectors and ports are designed to be more robust than the pins used on serial and parallel ports. Check however that the contacts have not become dirty or damaged by liquid. Also check that the cable has not been damaged in some way.

Most modern BIOS will have some (although very few) configurable options for USB. Through your CMOS Setup program it may be possible to disable USB support altogether or simply to disable support for older USB devices.

Many devices are USB 2 instead of the original USB standard. If you plug a high speed device into a low speed port, a warning message is displayed and the device will operate at low speed.

If a "Low Power Warning" message is displayed after plugging in a device, it means the device is trying to draw too much power over the bus and will be shut down. Connect the device to a power source before connecting the USB cable.

If there are intermittent problems with one or more devices, it could be that the power supply is overloaded. Try disconnecting some devices to see if the problem goes away. Intermittent problems can also be caused by long cable runs or interference from electromagnetic sources.

Another common issue is some sort of incompatibility with power management settings. If a USB device[196] causes problems or does not work after the computer has been put in standby, open **Device Manager** and select the device's property sheet. On the **Power Management** tab, disable **Allow the computer to turn off this device to save power** and **Allow this device to bring the computer out of standby**. If that seems to fix the problem, check for an updated driver for the device or for the USB hub (system chipset).

---

[196] This goes for many types of device, especially older devices running under Vista. Wi-Fi and network adapters often cause this sort of problem.

Page 464   IT Career FastTrack with CompTIA A+ Certification   © 2010 gtslearning

Module 4 Installation, Troubleshooting, and Maintenance | Troubleshooting Components

Troubleshooting Hard Drive Problems

Hard drives are most likely to fail due to mechanical problems either in the *first few months* of operation or after a *few years*, when they begin to reach the end of their useful life. Sudden loss of power can also damage a disk, especially if it is in the middle of a read/write operation. A hard drive that is failing will display the following symptoms:

- Bad sectors - when you run the CHKDSK program (see unit 2.6) it can test the surface of the hard disk. If more bad sectors are located each time the test is run, it is a sure sign that the disk is about to fail.

Tip
Use the Check Disk utility regularly to check that the drive is in good condition.

- Constant LED activity.

- Noise - a healthy hard disk makes a certain low-level noise when accessing the platters. A loud or grinding noise or any sort of clicking is a sign of a problem.

In this scenario, replace the disk as soon as possible to minimize the risk of data loss.

Hard disk not accessible

If the hard drive is not detected at boot (or if a second hard drive is not shown under Windows), first check that it is powering up. Drive activity is usually indicated by an LED on the front panel of the system unit case. If this is inactive, check that the drive has a power connector attached. If the PC has no LEDs, or you suspect that they may be faulty, it is usually possible to hear the hard drive spinning up.

Once you have determined that the drive is powering up try the following:

- If the system is not booting correctly from the hard drive, check that the boot sequence is set correctly in CMOS and that there are no removable disks in floppy or optical drives.

- Check the data cables are not damaged and that they are correctly connected to the drive and motherboard.

© 2010 gtslearning   IT Career FastTrack with CompTIA A+ Certification   Page 465

| Unit 4.5 | Module 4 Installation, Troubleshooting, and Maintenance |

- For a PATA drive, check that IDE drive jumpers are set to single/master/slave as appropriate.

- For a SCSI drive, check that the host adapter driver is working and that ID numbers and terminators are set correctly.

- If the drives are connected to a motherboard controller, check that it has not been disabled by a jumper or CMOS setting.

If a hard drive is detected by POST but not by Windows, there is probably a problem with the **file system**. Boot into the Recovery Console (see unit 4.3) and type C: at the command prompt. If this produces the error message **Invalid media type**, the disk has no valid file system structure on it. This may be caused by surface errors or by a virus. You may be able to recover from this by formatting the disk (at the expense of any data stored on the disk of course).

If you type C: at the command prompt and this produces the error message **Invalid drive specification**, the drive may have an invalid partition structure. You can check the drive's partition structure with the DISKPART utility.

1. Run the **DISKPART** utility then enter **SELECT DISK 0** at the prompt (or the number of the disk you want to check).

2. Type **DETAIL DISK** followed by **ENTER** to display configuration information for the disk.

```
Microsoft DiskPart version 5.1.3565

Copyright (C) 1999-2003 Microsoft Corporation.
On computer: JAMESV3

DISKPART> select disk 0

Disk 0 is now the selected disk.

DISKPART> detail disk

SEAGATE ST336607LW SCSI Disk Device
Disk ID: 6AAF6AAF
Type    : SCSI
Bus     : 2
Target  : 0
LUN ID  : 0

  Volume ###  Ltr  Label        Fs     Type       Size   Status     Info
  ----------  ---  -----------  -----  ---------  -----  ---------  --------
  Volume 1    C                 NTFS   Partition  17 GB  Healthy    System

DISKPART>
```

DISKPART program showing a hard disk partition structure

Module 4 Installation, Troubleshooting, and Maintenance	Troubleshooting Components

The utility should report that the partitions (or volumes) are **healthy**. If DISKPART reports that the hard disk has no partitions, the partition table may have become corrupted by a virus. You may be able to resolve this using CHKDSK and FIXBOOT or by partitioning and formatting the drive.

Note

If you can boot into Windows, use the Disk Management utility to view disk information (see unit 2.4). Do not experiment with DISKPART commands – you may destroy data on your disk(s).

Drive status

Each disk and drive displays status indicators in the Disk Management program. Disks can have the following status indicators:

- **Online** - the disk is OK.

- **Not Initialized** - when you add a new unpartitioned disk, a wizard runs prompting you to initialize, partition, and format the disk. If you cancel the wizard the disk will appear as Not Initialized - alt-click to start the wizard again.

- **Unreadable** - the disk is damaged. This message can be transitory so try alt-clicking the **Disk Management** tool and selecting **Rescan Disks**. If the disk is still shown as unreadable, you would have to use third-party tools to try to recover data from it.

- **Foreign** - if you configure a disk as dynamic on one computer, then install the disk in another computer, it will be marked as foreign. Alt-click the disk and select **Import Foreign Disk** to make it accessible to the system.

- **Offline / Missing** - a disk configured as dynamic cannot be read. This could be a transitory error but is more likely to indicate that the drive or I/O to the drive is damaged, a cable is unplugged, the disk has been switched off, and so on. There are two options:

  - ☐ If the disk can be restored, use the **Reactivate Disk** option to add it back to the array

  - ☐ If the disk cannot be restored, use the **Remove Disk** option

© 2010 gtslearning   IT Career FastTrack with CompTIA A+ Certification   Page 467

Unit 4.5 Module 4 Installation, Troubleshooting, and Maintenance

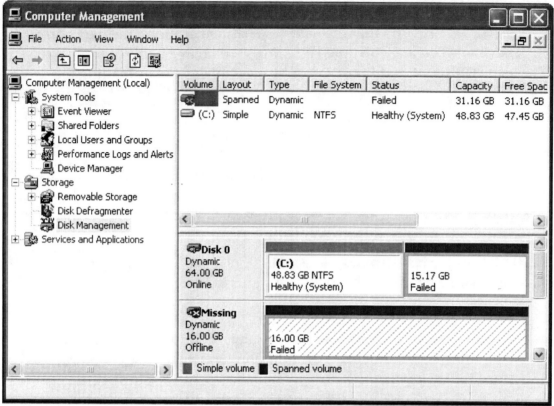

One of the disks underlying the spanned volume is missing and consequently the volume is marked as failed

Volumes (or partitions) can have the following status indicators:

- **Healthy** - the partition is formatted and ready to read and write data. **Healthy (System)** indicates that the partition or volume contains the OS files while **Healthy (Active)** represents the system volume. A drive may also display as **Healthy (At Risk)**, which means that a number of I/O errors are occurring - a good sign that the disk or controller is failing.

- **Failed** - this either indicates a damaged disk (basic) or a dynamic volume where the supporting disk drives are not available. You need to check the status of the devices (if cabling and power are OK the disk[s] or controller may have been damaged).

- **Formatting** - a user-initiated format is in progress. Wait for the format to complete before trying to access the partition or volume.

Module 4 Installation, Troubleshooting, and Maintenance   *Troubleshooting Components*

Formatted capacity

Another disk issue is that of capacity. A user may purchase a 300 GB disk and discover on formatting it that it is "only" 286 GB. Most disk vendors use decimal measurements to advertise the capacity of disk drives, as this results in a higher value[197]. Windows reports capacity using binary values, but with decimal units (the approved IEEE binary units are MiB and GiB but these are almost never used in practice). The "lost" capacity is due to this conversion error.

Low disk space

Windows warns the user when disk space is low (below 200 MB). If the disk continues to be filled up, system performance will be severely impacted.

You can use the **Disk Cleanup** program (see unit 2.6) to free up space but the user may have to take manual steps, such as moving or deleting files, uninstalling unnecessary applications, and so on.

Troubleshooting Other Storage Device Problems

Troubleshooting failures in RAID hardware

The precise process for managing a disk failure with a hardware array will be dependent on the vendor that supplied the array and the configuration being supported. All array controllers will be capable of generating an event to the OS system log and perhaps of generating an alert message for the administrator. If the array supports hot swapping, then the new disk can simply be inserted into the chassis of the computer or disk chassis. The RAID controller should recognize this fact and start to resynchronize the disks.

---

[197] The decimal definition of mega or giga is 1000 while the binary definition is 1024; dividing a value by 1000 rather than 1024 can make the drive seem much larger than it really is, especially when you get to drives of 100 GB+ capacity.

© 2010 gtslearning   IT Career FastTrack with CompTIA A+ Certification   Page 469

| Unit 4.5 | Module 4 Installation, Troubleshooting, and Maintenance |

Note

When hot swapping a faulty disk out, take extreme caution not to remove a healthy disk from the array as making a mistake could cause the array to fail, depending on the configuration. Disk failure is normally indicated by a red LED. Always make a backup beforehand.

Troubleshooting floppy drives

If you are unable to access the floppy drive, ensure that the power cable and data cable are correctly connected. Check that CMOS parameters are correct (they should be **1.44 MB 3.5"**), and that the floppy is enabled.

Check that the media is not causing the problem. If you are unable to access or format a floppy disk, try one from another source instead. Sometimes a whole box of floppy disks can be damaged or corrupted. If a disk can be accessed or formatted on another PC, then the disks are not damaged.

Floppy disk drives are cheap. If you have performed all of the above checks and the problem persists, it may be a good idea to replace the drive.

Troubleshooting optical drives

Optical drives such as CD, DVD, and Blu-ray drives can generally go for a long time between failures. This is because the part of the drive that reads the disc does not actually touch it. All reading (and writing with recordable and re-writable media) is done using lasers. This means that the read/write "heads" are not as likely to get dirty as with magnetic media drives such as floppy drives.

However, CDs and DVDs do get dirty and carry that dirt inside the optical drive. Special cleaning kits are available for cleaning optical drives if read/write problems are experienced. Most problems are related to dirt or scratches on the disc itself though.

Support for CD drives is built into Windows. If your CD drive is not able to read CDs at all, it is likely to be a hardware problem[198]. However, to take advantage of other features, such as optical writing, additional software and drivers may need to be installed.

---

[198] Older drives may have trouble reading recordable or rewritable media, though this is not common.

Page 470   IT Career FastTrack with CompTIA A+ Certification   © 2010 gtslearning

| Module 4 Installation, Troubleshooting, and Maintenance | Troubleshooting Components |

DVD-Video requires MPEG decoding hardware or software (codecs) to be installed for playback. This is supplied with Vista Home Premium and Ultimate editions; other versions of Windows require third-party software to be installed. Remember also that a DVD-ROM cannot be read from a CD-ROM drive.

There is currently no native support for Blu-ray in any version of Windows but the drive should be bundled with the appropriate codecs and software.

Tip

One common problem is where the OS or software program reports that it cannot locate a setup disc. This is usually because the drive letter has changed following installation of a second hard disk. You can reassign drive letters using the Disk Management program (see unit 2.4).

CD/DVD/BD writing

Where Windows does not support a particular recordable or rewritable format directly, third-party software is required. Windows 2000 does not support CD-R or CD-RW. Windows Vista supports recordable DVD but Windows XP does not.

Some writable media are not manufactured to the highest possible standards, so errors during CD or DVD write operations can be quite common. Check that you are using the write speed recommended for the brand of discs you have purchased. If the error is persistent however, it is not down to the media.

Most problems are connected to **buffer underruns**. On older devices, once the writing process starts, it cannot be paused. Therefore, if the OS does not supply data to the burner's buffer quickly enough, errors will be introduced into the disc's layout. The following solutions can usually be applied:

- Try burning discs at a lower write speed.

- Copy source files to the local hard disk (rather than removable or network drives).

- Do not use other applications when burning a disc.

The latest CD and DVD writers usually ship with buffer underrun protection.

Unit 4.5   Module 4 Installation, Troubleshooting, and Maintenance

Troubleshooting Peripheral Device Problems

Mouse and keyboard

The mouse and keyboard are very simple devices and require minimal troubleshooting.

- If the mouse pointer does not move, check the connection to the PC and then reboot. If a PS/2 mouse (or keyboard) is not connected properly at boot time, it will not function until the PC is rebooted.

- If the mouse pointer does not move properly, clean the internal rollers or lens.

- If neither keyboard nor mouse works, the connectors are probably plugged into the wrong PS/2 ports. Swap them over.

- If there is a "Key stuck" error at boot time, check for stuck keys or (more likely) something resting on the keyboard.

- If keys are getting stuck frequently, the keyboard needs cleaning.

- If typing produces unexpected characters, check that the correct input language is set and check that the system is not responding to speech input.

- If "special functions" on a device do not work (such as multimedia keys or third or fourth mouse buttons), check that the software and device drivers are installed and up-to-date.

- If a wireless device stops working, check that the batteries have not run flat. If the batteries are good, try rescynching the device to the controller.

Adapter cards

If an adapter card is not recognized after installation, the first thing to check is that it is compatible, the next that it is inserted correctly, and the last that there is no dirt affecting the connection between the contacts on the card edge and the slot.

If an adapter card stops working, try re-installing the driver then check for seating or dirt issues.

Page 472   IT Career FastTrack with CompTIA A+ Certification   © 2010 gtslearning

Display

If there is no image displayed on the monitor, check the following:

- Make sure that the monitor is plugged in and turned on. Check that the monitor is not in standby mode (press a key or cycle the power to the monitor to activate it).

- Check the connection between the video card and monitor. Make sure the cable is connected securely at both ends and is not loose. Make sure that the cable has not become stretched or crimped.

- Check the brightness and contrast controls. Make sure that they are turned up; a brightness control turned all the way down can make a monitor appear to be dead when it is actually working.

- Try the monitor with a different PC and see if it works.

If there is a problem with image quality, such as a flickering or misshapen image or missing colors, try the following checks:

- Check the video cable connector. If a pin is bent and not lining up with the video card connector, this can cause a missing color.

- Check refresh rate and resolution settings for the video driver. If resolution is too high or refresh rate is too low this can cause the screen to flicker. Check using the **Display Properties** dialog box in Windows[199].

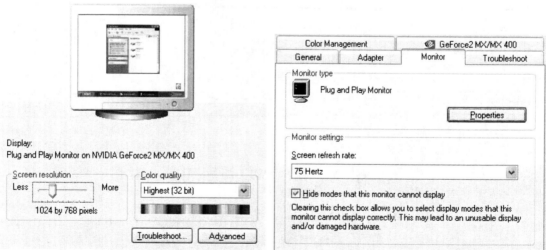

Screen resolution settings (left) and refresh rate setting (click Advanced then Monitor tab)

---

[199] In Vista, you adjust this via Personalization > Display Settings.

| Unit 4.5 | Module 4 Installation, Troubleshooting, and Maintenance |

- If video playback does not work, try lowering or disabling hardware acceleration (using the slider on the **Troubleshoot** tab). If this solves the problem, check for an updated display driver.

- If the screen image is misshapen, try adjusting it using the monitor's image control knobs.

- Low resolution or color depth makes the image look blocky or grainy. If you start the computer in safe mode the image may look like this if SVGA drivers are not loaded.

- If the image on a CRT is fuzzy, try using the Degauss button to discharge static electricity or cycling the power (degaussing the monitor will cause it to make a Tunng! noise). Make sure that no electrical devices are positioned near the monitor (for example, unshielded powered speakers or a desktop fan).

- If an LCD panel has stuck (constantly bright) pixels, and the panel cannot be replaced under warranty, these can sometimes be "reactivated" by gently pressing or tapping the affected area of the screen with a stylus or similar plastic object (though there is the risk of causing further damage or scratching the screen). "Dead" pixels cannot usually be fixed.

In terms of 3D graphics performance (especially with computer games), you need to ensure the card is one that is capable of playing the game and that the latest driver and version of DirectX are installed. If there are still issues with frame rates (the speed at which images are displayed), try disabling video effects or using a lower resolution. Make sure that you are using the correct (and latest) drivers for your video card. The FAQs will list any issues with particular applications that the driver addresses.

| Sound cards |

If there is a problem related to playing or recording sound, try the following:

- Ensure that all equipment is plugged into the correct connectors and that the speaker volume knob is adjusted correctly.

- If audio CDs do not playback smoothly, ensure that an audio cable from the CD drive is connected to the sound card.

- If there is interference on recorded sound, try locating the sound card away from other components (such as fans or disk drives). Check for possible sources of interference (such as power cables).

- On legacy systems, check for resource conflicts (sound cards were notorious for causing problems on early PCs, but Plug-and-Play devices should pose no such problem).
- Check the software volume control using the icon in the Windows taskbar.
- Check **Sound** properties from the Control Panel. If there are multiple audio input devices installed (such as a sound card and a webcam with microphone), it can be confusing as to which device is being used at any one time.

Sound and Multimedia properties - use the Audio tab to select default devices

Summary

To troubleshoot, try to categorize a problem and learn the common symptoms and causes for power, boot, thermal, motherboard/CPU/memory, I/O, and disk errors. If available, use diagnostic utilities to identify hardware problems.

Unit 4.6   Module 4 Installation, Troubleshooting, and Maintenance

---

Unit 4.6 Upgrading and Troubleshooting Laptops

CompTIA A+ Essentials Objectives

☐ **701.2.4 Given a scenario, explain and interpret common laptop issues and determine the appropriate basic troubleshooting method**
Issues (Power conditions, Video, Keyboard, Pointer, Stylus, Wireless card issues) • Methods (Verify power [e.g. LEDs, swap AC adapter], Remove unneeded peripherals, Plug in external monitor, Toggle Fn keys or hardware switches, Check LCD cut-off switch, Verify backlight functionality and pixilation, Check switch for built-in Wi-Fi antennas or external antennas)

CompTIA A+ Practical Application Objectives

☐ **702.1.3 Given a scenario, install, configure, detect problems, troubleshoot and repair/replace laptop components**
Components of the LCD including inverter, screen and video card • Hard drive and memory • Disassemble processes for proper re-assembly (Document and label cable and screw locations, Organize parts, Refer to manufacturer documentation, Use appropriate hand tools) • Recognize internal laptop expansion slot types • Upgrade wireless cards and video card • Replace keyboard, processor, plastics, pointer devices, heat sinks, fans, system board, CMOS battery, speakers

---

Upgrading Laptops

Laptops feature fewer user-replaceable components than desktops. That said, laptop components and designs have become better standardized (though using components sourced from the laptop vendor is still recommended). Basic upgrade options, such as memory and disks, have become much simpler as it reduces warranty support costs for the vendors.

Adding and removing laptop peripherals

Adding and removing external peripherals on a laptop is just a case of plugging or unplugging the connector into the correct type of socket. For PC cards and media bay devices, there is generally a release catch to push in. Almost all devices support Plug-and-Play and are hot swappable.

Power supply

If you need to replace the power supply (AC adapter or battery pack), it is best to get the manufacturer's recommended model, though universal AC adapters are available. These typically ship with a number of DC power connectors, which vary quite widely in size. They also have variable voltage settings. You must set the voltage correctly before plugging it in.

Page 476   IT Career FastTrack with CompTIA A+ Certification   © 2010 gtslearning

Note that the power output of adapters and batteries can vary, so using an adapter designed for an ultra-mobile model probably won't work with a desktop replacement, even if it's the same brand. A 90W adapter should be sufficient for most uses, but always check the documentation carefully[200].

Battery packs are often available in different sizes (6-cell and 9-cell for instance). Extra battery capacity can be obtained by purchasing a second battery pack.

The pack supplied with a laptop should be sufficient to drive the internal components and common peripherals. If you experience power problems, connect fewer peripherals at any one time or use external power sources for them, lower the screen brightness, use throttling features of the CPU and graphics card, and disable devices such as a Wi-Fi card or Bluetooth adapter.

Charging a battery

Before inserting or removing the battery pack, you must always turn the machine off and unplug it from the AC wall outlet. A portable battery is usually removed by releasing catches on the back or underside of the computer or in a media bay.

Replacing the battery on an HP Pavilion laptop

A portable computer's battery can be charged in three ways:

---

[200] Power output (W) is the output voltage (V) multiplied by output current or amperage (I).

Unit 4.6

Module 4 Installation, Troubleshooting, and Maintenance

- Plug the computer into an AC wall outlet with the computer turned off. This method is called a quick charge. It takes about 2.5 hours to fully charge a flat battery.

- Charge the battery while the computer is plugged into an AC wall outlet and turned on. This charge method is slower because the primary use of power is for operating the PC, rather than for charging the battery. It can take several hours to charge a battery while the machine is turned on.

- Use a battery charger. This method charges the battery while it is not in the computer, but involves purchasing an extra charging unit.

To maximize battery life, different battery types require different charging regimes. Always consult the manufacturer's instructions for obtaining optimal battery life for a specific product. Old NiCad batteries suffered from a "memory effect", where if the battery is set to recharge without being fully discharged, a portion of the battery's capacity is lost permanently.

Conversely, modern Li-ion batteries should *not* be allowed to fully discharge, as this reduces battery life. They benefit from regular charging and cannot be over-charged[201]. Li-ion batteries are also sensitive to heat. If storing a Li-ion battery, reduce the charge to 40% and store at below 20°C.

Note
All batteries hold less charge as they age and typically have a maximum usable life of around 2-3 years. If you attempt to charge a battery and the charge indicator does not show a full charge, you may need to purchase a new battery.

Working inside the chassis

As with desktops, take anti-static precautions when working with static-sensitive components. There are a few other things you should note that make servicing laptops different from desktops:

- Laptops use smaller screws than are found on desktops. You may find it useful to obtain a set of jeweler's screwdrivers. It is also much easier to *strip* the screws (remove the notch for the screwdriver) - take care!

---

[201] Li-ion batteries have circuitry to prevent over-charging because they will explode if over-charged. However, some degree of caution should be exercised when leaving batteries to recharge unattended (for example, overnight) as this circuitry has been known to fail. Do not leave a battery charger close to flammable material and ensure there is plenty of ventilation around the unit.

- Disconnect the AC power *and* remove the battery before opening the chassis.

- Read the vendor's service documentation carefully to familiarize yourself with the location of components and procedure for disassembling the chassis.

Adding and removing memory and expansion cards

Memory and mini PCI/PCIe adapter slots are usually made accessible via screw panels on the underside of the chassis though for some laptops you may need to remove the keyboard (see below). The connectors can usually be flipped up and down to allow easy insertion and removal.

Adding a mini PCI card (left) and accessing memory modules (right)

Upgrading the hard drive

A laptop typically supports one 2.5" internal hard drive, with extra storage being plugged in via a media bay or attached to a PC Card, ExpressCard, or USB port.

The internal drive may be screwed into the chassis or you may have to remove the keyboard to access it. It typically plugs into a combined data and power connector (there is no cable).

| Unit 4.6 | Module 4 Installation, Troubleshooting, and Maintenance |

Upgrading the CPU and graphics adapter

Some laptop CPUs (using **Ball Grid Array [BGA]** sockets) are soldered to the motherboard and therefore not upgradeable.

Laptops often use an **integrated** graphics adapter (as part of the system chipset), especially at the lower end of the market. Integrated graphics can be advantageous in terms of battery life and cooling. However, if a laptop is designed to work as a media center or games machines, only **dedicated** graphics will provide sufficient performance.

Cheaper graphics adapters may also feature a limited amount of on-board memory (or none at all[202]). In this scenario, they share system memory with the CPU. Obviously, this decreases the amount of system memory available.

Few graphics cards are actually *upgradeable*, though they may be *replaceable*. This is because high-end cards tend to have specific power and cooling requirements and a modular approach is not possible given the limited space available.

To access components such as the CPU and graphics card, you need to disassemble the laptop. The general process is as follows, though do be aware that you need to obtain the specific steps for the brand and model of laptop you are upgrading or repairing.

1. Make a backup of data stored on the system drive.

2. As you would for a PC, lay out your work area with any tools and reference material you will need and take anti-static precautions.

3. Disconnect peripheral devices and PCMCIA / PCI Express cards and eject discs from drives.

4. Disconnect the AC power **and** battery. Hold down the power button for a few seconds to ensure the circuits are completely de-energized.

5. Turn the unit upside down. Make a diagram of the screw locations.

Tip

A useful tip is to take a photo of the underside of the laptop and print it out. As you remove screws, tape them to the relevant point in your picture. This ensures you will not lose any and will know which screw goes where.

---

[202] Typically integrated adapters share memory. Most (but not all) dedicated adapters have on-board RAM.

6. Open any compartments on the underside of the laptop and remove the Field Replaceable Units (FRU - these should include the hard drive, memory, and possibly the optical drive and mini adapter cards also).

Tip

Store components that you remove in protective anti-static packaging.

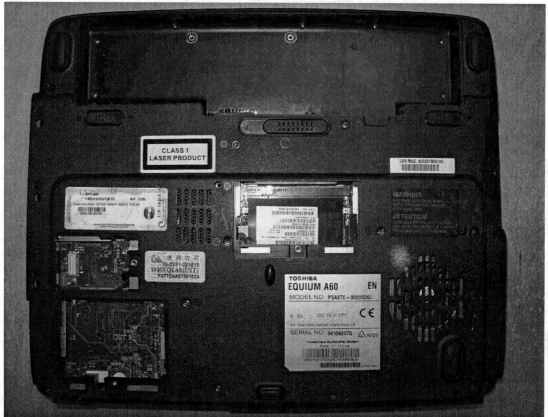

Remove the battery, any add-in cards, and the hard drive then unscrew the case, making a careful note of which screw goes where

7. Remove the screws holding the chassis together and put them somewhere safe.

8. Flip the laptop over again and remove the plastic bezel at the top of the keyboard. This might be difficult but take care not to snap it.

9. Unscrew the keyboard and partially lift it (carefully!) Disconnect the cable that attaches it to the motherboard then fully remove the keyboard.

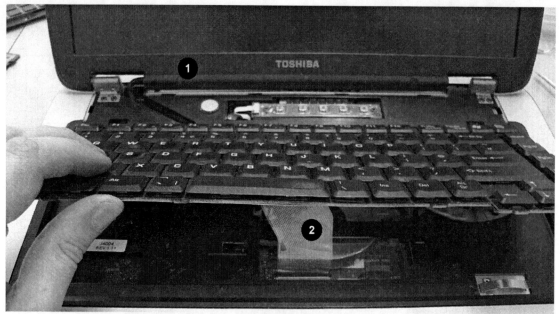

1) Unclip the plastic bezel (carefully) then 2) unscrew the keyboard and lift to disconnect

10. Disconnect the LCD cable and LCD power connector connecting the display to the motherboard then lift off the display.

11. Remove any internal drive cages or heat pipes covering the components you want to replace. As with a desktop, make a careful note of how fan power connectors are attached.

Disconnect the LCD cable making a note of how it is connected then remove the lid and display assembly from the motherboard

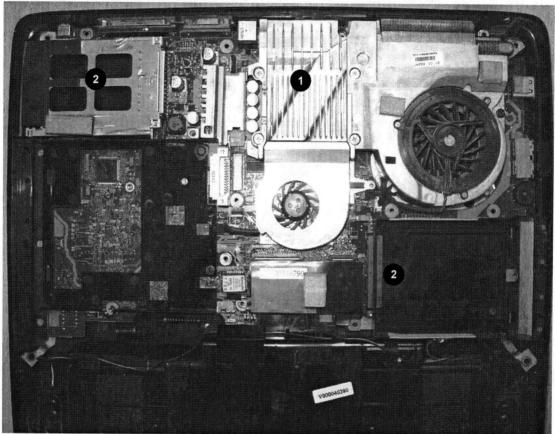

Remove the heatsink and fan assembly (1) and drive / adapter card bays (2) to access components on the motherboard, such as CPU, graphics, and CMOS battery

Replace devices such as the keyboard, touchpad, motherboard, heat pipe, fans, CMOS battery, and speakers using vendor-supplied parts.

Troubleshooting Laptops

Many of the standard PC troubleshooting procedures also apply to laptops. The following topics cover some laptop-specific troubleshooting issues.

Verifying power

If there is a power problem, first establish how the laptop *should* be operated and confirm that this procedure is being followed. For example, some laptops require that a battery be present, even on AC power; others may not work on AC power if the battery is completely discharged.

If working from the battery, first check that it is inserted correctly and seated properly in its compartment. A solid green LED may be present to indicate when the laptop is running on battery power (or an LED may simply show when a battery is being charged).

If the battery is properly inserted and still does not work, it is most likely completely discharged. If the battery will not hold a charge, it could be at the end of its useful life[203]. You can test this by using a "known good" battery; if this does not work then there is something wrong with the power circuitry on the motherboard.

If you experience problems working from AC power, first test the outlet with a "known good" device (such as a lamp). Next check that an LED on the AC adapter is green; if there is no LED, check the fuse on the plug and if available, try testing with a "known good" adapter.

If this does not work, inspect the DC socket on the laptop for any sign of damage. You can also use a multimeter to check the output of most types of AC adapter.

1. Set the meter up to test for the appropriate voltage range (the expected voltage will be printed on the adapter label).
2. Insert the red probe into the middle of the DC jack.
3. Turn on the multimeter.
4. Touch the black probe to the metal part of the outside of the DC jack.

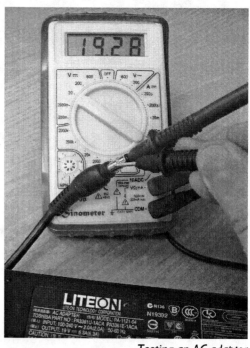

Testing an AC adapter

> **Warning**
> Take care not to touch the two probes together! Also, do not push the red probe too far into the DC jack. If you short the jack you could damage the adapter.

---

[203] You may be able to recondition a battery so that it holds a charge for longer (typically done by putting it through complete discharge and recharge cycles). Also check for BIOS updates for the laptop. Updates often improve battery management routines.

| Module 4 Installation, Troubleshooting, and Maintenance | Upgrading and Troubleshooting Laptops |

If there are too many devices connected to the laptop, the power drain may cause unexpected lockups or reboots. Try removing devices to see if the problem goes away.

Display problems

The components most likely to fail on an LCD screen are the backlight and inverter[204]. The backlight is a fluorescent bulb that illuminates the image, making it bright and clear. The inverter supplies the correct voltage to the backlight.

If the display has been flickering or if the image is very dim, but still present, suspect a problem with the backlight or inverter rather than the LCD itself.

The display panel is only likely to need replacing if it gets physically damaged.

The backlight, inverter, or screen on a laptop can be replaced by unscrewing the plastic bezel (the screws will be concealed by rubber stoppers). Take care not to damage the connectors once the panel has been freed from its housing.

1. To identify a problem with the backlight, first check that the laptop is set to use the built-in display not an external monitor (toggle the appropriate Fn key [usually **FN4** or **FN8**]).

2. Check that the cut-off switch (either a small plastic pin near the hinge connecting the TFT to the rest of the chassis or the catch that secures the lid) is not stuck. When it is depressed, power to the backlight may be switched off.

3. Next, check that the video card is good by using an external monitor (alternatively, there should be a very dim image on the TFT if the graphics adapter is functioning but the backlight / inverter has failed).

4. Next, check that power management settings in Windows or CMOS are not set to an energy saving mode that disables or dims the backlight. Note that power saving features are likely to dim the brightness automatically when on battery power.

5. If all these tests are negative, either the backlight, inverter, or cable have failed. An inverter can be tested using a bulb or multimeter, but at this point you will probably need to book the laptop in for repair or use it with an external monitor only.

---

[204] As you may know if you have fluorescent lighting at home, the inverter is more likely to fail than the tube itself.

| © 2010 gtslearning | IT Career FastTrack with CompTIA A+ Certification | Page 485 |

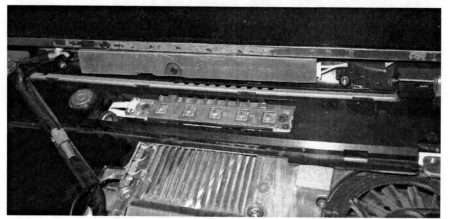
Access the backlight and inverter by removing the bezel around the TFT

If the display is damaged (if it has been bent or dented for example), this can cause pixilation problems (areas of the image break down with mis-coloring, blockiness, or jaggedness).

> **Tip**
> TFTs are best used at the native resolution. Any other resolution will produce some fuzziness in the image, which isn't a sign of a fault in the screen itself. Also, fast changing images (such as those produced by video playback) can produce artifacts on low quality screens.

When updating the driver for a display adapter, check whether the laptop vendor has released their own driver. Laptops often contain OEM (Original Equipment Manufacturer) versions of graphics adapters and you need to use the system vendor's driver rather than the retail driver.

Input device problems

As with desktops, the main problem with keypads tends to be stuck keys. If there is debris under a key, try cleaning with compressed air. If the laptop has been serviced recently and the keyboard has stopped working, check that the connector has not been dislodged (some service operations require the keyboard to be removed).

Be aware that the Function (Fn) keys can often be used to disable devices, such as the wireless adapter. If such a device is not working, check that it has not been disabled by accident.

Another issue is with using an external keyboard and experiencing problems with the Function key being locked. This can typically be solved by turning off Num Lock on the external keyboard.

The main problem with a stylus or touchpad tends to be synchronizing the input to the on-screen cursor. If the input device does not seem to be controlling the cursor properly (for example if clicking selects an unexpected part of the screen), check that the latest driver is installed then complete the synchronization procedure (for example, for a stylus this usually involves touching the corners of the screen while in sync mode).

Another problem is where the touchpad is configured to be too sensitive and typing causes vibrations that move the cursor (for example, if the cursor "wanders" across the screen or the cursor "jumps about" when typing). Install up-to-date drivers and configure input options to suit the user.

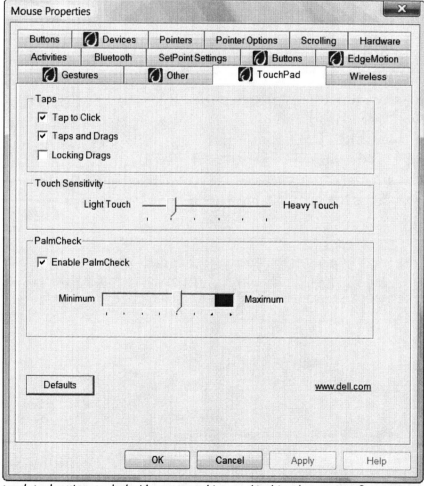

Configure appropriate touch pad settings to deal with unexpected input - this driver has settings for sensitivity, gesture control, special areas of the pad, and so on

Unit 4.6   Module 4 Installation, Troubleshooting, and Maintenance

Communications problems

Wireless input and communications devices can experience trouble with
interference. Infrared devices tend to be more problematic than radio-based
ones. If moving the two devices closer together solves the problem, then the
issue is range. If moving from side-to-side or up-and-down helps, then the
issue is directional and the signal could be blocked by something.

Note

The radio antenna wire for a laptop will either be located on an add-in card
or built into the case (normally into the screen).

As mentioned above, check that the adapter has not been disabled using a
Function key or software. Each device will have an LED on the chassis
showing whether it is enabled or not.

Summary

Laptop components designed to be upgraded (typically the disk, memory,
wireless adapter, and modem) can usually be accessed quite easily via screw-
down panels. Components such as the CPU and graphics card may not be
upgradable and the graphics card may use shared system memory, reducing
the amount of "general" memory available. Learn the typical scenarios and
responses for laptop troubleshooting.

Tip

To review what you have learned in this chapter, you should now visit the
course website. This contains review questions and bonus material to help
you to learn more and practice the topics covered in this unit.

Page 488   IT Career FastTrack with CompTIA A+ Certification   © 2010 gtslearning

Module 5 Networks and Printing — Networks and Printing

Module 5 Networks and Printing

A **network** is two or more computer systems linked together by some form of transmission medium that enables them to share information. The network technology is what connects the computers, but the purpose of the network is to provide services or resources to its users. These services may include access to shared files and folders, printing, and database applications.

Network components

Despite variations in size and design all networks have certain components in common. The key elements include the **transmission medium**, the **clients**, and the **servers** that hold the shared data.

- Transmission Media - information must be transferred using some form of media. Typically, this takes the form of cabling but wireless media using technologies such as infrared, microwave, and radio can provide the same function.

- Protocol - a set of rules enabling systems to communicate. A single network will involve the use of many different protocols. A protocol defines the format in which data can be exchanged.

- Node - a node is any device (such as a workstation, server, or printer) that can communicate on the network; host is often used to mean the same thing.

- Segment - part or unit of a larger network that is linked by a connectivity device, such as a switch or router.

- Backbone - high bandwidth link between segments of a network.

Network clients

Network **clients** are computers on the network that allow users to request shared resources on the servers. Client computers are often referred to as workstations.

© 2010 gtslearning — IT Career FastTrack with CompTIA A+ Certification — Page 489

| Module 5 | Module 5 Networks and Printing |

Network servers

Network services are the functions provided by the network and utilized by network clients. A **server** provides shared resources on the network and allows clients to access this information. There are a number of different types of server:

- **File and Print Servers** share resources amongst clients.

- **Application Servers** provide centralized processing - for example, database platforms such as SQL Server and Oracle.

- **Messaging Servers** provide email, instant messaging, and VoIP functionality.

- **Network Servers** provide services to support the network infrastructure, such as name resolution, authentication, or routing between networks.

One machine might provide some, or even all, of these functions. In larger networks, machines may be dedicated to a subset of these functions.

The internet

Most businesses and many home users now depend on having internet connectivity, so that they can access services such as web pages and email.

The internet now consists of thousands of networks in locations around the world. The major infrastructure of the internet is made up of very high bandwidth backbones connecting **Network Access Points (NAP)**. These backbones and NAPs are created by government, academic, and commercial organizations and typically organized on national and international levels. Below these backbones are many smaller regional and local networks, connected to a NAP either directly or through intermediate networks.

The development of **browsers** and the **World Wide Web** plus internet email in the early 1990s turned the internet into a user-friendly environment and it soon began to attract commercial interest, with the establishment of the first e-commerce sites and webstores. In the present time, the internet has become a cornerstone of business marketing, advertising, and sales and is increasingly dominating leisure activities too (the "Web 2.0" phenomenon of social networking, blogging, and video).

Page 490   IT Career FastTrack with CompTIA A+ Certification   © 2010 gtslearning

Module 5 Networks and Printing	Networks and Printing

Internet standards organizations

A number of organizations, working groups, and committees oversee internet administration and standards approval. Membership of these bodies is drawn from commercial, academic, and government institutions as well as a few private individuals.

- **Internet Society (ISOC)** - a professional membership organization providing comment on policy and practice and having oversight of IAB.

- **Internet Architecture Board (IAB)** - responsible for the overall architecture of the internet, with oversight of IETF.

- **Internet Engineering Task Force (IETF)** - responsible for development of protocols, standards, and best practice. IETF is split into a number of working groups. Standards are published as RFCs (Request For Comment) at www.faqs.org/rfc.

- **World Wide Web Consortium (W3C)** - develop standards (or recommendations) for the web (such as HTML, XML, and CSS).

- **Internet Assigned Numbers Authority (IANA)** - allocation of IP addresses and maintenance of the top-level domain space[205]. IANA is currently run by **Internet Corporation for Assigned Names and Numbers (ICANN)**. Responsibility for subdomains is licensed to accredited registrars. ICANN allocates addresses to regional registries who then allocate them to local registries or ISPs (Internet Service Provider). The regional registries are APNIC (Asia/Pacific), ARIN (North America), LACNIC (Latin America), and RIPE NCC (Europe, Central Asia, and the Middle East), and AfriNIC (Africa).

---

[205] IP addresses identify networks and computers (hosts) on the internet while domain names allow plain English names to be given to IP addresses (see unit 5.1).

Unit 5.1 | Module 5 Networks and Printing

Unit 5.1 Networking Fundamentals

CompTIA A+ Essentials Objectives

- **701.4.1 Summarize the basics of networking fundamentals, including technologies, devices and protocols**
  Bandwidth and latency • Protocols (TCP/IP, NETBIOS) • Full-duplex, half-duplex • Basics of workgroups and domains • Common ports: HTTP, FTP, POP, SMTP, TELNET, HTTPS • LAN / WAN • Basics class identification

Workgroups and Domains

A **server** is a computer that hosts **resources**, such as disk space, printers, and applications. A **client** is a computer that accesses those resources.

In a **peer-to-peer** network, each computer (or workstation) can act both as a server and as a client. Control of resources is essentially *distributed* between the users of each computer. Under Windows, this type of network is described as a **workgroup**.

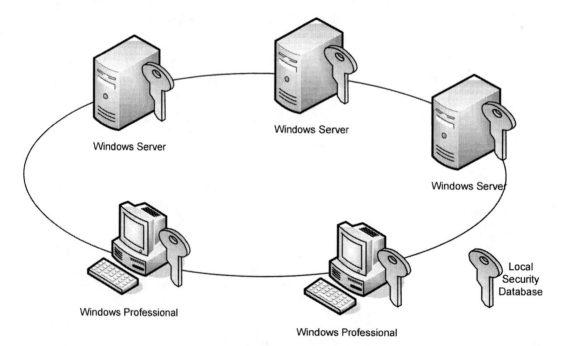

Peer-to-peer (workgroup) security accounts are all stored locally

Module 5 Networks and Printing	Networking Fundamentals

A workgroup is quite simple to set up, but unreliable and difficult to organize. For example, a user could switch off their machine while someone else was accessing it. There is also no good means of deciding who should have access to the network. It is also difficult to grow the network, as when a machine or new user is added all the other machines have to be "informed" about it.

A **client-server** network addresses these problems by locating all shared resources on dedicated server computers, controlled by network administrators. This network model is centralized, robust, scalable, and secure.

Client computers can either be ordinary PCs or low-cost **thin clients**. An ordinary PC allows applications to be installed locally to access data shared on the server whereas a thin client runs software hosted on the server. The thin client model goes in-and-out of fashion in IT quite regularly but is currently receiving a boost from the **cloud computing** model, where server and IT infrastructure is owned and managed by a third-party (the "cloud") and the client uses a low-cost computer to access applications on a use-basis.

Tip

Not all real-world networks are completely peer-to-peer or completely client-server. Some networks use a mixture of both approaches.

Windows domains

Under Windows, a client-server network is described as a **domain**. To create a domain, you need one or more Windows servers configured as **domain controllers**. The domain controllers store a database of network information called **Active Directory**. This database stores user, group, and computer objects. The database can be replicated between the domain controllers. The domain controllers are responsible for providing authentication services to users as they attempt to logon to the network. The network designer will designate as many as are needed to provide a timely and reliable logon service.

Domain controllers and member servers[206] are controlled by network administrators, who define client computers and users permitted to access resources.

---

[206] Member servers are any server based systems that have been configured into the domain, but do not maintain a copy of the Active Directory database and are therefore unable to provide logon services. Because the user validation process consumes resources, most servers are configured as member servers rather than domain controllers. They will provide file and print and application server services (such as Exchange for email or SQL Server for database or line-of-business applications).

© 2010 gtslearning   IT Career FastTrack with CompTIA A+ Certification   Page 493

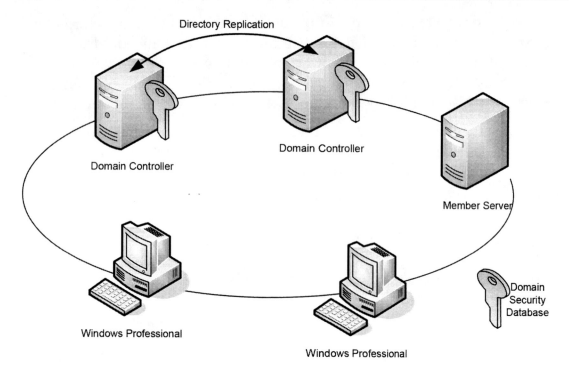

Active Directory security accounts are stored and managed from a domain controller

Network Operating Systems

Desktop operating systems such as Windows 2000 Professional or Windows XP can act as servers in a workgroup, but they are restricted in terms of the number of inbound connections they can support[207]:

- 5 connections - Windows XP Home and Windows Vista Home Basic.

- 10 connections - Windows 2000 Professional, Windows XP Professional / MCE, Windows Vista Home Premium / Business / Ultimate.

Windows Server editions represent the **Network Operating System (NOS)** products in Microsoft's OS suite. Server editions support more processors and memory and come with software to facilitate networking, such as routing, addressing, and client management (Active Directory). The number of allowed connections is determined by the **Client Access Licenses (CAL)** installed (see unit 2.1 for more notes on Windows licensing).

The main versions of Windows Server are:

---

[207] This does not affect the maximum number of clients on the network just the number of clients that can simultaneously open a connection to the PC. A connection would be opening a shared file or accessing a shared printer.

Module 5 Networks and Printing

Networking Fundamentals

- Windows 2000 Server - this comes in Standard, Advanced, and DataCenter editions. The main distinction between the editions is the number of processors and amount of memory supported.

- Windows Server 2003 - this comes in Standard, Enterprise (the equivalent of Windows 2000 Advanced Server), DataCenter, and Web editions. The Web edition is optimized to run Microsoft Internet Information Services (IIS) web server rather than perform ordinary network functions.

- Windows Server 2008 - this comes in similar editions but there is more support for virtualization (running multiple instances of a server OS on a single server computer) via the Hyper-V edition.

- Windows Small Business Server (2000, 2003, and 2008) - this features a simplified management interface compared to the equivalent Standard product and is bundled with several application servers (notably Exchange for email and SQL Server for database applications).

Other operating systems can also be used for network servers. The main ones include Linux, UNIX, and Mac OS X Server. These servers all support Windows clients, either using client software or open standard protocols (TCP/IP).

Network Technologies and Protocols

A network is made by creating communication pathways between the devices on the network (referred to as nodes or hosts). Communications pathways are implemented using an **adapter** installed in the host to transmit and receive signals and network **media** between the hosts to carry the signals. There are two main types of communications media:

- Wired networking uses cabling (copper wire or fiber optic) to connect nodes.

- Wireless networking uses electromagnetic waves (radio or infrared signals) to transmit signals.

Bandwidth

The main characteristic of network media is its **bandwidth**. This is the amount of data that can be transferred across the media in a given amount of time. One method used to increase bandwidth is **signaling speed**.

© 2010 gtslearning

IT Career FastTrack with CompTIA A+ Certification

Page 495

Signaling speed is measured in MHz (millions of clock cycles per second). If one bit of data can be sent per clock cycle then a signaling speed of 10 MHz allows: 1 bit/cycle x 10,000,000 cycles/second = 10 Mbps.

Full and half-duplex

Networking equipment can either be **half-duplex**, meaning that it can transmit and receive but not at the same time, or **full duplex**, meaning that it can transmit and receive at the same time.

Latency

Many networks are now used for "real-time" data, such as Voice over IP, video conferencing, or online gaming. Real-time data is sensitive to **latency**. Latency is the time it takes for a signal to reach the recipient. A video application can support a latency of about 80ms, while typical latency on the internet can reach 1000ms at peak times. Latency can be controlled by using Quality of Service (QoS) technologies, so that the real-time data is prioritized over other types.

Other important characteristics are range (the distance a signal can travel), cost, and susceptibility to eavesdropping (intercepting signals).

LAN and WAN

One basic distinction between types of network is between **Local Area Networks (LAN)** and **Wide Area Networks (WAN)**. A LAN is typically a single site or several sites connected by high-speed backbones. Any network where the nodes are within about 1 or 2 km (or about 1 mile) of one another can be thought of as "local".

WANs are usually thought of as relying on some intermediate network (such as the internet or phone system) to connect geographically diverse LANs. A network where remote users "dial-in" is also a type of WAN.

Below a LAN, the concept of a **Personal Area Network (PAN)** has gained some currency with the profusion of wireless and cellular connection technologies in the last few years.

Between LANs and WANs there are some designations for intermediate-size networks, such as **CAN (Campus)** and **MAN (Metropolitan)**.

Addressing and protocols

Network signals must be packaged in such a way that each computer is able to understand them. Also, each host must have a means of recognizing the location of other hosts on the network. These functions are provided by a network **protocol**. A network protocol identifies each host on the network using a unique address. It also defines a **packet** structure. A packet is a wrapper for each data unit transmitted over the network. A packet generally consists of a **header** (indicating the protocol type, source address, destination address, error correction information, and so on) and a **payload** (the data).

> **Tip**
> Networks use multiple protocols. The packet from one protocol can be wrapped within the packet from another (encapsulation).

Addressing and protocols are best understood with reference to the **OSI (Open Systems Interconnect) model**. This tool helps to design and troubleshoot networks. The OSI model conceptualizes network functions at seven layers.

Each layer communicates with its equivalent or "peer" layer on the other host via the lower layers of the model. Each layer *provides* **services** for the layer *above* and *uses* the services of the layer *below*.

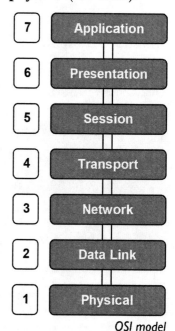

OSI model

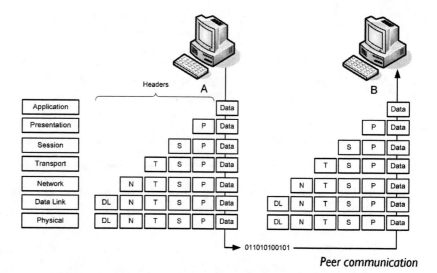

Peer communication

When a message is sent from one host to another, it travels down the stack of layers on the sending host, reaches the receiving host using the transmission media, and then passes up the stack on this host. At each level (except the physical layer) a **header** is added. These headers are read by the corresponding layer on the other host and provide control information.

Physical and data link layer protocols

In the OSI model, the **Physical (PHY)** layer represents the network media (such as wired or wireless) and devices (such as a network adapter). At this layer, the media uses a particular type of **signaling** to represent the 1s and 0s of binary computer data.

The **Data Link** layer represents ways of transferring data between devices. It organizes the stream of signals transmitted at the physical layer into units called **frames**. Frames allow signals to be **addressed** to a particular device and provide error checking, to ensure the integrity of the data.

Typical structure of a frame

At this layer, **addressing** means allocating a unique ID to each device (network adapter)[208].

Under the widely used IEEE 802.2 standard, this unique ID is a 48-bit number expressed in hexadecimal (00-01-E6-50-97-21 for example [remember that each hex digit can represent 4 binary digits]) called the **Media Access Control (MAC)** address. This number is hard-coded into the adapter by the device vendor.

There are various complementary standards supporting 802.2, each defining a different method of using different network media. The most popular cabled local network standard is 802.3 (Ethernet).

Network and transport protocols

PHY and Data Link standards and protocols establish a physical connection between computers and a format for exchanging signals carrying data.

---

[208] The network adapter works at both layers 1 and 2 of the OSI model. It physically transmits and receives signals but it also handles addressing and framing.

The next two layers in the OSI model, Network and Transport, define the services that are used to identify individual networks and the format of data packets transferred between computers. The basic function of the network layer is **routing** packets between networks; the basic function of the transport layer is **controlling** the flow of packets between nodes.

At this level, the overwhelming majority of networks use TCP/IP to perform these functions, though IPX / NWLink and NetBEUI also have roles to play in some older networks.

TCP/IP

Transmission Control Protocol / Internet Protocol (TCP/IP) is actually a suite of complementary protocols, working from the network layer (IP protocol) to the application layer (protocols such as HTTP [web] or SMTP [email]).

TCP/IP was originally developed by the US Department of Defense but is now an open standard to which anyone may contribute. Developments are implemented through the **Internet Engineering Task Force (IETF)**, which is split into a number of working groups. Standards are published as RFCs (Request For Comment) at www.faqs.org/rfc.

TCP/IP is a packet-based protocol. This means that a data message is split into numerous small packets. Smaller packets have a better chance of being delivered successfully and are easier to resend if lost or damaged.

Devices called **routers** choose the paths that packets take around the network from source to destination. To prevent packets travelling around the network indefinitely looking for a path, TCP/IP gives each packet a life span known as **Time To Live (TTL)**.

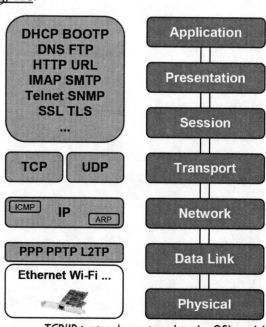

TCP/IP protocols compared to the OSI model

| Unit 5.1 | Module 5 Networks and Printing |

Internet Protocol and IP addressing

The core protocol in TCP/IP is the **Internet Protocol (IP)**, which provides network identification and addressing. **IP addresses** are used to identify each device (host).

An IP address is a 32-bit binary value. To make this value easier to enter in configuration dialogs, it is expressed as four decimal numbers separated by periods (172.16.11.200 for instance). Each number represents a byte value (that is, an 8-character binary value, also called an octet, or a decimal value between 0 and 255). This is referred to as **dotted decimal notation**.

Along with the IP address, each host must also be configured with a **subnet mask**. This is combined with the IP address to determine the identity of the network to which the host belongs.

The subnet mask contains a "1" where the matching bit in the IP address is part of the network ID and a "0" where the matching bit is a host ID.

Under the system of **classful addressing**, the subnet mask is always a whole octet, allowing for three possible masks (255.0.0.0, 255.255.0.0, and 255.255.255.0). These masks are used with ranges of IP addresses, divided into three classes (A, B, and C) based on the value of the first octet in the IP address.

Class	First Octet	Default Mask
A	1-126	255.0.0.0
B	128-191	255.255.0.0
C	192-223	255.255.255.0

So, using our example IP address of 172.16.11.200 you should be able to see that it is a Class B address and would be used with the subnet mask 255.255.0.0. This means that the network ID is "172.16" and the host ID is "11.200".

Classful addressing does not make optimum use of the total number of available IP addresses. In practice, addresses are more likely to use classless or **variable length subnet masks**. For example, the default class B subnet mask is 16 bits long. If you wanted to define some mini networks (subnets) within a class B address series, you could define a 20-bit mask. This would be expressed in decimal as 255.255.240.0. The network could also be referred to in classless notation as 172.16.0.0 /20.

Page 500   IT Career FastTrack with CompTIA A+ Certification   © 2010 gtslearning

Module 5 Networks and Printing — Networking Fundamentals

You may have noticed some missing ranges in the list of first octets in the table above. The dotted decimal representation of the IP address can theoretically range between 0.0.0.0 and 255.255.255.255. However, a number of IP addresses are reserved or perform special functions.

- Private address ranges - for networks not directly connected to the internet
    - 10.0.0.0 to 10.255.255.255 (Class A private address range)
    - 169.254.0.0 to 169.254.255.255 (used by APIPA)
    - 172.16.0.0 to 172.31.255.255 (Class B private address range)
    - 192.168.0.0 to 192.168.255.255 (Class C private address range)
- Loopback address - used to test TCP/IP functionality on a host (IP routes the transmission straight back to the host)
    - 127.0.0.0 to 127.255.255.255
- Multicast addresses (Class D) - these can be used by a single host to broadcast to multiple hosts
    - 224.0.0.0 to 239.255.255
- Reserved addresses - use of these addresses is not permitted
    - 0.0.0.0 to 0.255.255.255
    - 128.0.0.0 to 128.0.255.255
    - 191.255.0.0 to 191.255.255.255
    - 192.0.0.0 to 192.0.0.255
    - 223.255.255.0 to 223.255.255.255
    - 240.0.0.0 to 255.255.255.255 (Class E)

IP Version 6

The addressing scheme discussed above is for IP version 4 (the version currently in use). Because it is feared the global supply of IP addresses will run out, a new version of IP addressing (version 6) is being proposed. An IPv6 address is a 128-bit number (contrast with the 32-bit number used in v4).

Unit 5.1   Module 5 Networks and Printing

This number is expressed in **hexadecimal** notation. For example: 2001:0db8:0000:0000:0abc:0000:def0:1234. Even this is quite cumbersome, so where a double-byte contains leading zeros, they can be ignored. In addition, *one* contiguous series of zeroes can be replaced by a double colon place marker. Thus the address above would become: 2001:*db8*::*abc*:0:def0:1234

An IPv6 address is divided into two main parts: the first 64 bits are used as a network ID while the second 64 bits designate a specific interface.

ARP and ICMP

Also working at the network layer, the **Address Resolution Protocol (ARP)** converts IP addresses to MAC addresses and vice versa and the **ICMP (Internet Control Message Protocol)** is used for diagnostic and troubleshooting tools, such as PING or TRACERT.

TCP and UDP

A layer 3 protocol like IP attempts to deliver data packets to the correct address but does not attempt to make any guarantee that it will do so correctly. This raises a problem for any application that wants to use data in the packet! The transport layer (layer 4) provides the solution to this problem. In TCP/IP it is implemented by one of two protocols.

- **TCP (Transmission Control Protocol)** - provides reliable, connection-oriented transfer of packets. This is used by most TCP/IP applications, including HTTP (web) and email, where lost packets would mean corrupted data and application errors.

- **UDP (User Datagram Protocol)** - provides connectionless, unreliable transfer of packets. This is faster and more efficient and is used in time-sensitive applications, such as speech or video, where a few missing or out-of-order packets can be tolerated.

TCP/IP applications (such as HTTP for web services or POP3 for email) use a unique identification number called a **port**. Port numbers are assigned by the **Internet Assigned Numbers Authority (IANA)**. Enabling and disabling ports is an important part of configuring a **firewall**, to ensure that only valid application protocols are allowed. Some of the "well-known" port numbers are listed below:

Page 502   IT Career FastTrack with CompTIA A+ Certification   © 2010 gtslearning

Port Number	Process Name	Description
20	FTPDATA	File Transfer Protocol - Data
21	FTP	File Transfer Protocol – Control
22	SSH	Secure Shell
23	TELNET	Telnet
25	SMTP	Simple Mail Transfer Protocol
53	DNS	Domain Name Service
69	TFTP	Trivial FTP
80	HTTP	HTTP
110	POP3	Post Office Protocol version 3
119	NNTP	Network News Transfer Protocol
123	NTP	Network Time Protocol
139	NetBIOS	Session port
143	IMAP4	Internet Mail Access Protocol
389	LDAP	Directory Access Protocol
443	HTTPS	HTTP Secure

A port number plus the IP address form a **socket**. A socket provides an endpoint to a connection and two sockets from a complete **path**.

TCP/IP application protocols

The TCP/IP suite encompasses a large number and wide range of protocols that perform functions at the session, presentation, and application layers of the OSI model as a generic application layer. Some of the principal protocols amongst these are discussed below.

HTTP and HTML

HyperText Transfer Protocol (HTTP) is the basis of the World Wide Web. HTTP enables clients (typically web browsers) to request resources from an HTTP server. A client connects to the HTTP server using an appropriate TCP port (the default is port 80) and submits a request for a resource, using a special address called a **Uniform Resource Identifier (URI)**[209]. The server acknowledges the request and returns the data.

---

[209] The term URI is preferred to URL. The use of URL (Uniform Resource Locator) is deprecated in standards documentation but is still in widespread popular use. A URL is a particular type of URI describing the location of a resource.

© 2010 gtslearning   IT Career FastTrack with CompTIA A+ Certification   Page 503

Most organizations have an online presence, represented by a website. In order to run a website, it must be hosted on an HTTP server connected to the internet. Typically, an organization will lease a server or space on a server from an ISP. Larger organizations or SMEs with good technical skills may host websites themselves.

Web servers are not only used on the internet however. Private networks using web technologies are described as **intranets** (if they permit only local access) or **extranets** (if they permit remote access).

HTTP is usually used to serve **HTML** web pages, which are plain text files with coded tags (**HyperText Markup Language**) describing how the page should be formatted. A web browser can interpret the tags and display the text and other resources associated with the page (such as picture or sound files). Another powerful feature is its ability to provide **hyperlinks** to other related documents.

HTTP also features a forms mechanism (POST) whereby a user can submit data from the client to the server. The functionality of HTTP servers is also often extended by support for scripting and programmable features (web applications). Technologies such as scripting or integration with databases greatly enhance functionality but also significantly increase security risks[210].

Domain names

Every host on the internet has a unique, 32-bit, IP address. However, these addresses are difficult to remember, so an alternative addressing method, known as a **Fully Qualified Domain Name (FQDN)** has been developed.

The domain name does not replace the IP address but provides a user-friendly way of reaching the host. A series of inter-linked databases, known as **Domain Name Servers (DNS)** provide cross-referencing between IP addresses and domain names.

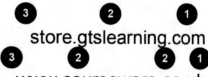

Parts of two FQDNs with 1) Top level domain; 2) Subdomain; 3) Local domain

---

[210] You will often see the term "Web 2.0" (originated and owned by O'Reilly Media) used to describe new web applications, such as social networking sites like MySpace, Facebook, blogs, podcasts, and so on.

The domain name structure follows a fixed hierarchy, with the top level of the hierarchy shown to the right of the name. The information becomes more specific as you move to the left. Each name has an entry in the domain name server that provides its IP address. Domain name servers cannot hold all names, but they can refer to other servers, using the top-level domain to locate a suitable server.

Top-level domain names are registered centrally. They describe the nature of the organization or the country in which it is located. Some examples include:

Domain Name	Description
edu	Educational and research institutes
gov	Government agencies
mil	Military institutions
net	Network companies (ISPs)
com	Commercial organizations
org	Other organizations
uk	United Kingdom
au	Australia
jp	Japan

The **subdomain** identifies a company, organization, or even an individual. The name has to be unique and officially registered (a process that is normally handled by your ISP).

Local domains are specified within the organization (for example, to identify a server located in the sales department of a company). The **www** local domain part is a common alias to indicate that the resource is a web server.

Uniform Resource Identifier

Resources on the internet are accessed using an identifier known as a **Uniform Resource Identifier (URI)**. The URI contains all the information necessary to identify and (in most cases) access an item.

http://store.gtslearning.com/comptia/index.htm

URI with 1) Protocol; 2) FQDN; 3) File path

- The protocol describes the access method or service type being used.

Unit 5.1   Module 5 Networks and Printing

- The host location is represented by a Fully Qualified Domain Name (FQDN). The FQDN is not case sensitive.

- The file path specifies the directory and file name location of the resource (if required). The file path may or may not be case-sensitive, depending on how the server is configured.

SSL / TLS

One of the critical problems for the provision of early e-commerce sites was the lack of security in HTTP. Under HTTP, all data is sent unencrypted and there is no authentication of client or server.

Secure Sockets Layer (SSL) was developed by Netscape and released as version 3.0 in 1996 to address these problems. SSL proved very popular with the industry and is still in widespread use. **Transport Layer Security (TLS)** was developed from SSL and ratified as a standard by IETF. TLS is now the version in active development, with 1.1 as the latest version[211].

SSL/TLS works as a layer between the application and transport layers of the TCP/IP stack (in OSI terms, at the session layer). It can be used to encrypt TCP connections (but not UDP). It is typically used with the HTTP application (referred to as **HTTPS** or **HTTP Over SSL** or **HTTP Secure**) but can also be used to secure other TCP/IP application protocols.

> **Tip**
>
> HTTPS operates over port 443 by default. HTTPS operation is indicated by using https:// for the URI and by a padlock icon shown in the browser.

Essentially, a server is assigned a **digital certificate** by some trusted **Certificate Authority**. The certificate proves the identity of the server (assuming that the client trusts the Certificate Authority[212]). The server uses the digital certificate and the SSL/TLS protocol to encrypt communications between it and the client. This means that the communications cannot be read or changed by a third party.

---

[211] SSL and TLS are not interoperable (that is, a client supporting only SSL 3.0 could not connect to a server supporting only TLS 1.0). SSL 3.0 is still the most widely supported version.

[212] It is also possible to install a certificate on the client so that the server can trust the client. This is not often used on the web but is a feature of Virtual Private Networks (VPNs).

Electronic mail (email)

Email is a messaging system that can be used to transmit text messages and binary file attachments encoded using **Multipurpose Internet Mail Extensions (MIME)**. The client software sends a message to the mail server, using a protocol called **Simple Mail Transfer Protocol (SMTP)**. The server software does not *deliver* the messages to the client software because the recipient may not be logged on or the destination host may be turned-off.

Instead, mail is held in the mailbox on the mail server, waiting for the client to connect and pick it up. The protocols that provide mailbox access are the **Post Office Protocol (POP)** and the **Internet Mail Access Protocol (IMAP)**[213].

Email is arguably the single most important service on the internet, as it has become the standard means of communication for most organizations. Users can send messages more or less instantaneously to anywhere in the world without incurring the cost of international telephone calls.

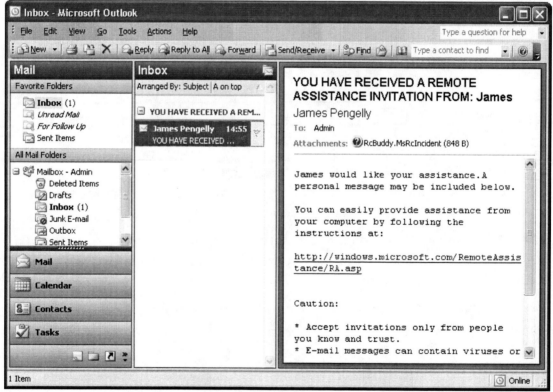

Outlook email client

---

[213] POP3 is more widely implemented, but IMAP provides extra features, such as support for mail folders other than inbox on the server and calendar functionality.

Email systems have been available since the early days of computing, but the facilities now available make it one of the most versatile and accessible methods of communication. As with most TCP/IP applications, the main drawback of email is that it is not secure. To maintain confidentiality, the sender and recipient must agree to use an encryption system. The main products are **Pretty Good Privacy (PGP)** and **Secure MIME (S/MIME)**.

Internet email addresses

An internet email address comprises two parts; the user name (local part) and the domain name, separated by an @ symbol. The domain name may refer to a company or an ISP (for **david.martin@gtslearning.com** or david.martin@aol.com). Different mail systems have different requirements for allowed and disallowed characters in the local part. The local part is supposed to be case-sensitive, but most mail systems do not treat it as such.

An incorrectly addressed email will be returned with a message notifying that it was undeliverable. Mail may also be rejected if it is identified as spam or if there is some other problem with the user mailbox (such as the mailbox being full).

File Transfer Protocol (FTP)

FTP (File Transfer Protocol) is part of the TCP/IP suite and used extensively for making files available over the internet. An FTP server is typically configured with a number of public directories (accessed anonymously) and private directories, requiring a user account.

FTP is more efficient compared to email file attachments or HTTP file transfer, but has no security mechanisms. All authentication and data transfer is communicated as plain text.

Most browsers include a FTP program and shareware is available to download from the internet.

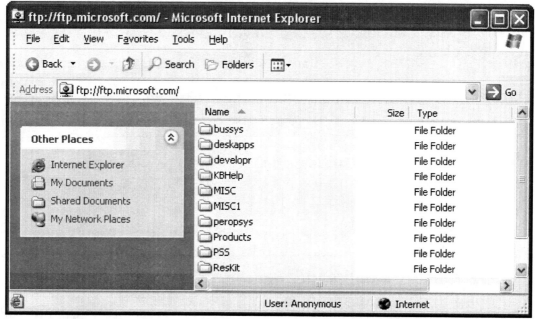

Browsing a FTP site using Internet Explorer

Instant Messaging

Instant messaging is a popular real-time text messaging tool. Instant messaging allows the exchange of text messages with other contacts on your messaging list. Instant messaging also supports file exchanges. The widespread use of webcams means that video messaging is becoming just as easy and popular. Many clients also support **Voice over IP (VoIP)** calling.

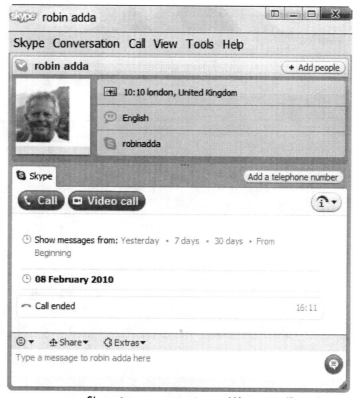

Skype instant messaging and Voice over IP application

Unit 5.1 — Module 5 Networks and Printing

Online conferencing can be established using a variety of tools, including audio and video, but also text messaging, whiteboard, presentation tools, and remote desktop.

NetBEUI / NetBIOS

NetBIOS (Network Basic Input / Output System) provides software programmers with an easy means of accessing and utilizing network resources.

IBM first introduced the **NetBEUI (NetBIOS Extended User Interface)** protocol suite in 1985 for its PC networks. NetBEUI was, for some years, Microsoft's preferred protocol for its LAN Manager and early NT products. Later versions of NT (3.5x and onwards) switched to Microsoft's own implementation of TCP/IP. NetBEUI is a *non-routable* protocol, meaning that it can only be used on a single network and cannot make use of a device such as a router to send information to another network.

Originally, NetBIOS and NetBEUI were considered one protocol but the NetBIOS component was separated for use with other protocols (such as TCP/IP). However, security vulnerabilities mean that NetBIOS is best disabled unless legacy OS and applications must be supported.

Summary

Make sure you know the different types and capabilities of network models such as workgroups and domains. Try to understand the OSI model and how it relates to practical network technologies and protocols. Focus on learning the different protocols in the TCP/IP suite, as these are critical to configuring and troubleshooting most networks.

Tip

To review what you have learned in this chapter, you should now visit the course website. This contains review questions and bonus material to help you to learn more and practice the topics covered in this unit.

Module 5 Networks and Printing   *Installing and Configuring Local Networks*

Unit 5.2 Installing and Configuring Local Networks

CompTIA A+ Essentials Objectives

☐ **701.4.1 Summarize the basics of networking fundamentals, including technologies, devices and protocols**
Basics of configuring IP addressing and TCP/IP properties (DHCP, DNS) • Hub, switch and router

☐ **701.4.2 Categorize network cables and connectors and their implementations**
Cables (Plenum / PVC, UTP [e.g. CAT3, CAT5 / 5e, CAT6], STP, Fiber, Coaxial cable) • Connectors (RJ45, RJ11)

☐ **701.4.3 Compare and contrast the different network types**
Wireless (All 802.11 types, WEP, WPA, SSID, MAC filtering, DHCP settings) • Bluetooth

CompTIA A+ Practical Application Objectives

☐ **702.3.2 Install and configure a Small Office Home Office (SOHO) network**
Connection types (Wireless [All 802.11, WEP, WPA, SSID, MAC filtering, DHCP settings], Routers / Access Points [Disable DHCP, Use static IP, Change SSID from default, Disable SSID broadcast, MAC filtering, Change default username and password, Update firmware], LAN [10/100/1000BASE-T, Speeds], Bluetooth [1.0 vs. 2.0]) • Physical installation (Wireless router placement, Cable length)

☐ **701.5.2 Summarize the following security features**
Wireless encryption (WEPx and WPAx, Client configuration [SSID])

Installing a Local Network

There are several ways to set up a LAN, depending on the number of computers to be connected and the level of reliability and security required. The main components of a **SOHO (Small Office Home Office)** type LAN are:

- Cabling - typically UTP patch cords.

- Network adapters - wired (Ethernet) or wireless (Wi-Fi).

- Switch / access point - providing communications between computers on the LAN.

- Router - providing a link to the internet.

Very often, the router and switch / access point will be combined in a single multifunction device.

© 2010 gtslearning   IT Career FastTrack with CompTIA A+ Certification   Page 511

Unit 5.2   Module 5 Networks and Printing

Ethernet cabling

Ethernet is by far the most popular wired local networking standard. Ethernet standards are maintained by the IEEE. Ethernet is a complex set of standards, specifying different ways of providing network solutions at the physical and data link layers of the OSI model. However, there are four broad "types" of Ethernet, defined in the **IEEE 802.3** standards documentation:

- 10 Mbps (10BASE-) - this is the original standard, specifying cabling and connectors for twisted-pair, coax, and fiber optic products.

- Fast Ethernet (100BASE-) - twisted-pair and fiber optic implementations of 100 Mbps LANs.

- Gigabit Ethernet (1000BASE-) - twisted-pair and fiber optic implementations of 1000 Mbps LANs. This has replaced Fast Ethernet as the "standard" for a typical network.

- 10G Ethernet (10GBASE-) - 10 Gbps connections for LANs and WANs using fiber optic or copper wire.

The basis of Ethernet is a network wired using copper or fiber optic cable in a "star" topology. Each device is connected to a switch (the center of the "star"). Each node is identified uniquely by its MAC address.

Unshielded Twisted Pair (UTP)

Unshielded Twisted Pair (UTP) is a type of copper cabling used for computer networking. The most widely used sort comprises four copper conductor "pairs"[214]. Each conductor has an insulating sheath. Each pair of conductors is twisted, which reduces interference between the wires (**crosstalk**) and from other electromagnetic sources (**Electromagnetic Interference [EMI]**). The four pairs are covered by a protective outer jacket.

The number of twists is one factor in determining the bandwidth of the cable. UTP cable is rated for different Ethernet applications according to "cat" specifications, defined in the **TIA/EIA-568-B Commercial Building Telecommunications Cabling Standards**.

UTP cable

---

[214] Another type of UTP is used for telephone wiring. Telephone wiring is typically 2-pair rather than 4-pair.

Page 512   IT Career FastTrack with CompTIA A+ Certification   © 2010 gtslearning

Cat	Frequency (MHz)	Capacity (Mbps)	Max. Distance	Ethernet Standard
3	16	10	100m (328ft)	10BASE-T
5	100	100	100m (328ft)	100BASE-TX (Fast Ethernet)
5e	100	1000	100m (328ft)	1000BASE-T (Gigabit Ethernet)
6	Up to 250	1000+	100m (328ft)	1000BASE-T (Gigabit Ethernet)
		10 Gbps	55m (180ft)	10GBASE-T (10G Ethernet)
6a	Up to 250	10 Gbps	100m (328ft)	10GBASE-T (10G Ethernet)

RJ-45 (left) and RJ-11 (right) connectors

Cat5e[215] or Cat6 would be the current choice for a new network installation.

Ethernet installations using UTP cabling use RJ-45 (8P8C) connectors.

In order to achieve throughput for Gigabit (or even Fast) Ethernet, the correct installation of the cable is as important as obtaining cabling and connectors rated at Cat5e or Cat6.

The smaller RJ-11 connectors are used with 2-pair cables. RJ-45 is by far the most common type of connector in use for network data cabling, while RJ-11 connectors are frequently used for telephone systems.

Cabling design for small LANs

A very small LAN may simply utilize flexible UTP patch cords of up to about 10m (30 feet) in length in conjunction with a 4-port switch / router. Computers outside the range of the wired LAN may use wireless links. Wireless links may be deployed anyway to avoid unsightly patch cords.

4-port Ethernet switch for small offices or homes (the device is also an ADSL router and wireless access point)

Note
While patch cords are designed to be flexible, do not bend them unnecessarily or excessively as this may reduce performance.

---

[215] Cat5 cable is no longer available. Cat5e is tested at 100MHz (like Cat5 was) but to higher overall specifications for attenuation and crosstalk, meaning that the cable is rated to handle Gigabit Ethernet throughput.

Commercial offices are more likely to use **structured cabling**. This means that the UTP cable is usually wired in a similar way to telephone systems.

An Ethernet segment using twisted-pair cabling can be up to 100m (328 feet). This means there must be no more than 100m of cabling between the switch and the computer. For structured cabling, within this overall limit, there is a distinction between **solid** and **stranded** cabling. Solid cabling uses a single thick wire per conductor. Stranded cabling uses multiple thin wires wrapped around one another.

In a structured cable installation, a patch cable made of stranded cabling is connected from the network adapter in the PC to an **RJ-45 wall port**. Solid cable from this port is then taken through ducting to a communications room where it is connected to a socket on a **patch panel**.

Note
Local fire regulations may require the use of special types of cable for specific situations; for example, the use of plenum cable in plenum spaces (the space above false ceilings in an office). Plenum cable is designed to be fire resistant and uses Teflon coatings so it produces a minimal amount of smoke. PVC insulation should be avoided as this produces poisonous gas when burned.

Another patch cord from the patch panel connects to a **switch**.

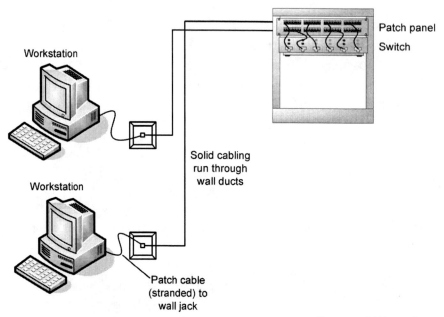

Structured Wiring System

The overall segment length should be no more than 100m and lengths of patch cord should be no more than 10m overall.

In a larger network, multiple switches may be connected via a **backbone**.

In this scenario, a **WAN router / DSL modem** might also be connected to a switch port for internet connectivity or it might be connected to a **proxy server**, which would handle all internet traffic for client workstations on the LAN.

Hubs and switches

A **hub** is one type of device used to implement a star topology. The hub contains a number of ports (typically between 4 and 48) to provide connections for network devices. A hub (operating at layer 1 of the OSI model) simply ensures that all devices receive signals put on the network.

A **switch** is an improved version of a hub (operating at layer 2). Switches are used to reduce the effect of **contention** on network performance. Contention arises in hub-based Ethernet because all communications are received by all computers connected to the hub. A lot of the communications are unnecessary and a lot of them "collide", slowing the network down. The network segment in which these collisions occur is called a **collision domain**.

HP ProCurve 12-port switch

The switch allows a device to utilize the full capacity of the network, rather than sharing it with other devices. The switch creates a temporary **virtual circuit** between the two devices that are attempting to communicate. In effect, the two computers are in their own collision domain and as the link is full duplex no collisions can in fact occur. This is referred to as **microsegmentation**.

For other devices, the network appears free, so they are able to send communications at the same time using the full bandwidth of the network media.

> **Tip**
>
> In practice, hubs are now obsolete. You are very unlikely to come across any. The vast majority of Ethernet networks are implemented using switches. Gigabit Ethernet can *only* run using switches.

Network adapter

Network adapters, also known as **Network Interface Cards (NICs)**, move data between the computer and the network media. Most motherboards ship with an onboard LAN adapter, but a NIC may also be installed into any free expansion slot. NICs operate at layers 1 and 2 of the OSI model. At layer 1 (PHY), the transceiver in the card sends and receives signals over the cable. At layer 2 (Data Link), the card driver handles addressing and framing (packaging the data into standard units). Each network card has a unique hexadecimal identifier, known as the **MAC address**[216], which is used to make sure that the messages arrive at the correct destination.

Most computers have a network adapter already installed as part of the motherboard's chipset. However, there may be occasions when you do need to install an adapter card (or **Network Interface Card [NIC]**) or need to upgrade an adapter to use a different type of network, bandwidth, or cabling.

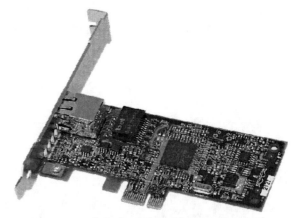

Broadcom PCIe Gigabit Ethernet adapter

When selecting a card, you must match the card to the technologies used on the network and host PC:

- Bus Type - the card must be fitted to a spare expansion slot in the PC (either PCI or 1x PCIe).

- Network Type - typically this will be Ethernet. With Ethernet, the card should support the speed of the network (Fast or Gigabit Ethernet). Most cards are "combos" that support a range of speeds (100/1000 for example).

---

[216] A MAC address is a 48-bit number, expressed in 12 hex numerals (for example, 00-01-E6-50-97-21). The first half is the ID of the adapter's manufacturer. The second half is a unique serial number assigned by the manufacturer.

- Transceiver and connector - most Ethernet cards are designed to support twisted-pair with an RJ-45 (8P8C) connector. Other types include older coaxial cards (BNC connector) and fiber optic (a range of possible connectors)[217].

- Other features - a card that supports **Pre-boot Execution Environment (PXE)** means that a computer can boot from a server rather from disk. The network adapter and computer BIOS must support PXE (**Network** will appear as a boot option in the computer's CMOS Setup program). PXE also supports **Wake-on-LAN**, which enables a remote administrator to switch on the PC via a "magic packet" broadcast from a network server. There must be motherboard and PSU as well as a compatible NIC.

Physically installing the card is a simple task. Just add it to the spare slot and restart the computer to install the card drivers using the **Found New Hardware** wizard.

Most adapters will also **auto-negotiate** network settings such as signaling speed and half- or full-duplex operation. If these settings do need to be configured manually, locate the adapter in **Device Manager**, alt-click and select **Properties**, then update settings using the card's driver software.

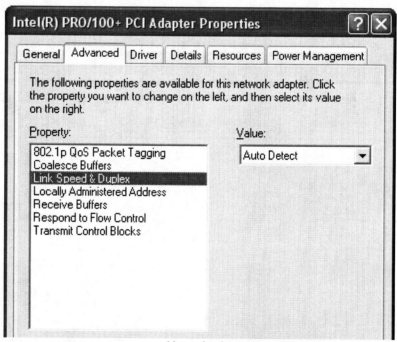

Network adapter properties in Device Manager

---

[217] There are some old combo cards to support both twisted-pair and coaxial connectors at 10 Mbps, but no cards support both twisted-pair and fiber optic.

Router

A **router** is a Layer 3 (Network) device that connects multiple networks and routes packets from one network to another. An **internetwork** is composed of **subnets** (or **subnetworks**) which are identified by a unique **network address**.

HP Procurve router with different types of Ethernet and WAN interfaces

A router has two main functions:

- *Divide* a single physical network into multiple logical networks (subnets) - this is useful for security and performance reasons.

- *Join* a network using one type of media with a network using different media. A typical example is to join a LAN to a WAN, such as the internet.

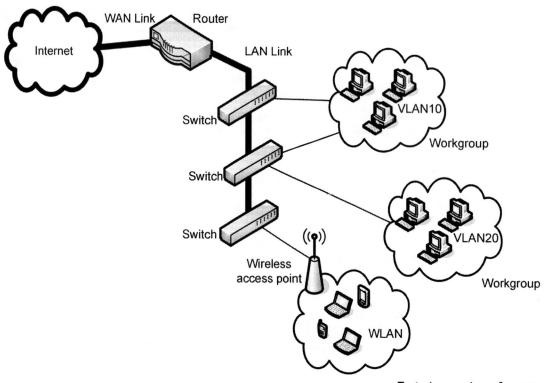

Typical network configuration

Module 5 Networks and Printing

Installing and Configuring Local Networks

The graphic above shows a simplified example of a typical network configuration. Switches provide ports and Virtual LANs (logical groupings of clients) for wired and (via an access point) wireless devices. Traffic between these logical networks is controlled by the router while the WAN ports on the router provide access to the internet.

On a small network, the principal use of a router will be to access the internet. Small Office Home Office (SOHO) routers combine the functions of a DSL modem, router, 4-port LAN switch, and wireless access point to provide network connectivity for small groups of computers.

Other cable types

Most local networks use UTP but there are some other cable types that you should be aware of.

Shielded Twisted Pair (STP)

When twisted pair cabling was first used it was mostly **shielded** (*each* pair had a braided shield) because of its greater resilience to EMI and eavesdropping. This makes the cable heavier, thicker, more expensive, and more difficult to install (the cable must be grounded). **Screened** cable has a thin outer foil or braided shield surrounding all pairs. This type of cable is known as **Foil Twisted Pair (FTP)** or **Screened Twisted Pair (ScTP)**. Screened cable is used in "noisy" environments such as factories where industrial equipment could disrupt the electrical signals passing through the wires. Screened cable may also be used for extra security (it is more resistant to someone intercepting the signals [eavesdropping]).

Fiber optic cable

Copper wire carries electrical signals, which are subject to **interference** and **attenuation** (the reduction of signal quality over distance). Fiber optic cable uses pulses of infrared light for signaling, which are not susceptible to interference, cannot be intercepted (eavesdropped), and suffer far less from attenuation. Consequently, fiber optic cabling supports much higher bandwidth (multiple gigabits per second) and longer cable runs (measured in kilometers rather than meters).

© 2010 gtslearning

IT Career FastTrack with CompTIA A+ Certification

Page 519

An optical fiber consists of an ultra-fine core of glass to carry the light signals surrounded by glass or plastic cladding, which guides the light pulses along the core (a process called Total Internal Reflection), and a protective coating. A fiber optic cable usually consists of two fibers (one for upstream and the other for downstream) contained in a protective jacket and terminated by a connector.

There are two types of optical fiber:

- Single mode (SMF) - has a smaller core (about 9 microns) and a longer wavelength light generated by a laser. Single mode cables are more expensive but support cable runs of many kilometers, depending on the quality of the manufactured cable.

- Multi-mode (MMF) - has a larger core (62.5 or 50 microns) and shorter wavelength light, generated by LEDs, transmitted in multiple waves of varying length. As it uses LEDs (not lasers) and is easier to manufacture, multi-mode cabling is cheaper. However, it does not support such long distances (up to about 500m for most applications) and so is more suitable for LANs than WANs.

The Ethernet standards specify several different implementations of a fiber optic LAN or WAN:

Standard	Speed	Max Length	Cable Type
10BASE-FL	10 Mbps	2 km	MMF
100BASE-FX (FDDI)	100 Mbps	2 km	MMF
1000BASE-SX	1 Gbps	550 m	MMF
10GBASE-SR	10 Gbps	82 m	MMF
10GBASE-LR	10 Gbps	10 km	SMF
10GBASE-ER	10 Gbps	40 km	SMF

Coaxial cable

Unlike twisted-pair, **coaxial** (or **coax**) cable contains a single conductor (either solid or stranded copper wire), encased in a plastic or rubber insulator. A wire or foil braid is wrapped around the insulator to reduce EMI and the whole thing is wrapped in a protective jacket.

Coax cable

Early types of Ethernet specified standards for two grades of coax cable:

- Thicknet (10BASE-5) uses RG-8 standard cable[218]. This was used mostly for network backbones as it supports long cable runs (up to 500m/1640ft). Connections are made using a vampire tap (a transceiver that pierces the cable to connect to the core) with an AUI (Attachment Unit Interface) 15-pin port.

- Thinnet (10BASE-2) uses RG-58 cable. While more flexible and easier to install than thicknet, it does not support long cable runs (185m/610ft). Connections are made using a BNC twist-and-lock bayonet style connector.

Supporting only 10 Mbps networks means that coax for Ethernet use is obsolete. However, it is still used for AV (audio-visual) applications (RG-6) and for connecting a cable "modem" to the provider's fiber optic network for broadband internet (typically also RG-6, though it depends on the network).

Configuring a Local Network

Having installed the network cabling and infrastructure, the next step is to configure Windows clients to connect to the network.

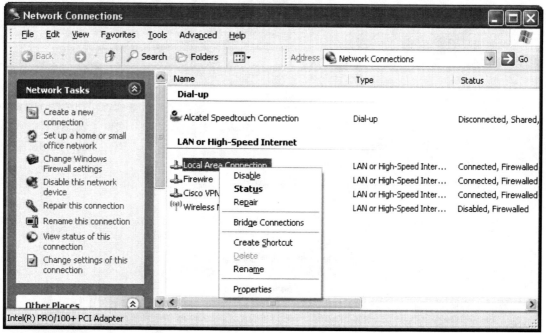

Network Connections

---

[218] RG stands for Radio Grade.

In Windows XP, you can configure the adapter via the **Network Connections** applet (**Network and Dial-up Connections** in Windows 2000). The network adapter will be listed as "Local Area Connection" (though you can rename it if you prefer). Alt-click the adapter and select **Properties** to configure settings or **Status** to view information about the connection. In Vista, select **Start**, alt-click **Network** and select **Properties**, select **Manage network connections**[219], then alt-click the adapter and select **Properties**. From the **Properties** dialog, you can add or configure the appropriate service, protocol, or client.

- **Clients** provide connections to types of file servers, such as Linux/UNIX, Mac OS X, or Windows.

- **Protocols** provide the format for addressing and delivering data messages between systems, the most widely adopted being TCP/IP.

- **Services** allow your machine to make resources available to other hosts over the network.

By default, **Client for Microsoft Networks**, the **TCP/IP** protocol, and the **File and Print Sharing for Microsoft Networks** service are installed[220].

You can add or configure the appropriate service, protocol, or client by alt-clicking the adapter and selecting **Properties**.

Network Connection Properties

---

[219] This is the long route; the short route is to enter NCPA.CPL into the search box.

[220] Checked items are described as being "bound" to an adapter. When installing a new protocol or service, check that it is only bound to adapters that should be using that protocol or service.

By default, Windows Vista is installed with *both* TCP/IP version 4 and TCP/IP version 6. The network adapter automatically uses the appropriate version of the protocol depending on the network it is connected to. Vista also comes with **Link-layer Topology Discovery** protocols, which provide the network mapping and discovery functions in the Vista **Network and Sharing Center**.

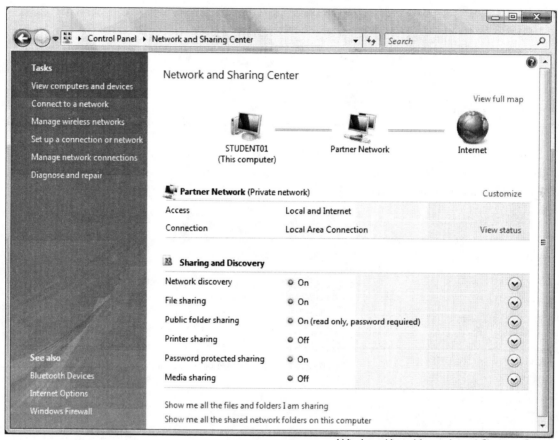

Windows Vista Network and Sharing Center

Configuring TCP/IP

Configuring TCP/IP is simply a case of entering the correct **IP address**, **subnet mask** and (optionally) the address of a **gateway** (that is, a router that can contact other networks):

- IP Address - used to identify each interface. It is entered as four decimal numbers separated by periods (e.g. 172.16.11.200). The IP address identifies both the network to which the interface is attached and also its unique identity on that network. IP addresses are required for ALL interfaces.

- Subnet Mask - used in conjunction with the IP address to determine whether another interface is located on a local or remote network. A subnet mask is required for ALL interfaces.

- Default Gateway - the IP address of the router to which packets destined for a remote network should be sent by default. This setting is not compulsory but failure to enter a default gateway would limit the interface to communication on the local network only.

On a Windows network, there are a few other factors to take into account however.

DHCP and APIPA

Configuring IP addresses and other TCP/IP network information manually raises many difficult administrative issues and makes incorrect configuration of one or more hosts more likely.

To avoid manually configuring all devices, a **DHCP (Dynamic Host Configuration Protocol) Server** may be used to allocate IP addresses and other settings automatically. The workstation contacts the DHCP Server as it starts up and is allocated a **lease** for an IP address. Settings such as default gateway, DNS, and WINS servers may be passed to the workstation at the same time.

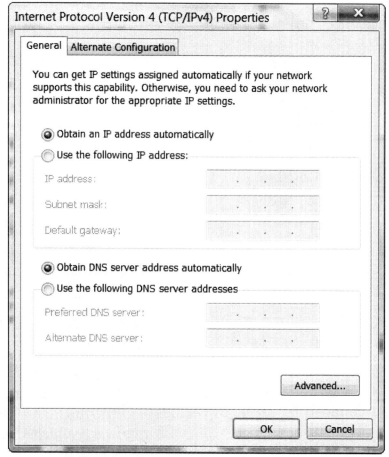

Configuring a NIC to obtain an address automatically (use DHCP)

| Module 5 Networks and Printing | *Installing and Configuring Local Networks* |

A DHCP server might be configured on a Windows Server or an internet connectivity device, such as a SOHO router.

Windows hosts also have a "fallback" mechanism for when the computer is configured to use a DHCP server but cannot contact one. In this scenario, the computer selects an address at random from the range 169.254.*x.y*. This is called **Automatic Private IP Addressing (APIPA)**.

When a host is using an APIPA address, it can communicate with other hosts on the same network that are using APIPA but cannot reach other networks (or communicate with hosts that have managed to obtain a valid DHCP lease).

DNS and WINS

A **Domain Name System (DNS)** server provides name resolution on the internet and on Microsoft Active Directory networks. To use a DNS, its IP address must be added to the DNS search order.

> **Warning**
>
> **DNS is a critical service in terms of security. Make sure you use only DNS servers that you know to be operated reliably and securely. On the internet, you would use those provided by your ISP.**

The **Windows Internet Naming Service (WINS)** provides a mechanism for resolving NetBIOS computer names to IP addresses. This service is generally only required to support older Windows clients (Windows NT or Windows 9x). WINS configuration allows primary and secondary WINS server addresses to be entered.

Configuring TCP/IP on a network adapter

TCP/IP can be configured through the network connection's **Properties** dialog. By default, Windows machines obtain an IP address dynamically, but you can configure a manual IP address and **Advanced** options, including DNS and WINS settings, if necessary.

1. From the **General** tab, under **Connections**, select **TCP/IP** and click **Properties**.

© 2010 gtslearning   IT Career FastTrack with CompTIA A+ Certification   Page 525

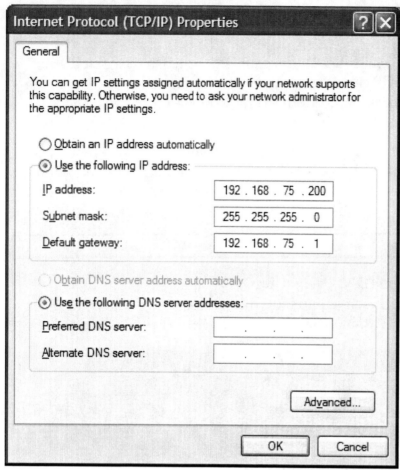

2. To use DHCP, select **Obtain an IP address automatically**. Alternatively, to enter an IP address manually, check **Use the Following IP address**.

3. Type in your **IP address** and **Subnet mask**.

TCP/IP Properties

4. Enter a **Default gateway** address to the IP of a router machine on the local subnet.

5. Enter the IP addresses of DNS servers (check with your ISP or network administrator for these addresses).

Configuring advanced TCP/IP settings

Advanced settings are split over three tabs[221]:

- **IP Settings** - configure additional IP addresses and gateways (not typically required on a desktop machine).

---

[221] In Windows 2000/XP there is a fourth Options tab to configure IP Security (IPSec) and TCP/IP filtering as a means of securing and firewalling the connection. In Windows XP/Vista, IP filtering is performed more easily by the Windows Firewall.

- **DNS** - add DNS server addresses and other advanced information.
- **WINS** - add WINS server addresses and choose whether to run NetBIOS over TCP/IP.

Alternate TCP/IP configuration

Windows XP/Vista also allow you to define an **alternate configuration** for a machine if it cannot contact a DHCP server and using APIPA is unsuitable. This is useful in the scenario that you have a laptop computer connecting via DHCP in a corporate network but requiring a static IP address on the user's home network.

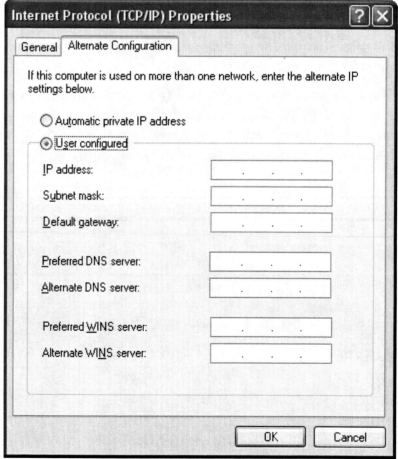

TCP/IP Alternate Configuration

To set up the alternate configuration, set the **General** tab option to use **Obtain an IP address automatically**. Click the **Alternate Configuration** tab and select **User configured**. Enter the static IP addressing information.

Unit 5.2

Module 5 Networks and Printing

Installing and Configuring a Wireless Network

"Wireless" encompasses a whole range of connectivity products and technologies, from personal area networking to internet connectivity.

Most wireless technologies use radio waves as transmission media. Radio systems use a transmitter and a receiver tuned to a specific frequency for the transfer of signals. The range of broadcast radio frequencies (RF) extends from 10 KHz to 30 GHz. Frequencies are subdivided into bands from very low to ultra high. FM radio and television signals are broadcast in the Very High Frequency band (30-300 MHz).

The use of the radio spectrum is regulated by national governments and (to some extent) standardized internationally by the **International Telecommunications Union (ITU)**. Use of a frequency requires a license from the relevant government agency. The license ensures no one else can transmit that frequency within a particular area.

There are however, unregulated frequencies that do not require a license. For example, 2.4 GHz is unregulated on an international basis but there is a limit on power output, which means coverage is restricted. Many wireless networking products operate in these unregulated ranges.

Wi-Fi

"Wireless networking" is generally understood to mean the IEEE's 802.11 standards for **Wireless LANs (WLAN)**, also called **Wi-Fi**. There are four main versions of the standard, as summarized below:

Standard	Data Transfer Rate (Max)	Typical Indoor Range	Frequency
802.11b	11 Mbps	38m (125 feet)	2.4 GHz
802.11g	54 Mbps	38m (125 feet)	2.4 GHz
802.11a	54 Mbps	35m (115 feet)	5 GHz
802.11n	290 Mbps (Single Channel) 600 Mbps (Bonded Channels)	70m (230 feet)	2.4 / 5 GHz

802.11b and 802.11g have proved the most successful (802.11g provides an upgrade path for older 802.11b devices). 802.11a is incompatible with the other two and not as widely adopted, but does use a less "crowded" frequency and is considered less susceptible to interference.

Page 528   IT Career FastTrack with CompTIA A+ Certification   © 2010 gtslearning

Module 5 Networks and Printing

Installing and Configuring Local Networks

The disadvantage of the higher frequencies used by Wi-Fi is that they lack penetrating power and there can be interference from other, nearby unregulated devices. The 2.4 GHz band in which 802.11g operates is split into 14 **channels** each about 20 MHz wide; selecting a different channel can help to overcome interference from other, nearby devices and networks[222].

The 802.11n high bandwidth standard was published in October 2009, though there were numerous "draft-N" products on the market before that. The key to increasing range and bandwidth in 802.11n is multiplexing the signals from 2-4 separate antennas (**Multiple-Input-Multiple-Output [MIMO]**)[223].

Another change is the option to use two adjacent 20 MHz channels as a single 40 MHz channel (**bonding**). 802.11n products can also use channels in the 2.4 GHz band or the 5 GHz band, though the 5 GHz band is preferred for optimal bandwidth (to avoid interference with existing 2.4 GHz networks and devices).

It is important to ensure that all devices (access points and wireless adapter cards) and software (the operating system or vendor-supplied utility) support the same standard. Some devices can operate in mixed mode (that is, support more than one standard), but you should note that the performance of the *whole* WLAN will be reduced to that of the weakest standard. For example, if you operate an 802.11b/g access point, and an 802.11b client joins the network, *all* clients will operate at 802.11b data rates.

802.11i defines an improved security protocol for use with wireless connections. It replaces the flawed WEP (Wired Equivalent Privacy) protocol with WPA (Wi-Fi Protected Access [version 2]).

Configuring wireless connections

More and more networks are employing wireless devices, either to replace cabling or to allow wireless devices to communicate on a wired network. Wireless links are a particularly effective way to allow visitors to an office get internet access.

---

[222] In the US, only use of 11 channels is licensed so most devices only support 11 channels, as they are manufactured for the US market.

[223] The configuration of 802.11n devices is identified by AxB:C notation, where A is the number of transmit antennas, B is the number of receive antennas, and C is the number of simultaneous transmit and receive streams. The maximum possible is 4x4:4 but at the time of writing the best available access points are 3x3:3 with other common configurations being 2x2:2 or 3x3:2.

© 2010 gtslearning

IT Career FastTrack with CompTIA A+ Certification

Page 529

To implement a **Wireless LAN (WLAN)** in **infrastructure mode**[224], a **Wireless Access Point (AP)** acts as a connection between the cabled network and the wireless devices (**stations**).

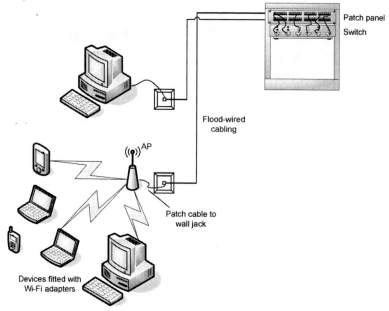

WLAN configuration in infrastructure mode

On a mixed network, the AP acts as connection between the cabled network and the wireless devices. The AP is normally attached to the LAN using standard cabling and transmits and receives network traffic to and from wireless devices. Each client device requires a wireless adapter compatible with the standard(s) supported by the access point (for example, 802.11b or 802.11g). A wireless adapter can be installed as an expansion card or a USB device.

All wireless devices operating on a WLAN must have the same network name (**Service Set Identification** or **SSID**) and security settings.

WLAN security

Wireless connections require careful configuration to make the connection and transmissions over the connection secure. The main problem with wireless is that because it is "over the air" there is no way to contain the signal. Anyone with a suitably equipped laptop or RF (Radio Frequency) scanner can intercept the signals. If the proper security has not been put in place, this could allow the interception of data or the unauthorized use of the network.

---

[224] Wireless devices can also be configured in **ad hoc** mode. This is a peer-to-peer type arrangement. Instead of communicating through an access point, the wireless devices establish communications directly with one another.

| Module 5 Networks and Printing | *Installing and Configuring Local Networks* |

Tip

"War driving" is the practice of driving around with a wireless-enabled laptop scanning for insecure WLANs.

Some security problems and solutions are listed below:

SSID

The **Service Set ID (SSID)** is like a front door key for the WLAN. Vendors use default SSIDs for their products to make connectivity (too) simple. The SSID should be changed to something unique to your network. Disabling broadcast of the SSID prevents any adapters not configured to connect to the name you specify from finding the network. This provides an extra margin of privacy[225].

Security protocols

The crucial step in enforcing wireless security is to enable **encryption**. There are three schemes:

- **Wired Equivalent Privacy (WEP)** is supported on old and new devices. However, the encryption system (based on the **RC4** cipher) is flawed. There are many tools available to crack WEP security[226].

- **Wi-Fi Protected Access (WPA)** fixes most of the security problems with WEP and adds the ability to *authenticate* to a network using the 802.1X security model (see below). WPA still uses the RC4 cipher but adds a mechanism (**TKIP [Temporal Key Integrity Protocol]**) to make it stronger.

- **WPA2** is fully compliant with the 802.11i WLAN security standard. The main difference to WPA is the use of **AES (Advanced Encryption Standard)** for encryption. AES is much stronger than RC / TKIP[227].

---

[225] Hiding the SSID does **not** secure the network; you must enable encryption. Even when broadcast is disabled, the SSID can still be detected using packet sniffing tools (software that can inspect the contents of network data packets).

[226] Under WEP version 1, you can select from different key sizes (64-bit or 128-bit). A larger key size makes it more difficult to attack the security system. WEP version 2 enforces use of the 128-bit key, but is still not considered secure. Tools used to crack WEP security include aircrack, AirSnort, and WEPCrack.

[227] The only reason not to use WPA2 is if it is not supported by adapters, APs, or operating systems on the network. In many cases, devices will be compatible with a firmware or driver upgrade. There is an update for Windows XP SP2 to support WPA2 but it is not supported under Windows 2000.

| © 2010 gtslearning | IT Career FastTrack with CompTIA A+ Certification | Page 531 |

| Unit 5.2 | Module 5 Networks and Printing |

Authentication

In order to secure a network, you need to be able to confirm that only valid users are connecting to it. WLAN authentication comes in three types:

- **Open** - this means that no authentication is required to join the network.

- **Pre-shared key (PSK)** - this is the key that is used to encrypt communications. It is generated from a passphrase, which is like a long password. The main problem is that distribution of the key or passphrase cannot be secured properly and users may choose an insecure phrase (or even leave it set to the device default). The advantage is that it is simple to set up. This is the only type of authentication available for WEP and is suitable for personal networks and workgroups using WPA.

- **802.1X** - WPA can also implement 802.1X (or **EAP [Extensible Authentication Protocol]**) authentication. The AP passes authentication information to a RADIUS server on the wired network for validation[228]. The authentication information could be a user name and password or could employ smart cards or tokens. This allows WLAN authentication to be integrated with the wired LAN authentication scheme. This type of authentication is suitable for client-server networks.

Other wireless security issues

The following steps can also be taken to provide additional security measures:

- **Firewall** wireless connections - MAC filtering allows access to network resources by specific devices only (a network adapter's **MAC address** is a unique hardware ID)[229]. Another option is to install a firewall between the access point and the network (see unit 5.6 for more information about firewalls).

- **DHCP** - some extra security can be gained by disabling DHCP on the access point. Of course, this means that TCP/IP settings have to be allocated and configured manually on the devices, which adds a lot of administrative overhead.

---

[228] RADIUS (Remote Authentication Dial-in User Service) allows different types of remote access technologies to be unified in a single infrastructure. You can also use different authentication technologies, such as smart cards, biometric ID, and so on. This conforms to the 802.1X framework.

[229] Note that this is difficult to manage and only really practical on a small network. Also it is quite simple to spoof a MAC address. WPA2 with 802.1X authentication is enough security for most networks.

Page 532   IT Career FastTrack with CompTIA A+ Certification   © 2010 gtslearning

| Module 5 Networks and Printing | Installing and Configuring Local Networks |

- **Firmware / driver** - keep the firmware and driver for the AP and wireless adapters up-to-date with the latest patches. This is important to fix security holes and to support the latest security standards, such as WPA2.

- **Configuration password** - vendors ship access points with a default management password (such as "admin" or "default"). Always change this password when installing the equipment to something more secure.

- **Unauthorized access points** - network security can be compromised by attaching an AP to the network. Apart from physically inspecting network ports regularly, a war driving tool such as NetStumbler or Kismet can be used to scan for wireless networks in the area.

Configuring an access point

To configure an access point, you normally connect a PC or laptop to one of the LAN ports on the AP. Set the PC to obtain an IP address automatically and it will be assigned one by the DHCP server in the AP. Use a browser to open the management console on the AP's default IP address (usually 192.168.0.1 or 192.168.1.1).

The following example shows configuration settings on a 3Com OfficeConnect wireless AP, designed for Small Office Home Office applications (SOHO).

Having checked the box to enable wireless communications[230], you can adjust the following settings from the default.

- Channel - you would change this if you experience a weak connection caused by interference from other devices.

- SSID (Service Set ID) - a name for the WLAN. This can be up to 32 characters and must be different to any other networks nearby.

> **Note**
>
> Do not leave the SSID setting to the default.

- SSID Broadcast - disabling this prevents any adapters not configured to connect to the SSID you specify from finding the network.

---

[230] It is best practice not to enable services you do not need, especially on a multifunction device such as this. Most devices are now shipped in "security-enabled" configurations, meaning that you explicitly have to choose to enable services that you want to run.

© 2010 gtslearning   IT Career FastTrack with CompTIA A+ Certification   Page 533

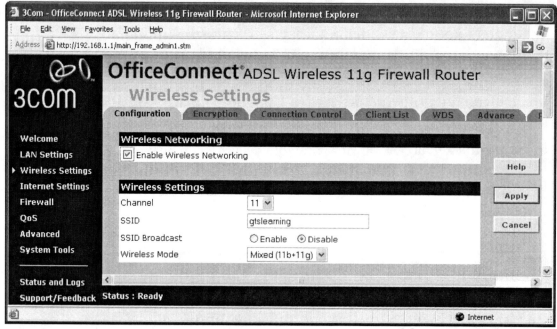

3Com wireless AP configuration

- Wireless mode - enable compatibility for different 802.11 devices.

To prevent snooping, you should enable encryption on the connection:

On the **Encryption** tab, select the highest security mode supported by devices on the network.

- **WEP (Wired Equivalent Privacy)** - this is an older standard. WEP is flawed and you would only select this if compatibility with legacy devices and software is imperative.

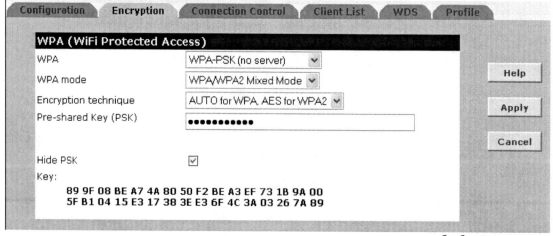

Configuring encryption

Module 5 Networks and Printing | *Installing and Configuring Local Networks*

- **WPA (Wi-Fi Protected Access) with Pre-shared Key (PSK)** - WPA is the current standard offering much better security. You can choose between TKIP or AES encryption (AES is considered to be stronger).

- **WPA with RADIUS** - if the network has a RADIUS server, this can be used to provide secure authentication and encryption. You would enter the IP, port, and key for the server.

Unless using a RADIUS server, you would also generate a secret key (PSK), using a passphrase (password). The key is a long number, expressed in hex. The same key must be configured on client adapters to enable them to connect.

Note

Choose a strong passphrase and keep it secret. In order to generate strong key, use a longer phrase than you would for a normal password.

Updating firmware

Firmware updates may be required to support a new standard (WPA2 for instance) or to improve security or reliability. You should download the latest firmware from the vendor's site, taking care to check that it matches the model and possibly also the series of your access point. This information should be printed on a sticker on the underside or back of the unit.

When you have downloaded the firmware, open the device's management console. There may be an option to back up the current configuration. Sometimes a configuration backup cannot be applied with the new firmware though, in which case you should make sure you have made a note of all the settings. Find the option to update firmware (in our example, it is in **System Tools > Upgrade**).

Do not power off the device while the firmware is being installed.

Warning

Installing the wrong firmware or a failed firmware update can render a device completely inoperable ("bricked").

When the new firmware has been applied, restore the system configuration, either from your backup or manually - remember to change the system administration password! Verify functionality by testing the connection.

© 2010 gtslearning | IT Career FastTrack with CompTIA A+ Certification | Page 535

Configuring a wireless client

The wireless adapter can either be configured using the manufacturer supplied software or by Windows.

> **Tip**
>
> If Windows is controlling the device and you want to use the supplied software (or vice versa), under the adapter's properties, uncheck (or check) **Use Windows to configure settings** (on the **Wireless Networks** tab). The **Wireless Zero Configuration** service (**WLAN AutoConfig** in Vista) should also be running.

Configuring a client using Windows XP

Open the **Network Connections** applet or the **Wireless Network Setup Wizard**. If the AP is set to broadcast the SSID, then the network will appear in the list of available networks. The bars show the strength of the signal and the lock icon indicates whether the network uses encryption. To connect, select the network then enter the pre-shared key (or log on in the specified way if using RADIUS).

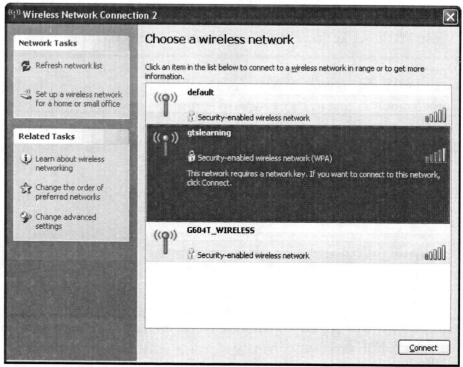

Browsing available networks under Windows XP

> **Note**
> Do not connect to an untrusted wireless network!

To connect to a "hidden" network, open the network adapter's property sheet and click the **Wireless Networks** tab. Under **Preferred networks**, click **Add**.

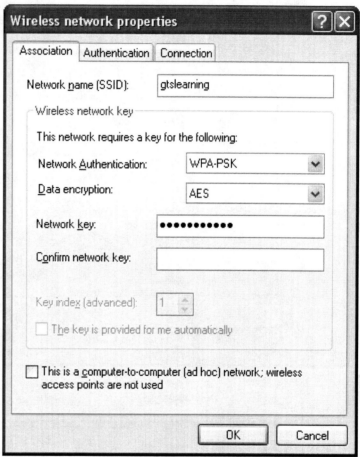

Configuring a WLAN connection

Enter the SSID, select an authentication method (such as WPA-PSK), and enter the key or other authentication information.

Configuring a client using Windows Vista

In Vista, the process is similar - you can either choose **Start > Connect To** or alt-click the network status icon in the notification area and select **Connect to a network**.

If the WLAN is not shown (if SSID broadcast is disabled), click **Set up a connection or network**. Otherwise, double-click a network name.

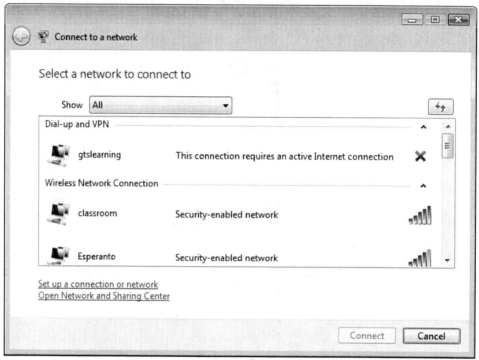

Connecting to a network using Windows Vista

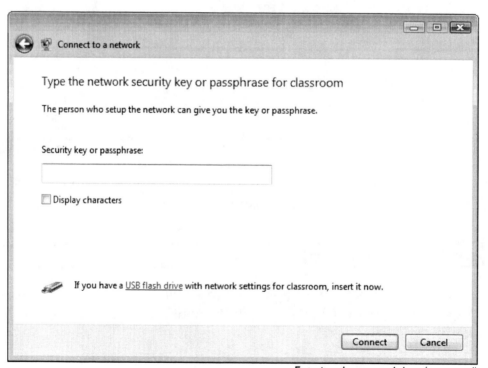

Entering the network key (password)

Enter the PSK and click **Connect**.

When you connect to a new network, you are prompted to set its **Location**. If the link is configured as **Public**, your computer is hidden from other computers on the same network and file sharing is disabled. If it is configured as **Private** (home or work), the computer is discoverable and file sharing is enabled.

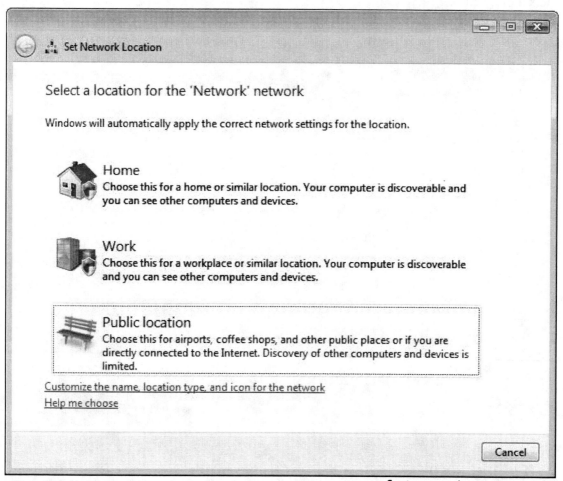

Setting network security properties

To change the location defined for a network, open the **Network and Sharing Center** and click the **Customize** link.

Configuring a client using third-party software

Under Windows 2000, you must use third-party software to configure the wireless link. You may also prefer to use the software provided with your adapter rather than the Windows configuration tool.

In the screenshot (which shows the configuration software for a wireless adapter), you would click **PC->PC** for ad hoc mode and **PC->AP** for infrastructure mode. To configure an ad hoc network, you would change the configuration settings on the adapter (using the **Configuration** menu).

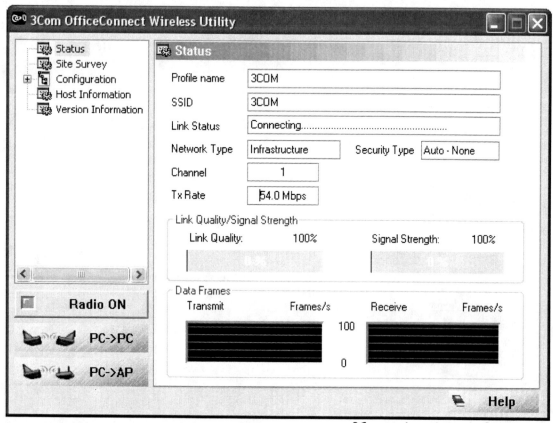

3Com wireless adapter configuration tool

Maximizing signal strength

A device supporting the Wi-Fi standard should have a maximum indoor range of up to about 38m (125 feet) - or a bit more for "N" equipment) - though the weaker the signal the lower the data transfer rate.

Radio signals pass through solid objects, such as walls, but can be blocked by particularly dense or thick material and metal. Other radio-based devices can also cause interference[231]. To minimize interference, position the AP as high as possible and change the channel from the manufacturer default. On the device, point the antenna towards the AP if possible. You can check signal strength by pointing to the WLAN icon on the taskbar.

Checking signal strength in Windows XP

If signals are particular weak, you can obtain **wireless range extenders** (repeaters) or add multiple APs to the network. A wireless range extender is basically a "dumb" AP; it picks up signals from (and signals intended for) the AP it is linked to and retransmits them. The main advantage is that the extender itself does not need to be plugged into a network port[232]. The main disadvantage is that the extra range comes at the cost of reduced speed, as there is more error correction involved.

A single access point may nominally support up to 50 clients. However, to obtain acceptable performance, somewhere between 10 and 25 clients is more realistic, depending on the amount of bandwidth and coverage required.

Bluetooth

Bluetooth is another radio-based technology. Bluetooth has been specifically designed to fit into small devices and require very little power. This makes it ideal for communication between devices such as cellphones and laptops or a wireless mouse and a desktop computer or even a wireless hands-free headset and a cell.

---

[231] Bluetooth uses the same frequency range as Wi-Fi but a different modulation technique, so interference is possible but not common. Other examples are microwave ovens, cordless phones, and baby monitors.

[232] You can also use an ordinary access point as a repeater but the same limitation on throughput applies. This works best if the access points are the same model (configure the Wireless Distribution System on the APs). The advantage of a range extender is that it may come with a unidirectional antennae; useful if you want to extend the signal to a specific "dead spot".

Bluetooth is quoted to work at distances of up to 10 meters (30 feet) for Class 2 devices or 1 meter (3 feet) for Class 3 devices[233]. Bluetooth is limited to speeds of about 1 Mbps. Devices supporting the **Bluetooth 2.0 - Enhanced Data Rate [EDR]** standard have a maximum transfer rate of 3 Mbps.

Windows XP SP2 and Vista include support for Bluetooth devices. You can manage devices using the **Bluetooth Devices** applet in Control Panel. Earlier versions of Windows require the device vendor's management software to be installed.

Bluetooth Devices

To add a new device you will typically need to put it into **discoverable** mode. On devices such as mice and keyboards this is normally done by pressing a small recessed switch. Do this and click **Add device** in the Bluetooth dialog and Windows should detect and install the device using the usual Hardware Wizard.

---

[233] There are also Class 1 devices that work at a range of 100m but these are restricted to industrial applications.

Module 5 Networks and Printing

Installing and Configuring Local Networks

Bluetooth security

Bluetooth devices have their own security issues, summarized below:

- Device discovery - a device can be put into discoverable mode meaning that it will connect to any other Bluetooth devices nearby. Unfortunately, even a device in non-discoverable mode is quite easy to detect.

- Authentication and authorization - devices authenticate ("pair") using a simple passkey configured on both devices. This should always be changed to some secure phrase and never left as the default. Also, check the device's pairing list regularly to confirm that the devices listed are valid.

- Malware - there are various "proof-of-concept" Bluetooth worms and application exploits. There are also vulnerabilities in the authentication schemes of some devices. Read the relevant security bulletins and keep devices updated with the latest firmware.

Summary

You need to learn the features and capabilities of network media and hardware. Low-level network adapter functions (such as network type, speed, and duplex settings) are usually configured via the properties sheet in Device Manager.

Protocol and client software are configured via the adapter properties in Network Connections. Make sure you know the configuration settings for TCP/IP and the function of DHCP and DNS servers.

A wireless network can either be configured using the adapter vendor's software or with the Windows Wireless Zero Configuration service. You can use a wizard to detect available networks or configure the adapter properties manually (in Network Connections) to connect to a specific network. Wireless devices used to suffer from poor security standards and practices, but the latest devices feature much improved systems, if properly enabled. Make sure that you understand the different encryption and authentication standards that can be configured for wireless networking.

Tip

To review what you have learned in this chapter, you should now visit the course website. This contains review questions and bonus material to help you to learn more and practice the topics covered in this unit.

© 2010 gtslearning

IT Career FastTrack with CompTIA A+ Certification

Page 543

Unit 5.3   Module 5 Networks and Printing

Unit 5.3 File Sharing and Data Security

CompTIA A+ Essentials Objectives

☐ **701.3.2 Given a scenario, demonstrate proper use of user interfaces**
My Network Places

☐ **701.5.2 Summarize the following security features**
BIOS Security (Drive lock, Passwords, Intrusion detection, TPM) • Password management /
password complexity • Locking workstation (Hardware, Operating system)

CompTIA A+ Practical Application Objectives

☐ **702.2.2 Differentiate between Windows Operating System directory structures
(Windows 2000, XP and Vista)**
Offline files and folders

☐ **702.4.2 Implement security and troubleshoot common issues**
Operating systems (Local users and groups: Administrator, Power Users, Guest, Users, Vista
User Access Control [UAC], NTFS vs. Share permissions [Allow vs. deny, Difference between
moving and copying folders and files, File attributes], Shared files and folders [Administrative
shares vs. local shares, Permission propagation, Inheritance], System files and folders, Encryption
[BitLocker, EFS], User authentication) • System (BIOS security [Drive lock, Passwords, Intrusion
detection, TPM])

Configuring Network Clients

A protocol provides addressing and the basic communication mechanism for
a network connection. You must also configure the adapter with the
appropriate network **client** and **service** software.

Windows client software

The Windows client allows the workstation to connect to workgroup or Active
Directory domain networks (though the latter functionality is disabled in
Home and Media Center Editions of Windows XP and Home editions of
Vista).

Page 544   IT Career FastTrack with CompTIA A+ Certification   © 2010 gtslearning

Through the **Computer Name** tab[234], an administrator can view the current network computer name and domain or workgroup membership details. In addition, a user with appropriate privilege can edit these details.

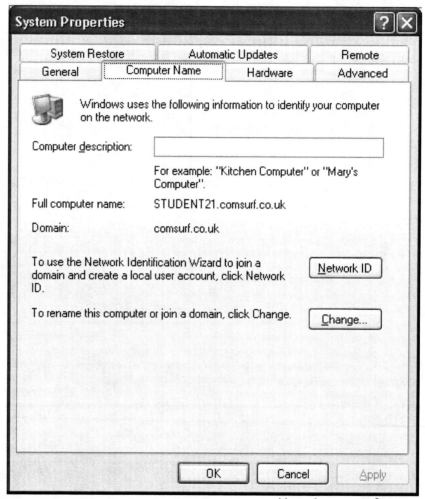

Network name configuration

---

[234] Under Windows 2000, the equivalent tab is **Network Identification**. It has a simple **Properties** button to let you change the computer name and workgroup/domain membership. Under Windows Vista, network information is shown on the System home page and you click **Change Settings** to show the Computer Name dialog.

The **Network ID** button provides a wizard driven method for configuring these properties. Alternatively, by clicking on the **Change** button, domain or workgroup membership can be reconfigured[235].

From the **Computer Name Changes** dialog, you can add the computer to a domain or back to a workgroup.

By clicking **More**, you can view the DNS suffix of the computer. The DNS suffix can also be configured via DHCP on a per connection basis.

Network identification - domain details

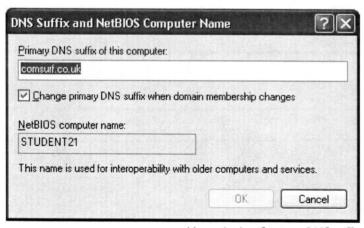

Network identification - DNS suffix

The DNS suffix of the computer represents, in conjunction with the computer name, the **Fully Qualified Domain Name (FQDN)** of the computer.

For example, if the domain is **gtslearning.local** and the computer name is **sales**, the FQDN is **sales.gtslearning.local**.

---

[235] The workgroup name is largely cosmetic - any Windows computer that is not part of a domain can "see" any other Windows computer on the same local network though in some versions the workgroup helps to provide logical groupings of computers.

The name must be unique within the domain or workgroup, cannot be all numbers, cannot contain spaces, cannot start with a period (.) or hyphen, and cannot contain any special characters. Windows Server DNS supports computer names of between 2 and 24 characters but the name could be longer on a workgroup[236].

My Network Places

Having connected the computer to the network using the appropriate hardware, protocol, and client settings, you should then be able to access shared resources on the network. Network resources are browsed via **My Network Places** (just "Network" in Vista).

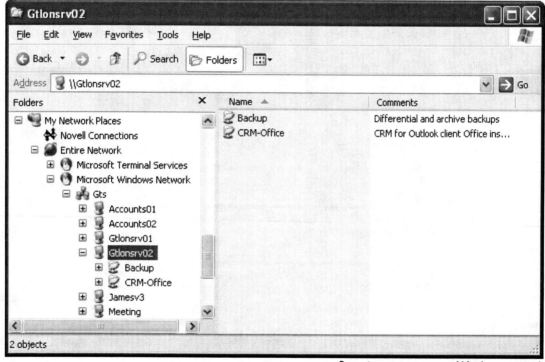

Browsing resources on a Windows network

The network object shows computers (servers) and the shared resources (folders / files and printers) available on them.

---

[236] To be compatible with older NetBIOS networks, the name should be up to 15 characters in length (though Windows will generate a NetBIOS-compatible name automatically if necessary) - it is not a good idea to use a name longer than 15 characters in any case. Under NetBIOS, a hidden 16th character represents the service type (such as workstation or server).

You can also access a shared folder or printer using **Universal Naming Convention (UNC)** syntax (*ComputerName**Path*), where *ComputerName* is the host name, FQDN, or IP address of the server and *Path* is the folder and/or file path to the resource.

Shared folders can also be **mapped** as network drives, making them accessible from **(My) Computer** via a drive letter. To do this, alt-click the share and select **Map Network Drive**. Select a drive letter and keep **Reconnect at logon** checked, unless you want to map the drive temporarily. Alternatively, you can alt-click **(My) Network (Places)** and select **Map Network Drive** or select the command from the **Tools** menu.

Mapping a network drive

To remove a mapped drive, alt-click the **(My) Computer** or **(My) Network (Places)** object and select **Disconnect Network Drive**.

Shared printers show up in the **Printers** folder under the computer object. To use a printer, alt-click it and select **Connect**.

Module 5 Networks and Printing   *Installing and Configuring Local Networks*

Security Policies

A "security policy" can mean either the rules that an organization puts in place to make employees use IT systems in a secure way and deal with incidents or (in a more technical sense) the rules enforced by an operating system to restrict what users can and cannot do on the system.

In a Windows domain network, this second type of security policy is enforced by **Group Policy Objects (GPO)**. For a standalone Windows machine or a computer that is part of a workgroup, the **Local Security Policy** determines these rules.

The basis of enforcing these rules is identifying (authenticating) the user and determining their access privileges on the system. This is achieved through the system of user and group accounts.

User and group accounts

A **user account** ensures that the identity of someone using a computer is validated by the operating system at log on. As described in unit 3.4, this validation is typically achieved by entering a user account name and a secret password, though extra security can be enforced using some sort of smart card or biometric authentication.

User accounts are linked to a **profile**, which contains desktop configuration settings, Start menu customizations, and other per-user information stored in the registry. The profile also contains document data folder and application configuration and settings folders relevant to that user. User profiles are stored in the **Documents and Settings** folder (Windows 2000/XP) or **Users** folder (Windows Vista).

User accounts can be assigned directly to security policies but if there are a large number of users this can be difficult. Administration is simplified by the use of **group accounts**. A user can belong to one or more group accounts and inherit security permissions through privileges allocated to the groups.

© 2010 gtslearning   IT Career FastTrack with CompTIA A+ Certification   Page 549

| Unit 5.3 | Module 5 Networks and Printing |

For a standalone or workgroup computer, local user and group accounts are stored in the **Security Account Manager (SAM)** database (part of the registry) and configured using the **Local Users and Groups** snap-in for the Computer Management console or the **User Accounts** applet in Control Panel. On a domain, accounts are managed on the server using **Active Directory Users and Computers**.

Built-in groups

All Windows machines have built-in groups. Built-in groups are given a standard set of rights that allow them to perform appropriate system tasks.

Home editions of Windows XP / Vista allow the use of two groups only:

- Limited / standard user.

- Computer administrator.

For Windows Professional / Business, the principal built-in local groups are as follows:

Group	Notes
Administrators	Members of this group are able to perform all system management tasks.
Power Users[237]	Members of this group receive some administrative privileges. They are able to add and modify users and share resources. They cannot back up or restore directories or add and remove devices.
Backup Operators	Backup operators are able to back up and restore folders and files without requiring specific permissions to access them.
Users	All new users are automatically added to this group. The group is able to perform most common tasks, such as shutting down the workstation, running applications, and using printers[238].
Guests	This group has only limited rights; for example, members can browse the network and internet and shut down the computer but cannot save changes made to the desktop environment.

---

[237] Power Users is there to provide support for legacy applications. In general, you should not use this group. This group is no longer provided in Windows Vista.

[238] Vista allocates some more rights to the Users group than 2000/XP. For example, ordinary users can change the time zone and install a local printer.

Page 550   IT Career FastTrack with CompTIA A+ Certification   © 2010 gtslearning

| Module 5 Networks and Printing | Installing and Configuring Local Networks |

Windows also includes built-in **system groups**. Their membership cannot be changed, as it is dependent on what users are doing at the time. Some of the important system groups are as follows:

Group	Notes
Everyone	All users who access the computer are members of the group Everyone. This includes users who have not been authenticated and who are accessing the computer as a guest.
Authenticated Users	All users who access the computer and have a valid user account.
Creator Owner	The Creator Owner group includes the account of the resource owner. Normally the creator of a resource is the owner but administrators (and other users who have been allowed to do so) are able to take ownership.
Interactive	This group contains the user account of the person currently working locally at the computer.
Network	This group contains the user account(s) of any users currently connected to the computer over a network.

System groups may be given permission to access resources. The default permission for most files and folders is **Full Control** for the group **Everyone**. This permission should usually be removed and replaced with something more secure.

Administrator user account

The **Administrator** account can perform all management tasks and generally has very high access to all files and other objects in the system. The Administrator account is the default member of the Administrators group and inherits its permissions from this group.

You should restrict use of this account, using a regular user account when appropriate, and only log in as **Administrator** for specific tasks. It is also good practice to rename the account, to make the computer harder to "hack".

When Windows XP is installed to a non-domain computer, the Administrator account is "hidden" and replaced by a named account created during setup. Unfortunately, this hidden Administrator account is sometimes set up with a blank password! It is good practice always to apply a password to this account (you can log on to it by pressing **CTRL+ALT+DEL** at the Welcome screen[239]).

---

[239] In Windows Vista Home Edition you can only log on to the Administrator account in Safe Mode.

| © 2010 gtslearning | IT Career FastTrack with CompTIA A+ Certification | Page 551 |

Under Windows Vista, the Administrator account is disabled by default. The setup procedure creates an account with administrative privileges.

In Vista, accounts with administrative privileges are mediated by **User Account Control (UAC)**. UAC supports the principle of **least privilege**; that is users should have only sufficient permissions required to perform tasks and no more. Under UAC, even if an account has administrative privileges, the account holder must manually confirm use of them. Depending on the security policy in force, this could simply mean clicking **Continue** at the UAC prompt or having to re-authenticate.

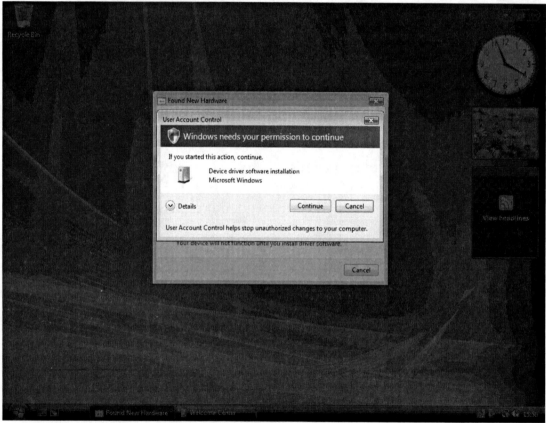

UAC requiring confirmation of the use of administrator privileges

Conversely, when logged on as an ordinary user, any task that requires administrative privileges can be performed by supplying the credentials through UAC, rather than having to log off and log back on as an administrator.

Guest user account

The **Guest** account has very limited access. Generally you should disable this account (its default condition) and establish a proper user account for each user accessing your system. If the account is enabled, then any user attempting to access your computer who does not hold their own user account or know a password for one, will be connected using the guest account credentials.

Creating user accounts

Most users will be configured with ordinary User accounts. These accounts allow limited configuration of the local computer (changing the display theme or input device settings for instance) and can be configured with permissions to access folders and files.

User Accounts applet

In Windows XP/Vista, the **User Accounts** applet in Control Panel allows users to manage their accounts. Users can manage local and network passwords and choose a picture to represent them on the log on screen.

User Accounts applet in Windows Vista

Administrators can create and delete accounts or change the type of account (between administrator and user). In Vista, you can also configure UAC from here.

Local Users and Groups snap-in

In all professional / business versions of Windows, the **Local Users and Groups** management console provides an advanced interface for managing both user and group accounts. This is the only interface available in Windows 2000. It is not available in home editions of XP or Vista.

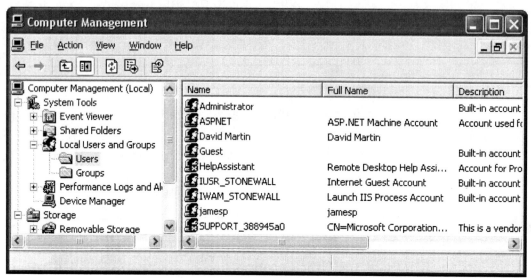

Local Users and Groups Snap-in

To create a new user here, open the **Computer Management** console then open **Local Users and Groups**. Alt-click on the **Users** folder and select **New User**.

Enter the following information:

Setting	Use
User name (required)	The user name may be up to 20 characters and should not contain " \ / [ ] : ; , + * ? < > The user name must be unique. This can cause problems in large domains so a system for dealing with duplicate names is required; for example, JohnS1 and JohnS2. User names are not case sensitive.
Full name (optional)	This should include the first and last name, and any middle initials if required.
Description (optional)	May be used to describe the user's job role.
Password (optional but recommended)	Passwords may be up to 128 characters (at least 8 is recommended). Passwords are case sensitive. Avoid passwords that simply use words; include upper and lower case letters, punctuation, and numbers.
User must change password at next logon	A useful way to ensure that the administrator assigned password is reset by the user when they first access the account.
User cannot change password	Generally users control their own passwords, but for some user accounts it is preferable for the administrator to control the password.
Password never expires	A useful option which overrides the local security policy to expire passwords after a fixed number of days. This option should be selected for system accounts, such as those used for replication and application services.
Account is disabled	Prevents use of the account. Acts as an alternative to deleting an account.

When you click **Create**, Windows creates the user and adds it to the **Users** group automatically.

Modifying a user account

To set user properties, alt-click on the **user name** and select **Properties**. This menu also provides options to **Set Password**, **Delete**, and **Rename** users.

The **General** page for user account properties allows the administrator to change the settings described above. It has an additional option that can be used to unlock an account that has exceeded the maximum number of attempts at entering the correct password.

Other settings that can be configured include membership of groups (using the **Member Of** tab), and profile settings for the logon script, user profile, and home folder location.

Renaming a user account

To rename a user account, select the account name, then alt-click and choose the **Rename** option.

A renamed account retains all the properties of the original account and also retains access to system resources.

Deleting a user account

To delete an account, select the account name and either press the DELETE key or choose **Delete** from the context menu.

Windows uses an **SID** (Security ID) to uniquely identify each user and group. A warning message is displayed to remind you that this account identifier is unique. Even if you recreate another account with exactly the same user name, the identifier created is still different. The new account cannot assume any access to system resources that were assigned to the original.

Disabling an account prevents it from being used, but allows the account to be reactivated if required.

Creating local groups

Windows Professional / Business editions allow you to create **local** groups. Like local users, groups reside in the security database of the local computer. Only local users from the *same computer* can be added as members of the local group. Local groups can only be assigned permissions to resources that are located on the same computer.

Page 556   IT Career FastTrack with CompTIA A+ Certification   © 2010 gtslearning

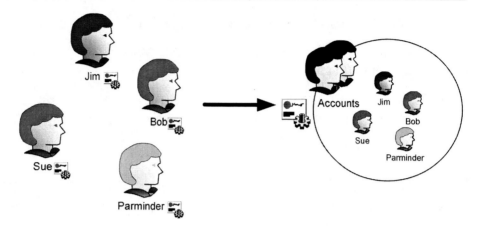

Simplifying administration using groups

Local groups should only be used when the Windows machine is part of a workgroup; for domain environments, security groups will be created on the domain controllers.

Group Properties

| Unit 5.3 | Module 5 Networks and Printing |

The **Local Users and Groups snap-in** is used to create and manage groups.

A unique name must be entered when creating the group. This can be up to 256 characters and can contain any character except \.

You can add or remove group members as required from this page. You can also modify a user's group membership using the **User Properties > Member of** page.

Password management

For a system to be secure against attack, "strong" passwords are required. Attackers often use **password cracker software**, which can identify a password by matching it to popular words and phrases or through a **brute force** attempt at every possible combination. Attackers may investigate the background of their prey to seek out likely passwords (dates of birth, children's names, make of car, favorite teams, and so on). Once an attacker obtains a password, s/he can gain access to a system posing as that person.

The following rules make passwords difficult to guess or crack:

- A longer password is more secure - around 7-9 characters is suitable for an ordinary user account. Administrative accounts should have longer passwords (14 or more characters).

- No single words - better to use word and number/punctuation combinations.

- No obvious phrases in a simple form - birthday, user name, job title, and so on.

- Mix upper and lowercase (assuming the software uses case-sensitive passwords).

- Use an easily memorized phrase - underscored characters or hyphens can be used to represent spaces if the operating system does not support these in passwords.

Tip

As long as it is not an obvious phrase, a long password is generally better than a complex one in terms of providing adequate security and being memorable. If a password is so complex that the user resorts to writing it down, it is not really that secure.

Page 558   IT Career FastTrack with CompTIA A+ Certification   © 2010 gtslearning

| Module 5 Networks and Printing | *Installing and Configuring Local Networks* |

- Do not write down a password or share it with other users.

- Change the password periodically.

The main problem with passwords is that they are prone to user error; selecting weak passwords, writing them down, and so on. Some types of behavior can be improved by system policies. For example, you can enforce password length and complexity requirements using the Windows **Local Security Policy** (in **Administrative Tools**). Other types of behavior need training (and possibly disciplinary measures!) to enforce.

Another concern is management of multiple accounts. A typical user might be faced with having to remember tens of logons for different services at work and on the internet and resort to using the same password for each. This is very insecure, as your security becomes dependent on the security of these other (unknown) organizations.

In a Windows **domain**, password management can be mitigated by applications that are compatible with the **Kerberos** authentication mechanism used by the domain. This is referred to as **single sign on**. Users must be trained to practice good password management (at the very least not to re-use work passwords for web accounts).

Configuring Data and File System Security

Security policies protect the system against unauthorized actions by users (such as installing software or hardware without permission). Another set of rules can be configured for protecting data files. These rules require that the volume be formatted using NTFS. FAT does not support secure data access.

NTFS permissions

NTFS permissions are file (and folder and printer) attributes stored in an **Access Control List (ACL)** associated with the object. Permissions are granted to group or user accounts. This controls whether (for instance) a given user can open a file, open and modify a file, or not open the file at all.

Permissions are configured via the **Security** page of the object's **Properties** dialog. For each account (group or user), **Allow** or **Deny** permissions are set on the object's attributes. If no permissions are set for a user account, access is denied by default. The permissions that may be set for folders are:

| © 2010 gtslearning | IT Career FastTrack with CompTIA A+ Certification | Page 559 |

Permission	Allows
Read	View files and subfolders including their attributes, permissions, and ownership.
Write	Create new folders and files, change attributes, and view permissions / ownership.
List	View the names of files and subfolders.
Read & Execute	Pass-through folders for which no permissions are assigned, plus read and list permissions.
Modify	Includes Read/Execute and Write permissions, as well as the ability to rename and delete the folder.
Full Control	All the above, plus changing permissions, taking ownership, and deleting subfolders and files.
Deny	This overrides any other permission.

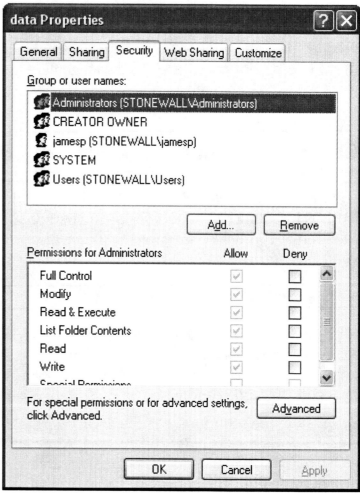

NTFS folder permissions

Module 5 Networks and Printing | *Installing and Configuring Local Networks*

The permissions that may be set for files are:

Permission	Allows
Read	Read the contents of the file and view attributes, ownership, and permissions.
Write	Overwrite the file and view attributes, ownership, and permissions.
Read & Execute	Read permissions, plus the ability to run applications.
Modify	Includes Read/Execute and Write permissions, as well as the ability to rename and delete the file.
Full Control	All the above, plus changing permissions and taking ownership.
Deny	This overrides any other permission.

The permissions that may be set for printers are:

Permission	Allows
Print	Use the printer to print documents.
Manage Printers	Print documents, adjust printer settings, change sharing status, pause and restart the printer, change spooler settings, and so on.
Manage Documents	Control the print queue.
Deny	This overrides any other permission.

There are various rules governing the rights granted to a user if permissions are assigned from multiple sources. In summary, the basic rules are:

- A user has the *most effective* permissions obtained from membership of any groups. For example, if membership of one group gives the user Read access and membership of another group allows Write access, the user will have Write access. The exception to this is Deny, which overrides any other permission (so if the user were added to a third group where the Deny permission was defined, the user would be denied access to the object).

- Permissions set on a folder propagate to subfolders and files (inheritance), unless specified otherwise (using the Advanced settings page).

  Uncheck the **Inherit from** box then choose whether to **Copy** existing permissions or **Remove** them. You can then modify the permissions on this folder independently of its parent.

  Conversely, to apply security settings for the current folder to all child objects (permission propagation), check the **Replace permission entries** box.

Unit 5.3　　　　　　　　　　　　　　　　　　　　　　Module 5 Networks and Printing

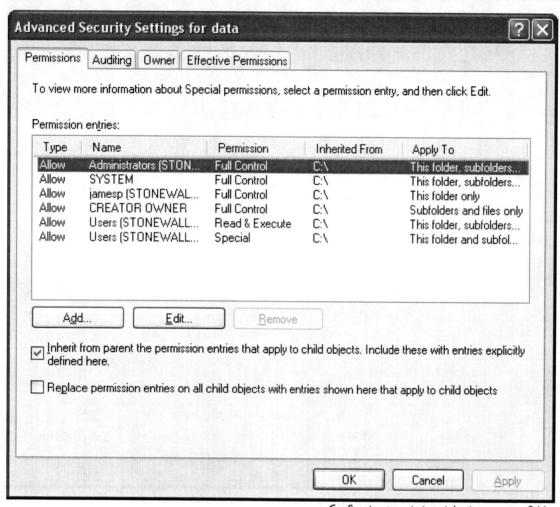

Configuring permissions inheritance on a folder

- When combined with network share permissions (see below), the most *restrictive* permissions apply. However, share permissions *do not* apply to local access.

Moving and copying NTFS files and folders

The behavior of NTFS permissions when moving and copying files under Windows is summarized in the table below:

Action	Effect
Moving files and folders on the same NTFS volume	Write permission is required for the destination folder and Modify for the source folder. NTFS permissions are retained.
Moving files and folders to a different NTFS volume	Write permission is required for the destination folder and Modify for the source folder. NTFS permissions are inherited from the destination folder and the user becomes the Creator/owner.
Copying files and folders on the same NTFS volume or different NTFS volumes	Write permission is required for the destination folder and Read for the source folder. NTFS permissions are inherited from the destination folder and the user becomes the Creator/Owner.
Moving files and folders to a FAT or FAT32 partition	Modify permission is required for the source folder. All permissions and NTFS attributes (such as encryption) are lost, as FAT does not support permissions or special attributes.

Share permissions

In order to make an object such as a printer or folder available over the network, it must be **shared**. As they only work over the network, share permissions can be applied on NTFS *and* FAT file systems. To share an object, alt-click it and select **Sharing and Security**. Enter a share name and an optional comment[240].

You can also restrict simultaneous access to a specified number of users (to protect network bandwidth) and configure share permissions.

Windows provides four levels of share permissions:

- **Full Control** – allows users to read, edit, create, and delete files and subdirectories, and to assign permissions to other users and groups.

- **Change** – this is similar to full control but does not allow the user to set permissions for others.

- **Read** – users are permitted to connect to the resource, run programs, and view files. They are not allowed to edit, delete, or create files.

- **Deny** – this overrides any other permission the user receives as an individual or member of a group.

---

[240] If the object is on an NTFS drive, Full Control permission is required to share it; if the object is on a FAT drive, any local user can share it.

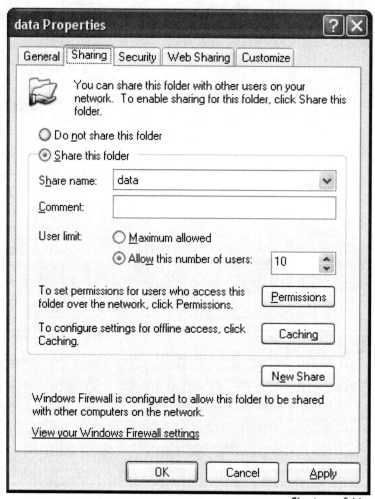

Sharing a folder

As described above, when the folder is accessed over the network, share permissions are combined with any NTFS permissions set to determine the user's access rights (the *most restrictive* set of permissions apply).

Offline files

Offline Files[241] is a feature that caches data from a network file server locally. When the computer is disconnected from the network, the user can continue to access the files. When the computer connects again, a synchronization process occurs to copy changes made locally to the network again and deal with any conflicts (if both the network and local versions have been modified, you need to decide which versions to keep).

---

[241] It is called Offline Folders in Windows 2000 – both folders and individual files can be made available however.

Tip

Offline files is available in Windows 2000/XP Professional and Windows Vista Business/Enterprise/Ultimate. It is not available in the home editions of XP/Vista.

Using offline files in Windows 2000 / XP

In Windows 2000 / XP, you need to configure **Offline Files** via the tab in the **Folder Options** dialog[242].

Check the box to **Enable Offline Files** then set the options for synchronizing and managing disk space used.

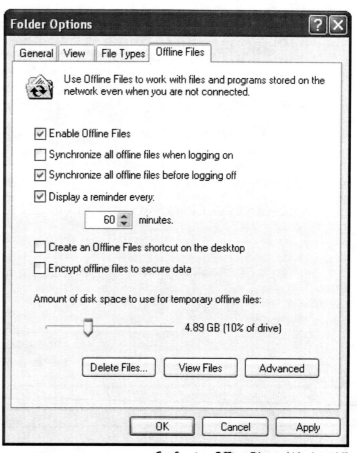

Configuring Offline Files in Windows XP

To set up offline files, just alt-click the folder or file on the network and select **Make available offline**. Offline files are shown in Explorer with a sync icon. Notifications are displayed on the taskbar when you are offline or when data is being synchronized. You can use this icon to synchronize manually.

Offline Files management icon

A dialog is displayed when a file has been modified in both locations. This lets you choose whether to keep one or both versions.

---

[242] In Windows XP, you also need to disable Fast User Switching. To do this, open the User Accounts applet and select "Change the way users log on and off".

Unit 5.3 Module 5 Networks and Printing

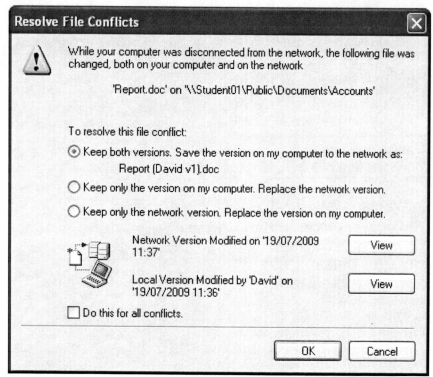

Resolving synchronization file conflicts

Tip

Offline access can also be set up on the server side if the file server is running Windows Server. This is referred to as automatic caching.

Using offline files in Windows Vista

Offline Files is enabled by default in Windows Vista and configured via its own **Control Panel** applet. There is also a **Sync Center** applet for managing the offline files themselves.

There are changes to the way caching works so that a user cannot consume all their disk space by making an excessive number of files available offline permanently.

Folder setup for offline access

Module 5 Networks and Printing — Installing and Configuring Local Networks

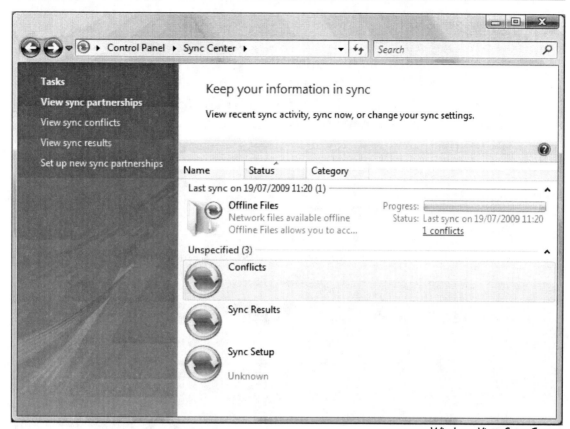

Windows Vista Sync Center

Offline files and slow links

Offline Files can suffer performance problems over a slow link, such as dial-up or VPN. Windows can detect a slow link and switch to using the local copy but the value defined as "slow" is 64 Kbps in Windows 2000/XP and unconfigured in Vista! If your network uses slow links, these values have to be reconfigured via group policy (a feature of Windows Domains) to make offline files work efficiently.

Vista does put **Work Offline** and **Sync** buttons on the Explorer bar so that the user can control the connection state manually.

Administrative shares

If you add a $ sign at the end of the share name, it will be hidden from general browsing but can still be accessed via the command line or by mapping a drive to the share name. Windows automatically creates a number of hidden **administrative** shares, including the root drive (C$) and the system folder (ADMIN$).

Managing shared folders

The **Shared Folders** snap-in (available through the Computer Management console) lets you view all the shares configured on the local machine as well as any current user sessions and open files

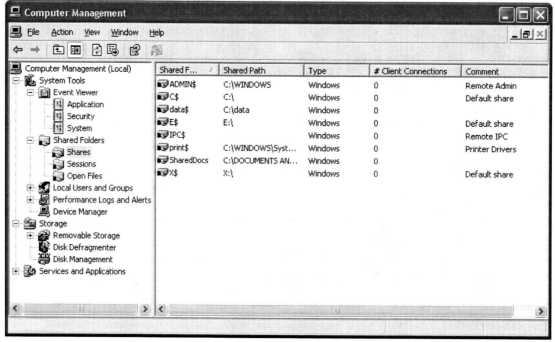

Managing shared folders

Windows XP Simple File Sharing

When you install Windows XP on a standalone or workgroup computer, it defaults to using a much simpler data access method called **Simple File Sharing**. Documents designed to be shared between all users of the computer should be stored in the **Shared Documents** folder (the **All Users** object's document folder).

Network users can be granted access to a folder (or printer) using the **Sharing** tab. Access can be granted as read-only or with change permissions but cannot be restricted on a per-user or per-group basis.

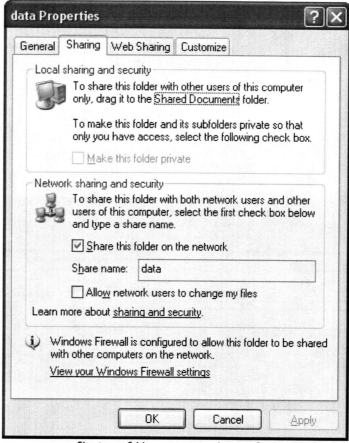

Sharing a folder on a network using Simple File Sharing

To enable or disable simple file sharing under Windows XP Professional[243], from the **Tools** menu of Explorer select **Folder Options**. On the **View** tab, check or uncheck the **Use simple file sharing** box, then click **OK**.

---

[243] Simple File Sharing is enabled by default unless the computer is joined to a domain or has been upgraded from Windows 2000. Simple File Sharing cannot be turned off in Windows XP Home edition.

Windows Vista Network and Sharing Center

Vista's "simple" file sharing model is based around the **Network and Sharing Center**. Whenever a new network link is detected, Vista prompts you to define it as **Public** or **Private** (**Home** or **Work**). The former option disables file and printer sharing and network discovery on the link.

You can customize the sharing options to include printers, disable password-protected sharing[244], and so on.

Like XP, Vista has a pre-defined folder for sharing files (the **Public** folder), which is available to all users of the PC and to network users if the network type is **Private**. You can share other folders by alt-clicking and selecting **Share**, which starts a wizard to help you to configure the appropriate settings. If you want to disable the wizard and use the advanced interface, open **Tools > Folder Options > View** and uncheck the **Use Sharing Wizard** box.

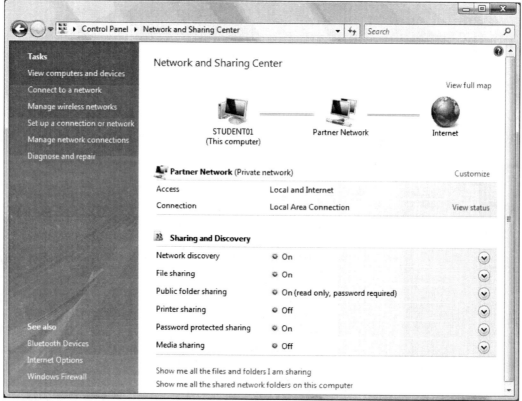

Windows Vista Network and Sharing Center

---

[244] For password-protected sharing, network users must have an account configured on the local machine. This is one of the drawbacks of workgroups compared to domains. Either you configure accounts for all users on all machines, use a single account for network access (again, configured on all machines), or disable security entirely (use the Everyone group).

Module 5 Networks and Printing

Implementing System Security

Windows' security mechanisms can protect data when it is accessed via Windows or over a network but not if a hard drive is physically removed from the computer.

BIOS security

BIOS security is important because an intruder could use a foreign OS (such as Live Linux) to boot the computer and gain access to data on the hard disk (or install malware). Different BIOS software will provide different support for BIOS passwords. There are usually at least two passwords, though some systems may allow for more:

- **Supervisor / Administrator** - protect access to the CMOS setup program.
- **User** - lock access to the whole computer. This is a very secure way of protecting an entire PC as nothing can be done until the POST has taken place. The only real way of getting around this would be to open the PC and reset the CMOS memory, which isn't very easy to do.

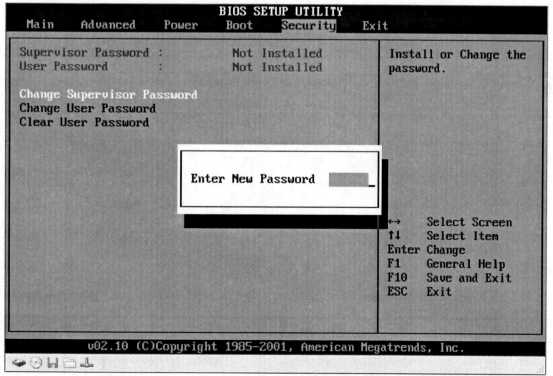

Configuring a supervisor or user BIOS password

Unit 5.3   Module 5 Networks and Printing

- **Drive lock** - there are generally three options for securing access to the disk specifically (rather than the PC generally):

  ☐ Configure and store the password in the PC firmware; this means that the disk is unusable except with the designated computer.

  ☐ Store the password in the disk firmware; this is configured in conjunction with a compatible PC BIOS and means that the disk is transferrable between computers with a compatible BIOS.

  ☐ Use Full Disk Encryption (FDE) to encode the contents of the drive as well as password-protecting it. The selected password is used as the basis of the encryption key. Again, this requires a hard drive and BIOS compatible with the same FDE product.

Note

In most cases there is some sort of recovery mechanism. This might involve the BIOS supervisor password or a password recovery disk.

Trusted Platform Module

Trusted Platform Module (TPM) is a specification for hardware-based storage of digital certificates, keys, hashed passwords, and other user and platform identification information. Essentially it functions as an embedded smart card (see unit 3.4).

Each TPM microprocessor is hard-coded with a unique, unchangeable key (the **endorsement key**). During the boot process, the TPM compares hashes of key system state data (BIOS, boot loader, and OS kernel) to ensure they have not been tampered with.

Hardware locks

Workstations may also need to be locked down from a hardware point-of-view. For example, many companies remove disk drives or use lockable face plates to prevent access. With the proliferation of USB removable media though, this gets more and more difficult to do without impacting ordinary use.

Page 572   IT Career FastTrack with CompTIA A+ Certification   © 2010 gtslearning

Kensington cable lock installed on an HP laptop docking station

A computer chassis can also be installed with sensors to report intrusion detection (if the chassis or lockable faceplate is opened) to management software. Some BIOS can also lock the workstation automatically if an intrusion is detected, requiring a supervisor to log on with the relevant password to unlock it again.

Locking the desktop

One problem with the logon system is that once logged on, the system trusts the workstation implicitly. If a user leaves the workstation unattended, someone else could perform actions as though they were that user (a so-called "lunchtime attack"). To prevent the possibility of this happening, users should be trained to **lock** the workstation whenever they leave it.

There are various means of doing this, depending on the version of Windows.

- Under Windows 2000, press **CTRL+ALT+DEL** and select the **Lock Computer** option.

- Under Windows XP, you can also press **WINDOWS+L**.

- In Windows Vista, there is also a **Lock Computer** icon on the Start menu.

Another way of locking the computer is to set the screen saver to password protect on resume.

Encrypting File System (EFS)

If a hard drive is stolen, the attacker can circumvent NTFS permissions quite simply by "taking ownership" of the files or by accessing the data using a foreign OS such as Linux. Encrypted files are not vulnerable to this attack.

File encryption can only be applied on NTFS volumes. FAT does not support encryption.

Unit 5.3   Module 5 Networks and Printing

To encrypt an object, open its **Properties** dialog box and click **Advanced**. From the **Advanced Attributes** dialog, check the **Encrypt** box.

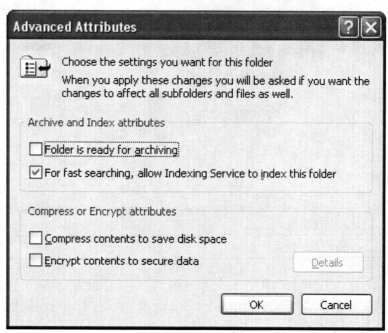

Advanced Attributes for a folder

Only the user that encrypted the file or folder will be able to open, move, or copy it[245]. Other users will receive an "Access Denied" message.

> **Warning**
> You should NEVER encrypt system files as the keys to decrypt such files will not be available during the file system initialization sequence. Failure to observe this rule will render the system unusable.

You *can* encrypt individual files but it is better practice to encrypt folders. When files are copied or moved, they should normally retain their encryption key, but if the user copies the file to a non-NTFS volume, the copy will not be encrypted (other users cannot copy the file to a non-NTFS drive to subvert the encryption however). There are also some other circumstances that can remove the encryption (such as copying a file into a folder that is not encrypted or copying the file over a network).

---

[245] Under Windows XP (not Windows 2000), access can be shared on a file-by-file basis by viewing the file's Advanced Attributes box then clicking the Details button.

Module 5 Networks and Printing

Installing and Configuring Local Networks

The encrypting and decrypting key is linked to the user's account. If the account is damaged or deleted, the data will be *unrecoverable*. In order to protect against this, you should configure a **recovery agent** (that is, an account with permission to recover encrypted files)[246].

Drive encryption

Drive encryption means that the entire contents of the drive (or volume), including system files and folders, are encrypted. Windows Vista supports drive encryption in the BitLocker product, bundled with the Enterprise and Ultimate editions.

> **Tip**
>
> Third-party disk encryption products are available for other versions and editions of Windows.

BitLocker requires the secure storage of the key used to encrypt the drive contents. Normally, this is stored in a **Trusted Platform Module (TPM)** chip on the computer motherboard[247] but it is also possible to use a removable USB drive. As part of the setup process, you also create a recovery password or key. This can be used if the disk is moved to another computer or the TPM is damaged.

BitLocker also requires an unencrypted system volume of 1.5 GB to store the boot files (if the boot files are encrypted, the computer cannot boot)[248].

Volumes other than the one containing the OS files can also be encrypted. In the original version of Vista, this was only possible at the command-line, but SP1 adds the option to do so through the BitLocker control panel.

---

[246] On a domain, recovery agents are created automatically. In a workgroup, you need to generate a certificate then configure an agent through the Local Security Policy. The recovery agent's key should be removed from the PC and stored on a disk in a secure location. Check the online help for details.

[247] You may need to enable the TPM chip via the CMOS Setup before it can be used. Many vendors ship the computer with TPM disabled. The chip must be version 1.2 or better. It is also more secure if the BIOS supports a pre-boot authentication environment. This means that you enter a PIN or password before the computer boots to validate your identity.

[248] If Windows has been installed on a single volume encompassing the whole disk, the BitLocker Drive Preparation Tool is available from Microsoft to shrink the boot volume and create the 1.5 GB system volume.

© 2010 gtslearning

IT Career FastTrack with CompTIA A+ Certification

Page 575

Unit 5.3   Module 5 Networks and Printing

Summary

Windows network client settings are configured via the Computer Name tab in System Properties (Network Identification tab in Windows 2000). Network resources can be browsed using My Network Places (or "Network" in Vista).

Security accounts and privileges (permissions) are central to the Windows security model, especially on a domain (server) network. Make sure you understand the elements of good practice: limiting use of administrative accounts, good password management, and effective security policies.

Data security can be enforced using a combination of NTFS file and folder permissions and network share permissions. Make sure you understand the different access levels and how permissions interact. Note that Windows XP and Vista can operate with a simplified sharing model in standalone and workgroup configurations.

System security mechanisms protect data even if it is removed from the protection of the operating system. Typical measure include BIOS passwords and file and disk encryption (as well as making the computer difficult to steal).

Tip

To review what you have learned in this chapter, you should now visit the course website. This contains review questions and bonus material to help you to learn more and practice the topics covered in this unit.

Page 576   IT Career FastTrack with CompTIA A+ Certification   © 2010 gtslearning

Module 5 Networks and Printing   *Configuring Internet Access*

Unit 5.4 Configuring Internet Access

CompTIA A+ Essentials Objectives

☐ **701.4.1 Summarize the basics of networking fundamentals, including technologies, devices and protocols**
Identify Virtual Private Networks (VPN)

☐ **701.4.3 Compare and contrast the different network types**
Broadband (DSL, Cable, Satellite, Fiber) • Dial-up • Cellular

CompTIA A+ Practical Application Objectives

☐ **702.3.2 Install and configure a Small Office Home Office (SOHO) network**
Connection types (Dial-up, Broadband [DSL, Cable, Satellite, ISDN], Cellular)

Internet Connection Types

For most homes and businesses, internet access is a critical service; as important as power, water, and telephone links. Most home users and businesses use an **Internet Service Provider (ISP)** to facilitate the link between their network (LAN) and the internet. Internet access is then a question of how you join the LAN to the ISP's network (or Point of Presence).

Dial-up

Dial-up connections refer to those made by sending digital data converted to analog signals over the telephone network.

Much of the communications network in developed countries (the **Public Switched Telephone Network [PSTN]**) has been upgraded to use high-bandwidth digital fiber optic cabling but the last part of the network, the wiring from the telephone company's switch to domestic residences (the local or subscriber loop), is still voice-grade 2-pair copper cable (**Plain Old Telephone Service [POTS]**).

As described in unit 1.5, a **modem** can convert digital computer data to an analog waveform representing the 1s and 0s in the data for transmission as a sound wave over the telephone network (modulation). The modem on the receiving computer demodulates the signal and responds with its own data message.

© 2010 gtslearning   IT Career FastTrack with CompTIA A+ Certification   Page 577

| Unit 5.4 | Module 5 Networks and Printing |

The **Point-to-Point Protocol (PPP)** is typically used to *encapsulate* the network protocol (which will usually be TCP/IP). PPP also provides a mechanism to authenticate the user and manage the connection between the two computers.

For a number of years, this was the primary means of accessing the internet or making a remote connection to an office computer. Dial-up access only supports low bandwidth connections (up to 56 Kbps). Making a data connection prevents the phone line being used for voice communications.

ISDN (Integrated Services Digital Network)

ISDN (Integrated Services Digital Network) is a fully digital version of the local loop, standardized by the ITU. It has been provided by telecommunication companies since the 1980s. ISDN is a digital circuit-switched technology for voice, video, and data (hence "integrated services"). ISDN makes use of existing copper telephone wiring (if the wiring is of sufficient quality).

ISDN is a dial-up service billed for by line rental and per-minute usage. The most common uses of ISDN are for interconnection of LANs and remote users (teleworkers) to businesses.

Typically, consumer ISDN is provided as a **Basic Rate Interface (BRI)**, with two "B" channels of 64 Kbps each[249]. One channel can be used for voice and the other for data simultaneously or both channels can be used for data. An ISDN terminal adapter is required to interface with the PC.

"Business" ISDN, or **Primary Rate Interface (PRI)**, provides more channels for higher bandwidth; 1.5 Mbps in the US and Japan or 2 Mbps in Europe[250].

Although ISDN is a dial-up technology, it is capable of establishing a circuit connection in less than 1 second. This means that many applications that time-out when using the analog modems can be used with ISDN.

Much of the switching technology of ISDN remains in use in terms of the telecommunications core network but as a WAN access method for subscribers it has largely been superseded by DSL and cable. It remains a good solution outside metropolitan areas where these other services may not be available.

---

[249] A third "D" channel of 12 Kbps provides connection control information.

[250] Digital line bandwidth is rated according to the T-carrier (US and Japan) or E-carrier (Europe and Australia) system. Primary rate ISDN is comparable to T1 or E1. Another option is to rent a private leased line, providing greater security.

| Page 578 | IT Career FastTrack with CompTIA A+ Certification | © 2010 gtslearning |

Module 5 Networks and Printing   *Configuring Internet Access*

Broadband

In recent years, several different high-bandwidth internet access methods have established themselves as replacements for dial-up and ISDN, both for domestic use and in small to medium enterprises. These services are described as "broadband" because different signals (voice and data for instance) are carried over the same media simultaneously[251].

DSL

Digital Subscriber Line (DSL) is a technology for transferring data over voice-grade telephone lines. The connection is "always on", meaning that there is no need to dial to initiate access and no call charges are incurred.

There are various "flavors" of DSL, with the most popular being **Asymmetric DSL (ADSL)**, which restricts upload speeds dramatically (from a half to an eighth of the download speed). ADSL is also packaged in a number of bandwidths, from 512 Kbps up to about 8 Mbps. Often service providers impose usage restrictions to limit the amount of data downloaded per month. Actual speed may be affected by the quality of the cabling in the consumer's premises and between the premises and the exchange and also by the number of DSL users connected to the same exchange (contention).

DSL is not available in all areas. The customer's premises need to be within about 3 miles of a DSL-enabled telephone exchange.

ADSL2 supports higher data rates (up to 12 Mbps downstream and 1 Mbps uplink) and slightly greater range (about 5% extra). ADSL2+ offers downlink speeds up to about 24 Mbps but this sort of bandwidth can only be expected from within a mile or so of the exchange.

Symmetric versions of DSL offer the same uplink and downlink speeds. These are of more use to businesses and for VPN links, where more data is transferred upstream than with normal internet use.

Depending on the equipment used by the ISP, the data link protocol used for DSL may be **PPP over Ethernet (PPPoE)** or **PPP over ATM (PPPoA)**.

---

[251] Most people understand broadband to mean "more bandwidth" but there is no definition of how much bandwidth constitutes broadband.

| Unit 5.4 | Module 5 Networks and Printing |

Hybrid Fiber Coax (HFC)

A cable internet connection is usually available along with a cable telephone/television service (**Cable Access TV [CATV]**). These networks are often described as **Hybrid Fiber Coax (HFC)** as they combine a fiber optic core network with coax links to customer premises equipment, but are more simply just described as "cable".

Cable supports downlink speeds of up to 50 Mbps and uplinks of up to 30 Mbps, but in practice, consumer and small business services are offered at the same sort of asymmetric speeds as ADSL.

Cable also suffers from contention ratio as the bandwidth is shared with users on the same loop.

FTTx

The major obstacle to providing really high bandwidth to consumers and small businesses is in the "last mile", where the wiring infrastructure is generally not good. The projects to update this wiring to use fiber optic links are referred to by the umbrella term "Fiber to the X" (FTTx).

The most expensive solution is **Fiber to the Premises (FTTP)** or its domestic variant **Fiber to the Home (FTTH)**. The essential point about both these implementations is that the fiber link is terminated on Customer Premises Equipment.

Other solutions can variously be described as **Fiber to the Node (FTTN)** or **Fiber to the Curb (FTTC)**. These retain some sort of copper wiring (twisted pair or coax) while extending the fiber link to a communications cabinet servicing multiple subscribers.

Such "pure" fiber solutions are not widespread and generally carry a price premium above other types of internet access.

Satellite

The widespread use of satellite television receivers allows for domestic internet connectivity services over satellite connections. Satellite services for business are also expanding, especially in rural areas where DSL or cable services are unlikely to be available. Bandwidth is similar to ADSL.

Module 5 Networks and Printing   *Configuring Internet Access*

Satellite connections experience quite severe **latency** problems as the signal has to travel over thousands of miles more than terrestrial connections, introducing a delay of up to 900 ms (compared to 200 ms or less for earth-bound connections; latency on the uplink is even greater). This is an issue for real-time applications, such as video-conferencing, VoIP, and multi-player gaming.

Cellular

A cellular (or mobile)[252] phone makes a connection using the nearest available transmitter (cell or base station). The transmitter connects the phone to the cellular and telephone networks. Transmitter coverage in many countries is now very good, with the exception of remote rural areas. Signals can also be blocked by thick walls and devices that cause radio interference.

A cellphone uses digital communications for basic functions such as voice communications and text messaging (SMS [Short Message Service]) and can also support data-only transfer and internet access. There are three digital standards:

- 2G (2nd generation) - typically **GSM (Global System for Mobile Communication)**-based phones. These offer low connection speeds, from about 9.6 to 14.4 Kbps. There are other 2G technologies, but GSM is the most widespread and provides the best support for roaming (using a phone in different countries)[253].

- 2.5G - this describes technologies falling between 2G and 3G. Access to the internet is enabled through **GPRS (General Packet Radio Services)**, supporting speeds from about 32-48 Kbps and allowing simultaneous data transfer and voice calls. Higher transfer rates can be achieved using technologies such as HSCSD and EDGE.

- 3G - this is the latest set of standards and technologies, implemented in a many countries (though coverage tends to be limited to cities). There are two main 3G internet access technologies:

  - HSPA (High Speed Packet Access), supporting speeds up to about 14 Mbps.

---

[252] In the US, the terminology is cellphone (or simply "cell"). In the UK and most other English-speaking countries the term "mobile" is used.

[253] GSM operates over four different frequencies (850, 900, 1800, and 1900 MHz). If you need to use a phone internationally, obtain one that is tri- or quad-band for the best coverage.

© 2010 gtslearning   IT Career FastTrack with CompTIA A+ Certification   Page 581

□ CDMA2000 EV-DO (Enhanced Version-Data Only) - each channel supports a 3.1 Mbps downlink and 1.8 Mbps uplink; multiple channels can be aggregated to support higher speeds.

A smartphone or PDA with a Wi-Fi adapter can also use an AP for internet connectivity. Conversely, an HSPA / EV-DO adapter fitted in the laptop (or connected as a USB dongle or ExpressCard) enables the laptop to use cellular broadband internet access using the selected telecom provider's network.

Installing and Configuring Internet Connections

There are many different internet access technologies and different ways of using those technologies depending on the number of workstations connecting from the site. On corporate LANs, workstations are generally connected to the internet via a router, which in turn will use a leased line[254], DSL, or cable connection. The router provides **Network Address Translation (NAT)**, meaning that the internal network can use private IP addresses. This adds a measure of security and is much simpler to configure. The clients' TCP/IP settings will be configured using DHCP.

A single computer might use any type of connection with the connectivity device (modem, DSL adapter, or cable modem) connected as a peripheral device[255].

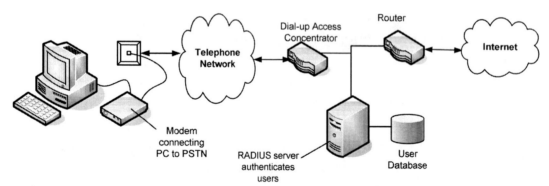

Internet access for a standalone PC via an ISP

The client's TCP/IP settings will generally be dynamically allocated by the ISP, though in some cases the ISP may provide a static address.

---

[254] A leased line is a communications link made available privately to a single company. This allows for high bandwidth with no contention but is correspondingly expensive.

[255] Dial-up modems are often fitted as internal adapters. External modems and most other adapters are connected via USB, with the exception of cable "modems", which use an Ethernet port.

Module 5 Networks and Printing | Configuring Internet Access

This type of connection can also be shared between a number of networked computers (in Windows, **Internet Connection Sharing** can be enabled to facilitate this).

Another popular option for home networks using DSL or cable is to use a device that combines the function of a DSL/Cable adapter with that of a switch and router. In this scenario, TCP/IP is configured on the device (using settings provided by the ISP), which uses DHCP to set the clients' configuration.

Internet Service Providers

Internet Service Providers (ISPs) offer connections to and from the internet. Most ISPs also offer website and email hosting and domain name registration.

There are a number of issues that should be taken into consideration when selecting a service provider. These are summarized as follows:

Factor	Notes
Price	Connection fee (including equipment costs).
	Tariff scales[256].
Services	Range of access methods (dial-up, DSL, satellite, leased line).
	Security facilities, such as firewalls.
	Permanent (static) IP address(es) for the connection[257].
	Online services such as magazines, games, financial information.
	Domain name registration, web space, email hosting, web design, server-side features, and so on.
	Other services, such as telephone/TV for home users or VoIP for business.
Customer service	Availability of help and support. Assistance with network configuration.
Available bandwidth	A service provider either has a direct connection to the internet or borrows some bandwidth from a larger provider. The amount of bandwidth available to your service provider determines the effective performance of your connection.
Reliability	Monthly uptime for the connection and time-to-fix for outages.

---

[256] Most ISPs offer tiered products with different levels of bandwidth (for example, Home User, Home-Office, Small Business, Enterprise). Some services may involve a monthly download limit (cap).

[257] Allowing you to host a web services from your own machine. Services such as ADSL are asynchronous, meaning that upload is much slower than download. This means that large-scale services cannot be supported as the site would run too slowly. However, some access is very useful for intranet and extranet functions, such as VPN, Outlook Web Access/Outlook Mobile Access, or a company intranet site. From a hobbyist point-of-view, a static IP address is useful for online gaming.

© 2010 gtslearning | IT Career FastTrack with CompTIA A+ Certification | Page 583

| Unit 5.4 | Module 5 Networks and Printing |

Installing modems

The term "modem", meaning Modulator / Demodulator, originally referred to a device that converts between analog and digital signals (modulation and demodulation). The term "modem" is now widely used to refer to any type of SOHO remote connectivity appliance, even when such appliances do no actual modulation. These include DSL, cable, and satellite "modems".

Creating a dial-up networking connection in Windows XP

Most laptops still come with built-in modems and they are also widely available either as adapter cards for PCs or external devices, connected via a serial or USB port. The modem is connected to an analog phone point by 2-pair cable (typically a flat "silver satin" cable) with RJ-11 connectors[258].

Regardless of the physical interface, the modem must be installed to one of the computer's software COM ports. The modem must also be configured with the local dialing properties, such as dial or pulse tone, access prefix for an outside line, area code, and so on.

Connections to remote modems can then be configured by entering the remote modem's telephone number and other connection properties, such as protocol and authentication information.

Creating a dial-up networking connection in Windows XP

To configure dialing properties in Windows XP, in Control Panel, open **Phone and Modem Options**. Select an existing location and click **Edit** or click **New** to create new dialing rules.

Enter a name to describe the location, choose the correct country and area code, then select any appropriate dialing rules:

- Outside line and carrier code - enter any numbers required to access an outside line or call carrier.

- Call waiting - this can interfere with the connection and should be turned off using the appropriate code.

- Tone or pulse dialing - check with your phone company.

---

[258] In the UK, the phone jack uses a BT connector (BS 6312) rather than RJ-11.

| Page 584 | IT Career FastTrack with CompTIA A+ Certification | © 2010 gtslearning |

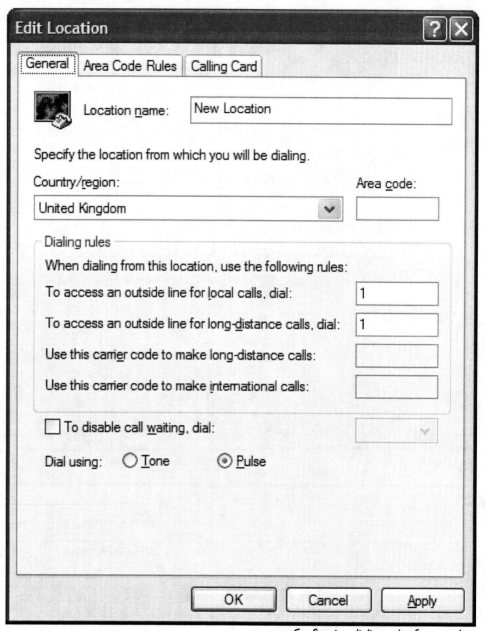

Configuring dialing rules for a modem

To configure a new internet link using the modem, in Control Panel, open **Network Connections**. Click **Create a new connection** (or select **File > New Connection**). Choose **Connect to the Internet** then select your modem and enter the dialing and connection information for the ISP's internet access server.

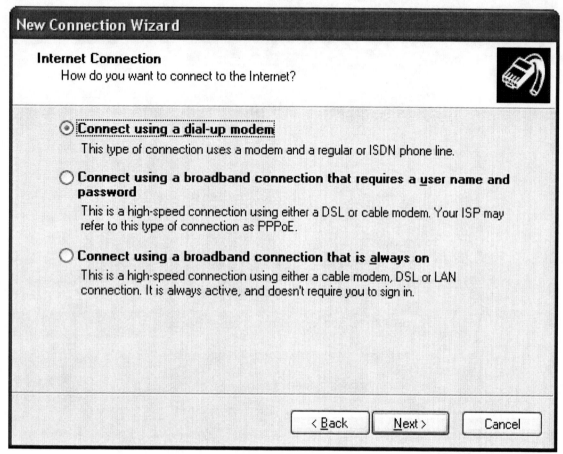

New Connection Wizard

Creating a dial-up networking connection in Windows Vista

Select **Start > Connect To > Set up a Connection or Network > Set up a dial-up connection**.

Enter the configuration information and click **Connect** and complete the connectivity test. To modify the connection properties, use the icon in the **Network Connections** applet.

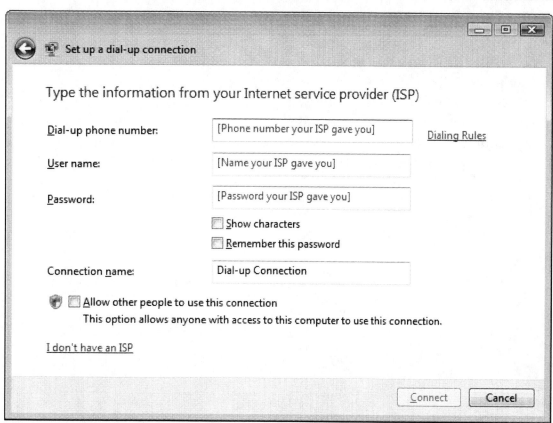

Configuring a dial-up connection in Windows Vista

Installing ISDN adapters

An ISDN connection would typically be facilitated through a **Terminal Adapter (TA)**. The terminal adapter may be an external appliance or a plug-in card for a PC or compatible router. The TA is connected to the ISDN network via an **NT1** device (Network Terminator). The NT1 would either be incorporated into the TA or provided as an external device (in which case the TA and NT1 are connected via the "S/T" port). The "U" port on the NT1 is connected to the ISDN wall jack.

The ISDN-enabled router may then either be connected to a switch or support direct connections from ISDN devices[259].

---

[259] A separate NT1 appliance can provide a connection for up to 7 devices (referred to as Terminal Equipment [TE]). TE1 devices can connect directly to the NT1; TE2 devices require a Terminal Adapter, as described above.

Installing DSL modems and routers

A DSL adapter is installed as some sort of combined router and switch (and generally with a wireless AP built in too). These **multifunction network devices** are now ubiquitous in the SOHO market. They provide Ethernet ports for connection to computers and switches on the LAN and a WAN port for connection to the phone line (utilizing a short length of silver satin cable with RJ-11 connectors). Alternatively, a USB adapter can be installed to make the connection for a single PC.

WAN port (left) and 4xEthernet ports on a Netgear wireless router/DSL modem

A filter (splitter) must be installed to separate voice and data signals. These can be self-installed on each phone point by the customer.

The ISP may supply a setup CD to configure the connection. Alternatively, the 3Com DSL router shown below provides a browser interface for configuring the relevant settings. With the PC connected to the router via one of the RJ-45 ports and the router connected to the phone point via its RJ-11 (WAN) port, power on the router and once it has completed startup, use a browser on the PC to access the IP address for its configuration page (typically http://192.168.1.1).

Self-installed DSL splitter

Log in using the default password. You can then configure the router using the pages provided (most devices have a wizard-driven process to configure basic settings, which you can obtain from your ISP). **Make sure you change the default password to something more secure.**

Module 5 Networks and Printing — Configuring Internet Access

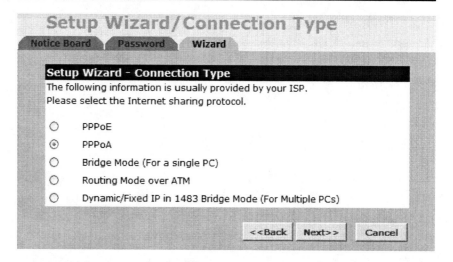

Configuring ADSL connection settings for an ISP using PPPoA (ATM)

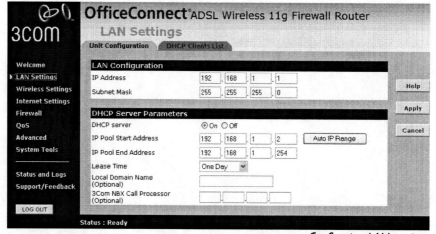

Configuring LAN settings

You can also adjust LAN settings, such as the router's default IP address (it is a good idea to change this for security reasons) and disable or reconfigure the DHCP server. Most of these router devices also ship with a firewall. See unit 5.6 for notes on configuring these.

Hybrid Fiber Coax (HFC) / cable modems

Installation of a cable modem follows the same general principles as for a DSL modem. Generally, the cable modem is interfaced to the computer through an Ethernet or USB adapter and with the access provider's network by a short segment of coax.

Cellular

Cellular internet access refers to using an adapter to link to a cellular phone provider's network via the nearest available transmitter (base station). If the transmitter supports 3G, the adapter will use HSPA (or EV-DO in the US) with a link speed of up to about 14 Mbps. If no 3G transmitter is available, it will default to a lower speed technology such as EDGE, GPRS, or CDMA-one.

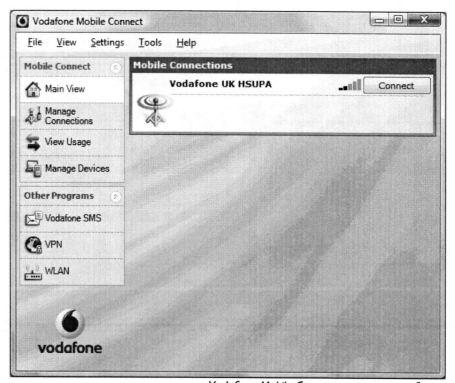

Vodafone Mobile Connect management software

Module 5 Networks and Printing   *Configuring Internet Access*

The HSPA / EV-DO adapter can be fitted as a USB device or (on laptops) as an internal mini-PCIe card or PCI Express card. The advantage of the latter is that they do not protrude from the chassis; USB adapters are quite unwieldy.

Once the vendor's software has been installed, plug in the adapter and it will be detected and configured automatically. You can then use the software to open a connection, check signal strength, view usage, and so on.

Satellite

To create a satellite internet connection, the ISP installs a satellite dish (antenna) at your premises and aligns it with the orbital satellite. The antenna is connected via coaxial cabling to a **DVB-S (Digital Video Broadcast Satellite)** modem. This can be installed in the PC as a PCI card or as an external box connected via a USB or Ethernet port.

Configuring the Browser

Browser software can connect to the internet in three ways:

- Using a dial-up connection.
- Using a proxy server.
- Via a router across a LAN or a WAN.

Use the connection settings for the browser to select the required option (in **Internet Explorer** these are accessed through **Tools > Internet Options > Connections** tab or through **Internet Options** in **Control Panel**).

Connecting using a dial-up connection

Click **Add** to configure a new dial-up connection then select either the **Dial whenever a network connection is not present**[260] or **Always dial my default connection**. If the connection selected in the **Dial-up Settings** box is not the default, click **Set Default**.

---

[260] You would typically select this option for a laptop computer that connects via the LAN in the office but a modem elsewhere.

© 2010 gtslearning   IT Career FastTrack with CompTIA A+ Certification   Page 591

Unit 5.4 Module 5 Networks and Printing

The next time the browser software starts, it uses the dial-up connection to access the ISP (unless it is configured to check for a connection over the local network).

Dial-up connection settings

Connecting using a proxy server

Many companies use a **proxy server** as a gateway to and from the internet. A proxy server can be used to improve both performance and security. User machines pass internet requests to the proxy server, which forwards them to the ISP.

1. From the **Connections** tab, click **LAN Settings**.

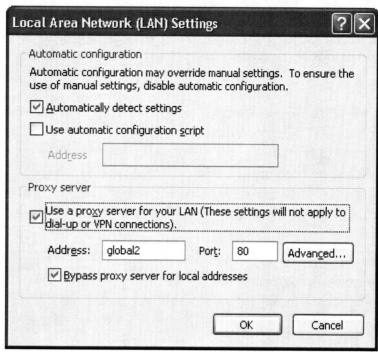

Configuring proxy internet access

2. Check **Use a proxy server**. Enter the IP address or name of the proxy server and other settings required.

Using a router

To use a router, you simply need to configure the **Default gateway** parameter in TCP/IP properties for the local network adapter (though more typically, this would be configured automatically using DHCP). The browser will use this connection when you select **Never dial a connection** or **Dial whenever a network connection is not present**.

Internet Connection Sharing (ICS)

Under Windows, workgroup computers can make use of a single dial-up internet connection. The machine with the internet adapter or modem is the host.

Note that this feature is intended for small home and office networks only. The network cannot have a DHCP server (the host system itself becomes a DHCP server). The IP address of the host machine is set to **192.168.0.1**.

To enable ICS under Windows XP/Vista[261], on the host machine, check the **Allow other network users to connect through this computer's internet connect** box on the **Advanced** tab of the adapter's properties sheet (or the **Sharing** tab in Vista).

Configure client machines to obtain an IP address automatically.

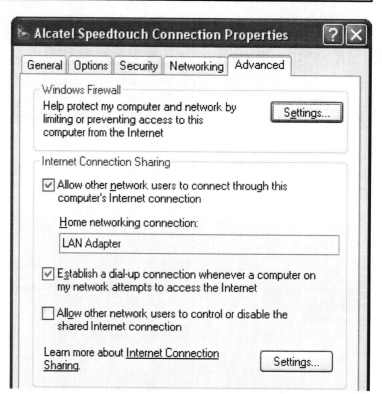

Internet Connection Sharing

Virtual Private Networks

A **Virtual Private Network (VPN)** connects the components and resources of two (private) networks over another (public) network.

The internet provides a pretty cost effective way of connecting both users to networks and networks to networks. Rather than a user direct-dialing your server, which is private but expensive, the user connects to an **Internet Service Provider (ISP)**, which is cheap, but public.

A VPN is a "tunnel" through the internet (or any other public network). It uses special connection protocols and encryption technology to ensure that the tunnel is secure and the user is properly authenticated. Once the connection has been established, to all intents and purposes, the remote computer becomes part of the local network (though it is still restricted by the bandwidth available over the WAN link).

---

[261] Under Windows 2000, check the **Enable ICS for this connection** box on the **General** or **Sharing** tab of the internet adapter's properties sheet.

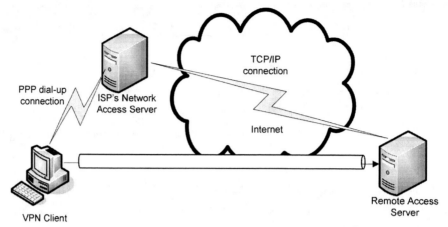

Remote access VPN

The figure above describes a "remote access" topology, where a single remote user (or perhaps several remote users but at different locations) join the network. VPNs can also be configured in a "site-to-site" topology. This model connects two or more local networks, each of which runs a VPN gateway (or router).

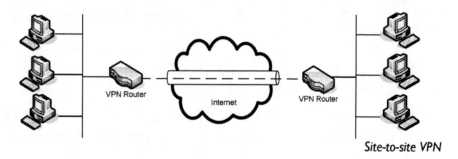

Site-to-site VPN

Summary

Make sure you know the characteristics of internet access methods such as dial-up, ISDN, ADSL, cable, satellite, and cellular.

Use the Internet Connection Wizard to set up different types of internet connection. With dial-up connections, configure the modem and dialing properties using Device Manager and the Phone and Modem applet in Control Panel. A SOHO router can be configured using the web management interface. You also need to configure the browser to use the appropriate connection (open the Internet Options applet).

Unit 5.5 Troubleshooting Network Links

CompTIA A+ Essentials Objectives

☐ **701.3.2 Given a scenario, demonstrate proper use of user interfaces**
Command prompt utilities (PING, IPCONFIG)

☐ **701.4.1 Summarize the basics of networking fundamentals, including technologies, devices and protocols**
Status indicators

CompTIA A+ Practical Application Objectives

☐ **702.1.4 Given a scenario, select and use the following tools**
Cable testers

☐ **702.2.1 Select the appropriate commands and options to troubleshoot and resolve problems**
IPCONFIG (/all /release /renew) • PING (-t -l) • TRACERT • NSLOOKUP

☐ **702.3.1 Troubleshoot client-side connectivity issues using appropriate tools**
TCP/IP settings (Gateway, Subnet mask, DNS, DHCP [dynamic vs. static]) • Characteristics of TCP/IP (Loopback addresses, Automatic IP addressing) • Tools - use and interpret results (PING, TRACERT, NSLOOKUP, NETSTAT, IPCONFIG)

Network Troubleshooting Theory

When testing network connectivity, it helps to apply a methodical process. Think of components that could go wrong in terms of layers:

- Cabling / media - damaged cables or connectors, poor quality cabling, and interference.

- Network adapter - check that the device is recognized and supports the network product, speed, and configuration.

- Switch - damage or wrong configuration. A problem will usually be manifested when multiple users cannot connect, though it is possible that one port only has failed.

- Protocol - check that the necessary protocols and client software are installed and configured correctly. Check that expected services are installed and correctly configured on the server.

Module 5 Networks and Printing

Troubleshooting Network Links

- Routing - check that the router (default gateway) address is correctly configured on the client (if one client cannot connect) or check configuration settings on the router (if many clients cannot connect). Also consider the impact of firewalls installed between the two networks and whether these are blocking traffic.

- Name resolution - as for routing, check the configuration on the client (problem restricted to one workstation) or the server (problems on many workstations).

- Security - log on (password input), authentication, and permissions.

Start from either end - but note that problems occur more often at the top than the bottom!

Troubleshooting Network Hardware

Remember to test simple things first. It may sound obvious, but if a single computer is unable to connect to the network, the first thing you should check is whether the network cable is properly connected. If you can discount basic configuration errors such as an unplugged cable, some methods for solving common problems are discussed below.

Product indicators

Network components such as network adapters, hubs, switches, and routers provide Light Emitting Diodes (LEDs) to indicate the status of the device. The number of LEDs and their meaning will vary considerably from vendor to vendor. The user guide provided with the device usually explains their function. For example, the Intel PRO/1000 network card provides two LEDs (ACT/LNK and 10/100/1000). The link LED provides the following information:

LED Status	Indicating
On	Active connection between adapter and hub (driver must be loaded).
Off	No connection between adapter and hub (check cable, hub, and adapter).
Flashing	Data activity.

© 2010 gtslearning

IT Career FastTrack with CompTIA A+ Certification

Page 597

The other LED indicates the connection speed (Off=10, Green=100, Yellow=1000). An orange light on this LED indicates a problem with the speed settings selected. The card comes with a diagnostic tool (accessible via the property page in **Device Manager**) to assist troubleshooting.

Hubs and switches usually provide the same sort of indicators. A device such as a SOHO router will have status indicators for LAN ports, WAN port, wireless access, and so on.

Intel PRO/1000 status indicators 1) ACT/LNK (activity / link indicator); 2) 10/100/1000 (speed indicator)

Checking the status of the connection

In Windows 2000/XP, each network adapter has a **Status** page, viewable by alt-clicking the icon in **Network Connections** and selecting **Status** or by clicking the icon if it is displayed in the notification area.

The **General** page shows the connection speed and activity; for a wireless connection it will also show an approximation of the signal strength (Excellent, Very Good, Good, Low, or Very Low). Under Windows XP, the **Support** page shows the TCP/IP configuration.

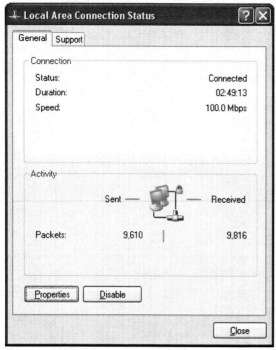

Network connection status

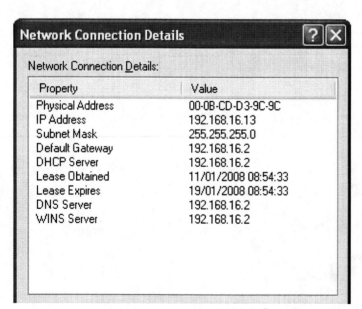

Network Connection Details

Click the **Details** button to show extra information, including the physical network adapter address (MAC).

The **Repair** button forces Windows to attempt to repair the connection by contacting a DHCP server.

You can also show a network connection status icon in the **notification area** (check the option on the adapter's property page). Pointing to the notification area network status icon displays summary information or you can click it to open the **Status** page.

In Vista, you can view network details and status information from the **Network and Sharing Center**.

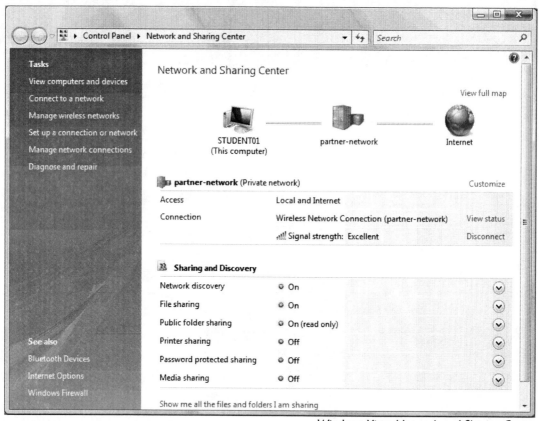

Windows Vista Network and Sharing Center

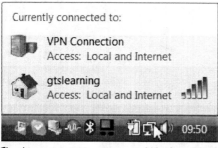

Checking connection status in Windows Vista

Vista only shows a single network connection icon in the notification area. Point to the icon to view the status of each link or open the Network and Sharing Center.

Troubleshooting a dial-up modem

If a modem cannot make a connection, the line may be busy, the remote modem might not be connected or receiving calls, or you may be dialing the wrong number.

When you have confirmed the number, try repeating the call later or contact whoever is operating the remote server to find out if there is a problem[262].

If the modem cannot get a dial tone, connect an ordinary phone handset to the line and check for a tone. If there is a tone, check the modem cabling; if there is no tone, report the fault to the phone company.

> **Note**
> Check that the modem has not been plugged into a digital telephone port. Digital ports are used in most company networks and many hotels. Without overcurrent protection, the digital signaling may damage the modem.

If the modem makes a connection, but it is slower than expected or "drops out" frequently, there may be a problem with the telephone cabling. Connect an ordinary phone handset, dial a number, and listen to see if you can detect any audible noise. Also check the modem properties from Device Manager. You can reduce the line speed and query the modem (to ensure that it is installed and working properly).

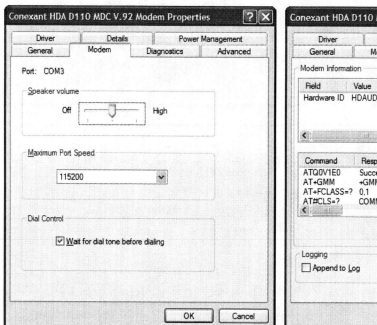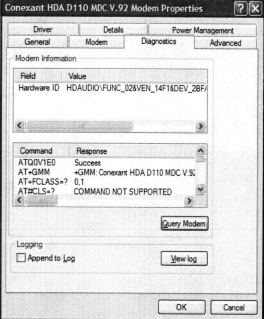

Viewing modem properties from Device Manager - use the Modem tab to set the port speed and Diagnostics tab to query the modem

---

[262] On a private network, the remote server may only accept connections at certain times of day and may limit the maximum number of inbound connections.

Testing cabling

The simplest way to test patch cable is to substitute with a known-good cable. Unfortunately, it is not possible to do this with conduit cable. To test cable infrastructure[263], you need to use a cable tester device.

- **Multimeter** - a multimeter with a built-in cable tester can be used to test continuity (that is, for breaks in the cable) cheaply. Such devices normally have RJ-45 and RJ-11 ports.

- **Tone generator and probe** - a network tone generator and probe are used to trace a cable from one end to the other. This device is also known as a **Fox and Hound**. The tone generator is used to apply a signal on the cable to be traced where it is used to follow the cable over ceilings and through ducts.

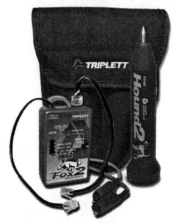

Triplett Fox and Hound

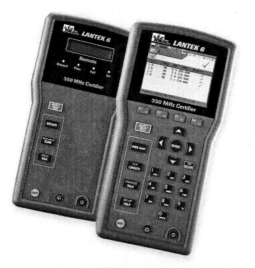

LANTEK Advanced cable certifier

- **Time Domain Reflector** - these devices are able to locate open and short circuits, kinks/sharp bends, and other imperfections in cables that could affect performance.

- **Advanced testers / certifiers** - provide detailed information on the physical and electrical properties of the cable. For example, they test and report on cable conditions, crosstalk, attenuation, noise, resistance, and other characteristics of a cable run.

On all but the smallest networks, cabling should be run through conduit to prevent damage (or even eavesdropping). Unused network jacks should be disabled (that is, not connected to a port on a hub or switch) to prevent the attachment of unauthorized equipment.

---

[263] Damage to infrastructure cable is fairly rare, unless it was not installed properly. Inspect jacks and cable runs for signs of visible damage first.

Module 5 Networks and Printing   *Troubleshooting Network Links*

Similarly, hubs and switches should be located in a secure room (typically both the room and the cabinet containing the network equipment are kept locked).

Troubleshooting wireless connections

Firstly, check the configuration and compatibility of the devices used. For example, an older wireless adapter may only support 802.11b and be unable to communicate with an AP configured for 802.11g operation.

Tip

Remember that all devices perform to the standard of the lowest specification device on the network.

The signal from radio-based devices weakens considerably the farther apart the devices are. If you cannot establish a connection, try moving the devices closer together. If you still cannot obtain a connection, check that the security and authentication parameters are correctly configured on both devices. If a device is within the supported range but the signal is very weak or you cannot get a connection, there is likely to be interference from another radio source broadcasting at the same frequency (try adjusting the channel that the devices use), interference from a powerful electromagnetic source (such as a motor or microwave oven), or the signal is being blocked by something. Radio waves do not pass easily through metal or dense objects (such as a crowd of people). Try angling or repositioning the device or antenna to try to get better reception.

Tip

Position wireless access points as high as possible to get the best reception.

Infrared devices require line-of-sight so check that nothing is blocking the signal. The beams are also easily diluted by bright sunlight. You should also check that the photoreceptors on the devices are clean.

Tip

With portable devices, also check that the battery has not run down. Devices may need to be re-synched; this can normally be done by holding down a recessed button on each device for a number of seconds.

© 2010 gtslearning   IT Career FastTrack with CompTIA A+ Certification   Page 603

Unit 5.5   Module 5 Networks and Printing

Troubleshooting TCP/IP

There are a number of command-line tools for testing and troubleshooting TCP/IP connections.

Viewing IP configuration (IPCONFIG)

In Windows, TCP/IP configuration information is displayed using the IPCONFIG command line utility. Used without switches, IPCONFIG displays the IP address, subnet mask, and default gateway (router) for all network adapters to which TCP/IP is bound.

```
C:\WINDOWS\system32\cmd.exe                                          _ □ ×

C:\>ipconfig

Windows IP Configuration


Ethernet adapter Wireless Network Connection 2:

        Media State . . . . . . . . . . . : Media disconnected

Ethernet adapter LAN Adapter:

        Connection-specific DNS Suffix  . :
        IP Address. . . . . . . . . . . . : 192.168.1.2
        Subnet Mask . . . . . . . . . . . : 255.255.255.0
        Default Gateway . . . . . . . . . : 192.168.1.1

C:\>ipconfig /renew "LAN Adapter"

Windows IP Configuration


Ethernet adapter Wireless Network Connection 2:

        Media State . . . . . . . . . . . : Media disconnected

Ethernet adapter LAN Adapter:

        Connection-specific DNS Suffix  . :
        IP Address. . . . . . . . . . . . : 192.168.1.2
        Subnet Mask . . . . . . . . . . . : 255.255.255.0
        Default Gateway . . . . . . . . . : 192.168.1.1

C:\>
```

Using IPCONFIG

Typical IPCONFIG arguments are:

- **IPCONFIG /all** - display detailed configuration, including DHCP, DNS and WINS servers, MAC address, and NetBIOS status.

Page 604   IT Career FastTrack with CompTIA A+ Certification   © 2010 gtslearning

| Module 5 Networks and Printing | Troubleshooting Network Links |

- **IPCONFIG /release** *AdapterName* - releases the IP address obtained from a DHCP Server, so that the network adapter(s) will no longer have an IP address.

- **IPCONFIG /renew** *AdapterName* - forces a DHCP client to renew the lease it has for an IP address.

- **IPCONFIG /showdns** - displays the DNS resolver cache.

- **IPCONFIG /flushdns** - clears the DNS resolver cache.

Omitting the *AdapterName* argument releases or renews **all** adapters. If *AdapterName* contains spaces, use quotes around it (for example, IPCONFIG /renew "Local Area Connection").

You would use IPCONFIG to determine that the adapter has been correctly configured. IPCONFIG can resolve the following questions:

- Is the adapter configured with a static address? Are the parameters (IP address, subnet mask, default gateway, and DNS server correct)?

- Is the adapter configured by DHCP? If so:

  - An address in the range 169.254.x.y indicates that the client could not contact a DHCP server and is using **Automatic Private IP Addressing (APIPA)**

  - A DHCP lease can be static (always assigns the same IP address to the computer) or dynamic (assigns an IP address from a pool) - has the computer obtained a suitable address and subnet mask?

  - Are other parameters assigned by DHCP correct (default gateway, DNS Server, and so on)?

If any of these results are negative, you should investigate either communications between the client and the DHCP server, the configuration of the DHCP server, or whether multiple DHCP servers are running on the network (and the client has obtained the wrong configuration from one).

PING

The **Packet InterNet Groper (PING)** utility is a command line diagnostic tool used to diagnose link failures.

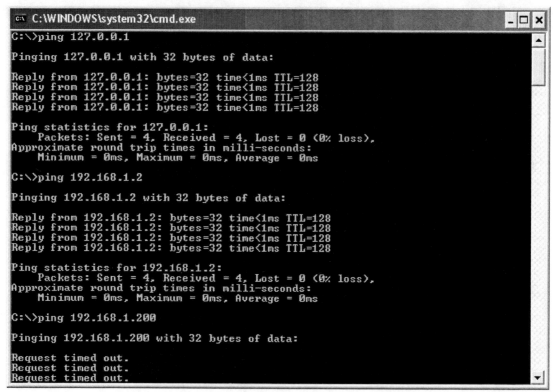

Using PING

Follow these steps to verify the configuration of a computer and test connections:

1. Ping the loopback address to verify that TCP/IP is installed and loaded correctly:
   PING 127.0.0.1

2. Ping the IP address of your workstation to verify that it was added correctly, and to check for possible duplicate IP addresses.

3. Ping the IP address of another workstation to test local subnet connectivity.

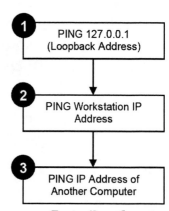

Testing IP configuration

Module 5 Networks and Printing   *Troubleshooting Network Links*

To test routing, you should proceed to ping the default gateway (router) then a machine on the remote network. You can also ping DNS names (PING gtslearning.com for example) or FQDNs (PING sales.gtslearning.com for instance). This will not work if a DNS server is not available. Type PING /? to view available switches.

If PING is successful, it responds with the message **Reply from *IP Address*** and statistics. If PING is unsuccessful, one of two messages are commonly received:

- **Destination unreachable** - there is no routing information (that is, the local computer does not know how to get to that IP address). If the host is on the same network, check physical cabling, infrastructure devices such as the switch, and TCP/IP configuration. If the host is on another network, check the TCP/IP configuration and router.

- **No reply (Request timed out)** - the host is unavailable or cannot route a reply back to your computer. If the host is running, try using TRACERT (see below).

Ping can be used with a number of switches. You can adjust the TTL (-i) and timeout (-w) and force the use of IPv4 (-4) or IPv6 (-6) when pinging by host name. With IPv4, you can also use loose (-j) or strict (-k) source routing (sending packets via a predetermined route). The -a switch performs name resolution. Also, -t continues to ping host until interrupted (CTRL+C).

Two other switches are used to test the MTU path between two hosts. Each host and any intermediate routers and network segments are configured with a maximum packet size (Message Transfer Unit [MTU]). Normally, when a router receives a packet that is too big, it responds with an error message. Some routers may not respond correctly or a firewall may block the error message, and so packets sent via that route are lost.

You can use ping with the -f and -l *nn* switches to simulate packets with a given MTU and therefore work out the maximum permissible packet size. The -f switch prevents routers from fragmenting the packets (breaking them into smaller chunks) and the -l switch sets the size of the packet in bytes. When working out the size to send, you need to know the smallest MTU used along the network path. For Ethernet, this is 1500 bytes but on a WAN it may be less. You then need to subtract 28 bytes from that number as this is the size of the ICMP packet itself. Therefore, to test an Ethernet path, you would enter: PING *x.x.x.x* -f -l 1472.

© 2010 gtslearning   IT Career FastTrack with CompTIA A+ Certification   Page 607

TRACERT

The **TRACERT** command line utility is part of the TCP/IP protocol suite. It is used to trace the route a packet of information takes to get to its target. For example, you might type the following: **TRACERT 10.0.0.1**

This command would return details of the route taken to find the machine or device with the IP address of 10.0.0.1. TRACERT can also be used with a domain name or FQDN, such as: **TRACERT gtslearning.com**

If the host cannot be located, the command will eventually timeout but it will return every router that was attempted.

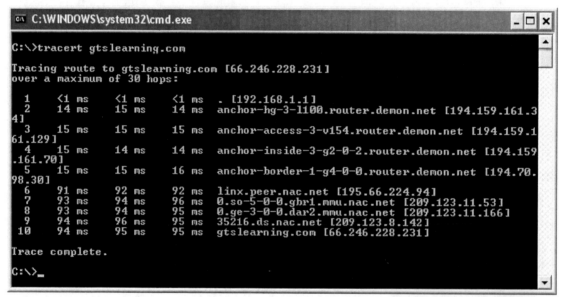

Using TRACERT

The output shows the number of hops, the ingress interface of the router or host (that is, the interface from which the router receives the ICMP packet), and the time taken to respond to each probe in milliseconds (ms).

You can use the **-d** switch to suppress name resolution, **-h** to specify the maximum number of hops (the default is 30), and **-w** to specify a timeout in milliseconds (the default is 4000). The **-j** option allows you to specify preferred routers (loose source routing).

> **Note**
> PING and TRACERT use Internet Control Message Protocol (ICMP) traffic. A firewall may be configured to block this traffic to prevent network snooping.

Module 5 Networks and Printing | Troubleshooting Network Links

Troubleshooting DNS with NSLOOKUP

If you identify a problem with name resolution, you can troubleshoot DNS with the **NSLOOKUP** command, either interactively or from the command prompt.

- **NSLOOKUP** *ComputerName* -*DNSServer* -option

ComputerName can be either a host name or an IP address. *DNSServer* is the DNS server to use (the default DNS server is used if this argument is omitted). **-option** is an NSLOOKUP subcommand. Refer to Windows Help for more information on NSLOOKUP subcommands.

NSLOOKUP can perform specific query types and output the result to a text file for analysis. If you do not use any arguments, NSLOOKUP is started in *interactive* mode.

Some items to remember about interactive mode:

- To interrupt interactive commands at any time, press **CTRL+C**.

- To view subcommands, type **HELP** or **?**.

```
C:\WINDOWS\system32\cmd.exe - nslookup

Microsoft Windows XP [Version 5.1.2600]
(C) Copyright 1985-2001 Microsoft Corp.

C:\Documents and Settings\James Pengelly>nslookup
Default Server:
Address:  192.168.1.1

> set querytype=mx
> microsoft.com
Server:
Address:  192.168.1.1

Non-authoritative answer:
microsoft.com    MX  preference = 10, mail exchanger = mailb.microsoft.com
microsoft.com    MX  preference = 10, mail exchanger = mailc.microsoft.com
microsoft.com    MX  preference = 10, mail exchanger = maila.microsoft.com

mailc.microsoft.com        internet address = 131.107.115.214
mailc.microsoft.com        internet address = 205.248.106.32
maila.microsoft.com        internet address = 205.248.106.64
maila.microsoft.com        internet address = 131.107.115.212
mailb.microsoft.com        internet address = 205.248.106.30
mailb.microsoft.com        internet address = 131.107.115.215
>
```

Using nslookup to discover mail (MX) records for a domain

- By default, host name (A) records will be returned; use the **set type=xx** command to display different records (for example, **set type=mx** returns mail server records for the domain).

- To exit, type **EXIT**.

© 2010 gtslearning | IT Career FastTrack with CompTIA A+ Certification | Page 609

Unit 5.5   Module 5 Networks and Printing

- To treat a built-in command as a computer name, precede it with the escape character (\\).

- An unrecognized command is interpreted as a computer name.

HOSTS and LMHOSTS files

Prior to the use of DNS servers, name resolution was performed using a file containing name to IP address mappings. An example HOSTS file would contain entries such as:

```
# Example HOSTS file - this line is a comment
128.103.100.1        toad
178.143.216.47       ratty
12.11.97.104         mole
```

HOSTS is still sometimes used to troubleshoot name resolution services. If you suspect a name resolution problem, you can add the IP address mapping to the file; if you can then ping by host name, it suggests a problem with the DNS server.

The LMHOSTS file performs the same function for NetBIOS (WINS) name resolution.

The files are stored in **%SystemRoot%\System32\Drivers\etc**.

The files are also a target of malware or attackers attempting to compromise the computer (administrative privileges are required to modify them). An attacker could place a malicious IP to name mapping in HOSTS to perform a "pharming" attack (attempting to harvest logon details using a counterfeit website).

NETSTAT

NETSTAT can be used to investigate connections on your machine. These connections are established by checking for ports which are active, or merely listening for connection attempts. The following switches can be used:

- **-a** displays all the connections and listening ports.

- **-e** displays Ethernet statistics.

- **-n** displays port's number in numerical format.

Page 610   IT Career FastTrack with CompTIA A+ Certification   © 2010 gtslearning

- **-p** *proto* displays ports by protocol (TCP or UDP).
- **-r** shows the routing table.
- **-s** shows per protocol statistics.

The utility can also be set to run in the background by entering **NETSTAT** *nn*, where *nn* is the refresh interval in seconds (press **CTRL+C** to stop).

Displaying open connections with NETSTAT

Summary

Make sure you know the main tools used to troubleshoot physical network connections, including inspecting product indicators such as LEDs. Adapters have a Status information page allowing you to check the connection speed and address parameters (plus signal strength for a wireless adapter).

You can use a number of command utilities to test and troubleshoot TCP/IP. Make sure you know when and how to use each of these utilities.

Tip
To review what you have learned in this chapter, you should now visit the course website. This contains review questions and bonus material to help you to learn more and practice the topics covered in this unit.

Unit 5.6 | Module 5 Networks and Printing

Unit 5.6 Troubleshooting Network Applications

CompTIA A+ Essentials Objectives

☐ **701.3.2 Given a scenario, demonstrate proper use of user interfaces**
Command prompt utilities (TELNET)

CompTIA A+ Practical Application Objectives

☐ **702.2.1 Select the appropriate commands and options to troubleshoot problems**
NET

☐ **702.3.1 Troubleshoot client-side connectivity issues using appropriate tools**
TCP/IP settings (NAT [private and public]) • Mail protocol settings (SMTP, IMAP, POP) • FTP settings (Ports, IP addresses, Exceptions, Programs) • Proxy settings (Ports, IP addresses, Exceptions, Programs) • Tools - use and interpret results (NET USE, NET /?, TELNET, SSH) • Secure connection protocols (SSH, HTTPS) • Firewall settings (Open and closed ports, Program filters)

☐ **702.3.2 Install and configure a Small Office Home Office (SOHO) network**
Connection types (Routers / Access Points [Firewall], Basic VoIP [consumer applications] • Basics of hardware and software firewall configuration (Port assignment / setting up rules (exceptions), Port forwarding / port triggering)

Troubleshooting Client Connectivity

The TCP/IP and Microsoft utilities listed in unit 5.5 can be used to troubleshoot many low-level connectivity issues. For example, you can use PING and TRACERT to ensure a link is up-and-running, IPCONFIG to check the client configuration, and NETSTAT to investigate what connections (ports) are open.

Many client issues however are ones of configuration. You may need to investigate settings in the application itself to diagnose and solve the problem.

Troubleshooting Firewalls

A firewall restricts access to a computer or network to a defined list of hosts and applications. Basic **packet filtering** firewalls work on the basis of filtering network data packets as they try to pass *into* or *out of* the machine. Filters can be applied to IP addresses, to TCP or UDP ports (for applications such as HTTP or SMTP), or to executable files installed on the local machine.

Page 612 | IT Career FastTrack with CompTIA A+ Certification | © 2010 gtslearning

A more advanced firewall (**stateful inspection**) can analyze the *contents* of network data packets (so long as they are not encrypted) and block them if any suspicious signatures are detected and identify *patterns* of activity.

A **hardware** firewall is a dedicated router appliance with the firewall installed as **firmware**. A **software** firewall is installed as an application on a workstation or server. Hardware firewalls are generally more secure. A software firewall is exposed to attacks on the underlying operating system (though hardware firewall firmware can contain vulnerabilities too). Most DSL routers also feature a built-in firewall, configured via the web management interface.

Configuring a firmware-type firewall on a 3Com ADSL router

An organization may deploy one or more hardware or software firewalls at strategic locations on the network to filter traffic. The most obvious location for a hardware firewall is between the private network and the internet[264]. A simple **personal** firewall may be installed on a local machine to protect it. Windows XP and Vista both feature such a firewall. There are also numerous third-party personal firewalls.

---

[264] There are lots of ways of configuring firewalls for network protection. The simplest is a single firewall router that manages the transfer of traffic between the public (internet) and private networks. More advanced configurations create some sort of Demilitarized Zone (DMZ) of semi-trusted hosts that require internet connectivity. This configuration can be accomplished using more than one firewall router or a multi-homed router (one with more than one network adapter).

Configuring SOHO router firewalls

SOHO routers may come with quite sophisticated firewalls. For example, the one shown below supports Denial of Service (DoS) detection (DoS is a type of attack aiming to disrupt a router by overloading it), content filtering (blocking sites based on filters for foul language, obscenity, excessive advertising, and so on), URI filtering, and time-of-day connection restrictions.

However, the core function of a firewall is its **Access Control List (ACL)**. This specifies inbound and outbound rules allowing or denying particular applications (as identified by their port number) to contact particular hosts (as identified by their IP address). In this firewall, inbound rules are configured on the Server Control tab while outbound rules are configured on the PC Privileges tab.

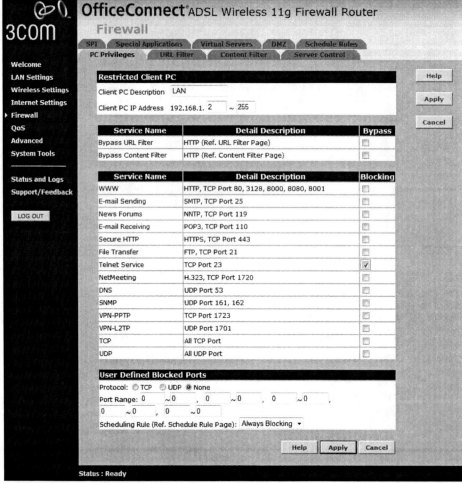

Configuring client access (outbound) permissions (access to Telnet has been blocked but all other ports are permitted)

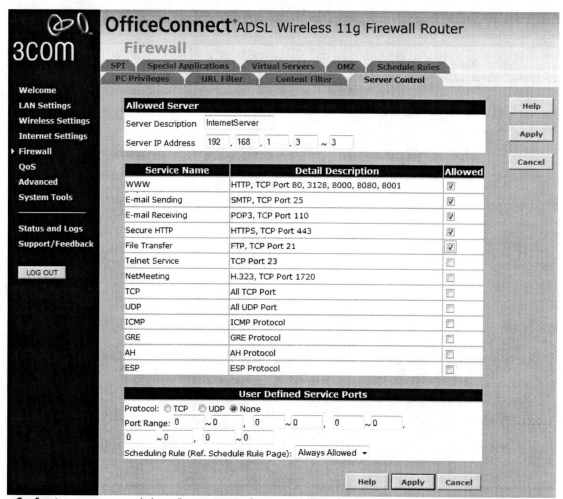

Configuring server access (inbound) permissions (access to HTTP, SMTP, POP3, HTTPS, and FTP are permitted but all other ports are blocked)

Network Address Translation

One of the functions of a router firewall is to translate between the private addressing used on the LAN and the public scheme used on the internet. The router converts the client's private IP address into a valid public address using **Network Address Translation (NAT)**. As well as making IP configuration easier, this protects the clients in the local network from direct access across the internet (all traffic has to be channeled through the router).

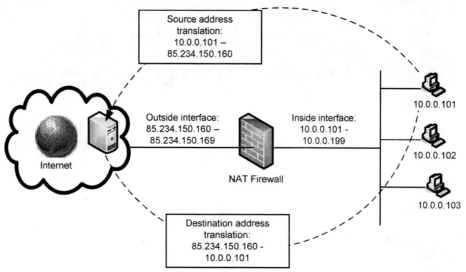

Network Address Translation

A typical SOHO router uses a type of NAT called **Port Address Translation**. The ISP typically allocates a single IP address to the subscriber, which is assigned to the router's external interface. When an internal client connects to the internet, the router assigns the connection a port number and uses that to track the connection.

For example, say two hosts (10.0.0.101 and 10.0.0.102) initiate a web connection at the same time. The NAT service creates two new port mappings for these requests (10.0.0.101:61101 and 10.0.0.102:61102). It then substitutes the private IP for the public IP and forwards the requests to the public internet. It performs a reverse mapping on any traffic returned using those ports, inserting the original IP address and port number, and forwarding the packets to the internal host.

Port forwarding / port triggering

When NAT is deployed, hosts on the internet can only "see" the router and its public IP address. If you want to run some sort of server application from your network and make it accessible to the internet, you need to set up **port forwarding**. Port forwarding means that the router takes requests from the internet for a particular application (say, HTTP / port 80) and sends them to a designated host on the LAN.

In our router / firewall example, this is configured on the **Virtual Servers** tab:

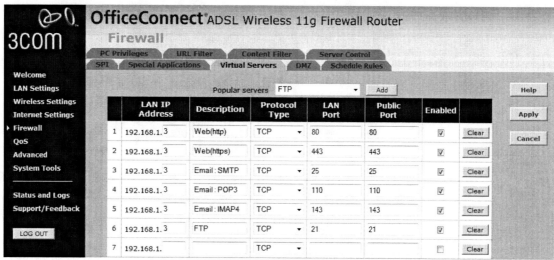

Configuring port forwarding for various applications

Port triggering is used to set up applications that require more than one port. Basically, when the firewall detects activity on outbound port A destined for a given external IP address, it opens inbound access for the external IP address on port B for a set period.

Configuring and troubleshooting software firewalls

A **software** (or **personal**) firewall might be deployed instead of or in addition to the network (router) firewall. Having two firewalls is more secure; if one firewall is not working or misconfigured, the other firewall might prevent an intrusion. The downside is complexity; you must configure rules in two places and there are two things that could be blocking communications when you come to troubleshoot connections.

Windows XP SP2 and Windows Vista ship with a personal firewall that can manage inbound connections. Most anti-virus software also ships with a firewall, some of which may enable rules for both inbound and outbound traffic, or you can just configure outbound rules on the router firewall.

> **Note**
> Do not enable more than one personal firewall. A personal firewall combined with a network firewall can work well but two personal firewalls will not.

Open the **Windows Firewall** applet in Control Panel to configure it. The firewall can be enabled or disabled on a per-connection basis. The **Exceptions** tab lets you configure which application processes (**program filters**) or network ports are permitted to accept connections from the internet. When a new program attempts to accept an internet connection, a warning is displayed prompting the user to allow or block the program.

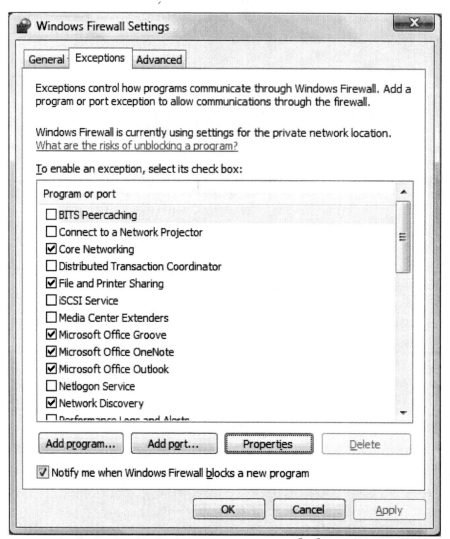

Configuring Windows Firewall

Tip

In Vista, the firewall is automatically configured depending on the type of network you specify a link as. A public network means that file sharing and computer discovery are disabled while a private network means they will be enabled by default.

> **Note**
>
> In order to work properly, a personal firewall needs to be bound to the network connection. If you open the connection properties, you will see the firewall service as a checked item. Do not uncheck it!

The **Advanced** tab allows you to enable or disable the firewall on specified network connections and set up features such as logging or allowing troubleshooting tools (ICMP) to work.

Windows Vista Advanced Firewall

As mentioned above, the basic Windows Firewall can be configured to block inbound connections. Windows Vista ships with an add-in to the basic firewall (**Windows Firewall with Advanced Security**) that allows configuration of outbound filtering (as well as IPsec connection security and additional monitoring tools).

The Advanced Firewall can be configured through group policy on a domain; on a standalone workstation or workgroup, open the **wf.msc** management console (or enter "firewall" at the Search box).

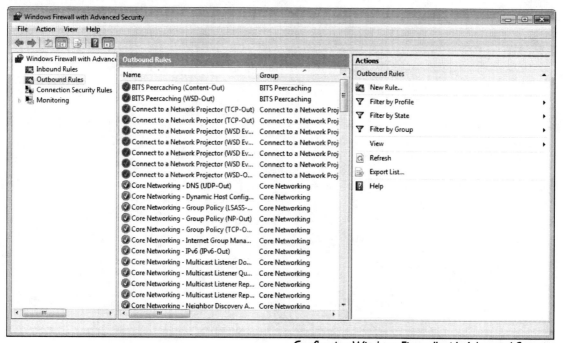

Configuring Windows Firewall with Advanced Security

| Unit 5.6 | Module 5 Networks and Printing |

Troubleshooting firewall configuration

If a network application is not working, one of the first things to check is whether a firewall at some point in the communications path is blocking access. Remember that access could be restricted because of the IP address, the type of application (port), or some characteristic of the data exchanged. Refer to the documentation for the firewall to work out how to configure its **Access List**.

With Windows Firewall, you would check that the program that is not working is listed and checked under the **Exceptions** tab. If it is not listed, click **Add Program** or **Add Port** as appropriate to allow access.

Network Address Translation (NAT) does not work well with some protocols (notably active FTP and the security protocol IPsec). These are not typically major issues for most subscribers and some routers have functionality to mitigate the problems (NAT Traversal).

Well-known ports

You should make sure you know the "well-known" default ports for TCP/IP applications. Some of the "well-known" port numbers are listed below:

Port Number	Process Name	Description
20	FTPDATA	File Transfer Protocol - Data
21	FTP	File Transfer Protocol - Control
22	SSH	Secure Shell
23	TELNET	Telnet
25	SMTP	Simple Mail Transfer Protocol
53	DNS	Domain Name Service
80	HTTP	HTTP
110	POP3	Post Office Protocol version 3
139	NetBIOS	Session port
143	IMAP4	Internet Mail Access Protocol
443	HTTPS	HTTP Secure
465	SMTPS	SMTP Secure
990	FTPS	FTP Secure
993	IMAPS	IMAP Secure
995	POP3S	POP3 Secure
3389	RDP	Remote Desktop Protocol

| Module 5 Networks and Printing | Troubleshooting Network Applications |

Troubleshooting Web Browsers

A **Web Browser** is required to access Web pages. A Web Browser is a software package that can retrieve and display information that has been formatted using HTML from an HTTP server.

Internet Explorer is by far the most popular web browser, but that popularity means that it is targeted ruthlessly by security researchers and hackers. This attention has led to a continual stream of security updates and patches to fix bugs and vulnerabilities.

Other web browsers, notably Firefox, Safari, Chrome, and Opera, are growing in popularity. However, inconsistent standards support in IE for things like CSS and Dynamic HTML[265] mean that many websites only support IE and using a different browser causes formatting problems[266].

As well as displaying Web pages, browsers have evolved to include support for additional internet services. A user can send and receive email, transfer files from an FTP server, and participate in newsgroups through the browser.

Connecting using a proxy server

Many companies use a **proxy server** as a gateway to and from the internet. A proxy server can be used to improve both performance and security. User machines pass internet requests to the proxy server, which forwards them to the ISP. The proxy may also cache pages and content that is requested by multiple clients, reducing bandwidth.

If a client cannot connect and a proxy server is deployed on the network, check that the browser is configured to use the proxy:

1. Open **Internet Options** and click the **Connections** tab.

    If a machine is connecting over the network, the **Never dial a connection** option should be selected. Otherwise, check that the dial-up connection is properly configured and that either **Dial whenever a network connection is not present** or **Always dial my default connection** are selected.

---

[265] CSS stands for Cascading Style Sheets; these and dynamic HTML are used to provide better formatting and interactivity than is available with ordinary HTML tags.

[266] Internet Explorer 8 has better standards support; in fact it includes a compatibility mode to display sites designed for IE6/7 properly!

| © 2010 gtslearning | IT Career FastTrack with CompTIA A+ Certification | Page 621 |

2. To configure a proxy server, click **LAN Settings**.

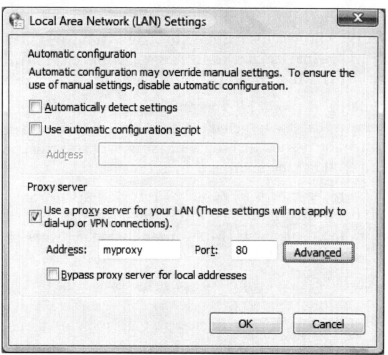

Configuring proxy internet access

3. If the proxy is configured to broadcast its settings, check the **Automatically detect settings** box. Otherwise, check **Use a proxy server**. Enter the IP address or name of the proxy server and other settings required.

4. Check the **Bypass proxy server for local addresses** if the proxy does not serve web pages on your local network (intranet).

5. If you want to specify different proxy servers for different applications (FTP or HTTPS for instance), click **Advanced**.

You can also use the **Advanced** dialog to configure exceptions - these would also need to be set up on the proxy server as allowing local access.

Tip
You can use the same sort of procedure for an application that uses different protocols through a proxy. For example, you can configure Windows Media Player to use a proxy server for streaming media protocols (RTSP) using Tools > Options > Network.

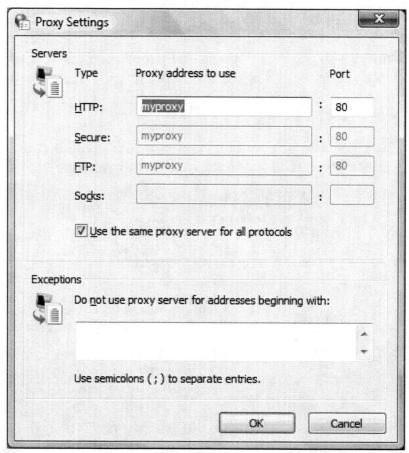

Advanced proxy settings

Configuring web browser security

The web browser (and in particular Internet Explorer) is one of the most well exploited *vectors* for infecting a system with malware or stealing information. As well as faults in the browser software itself, **web applications** can be vulnerable to faults in web server and database software and poor programming practice.

The following notes discuss Internet Explorer version 8 but the same general principles can be applied to securing other browsers.

Security zones

Protecting a computer against malicious use of web content means deactivating the use of such content on web pages or at least warning that some level of threat is present. However, this means that some websites may not display correctly.

Internet Explorer has a system of **zones**, for which you can set different security levels. The four security zones are as follows:

Use This Zone		To
	Internet	Browse safely with warnings when sites contain potentially unsafe content.
	Trusted Internet	Set minimum or no security protection.
	Restricted Internet	Set the highest level of security and prevent any active content from running.
	Intranet	Browse safely on a local network, with warnings when pages contain potentially unsafe content.

By default, all pages outside the local subnet appear in the **Internet** zone. You have to add sites to the **Trusted** and **Restricted** zones. The **Status** bar displays the icon for the zone you are currently browsing.

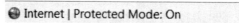

Security zone (Internet) shown on Status bar; the icon to the right shows whether items on the page that collect data about sites you have visited have been blocked

The following types of web page content could put a computer or data at risk while browsing the internet or because of downloading files.

Content	Description
.NET Framework, ActiveX Controls, Java, Scripting	These are used to provide interactive content and navigation tools on websites. You should disable this type of content on sites you do not trust.
Miscellaneous (Launch / Download files)	You may want to prevent programs from being downloaded or executed automatically, as such files could contain viruses.

By default, the Internet zone uses **Medium-High** settings. This blocks any active content that is unsigned (see "Digital Certificates" below) and prompts before running any potentially unsafe content.

To add sites to a particular zone or change the default settings, click the **Tools** button and select **Internet Options**. Click the **Security** tab.

Select the zone (**Trusted** or **Restricted**) to which you want to add a website, click the **Sites** button, and enter the address of the website.

Drag the slider or click the **Custom level** button to change the security settings for a zone.

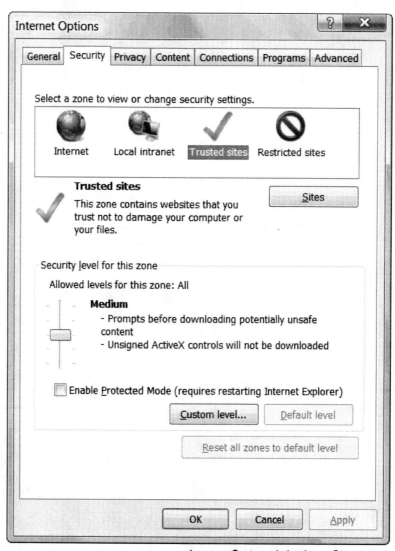

Internet Options dialog box - Security tab

Tip
When content is blocked, an Information Bar is displayed below the page tab. This informs that content has been blocked and may give an option to override the blocking.

Controlling cookies, pop-ups, and AutoComplete

Some websites collect information about you when you visit the site and store the data in a text file on your computer (a **cookie**). Such information might consist of which pages you visit and text you type into forms.

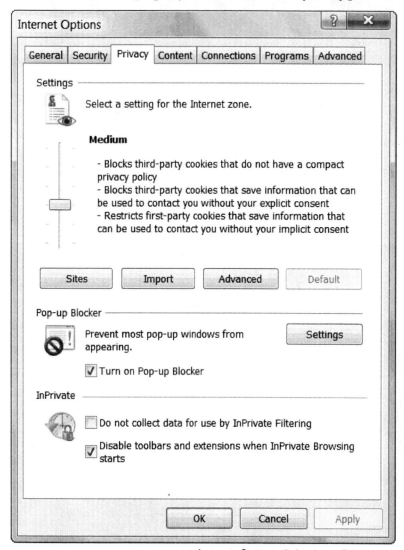

Internet Options dialog box - Privacy tab

Cookies cannot be used to spread viruses. However, you may prefer not to have this information stored on your computer. You can control the use of cookies by the websites you visit.

Use the **Privacy** tab in **Internet Options** to configure the cookie policy.

Drag the slider to set the level of privacy you want[267].

---

[267] These settings only affect the Internet zone. Internet Explorer blocks all cookies from sites in the Restricted zone and accepts all cookies from sites in the Trusted and Intranet zones.

Select	To
Block All Cookies	Prohibit use of new and existing cookies.
High	Block cookies from sites that do not have a compact privacy policy (that is, a privacy policy that is automatically readable by Internet Explorer). Also blocks cookies that store information that could identify you (such as your name or email address), unless the site prompts you to allow this.
Medium High	Much the same as above, but distinguishes between first-party and third-party cookies. Third-party cookies are created by or send data to a site other than the one you are viewing.
Medium / Low	Generally allows the use of first-party cookies. Third-party cookies are restricted but not blocked.
Accept All Cookies	Allow use of all cookies.

The new settings only affect the creation of new cookies. If you have visited sites using different settings, some cookies may already be stored on your computer. If you restrict cookies, a **Privacy Report** icon is displayed on the **Status** bar when cookies are blocked. Double-click the icon to see which cookies have been restricted.

You can also use this dialog to enable and configure the browser's pop-up blocker.

Another privacy issue is that Internet Explorer can be set to store information typed into forms, including passwords, and retains a history of browsed pages. Any user using a publicly accessible computer should be trained to check these settings and to clear the browser cache before logging off.

To configure whether form data is saved, click the **Settings** button next to **AutoComplete** on the **Content** tab of **Internet Options**.

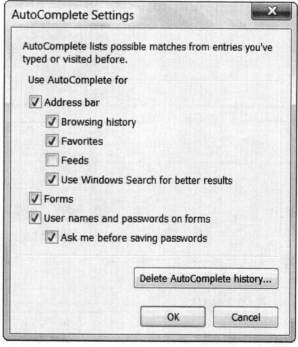

AutoComplete settings

You can check or uncheck the boxes to configure AutoComplete behavior and click the **Delete AutoComplete history** button to clear the cache.

To delete the browser history and cache, on the **General** tab, click **Delete**[268]. Check the items you want to get rid of then click **Delete**.

Tip
You can also use Internet Explorer's InPrivate mode, which deletes the cache automatically when you close the browser. Press CTRL+SHIFT+P or click the **Safety** button to start an InPrivate session.

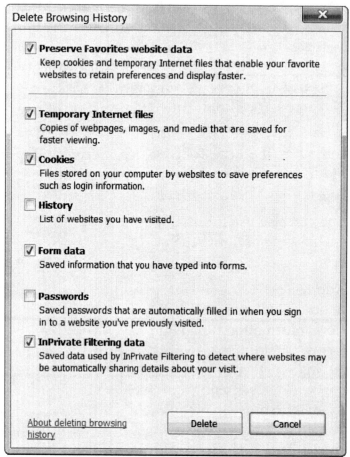

Clearing the browser cache

Digital certificates

When a web browser communicates with a secure (HTTPS) server, it installs the server's certificate to use its public key to encrypt communications[269]. Having a certificate is not in itself any proof of identity however.

---

[268] On this page you can also click the Settings button to configure the location of the cache file and how much disk space it can consume. It also allows you to view and delete any ActiveX objects that have been installed.

The browser and server rely upon a third-party - the Certificate Authority (CA) - to vouch for the server's identity. This framework is called **Public Key Infrastructure (PKI)**.

Internet Explorer is pre-installed with a number of **root certificates** that are automatically trusted[270]. These represent the commercial CAs that grant certificates to most of the companies that do business on the web.

When the user browses a site containing a new certificate (or attempts to run an application that has been signed using a code-signing certificate), Windows displays the certificate information and prompts the user whether to trust the certificate or not. If the certificate is trusted, it is added to the certificate store.

When you browse a site using a certificate, Windows displays the information about the certificate in the address bar:

- If the certificate is trusted, a padlock icon is shown. Click the icon to view information about the certificate and the Certificate Authority guaranteeing it.

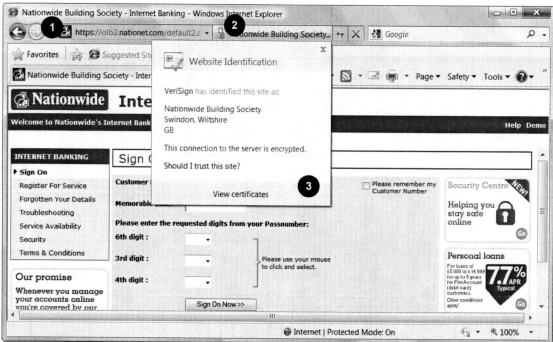

Browsing a secure site: 1) Check the domain name as highlighted in the address bar; 2) Only enter confidential data into a site using a certificate; 3) Click the padlock to view information about the certificate holder and the CA that issued it

---

[269] Remember that the public key cannot be used to decrypt a message. Only the linked private key can be used to do that. The private key must be kept secret.

[270] Root certificate updates are provided via Windows Update.

- If the certificate is highly trusted, the address bar is colored green. High assurance certificates go through an (even) more rigorous identity validation procedure.

- If the certificate is untrusted, the address bar is colored maroon and the site is blocked by a warning message. If you want to trust the site anyway, click through the warning.

> **Note**
> Digital certificates are also used to verify the identity of software publishers. If a certificate has not been issued by a one of the trusted root CAs, Windows will warn you that the publisher cannot be verified when you try to install an add-on or other type of application.

You can view, add, and remove certificates from the store using Internet Explorer. From the **Internet Options** dialog, click the **Content** tab, then select the **Certificates** button[271].

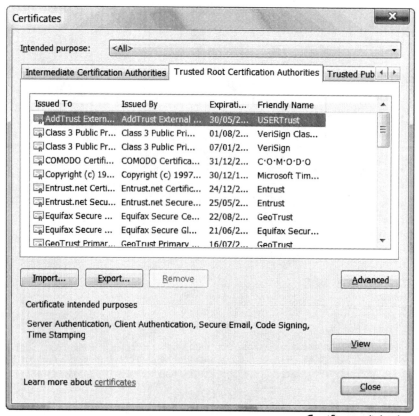

Certificates dialog box

---

[271] In Vista, you have to start Internet Explorer in administrator mode to install a certificate. To do this, alt-click the shortcut and select Run as administrator.

Module 5 Networks and Printing   *Troubleshooting Network Applications*

From here you can view (double-click), import, and remove certificates[272]. They are grouped by category using the tabbed headings (use the arrow buttons to navigate left and right). Note that the **Untrusted Publishers** tab is populated with any certificates that the user has chosen not to trust.

Anti-phishing controls

Another important step in validating the identity of a site is to confirm its domain name. One **phishing** trick is to use well-known subdomains as part of the address. For example, "amazon.phishing.com" has nothing to do with "amazon.com" but may fool the unwary into thinking it does. Internet Explorer highlights the registered domain part of the address so that you can verify it.

Internet Explorer also includes a phishing filter (SmartScreen), enabled by default, that blocks known phishing sites. If you suspect a site, you can select **SmartScreen Filter** from the **Safety** button and run a check on the site; you can also report suspected phishing sites.

Troubleshooting Email Clients

Email is a messaging system that can be used to transmit text messages and file attachments such as word processing documents, graphics, video, and sound. The client software sends a message to the mail server, using a protocol called **Simple Mail Transfer Protocol (SMTP)**, and the mail server forwards it to the recipient's mail server (using SMTP again). The server software does not *deliver* the messages to the client software for various reasons, such as:

- The recipient may not be logged on.

- The destination host may be turned-off.

Instead, mail is held in the mailbox on the mail server, waiting for the client to connect and pick it up. The SMTP protocol is not appropriate for this task; SMTP is only really useful for delivering mail to hosts that are permanently available and permanently connected to the network.

---

[272] As well as commercial third-party CAs, a Windows network might be set up with its own CA for issuing certificates for network use (smart card authentication, code-signing, and so on). A PC that is part of Active Directory will install certificates automatically but a computer outside AD might need them installing manually.

© 2010 gtslearning   IT Career FastTrack with CompTIA A+ Certification   Page 631

The protocols that provide mailbox access are the **Post Office Protocol (POP)** and the **Internet Mail Access Protocol (IMAP)**.

To configure an email account, you need the user name, password, and default email address, and incoming and outgoing server addresses from the ISP.

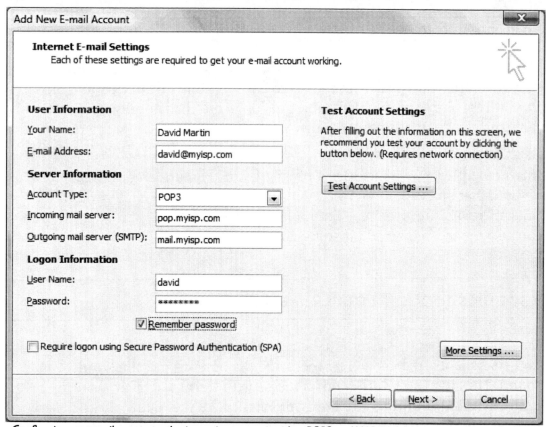

Configuring an email account - the incoming server is either POP3 or IMAP while the outgoing server is SMTP

To configure email access through a firewall, you should allow *outbound* connections to the mail server over port 25 (SMTP) and either port 110 (POP3) or port 143 (IMAP)[273].

> **Tip**
> POP3 is more widely implemented, but IMAP provides extra features, such as support for mail folders other than inbox on the server and calendar functionality.

---

[273] POP3S (port 995), IMAPS (port 993), and even SMTPS (port 465) can also be configured to run over SSL to make the connection secure.

Troubleshooting FTP

File Transfer Protocol (FTP) was one of the earliest protocols used on TCP/IP networks and the internet. The World Wide Web service has replaced most functions of FTP although only FTP allows you to copy files from a client computer to a server[274]. If your remote users need to do this, they must use FTP. FTP is also more efficient than HTTP for the transfer of files.

Also, if you have existing files that you want to make available to remote users, FTP is a simple service to install and maintain. Files made available through FTP can be in any format, including document, multimedia, or application files.

FTP clients

The FTP client may take a number of forms:

- Most installations of TCP/IP include a command line client interface. The commands PUT and GET are used to upload and download files respectively.

- Dedicated GUI clients allow you to connect to servers, browse directories and upload and download files.

- Internet browsers allow you to connect to an FTP service and download files. You use a **Uniform Resource Indicator (URI)** to connect to an FTP server; for example, **ftp://ftp.microsoft.com/**.

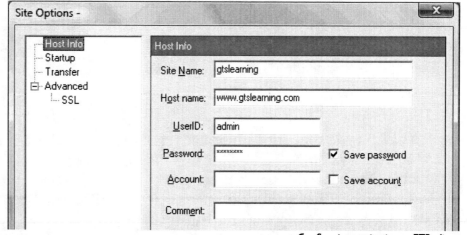

Configuring a site in an FTP client

---

[274] HTTP uploads can be facilitated using scripting or plug-ins.

Active versus passive FTP

A client connects to TCP port 21 on an FTP server (and a dynamically chosen high port number (N) on the client[275]). This **control port** is used to transfer commands and status information, but not for data transfer.

Data transfer can operate in one of two modes:

- In active mode, the client sends a PORT command specifying its chosen **data connection** port number (typically N+1) and the *server* opens the data connection between the chosen client port and port 20 on the server.

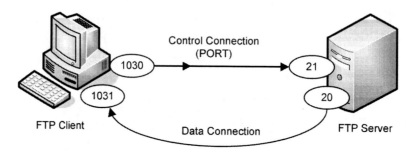

FTP in active mode

- In passive mode, the *client* opens a data port (again, typically N+1) and sends the PASV command to the server's control port. The server then opens a random high port number and sends it to the client using the PORT command. The *client* then initiates the connection between the two ports.

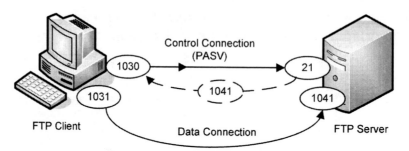

FTP in passive mode

Active FTP poses a configuration problem for some firewalls, as the server is initiating the inbound connection but there is no way of predicting which port number will be utilized. However, not all FTP servers and clients can operate in passive mode. If this is the case, check that firewalls installed between the client and server can support active FTP (stateful inspection firewalls).

---

[275] A high port number is 1024 or greater.

Module 5 Networks and Printing   Troubleshooting Network Applications

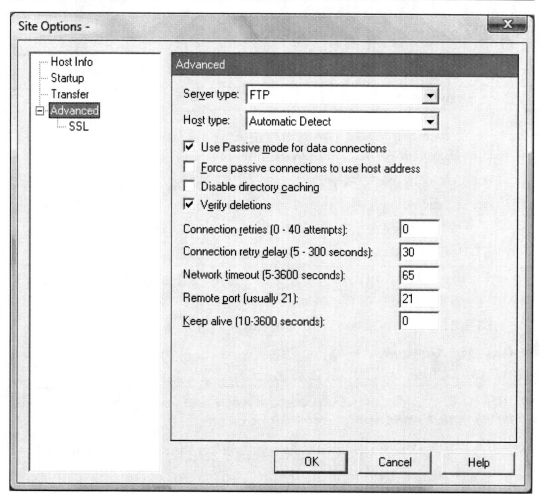

Configuring port and connection settings in an FTP client

Tip

Another problem is that the control connection can remain idle when the data connection is in use, meaning that the connection can be "timed out" by the firewall (or other routing device).

Unit 5.6   Module 5 Networks and Printing

NET, Telnet, and Secure Shell (SSH)

NET commands

There are a number of **NET** command utilities that can be used to view and configure shared resources on a Windows network.

- **NET USE** *DeviceName* *****ComputerName******ShareName* - connect to a network resource, such as a folder or printer. For example, to map the DATA folder on MyServer to the M: drive, you would enter:

    NET USE m: \\MyServer\data /persistent:yes

To redirect print output sent to LPT2 to a printer shared as "OfficePrinter" from MyServer, you would enter:

    NET USE lpt2: \\MyServer\officeprinter /persistent:yes

- **NET USE** *DeviceName* **/delete** - remove a connection (**NET USE * /delete** removes all connections).

- **NET USE** - view connections on the local computer; use **NET USE** *****ComputerName* to view connections on another computer.

- **NET VIEW ***ComputerName* - view shares on the specified computer.

- **NET STOP** *Service* - stops the named service. For example, to stop the printer service, you would enter:

    NET STOP spooler

- **NET START** *Service* - starts the named service.

- **NET PRINT ***ComputerName******QueueName* - shows the named print queue.

More uses of the commands listed above as well as other commands can be investigated using the online help (**NET HELP**).

The **netsh** commands are also enormously useful for configuring Windows network services and clients via the command line.

Page 636   IT Career FastTrack with CompTIA A+ Certification   © 2010 gtslearning

| Module 5 Networks and Printing | Troubleshooting Network Applications |

Telnet

Telnet is a command-line terminal emulation utility that supports a remote connection to another computer. When you connect, your computer acts as if your keyboard is attached to the remote computer and you can use the same commands as a local user.

One potential downside to Telnet is that you must know how to issue commands to the computer you have logged on to. The remote computer must also grant you access. In order to support Telnet access, the remote computer must run a service known as the Telnet Daemon. Under TCP/IP, this runs on TCP port 23. If you enter TELNET at a command prompt to start a new session, some of the basic commands you can use are listed below:

Command	Use
open *Host Port*	Starts a session with the host on that port. Host can either be a host name, FQDN, or IP address.
?	Displays help.
status	Check session status.
close	Ends the current session.
quit	Exits the telnet prompt.

One application of Telnet is router or switch configuration. The Telnet application is used to connect to the Telnet Daemon on the router and then command line instructions can be issued to configure it. However, as Telnet has no security mechanisms, other remote login and graphical management programs have largely replaced it.

Tip

Telnet is not installed by default in Windows Vista. You can add it using Programs and Features.

Telnet is sometimes still used for troubleshooting services such as SMTP or HTTP. For example, to connect to an SMTP server at the IP address 192.168.1.3 you would enter TELNET 192.168.1.3 25.

| © 2010 gtslearning | IT Career FastTrack with CompTIA A+ Certification | Page 637 |

| Unit 5.6 | Module 5 Networks and Printing |

```
Telnet vpc01                                                    _  □  X

220 vpc01 Microsoft ESMTP MAIL Service, Version: 6.0.2600.2180 ready at  Thu, 16
 Jul 2009 10:22:00 +0100
helo
250 vpc01 Hello [192.168.1.2]
mail from:test@domain.com
250 2.1.0 test@domain.com....Sender OK
rcpt to:user@myisp.com
250 2.1.5 user@myisp.com
data
354 Start mail input; end with <CRLF>.<CRLF>
subject:test message

Connectiivty test

250 2.6.0 <VPC01J5gjo17TdnfmYo00000001@vpc01> Queued mail for delivery
```

Telnet session with an SMTP server

SSH

Secure Shell (SSH) is an improvement on remote administration and file copy programs such as Telnet and FTP. SSH uses port 22. There are numerous commercial and open source SSH products available for all the major NOS platforms (UNIX, Linux, Windows, and Mac OS).

> **Tip**
>
> Windows Vista includes WinRS, which provides the same kind of secure remote command prompt as SSH.

Troubleshooting Voice-over-IP

Voice-over-IP (VoIP) packages voice communications as data packets, transmits them over the network, then reassembles the packets to provide two-way, real-time voice communication. The advantage of VoIP for general consumers is that the network providers have not yet found a model for charging "calls" placed in this way, though this situation is not likely to persist for too much longer. Another significant advantage (notably for call centre operations) is that data from calls can be recorded, tracked, routed, analyzed much more easily.

The main disadvantage of VoIP is that call quality can be patchy, especially if the network is congested (it is difficult to guarantee **Quality of Service [QoS]** over a public network such as the internet). There are a number of other drawbacks, including call security, compatibility with firewalls, making emergency calls, and integration with landline and cellphone networks.

Page 638   IT Career FastTrack with CompTIA A+ Certification   © 2010 gtslearning

There are numerous different ways of implementing VoIP, each with different protocols, which are often proprietary to a particular VoIP software vendor.

To implement VoIP to make calls from a computer in a typical Peer-to-Peer configuration, you need software (such as Skype) an internet connection, and usually a headset (more convenient than using PC microphone and speakers).

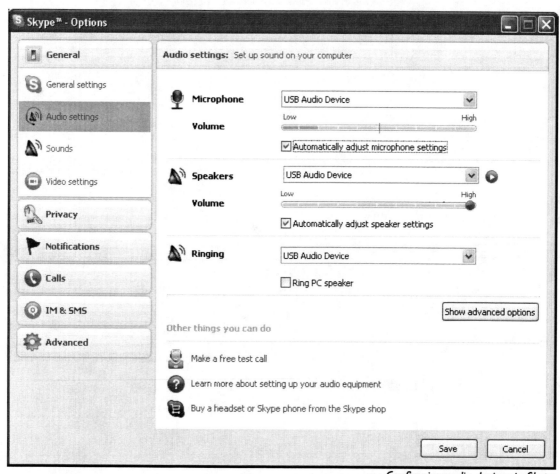

Configuring audio devices in Skype

You may also need to configure your firewall(s) to allow connections. If a proxy is deployed on the network, you can configure the VoIP application to communicate through it:

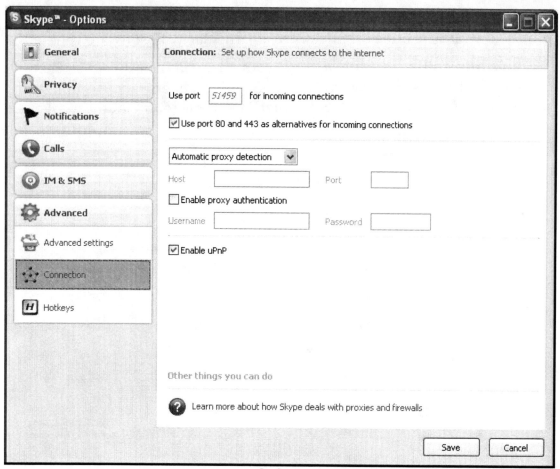

Configuring connection properties and proxy settings in Skype

VoIP calls can be placed from computer-to-computer or from computer-to-PSTN/cell phone. Calls can also be made from PSTN-to-computer, if a suitable access number is setup.

> **Tip**
> Only VoIP-to-VoIP calls are usually free from call charges. Receiving and making calls to and from traditional landlines and mobiles is chargeable.

VoIP call quality may be very badly affected if the network is busy (say, if one user is downloading a large file from the web at the same time as another user is making a call). You may be able to configure Quality of Service (QoS) on the router to prioritize the port used by the VoIP application over any other type of protocol.

Module 5 Networks and Printing　　　　　　　　　　　　　　Troubleshooting Network Applications

Calling a landline from Skype

On an enterprise level, many organizations have implemented VoIP using fully digital **Private Branch Exchanges (PBX)**[276].

Summary

Make sure you are familiar with the general procedures for configuring and troubleshooting firewalls and client applications (browsers, email software, FTP, and VoIP) plus the use of command tools to perform network administration (NET, Telnet, and SSH).

> **Tip**
> To review what you have learned in this chapter, you should now visit the course website. This contains review questions and bonus material to help you to learn more and practice the topics covered in this unit.

---

[276] The technology used to connect a business to the phone system and route calls within the organization.

Unit 5.7

Module 5 Networks and Printing

Unit 5.7 Configuring Malware Protection

CompTIA A+ Practical Application Objectives

☐ **702.4.1 Given a scenario, prevent, troubleshoot and remove viruses and malware**
Use anti-virus software • Identify malware symptoms • Quarantine infected systems • Research malware types, symptoms and solutions (virus encyclopedias) • Remediate infected systems • Update anti-virus software (Signature and engine updates, Automatic vs. manual) • Schedule scans • Repair boot blocks • Scan and removal techniques (Safe mode, Boot environment) • Educate end user

Malware Symptoms

Viruses are classified as software that attempts to self-replicate to other files, disks, computers, or networks. However, a virus's **payload** can be programmed to perform many different actions, so it is difficult to provide a definitive list of "virus"-like symptoms.

General symptoms

The following are examples of the symptoms that may indicate a virus infection:

- The computer fails to boot.

- Hard or floppy disks are reformatted.

- The file system becomes corrupt.

- The Master Boot Record (MBR) is corrupted.

- Individual files on hard drives or floppy disks may be corrupt.

- Date stamps and file sizes of infected files change.

- New executable files (EXEs and DLLS) appear in system folders.

- Strange messages or graphics appear on the screen.

- Security applications (anti-virus, firewall, Automatic Updates) stop working.

- Applications or Windows tools (Notepad for instance) stop working.

- Performance at startup or generally is very slow.

Page 642   IT Career FastTrack with CompTIA A+ Certification   © 2010 gtslearning

| Module 5 Networks and Printing | Troubleshooting Network Applications |

- Network performance is slow.

- Emails are sent automatically.

Any sort of activity or configuration change that was not initiated by the user is a good reason to suspect infection by a virus, worm, or Trojan.

Spyware, Adware, and the web browser

Malware often targets the web browser. Remember that malware is not always destructive. Malware such as adware and spyware is designed with commercial or criminal intent rather than to vandalize the computer system.

Common symptoms of infection by spyware or adware are pop-ups or additional toolbars[277], the home page or search provider changing suddenly, searches returning results that are different to other computers, slow performance, and excessive crashing (faults). Viruses and Trojans may spawn pop-ups without the user opening the browser.

Another symptom is redirection - this is where the user tries to open one page but gets sent to another. Often this may imitate the target page. In adware this is just a blunt means of driving traffic through a site, but spyware may exploit it to capture authentication details.

Software

Software other than Windows is often equally attractive for malware writers as not all companies are diligent in terms of secure coding. Software that uses browser plug-ins are often targeted; examples include Adobe's Reader software for PDFs and Flash Player.

If software from a reputable vendor starts crashing (faulting) repeatedly, suspect malware infection.

Trojans, rootkits, and botnets

Malware that tries to compromise the PC will try to create a communications channel with its "master". If the firewall is still working, you may see unfamiliar processes or ports trying to connect to the internet.

---

[277] The lines between useful utilities, adware, and spyware are not completely clear-cut but if something is there that the user (or IT department) did not explicitly sanction then it's best to get rid of it.

| © 2010 gtslearning | IT Career FastTrack with CompTIA A+ Certification | Page 643 |

| Unit 5.7 | Module 5 Networks and Printing |

> **Note**
>
> Remember that the most powerful malware can disguise its presence. For example, the NETSTAT utility shows ports open on the PC. A rootkit may replace NETSTAT with a modified version that does not show the ports in use by the rootkit.

One of the main criminal uses of Trojans is to install spamming software on the "zombie" PC. The software starts sending out spam emails. The software may do this surreptitiously to avoid detection; that is, it does not try to send thousands of messages in one go but a few messages every hour. Because the Trojan may have infected thousands or millions of PCs (a botnet), it is capable of delivering huge quantities of spam.

If a computer is being used to send out spam, the user is likely to receive bounces and non-deliverable messages from unknown recipients[278]. If the volume is large, they may receive complaints from other networks and from their ISP.

Another use of Trojans and rootkits is to scan other hosts for weaknesses and launch Denial of Service (DoS) attacks against networks. Most ISPs monitor the use of scanning tools and will warn you if they detect their use coming from your IP address.

> **Note**
>
> Trojans and rootkits are likely to try to disguise their presence. New breeds of rootkit try to occupy firmware for instance, so that not even shutting down the PC or re-formatting the hard drive will remove them. Sometimes the only way to diagnose such infections is to examine network traffic from the infected PC from a different machine.

| Virus alert hoaxes |

Hoax virus alerts are quite common. They are often sent as mass emails as a prank. Most advise you to forward the "alert" to everyone in your address book. Some hoax virus alerts describe a number of steps that you "must take" to remove the virus - following these steps may cause damage to your computer.

---

[278] This does not always indicate malware infection however; it could simply be that the spammer has spoofed the user's email address.

Information about virus hoax alerts from www.mcafee.com

If you have an anti-virus application, your anti-virus vendor may provide a virus alerting service. You can also check the vendor's site for a list of malware threats. You should use anti-virus software to remove a virus from an infected file. If anti-virus software does not work, you can look for further instructions from the vendor's website or contact your system administrator.

Researching malware

There are several websites dedicated to investigating the various new attacks that are developed against computer systems. Apart from the regular IT magazines, some good examples include www.cert.org, www.sans.org, www.schneier.com, and www.grc.com. The annual SANS "Top 20" security attack targets is one of the most useful starting points (www.sans.org/top20).

Anti-virus vendors also maintain malware encyclopedias ("bestiaries") with complete information about the type, symptoms, purpose, and removal of viruses, worms, Trojans, and rootkits.

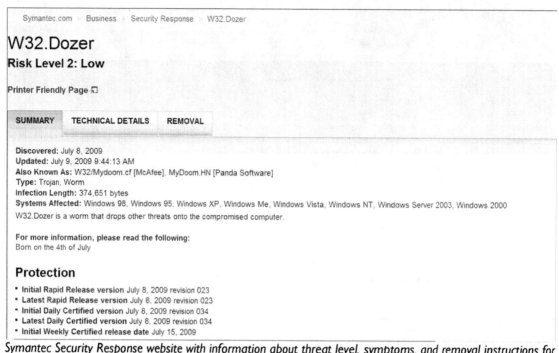

Symantec Security Response website with information about threat level, symptoms, and removal instructions for a typical worm

Preventing Malware Infections

There are numerous sources of malware infection[279], but the main ones are:

- Visiting "unsavory" websites with an unpatched browser, low security settings, and no anti-virus software.

- Opening links in unsolicited email.

- Infection from another compromised machine on the same network.

- Executing a file of unknown provenance - email attachments are still the most popular vector but others include file sharing sites, websites generally, attachments sent via chat / Instant Messaging, autorun USB sticks and CDs, and so on.

- Becoming victim to a "zero-day" exploit (that is, some infection mechanism that is unknown to software and anti-virus vendors).

A number of steps can be taken to reduce the risk and impact of malware infection:

---

[279] The route by which malware infects a computer is called the vector.

| Module 5 Networks and Printing | Troubleshooting Network Applications |

- Carry out regular backups that allow data to be recovered, in case of loss due to a virus infection.

- Apply operating system and application security patches.

- Do not allow users to bring in their own software programs. If necessary, measures such as removing (or disabling) drives can be used. Windows-based systems also allow the administrator to determine who can run new programs, install new software, or download files from the web. Use these rights effectively.

- Install and use an anti-virus package. The virus package must be kept up to date with updated **signatures** (or **definitions**), since viruses are continually being developed and the latest signatures offer the most protection.

- Select anti-virus software that scans automatically (on-access). This provides much more reliable protection against web and email attachment threats.

- Configure filtering on the messaging server - this will prevent most of the unsolicited messages (spam) arriving at the server from getting to the users' mailboxes.

- Do not log on with administrative privileges except where necessary. Limit administrative privileges to a few, selected accounts. Keep passwords for these accounts secure.

- Educate users about not running attachments - and supplement this with procedures that will prevent files, such as executables and Office macros, from being allowed to run. This could be accomplished (for instance) by only allowing digitally signed code to be executed.

- Audit system events (such as logons) and review logs for unusual activity.

- Establish a procedure for recovery following virus infection to minimize the spread and effect of a virus.

Routine procedures, such as applying critical and security patches to the OS and applications and updating virus definitions and malware threats in anti-virus software, should be automated where possible or performed according to a strict schedule. Try to find time to monitor security developments so that you are aware of new threat types and strategies or "zero-day" vulnerabilities (flaws that have not been fixed by a patch).

| Unit 5.7 | Module 5 Networks and Printing |

Training and educating users can be more problematic. You may well have to overcome resistance to end users accepting responsibility for security. The efforts of a single support technician are unlikely to make much difference. An organization needs to develop and enforce effective policies, backed up by disciplinary procedures to supplement training and education programs.

That said, there may be plenty of scope for you to educate users when you attend support incidents ("Once bitten, twice shy").

Anti-virus Software

Anti-virus (A-V) software uses a database of known virus patterns (**definitions**) plus **heuristic** malware identification techniques to try to identify infected files and prevent viruses from spreading. "Heuristic" means that the software uses knowledge of the sort of things that viruses do to try to spot (and block) virus-like behavior.

Typically the software is configured to run automatically when a user or system process accesses a file. The anti-virus software scans the file and blocks access if it detects anything suspicious. The user can then decide either to try to **disinfect** the file, **quarantine** it (block further access), or **delete** it.

The A-V scanner also runs at boot-time to prevent boot sector viruses from infecting the computer. Most types of software can also scan system memory (to detect worms), email file attachments, removable drives, and network drives.

The latest anti-virus software usually includes routines for detecting and removing Trojan software, as well as spam, adware, and spyware blockers.

More sophisticated viruses have mechanisms to try to defeat anti-virus software. Some examples of these strategies are:

- **Stealth** - the virus intercepts commands from anti-virus software and passes the software a clean version of the file; alternatively the virus may "jump" from file-to-file ahead of the virus scanner.

- **Modification** - anti-virus software mostly works by identifying known virus patterns (signatures). A polymorphic or metamorphic virus attempts to defeat this approach by changing itself (for example, by encrypting the virus code)[280].

---

[280] A metamorphic virus completely re-compiles itself to infect new files.

| Page 648 | IT Career FastTrack with CompTIA A+ Certification | © 2010 gtslearning |

Module 5 Networks and Printing   *Troubleshooting Network Applications*

- **Armor** - the virus code is protected, making it difficult for anti-virus software to analyze it.

- **Retrovirus** - the virus seeks to disable the anti-virus software.

- **Slow** and **sparse** infectors - these attempt to stay "under the radar" by replicating slowly.

The best anti-virus software contains routines to defeat these techniques.

Anti-virus (or anti-malware) software tends to come as either personal security suites, designed to protect a single host, or network security suites, designed to be centrally managed from a server console. Most anti-virus software is designed for Windows PCs and networks, as these are the systems targeted by most virus writers, but software is available for Linux and Apple Mac OS as well.

Some of the major vendors are Symantec (including the Norton brand), McAfee, Computer Associates (CA), Trend Micro (PC-cillin), Kaspersky, ESET (NOD32), and BitDefender.

Many anti-virus vendors offer applications that are specifically designed for the protection of organizations connected to the internet. For example, **Symantec Endpoint Protection** can be configured to download virus definitions and product updates to clients automatically, scan Microsoft Exchange and Lotus Notes messaging systems, and to protect against Trojans and spyware.

The following steps use Symantec Endpoint Protection as an example of scanning for viruses.

Scanning for viruses

1. Use the icon in the notification area (or Start menu) to open the anti-virus application.

2. Select the **Scan for threats** option then check the drives and/or folders that you want to scan.

3. You can choose between an "Active Scan" of commonly targeted folders and file types, a full scan, or a custom scan.

© 2010 gtslearning   IT Career FastTrack with CompTIA A+ Certification   Page 649

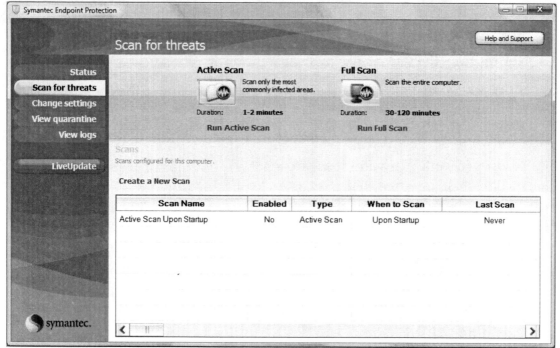

Symantec Endpoint Protection

On-access scanning

Almost all security software is now configured to scan **on-access**. This reduces performance somewhat but is essential to maintaining effective protection against malware.

> **Note**
> When configuring anti-virus software, it is vital to configure the proper exceptions. Real-time scanning of some system files and folders (notably those used by Windows Update) can cause serious performance problems.

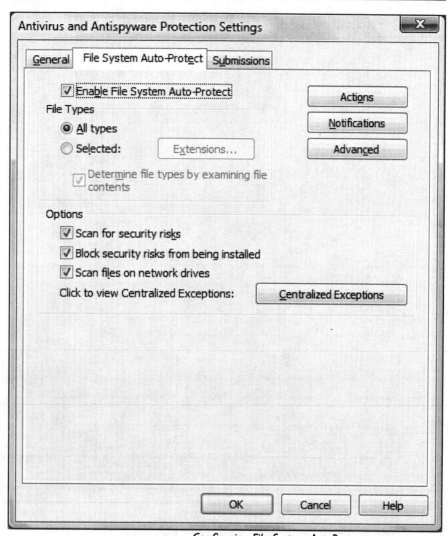

Configuring File System AutoProtect on-access scans

Note
Anti-virus software depends on services to run properly - make sure that these are not disabled.

Scheduled scans

Finally, all security software supports **scheduled scans**. These scans can seriously impact performance however, so it is best to run them when the computer is otherwise unused. Symantec Endpoint Protection performs an "Active Scan" at startup but the user can define any type of scan to run to a schedule of their own choosing:

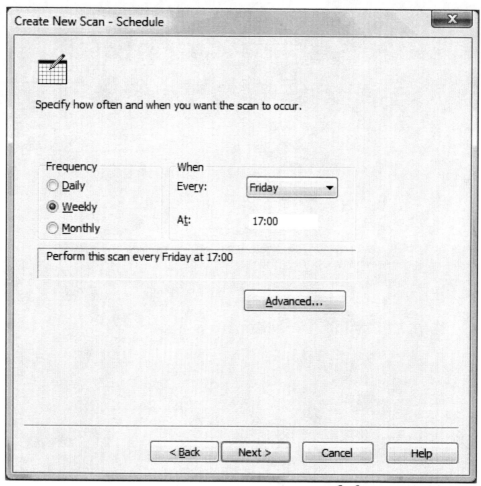

Configuring a scheduled scan

Updating anti-virus software

All anti-virus software must be updated regularly. Two types of update are generally necessary:

- Virus definitions / patterns - this is information about new viruses. These updates may be made available daily or weekly.
- Scan engine / components - this fixes problems or makes improvements to the scan software itself.

There is usually an option within the software program to download and install these updates automatically.

1. For example, with Symantec Endpoint Protection, click the **LiveUpdate** button from the status page.

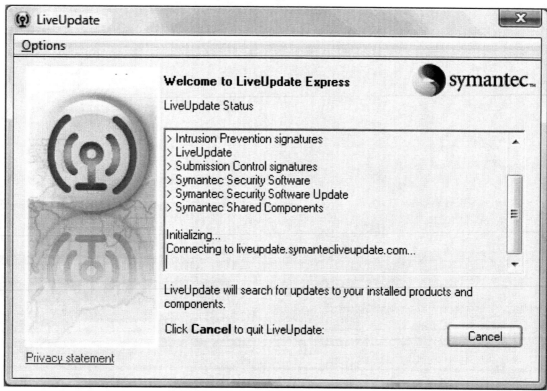

Symantec LiveUpdate

2. Follow the prompts to check the website for virus definition and program updates and download and install them.

Updates are also scheduled to take place daily by default, though this can be configured via the **Client Management** settings:

Note the options to retry and randomize the start time - this helps to ensure that an update will take place.

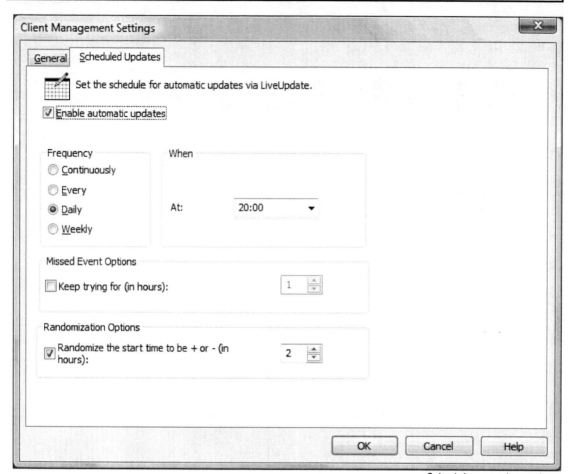

Scheduling regular updates

Quarantining and remediating infected systems

Malware such as worms propagate over networks. This means that one of the first actions should be to disconnect the network link.

If a file is infected with a virus, you can use anti-virus software to try to **remove** the infection (**cleaning**), **quarantine** the file (the anti-virus software blocks any attempt to open it), or **erase** the file. You can configure the action that software should attempt when it discovers malware as part of a scan:

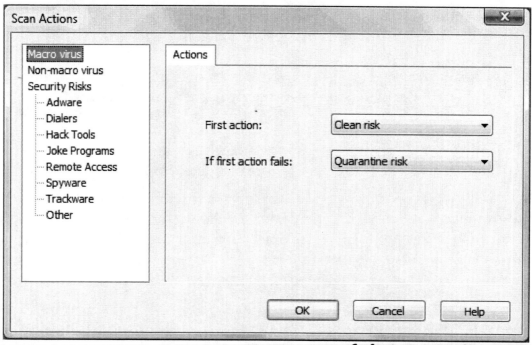

Configuring scan remediation options

Most of the time the software will detect the virus and take the appropriate action:

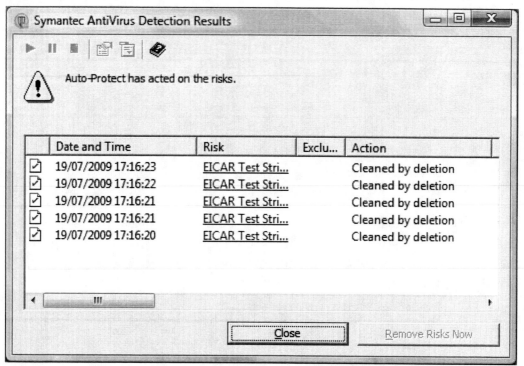

Detecting and remediating a virus infection

If you cannot clean a file, and have a backup copy, use it to restore the file. Check the files you restore to make sure that your backups are not infected.

> **Note**
> Also verify that system backups (such as System Restore points) are not infected.

The only other alternative is to remove the virus manually or reformat the machine, reinstall software, and restore data files from a (clean) backup.

For assistance, check the website and support services for your anti-virus software. In some cases, you may have to follow a further procedure to remove the virus or Trojan Horse (such as booting into Safe Mode or Recovery Console).

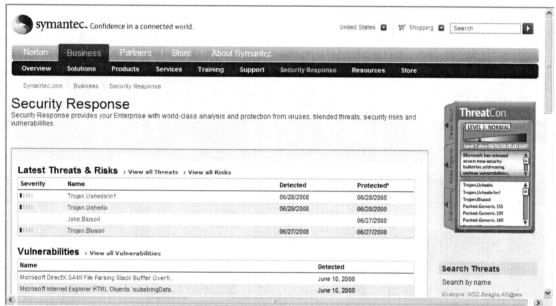

Symantec's Security Response portal showing current threat status, recent viruses and vulnerabilities, and search options for the malware database

Anti-virus software will not necessarily be able to recover data from infected files. Also, if a virus does disrupt the computer system, you might not be able to run anti-virus software anyway and would have to perform a complete system restore.

Removing Backdoor Applications

Anti-virus software may have routines for removing Trojans and rootkits, but the most secure way is to remove the computer from the network, re-partition and re-format the drives, then reinstall the OS, applications, and data from backup (provided you have a backup that was made before the installation of the backdoor).

It is also important to configure a firewall on the network to block outgoing communications. This makes it more difficult for the backdoor application to send data back to the attacker.

Most "anti-virus" software now combines the functionality of basic malware detection with the capabilities of previously stand-alone programs, such as personal firewall, adware or spyware detection, and intrusion detection.

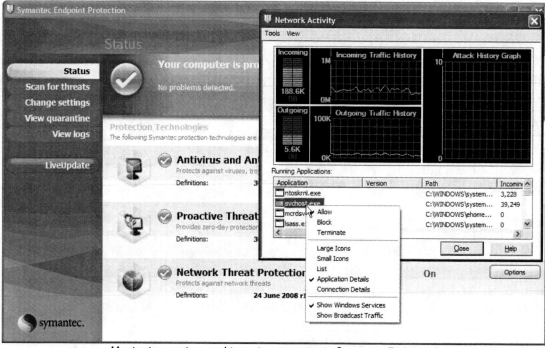

Monitoring services and intrusion attempts in Symantec Endpoint Protection security suite

| Unit 5.7 | Module 5 Networks and Printing |

Repairing Boot Blocks

One of the unwelcome actions that malware can perform is to damage the boot information on the hard drive. There are two sectors that are important here:

- The **Master Boot Record (MBR)** is located in the first sector of the first partition and contains information about the partitions on the disk plus some code that points to the location of the boot sector.

- The **Boot Sector** is located either on the sector after the MBR or the first sector of each other partition. It describes the partition file system (FAT or NTFS) and contains the code that points to the method of booting the OS (BOOT.INI on Windows 2000/XP or the Boot Configuration Database on Windows Vista).

Damage to these records results in boot errors such as "OS not found" or "Invalid drive specification". If this problem *has* been caused by a virus (it can also occur due to disk corruption or installing too many operating systems in multi-boot configurations), the best way to resolve it is to use the boot disk option in your anti-virus software. This will include a basic anti-virus scanner that may detect the virus that caused the problem in the first place.

If you don't have the option of using a recovery disk created by the anti-virus software, you can try to use the repair options that come with the Windows product disc. Do be aware that these may not work completely reliably if the system is still infected with a virus.

Note

Also note that these tools are not suitable for use with multi-boot configurations if one of the other OS has created a non-standard partition table.

Repairing the boot block under Windows XP / 2000

1. Boot from the product disc, choose the **Repair** option, then launch the Recovery Console and log on using the local Administrator account credentials.

2. Enter **MAP**.

Page 658   IT Career FastTrack with CompTIA A+ Certification   © 2010 gtslearning

| Module 5 Networks and Printing | Troubleshooting Network Applications |

This will provide information about the drives available to the computer and the parameters you will need to use.

3. Enter FIXBOOT *x:*, where *x* is the drive letter of the partition containing the boot sector you want to repair.

4. Optionally, also enter FIXMBR *\Device\Harddisk0*, where *\Device\Harddisk0* is the device you want to repair.

```
Microsoft Windows XP(TM) Recovery Console.

The Recovery Console provides system repair and recovery functionality.

Type EXIT to quit the Recovery Console and restart the computer.


1: C:\WINDOWS

Which Windows installation would you like to log onto
<To cancel, press ENTER>? 1
Type the Administrator password: ********
C:\WINDOWS>map

C: NTFS        49999MB      \Device\Harddisk0\Partition1
A:                          \Device\Floppy0
D:                          \Device\CdRom0

C:\WINDOWS>fixboot c:

The target partition is C:.
Are you sure you want to write a new bootsector to the partition C: ? y
The file system on the startup partition is NTFS.

FIXBOOT is writing a new boot sector.

The new bootsector was successfully written.


C:\WINDOWS>_
```

Using fixboot in the Recovery Console

5. Type EXIT to leave the Recovery Console and restart the PC.

Repairing the boot block under Windows Vista

1. Boot from the product disc and choose the **Repair** option.

2. First, use the **Startup Repair** option. If this does not work, choose the **Command Prompt** option.

3. Enter BOOTREC /fixboot.

4. Enter BOOTREC /fixmbr.

5. Restart the PC.

Windows Defender

Windows Vista ships with the anti-spyware program **Windows Defender**. This provides protection against programs that might try to modify the web browser or startup programs, display excessive pop-ups, or try to track web activity but is not an anti-virus or anti-Trojan tool.

If you have anti-virus software, you may want to disable Windows Defender as the two may conflict. To do so, open **Windows Defender** from Control Panel and select the **Tools** option. Click **Options** then scroll to the bottom of the dialog and uncheck **Use Windows Defender** (under Administrator Options).

Windows Defender

Parental Controls

Windows Vista also ships with a **Parental Controls** tool, which can be configured from Control Panel. You can activate controls on a per-account basis and configure things such as time of day restrictions on using the computer, web content filters, and blocking access to games and programs.

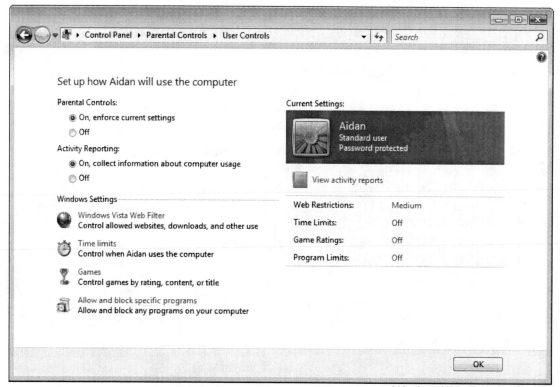

Windows Vista Parental Controls

Summary

You should be able to identify the typical effects of malware infections and recognize the different ways malware infects a computer or network. Make sure you understand the characteristics of properly configured anti-virus software and the procedures to clean infected systems.

Unit 5.8 Module 5 Networks and Printing

Unit 5.8 Printers

CompTIA A+ Essentials Objectives

□ **701.1.11 Install and configure printers**
Differentiate between printer types (Laser, Inkjet, Thermal, Impact) • Local vs. network printers • Printer drivers (compatibility) • Consumables

□ **701.2.2 Given a scenario, explain and interpret common hardware and operating system symptoms and their causes**
OS related symptoms (Windows specific printing problems [Print spool stalled, Incorrect / incompatible driver])

□ **701.2.3 Given a scenario, determine the troubleshooting methods and tools for printers**
Manage print jobs • Print spooler • Printer properties and settings • Print a test page

CompTIA A+ Practical Application Objectives

□ **702.1.5 Given a scenario, detect and resolve common printer issues**
Symptoms (Paper jams, Blank paper, Error codes, Out of memory error, Lines and smearing, Garbage printout, Ghosted image, No connectivity) • Issue resolution (Replace fuser, Replace drum, Clear paper jam, Power cycle, Install maintenance kit [reset page count], Set IP on printer, Clean printer)

□ **702.2.2 Differentiate between Windows Operating System directory structures (Windows 2000, XP and Vista)**
Fonts

□ **702.2.4 Evaluate and resolve common issues**
Operational Problems (Windows specific printing problems, Print spool stalled, Incorrect / incompatible driver form print)

Windows Print Process

Printing has always been associated with PC use. Reading from a screen is difficult compared to reading from paper. Printers also meet the need to keep hard copy records of important data. At home, printer sales have been boosted by the popularity of digital cameras.

The **print process** determines how a printer creates images on paper given output from an application. Windows applications that support printing are typically **WYSIWYG (What You See Is What You Get)**, which means that the screen and print output are supposed to be the same. To achieve this, several components are required:

Page 662 IT Career FastTrack with CompTIA A+ Certification © 2010 gtslearning

Module 5 Networks and Printing   *Printers*

- The **print driver** provides an interface between the print device and Windows.

- Support for one or more **print languages** determines how accurate the output can be.

- The **technology** used by the print device determines the quality, speed, and cost of the output.

The basic process of printing to a local printer in Windows 2000/XP is as follows:

1. When the user selects the **Print** command using a local printer, the Windows **Graphics Device Interface (GDI.EXE)** calls the printer's driver.

2. GDI and the print driver translate the application's print commands into commands understood by the printer.

3. The resulting **print job** is stored as a file in the printer's spool folder (**%SystemRoot%\System32\Spool\Printers**). The print job is usually collated in one of two formats:

   □ **EMF (Enhanced Metafile)** - a small, efficient, printer-independent file type. The application and GDI create a partial print job then quickly release control of the application back to the user, while the print job is completed in the background. The printer must support EMF (or **Advanced Printing Features**) for this to work.

   □ **RAW** - this file type differs depending on your printer. RAW files must be fully formatted for the printer and so spooling takes longer.

4. The **print processor** (WINPRINT.DLL) converts the spooled file into a format that can be sent to the print device.

5. The **print monitor** (typically LOCALMON.DLL) transmits the print job to the printer and provides status information.

6. Most print devices have their own memory and processor and possibly even disk space, enabling the print job to be transmitted more quickly and reliably. If a problem is encountered during printing, the printer sends a status message back to the print monitor, informing the user.

© 2010 gtslearning   IT Career FastTrack with CompTIA A+ Certification   Page 663

| Unit 5.8 | Module 5 Networks and Printing |

Users can also print to network printers. In this case, a redirector service on the local computer passes the print job from the locally spooled file to the spooler on the print server (the computer to which the network printer is connected). Note that a print driver for the network device must be installed locally.

Windows Vista features a new printing system with better support for color management and effects such as gradients and transparency. Display and print functions are handled by **Windows Presentation Foundation**[281]. The print job is formatted and stored as an **XML Print Specification (XPS)** file. This may then either be output directly to an XPS-compatible print device or rendered using the older GDI process (to support legacy devices).

Printer Technologies

A **printer technology** is the mechanism used to make images on the paper. The most common technologies for general home and office use are inkjet (or ink dispersion) and laser, though others are used for more specialist applications. Some of the major vendors include HP, Epson, Canon, Xerox, Brother, OKI, Konica/Minolta, Lexmark, Ricoh, and Samsung. The following criteria are used to select the best type and model of printer:

- **Speed** - the basic speed of a printer is measured in Pages Per Minute (ppm). You will see different speeds quoted for different output (for example, pages of monochrome text will print more quickly than color photos).

- **Connections** - almost all printers support USB, but printer models designed for workgroups also support network connections, usually at a higher cost than standard models. Wireless connections may also carry a price premium.

- **Image quality** - the basic measure of image quality is the maximum supported resolution, measured in dots per inch (dpi)[282]. The minimum resolution for a monochrome printer should be 600 dpi. Photo-quality printers start at 1200 dpi. Resolution is not the only factor in determining overall print quality however (especially with color output). When evaluating a printer, obtain samples to judge text and color performance.

---

[281] Though by default, legacy applications not compatible with WPF revert to GDI.

[282] Printer dots and screen image pixels are not equivalent. It requires multiple dots to reproduce one pixel at an acceptable quality. Pixel dimensions are typically quoted in Pixels Per Inch (ppi) to avoid confusion. Also vertical and horizontal resolution are often different, so you may see figures such as 2400x600 quoted. The horizontal resolution is determined by the print engine (that is, either the laser scanning unit or inkjet print head); vertical resolution is determined by the paper handling mechanism.

| Page 664 | IT Career FastTrack with CompTIA A+ Certification | © 2010 gtslearning |

Module 5 Networks and Printing   *Printers*

Tip

Image quality needs to be matched to use. The best quality will be correspondingly expensive.

- **Paper handling** - this means the type of paper or media that can be loaded. It may be important that the printer can handle labels, envelopes, card stock, acetate, and so on. The amount of paper that can be loaded and output is also important in high volume environments[283].

- **Total Cost of Ownership (TCO)** - this is the cost of the printer over its lifetime, including the cost of replacement components and consumables. It is important to know how a printer will be used to work out TCO.

- **Options** - additional memory, duplex (double-sided) printing, large format (A3 and greater), finishing (collating jobs to different output bins, binding, stapling, and so on). These options may be default or additional extras.

- **Multi-Function Device (MFD)** - many print devices are multi-function, combing print with scanning, copying, and fax capability.

Laser printers

Laser printers are the most popular printer technology for office applications because they are cheap (both to buy and to run), quiet, fast, and produce high quality output. There are both grayscale and color models[284].

A laser printer works by fixing a fine powder called **toner** to the page surface. The toner is applied using electrostatic charging then fixed using high heat and pressure, creating a durable printout that does not smear or fade.

A laser printer operates on the whole image as a single item. This means that laser printers need quite sophisticated processors and large amounts of RAM. As soon as all the data for one page has been received by the printer, it is broken down into a series of single-dot strips in a process known as **rasterizing**. This creates a bitmap image of the page in the printer's memory.

---

[283] Overloaded output trays will cause paper jams. If the output tray is low capacity, this could happen quite quickly in a busy office.

[284] Color laser printers were once expensive specialist devices but prices have fallen considerably. They are still more expensive to run and slower than grayscale models though.

© 2010 gtslearning   IT Career FastTrack with CompTIA A+ Certification   Page 665

HP LaserJet printer

Once rasterizing is complete, the physical process of printing the page begins.

- **Preparation (Cleaning)** - laser printers contain a photosensitive drum, known as the **Organic PhotoConductor (OPC)** drum[285]. To begin the printing cycle, the OPC drum is cleaned to remove any remaining toner particles using a cleaning blade, roller, or brush resting on the surface of the drum. Any residual electrical charge is removed using a discharge lamp.

- **Electrostatic Charging (Conditioning)** - when not exposed to light, the OPC drum's coating can hold a very high electrostatic charge. Using its primary corona wire or charge roller[286], the laser printer applies a *high uniform negative charge* (around -500 to -600V) to the OPC drum. The strength of the charge determines the overall darkness of the image (a stronger charge attracts more toner at the development stage).

- **Laser Imaging (Writing)** - the surface coating of the OPC drum loses its charge when exposed to light. A laser directed through an array of mirrors removes the charge selectively, line-by-line, as the drum rotates[287]. As the laser receives the image information, it fires a short pulse of light for each dot in the raster.

---

[285] A photoconductor is a metal whose conductivity increases when exposed to *radiation* (light). In the *dark* therefore, the drum can hold an electrostatic charge.

[286] Newer models of printers use charge rollers rather than wires as these produce less ozone as a by-product.

[287] Cheaper printers use an array of Light Emitting Diodes (LEDs).

| Module 5 Networks and Printing | Printers |

The pulsing light beam is reflected by a rotating polygonal mirror and through a system of lenses onto the OPC drum. The OPC ends up with a whole series of raster lines with charge / no-charge areas that represent an electrostatic impression of the image to be printed.

- **Image Development** - laser toner is composed of a fine metallic compound bound together with powdered dyestuff. The toner is fed evenly onto a magnetized roller (the **developer roller**) from a hopper. The developer roller is located very close to the OPC drum and has the same *high uniform negative charge*. Under normal circumstances, there would be no interaction between the two parts but because the charge has been selectively removed from the OPC drum, toner is attracted to the non-charged areas and sticks to the surface. The OPC drum, now coated with toner in the image of the document, rotates until it reaches the paper.

- **Image Transfer** - the paper is picked up from the paper tray and pulled through the printer by the **registration rollers** to pass between the OPC drum and another high-voltage part (the **secondary [transfer]** corona wire or roller). The transfer roller applies a *strong positive charge* on the paper, which attracts the negatively charged toner from the OPC drum onto the paper. As the paper leaves the transfer assembly, a **static eliminator strip** removes any remaining charge from the paper, which might otherwise cause it to stick to the drum or curl as it enters the fuser unit.

Tip

The entire laser printer cycle takes place in one smooth sequence but, since the OPC drum's circumference is smaller than a sheet of Letter paper, writing, development, and transfer are repeated 2-4 times (according to size) per page.

- **Fusing** - the paper continues past the OPC drum and passes between a hot roller and a pressure roller so that the toner is fused, or melted, onto the surface of the paper. The hot roller is a metal tube containing a heat lamp; the pressure roller is typically rubber. Both rollers have a Teflon coating to prevent toner from sticking to them.

When the paper has passed through the fuser, if a duplex unit is installed, it is turned over and returned to the developer unit to print the second side. Otherwise, the paper is directed to the selected output bin using the exit rollers.

© 2010 gtslearning   IT Career FastTrack with CompTIA A+ Certification   Page 667

Color laser printers

Color laser printers, once very highly priced and positioned at the top end of the market, are becoming more affordable, with medium quality, entry-level models priced competitively against inkjet equivalents. Color lasers use separate color toner cartridges (Cyan, Magenta, Yellow, and Black) but employ different processes to create the image (some may use four passes to put down each color; others combine the colors on a plate and print in one pass).

Inkjet printers

Inkjets (or more generally **ink dispersion** printers) are often used for good-quality color output. Inkjets are typically cheap to buy but expensive to run, with high cost consumables such as ink cartridges and high-grade paper. Compared to laser printers, they are slower and often noisier, making them less popular in office environments, except as a cheap option for good quality color printing.

Color images are created by combining four inks (Cyan, Magenta, Yellow, and Black [K]). The inks are stored in separate reservoirs, which may be supplied in single or multiple cartridges.

There are a wide range of inkjet printers, ranging from cheaper desktop models, through "prosumer" high quality photo printers, to large format, commercial print solutions. Higher quality printers feature additional ink colors (light magenta and light cyan).

HP DeskJet (left) 4-colour inkjet printer and DesignJet (right) 6-colour, large format printer

Module 5 Networks and Printing

Printers

Inkjet print process

Inkjets work by firing microscopic droplets of ink (about 50 microns in size) at the paper. The process creates high quality images, especially when specially treated paper is used, but they can be prone to smearing and fading over time.

There are two types of inkjet print process:

- Thermal (called Bubblejet by Canon) - the ink at the nozzle is heated, creating a bubble. When the bubble bursts, it sprays ink through the nozzle and draws more ink from the reservoir.

- Piezoelectric - the nozzle contains a piezoelectric element, which changes shape when a voltage is applied. This acts like a small pump, pushing ink through the nozzle and drawing ink from the reservoir. The piezoelectric print process is patented by Epson.

Inkjet printers are line printers (where laser printers are page printers) because they build up the image line-by-line (or at least, row-by-row). A stepper motor moves the print head across the page, advancing a tiny amount each time. On some types of printer, ink is applied when the print head moves in one direction only (unidirectional); on others, ink is applied on both the "outward" and "return" passes over the page (bidirectional). When a line or row has been completed, the stepper motor advances the page a little bit and the next line or row is printed.

If the printer has been idle for some time (or when it is first started up), it applies a cleaning cycle to the print head to remove any dried or clogged ink. This means pushing ink through all the print heads at once then wiping it away to collect in a waste ink spittoon. The cleaning cycle can also be invoked manually through the printer control panel or driver.

Dot matrix printers

A **dot matrix** printer produces output by firing pins (also known as print wires) in a print head at an inked ribbon, which touches and leaves marks on the paper (dot matrix printers are described as **impact** printers).

Desktop dot matrix printers are no longer widely deployed, but where they are used it is typically for specialist functions such as printing invoices, payslips, and the like on continuous, tractor-fed paper. Portable models are still quite widely used for printing receipts.

© 2010 gtslearning   IT Career FastTrack with CompTIA A+ Certification   Page 669

The pins are contained in a device called the **print head**, which is secured to a moving carriage that sweeps across the paper. The pins are moved, or fired, by coils of wire called solenoids. When a coil is energized, it forms a strong electromagnet that causes the metal firing pin to move sharply forwards, striking the ribbon. A strong permanent magnet moves the pins back into their resting position immediately after firing.

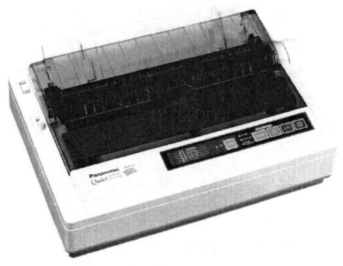

Dot matrix printer

The output quality of a dot-matrix printer is largely governed by the number of pins in the print head. Most modern printers use 9-pin or 24-pin print heads. The latter offer a much-improved print quality. More sophisticated printers may use 48-pin print heads, although if you require this level of quality, it is more common to use an inkjet or laser printer.

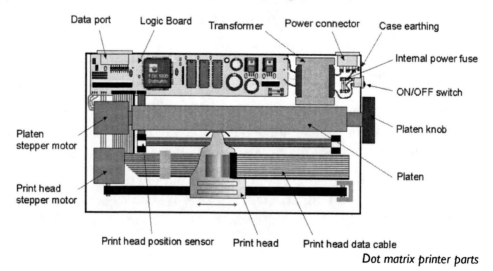

Dot matrix printer parts

A platen gap lever is often fitted to printers capable of printing on multi-part stationery. This lever adjusts the gap between the print head and the platen to accommodate different thickness of paper. Incorrect adjustment of the platen gap can cause faint printing (gap too wide) or smudging (too narrow). On more sophisticated printers, the platen gap is adjusted automatically.

Thermal transfer printers

Laser and inkjet printers dominate the market for print devices but other types of printer fill niche positions.

Portable or small form factor thermal transfer printers are used for high volume bar code and label printing and also to print receipts. They work using a heat transfer process similar to laser printers, but without the use of toner. There are two types:

- Direct thermal - a print head selectively heats areas of specially coated paper to form the image.

- Thermal wax - "ink" from a wax-based ribbon is melted onto the paper by the print head.

HP Point-of-Sale solution with bar code reader and thermal receipt printer

Devices typically support 200-300 dpi, with some models able to print one or two colors (typically red and/or blue). Print speeds are measured in inches per second.

As with other PC peripherals, USB is the dominant printer interface.

Unit 5.8   Module 5 Networks and Printing

Installing and Configuring Printers

Printer interfaces

Like any other peripheral device, a printer uses an I/O interface to connect to the computer:

- USB - most printers use USB for local connectivity.

- Network - some printers come with a wired or wireless network adapter and print server and can be attached directly to the network. A printer can also be networked by attaching it to a server then sharing it.

- Wireless - a printer may support local connections via a Bluetooth or infrared port or use wireless networking.

- Flash memory card - some printers come with a memory card reader and can print directly from memory cards.

- Parallel - older printers use the parallel interface.

Installing a local printer

Installing a local Plug-and-Play compatible printer is simple.

1. Install the printer driver and software using the vendor's disk or setup file downloaded from their website.

2. Connect the printer to the computer using a suitable adapter, plug it into mains power and switch it on.

3. The Windows **Add Printer Wizard** will run, allowing you to configure the printer's device driver.

4. When the printer is installed, check the printer setup and default options and test by printing a test page.

Operating system printer drivers must be installed for a printer to function correctly. If the device is not detected automatically, drivers can be installed in Windows using the **Printers** folder, and the **Add Printer Wizard**.

Page 672   IT Career FastTrack with CompTIA A+ Certification   © 2010 gtslearning

Configuring network properties

A network printer needs to be configured so that it has a valid address. On a TCP/IP network, you might set the printer to obtain an address automatically via a DHCP server or configure it with a static IP address and subnet mask.

Most printers provide a mechanism for locally configuring the printer. Usually, this is by means of a menu system which you navigate by using an LCD display and adjacent buttons on the front of the printer.

Configuring the IP address via the printer's front panel

This method is suitable for small office environments where you have few printers to manage. It is also useful in troubleshooting situations when the printer is inaccessible from the network. However, the printer vendor will usually supply a web-based utility to discover and manage their printers while more advanced management suites are available for enterprise networks.

Unit 5.8   Module 5 Networks and Printing

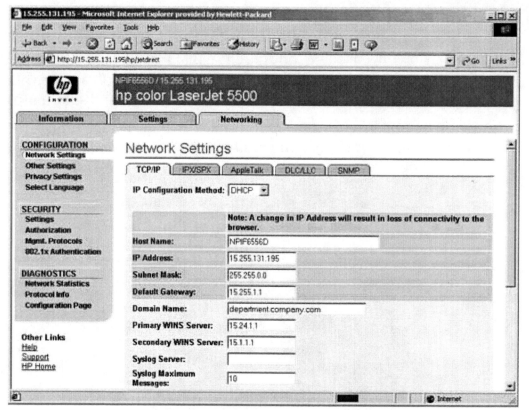

Managing an HP printer using a browser

| Installing a network printer |

An ordinary user can connect to a network printer (assuming that the printer administrator has given them permission to use it). The simplest way of doing this is to browse through the network resources using **(My) Network (Places)** then alt-click the required printer and select **Connect**.

Alternatively, you can use the **Add Printer Wizard**. Having selected **Network printer** on the initial page, you can then select how you want to locate the printer.

If you know the name or location of the printer, you can enter it into the boxes. Otherwise, select **Connect to this printer**, leave the box blank, and click **Next**. On the next page, expand the directory to locate the printer.

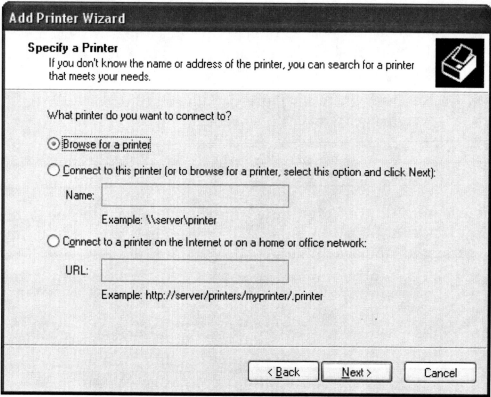

Add Printer Wizard - connecting to a network printer

The remainder of the pages allow you to name the device, set it as the default, and print a test page.

Upgrading a printer

Many printers support add-on accessories such as a hard drive, memory, network adapters, duplex unit, binding unit, extra paper handling trays, and so on. These upgrades are simple to perform, but remember basic procedures:

1. Check the compatibility of optional devices with your printer model when ordering.
2. Unpack the device carefully and inspect it for damage or missing parts before proceeding with the installation.
3. Read the installation instructions carefully before proceeding.
4. Disconnect the power supply to the device.
5. Take anti-static precautions if handling static-sensitive components such as memory or circuit boards.

6. If necessary, update the printer firmware or driver using a setup program downloaded from the manufacturer's website and verify in the property sheet that the upgrade has been recognized and is enabled.

7. Test the upgrade and the device after installation to check that everything is working as it should.

Configuring printers

In Windows XP, printers are installed and configured using the **Printers and Faxes** folder (though these are separate applets in Windows 2000 and in Vista the folder is just called **Printers** but does still contain fax devices).

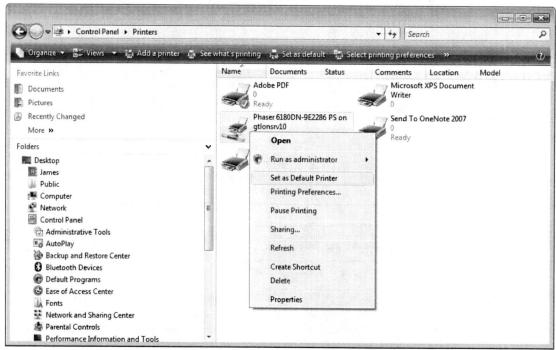

Choosing a default printer through the Printers folder

Opening a printer object displays its print queue while the shortcut menu allows the selection of the default printer and configuration of sharing, properties, and printing preferences.

Module 5 Networks and Printing

Printer properties and preferences

A local printer can be managed using **Printer Properties** and **Printing Preferences**. To get either dialog, alt-click the printer icon in the **Printers and Faxes** folder.

Properties allows you to update the driver, print to a different port, configure sharing and permissions, set basic device options (such as whether a duplex unit is installed), and configure default paper types for different feed trays. This dialog also lets you print a test page (off the **General** tab).

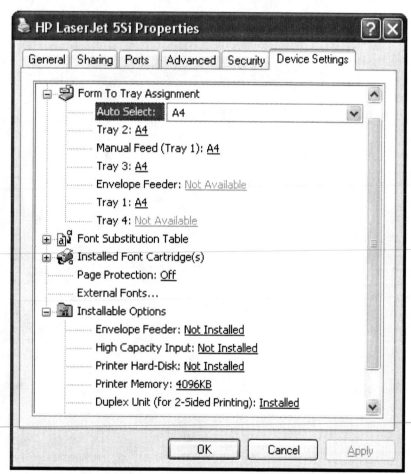

Printer properties

Preferences sets the **default** print options.

These settings can also be changed on a **per-job** basis by clicking the **Properties** button in the *application's* **Print** dialog.

Alternatively, the printer may come with management software that you can use to change settings.

Some of the common printing options are listed below.

Form tray

Most printers have more than one tray. Typically, there is at least one automatic sheet feed and one manual feed. Different trays may be capable of handling different paper (media) types. For example, the manual tray might be able to handle card or acetate that cannot run through the automatic tray; or one tray might be able to handle A3 paper.

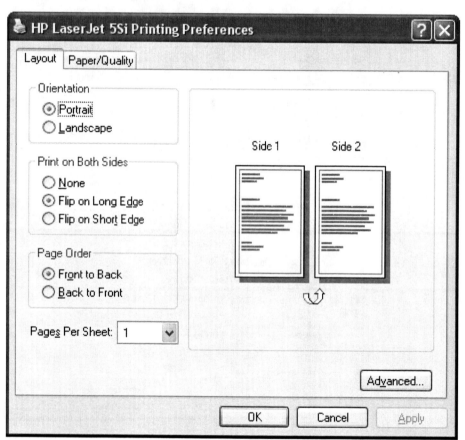

Printing preferences

Form-to-Tray assignment allows you to specify what media (paper type) is loaded in which tray. One tray can be set as the default (paper source), but the user can select a different tray (and media) using the **Properties** button in the *application's* **Print** dialog.

Module 5 Networks and Printing   *Printers*

Paper orientation

This is normally set to Portrait (taller than wide) by default. Landscape orientation can be selected on a per-job basis.

Duplex operation

Duplex means that the printer can print both sides of a sheet in one operation. Typically a duplex unit must be installed and enabled for this capability. Duplex pages can be flipped on the long or short edge.

> **Tip**
>
> It's best to turn off the duplex option when printing to labels. Typically, using duplex reverses the side that should be placed facing up, and this confuses most users.

Paper scaling

If a document has been designed at one page size but is to be printed to different size media, the job can be scaled to fit. Scaling (or zoom) is usually configured via the *application's* **Print** dialog. Another common option is to print multiple page images on one sheet, allowing for bookfold printing.

Economy mode

Most printers have an ink/toner-saving mode for draft output.

Copy count and collation options

The *default* copy count is best left set to 1, unless you want to waste a lot of paper. Collation refers to how multiple copies of multi-page documents are printed. You can either print by page (that is, all copies of page 1 then all copies of page 2, and so on) or by document (all pages in copy 1 then all pages in copy 2, and so on).

© 2010 gtslearning   IT Career FastTrack with CompTIA A+ Certification   Page 679

| Unit 5.8 | Module 5 Networks and Printing |

Printer control languages

A printer control language is the instructions that the printer can use to create an image on the page (for most printers, this means the placement of dots on the paper). Typically, one of two languages is used:

- **PostScript** - developed by Adobe, this is a powerful language capable of creating accurate, device-independent output. This means that two different printer models will produce exactly the same output from the same print file. There are three levels of PostScript. Most printers will support level 3, but some may only support level 2.

  Most high-end printers support PostScript but cheaper printers do not, as it is a complex language, requiring a powerful print processor and plenty of memory installed on the device.

  One advantage of PostScript is that print processor functions are handled by the print device, reducing the load on the PC. PostScript features can be configured via the Advanced Printing Preferences page.

- **PCL (Printer Command Language)** - this is a simpler language, developed by HP for their LaserJet and DeskJet printer ranges, but also supported on many non-HP printers. There are several versions of PCL (PCL 3, PCL 5, PCL 5e, PCL 5C(olor), and PCL 6).

- **Graphics Device Interface (GDI)** - the cheapest printers simply use Windows' GDI language to create print jobs. Windows XP supports GDI+, which has improved support for transparency, gradients, and the JPEG and PNG picture file formats. Vista uses a new print subsystem (**XML Print Specification [XPS]**) but retains backwards compatibility for GDI-based applications.

- **Plain Text Spooling** - another option is to spool a job as **plain text**, meaning that the device's default options for font, margins, orientation, and so on are used.

Page 680   IT Career FastTrack with CompTIA A+ Certification   © 2010 gtslearning

Module 5 Networks and Printing	Printers

A printer vendor may release two drivers for a printer; one supporting PostScript and one supporting PCL. You should install the driver that provides the best compatibility with the applications you use to print. Design and publishing applications will probably work best with PostScript while more general office and database software may work better with PCL. PCL is also likely to be faster than PostScript, unless the printer is very highly specified.

You can also install both drivers. Either install the printer twice (one with the PS driver and one with the PCL driver; make sure you use descriptive names) or change the driver used by opening the printer's property sheet and selecting a new driver on the **Advanced** tab.

Features of command languages

Printer control languages support the following features:

- **Scalable fonts** - originally, characters were printed as bitmaps. This meant that the character could only be printed at sizes defined in the font. Scalable fonts are described by vectors[288]. All Windows printers support scalable TrueType fonts[289]. PostScript compatible printers will also support PostScript *outline* fonts.

- **Color printing** - the color model used by display systems is different to that used by printers (additive versus subtractive[290]). A color model provides an accurate translation between on-screen colors and print output and ensures that different devices produce identical output. Only PostScript supports a full range of professional color correction features but PCL and GDI are sufficient for desktop applications.

- **Vector graphics** - as with fonts, scalable images are built from vectors, which describe how a line should be drawn, rather than providing a pixel-by-pixel description, as is the case with bitmap graphics.

---

[288] A bitmap font consists of a number of dot-by-dot images of each character at a particular font size. A vector font consists of a description of how each character should be drawn.

[289] In fact, many fonts are now OpenType. OpenType is an extension of TrueType. OpenType offers portability between Windows and Mac OS, better character (Unicode) support, and more advanced typographic options.

[290] An additive model combines differently colored transmitted light (Red, Green, and Blue for instance) to form different shades. A subtractive model works using the reflective properties of inks (Cyan, Magenta, and Yellow [plus Black ink for "true" blacks]).

© 2010 gtslearning	IT Career FastTrack with CompTIA A+ Certification	Page 681

| Unit 5.8 | Module 5 Networks and Printing |

Maintaining Printers

As devices with moving parts and consumable items that deplete quickly, printers need more maintenance than most other computer devices.

Printers generate a lot of dirt (principally paper dust and ink/toner spills) and consequently require regular cleaning. Consumable items also require replacing frequently under heavy use.

Tip

For best results and to stay within warranty, use branded supplies designed for the specific model of printer.

Cleaning

A printer should be kept free of dust and paper debris using an approved vacuum cleaner. Cleaning of parts such as rollers and print heads should also take place according to the manufacturer's schedule.

- Unplug the printer before cleaning or performing routine maintenance.

Warning
The inside of a laser printer may be hot - take care - especially when handling the fuser unit.

- Use a damp cloth to clean exterior surfaces.

- Wipe dust and toner from inside the case with an approved toner cloth or toner vacuum[291]. DO NOT use an ordinary domestic vacuum cleaner. Toner is conductive and can damage the motor. Toner is also so fine that it will pass straight through a normal dust collection bag and back into the room.

Note

If toner is spilt on skin or clothes, wash it off with COLD water. Hot water will open the skin's pores and push the toner into the skin.

---

[291] Manufacturers recommend not trying to clean inside the case of an inkjet as you are likely to do harm for no real benefit. The outside of the printer can be cleaned using a soft damp cloth.

Page 682   IT Career FastTrack with CompTIA A+ Certification   © 2010 gtslearning

Module 5 Networks and Printing   *Printers*

Paper

The printer will report when a tray runs out of paper. When loading new paper, remember the following guidelines:

- Use good quality paper designed for use with the model of printer that you have and the printing function. Laser printers work best with standard weight copier paper (60-90gsm [60-90 bond]) while inkjets works best with their own type of paper. There is inkjet paper for "ordinary" printing and special glossy paper for photo printing.

- If using heavier paper stock or labels, check the printer can use it and make sure you put the paper in the appropriate feed tray. You should also select the media type in the Print dialog so that the print process is configured properly.

- Do not overload a paper tray.

- Do not use creased or dirty paper.

- Keep paper in its packaging until it is ready to use.

Some dot-matrix printers can be used with either **plain** or **tractor-fed** paper:

- **Plain paper** is held firmly against the moving roller (the platen), and is pulled through the mechanism by friction as the platen rotates. A cut-sheet feeder may be added to some printers to automate the process of providing the next page.

- **Tractor-fed** paper is fitted with removable, perforated side strips. The holes in these strips are secured over studded rollers at each end of the platen. This type of paper is more suitable for multi-part stationery as there is less chance of skewing or slippage since the end rollers fix the movement of the paper.

You will also need to deal with paper jams. The printer's status panel will indicate what area of the printer is jammed. Check the instruction manual to find out how to remove any components that might prevent you from removing the paper.

Note

Do not allow a jammed page to rip! If a page is stuck in the fuser or developer unit, look for a release mechanism or lever. If a printer experiences multiple paper jams, look at the quality of media being used or inspect components for wear.

© 2010 gtslearning   IT Career FastTrack with CompTIA A+ Certification   Page 683

Driver and firmware updates

A driver update may also be necessary to fix operational or performance problems or provide support for optional components.

1. To update a driver, log on as administrator and download the file from the manufacturer's website and save it to a folder on your computer.
2. Open the printer's property sheet and click the **Advanced** tab.
3. Click the **New Driver** button then click **Have Disk** and browse for the file you downloaded.

Most manufacturers periodically bring out firmware updates for their printers. Firmware is the software stored on the printer itself. By updating the firmware you can get rid of bugs, generally increase the reliability of the printer, and even increase the speed of printing.

Firmware updates can usually be run directly from the computer that the printer is attached to or using network management software. Simply run the firmware update software on the computer and the new firmware will be sent to the printer and installed automatically. The printer will probably need to be cycled off and on to ensure that the update has worked.

Replacing a toner cartridge

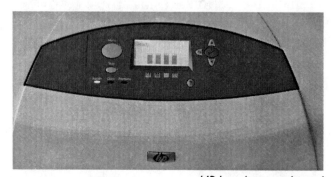

HP LaserJet control panel

When toner is low, the printer will display a status message advising you of the fact. Frugal departments may continue printing until the actual output starts to dip in quality[292].

The OPC drum in the toner cartridge is light-sensitive. If you remove it, place it in its storage bag or in a dark area. Remove the OPC drum for as short a time as possible.

---

[292] Removing the cartridge and shaking gently from side-to-side can help to get the most out of it.

To replace the toner cartridge[293], turn off the printer and remove the old cartridge by opening the relevant service panel and pulling it out. Place the cartridge in a bag to avoid shedding toner everywhere.

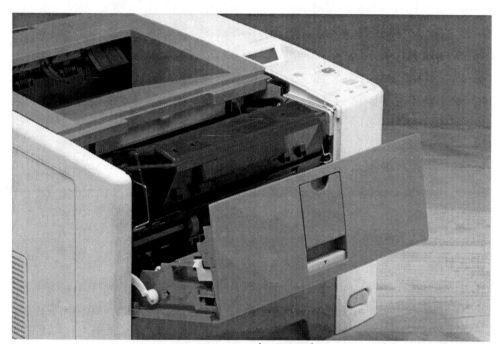

Accessing the toner cartridge on an HP LaserJet

Take the new cartridge and remove the packing strips as indicated by the instructions. Insert the cartridge, close the service panel, turn on, and print a test page.

If possible, dispose of old cartridges by recycling them.

Replacing a maintenance kit

A **maintenance kit** is a set of replacement feed rollers and a new fuser unit. The feed rollers guide paper through the printer assembly. When they begin to wear out, paper jams become more frequent. Wear on the fuser or rollers is also evidenced by persistent marks on print output or excess toner "blobs" appearing on sheets.

Replacement of the maintenance kit is guided by the printer's internal record of the number of pages that it has printed (page count). The printer's status indicator will display the message "Maintenance Kit Replace" at this point.

---

[293] Color lasers will usually have four cartridges for the different colors, which can be replaced separately.

Before replacing the kit, turn off the printer, disconnect from the power supply, open the service panels, and allow it to cool (the fuser unit becomes extremely hot and may cause burns). Remove the old fuser and rollers and clean the printer. Install the fuser and new rollers (don't forget to remove the packing strips), following the instructions carefully.

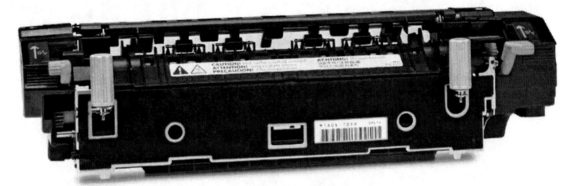

Fuser unit for HP LaserJet

Once you have replaced the maintenance kit, start the printer up and print a test page to check functionality. Use the property sheet or the printer's control panel menu (for example, the Configuration menu on an HP printer) to reset the page count to zero.

As with toner cartridges, try to use a recycling program to dispose of the fuser unit in an environmentally responsible manner.

Replacing inkjet cartridges

The replaceable print components for an inkjet depend on the printer model. Some have multiple cartridges for different colors; some have a single cartridge. Thermal inkjet cartridges often incorporate a replacement print head; on piezoelectric models, the print head is usually part of the printer (fixed).

When the inkjet's driver software determines that a cartridge is empty, it will prompt you to replace it.

Check the printer's instruction manual for the correct procedure, but in general you will complete the following steps:

1. Put the printer into cartridge replacement mode (there'll be a button that you need to depress for a number of seconds).

2. Unlock the old cartridge and lift it out of the mechanism. Put the old cartridge in a bag, ready for recycling.

3. Take the new cartridge and remove the *packing* strip (typically yellow). Do **not** remove the ink well strip (typically white). Do not touch the ink nozzles or the copper contacts.

4. Drop the cartridge into place and lock down.

5. Press the button to restart the printer. Wait for the charging process to complete (about a minute) then print a test page.

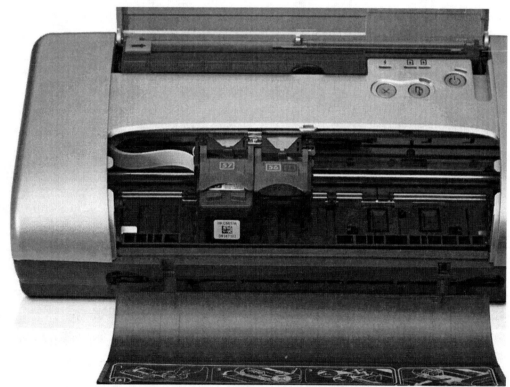

Replacing ink cartridges on an HP DeskJet

Refilling inkjet cartridges

Refilling cartridges is cheaper than replacing them, but goes against all the manufacturers' advice. To refill a cartridge, you inject ink from the refill kit into the old cartridge. Typically you have to do this soon after the cartridge runs out or dried ink makes it unusable. You may also have to flash the controller chip on the cartridge to get the printer's driver software to recognize that it is not empty.

Unit 5.8   Module 5 Networks and Printing

Other inkjet maintenance operations

Two other operations may be required periodically:

- Print head alignment - if output is not aligned correctly, use the print head alignment function from the printer's property sheet to calibrate the printer. This is typically done automatically when you replace the ink cartridges.

- Print head cleaning - a blocked or dirty nozzle will show up on output as a missing line. Use the printer's cleaning cycle (accessed via the property sheet or control panel) to try to fix the problem[294].

Dot matrix consumables

A dot matrix printer will have some form of replaceable **ribbon**. Older-style printers used to have a two-spool ribbon, the same as that found on typewriters. However, most units now have a cartridge device that slots over or around the carriage of the print head. These integrated ribbons simplify the design of the printer because they can be made as a complete loop moving in one direction only. The two-spool design requires a sensor and reversing mechanism to change the direction of the ribbon when it reaches the end.

Troubleshooting Printers

Remember to test obvious things first: is the printer switched on and loaded with paper? Is the connection between the printer and PC good? Can you print a test page using the printer control panel and from Windows?

Online versus offline

If documents do not print, one of the first checks should be that the printer is switched on and "online". A printer can be taken offline quite easily by pressing the button on the control panel. Often this happens quite by accident. A printer may also go offline because it is waiting for user intervention or because it has received corrupt print job data. Also check the connection between the host PC and printer.

---

[294] If it does not work, there are various inkjet cleaning products on the market.

Page 688   IT Career FastTrack with CompTIA A+ Certification   © 2010 gtslearning

Also check environmental conditions - a printer may malfunction if it overheats. Check that there is plenty of space around the printer for air to circulate (especially around the vents on the printer case) and that the environment is not excessively hot.

Remember to ask: "What has changed?" It is important to establish whether something has never worked or has just stopped working. If something never worked, then there has been an installation error; if something has stopped working, look for a configuration change or maintenance issue.

Error codes

If the printer detects an internal problem, it should display an error code on its control panel. There should be a numeric code plus a general description of the error ("Out of memory" for instance). Look the error code up in the printer's service documentation to identify the problem.

If there is a software-related problem, there should be an error message or alert displayed in Windows and an event in the application log. Use that information to try to track down the source of the error.

Windows print queue troubleshooting

If a particular job will not print, double-click the printer to open its print queue and try restarting the job. If that does not work, delete it and try printing again. Transient problems can often be solved by cycling the power on the printer. Check the volume holding the spool file on the print server to ensure there is enough disk space. For a network printer, check the network connections between the client and the print server and between the print server and the print device.

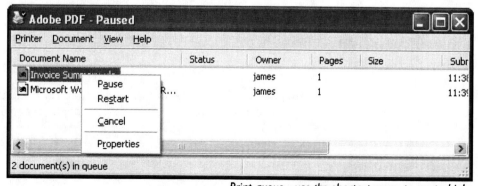

Print queue - use the shortcut menu to control jobs

If you cannot delete a job (if the print queue is stalled), you will need to stop the **Print Spooler** service (either use the **Services** snap-in or enter the command NET STOP SPOOLER at the command prompt), delete the spooled file from **%SystemRoot%\System32\Spool\Printers**, then restart the service (again, either use the **Services** snap-in or run NET START SPOOLER).

Printer driver

If a print job contains high-resolution graphics or multiple pages and printing is very slow, bear in mind that the printer may not have sufficient resources to handle the job. If there are persistent problems with printing from a specific application, check the vendor's troubleshooting website to determine whether a driver update will fix the problem.

If a print job is garbage (if it emits many pages with a few characters on each), cancel the job and clear the print queue then cycle the power on the printer (leaving it off for 30 seconds to clear the memory) and try to print again. If the problem persists, update the printer driver and check that the printer is set to use the correct control language (PCL or PostScript). You can also try changing the spool type from EMF to RAW, using the printer's **Advanced** property page or disabling spooling (select **Print directly to printer**).

If printing is slow, use the **Advanced** property page to choose the **Start printing immediately** option. You can also try changing the spool format from RAW to EMF (click the **Print Processor** button from the **Advanced** page).

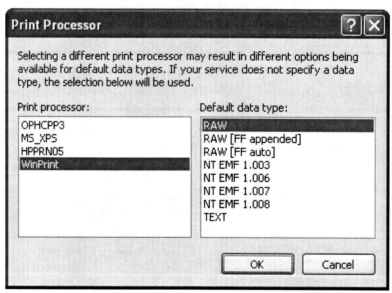

Changing print processor settings

Module 5 Networks and Printing   *Printers*

Use the printer's property sheet to print a test page. If the test page prints successfully, then the problem is related to the print function of a particular application[295]. Try printing a different file from the same application; if this works then you know that the problem is specific to a particular file.

One of the first options when trying to remedy most types of software print problem is to update the driver to the latest version or use a different driver (PostScript rather than PCL for instance).

Also check that the correct job options have been set (media type, input tray, duplex printing, monochrome or color, economy mode, and so on). Remember that print properties set through the application (**File > Print > Properties | Print Setup**) override those set as the default (either through the Printer object in Windows or through the device control panel).

Fonts

If the characters in a document are different from those expected or if strange characters appear in an otherwise normal print, check that **fonts** specified in the document are available on the workstation and / or printer. The software application should indicate whether the specified font is available or whether it is substituting it for the nearest match.

To view fonts installed on the workstation, open the **Fonts** applet in **Control Panel**. Each font **family** (such as Arial) often comes with a number of **variants** (such as Bold or Italic). If you open a font icon, a preview of the font at different sizes is shown.

If a font is not shown here, use the **File** menu to locate and install it. Fonts are usually located in **c:\Windows\Fonts** but some font manager applications may store fonts in another location.

---

[295] If the test page does not print, try using the printer's control panel to print it. If this works, there is some sort of communication problem between the print device and Windows.

© 2010 gtslearning   IT Career FastTrack with CompTIA A+ Certification   Page 691

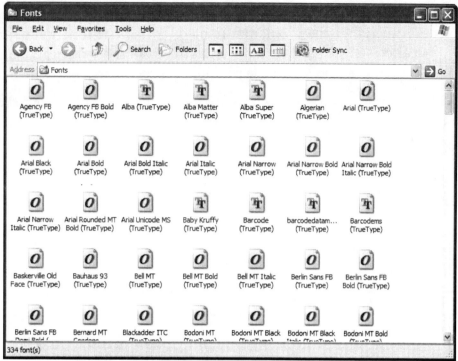

If characters do not appear correctly, check that the proper fonts are installed

> **Note**
> Most fonts require a license - you should not copy them between workstations with making the proper licensing arrangements.

A PostScript printer may use internal fonts in preference to those installed on the PC. Check **Printing Preferences** to confirm that the printer is not using font substitution.

Print device troubleshooting

Problems with a print device generally fall into one of three categories:

- **Paper jam** - this is usually caused by inappropriate media or overloading.
- **Faint output** - assuming the user has not set the option for draft output, this indicates that the ink or toner needs replacing.
- **Blank pages** - this is usually an application or driver problem, but could indicate that an ink or toner cartridge has been installed without removing its packing seals.

| Module 5 Networks and Printing | Printers |

- **Skewed output** - check that the paper is inserted correctly and that media guides are well-positioned (not to tight and not too loose).

There are also certain common problems with the different types of printer.

Laser printer troubleshooting

- **Faint output** - as well as the simple causes listed above, such as low toner or density setting, this could be a sign that the OPC drum is worn out or damaged (though with an integrated cartridge, the toner tends to run out well before this happens).

- **Blank pages** - again, given the simple causes, this could also be a sign that the transfer roller (or secondary corona wire) is damaged (the image transfer stage fails).

- **White stripes** - this indicates either that the toner is poorly distributed (give the cartridge a gentle shake) or that the transfer roller is dirty or damaged.

- **Black stripes or whole page black** - indicates that the primary transfer roller is dirty or damaged or that the High Voltage Power Supply to the developer unit is malfunctioning.

- **Toner specks** - if the output is "speckled", loose toner may be getting onto the paper. Clean the inside of the printer using an approved toner vacuum.

- **Persistent marks** - often due to dirty feed rollers (note that there are rollers in the toner cartridge and fuser unit too) or a damaged or dirty OPC drum.

- **Output that smudges easily** - indicates that the fuser needs replacing.

- **Wavy or wrinkled output** - make sure the paper is inserted correctly (try turning the stack over).

- **Ghosted image** - this is a sign that the OPC drum has not been cleaned properly. The drum is smaller than the size of a sheet of paper, so if the image is not completely cleared it will repeat as a light "ghost" or dark "shadow" image farther down the page. Images may also appear from previous prints. Try printing a series of different images and see if the problem resolves itself. If not, replace the OPC drum / toner cartridge.

© 2010 gtslearning   IT Career FastTrack with CompTIA A+ Certification   Page 693

| Unit 5.8 | Module 5 Networks and Printing |

- **Paper jams** - if the media and pickup rollers are good and if the jam occurs within the OPC assembly but before the image is fused, the cause could be a faulty **Static Eliminator Strip**. Normally, this removes the high static charge from the paper as it leaves the transfer unit. If the strip fails, the paper may stick to the drum or curl as it enters the fuser unit.

Inkjet printer troubleshooting

Lines running through printouts indicate a dirty print head or blocked ink nozzle, which can usually be fixed by running a cleaning cycle. Most other print quality problems (output that smears easily, wavy or wrinkled output, or blurry output) is likely to be a media problem. As with laser printers, persistent marks on output probably indicate a dirty feed roller.

If the print head jams, the printer will probably display a status message or show a flashing LED. Try turning the printer off and unplugging it then turning it back on. Inconsistent color output indicates that one of the ink reservoirs is running low (or that a print head for one of the color cartridges is completely blocked). If a document does not print in color, check that color printing has actually been selected.

Dot matrix printer troubleshooting

Lines in the output indicate a stuck pin in the print head. Output can also be affected by the platen position (the platen adjusts the gap between the paper and the print head to accommodate different paper types).

Summary

It is important to have a good understanding of the steps and components in the laser and inkjet print processes and the sort of consumables and options associated with each type of device.

Printer installation is quite straightforward, but make sure you know how to access the different configuration options and printing preferences.

Make sure you understand the basic maintenance processes for lasers and inkjets. Troubleshooting printing is a case of diagnosing a specific output problem (print quality) or interpreting an error message.

Module 6 Taking the Exams   *Taking the Exams*

Module 6 Taking the Exams

When you think you have learned and practiced the material sufficiently, you can book a time to take the test.

Preparing for the Essentials Exam

Questions in the exam are weighted by domain area as follows:

A+ Certification Essentials Domain Areas	% of Examination
1.0 Hardware	27%
2.0 Troubleshooting, Repair, and Maintenance	20%
3.0 Operating System and Software	20%
4.0 Networking	15%
5.0 Security	8%
6.0 Operational Procedure	10%

Because there are 100 questions in the exam, you should expect to see 27 questions on hardware, 21 on operating systems, 15 on networks, and so on.

As you can see, almost half the questions are on basic hardware and operating systems topics; the other half are on installation and troubleshooting, networking, security, and safety and professionalism (operational procedure). We've tried to balance this course to reflect the percentages in the exam so that you have learned the correct level of detail about each topic to comfortably answer the exam questions.

Read the following notes to find out what you need to do to register for the exam and get some tips on what to expect during the exam and how to prepare for it.

There are two practice tests for the Essentials exam available on the support website. Each test contains 100 questions and the same domain weightings as the actual exam.

© 2010 gtslearning   IT Career FastTrack with CompTIA A+ Certification   Page 695

When you think you have studied enough and know the material quite well, take one of the practice tests. To access the exams on the support site, click the **Exam** link in the navigation bar. If you score less than 95%, you probably need to do more study. You need about 85% to pass the actual exam so you should make sure you can exceed that target comfortably before booking the test.

Exam
220-701
220-702

Preparing for the Exams

This section contains information about the exam and links to the practice tests.

Questions in the exam are weighted by domain area as follows:

Domains	701 Weighting	702 Weighting
Hardware	27%	38%
Troubleshooting, Repair, and Maintenance	20%	-
Operating System and Software	20%	34%
Networking	15%	15%
Security	8%	13%
Operational Procedure	10%	-

When you are preparing for the either exam, you can check the key units to revise and complete bonus review questions using the links on the left.

Visit www.aplus-fast.com to complete practice exams

Take the second practice test for extra confirmation that you have done enough preparation.

The Exam area of the support site also contains an exam walkthrough, study notes to help identify the key units to revise for either exam, and extra review questions.

Module 6 Taking the Exams   *Taking the Exams*

Registering for the Exam

Two commercial organizations currently administer the CompTIA
Certification exams - VUE and Prometric. You can locate a test center using
the links on CompTIA's website:
certification.comptia.org/resources/registration.aspx

> **Note**
>
> You can obtain a discount on the full cost of the exams by purchasing a
> voucher from gtslearning. The voucher may be used to book an exam at a
> Prometric test center. Visit **www.aplus-fast.com** and register to buy your
> discounted exam voucher.

- Log on to VUE (www.pearsonvue.com/comptia) or Prometric
  (www.prometric.com/CompTIA/default.htm)

- Register your details to create an account.

- To book a test, log in using your account credentials then click the link to
  schedule an appointment.

- The testing program is CompTIA and the exam is 220-701.

- Use the search tool to locate the test center nearest you then book an
  appointment.

- If you have purchased the voucher available with this course, enter the
  voucher number to pay for the exam - remember that the voucher can only
  be used with Prometric. Otherwise, you can pay with a credit card.

- When you have confirmed payment, an email will be sent to the account
  used to register confirming the appointment and directions to the venue.
  Print a copy and bring it with you when you go to take your test.

Arriving for the Exam

- Arrive at the test center at least 15 minutes before the test is scheduled.

- You must have two forms of ID - one with picture, both with signature,
  preferably with your private address (driving license, passport, and so on).

- Books, calculators, laptops, PDAs, cellphones, or other reference materials
  are not allowed.

© 2010 gtslearning   IT Career FastTrack with CompTIA A+ Certification   Page 697

| Module 6 | Module 6 Taking the Exams |

- You will be given a pad and marker to make notes but you must not attempt to write down questions or remove anything from the exam room.

- It is CompTIA's policy to make reasonable accommodations for individuals with disabilities.

- The test center administrator will demonstrate how to use the computer-based test system and wish you good luck. Check that your name is displayed, read the introductory note, and then click the button to start the exam.

Taking the Essentials Exam

- There are 100 questions which must be answered in 90 minutes. The passing score is 675 on a scale of 100-900.

- Read each question and its option answers carefully. Don't rush through the exam as you'll probably have more time at the end than you expect.

- At the other end of the scale, don't get "stuck" on a question and start to panic. You can mark questions for review and come back to them.

- As the exam tests your ability to recall facts and to apply them sensibly in a troubleshooting scenario, there will be questions where you cannot recall the correct answer from memory. Adopt the following strategy for dealing with these questions:

    □ Narrow your choices down by eliminating obviously wrong answers.

    □ Don't guess too soon! You must select not only a *correct* answer, but the *best* answer. It is therefore important that you read all of the options and not stop when you find an option that is correct. It may be impractical compared to another answer.

    □ Utilize information and insights that you've acquired in working through the entire test to go back and answer earlier items that you weren't sure of.

    □ Think your answer is wrong - should change it? Studies indicate that when students change their answers they usually change them to the wrong answer. If you were fairly certain you were correct the first time, leave the answer as it is.

Page 698 · IT Career FastTrack with CompTIA A+ Certification · © 2010 gtslearning

Module 6 Taking the Exams | Taking the Exams

- Don't leave any questions unanswered! If you really don't know the answer, just guess.

- The exam may contain "unscored" questions, which may even be outside the exam objectives. These questions do not count towards your score.

- The exam questions come from a regularly updated pool to deter cheating. Do not be surprised if the questions you get are quite different to someone else's experience.

Good Luck!

After the Exam

- A score report will be generated and a copy printed for you by the test administrator.

- The score report will show whether you have passed or failed and your score in each section. Make sure you retain the report!

- Once you have passed both exams (Essentials plus the Practical Application 702 exam, a certificate and ID card should be with you in 4-6 weeks.

- If 8 weeks have passed after taking your exam and you haven't received a copy of your certificate, contact questions@comptia.org.

- You can use your Career ID to track your certification progress on CompTIA's website (certify.comptia.org), order duplicate certificates, and download certification logos in various image file formats.

© 2010 gtslearning | IT Career FastTrack with CompTIA A+ Certification | Page 699

Module 6   Module 6 Taking the Exams

Taking the Practical Application Exam

Questions in the 220-702 "Practical Application" exam are weighted by domain area as follows:

A+ Certification Practical Application Domain Areas	% of Examination
1.0 Hardware	38%
2.0 Operating Systems	34%
3.0 Networking	15%
4.0 Security	13%

Tip

If you are confident, there is nothing to stop you from scheduling both exams on the same day. The benefit of leaving a gap between the exams is that you can use insights gained from the first exam to help with the second. As this is likely to be the first IT certification exam you have taken, it is probably best to take a cautious approach. There is no time limit between passing one exam and taking the other. You could also take the Practical Application exam *before* the Essentials exam, if you really wanted to.

When it comes to preparing for the 220-702 CompTIA A+ Practical Application exam, you should review the material in modules 1-5, paying more attention to the Practical Application objectives listed at the start of each unit.

As with Essentials, there are two practice tests for the Practical Application exam available on the support website. Each test contains 100 questions and the same domain weightings as the actual exam. The passing score for the Practical Application exam is 700 on a scale of 100-900.

When you think you have studied enough and know the material quite well, take one of the practice tests. If you score less than 95%, you probably need to do more study. You need about 85% to pass the actual exam so you should make sure you can exceed that target comfortably before booking the test.

Take the second practice test for extra confirmation that you have done enough preparation.

The process for booking the test is much the same as for the Essentials exam, except that you will already have registered your details with Prometric or VUE (make sure to book the exam using the same account). You should also input your CompTIA Career ID (printed on your Essentials score report).

Page 700   IT Career FastTrack with CompTIA A+ Certification   © 2010 gtslearning

Module 7 Career Advice

Module 7 Career Advice

CompTIA A+ Certification is a great thing to have to prove to employers that you know a lot about PC support, but it is not a golden ticket into employment. To get a job, you need to know where to look, how to write a good resume and application letter, how to prepare for an interview, and generally how to impress potential employers.

This module contains tips to help you do this. There are also sample job-hunting resources, such as a resume and covering letter, on the support website (www.aplus-fast.com). To access these tools, click the **Your Career** link in the **Resources** menu on the left.

Making a Career Plan

To make a career plan, first you need to think about where you are and where you want to be. Then you identify the steps you need to take to get from one situation to the other.

No job experience

It is likely that you will not have any formal job experience. However, becoming A+ Certified is an excellent way to demonstrate that you have the necessary skills and that you have the enthusiasm to pursue a career in this area. If you have completed the practical activities suggested on the CD, you will also have some evidence of practical experience.

Already working in the IT industry

If you work in the IT industry in a customer services or administrative role, you may want to move into or up to a support role. Becoming A+ Certified is an excellent way to demonstrate that you have the necessary *skills* and *enthusiasm* to pursue a career in this area. You should also be able to demonstrate customer service skills from your current job.

Module 7   Module 7 Career Advice

If you are already working in PC support and want to move further up the ladder, your job experience and A+ Certification will serve you well in proving that you have acquired basic skills and aptitudes. In a Help Desk environment, there might be scope for you to be promoted to Senior Technician level. Alternatively, you may look at Network Support or an applications or programming role.

For any of these options, you are going to need to acquire the relevant technical skills and possibly certifications. More information on these can be found under the "Career Paths" topic below.

Working in another industry

IT is a popular career choice for many "job changers". As described above, you can use A+ as evidence of your aptitude and enthusiasm for IT support and use your career to date as evidence of your skills in communication and professionalism.

IT Support Job Roles

IT support is provided in a number of ways. In planning your career, you should first recognize the range of organizations that recruit IT support staff and the sort of job roles available within each.

IT technicians

"IT Technician" describes the "traditional" PC service role, where a technical support department provide assistance to a number of users. Typically this involves both remote and client-facing support. Apart from technical support within medium-size and large companies[296], this role is also important to the third-party IT support service industry. These businesses range widely in size and turnover, from sole traders to stock market listed companies.

---

[296] IT support technicians working in smaller companies are likely to need a broader range of skills (including server and network management).

Page 702   IT Career FastTrack with CompTIA A+ Certification   © 2010 gtslearning

| Module 7 Career Advice | Career Advice |

PC technicians need to demonstrate a full range of technical skills. Apart from troubleshooting and maintenance, typical activities are completing hardware and OS upgrades, performing simple network configuration, and training and supporting users.

Apart from PC technicians, the CompTIA A+ skill set is also useful to those in a PC or software sales role. Sound technical knowledge enables sales staff to discuss benefits of products authoritatively and understand client needs.

PC support and application support are typically the entry-level positions within an IT support department or help desk. Roles may be divided between two levels, with senior technicians taking more responsibility in resolving problems, taking decisions, making recommendations, and providing team leadership.

More senior roles take responsibility for network support and then network and application service design and management.

Remote support

Remote support is now a specialist function within many IT support departments and contact centers[297]. This type of role is increasingly important as more and more software and hardware vendors realize that providing cost-effective technical support is a key product differentiator. Managed services IT providers also use remote support to proactively manage a customer's IT infrastructure, rather than responding to support incidents.

Traditionally, remote support was very much telephone-based. However, the technologies available for remote configuration have improved to the extent that many incidents are now dealt with using email or chat messaging plus Remote Assistance-style tools (see unit 2.3). These tools are highly cost-effective, greatly reducing the number of incidents that require a site visit.

In terms of technical skills, remote support is more focused on software troubleshooting and configuration.

---

[297] Technicians are usually graded, with Level 1 techs providing telephone and remote support and more experienced Level 2 techs handling any desk-side or client-facing jobs.

© 2010 gtslearning   IT Career FastTrack with CompTIA A+ Certification   Page 703

Contact centers

A **contact center** (or **help desk**) is a division responsible for receiving, initiating, and managing customer contacts. A contact center may be a unit within a business or may be a business in itself. The concept of a contact center is to provide a proper framework for the supply of services to customers.

The benefits of contact centers are:

- Well-advertised and recognized single point-of-contact for customers (telephone number, email, website).

- Documented mission statements, call management procedures, customer service standards, and quality assurance.

- Professional customer services personnel trained in the range of competencies required and able to respond to requests in a courteous and positive manner.

- Use of technology to implement and manage support calls and documented Customer Relationship Management (CRM).

- Efficient use of staff and equipment resources, resulting in cost savings for the company.

Contact center job roles are usually divided between:

- Customer service operators - take initial contacts, deal with basic queries, or direct calls to appropriate service area.

- Analyst / Service Technician - provide advice and troubleshooting. This role may be graded between first and second line support.

Service technician

- Team leader - responsibility for leading and motivating a team or department. Managers must demonstrate a variety of skills, including being able to recruit, develop, and motivate staff, design efficient procedures and operations, monitor and evaluate service quality and performance, and deal with change and crisis.

Module 7 Career Advice   Career Advice

- Contact Center Manager / Operations Manager - the senior role within the contact center, with responsibility for setting policy, managing the budget, managing day-to-day operations, providing staff and equipment resources, and ensuring compliance (adherence to legal requirements).

Managed services

Managed Services companies provide a completely outsourced IT solution to businesses. The advantage for the business is that it does not need to retain in-house expertise or employees.

Managed services typically use remote support to handle monitoring and basic troubleshooting and configuration of computer systems. Site visits may be required for new installations or complex troubleshooting, but the focus is on proactively managing the IT infrastructure rather than responding to incidents.

Depot technicians

The depot (or bench) technician role is one that involves the least direct client contact. Depot technicians will perform PC troubleshooting, maintenance, and optimization that cannot be performed in the field. Consequently, the emphasis is on hardware systems building, troubleshooting, and maintenance skills.

This role may exist as a specialist part of the support services in larger companies but most jobs are with PC and hardware vendors.

Self-employed technicians

Starting your own business is another IT support career option. There is a huge market for assisting home users and small businesses with new PC sales and troubleshooting. As with any small business though, you need to be able to handle marketing, accounting, and legal issues to make the business successful, in addition to developing your technical and customer service skills.

© 2010 gtslearning   IT Career FastTrack with CompTIA A+ Certification   Page 705

Searching for Vacancies

To summarize from the section above, you will be searching for vacancies such as "PC Support Technician", "PC Engineer", "Support Engineer", "Support Specialist", or "Systems Administrator" for hands-on roles or "Help Desk Technician" or "Call Center Technician" for remote support roles.

The most likely recruiters are medium to large companies with internal support departments or third-party IT support specialists of any size.

A simple approach to job seeking is to sign on with recruitment agencies. Many companies use agencies to handle recruitment so you may find that job adverts are placed by an agency anyway. Make sure you choose agencies that specialize in IT support.

The next simplest option is to browse advertised vacancies and post your resume to a recruitment website. Some popular sites include itjobs.com, careerbuilder.com, computerjobs.com, hotjobs.com, and monster.com. You should also look at the job ads in local newspapers.

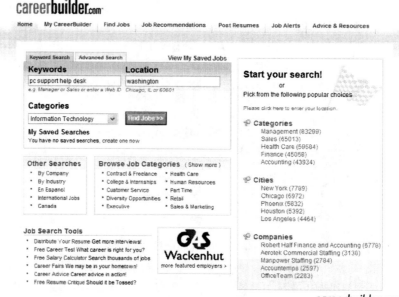

careerbuilder.com

If these approaches do not turn up anything, you can try the following:

- Ask family, friends, and educators for contacts or introductions.
- Approach local companies speculatively (see "Cold calling employers" below).

Module 7 Career Advice

Career Advice

Approaching Employers

When you respond to a vacancy you have seen advertised, you will normally submit your resume (with a covering letter) or possibly complete an application form and might then attend an interview.

Resume

Your resume is the key tool to get you into work. A resume is a description of your skills and career history. You must make sure that your resume is factually correct, contains no spelling or grammar errors, advertises the skills and experience employers will be interested in, and has a simple and attractive layout. Your resume should be no longer than 2 pages. If you do not have much previous experience, use a 1 page resume rather than trying to "pad out" to 2 pages. You can either organize a resume to focus on career history or on skills. As you are probably entering the job market for the first time, the latter approach is probably best. The typical layout is as follows:

- Personal details - make sure your name and contact details (address, telephone, and email) are clearly printed. Do *not* include your date of birth, marital status, gender, or a photograph.

- Profile - this explains why you are looking for a job in IT support. Try to tell your *story* to make yourself interesting to employers. The profile should explain what skills and relevant experience you have gained in the past, why you are a great candidate for an IT support position now, and how you plan to develop your career. Given all this, the profile must also be short (no more than 4-5 lines).

- Key skills / qualifications - key skills should be presented as 4-5 bullet points, each of a single line. Your A+ qualification should be top of the list. Other key skills should relate to what an employer says they are looking for in their job advert or other skills you have that could be valuable (such as speaking foreign languages).

- Achievements - in a 2-page resume or if your career history is short and not relevant to the post you are seeking, present a list of 4-5 key achievements that demonstrate that you have some of the *experience* that will be relevant to the prospective employer. Achievements should also demonstrate that you can *use* your skills effectively.

© 2010 gtslearning

IT Career FastTrack with CompTIA A+ Certification

Page 707

| Module 7 | Module 7 Career Advice |

- Career history - a list of significant employment and/or voluntary work in reverse chronological order. List the job title, company, date, and key achievements. Do not try to make inflated claims for minor jobs but do try to show that you have gained at least some experience in all the areas that will interest prospective employers (specific IT experience, team working, and customer support).

> **Tip**
>
> In a career-focused resume, career history will come before key skills. If there are long gaps (over 1 month) in your employment history, try to find ways to explain them in your resume (for example, show that you were doing voluntary work or travelling). Be prepared to be asked about gaps at an interview.

- Education - list academic education, with the name of each school or college, dates attended, and key qualifications. Also list any relevant professional training.

- Hobbies - only list hobbies if you have spare space and they are genuinely interesting, reflect some genuine achievement, or demonstrate your character.

- References - you do not need to include previous employer or character references unless specifically requested by the prospective employer. Do state that references can be provided on request.

> **Tip**
>
> You will need 2-3 references and cannot use members of your family. If you do not have a previous employer, ask educators or friends of good professional standing. Give your referees a copy of your resume.

When you have finished your resume, hold it at arm's length for 10 seconds - what part of it stands out? Does the resume make it clear that you want a career in IT support and have skills (A+ Certification) and some experience? Get other people to give you their opinion about your resume and ideally to help you check it for any mistakes.

When you print your resume, use good quality paper (*not* colored) and a decent printer (it is probably worth getting copies printed professionally). If you submit your resume online or by email, Microsoft Word, RTF, or PDF format is probably best. If submitting an electronic file, stick to common fonts to avoid formatting problems.

Module 7 Career Advice   *Career Advice*

If you post your resume to recruitment websites, remember to re-upload it each week so that employers know you are still in the job market.

Application forms

The challenge of an application form is to leverage the material in your resume to the format required by the form.

When completing a form by hand (required by some employers), print and fill out a draft copy first and work on it until you are happy with the text. Spell check what you have written carefully.

Covering letter

A resume or application form should normally be accompanied by a covering letter, especially if applying for a job speculatively. The covering letter should be hand-written if this is specifically requested by the employer (unlikely for jobs in IT support).

The purpose of a covering letter is to show that you want the job, that you are interested in the company, and to draw out the key skills and achievements from your resume that demonstrate that you are a capable candidate for the job. The covering letter should fit on one page and consist of 3-4 paragraphs of 4-5 lines.

Cold calling employers

If you do not see many vacancies advertised, you may wish to approach companies speculatively by cold calling them. This is very hard work and you must prepare to face many rejections, but it does demonstrate your commitment and confidence.

1. Make a list of likely companies in your area. Remember the companies with the most potential are likely to be medium to large companies with internal support departments or third-party IT support specialists of any size. You should be able to locate third-party IT support companies via the yellow pages and the larger companies close to where you want to work should be quite easy to identify.

© 2010 gtslearning   IT Career FastTrack with CompTIA A+ Certification   Page 709

Module 7	Module 7 Career Advice

Tip

Be methodical when cold calling companies. Make sure you make a note of who you have called already!

2. Research the company using their website - find out what they sell and who to. If possible, find out who is responsible for recruitment (obviously also check if they are advertising any jobs!)

3. Phone the company and ask the receptionist who (if anyone) manages IT or computers or computer support in the company. Make sure you get their name (correctly spelled) and job title. Remember to thank the receptionist.

Tip

You want to try to approach the person responsible for IT support rather than an HR manager.

4. Adapt your resume and covering letter to write a speculative application to work with the company in a support role. Make it clear in the letter that you have researched and understand their business.

5. Follow-up the letter (around 3-5 days after sending it) by calling the IT or support manager. Ask if they have had a chance to look at your resume and whether any opportunities are available, now or in the future. If there are no opportunities, ask whether they know of any other firms that might have openings and whether you can use their name to approach them (a referral).

Preparing for interview

To prepare for an interview, you should anticipate what questions you will be asked. Interview questions will focus on the skills and required experience that are listed in the job advert. The interviewer(s) will want either evidence of previous experience or to be convinced that you are competent enough to learn quickly and to assess your character and personality.

Interviewers are also likely to ask questions based on your resume - for example, "I see you have A+ Certification but you haven't worked in IT support before - do you have any practical experience of maintaining PCs?" They may also ask questions designed to confirm that you really have the skills and experience that you are claiming.

Page 710   IT Career FastTrack with CompTIA A+ Certification   © 2010 gtslearning

Module 7 Career Advice   Career Advice

Some of the standard questions to prepare answers for include:

- Why do you want this job? / Why do you want to work for this company?

- What are your strengths and weaknesses?

- How would you cope with…?

Prepare and memorize 4-5 little scenarios that demonstrate practical experience of IT troubleshooting, configuring or specifying a computer system, dealing with customers, working on a team, showing resourcefulness when faced with a problem, and dealing with a difficult or challenging situation. These should be things you have actually done - do not make anything up. You should be able to deploy these scenarios to answer most of the questions you will be asked. Try not to repeat yourself.

Show that you understand the realities of working in support and that you have taken the time to research the prospective employer's business. Your weakness is likely to be obvious (lack of professional experience), but show that you understand that and are resourceful enough to have acquired skills in other ways and that you can learn quickly.

Tip

A lot of people with no professional experience will say they have experience from helping with friends' and family's PCs. If you have to rely on this type of experience, be specific about what sort of problems you have fixed and make it clear that you also understand that professional IT support is more pressured environment.

Also prepare any questions you might have about the post, both in terms of responsibilities and pay and benefits. These may be covered in the course of the interview, but you will also be asked if you have any questions. Only ask a *good* question; do not ask one for the sake of it.

On the day of the interview, dress smartly and check your appearance in a mirror. Make sure you arrive on time. Bring a couple of copies of your resume with you.

When you walk in, keep your head up and make eye contact with the people in the room. Shake hands and introduce yourself. When you answer questions, try to keep making eye contact. Sit up and try not to fidget but do use hand gestures to reinforce what you are saying.

At the end of the interview, get up and shake hands with each interviewer, thanking them for their time.

© 2010 gtslearning   IT Career FastTrack with CompTIA A+ Certification   Page 711

Module 7   Module 7 Career Advice

Career Paths

PC support is an entry-level position with the field of IT job opportunities.
You should start to think early about how to progress your career.

Network support

A typical route from PC support is into network support. **CompTIA's
Network+** certification provides an entry-level qualification. Most network
support technicians and engineers will progress to **Microsoft Certified
Systems Administrator (MCSA)** or **Microsoft Certified Systems Engineer
(MCSE)** for the Windows Server 2003 track or **Microsoft Certified IT
Professional (MCITP)** for the Windows Server 2008 Server Administrator /
Enterprise Administrator track. A+ and Network+ can count towards
obtaining these. Other options include **CCNA** and **CCNP** (for supporting
Cisco networks) or Linux professional qualifications (such as **LPI**).

Security is an increasingly important specialization, both within network
support and for specific job roles within IT. **CompTIA's Security+** certification
provides an entry-level qualification.

Application support

Application support means assisting users with software applications and
troubleshooting errors. The **Help Desk Analyst (HDA)** qualification validates
general support skills. **MCITP Support Technician** certifications are available
for those providing enterprise and consumer support for Windows desktop
software. More specialized support is provided for database applications
customized to a particular function (Line of Business applications). At this level,
there are numerous vendor certifications for different application products.

Management

If you have any leadership ability, you may move into some sort of
management role. Most organizations have a defined role for team leaders
with line managers above them. There are many management qualifications,
but to get on this career path you need to demonstrate the ability to make
decisions, motivate others, and plan effectively.

Page 712   IT Career FastTrack with CompTIA A+ Certification   © 2010 gtslearning

Index

⅛

⅛" Connector 95

1

10BASE Standards 512

3

3.5" Diskette 59
32-bit CPU 38
3DNow! 37

6

64-bit CPU 38

8

802.1X 532
8mm Tape 67

A

AC Adapter 125, 476
Access Control 550
Access Control List 559
Access Point 529, 530, 614
Access Time 61
Accident 293
Accounting 319
ACL 614
ACPI 230
ACR 26
Acronyms 267
Active Listening 268
Active Partition 189
Adapter Card 76, 89, 95, 368, 391, 472
Adapter Cards 22
Add Hardware Wizard 431
Add or Remove Programs ... 223
Address Bus 40
Addressing 497, 523
Administrative Share 568

Administrative Tools 180, 242
Administrator Account 549, 550, 551
Advanced BIOS Settings 455
Advanced Startup Options .. 403
Adware 643
Aero 142, 257
AGP 24, 368
Air Quality 334
Alerts 445
Allocation Unit 191
Alternate Configuration 527
AMD 44
AMR 26
Analyzing Problems 285
Answer Files 167
Antenna 488, 528, 529
Anti-static Precautions 301, 302, 303, 304
Anti-virus Software 648, 649
APIPA 524, 525
Apple 148
Application Compatibility ... 127, 226, 227
Application Management 223
Application Problems 437
Archive Attribute 215, 347
ARP 502
Aspect Ratio 86
ASR 412
Assessing Problems 285
ATA 29
Athlon 44
Athlon 64 45
Attended Installation 152
Attribute 215
ATX 15
ATX12V 106
Audio Connector 95
Audio Device 95
Audio Inspection 285
Auditing 319
Authentication 317, 532
Authorization 314
AutoComplete 627

Automatic Address Assignment
.... 525
Automatic Updates 340
Auto-restart Errors 428
Auto-switching 104, 125

B

Backdoor 657
Background Processes 248
Backlight 485
Backup 326, 345
  System 410
Bandwidth 495
Bank 56
Bar Code Reader 80
Baseline 238
Batch File 252
Battery 126, 309, 476, 477
BCD 400
Biometric Devices 80, 318
BIOS 21, 401
BIOS Security 571
BIOS Updates 343
Bit 11
BitLocker 575
Blackout 305
Blank Paper 692
Blanking Plate 368
Bluescreens 428, 458
Bluetooth 124, 541, 543
Blu-ray 66
Body Language 270
Boot Environment 658
Boot Media .. 152, 393, 411, 417
Boot Problems 417
BOOT.INI 394, 397, 398
BOOTREC 409
Botnet 643
Broadband 579
Brownout 305
Browser 621
Browser Cache 626
BTX 15
Bus Architecture 22
Bus Slots 18, 23, 24, 26

Index

Bus Speed........39, 354, 376, 386

C

CA.................................628
Cable Certifier.....................602
Cable Internet Access...........580
Cable Length 513
Cable Modem.....................590
Cabling.............................602
Cache.................21, 39, 256
Capacitor 14
Capture Card.......................101
Cases.................................15
CD (CHDIR).......................205
CD / CD-R / CD-RW..... 62, 63, 361
CD Problems.......................470
Cellular.................124, 581, 590
Centronics...........................72
Certificate Authority.............316
Changing Default Access Point
Credentials.........................533
Channel 533
Chassis...............................15
Check Disk 255
Chipset 20
Classful Subnet....................500
Classification of Information 325
Cleaning Computer
Components.........336, 337, 338
Cleaning Printers 682
Cleaning Products 335
Clear Paper Jam 683
Client.................................489
Client Options 544
Client-Server 492
Clock Speed.........................39
Cluster...............................191
CMD.................................178
CMOS.......................21, 401
CMOS Battery.....................457
CMOS Setup.......................455
CNR..................................26
Coaxial Cable......................520
Command Prompt................178
Communication 267
Communications Devices 81
Communications Problems.488, 597

Complaints 278
Compliance...........................313
Component Video..................92
Components 18
Computer Management 180
Computer Name..................544
Conductor 14
Confidentiality......................275
Configuring Displays 371
Configuring Drives................362
Configuring Input Devices ...386
Configuring Multimedia Devices
....386
Connection Status.................598
Contact Centers....................704
Contrast Ratio 86
Control Panel.......................174
Cookie................................626
Cooling Devices 108, 378
COPY.................................213
Copy Backup 347
Cordless Phone Interference
....304
Core i7................................44
Counter 243
CPU.........34, 35, 117, 378, 480
CPU Problems.......................458
CPU Sockets 46
Creating Folders...........198, 207
CRM..................................704
CRT 83
Cultural Sensitivity................276
Current...............................14

D

DAT...................................67
Data Protection....................313
Data Wiping..........................327
Daughter Board.....................15
DDR SDRAM........................53
DDS...................................67
Deconstruction.....................326
Default Gateway...........523, 593
Defragmenter.......................253
DEL...................................211
DEP...................................41
Deployment.........................167
Desktop 15, 130, 136, 141
Device Installation........430, 431

Device Manager....................433
Device Removal....................436
DHCP...........524, 525, 527, 532
Diagnostic Tools 421, 447
Dial-up...............................577
Dial-up Networking.............591
Dial-up Problems.................600
Differential Backup...............347
Difficult Situations................278
Digital Camera......................99
Digital Certificate.316, 318, 628
Digital Video Recorder.......101
Digitizer 119, 486
DIMM 51
Diode 14
DIR 206
Directory Structures............193
DirectX 222
Disabling DHCP 532
Disinfecting Viruses 654
Disk Boot Order..................401
Disk Cleanup.......................254
Disk Management.........192, 250
Display Problems..........473, 485
Disposal 309
Distractions.........................276
DLT 67
DNS.............504, 523, 525, 609
Docking Station.....................123
Documentation Resources. 289, 291
Documenting Activities........289
Documenting Services..........270
Documents and Settings......194
Domain 154, 493
Domain Controller..............154
Domain Name 504
DOS..................................128
Dot Matrix Printer..............669
Double-sided Memory 56
Dr. Watson 441
Dress Code..........................270
Drive Controller...................28
Drive Encryption..................575
Drive Imaging........................168
Drive Lock...........................571
Drive Preparation 153, 189, 362
Drive Status 467
Driver.................171, 430, 431
Driver Signing 432

Page 714   IT Career FastTrack with CompTIA A+ Certification   © 2010 gtslearning

Index

Driver Updates.....................343
DSL..........................579, 588
Dual Monitors......................374
Dual-channel.........................56
Dual-core.............................37
Duplex Printing..................679
Duplexing............................364
Duron.................................44
DVB.................................101
DVB-S..............................591
DVD / DVD±R / DVD±RW 62,
64, 361
DVD Problems....................470
DVI..................................92
Dynamic Disks....................366

E

EAP.................................532
ECC..................................57
EDIT................................210
Educate Users.....................646
EFS.................................573
EIDE.................................29
Electrical Interference . 512, 596
Electrical Safety..................296
Email.....................507, 508, 631
EMF.................................662
EMI...................304, 512, 596
Empathy............................269
Encryption....................315, 573
EnergyStar........................230
Environment.........298, 309, 332
Equal Opportunities..............313
ERD..................................411
Error Codes........................689
Error Reporting...................441
eSATA.................................30
Escalation...................273, 287
ESD.............301, 302, 303, 304
Ethernet........................512, 513
EULA................................129
Evaluating Results................287
Event Logging......................421
Event Viewer.........180, 421, 423
Excessive Heat.....................445
EXPAND.............................216
Expansion Bus.......................22
Expansion Slot.....................368
ExpressCard........................122

Extended Partition...............189
Extension...........................208
Extension Magnet.................330
External Cache Memory.........21
External Drive.......................62
External Monitor..................485
Eyestrain...........................298

F

Failed Volume.....................467
Fan.................................109
FAT.................................190
FDD.............................59, 361
FDD Problems.....................470
Fiber Optic Cable................519
File.........................208, 213
File and Settings Wizard.......165
File Attribute.....................215
File System ... 189, 250, 256, 559
Filenames..........................208
Fire Safety........................294
Firewall.........317, 532, 612, 614
Firewire.............75, 392, 464
Firmware.................21, 343, 535
Fixed Input........................104
Fixed-input........................125
Flash Memory.......................68
Flip3D.............................142
Fob.................................318
Folder..............................193
Folder Options............200, 569
Fonts..............................691
Foreign Disk......................467
Form Tray.........................678
FORMAT..............................192
Formatting Volume...............467
Fox and Hound....................602
FQDN................................504
Front Panel Connector........384
FSB..................................20
FTP.........................508, 633
FTTx...............................580
Full Backup........................347
Full Duplex........................496
Function Keys......................119
Fuse.............................14, 296
Fuser..............................685

G

Game Pad......................80, 390
Garbage Printout.................690
Gateway............................523
GB..................................11
GDI...........................662, 680
Gesture Control....................79
Ghosted Image....................693
GPO.................................549
GPU..................................91
Graphics Adapter.................370
Group..............................549
Group Account.....................556
Guest..............................549
Guest Account..............550, 553
GUI.................................128

H

HAL.................................171
Half-duplex........................496
Hand Tools........................330
Hardware..........................444
Hardware Compatibility.......151
Hardware Deconstruction...326
Hardware Lock.....................572
Hardware Profile.................436
HCL.................................146
HDD.......60, 118, 356, 359, 360
HDD Problems.....................465
HDMI................................92
Health and Safety.........293, 313
Healthy Volume...................467
Heat Pipe..........................110
Heat Spreader.....................110
Heatsink...........................108
HELP................................178
Help and Support.................289
Help Desk.........................704
Hertz...............................13
Hexadecimal........................12
Hibernate..........................230
Hidden Attribute..................215
High Definition...................101
High Voltage Service Area...304
Hoax..............................644
Host Adapter.......................31
Host Name.........................523
HOSTS..............................610

Index

Hot Swappable......................219	Insulator..................................14	LCD...84
HTML..503	Intel...42	LCD Cut-off........................485
HTTP..503	Internal Drive........................60	Least Privilege.....................551
HTTPS.........................506, 628	Internet..................................490	LGA...46
Hub 513, 515	Internet Cache......................626	Lifting......................................297
Humidity.................................304	Internet Connection 582	Line Conditioner.................305
HyperThreading.....................36	Internet Explorer 591, 623	Lines in Printout..........693, 694
	Intrusion Detection 572	Link...26
I	Inverter 485	Linux..147
	IP Address 500, 523	Liquid Cooling Systems........110
I/O Device 76	IP Address Filtering..............317	LMHOSTS 610
I/O Interfaces 71	IP Version 6...........................501	Local Share...........................570
I/O Problems...........................462	IPCONFIG................................604	Local Users and Groups 553,
IAB..491	IRQ 219	554
IANA..491	ISA...368	Local versus Network Printing
ICANN.......................................491	ISDN..............................578, 587	664
ICMP 502, 606	ISOC...491	Lock Workstation.................573
ICS..593	ISP 583	Locking Workstation... 314, 321
ID...31		Lockup Problems 429
IDE 29	**J**	Logical Drive..........................189
Identifying Problems.............285		Loopback Address 606
IEEE 1284 72	Jargon......................................267	Loopback Test.......................462
IEEE 1394 75	JBOD 366	
IEEE 802.11 528	Joystick.............................80, 390	**M**
IEEE 802.2 498	Jumper settings 384	
IEEE 802.3 512		MAC Address........498, 516, 532
IETF...491	**K**	MAC Filtering 532
Image...415		Mac OS 148
Imaging.............................152, 362	K5 / K6......................................44	Magnets....................................304
IMAP 507, 631	KB 11	Mail Protocol Settings 631
Incident Reporting.................319	Kernel.......................................170	Mail Servers............................507
Incompatible Driver 680, 690	Keyboard 76, 388	Maintenance Kit.....................685
Incremental Backup...............347	Keyboard (Laptop)................482	Malware 323
Index Settings.........................262	Keyboard Problems 472	Malware Symptoms................642
Index, Value Of 292	Keyboard Regionalization 388	Manual Handling.....................297
Infrared.....................................124	Keyboards and Languages....234	Map Network Drive.............547
Inheritance..............................561	Knowledge Base 290, 291	Materials Safety......................300
Inkjet Printer 668	KVM Switch..............................78	MB..11
Input Device 76		MBR..............................189, 658
Input Device Problems 486	**L**	MD..207
Installation Methods..... 152, 154		Media Bay 118
Installing Components..........353	L1 / L2 Cache..........................39	Media Center.........................101
Installing Display Devices 370	LAN 496, 594	Memory 50, 118, 376, 479
Installing Drives.....................354	LAN Speed 512	Memory Address....................219
Installing Input Devices 386	Lane 26	Memory Card 68
Installing Memory 376	Laptop Problems 483	Memory Card Reader 361
Installing Multimedia Devices	Laptops............................117, 476	Memory Chips.........................55
....386	Laser Printer 665	Memory Problems 461
Instant Messaging...................509	Last Known Good.................404	Memory Sharing 480
Instruction Set.........................38	Latency............................21, 496	Memory Slots...............18, 376

Page 716   IT Career FastTrack with CompTIA A+ Certification   © 2010 gtslearning

Index

MicroATX 17
Microwave Interference 304
MIDI 95, 97
Mini PCI 122
Mini-DIN 71
Mirroring 364
MMC 182
MMX 37
Modem 81, 577, 584
Modem Problems 600
Motherboard 15, 385
Motherboard Components ... 18
Motherboard Problems 458
Mount Point 204
Mouse 77, 387
Mouse Problems 472
MOVE 213
Moving Parts 298
MSCONFIG 248
MSDS 300
MSINFO32 221
MTBF 61
MT-RJ 519
Multifunction Network Device
.... 588
Multimedia Connector 95
Multimeter 449, 602
Multi-monitor Settings 374
Multi-touch 79
My Computer 176
My Network Places 544, 547

N

NAT 615, 620
Native Resolution 86
Navigating Directories 198, 205
NET Commands 636
NetBEUI 510
NetBIOS 510
Netbook 115
NETSTAT 610
Network 489, 492, 511
  Adapter 516
  Browsing 547
  Cabling 577
  Client software 544
  Configuring client 154, 540
  Configuring wireless client...536, 537
  Domain 154
  Installing 516
  Models 492

Permissions 563
Physical installation 513
Printing 673
Protocols 498, 521
Sharing 563
TCP/IP configuration 525
Troubleshooting..........596, 597, 604
Wireless 528
Workgroup 154
Network Adapter 81, 521
Network and Sharing Center
................................523, 570
Network Connections.521, 584
Network Operating System 494
Network Printer 674
NIC 516
NLX 17
No Connectivity Problem ... 688
Noise 446
Non-parity Memory 57
Northbridge 20
Notification Area 131, 136
NSLOOKUP 609
NTBACKUP 345, 350
NTBOOTDD.SYS 394, 397
NTDETECT.COM.......394, 397
NTFS 190
NTFS Permissions 559
NTLDR 394, 397
NTSC 101
NTUSER.DAT 195
NX 41

O

Odors 446
OEM 705
Offline Disk 467
Offline Files 564
Onchip Cache 39
Online Conferencing 509
Open and Closed Ports 614
Operating Environment 332
Opteron 45
Optical Drive 62
OSI Model 497
Out of Memory Error 690
Output Voltage 106, 125
Overclocking 39
Ownership 273

P

Page Count 685
Pagefile 257
PAL 101
Paper 683
Paper Jam 692
Parallel Port 72
Parental Controls 661
Parity Memory 57
Partition 189
Passive Protection Device....305
Passphrase 533
Password 156, 317
Password Management 558
PATA 29, 354, 356
Patch Panel 513
PBX 638
PC 9
PC Technicians 702, 703, 705
PCI 23, 368
PCI Express 26
PCIe 368
PCL 680
PCMCIA 121
PDA 115
Peer-to-Peer 492
Pen 389
Perform Backups 283, 345
Performance Information and
Tools 223, 260
Performance Monitor ..242, 246
Performance Options 257
Peripheral Device 219
Permission Propagation 561
Permissions 559, 562
PGA 46
Phenom 45
Phishing 324, 631
Phone and Modem Options.584
Physical Address 498
Physical Safety 297
Physical Security 571
PING 606
Pixilation 485
PKI 316, 628
Plan of Action 288
Plastics 481, 482
Plenum Cable 513
Plug-and-Play 218

Index

Point Stick................................119
POP..............................507, 631
Pop-up Blocker.....................626
Port Assignment...................614
Port Filtering........................317
Port Forwarding....................616
Port Replicator......................123
Port Triggering......................616
Ports....................................620
Positive Attitude...................266
POST Error Codes................455
POST Problems.....................453
PostScript.............................680
Power........................... 14, 305
Power Cycle..........................690
Power Management..............230
Power Options............. 231, 232
Power Problems........... 448, 483
Power Rating.........................105
Power Strip...........................296
Power Supply Tester............452
Power User Account............550
PPP.....................................577
Pre-shared Key............. 532, 533
Preventative Maintenance...330,
331, 335, 338, 339
Preventative Measures..........288
Primary Partition...................189
Print Process.........................662
Print Spooler................ 662, 689
Print Test Page.....................674
Printer Installation................672
Printer Interfaces.................672
Printer Preventative
Maintenance...........................682
Printer Troubleshooting.......688
Printer Types664, 665, 668, 669
Printer Upgrades...................675
Printing Preferences.............677
Privacy.......................... 313, 626
Problem Management...........283
Problem Reports and Solutions
....442
Process Management............439
Product Activation................157
Product Indicators................597
Professionalism.....................270
Profile..................................549
Program File Locations 194, 223
Program Filter.......................617

Programs and Features..........225
Projector................................85
Property (Respect For)........275
Proprietary Power Supplies. 106
Protocol................................497
Proxy Server........................592
Proxy Settings.......................621
PS/2......................................71
PSU................... 104, 106, 382
PSU Connectors...................106
PXE......................................169

Q

Quality Assurance.................277
Quarantining Infected Systems
....654
Questioning the Obvious.....285
Questioning Users.................286

R

RADIUS.................................533
RAID............354, 363, 365, 469
RAM......................................50
RAW.....................................662
RD.......................................207
RDRAM.................................52
Read-only Attribute..............215
ReadyBoost...........................259
Reboots.................................429
Recovery Console.................408
Recovery Disc / Partition.....416
Recycle Bin............................211
Recycling...................... 309, 326
Refresh Rate................... 86, 373
Regional and Language Options
.... 234, 388
Registered Memory...............58
Registry....................... 172, 425
Reliability and Performance
Monitor.................................247
Remediating Infected Systems
....654
Remnant Removal.................327
Remote Assistance................185
Remote Desktop....................183
Remote Support....................703
Removable Storage..........67, 68
Removing Components.........353

Removing CPU.....................378
Removing Drives...................354
Removing Input Devices......386
Removing Memory...............376
Removing Multimedia Devices
....386
Removing PSU......................382
Removing Unnecessary Devices
....483
REN......................................215
Repair Install.........................416
Repair Tools..........................330
Repairing Boot Blocks..........658
Replacing Drum....................684
Replacing Fuser....................685
Researching Ideas......... 287, 289
Researching Malware............645
Reset Page Count.................685
Resistance..............................14
Resistor.................................14
Resolution.......................86, 373
Resource Conflict.................463
Respect.................................275
Restore Point.......................404
Restoring Data.......................351
Restricted Spaces..................314
RFC......................................491
RFI..304
RIMM....................................52
RIS.......................................169
Riser Card.............................15
RJ-11....................................81
RJ-45..............................81, 512
Rootkit...................... 324, 643
Router.................518, 593, 614
RS-232...................................73
RSI......................................298
Run.......................................178

S

S/PDIF...................................95
Safe Mode..................... 403, 656
Safely Remove Hardware ... 220,
392, 476
Safety Hazards......................293
Sag.......................................305
SAM......................................549
SATA...................30, 354, 359
Satellite...................... 580, 591

Index

Scan.................................318
Scheduled Scans.....................651
Screen Size.........................86
Screwdrivers........................330
Script..............................252
SCSI....................31, 354, 360
SD Card.............................68
SDRAM...............................51
Search Utility......................201
SECC................................46
Sector...........................59, 60
Secure Connection Protocols
...................................628
Security Policy.....................549
Security Zone.......................624
Self Test...........................453
Semiconductor.......................14
Sempron.............................44
Serial Port.........................73
Server.........................490, 492
Service.............................228
Service Level Agreement.............277
Service Pack...................340, 342
Service Problems....................438
Setting IP on Printer...............673
Setting Up Rules (Firewall)..614
Setup.....................154, 159, 160
Setup Log...........................159
Setup Manager.......................167
SFC.................................424
SFF.................................15
Share Permissions..............562, 563
Shared Documents....................569
Shared Folders......................568
Shipping............................338
SID.................................556
Sidebar........................143, 264
Signal Strength.....................540
Signaling...........................13
Signed Drivers......................432
SIMD................................37
Simple File Sharing.................569
Simple Volume.......................366
Single-sided Memory.................56
Slang...............................267
Sleep...............................230
Slot................................46
Slot Cover..........................368
SMART...............................61
Smart Card..........................318

Smartphone..........................115
Smeared Printout............693, 694
SMP...........................37, 381
SMTP.........................507, 631
Social Engineering..................320
Sockets.............................46
SO-DIMM.............................118
Software Diagnostic Test....447
Software Firewall..........612, 617
SOHO................................511
Solid State Drive...................68
Sound Card.....................95, 390
Sound Problems......................474
Sound Recording.....................98
Southbridge.........................20
Spam...............................325
Spanned Volume......................366
Speakers.......................97, 390
Speed (CPU)....................39, 460
Spills..............................338
Spyware...............324, 643, 660
SRAM...........................51, 55
SSD.....................69, 355, 360
SSE.................................37
SSH................................638
SSID..........................531, 533
SSL...........................506, 628
ST / SC / LC........................519
Standby.............................230
Start Menu............131, 136, 144
Startup.............................248
Startup Modes.......................403
Startup Problems....................428
Static Address......................525
Static Electricity..................301
Status Indicators...........445, 597
Storage.............................338
Storage Controller..................365
STP................................519
Striped Volume......................366
Striping.....................364, 365
Stylus..........79, 119, 389, 486
Subnet.............................523
Subnet Mask...............500, 523
SuperFetch..........................259
Surge..............................305
Surge Suppressor....................305
Surround Sound......................97
Suspend.............................230
SVGA...............................89

S-Video.............................92
Switch........................513, 515
SXGA...............................89
SYSPREP.............................168
System Attribute....................215
System Folders......................194
System Information..................221
System Limits........133, 139, 146
System Lockup.............429, 458
System Monitor......................238
System Performance....236, 237
System Properties...................176
System Requirements.132, 138, 146
System Resources..........218, 463
System Restore......................404
System Variables....................197
Systray.............................131

T

Tablet PC...........................114
Tape Drive..........................67
Tape Rotation.......................349
Task Manager...............239, 439
Task Scheduler......................251
Taskbar.................131, 136, 144
TCP................................502
TCP/IP.........499, 523, 525, 604
Telnet..............................637
Temperature................108, 333
Temporary Files.....................254
Temporary Internet Files.....626
Termination.........................31
Test Page............674, 677, 689
Testing Components..................287
Theory of Probable Cause...285
Thermal Compound..............108
Thermal Problems....................459
Thermal Transfer Printer.....671
Threats............................312
Throttling..........................40
Thumb Drive........................68
Time Domain Reflectometer
...................................602
TLS................................506
Tone Generator......................602
Toner..........................309, 684
Touch Screen........................79
Touchpad............................119

Index

Tower 15	UXGA 89	Monitoring 242, 246
TPM.................................572		Network browsing 547
TRACERT 608	**V**	Network configuration 154
Track.............................. 59, 60		Networking..............521, 544, 582
Track Point 119	Ventilation 333	Optimizing 239, 256
Transfer Rate..........................61	Verify Installation.................. 157	Preventative Maintenance 339
Transistor..............................14	Verifying Full System	Printing.............................. 662
Transportation 338	Functionality 288	Profiles 261
Trip Hazards..........................298	Verifying the Obvious...........283	Recovery 410
Trojan Horse.................324, 643	VGA...............................89, 92	Reporting............................ 441
Troubleshooting Client	V-hold................................. 88	Setup.........................154, 159
Connectivity 612	Video Adapter 89	System requirements..132, 138, 146
Troubleshooting Techniques	Video Recording.................... 101	Troubleshooting.................... 428
......282, 284, 417, 428, 444, 483	Video Sharing 480	Unattended installation............ 167
Troubleshooting Theory 283	Virtual Memory............. 172, 257	Upgrade 163
TV Tuner................................101	Virtualization Technology 41	Windows 2000 129
Tweezers................................330	Virus 323, 642	Windows 7.............................. 148
Twisted Pair Cable...............512	Virus Disinfection...................654	Windows Complete PC Backup
	Virus Encyclopedia 645	 415
U	Visible Damage 446	Windows Defender 145, 660
	Visual Inspection....................285	Windows Deployment Services
UAC...................... 145, 263, 551	VoIP 638	 169
UDF..................................190	Voltage 14	Windows Explorer 173, 198
UDMA 29	Voltage Regulator.....................106	Windows File Protection..... 424
UDP 502	Voltage Selector Switch 105	Windows Firewall 317, 617
UEFI.................................399	Volume................... 189, 366	Windows Messenger 509
Unattended Installation 167	VPN 594	Windows RE 409, 414
UNC 525	VRM....................................46	Windows System Image
Units....................................11		Manager 169
UNIX 147	**W**	Windows Update................. 340
Unsigned Drivers.....................432		Windows Vista 140
Unused Connections 532	W3C 491	Windows XP............... 133, 138
Updating Anti-virus Software	Wake on LAN 233	WINLOAD.EXE.................. 400
....652	WAN............................ 496, 594	WINS 523, 525
Updating Firmware...............535	Wattage 105, 125	Wireless..............124, 528, 530
Upgrade Considerations 163,	Web Browser 591, 621, 623	Wireless Problems............... 603
164, 166	Web Browser Security.........625	Wireless Router Placement 540
Upgrade Paths 163, 164, 166	Webcam.............................. 101	WLAN Security..................... 533
UPS................................. 305, 306	Welcome to Windows......... 157	Workflow........................... 325
URI 505, 508	WEP............................. 531, 533	Workgroup 154, 492
USB 74, 392, 464	Wi-Fi..............124, 528, 529, 530	Worm 323, 642
USB Drive............................. 68	Windows 128, 170	WPA........................... 531, 533
User 549	Accounts....................550, 553	Write-protect Tab................. 59
User Account.......317, 549, 553	Additional components............ 223	WUXGA 89
User File Locations...............194	Application management............ 223	
User Interface 131, 136, 141	Backup 345	**X**
User Profiles.........................261	Boot process........................ 393	
Using Static IP.......................532	Configuring 176, 180	x64...................................... 227
USMT.................................165	Desktop 136, 141	XCOPY.............................. 213
UTP....................................512	Device management 430	XD...................................... 41
	Diagnostic tools 403, 421	XGA.................................... 89
	Installation........................ 150	
	Licensing............................ 129	